User Interface Design for Virtual Environments:
Challenges and Advances

Badrul H. Khan
McWeadon Education, USA

Information Science
REFERENCE

Managing Director:	Lindsay Johnston
Senior Editorial Director:	Heather Probst
Book Production Manager:	Sean Woznicki
Development Manager:	Joel Gamon
Development Editor:	Joel Gamon
Acquisitions Editor:	Erika Gallagher
Typesetters:	Lisandro Gonzalez
Print Coordinator:	Jamie Snavely
Cover Design:	Nick Newcomer

Published in the United States of America by
Information Science Reference (an imprint of IGI Global)
701 E. Chocolate Avenue
Hershey PA 17033
Tel: 717-533-8845
Fax: 717-533-8661
E-mail: cust@igi-global.com
Web site: http://www.igi-global.com

Copyright © 2012 by IGI Global. All rights reserved. No part of this publication may be reproduced, stored or distributed in any form or by any means, electronic or mechanical, including photocopying, without written permission from the publisher. Product or company names used in this set are for identification purposes only. Inclusion of the names of the products or companies does not indicate a claim of ownership by IGI Global of the trademark or registered trademark.

Library of Congress Cataloging-in-Publication Data

User interface design for virtual environments : challenges and advances / Badrul H. Khan, editor.
    p. cm.
  Includes bibliographical references and index.
  Summary: "This book focuses on challenges that designers face in creating interfaces for users of various virtual environments, including coverage of various critical issues that have implications for user interface design from a number of different viewpoints"--Provided by publisher.
  ISBN 978-1-61350-516-8 (hardcover) -- ISBN 978-1-61350-517-5 (ebook) -- ISBN 978-1-61350-518-2 (print & perpetual access) 1. User interfaces (Computer systems) 2. Virtual reality. I. Khan, Badrul H. (Badrul Huda), 1958-
  QA76.9.U83U8375 2012
  006.8--dc23
                          2011045543

British Cataloguing in Publication Data
A Cataloguing in Publication record for this book is available from the British Library.

All work contributed to this book is new, previously-unpublished material. The views expressed in this book are those of the authors, but not necessarily of the publisher.

This book is dedicated to my late parents:

Mr. Lokman Khan Sherwani &

Mrs. Shabnom Khanam Sherwani

of

Khan Manzil, Pathantooly, Chittagong, Bangladesh.

List of Reviewers

Mauri Collins, *St. Rebel Design, LLC, USA*
Manish Gupta, *State University of New York at Buffalo, USA*
Kelee Plagis-Tsitsikaos, *Ph.D, InfotellVA, LLC, USA*

Table of Contents

Detailed Table of Contents

Chapter 1

Badrul H. Khan, McWeadon Education, USA

In the information digital society, the advancement of Information and Communication Technologies (ICTs) has created a broadened scope of sharing innovations globally by digital citizens. In this global digital society, individuals can learn and work individually or as a member of a team using various ICTs without being physically face-to-face with each other. How is it possible?

Chapter 2

Manish Gupta, State University of New York at Buffalo, USA
Rui Chen, Ball State University, USA

Virtual worlds are emerging as important socio-technical artifacts in contemporary society. Improvements in technology – both hardware and software performance and costs – have facilitated fast emergence of complex and near-real experience virtual worlds. Recent years have seen an unprecedented growth in number of users and corporations joining these virtual worlds. They have enabled unique business models in the digital economy and cast far-reaching impacts on the society spanning literature to leisure. The chapter analyzes 106 journal articles published in last decade to uncover a shift in focus of research on different aspects of virtual worlds. The chapter identifies six dominant themes of research on virtual worlds and then content-analyzes extant literature to show how these themes have emerged in research on virtual worlds. This presents unique insights into perceived relative importance of impact of different aspects of virtual worlds on individuals and organizations alike.

Chapter 3

Christina K. Curnow, ICF International, USA
Jeremy A. Henson, ICF International, USA
Robert A. Wisher, Naval Postgraduate School, USA

This chapter provides a preliminary framework for learner centered user interface design across a variety of training categories. To arrive at this framework, the authors explore (1) user interface design principles and the extent to which they apply to learning environments, (2) the learner centric psychological principles that should be included in the design of learner interfaces, and (3) methods by which training tasks are categorized. The overarching premise of the framework is that designs that are compatible with the psychology of learning promote learning, and ultimately performance, better than those that do not. This seemingly simple concept is sometimes in conflict with user interface design principles for other purposes, such as general purpose websites or marketing campaigns. The framework results in a notional configuration of 27 learner centered training interfaces, which are analyzed for their relevance to user interface design. The chapter concludes with a call for further research to determine best practices in learner interface design.

Chapter 4

This chapter investigates the potential of aesthetics in the design of Human-Computer Interaction (HCI). In particular, it aims to provide a means by which aesthetics can be applied in photorealistic Virtual Reality (VR) to create engaging experiences. Indeed, this chapter suggests that much can be gained from looking at the aesthetics of photorealistic VR content as opposed to solely looking at the more traditional HCI approaches that have mainly concentrated on the performance and efficiency issues of the technology. The chapter is motivated by the very notion that the aesthetic potential of photorealistic VR content is, and continues to be, underestimated whilst the emphasis on the development of newer and more efficient technologies to create engaging VR experiences increases. Challenging this, the author reports on the results of a comparative analysis performed on two photorealistic virtual environments. These results highlight how both aesthetic form and functionality – efficiency and performance issues – need to be considered in tandem in order to create engaging VR experiences. In demonstrating this, the chapter aims to not only successfully emphasize the experiential side of photorealistic VR, but also to advance the idea of the engaged interaction and in doing so, a new design drive for HCI.

Chapter 5

Virtual Environments are complex systems in that they involve the crucial concept of sharing. Users can share knowledge of each other's current activities, environments, and actions. In this chapter, the authors discuss about interaction interoperability, intended to mean the ability of two or more users to cooperate despite the heterogeneity of their interfaces. To allow such interoperability, formal methods to formalize the knowledge and middleware solutions for sharing that knowledge are required. After introducing the state-of-the-art solutions and the open issues in the field, the authors describe a system for providing interaction interoperability among multi-user interfaces. Rather than focusing on the de-coupling of input devices from interaction techniques and from interaction tasks, this chapter suggests integrating interactive systems at higher level through an interface standardization. To achieve this aim, the authors propose: i) an architectural model able to handle differences in input devices and interaction tasks; ii) an agent-based middleware that provides basic components to integrate heterogeneous user interfaces. The chapter also presents a case study in which an agent-based middleware is used to support developers in the interconnection of monolithic applications.

Chapter 6

Olga C. Santos, UNED, Spain & Cadius Community of Usability Professionals, Spain
Emanuela Mazzone, UNED, Spain & Cadius Community of Usability Professionals, Spain
Maria Jose Aguilar, Cadius Community of Usability Professionals, Spain
Jesus G. Boticario, UNED, Spain

This chapter presents the information architecture approach for the design of an administration tool for educators to manage educational oriented recommendations in virtual learning environments. In this way, educators can be supported in the publication stage of the e-learning life cycle after recommendations have been designed with the TORMES methodology. The chapter starts introducing relevant background information on recommender systems for e-learning and the rationale for the educators' involvement in the recommendation design process. Afterwards, the chapter comments on the information architecture that supports the user interface design process with user-centered design methods, including the goals to achieve in each of the steps defined. The chapter ends by discussing the application of this approach in different contexts.

Chapter 7

Serkan Özel, Bogazici University, Turkey

This chapter focuses on multiple representations and cognitive perspective about presenting information via different modes in user interface design. Research studies indicate that providing accurate representations increases users' recognition of information. Moreover, presentation of one concept in multiple modes improves concept acquisition. Developing an understanding of how concept acquisition occurs requires knowledge about cognitive information processing and brain functioning. Scientific studies related to brain functioning will enlighten the path in front of cognitive psychology while the cognitive psychology research will advance the knowledge base on information processing.

Chapter 8

Alex Stedmon, University of Nottingham, UK

Speech is the primary mode of communication between humans, and something most people are able to use on a daily basis in order to interact with other people (Stedmon & Baber, 1999). For over 70 years the potential to interact with machines using speech input has been possible (Ullman, 1987), however it still remains an elusive concept without widespread use or acceptance.

Chapter 9

Keysha I. Gamor, ICF International, USA

While the age old adage: "Build it and they will come" may ring true to some extent in many cases, it also begs the question: "...But will they come back?" Persistence can describe the continuously existing state of a virtual world, whether anyone is in it and using it or not; it remains as the last person left it. Persistence is a major affordance of virtual worlds—a central characteristic that sets it apart from any other learning medium available in the current instructional design toolkit. This chapter addresses the criticality of exploiting this attribute in order to design the optimal user interface for a meaningful, lasting learning experience in a virtual world.

Chapter 10

    Kambiz Badie, Research Institute for ICT (ITRC), Iran
    Mahmood Kharrat, Research Institute for ICT (ITRC), Iran
    Maryam Tayefeh Mahmoudi, Research Institute for ICT (ITRC), Iran & University of Tehran, Iran
    Maryam S. Mirian, Research Institute for ICT (ITRC), Iran & University of Tehran, Iran
    Tahereh M.Ghazi, Research Institute for ICT (ITRC), Iran and
    Sogol Babazadeh, Research Institute for ICT (ITRC), Iran

In this chapter, a framework is discussed for creating contents to help significant organizational tasks such as planning, research, innovation, education, development, et cetera be achieved in an efficient way. The proposed framework is based on an interplay between the ontologies of the key segments and the problem context using the linguistically significant notions for each key segment. Once a certain organizational task is faced these notions are adjusted to create a new content filling the new situation. In the chapter, an agent-based architecture is discussed to show how human interaction with his/her surrounding organization can be realized through using this framework.

Chapter 11

    Kanubhai K. Patel, Ahmedabad University, India
    Sanjay Kumar Vij, SVIT, India

Locomotion interface with unidirectional as well as omni-directional treadmills creates infinite surface by use of motion floors. But realization of the motion floors requires a bulky or complex drive mechanism, thereby restricting practical use of locomotion interfaces. Secondly, it presents a problem of stability, especially while using these interfaces for simulating virtual walking of visually impaired people for spatial learning through virtual environments. As a result, such devices induce a kind of fear psychosis leading to difficulties in exploring virtual environment and thereby in cognitive map formation. A design of locomotion interface which reduces to a minimum these constraints is presented by first undertaking a literature review of the material existing in the area of locomotion interfaces and computer science. This proposed design of a locomotion interface to the virtual environment for spatial learning is aimed at providing unconstrained walking plane for building improved cognitive map and thereby enhancing mobility skills of persons with limited vision. A major design goal is to allow visually impaired people to walk safely on the device with a limited size, and to give them the sensation of walking on an unconstrained plane.

Chapter 12

    Stephen R Quinton, University of New South Wales, Australia

In an era marked by rapid change and increasing reliance on digital technologies, there is much evidence to suggest that the learning preferences and goals of today's students have become distinctly different from those of the past. Taken as a whole, it is conceivable that education as we have known it over the past two hundred years is poised on the verge of entering into a new realm of possibilities that will revolutionise accepted views on the role and purpose of learning. If such claims are correct, a highly adaptive, systemic theory of learning may assist to explain the complexities and implications of the present (emergent) and future (unknown) challenges facing educationalists and learners in the coming decade.

This chapter presents a philosophical treatise on how the author envisions the design of electronic learning environments in the future. The uniqueness of the theory of learning to emerge from this exploration lies in its capacity to dynamically adapt and evolve in response to the changing expectations of the teacher and the changing learning needs of the student. It promotes the concept of a continuum of possibilities and opens the way to move beyond the application of a static approach to learning design that is limited in its capacity to satisfy the needs of all, to the adoption of a dynamic, highly adaptable approach that begins to address the specific learning goals of every individual. Thus, educationalists are encouraged to explore what might be possible and not be constrained by current assumptions on how electronic learning environments are currently designed.

Using the resistance literature as an underpinning theoretical framework, this chapter analyzes how Web designers through their daily practices, (i) adopt recursive, adaptive, and resisting behavior regarding the inclusion of social cues online and (ii) shape the socio-technical power relationship between designers and other stakeholders. Five vignettes in the form of case studies with expert individual Web designers are used. Findings point out at three types of emerging resistance namely: market driven resistance, ideological resistance, and functional resistance. In addition, a series of propositions are provided linking the various themes. Furthermore, the authors suggest that stratification in Web designers' type is occurring and that resistance offers a novel lens to analyze the debate.

There is increasing use of mobile devices around the world to conduct everyday business and to socialize. As a result, learners will be using mobile devices to access learning materials so that they can learn from anywhere and at anytime. Learning materials must be designed using proven instructional design models and learning theories. This will allow the learning system to provide flexibility in learning and to meet the needs of individual learners. In addition, good user interface design must be followed in mobile learning to allow learners to interact with the learning system and learning materials to facilitate learning from anywhere and at anytime.

Chapter 15

This chapter investigates issues associated with the design of an electronic textbook and describes metasystems learning design (MLD). MLD was founded by the Globalisation G- Anthropology A- Existentialism E paradigm (GAE). This paradigm argues the transition from closed pedagogical systems to more open educational systems. The core element of MLD is the pedagogy of a competence development triggered electronic textbook. The functionality of MLD is assured by a flexible and dynamic instructional strategy. This new strategy provides an operating framework both for teachers and for learners through self-regulation assessment.

The contents of this chapter are framed under three categories: the theoretical approach, pedagogy of competence development and practice. Conclusions are provided at the end.

Chapter 16

Other chapters in this book discuss the design and development of interfaces for virtual worlds. This chapter will discuss the instructional design aspects of designing learning in virtual worlds. The use of virtual worlds is a relatively new phenomenon in education and, like many innovations that have preceded them, they are a new and intriguing tool to be mastered by both student and instructor alike. While bounded by a computer screen, virtual worlds have many of the affective components of everyday life and familiar-looking environments, where real life rules pertain, can be created to transfer learning, and both formal and informal learning can take place (Jones & Bronack, 2007).

Chapter 17

The meme of the physical university is changing and moving swiftly, due mostly to virtual technological developments, towards the "multi-versity" where Higher Education Institutes will exist in both the real world and a virtual space: a term this chapter names "augmented education." Augmented education requires innovation in technology that can deliver new ways of learning. Therefore, virtual worlds that support effective experiential learning need to be designed beyond merely established real world replication. The concern for researchers and educational practitioners is the need to provide evidence-based frameworks for tasks of measurable complexity that result in verifiable learning in an augmented virtual world. In an attempt to develop a framework for science education this chapter summarizes the theoretical and technical progress of research in the iterative, leaner centered design of virtual tools and associated tasks for evidencing the processes of learning (witnessed as measurements of six cognitive processes and four knowledge dimensions) of participants communicating the programming of LEGO robots within a virtual world.

    Brenda Tyczkowski, University of Wisconsin Green Bay, USA
    Eric Bauman, Clinical Playground, LLC, USA
    Susan Gallagher-Lepak, University of Wisconsin Green Bay, USA
    Christine Vandenhouten, University of Wisconsin Green Bay, USA
    Janet Resop Reilly, University of Wisconsin Green Bay, USA

Initially designed for corporate use, the World Wide Web as it is now known surfaced in the early 1990s. Individual use grew rapidly in the 1990's, with "online users doubling or tripling every year" (When Guide, n.d.). Online degree granting educational programs slowly developed. An early fully online RN (Registered Nurse) to BSN (Bachelor of Science in Nursing) program was the Collaborative Nursing Program (CNP) in Wisconsin. The program, now called the "BSN@Home" program, started in 1995, to serve associate degree and diploma prepared nurses throughout the state of Wisconsin desiring a baccalaureate degree in nursing. This statewide program continues to be delivered collaboratively by five University of Wisconsin (UW) nursing programs (UW-Eau Claire, UW-Green Bay, UW-Madison, UW-Milwaukee, and UW-Oshkosh).

Preface

In the information digital society, the advancement of Information and Communication Technologies (ICTs) has created a broadened scope of sharing innovations globally by digital citizens. In this global digital society, people use electronic devices in almost everything they do: from brushing their teeth to driving a car. In this fast moving digital society, people are encountering newer features associated with emerging technologies including (but not limited to): computers, all kinds of appliances and machines, mobile communication devices, software applications, social media, and websites. With all these advances in emerging technologies coupled with fast paced lifestyles, people are increasingly overwhelmed with various electronic devices and services. What do users of these various digital devices and services really need? They need useable and adaptable interfaces to operate in these virtual environments.

When I was asked by IGI Global to edit this book on user interface design, I was very excited, honored, and intrigued. I was *excited* and *honored* because the themes and the purpose of the book fall under my forthcoming publication plan which is to author/edit eight different books using the eight dimensions of the *Virtual Learning Framework* (see below). I was *intrigued* as I do not claim to be an expert in interface design but as it is one of the eight dimensions. However, it took some convincing from the publisher and several of my colleagues who convinced me that my research and interest on critical issues associated with the design of open and distributed learning environments are definitely useful to the user interface design for virtual environments.

Since 1997, I have been studying the question *"What does it take to provide meaningful Virtual Learning Environments (VLEs) for learners worldwide?"* Through my research I found that numerous factors help to create a meaningful VLE, and many of these factors are systemically interrelated and interdependent. I clustered these factors into eight dimensions (institutional, management, technological, pedagogical, ethical considerations, interface design, resource support, and evaluation) and created *A Framework for Virtual Learning* (http://badrulkhan.com/framework). Designing interfaces for VLEs cannot be accomplished by addressing only the issues relevant to the interface design dimension. One must recognize the interrelationships and interconnectedness with the issues of the seven other dimensions of the Framework. Therefore, I have included chapters focusing on comprehensive issues of challenges and advances of VLEs in this book.

To some, the term "virtual environment" may sound as if it applies only to 3-dimensional virtual worlds, so I feel it is important to clarify that, in this book, VLEs include both two dimensional (2D) and three dimensional (3D) virtual spaces. Therefore, chapters in the book are inclusive of both kinds of virtual environments.

I am very fortunate to have researchers and practitioners involved in VLEs as contributors of this book. As the editor of this book, I took an open and democratic approach to solicit contributions. I sent e-mail messages to potential authors and also cross-posted a message to several listservs soliciting contributions for the book. As a result, I put together this book by incorporating works of talented individuals with unique backgrounds from around the globe. It should also be noted that there are many significant people involved in doing research in virtual learning who are not included in this book.

The *purpose* of this book is to provide the reader with a broad understanding of issues relevant to user interface design (one dimension of the Framework) of virtual environments. Chapters included in this book attempt to address various critical issues that have implications for user interface design, and offer a variety of points of view on those issues. Below, I present a brief description of each chapter of the book:

1. In the introductory chapter entitled "*Virtual Learning Environments: Design Factors and Issues,*" I argue that designing interfaces for VLEs cannot be accomplished by addressing only the issues raised based on the interface design factors. Other VLE factors (i.e., institutional, management, technological, pedagogical, ethical, resource support, and evaluation) are systemically interrelated and interdependent with interface design factors. Therefore, for a meaningful VLE design, it is very important to recognize the interrelationships and interconnectedness of factors in addressing issues conducive to learning.

2. **Gupta and Chen** (*Understanding Evolution of Virtual Worlds Research: A Content Analytic Approach*) present six dominant themes of research on virtual worlds and then content-analyze extant literature to show how several themes have emerged in research on virtual worlds. This presents unique insights into perceived relative importance of impact of different aspects of virtual worlds on individuals and organizations alike.

3. **Curnow, Henson, and Wisher** (*User Interface Designs, Task Categories and Training*) focus on a preliminary framework for learner centered user interface design across a variety of training categories. The overarching premise of the framework is that designs that are compatible with the psychology of learning promote learning and ultimately perform better than those that do not. The framework results in a notional configuration of 27 learner centered training interfaces, which are analyzed for their relevance to user interface design.

4. **Carroll** (*Exploring Past Trends and Current Challenges of Human Computer Interaction [HCI] Design: What Does This Mean for the Design of Virtual Environments?*) investigates the potential of aesthetics in the design of Human-Computer Interaction (HCI). In particular, the chapter aims to provide a means by which aesthetics can be applied in photorealistic virtual reality (VR) to create engaging experiences.

5. **Ciampi, Coronato, De Pietro, and Gallo** (*Architectural Models for Reliable Multi-User Interfaces*) describe a system for providing interaction interoperability among multi-user interfaces. Rather than focusing on the de-coupling of input devices from interaction techniques and from interaction tasks, they suggest integrating interactive systems at higher level through an interface standardization. The chapter also presents a case study in which an agent-based middleware is used to support developers in the interconnection of monolithic applications.

6. **Santos, Mazzone, Aguilar, and Boticario** (*Information Architecture for the Design of a User Interface to Manage Educational Oriented Recommendations*) presents the user centred design process of the administration tool for educators using a recommender system in virtual learning environments. The aim of this tool is to facilitate the involvement of educators when personal-

izing the learning experience for their students, in order to make the educative process as simple, meaningful, and efficient as possible.

7. **Özel** (*Utilizing Cognitive Resources in User Interface Designs*) focuses on multiple representations and cognitive perspective about presenting information via different modes in user interface design. Research studies indicate that providing accurate representations increases users' recognition of information. Moreover, presentation of one concept in multiple modes improves concept acquisition. Developing an understanding of how concept acquisition occurs requires knowledge about cognitive information processing and brain functioning.

8. **Stedmon** (*Designing Usable Speech Input for Virtual Environments*) provides guidelines derived from a number of sources that would appear to reinforce widespread common sense conventions and even anecdotal evidence for speech interface use. He emphasizes on the need to generate a much better understanding, from a user-centered perspective, and better organization of guidelines to make them more universally applicable.

9. **Gamor** (*Exploiting the Power of Persistence for Learning in Virtual Worlds*) addresses the criticality of using "persistence" in order to design a meaningful, lasting learning experience in a virtual world. The chapter examines how to optimize the user interface for "persistence" using sound instructional design strategies.

10. **Badie, Kharrat, Mahmoudi, Mirian, Ghazi, and Babazadeh** (*Ontology-Driven Creation of Contents: Making Efficient Interaction between Organizational Users and Their Surrounding Tasks*) discuss a framework to create contents for helping organizational tasks based on an interplay between the ontologies of the key segments and the problem context. The focal point in this regard is using the linguistically significant notions to be adjusted separately for each key segment once a certain organizational task is faced.

11. **Patel and Vij** (Unconstrained Walking Plane as Locomotion Interface to Virtual Environment) discuss how the design of a locomotion interface to the virtual environment for spatial learning is aimed at providing unconstrained walking plane for building improved cognitive map and thereby enhancing mobility skills of persons with limited vision. The structure of the interface, and control mechanism of the device are presented, and discussion of advantages and limitations of the interface is given.

12. **Quinton** (*Redefining the Role and Purpose of Learning*) presents a philosophical treatise on the design of electronic learning environments in the future. The uniqueness of the theory of learning to emerge from this exploration lies in its capacity to dynamically adapt and evolve in response to the changing expectations of the teacher and the changing learning needs of the student.

13. **De Kervenoael, Bisson, and Palmer** (*Are Web Designers Resisting the Inclusion of Social Cues When Creating Website User Interface?*) discuss how Web designers through their daily practices, (i) adopt recursive, adaptive and resisting behavior regarding the inclusion of social cues online and (ii) shape the socio-technical power relationship between designers and other stakeholders. Five vignettes case study with expert individual web designers are used. Findings point out at three types of emerging resistance, namely: market driven resistance, ideological resistance, and functional resistance.

14. **Ally** (*Designing Mobile Learning for the User*) discusses learning strategies for mobile learning, and provides several design principles for the development of mobile learning materials to maximize the amount learned and to meet the needs of the user.

15. **Railean** (*Issues and Challenges Associated with the Design of Electronic Textbook*) investigates issues associated with the design of electronic textbook and describes metasystems learning design (MLD). This paradigm argues the transition from closed pedagogical systems to more open educational systems. The core element of MLD is the pedagogy of competence development triggered electronic textbook. The functionality of MLD is assured by a flexible and dynamic instructional strategy. This new strategy provides an operating framework both for teachers and for learners through self-regulation assessment.

16. **Collins** (*Using a Blueprint in the Design of Instruction for Virtual Environments*) discusses the instructional design aspects of designing learning in virtual worlds. The chapter presents a relatively straightforward instructional design framework that stresses the alignment of learning outcomes, learning activities, and assessment/feedback.

17. **Vallance** (*Design and Robots for Learning in Virtual Worlds*) states that the meme of the physical university is changing and moving swiftly, due mostly to virtual technological developments, towards the "multi-versity" where Higher Education Institutes will exist in both the real world and a virtual space. This chapter summarizes the theoretical and technical progress of research in the iterative, leaner centered design of virtual tools and associated tasks for evidencing the processes of learning (witnessed as measurements of six cognitive processes and four knowledge dimensions) of participants communicating the programming LEGO robots within a virtual world.

18. **Tyczkowski, Bauman, Susan Gallagher-Lepak, Vandenhouten, and Reilly** (*An Interface Design Evaluation of Courses in a Nursing Program Using an E-Learning Framework: A Case Study*) present a case study that uses a checklist of interface design issues to conduct a formal analysis of the five core online courses taught in the BSN@HOME collaborative. Such an analysis was aimed at identifying strengths and areas for improvement of the program.

It is important to note that user interface design for newer and constantly emerging virtual environments will be challenging. However, sharing of knowledge among VLE researchers and practitioners about "what works and what does not work" provides useful guidance for advancing the field.

Hopefully, this collection of ideas and issues discussed by international authors will help practitioners understand various aspects of the meaningful design of VLEs and provide valuable guidance in creating VLEs for the target audience. I would appreciate hearing comments regarding this book.

Badrul H. Khan
McWeadon Education, USA

Acknowledgment

This book owes much to the encouragement and assistance of many people. First of all, I would like to thank Mauri Collins for her critical review and helpful feedback. I would also like to thank Kelee Plagis-Tsitsikaos and Manish Gupta for their review of several chapters.

I would also like to thank my well-wishers who believed in me and are very supportive of my ideas and visions, including: Joel Gamon, Development Manager and Lisandro Gonzalez, Production Assistant at IGI Global.

Finally, and most important, I thank my wife Komar Khan and my sons Intisar Sherwani Khan and Inshat Sherwani Khan for their continued support and encouragement.

Badrul H. Khan
McWeadon Education, USA

Chapter 1
Virtual Learning Environments:
Design Factors and Issues

Badrul H. Khan
McWeadon Education, USA

ABSTRACT

In the information digital society, the advancement of Information and Communication Technologies (ICTs) has created a broadened scope of sharing innovations globally by digital citizens. In this global digital society, individuals can learn and work individually or as a member of a team using various ICTs without being physically face-to-face with each other. How is it possible?

INTRODUCTION

Here is a quote from Wikipedia[1] that explains it well:

Internet and communication technology fostered de-coupling of space where events happen, and storage technologies facilitate de-coupling of time between a message being sent and received. These technologies build the environment for virtual work in teams, with members who may never meet each other in person. Communicating by telephone and e-mail, with work products shared electronically, virtual teams produce results without being co-located.

The term "virtual" has become synonymous with any activities done on the computer or on the Internet. It has been used in many fields to represent profession and activities. For example, lawyers who deliver legal services over the Internet may refer to themselves as "digital lawyers", "online lawyers", or "virtual lawyers." With more and more people logging onto the Internet, patients are consulting with a doctor without ever going to the doctor's office (Morales, 2002). These virtual professionals who work in virtual environments or cyberspace are capable of providing their services to more and more of their clients/patients than traditionally. Because of the 24/7 accessibility, both the providers and receivers enjoy flexible services. It is also very important to note that anyone who is interested in receiving ongoing professional development training in their fields, Virtual Learning Environ-

DOI: 10.4018/978-1-61350-516-8.ch001

Copyright © 2012, IGI Global. Copying or distributing in print or electronic forms without written permission of IGI Global is prohibited.

ments (VLEs) are becoming increasing available in almost all disciplines.

In this chapter, I would like to discuss the following:

- Virtual Learning Environments (VLEs)
- User Interface Design for VLEs
- Design Perspective for VLEs

VIRTUAL LEARNING ENVIRONMENTS

When "learning" is added to any specific delivery format or medium, it is generally expected that one can use the medium for learning. Now the question is: what does VLEs include? Does it only refer to three-dimensional (3D) environments like Second Life or games like World of Warcraft? Or does it also include the familiar two-dimensional (2D) environments of web pages and learning management systems (LMSs)? The answer is simple: it includes both 2D and 3D environments. As Russell (2010) notes VLEs are both two dimensional (2D) and three dimensional (3D) virtual spaces that include multiple interactive aspects including collaborative dialogic forums such as chat rooms, discussion boards, live audio, information dissemination, and presentation in multiple media including sound, video and animated graphics, and hyperlinks in the environment that link the learners throughout the learning experience.

However, the term "virtual environment" may be viewed differently by different people in different fields. In the Human Computer Interaction (HCI) community, it implies the use of a simulated environment, typically containing a 3D model allowing for user controlled navigation and dynamic view generation (Wann & Mon-Williams, 1996). However, Davies & Dalgarno (2008) note that VLE has increasingly become used to refer to web based learning resources that do not necessarily include any form of visual simulation (Dillenbourg, Schneider & Synteta, 2002).

The position taken in this book is that access to any digital learning content stored on servers/ disks or on the Internet is a part of the VLE. Thus, Computer-Assisted Instruction (CAI), Computer-Based Training (CBT), Web-Based Instruction (WBI), and Web-Based Training (WBT) are obviously part of the VLE. All LMSs create VLEs. As we are technologically advancing into 3D environments, VLEs are becoming highly engaging to learners as they respond to interactions in virtual worlds.

In this book, *a virtual learning environment (VLE) is defined as any digital learning space or environment where learning activities, opportunities, and experiences are designed based in appropriate learning theories and techniques, using various attributes of digital technologies to create meaningful environments for diverse learners where learning is fostered and supported.*

VLEs are open and distributed learning environments. According to Calder & McCollum (1998), "The common definition of open learning is learning in your own time, pace and place" (p. 13). Ellington (1997) notes that open and flexible learning allows learners to have some say in how, where, and when learning takes place. Saltzberg & Polyson (1995) noted that distributed learning is not synonymous with distance learning, but they do stress its close relationship with the idea of distributed resources:

Distributed learning is an instructional model that allows instructor, students, and content to be located in different, non-centralized locations so that instruction and learning occur independent of time and place. . . . The distributed learning model can be used in combination with traditional classroom-based courses, with traditional distance learning courses, or it can be used to create wholly virtual classrooms. (p. 10)

Because of the open and distributed nature of VLEs, learners enjoy greater flexibility in access to learning resources distributed in various loca-

Figure 1. Open and distributed learning

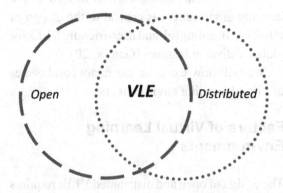

tions. Figure 1: Open and Distributed Learning graphically shows how an open and distributed educational system contributes to flexibility.

A clear understanding of the *open and distributed* nature of learning environments will help us create meaningful learning environments with increased flexibility (Khan, 2007).

USER INTERFACE DESIGN FOR VIRTUAL LEARNING ENVIRONMENT

User interface design is a dominant and critical factor for open and distributed learning environments such as VLEs where learners, instructors, support staff, learning content, and learning resources may not be located at the same place.

Who are the Users of VLEs?

Users of VLEs are human—the learners. Who are the creators of VLEs? The creators of VLEs are human—the designers. Therefore, *humans create VLEs for humans using technologies*. Once a VLE is created, learners or users follow the navigational cues or user interfaces to use the system. If interfaces are not designed meaningfully, the flow of learning is affected.

What are Interfaces?

Interfaces are where the interactions between things happen. When a power button on a TV set is pressed, the TV is turned on. "The buttons on the front of your television set, for example, are the interface between you and the electrical wiring on the other side of its plastic casing.[2] It like stimuli (i.e., TV button) and response (i.e., TV is turned on) must be coordinated meaningfully for a TV program to run. On a Website, "interface" refer to how the pages look, the navigation scheme, and how the pages work and interact with the visitors (Williams & Tollett, 2006).

What is User Interface Design for Virtual Learning Environments?

At the heart of user interface design is the "user" and the user is in the "driver's seat." Therefore, it is critical that users of any virtual environment be able to use the interface intuitively, regardless of cultural diversities (del Galdo & Nielsen, 1996). The goal of user interface design is to make the user's interaction as simple and efficient as possible, in terms of accomplishing user goals—what is often called user-centered design.[3] Therefore, in VLEs, the most important goal of designing a user interface is to reach learners more effectively (Cheon, & Grant, 2009; Pimentel, 1999). User interface design is the creation of a seamless integration of content and its organization, together with the navigational and interactive controls that learners use to work with the content (Jones and Farquhar, 1997).

DESIGN PERSPECTIVE FOR VIRTUAL LEARNING ENVIRONMENTS

In this global digital society, people use electronic devices in almost everything they do in their lives: from brushing their teeth to driving a car. In the fast moving digital society, people are encountering newer features associated with emerging technologies including (but not limited to): computers, appliances, machines, mobile communication devices, software applications, social media, and websites. With all these advances in emerging technologies, coupled with fast paced lifestyles, people are increasingly overwhelmed with various electronic devices and services. What do users of these various digital devices and services really need? They need useable and adaptable interfaces to operate in these digital environments. Interfaces are like signposts on highways guiding users to their destinations.

The linkage between a digital society and globalization has tremendous implications on the design of user-interfaces for various virtual environments. Reflecting on the global and cross cultural nature of today's world, user interface design for access to various VLEs should be based on the needs of cross culturally diverse global user population. The interface design should be user-centric. User interface design should strive to make the user's interaction with the technologies as simple, meaningful, and efficient as possible.

This book focuses on the challenges inherent in designing interfaces for various virtual environments. To overcome such challenges, a comprehensive understanding of various factors of virtual environments, and critical issues associated with them must be explored.

In this chapter, virtual environments conducive to learning (or VLEs) are considered. A VLE can be compared to a human activity system (Banathy, 1995). In a human activity system, *blood* flows through the *arteries* for the entire body to be functional. Similarly, in a learning activity system such as a VLE, *issues* are like blood flow whereas the *factors* are the arteries. For example, *navigation* is an interface design factor (see Table 1, 4.3) and *cross-cultural sensitivity* is one of the critical issues which should be incorporated into a VLE's interface for a smooth flow of learning activities for diverse learners. Therefore, address-

ing *issues* encompassing various *factors* of the learning environment is critical to the design of effective, meaningful, and user-friendly VLEs for globally diverse learners (Gamor, 2010)

We will now examine the factors and issues of virtual learning environments.

Factors of Virtual Learning Environments

The design of open and distributed VLEs requires a comprehensive understanding of *"What does it take to provide meaningful virtual learning environments for learners worldwide?* Since 1997, I have communicated with learners, instructors, administrators, and technical and other support services staff involved in virtual learning (in both academic and corporate settings) all over the world. I have researched virtual learning issues discussed in professional discussion forums, and I have designed and taught online and blended learning courses. I have surveyed online educators and students (Khan & Vega, 1997; Khan & Smith, 2007 and Khan, Cataldo & Bennett, 2007). Also, as the editor of *Web-based instruction (1997), Web-based training (2001), Flexible learning in an information society (2007),* and *Learning on demand: ADL and the future of e-learning (2010),* I have had the opportunity to work closely on critical virtual learning issues with more than 250 authors worldwide, who have contributed chapters to these books.

Through these activities, I have learned that virtual learning represents a paradigm shift, not only for learners, but also for instructors, administrators, technical, support services staff, and the institution. As we are accustomed to teaching and learning in a closed system like physical classrooms, the openness of virtual learning is new to us. To create effective VLEs for diverse learners, we need to jump out of our closed system mentality. We need to change our mindset. We need to be attentive to a variety of new and emerging issues of virtual environments, and address them

Table 1. Virtual learning framework

1. INSTITUTIONAL
1.1 Administrative Affairs
1.1.1 Needs Assessment
1.1.2 Readiness Assessment (Financial, Infrastructure, Cultural, and Content readiness)
1.1.3 Organization and Change (Diffusion, Adoption, and Implementation of Innovation)
1.1.4 Budgeting and Return on Investment (ROI)
1.1.5 Partnerships with Other Institutions
1.1.6 Program and Course information Catalog (Academic Calendar, Course Schedule, Tuition, Fees, and Graduation)
1.1.7 Marketing and Recruitment
1.1.8 Admissions
1.1.9 Financial Aid
1.1.10 Registration and Payment
1.1.11 Information Technology Services
1.1.13 Instructional Design and Media Services
1.1.14 Graduation Transcripts and Grades
1.2 Academic Affairs
1.2.1 Accreditation
1.2.2 Policy
1.2.3 Instructional Quality
1.2.4 Faculty and Staff Support
1.2.5 Class Size, Workload, and Compensation and Intellectual Property Rights
1.3 Student Services
1.3.1 Pre-enrollment Services
1.3.2 Orientation
1.3.3 Faculty and Staff directories
1.3.4 Advising
1.3.5 Counseling
1.3.6 Learning Skills Development
1.3.7 Services for Students with Disabilities
1.3.8 Library Support
1.3.9 Bookstore
1.3.10 Tutorial Services
1.3.11 Mediation and Conflict Resolution
1.3.12 Social Support Network
1.3.13 Students Newsletter
1.3.14 Internship and Employment Services
1.3.15 Alumni Affairs
1.3.16 Other Services
2. PEDAGOGICAL
2.1 Content Analysis
2.2 Audience Analysis

continued on following page

Table 1. Continued

2.3 Goal Analysis
2.4 Medium Analysis
2.5 Design approach
2.6 Organization
2.7 Methods and Strategies
2.7.01 Presentation
2.7.02 Exhibits
2.7.03 Demonstration
2.7.04 Drill and Practice
2.7.05 Tutorials
2.7.06 Games
2.7.07 Story Telling
2.7.08 Simulations
2.7.09 Role-playing
2.7.10 Discussion
2.7.11 Interaction
2.7.12 Modeling
2.7.13 Facilitation
2.7.14 Collaboration
2.7.15 Debate
2.7.16 Field Trips
2.7.17 Apprenticeship
2.7.18 Case Studies
2.7.19 Generative Development
2.7.20 Motivation
3. TECHNOLOGICAL
3.1 Infrastructure Planning (Technology Plan, Standards, Metadata, and Learning Objects)
3.2 Hardware
3.3 Software (LMS, Learning Content Management Systems (LCMS), and Enterprise Applications)
4. INTERFACE DESIGN
4.1 Page and Site Design
4.2 Content Design
4.3 Navigation
4.4 Accessibility
4.5 Usability Testing
5. EVALUATION
5.1 Assessment of Learners
5.2 Evaluation of Instruction and Learning Environments

continued on following page

Table 1. Continued

6. MANAGEMENT
6.1 Maintenance of Learning Environments
6.2 Distribution of Information
7. RESOURCE SUPPORT
7.1 Online Support
7.1.1 Instructional/Counseling Support
7.1.2 Technical Support
7.1.3 Career Counseling Services
7.1.4 Other Online Support Services
7.2 Resources
7.1.1 Online Resources
7.1.2 Offline Resources
8. ETHICAL CONSIDERATIONS
8.1 Social and Political Influence
8.2 Cultural Diversity
8.3 Bias
8.4 Geographical Diversity
8.5 Learner Diversity
8.6 Digital Divide
8.7 Etiquette
8.8 Legal Issues
8.8.1 Privacy
8.8.2 Plagiarism
8.8.3 Copyright

in the design of learning environments. That's the paradigm shift! In order to facilitate such a shift, and in response to the range of issues identified in my research, I created a *Framework for Virtual Learning*, also known as *a Framework for E-Learning* (Figure 2).

Through my research numerous factors were identified to help create a meaningful VLE, and many of these factors are systemically interrelated and interdependent. A systemic understanding of these factors can help us create meaningful VLEs. I clustered these factors into eight *dimensions* (institutional, pedagogical, technological,

Figure 2. The octagon framework for virtual learning

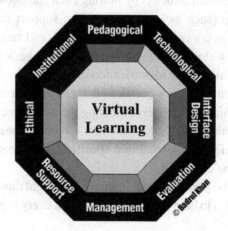

interface design, evaluation, management, resource support, and ethical considerations) to create the *Framework* (http://badrulkhan.com/framework). Designing interfaces for VLEs cannot be accomplished by addressing only the issues relevant to the interface design dimension. One must recognize the interrelationships and interconnectedness with the issues of the seven other dimensions of the Framework

Each dimension of the Framework is composed of a number of factors. Table 1 lists several factors under each dimension. It is important to note that the factors identified here are by no means exhaustive. As we learn more about VLEs, more factors may be added to the lists or existing factors may be modified based on research findings.

ISSUES OF VIRTUAL LEARNING ENVIRONMENTS

Each factor in Table 1 focuses on a specific aspect of a VLE. One could ask, *"What are the critical issues associated with many of these factors that can help in the design of meaningful VLEs?"*

There may be numerous issues within each factor of VLEs. These issues can be explored as *questions* that designers can ask themselves when planning a VLE. Each VLE project is unique. It is important to identify as many issues (in the form of questions) as possible by using the Framework's eight dimensions. One way to identify critical issues is by putting each stakeholder group (such as learner, instructor, support staff, etc.) at the center of the Framework and raising issues along the eight dimensions of the VLE. This allows the identification of many critical issues and answers questions that can help create a meaningful VLE. By repeating the same process for other stakeholder groups, a comprehensive list of issues related to a specific effort/ project can be compiled.

The purpose of the Framework's eight dimensions is to help focus and think about every aspect

of what is to be accomplished during the steps of the virtual learning design process. Therefore, it is important to review each of the eight dimensions of Framework, and explore the questions that should be asked with regard to the design of the VLE (Gamor, 2010; Gamor, 2011a), which can be a lesson, a course, or an entire program.

Since the focus of this book is on "interface design"—one of the eight dimensions of the Framework - let me present the following critical issues adopted from the *E-Learning Quick Checklist* (Khan, 2005a):

Page and Site Design

- Does the course use a consistent layout, including color, and the placement of titles and content on Web pages?
- Does the choice of graphics enhance the learners understanding of the site's purpose?
- Are colored graphics, if used, clearly interpretable when printed in black and white? (Note: Some users like to print out Web pages to read them later. With a black and white printer, a variety of different colors used in a graphic to distinguish critical parts and functions may not be visible in the print out.)
- Is the program attractive and appealing to the eye and soothing to the ear? (Note: Remember that different people may find different colors or fonts appealing.)
- Does the site use any icons that are difficult to remember? (Note: In using icons, we should ask "Is it clear what they represent?" "Do the icons support different cultures and languages?")

Content Design

- Check if the course uses any of the following ways to gain learner attention:
  - Novelty

- Animation
- Motion (e.g., animated GIFs)
- Captioned graphics
- Changes in brightness
- Contrast between object of interest and its surroundings
- Colors, sounds, and symbols that focus on specific content

- Check if the course uses any of the following ways to improve learner retention:
  - Sequenced screens
  - Meaningfully organized contents
  - Overviews
  - Consistent screen layout (consistent placement of title, graphic, textual contents, etc)
  - Chunked materials, presenting together when appropriate
  - Introductions and summaries
- Does the course follow the "one idea per paragraph" rule?
- Is the text chunked and presented in a way that enables scanning and comprehension? (Note: Throughout the course headings and sub-headings should be parallel, short, and logically connected so that readers can easily scan them.)
- How effectively is multimedia presentation components (e.g., text, graphics, animation, audio, video, etc.) used in the course to create meaningful learning?
- How effectively is the course content presented using proper grammar, punctuation, spelling and syntax (i.e., how are words put together to form phrases or sentences)?

Navigation

- Does the course provide structural aids (i.e., units, lessons, activities, etc.) to help learners navigate the course?
- Does the course provide a site map (i.e., a big picture of the course) to help learners navigate the course?

- To avoid bandwidth bottlenecks, are students asked to download large audio, video, and graphic files to their hard drives before the instructional events?
- Are all links clearly labeled, and do they serve an easily identified purpose, so that learners have enough information to know whether they should click a link?
- Do users have the option to "skip" or "turn off" any animation or media component in the course? (Note: They can be part of the design, but it is a client decision too.)
- Does the site contain so many internal links as to be distracting?
- Does the site contain so many external links as to be distracting?
- Does the course use a consistent color for both unvisited and visited links? (Note: The standard link colors such as 'blue' for unvisited links and 'reddish or purple' for visited links can be used on every page of the course site.)
- Is terminology used consistently throughout the course? (Note: If you use a term or word on one Webpage, use the same term throughout the course to avoid confusion.)
- Does the course indicate the size (e.g., 13k, 200k, etc.) of the multimedia files to be downloaded?
- Does the course have structural flexibility by providing students a choice of multiple pathways through the instruction?
- Does the course offer suggested pathways for the user? (Note: Learners tend to follow links in the course. Therefore, hyper-linking in pages should be well-thought out as they suggest pathways for users and should not lead to dead ends with no "Return" or "Home" buttons.)
- Does the course use consistent symbols and words as navigation aids? (Boshier, 1997)

Accessibility

- Is the VLE designed to be accessible by a wide user population?
- Are various accessibility barriers considered in the design of the course? (Note: VLEs can be run through accessibility testing software to repair barriers to accessibility and encourage compliance with existing accessibility guidelines, such as Section 508 http://www.section508.gov/ and the W3C's WCAG http://www.w3.org/TR/WCAG20/.)
- Does the course use alternate text for the images? (Note: The alternate text and descriptions for all non-text elements can be read aloud by software for synthesizing speech, and are essential for visually impaired learners.)
- Does the course provide captions or a script for audio content? (Note: People who cannot hear can read the audio content from the captions.)
- Can various screens of the course be resized to accommodate low-vision users? (Note: Even if the Web pages are designed to a specific screen size, the user can easily resize the screen by using the maximize or minimize option in the browser.)
- Are all the colors used on all screens of the course clearly distinguishable by the visually impaired?
- Can users who cannot use the mouse navigate through the e-learning materials using the keyboard instead?

Usability Testing

- Can users find answers to the most frequently asked questions on the course site within a reasonable amount of time?
- Do users know where they are and can navigate the site without guessing?

- Does the course use easy-to-understand terminology?
- Is the VLE designed so that users can easily get to a specific piece of content in no more than 3 clicks?

Designing interfaces for VLEs cannot be accomplished by addressing only issues raised based on interface design factors. As indicated earlier, many VLE factors encompassing the eight dimensions are systemically interrelated and interdependent. Therefore, for a meaningful VLE design, we must recognize the interrelationships and interconnectedness of these factors in addressing issues that impact learning.

Some VLE issues can be understood in terms of how they represent a distinctive overlap between two different dimensions. For example, with respect to the interface design and ethical factors related to designing VLEs for a cross-cultural population, consider following issues (in the form of questions) intertwined with two factors *4.3. Navigation* and *8.2. Cultural Diversity* (see Table 1)

- *When a page contains links to sites located in different countries with different cultures (where navigation or expression icons may differ from the learners' native culture), are there any cues on how to adjust to unfamiliar navigation or a different instructional environment?* (Boshier, 1997).
- *To improve cross-cultural verbal communication and avoid misunderstanding, does the VLE make an effort to reduce or avoid the use of jargon, idioms, ambiguous or cute humor, and spell out all acronyms on first appearance?* Jokes or humorous comments are easily misinterpreted and best avoided. For example, in Bangladesh, thumbs-up sign means to disregard someone but in other cultures, it means 'excellent or job well done'. These points need

to be noted while designing the interface (Khan, 2003).

- *To improve visual communication, is the VLE sensitive to the use of navigational icons or images?* For example, a pointing hand icon to indicate direction would violate a cultural taboo in certain African cultures by representing a dismembered body part. Using a right-pointing arrow for "next page" may mean "previous page" for Arabic and Hebrew language speakers, as they read from right to left.
- *Does the VLE use terms or words that may not be used by worldwide audiences?* For example, the term "sidewalk" is used in the US and "pavement/footpath" in the UK. When such a term is needed, we should include both forms for a diverse audience (e.g., Students should use the sidewalk [or pavement] rather than trample the grass.).
- *Is the VLE offered in a multilingual format?* Since text found in buttons or icons is harder to change, it is better not to include text within graphics when the VLE content may be translated into other languages.

Raise issues (in the form of questions) on all critical factors listed in Table 1 and explore how these issues impact VLE design. The purpose of raising many questions is to help designers think through their projects thoroughly. It doesn't mean that we will have all the answers or strategic solutions to all those issues, however discussing/addressing them makes us aware of what it takes to create a meaningful VLE. It is important to note that there might be other issues that we cannot think of or have not yet encountered. As more and more institutions offer VLEs worldwide, designers will become more knowledgeable about new issues within the eight dimensions of the VLE Framework (Table 1).

Various issues within the eight dimensions of the Framework were useful in several studies that were conducted to review virtual learning pro-

grams, resources, and tools (Bedard-Voorhees & Dawley 2008; Emami, H., Aqdasi, M. & Asousheh, A. 2008; Khan, Cataldo, Bennett & Paratore, 2006; Khan & Smith, 2006; Romiszowski, 2004; Singh, 2003; Chin & Kon, 2003; Kuchi, Gardner, & Tipton, 2003; Mello, 2002; Barry, 2002; Goodear, 2001; Khan, Waddill, & McDonald, 2001; Dabbagh, Bannan-Ritland, & Silc, 2001; Khan & Ealy, 2001; El-Tigi & Khan, 2001; Zhang, Khan, Gibbons, & Ni, 2001; Gilbert, 2002 and Kao, Tousignant, & Wiebe, 2000). More recent studies on the Framework can be found at: http://asianvu.com/digital-library/elearning/

To develop meaningful VLEs, interface design issues as well other issues encompassing the VLE Framework must be explored. The overall VLE design process must balance technical functionality and visual elements to create a system that is not only operational but also usable and adaptable to changing user needs.[4] Both theoretical and practical knowledge bases from learning design (e.g., Spiro et al., 2007; Wisher & Khan, 2010, Gamor; and Ally in this volume) and human-computer interaction (del Galdo & Nielsen, 1996; Hedberg et al, 2001; Krug, 2006) perspectives will guide the selection of appropriate learning strategies for the creation of meaningful VLEs. Several chapters in this book address such design issues and provide guidance and perspectives.

CONCLUSION

Advancement of Information and Communication Technologies (ICTs) with various emerging technologies in recent years has increasingly influenced the way we work, learn, and live. In every sector of our daily lives, we use many different technologies. With any new innovation, users of these emerging technologies will encounter challenges. As is the case with VLEs, learners or participants may encounter challenges in achieving their learning goals if the VLEs are not designed with the users' needs in mind.

To overcome such challenges, a comprehensive understanding of all factors and critical issues associated with them must be developed. Once the critical issues encompassing the various factors of VLEs are identified in its design, various learning strategies supported by appropriate learning theories and human–computer interaction (HCI) principles should be applied to provide meaningful learning environments with simple and efficient interfaces for learners to achieve their learning goals.

Designing open and distributed VLEs for globally dispersed learners is challenging; however, as more and more institutions offer VLE to learners worldwide, we will become more knowledgeable about what works and what does not work. We should try to accommodate the needs of diverse learners by asking critical questions along the eight dimensions of the VLE Framework. Questions may vary based on each VLE. The more factors within the eight dimensions of the Framework we explore, the more meaningful and supportive a learning environment we can create. Given our specific contexts, we may not be able to address all issues within the eight dimensions of the Framework, but we should address as many as we can in order to provide the most meaningful learning experiences for learners.

REFERENCES

Ally, M. (2011, in press). Designing mobile learning for the user. In Khan, B. H. (Ed.), *User interface design for virtual environments: Challenges and advances*. Hershey, PA: IGI Global.

Banathy, B. H. (1995). Developing a systems view of education. *Educational Technology, 35*(3), 53–57.

Barry, B. (2002). *ISD and the e-learning framework*. Retrieved January 24, 2003, from http://www.wit.ie/ library/webct/isd.html

Bedard-Voorhees, A., & Dawley, L. (2008). *Evaluating SL course experience: A learner's evaluation and faculty response*. Retrieved November 12, 2008, from http://www.aect.org/ SecondLife/08-archives.asp

Boshier, R., Mohapi, M., Moulton, G., Qayyum, A., Sadownik, L., & Wilson, M. (1997). Best and worst dressed web courses: Strutting into the 21st Century in comfort and style. *Distance Education, 18*(2), 327–348. doi:10.1080/0158791970180209

Calder, J., & McCollum, A. (1998). *Open and flexible learning in vocational education and training*. London, UK: Kogan Page.

Cheon, J., & Grant, M. M. (2009). Are pretty interfaces worth the time? The effects of user interface types on web-based instruction. *Journal of Interactive Learning Research, 20*(1), 5–33.

Chin, K. L., & Kon, P. N. (2003). Key factors for a fully online e-learning mode: A Delphi study. In G. Crisp, D. Thiele, I. Scholten, S. Barker & J. Baron (Eds.), *Interact, integrate, impact: Proceedings of the 20th Annual Conference of the Australasian Society for Computers in Learning in Tertiary Education*, Adelaide, 7-10 December 2003.

Dabbagh, N. H., Bannan-Ritland, B., & Silc, K. (2000). Pedagogy and Web-based course authoring tools: Issues and implications. In Khan, B. H. (Ed.), *Web-based training* (pp. 343–354). Englewood Cliffs, NJ: Educational Technology Publications.

Davies, A., & Dalgarno, B. (2008). Learning fire investigation the clean way: The virtual experience. In Hello! Where are you in the landscape of educational technology? *Proceedings ASCILITE Melbourne 2008*. Retrieved from http://www.ascilite.org.au/conferences/ melbourne08/procs/davies.pdf

del Galdo, E. M., & Nielsen, J. (Eds.). (1996). *International user interfaces*. New York, NY: John Wiley & Sons.

Dillenbourg, P., Schneider, D. K., & Synteta, P. (2002). Virtual learning environments. In A. Dimitracopoulou (Ed.), *Proceedings of the 3rd Hellenic Conference on Information & Communication Technologies in Education* (pp. 3-18). Kastaniotis Editions, Greece.

El-Tigi, M. A., & Khan, B. H. (2001). Web-based learning resources. In Khan, B. H. (Ed.), *Web-based training* (pp. 59–72). Englewood Cliffs, NJ: Educational Technology Publications.

Ellington, H. (1995). Flexible learning, your flexible friend. In Bell, C., Bowden, M., & Trott, A. (Eds.), *Implementing flexible learning* (pp. 3–13). London, UK: Kogan Page.

Emami, H., Aqdasi, M., & Asousheh, A. (2008). Key success factors in e-learning in medical education. *Journal of Medical Education, 12*(3), 81–89.

Gamor, K. (2010). What's an avatar? Identity, behavior, and integrity in virtual worlds for educational and business communication. In R. Proctor & K. Vu (Eds.), *Handbook of Human Factors in Web Design* (2nd edition). New York: CRC Press.

Gamor, K. (2011a). Signs and guideposts: Creating successful virtual world experiences. In G. Vincenti & J. Braman (Eds.) *Multi-User Virtual Environments for the Classroom: Practical Approaches to Teaching in Virtual Worlds*. Hershey, PA: IGI Global.

Gamor, K. (2011). Exploiting the power of persistence in virtual worlds. In Khan, B. H. (Ed.), *User interface design for virtual environments: Challenges and advances*. Hershey, PA: IGI Global.

Gilbert, P. K. (2002). *The virtual university an analysis of three advanced distributed leaning systems*. Retrieved February 24, 2004, from http:// gseacademic.harvard.edu/ ~gilberpa/homepage/ portfolio/ research/pdf/edit611.pdf

Goodear, L. (2001). *Cultural diversity and flexible learning*. Presentation of Findings 2001 Flexible Learning Leaders Professional Development Activity. South West Institute of TAFE. Australia. Retrieved February 24, 2004, from http://www. flexiblelearning.net.au/ leaders/events/pastevents/2001/ statepres01/papers/l_goodear.pdf

Hedberg, J. G., Brown, C., Larkin, J. L., & Agostinho, S. (2001). Designing practical websites for interactive training. In Khan, B. (Ed.), *Web-based training*. Englewood Cliffs, NJ: Educational Technology Publications.

Jones, M. G., & Farquhar, J. D. (1997). User interface design for Web-based instruction. In Khan, B. H. (Ed.), *Web-based instruction* (pp. 239–244). Englewood Cliffs, NJ: Educational Technology Publications.

Kao, D., Tousignant, W., & Wiebe, N. (2000). A paradigm for selecting an institutional software. In D. Colton, J. Caouette, & B. Raggad (Eds.), *Proceedings ISECON 2000, v 17* (p. 207). Philadelphia, PA: AITP Foundation for Information Technology Education.

Khan, B. H. (2003). Do we fit in the virtual education plan? *Daily Star, 4*(206). Retrieved November 23, 2010, from http://www.thedailystar.net/2003/ 12/24/d312241601108.htm

Khan, B. H. (2005). *Managing e-learning: Design, delivery, implementation and evaluation*. Hershey, PA: Information Science Publishing. doi:10.4018/978-1-59140-634-1

Khan, B. H. (2005a). *E-learning Quick checklist*. Hershey, PA: Information Science Publishing.

Khan, B. H. (Ed.). (2007). *Flexible learning in an information society*. Hershey, PA: Information Science Publishing.

Khan, B. H., Cataldo, L., Bennett, R., & Paratore, S. (2007). Obstacles encountered during e-learning. In Khan, B. H. (Ed.), *Flexible learning in an information society* (pp. 307–320). Hershey, PA: Information Science Publishing.

Khan, B. H., & Ealy, D. (2001). A framework for web-based authoring systems. In Khan, B. H. (Ed.), *Web-based training* (pp. 355–364). Englewood Cliffs, NJ: Educational Technology Publications.

Khan, B. H., & Smith, H. L. (2007). A program satisfaction survey instrument for online students. In Khan, B. H. (Ed.), *Flexible learning in an information society* (pp. 321–338). Hershey, PA: Information Science Publishing. doi:10.4018/9781599043258.ch030

Khan, B. H., & Vega, R. (1997). Factors to consider when evaluating a Web-based instruction course: A survey. In Khan, B. H. (Ed.), *Web-based instruction* (pp. 375–380). Englewood Cliffs, NJ: Educational Technology Publications.

Khan, B. H., Waddill, D., & McDonald, J. (2001). Review of Web-based training sites. In Khan, B. H. (Ed.), *Web-based training* (pp. 367–374). Englewood Cliffs, NJ: Educational Technology Publications.

Krug, S. (2006). *Don't make me think: A common sense approach to Web usability*. Berkeley, CA: New Riders.

Kuchi, R., Gardner, R., & Tipton, R. (2003). *A learning framework for information literacy and library instruction programs at Rutgers University Libraries. Recommendations of the Learning Framework Study Group*. Rutgers University Libraries.

Lohr, L., Falvo, D., Hunt, E., & Johnson, B. (2007). Improving the usability of web learning through template modification. In Khan, B. (Ed.), *Flexible learning* (pp. 186–197). Educational Technology Publications.

Maes, A., Van Geel, A., & Cozijn, R. (2006). Signposts on the digital highway. The effect of semantic and pragmatic hyperlink previews. *Interacting with Computers, 18*, 265–282. doi:10.1016/j.intcom.2005.05.004

Mello, R. (2002, June). 100 pounds of potatoes in a 25-pound sack: Stress, frustration, and learning in the virtual classroom. *Teaching With Technology Today, 8*(9). Retrieved February, 2004, from http://www.uwsa.edu/ttt/articles/mello.htm

Morales, T. (2002). *Virtual doctors: A growing trend avoid waiting at doctor's office*. Retrieved October 21, 2010, from http://www.cbsnews.com/stories/ 2002/06/21/earlyshow/ saturday/main513017.shtml

Pimentel, J. R. (1999). Design of net-learning systems based on experiential learning. *Journal of Asynchronous Learning Networks, 3*(2), 64-90. Retrieved June 11, 2002, from http://www.aln.org/publications/ jaln/v3n2/v3n2_pimentel.asp

Romiszowski, A. J. (2004). How's the e-learning baby? Factors leading to success or failure of an educational technology innovation. *Educational Technology, 44*(1), 5–27.

Russell, D. (Ed.). (2010). *Cases on collaboration in virtual learning environments: Processes and interactions*. Hershey, PA: IGI Global.

Saltzbert, S., & Polyson, S. (1995, September). Distributed learning on the World Wide Web. *Syllabus, 9*(1), 10–12.

Singh, H. (2003). Building effective blended learning programs. *Educational Technology, 44*(1), 5–27.

Spiro, R. J., Collins, B. P., & Ramchandran, A. R. (2007). Modes of openness and flexibility in cognitive flexibility hypertext learning environments. In Khan, B. H. (Ed.), *Flexible learning in an information society*. Hershey, PA: Information Science Publishing. doi:10.4018/9781599043258.ch002

Wann, J., & Mon-Williams, M. (1996). What does virtual reality NEED? Human factors issues in the design of three-dimensional computer environments. *International Journal of Human-Computer Studies, 44,* 829–847. doi:10.1006/ijhc.1996.0035

Williams, R., & Tollett, J. (2006). *The non-designer's web book: An easy guide to creating, designing, and posting your own website* (3rd ed.). Berkeley, CA: Peachpit Press.

Wisher, R., & Khan, B. H. (Eds.). (2010). *Learning on demand: ADL and the future of e-learning.* Alexandria, VA: Advanced Distributed Learning.

Zhang, J., Khan, B. H., Gibbons, A. S., & Ni, Y. (2001). Review of web-based assessment tools. In Khan, B. H. (Ed.), *Web-based training* (pp. 137–146). Englewood Cliffs, NJ: Educational Technology Publications.

ENDNOTES

1. http://en.wikipedia.org/wiki/Virtual_(computing)
2. http://download.oracle.com/javase/tutorial/java/concepts/interface.html
3. http://en.wikipedia.org/wiki/User_interface_design
4. http://www.facebook.com/pages/Interface-design/106221802749850?v=stream

Chapter 2
Understanding Evolution of Virtual Worlds Research:
A Content Analytic Approach

Manish Gupta
State University of New York at Buffalo, USA

Rui Chen
Ball State University, USA

ABSTRACT

Virtual worlds are emerging as important socio-technical artifacts in contemporary society. Improvements in technology – both hardware and software performance and costs – have facilitated fast emergence of complex and near-real experience virtual worlds. Recent years have seen an unprecedented growth in number of users and corporations joining these virtual worlds. They have enabled unique business models in the digital economy and cast far-reaching impacts on the society spanning literature to leisure. The chapter analyzes 106 journal articles published in last decade to uncover a shift in focus of research on different aspects of virtual worlds. The chapter identifies six dominant themes of research on virtual worlds and then content-analyzes extant literature to show how these themes have emerged in research on virtual worlds. This presents unique insights into perceived relative importance of impact of different aspects of virtual worlds on individuals and organizations alike.

INTRODUCTION

Virtual worlds (VWs) are Internet-based online communities where people interact with one another and to their online environments in a three-dimensional space. The number of individuals and companies joining virtual worlds has exponentially increased in recent years. A Gartner research report (2007) estimates that about 80 percent of active Internet users will be participating in one or more virtual worlds by the end of 2011. A report by Strategy Analytics (2008) predict that the percentage of registered users that will participate in virtual worlds will increase from 10% in 2008 to 27% by 2017, which will amount to about almost 1 billion users. For example, regis-

DOI: 10.4018/978-1-61350-516-8.ch002

Copyright © 2012, IGI Global. Copying or distributing in print or electronic forms without written permission of IGI Global is prohibited.

tered users in Linden Lab's "Second Life", one of the most popular virtual worlds, has grown from 230,000 residents in April of 2006 to 8.5 million residents in August of 2007 (Calongne and Bayne, 2007). There are several million inhabitants of these virtual worlds across globe – from every age group – that have made these virtual worlds their second home (Williams, et al., 2008; Woodcock, 2008). In addition to individuals and companies a large number of educational institutions and government agencies have also started to use the offerings of virtual worlds for their operations (Kim et al., 2008; Warmelink, 2009). A recent Gartner report predicts that 80% Fortune 500 companies and of individual Internet users will have presence in virtual worlds by 2011 (Wagner, 2007). Prior reports also reveal annual revenue of $100 million for Cyworld in 2005, $360 million for Entropia Universe in 2006, and $700 million for Second Life in 2007 (Tynan, 2007).

Virtual worlds have emerged as "*a rich and complex platform for research*" (Mennecke et al., 2007). Castronova (2006) suggests that large multiplayer games are "*social science research tools on the scale of the supercollider used by physicists*". They offer researchers a "*laboratory*" where people behave in ways that often are nearly identical to how they behave in the real world. As a consequence, virtual words offer scholars an interesting set of opportunities for examining social interaction, technology development, adoption and diffusion, business development and operations, and a vast array of other topics of interest to researchers in information systems and other branches of social science (Mennecke et al., 2007). Given the impact of virtual worlds on almost all aspects of our lives, it is critical that we understand how this technology can be leveraged in business and throughout society. In this paper, the authors review the status quo of the virtual worlds and discuss how this socio-technical artifact is transforming the real world. In particular, we examine the promise and potential

of virtual worlds and explore the challenges of the emergence of virtual worlds.

Many researchers are investigating the merits, costs and benefits that virtual worlds have as a "*field*" for experiments and how social, legal and businesses are impacted by virtual worlds. Recently, National Science Foundation awarded half-million-dollar grant to the university of Central Florida at Orlando and University of Illinois at Chicago to investigate and identify opportunities for social science and other researchers towards development of digital versions of real people using a wide array of available technologies including AI, imaging and virtual worlds (Tucker, 2007). Dr. John List, an economics professor, and Dr. David S. Abrams, an economist, have begun a project to find feasibility and other options of conducting social experiments in virtual worlds by observing people's behavior in virtual environments. Dr. List, who frequently conducts microeconomic field experiments, says conducting studies in virtual worlds are very cost-effective and convenient. However, he also says that it is still to be found out if people would behave similarly in online world as in real world for some of the tests that he is interested in (Foster, 2007).

It has become evident that the potential for research that these virtual worlds offer is unprecedented (Bainbridge, 2007). It has opened new methods and channels for research for social scientists and computer science researchers. Most of this can be attributed to the tremendously high rate of adoption of this phenomenon and to the nature and scope of socio-economic activities contained in them (Castranova, 2005). The study of social interactions and cultural dynamics has really come to closer observance than ever before (Noveck, 2004). Recognizing the importance of these social sites as strongly emerging social communities, academic research in and on them has tremendously increased (Ducheneaut et al, 2007; Steinkuehler and Williams, 2006). Researchers have looked into who are participating in these ventures, how and why aspects (Williams et al,

2008; Yee, 2006) on the interactions themselves. (Walther, 2006; Williams et al., 2006).

This chapter looks into a sample of virtual world research that is published in journals published by *Sciencedirect* database. Our assumption is that journals in other scientific databases such as Elsevier, IEEE, ACM, etc would also follow similar trends. We analyzed 106 journal articles in *Sciencedirect* database with publication date in last decade (2000-2010) that do research on virtual worlds. The chapter investigates the focus of research done on virtual worlds in the recent decade. The research has been categorized into six broad themes: social, legal and business, education and training, entertainment and utility, technology and security. We investigated how focus of overall research on virtual worlds has shifted during the decade using these six broad themes. The contributions of the chapter are manifold. First it provides a glimpse of a decade of research on virtual worlds in these six domains. Secondly, it shows how the focus of research has shifted across the themes which provides into insights into how importance of different aspects of virtual worlds have changed over time. For example, when virtual worlds were a new phenomenon and perhaps the end-user technology was not advanced or cheap enough for an efficient interactive experience due to limited resources on end-user machines, technology and security might have been the focus of most researchers. But as time passed and popularity of virtual worlds increased and as more users started to participate in these environments while technology also matured the focus of research shifted to understanding social interactions and to other areas. The organization of the chapter is as follows: The next section presents the background and related concepts. The third section presents discussions on the analysis of the results. The final section presents discussions and conclusions.

BACKGROUND AND CONCEPTS

Research on Virtual Worlds, in one way, has been going on since late 1980s by computer scientists and technologies in creating environments of virtual reality for training and rehabilitation programs. There are different streams of research that work on understanding and improving experiences within these virtual worlds. Most notably, involvement of social scientists, marketing and business researchers and information technology scientists have yielded most prolific research outputs.

Some of the most dominant themes of research have been on investigating why people are participating in virtual worlds, and mutual influence on the evolution of experiences. Last few years has seen a large number of companies starting their presence in virtual worlds which has facilitated development of research interests in understanding value creation for businesses and customers alike. The research has been categorized into six broad themes: social, legal and business, education and training, entertainment and utility, technology and security. Figure 1 illustrates these six high level themes and their constituent concepts. We have used this to explore the emerging areas of research and trend of virtual world research in last decade. For example, under theme of entertainment and utility, we have used keywords such as multimedia, games, uses, players, interactive, etc.

These keywords, for each theme, have been analyzed in extant literature to understand the trend.

Virtual worlds are bringing about fundamental and profound changes in patterns of social interaction, relationships and perceptions, which are allowing participants to communicate, establish relationships and acquaintances based on mutual interest rather than geographic proximity. They are eliminating social barriers caused by age, race, gender, geographical location and appearances. Virtual environments are providing a new social environment where youth are playing out issues such as sexuality, identity and a sense of

Figure 1. Emergent themes in extant virtual world's research

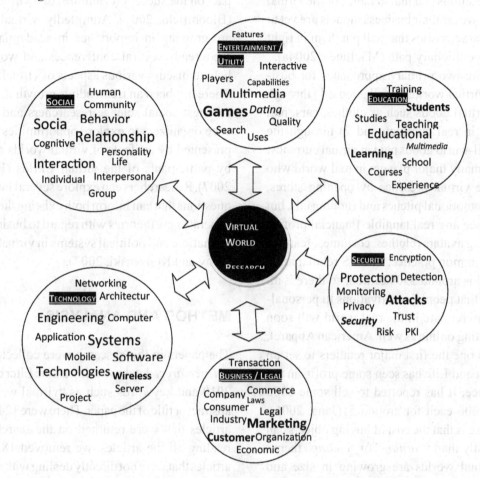

self-worth (Subrahmanyam et al., 2001). Also, Internet as has been considered one of the most important communication tools by adolescents (Gross, 2004).

It is estimated that the annual revenue for year 2009 will reach $12 billion (Greenemeier, 2007). Virtual commerce (the buying and selling of virtual goods) in Entropia is estimated to be around $1 million per day and the Universe had more than 580,000 registered accounts, and a 2006 turnover of more than $360 million (Furlonger, 2007). According to one estimate, at least 10 million people pay $15 and up a month to play these games (Hof, 2007). That's a big chunk of game operators' revenue. It has been found that gaming is not just a kids' thing. For example, 68 percent

of participants in major gaming worlds are over 35 (Cambridge, 2007)

Virtual commerce (the buying and selling of virtual goods) in Entropia is estimated to be around $1 million per day. This has made it a ripe environment for the development of financial frameworks and enterprises like lending and currency trading. Such virtual-world environments are equally fertile breeding grounds for less legitimate activity, like money laundering and tax evasion (Furlonger, 2007). Unfair financial gains and other advantages can be taken by online game players that are proficient in programming skills (MacInnes, 2004b). Even though it is evident that due to cheap labor costs, work ethics and acute business sense, Chinese virtual world operators are very profitable in their operations and maintenance of the virtual worlds. However their business models are yet to achieve characteristics that will put them in right business evolutionary path (MacInnes, 2004a).

There are two primary approaches for businesses in virtual worlds to sell goods: 1) through sales of virtual goods such as clothes, cars, real estate, etc in real currency and 2) through the sales of real-world goods paid in virtual currency. There are many major players in real world who have made virtual presence by opening stores, making promotional pitches and running ads, but are yet to see any real tangible financial profits. Customizing avatars (clothes, costumes, features etc.) is a common practice. The US retail market for apparel is around $300 billion, so there is all likelihood that people's motivations to personalize and differentiate in the real world will soon start reflecting online as well. American Apparel, which was one the first major retailers to set up shop in Second Life has seen some profits in the virtual space. It has reported to sell some 2000 items in 2006 each for around $1(Jana, 2006). The premise is that the cost of buying objects can be less costly than "*earning*" or "*coding*" them.

As virtual worlds are growing in size and population, high-stakes legal issues are constantly being raised. Virtual worlds have been the subject of legal scholarship to explore the applicability and legality of offline laws of property, taxation, crime, contract, and intellectual property. As more people are participating in virtual worlds, there is an increase in litigations and debates on the governance structure and on the questions such as to which extent the real-world laws should affect virtual worlds. Virtual worlds have brought to fore some very profound potential social, economic, ethical and policy implications that require further research and pose a lot of questions. Researchers rarely have the opportunity to watch systems emerge endogenously with the potential to succeed or fail. Additionally, there are opportunities to advise and inform the rules afforded to a virtual world and observe their im-

pact on the success (or failure) of a virtual world (Bloomfield, 2007). Admittedly, virtual worlds are growing in importance in academia. There are already several conferences and workshops held to discuss various aspects of virtual worlds. There has been an tremendous growth in interest amongst social science researchers and conference organizers to explore opportunities that are presented by artifacts of virtual worlds and also by participants of the virtual worlds (Herman, 2007). Researchers can explore several intriguing questions that can inform both existing theory and generate new theories with regard to business, information, and political systems in virtual worlds (Bray and Konsynski, 2007).

METHOD AND ANALYSIS

The papers in this research were collected from *Sciencedirect* database using a time filter of 2000-2010 and keywords such as "virtual worlds" in abstract or title of the paper. There were 124 journal articles that were returned on the search. After reading all the articles, we removed 18 journal articles that were not directly dealing with research on one or more aspects of virtual worlds. This left us with 106 journal articles in a span of 11 years including 2010. The journals included *Information & Management, European Management Journal, Decision Support Systems, Information Sciences, Computer Fraud & Security* and *Computer Communications* amongst others. Our assumption here is that the sample we collected from *Sciencedirect* database is representative of publications in other premier information systems related databases and journals. Over the years, we see (Figure 2) that the number of publications per year has consistently increased ($R^2 = 0.84$). We have extrapolated the numbers for 2010. As we can see in Figure 2, the 2000 only had 2 papers while in 2010, it has increased ten-fold to 22 (extrapolated).

The trend-line also shows a consistent growth in number of publications over years in last decade.

Figure 2. Number of publications from 2000 to 2010

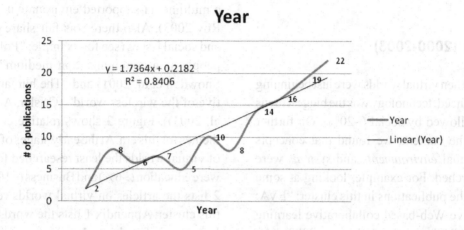

For our analysis we created three clusters for 11 years for our content analysis. We used *atlas.ti* version 6.0 to run content analysis on these three clusters of papers. Cluster 1 is for papers published between 2000 and 2003, cluster 2 for papers between 2004 and 2007; and cluster 3 for papers between 2008 and 2010 (including the years mentioned). On running content analysis on each cluster for word frequency, we uncovered broad themes for each cluster. We categorized these keywords in six themes as (i) social, (ii) legal and business, (iii) education and training, (iv) entertainment and utility, (v) technology and (vi) security. Certain keywords were categorized together into these six themes. Table 1 lists the keywords we used for each research theme. Next

Table 1. Keywords for each research theme

Research Theme	Keywords
SOCIAL	ACTIVITY, AVATAR, BEHAVIOR, BEHAVIORAL, CHILD, COGNITIVE, COLLABORATION, COLLABORATIVE, COMMUNICATION, COMMUNITY, ENVIRONMENT, EXPERIENCE, GROUP, HUMAN, INDIVIDUAL, INFLUENCE, INTERACTION, INTERACTIVE, LANGUAGE, LIFE, MEMBERS, NETWORK, PEERS, PEOPLE, PERSONAL, PERSONALITY, PRIVATE, PUBLIC, RELATIONSHIP, RIGHTS, ROLE, RULES, SOCIAL, SOCIETY, TEAM, TOOL
LEGAL & BUSINESS	BUSINESS, BUYER, COMMERCE, COMMERCIAL, COMPANIES, CONSUMER, COURT, CUSTOMER, ECONOMIC, FIRM, INDUSTRY, JURISDICTION, LAW, LEGAL, MANUFACTUR, MARKET, MARKETING, MEDIA, OPERATIONS, ORGANIZATION, PAYMENT, PRICE, PRODUCT, PRODUCTION, PUBLIC, TRANSACTION
EDUCATION & TRAINING	COURSE, EDUCATION, EDUCATIONAL, EXPERIENCE, KNOWLEDGE, LEARNING, MULTIMEDIA, SCHOOL, STUDENT, STUDY, SURVEY, TEACHING, TRAINING, VIDEO
SECURITY	ACCESS, ANONYMITY, ATTACK, ATTACKER, CONTROL, COPYRIGHT, CRIMINAL, DETECTION, ENCRYPTION, ID, MONITORING, PRIVACY, PROTECTION, REPUTATION, RISK, SECURE, SECURITY, TRUST
ENTERTAINTMENT & UTILITY	AVATAR, CAPABILITIES, CHARACTERISTIC, CHAT, DESIGN, EXPERIENCE, FEATURES, GAME, INDIVIDUAL, INTERACTION, INTERACTIVE, MEDIA, MULTIMEDIA, PLAYER, QUALITY, SEARCH, TOOL, USE, USEFUL, USER, VIDEO, VISUAL, VIDEO, VISUAL
TECHNOLOGY	APPLICATION, ARCHITECTURE, COMMUNICATION, COMPONENTS, COMPUTER, COMPUTING, DESIGN, DEVELOPMENT, DISTRIBUTED, ENGINEERING, IMPLEMENTATION, INTERFACE, IP, MODEL, NETWORK, NETWORKING, PERFORMANCE, PLATFORM, PROJECT, PROTOCOL, REQUIREMENTS, SERVER, SERVICE, SIMULATION, SOFTWARE, SYSTEM, TECHNICAL, TECHNOLOGIES, WIRELESS

we look at each cluster in detail and the dominant themes.

Cluster 1 (2000-2003)

In this era, when virtual worlds were just beginning to get introduced, technology was the biggest focus (~35%), followed by social (~20%). On further analyzing the content, we found that concepts such as virtual *environments* and *systems* were most researched. For example, looking at some of titles of the publications in this cluster: "EVA: an interactive Web-based collaborative learning environment" (Sheremetov and Arenas 2002), "An Internet virtual reality collaborative environment for effective product design" (Kan, Duffy et al. 2001), "A Web-based nomadic computing system" (Kindberg and Barton 2001) and "CyberCAD: a

collaborative approach in 3D-CAD technology in a multimedia-supported environment" (Tay and Roy 2003). Also there was fair share of human and social issues (see for example: "Pollen: using people as a communication medium" (Glance, Snowdon et al. 2001) and "The human perspective of the wireless world" (Crisler, Anneroth et al. 2003)). Figure 3 shows relative coverage of themes for this era. At the early stages of evolution of virtual worlds the least researched focus areas were education (~6%) and Business (~10%). Table 2 lists the articles on virtual worlds research in this cluster. Appendix 1 lists the words and their frequenceis for cluster 1.

There were other online systems that could have considered virtual worlds for a long time before this cluster's time, but it was around year 2000 that the "*systems achieved a superior level*

Figure 3. Research Focus areas for cluster 1

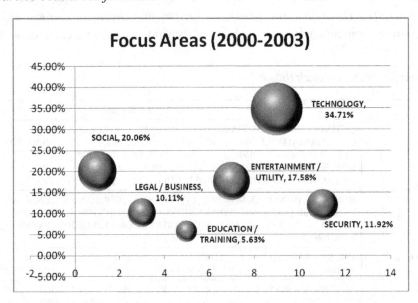

Table 2. Cluster 1 articles

Cluster 1 (2000 – 2003)
(Mott 2000; Peppard 2000; Saini, Saxena et al. 2000; Tibau 2000; Tomlinson 2000; Epstein and Klinkenberg 2001; Feridun and Krause 2001; Glance, Snowdon et al. 2001; Kan, Duffy et al. 2001; Kindberg and Barton 2001; Kotha, Rajgopal et al. 2001; Stuurman and Wijnands 2001; Yapp 2001; Hayes 2002; Prastacos, Söderquist et al. 2002; Saxby 2002; Sheremetov and Arenas 2002; Taxén and Naeve 2002; van Dam, Laidlaw et al. 2002; Crisler, Anneroth et al. 2003; Li, Khoo et al. 2003; Mohr 2003; Phan 2003; Tay and Roy 2003; Tewari, Youll et al. 2003)

of realism, opening up the way for new applications" (Komosinski, 2000; pp214). The technological advancements in computing artifacts such as communications and hardware significantly facilitated emergence of such systems. With the introduction of newer virtual worlds with enhanced performance, a wider range of applications and demands for next better offerings started to pour in. One element that is considered to be one of the biggest achievements in evolution of virtual worlds was the creation of natural and more relateable environments and interactive mechanisms (Maes, 1995; Reynolds, 1987), which was previously restricted due to absence of supporting hardware and models (Ficici and Pollack, 1998a, 1998b). This was the era when new commercial virtual world forms such as *There.com*, *Project Entropia* and *The Sims Online* seem were introduced to the world to compete with existing other new massively multi-player role-playing game worlds such as *Eve*, *Star Wars Galaxies*, *Neocron*, *Shadowbane*.

Cluster 2 (2004-2007)

This period witnessed a relatively significant increase in number of publications, around 60% more journal articles in the *Sciencedirect* database. The one focus area that saw the most growth was *legal and business* in which the content analysis reveals about 40% more coverage in the papers of this cluster. During these four years, due to immense adoption in the preceding years of cluster 1, the companies started to realize the benefits that these alternate worlds have to offer for almost all segments of their customer base. By this time, the worlds have matured and expanded enough for every age and economic group. It started to increasingly become an important channel for companies to communicate with existing and potential customers. These worlds provided businesses with newer and unique ways to allow customers to interact with their products and services (Lui et al., 2007, pp 77), while greatly

enhancing their knowledge about the products and services. These worlds gradually became great locations for companies to favorably showcase their new offerings while improving their brand reputation (Li et al., 2002; Suh and Lee 2005). The e-commerce tremendously benefited by the 3D simulated environments where customers spent time learning about new products and services (Bray and Konsynski 2007; Hemp 2006). By the end of this era companies even started accepting orders in virtual worlds for physical goods and services thereby supplementing and extending their business activities (Hof 2006). These virtual Worlds were, in turn, were making money from participation from individuals and companies. However, the leading virtual worlds of this cluster such as Active Worlds, Entropia Universe, There, Second Life and World of Warcraft had different revenue models. Some required a subscription fees (example World of Warcraft) while others made money by selling virtual goods or taking commission from the sales of virtual artifacts (example Second Life).

This is further supported by number of currency exchanges that are available. Increasing transactions in virtual currency mandates the existence of an exchange rate (Yamaguchi, 2004) that serves as an economic forum for exchanges and incentives. Not surprisingly, allowing in-world currency to be exchanged for real world currency has profound implications for the world operators' strategies (Lehdonvirta, 2005) and for the development of the virtual worlds themselves. Many of the well-known companies jumped on the back wagon to leverage the rising trend. There are more than 80 companies that have started to venture online for their brand presence, including Visa Europe, which is the latest one, (Rubach, 2007), Daimler-Chrysler, Coca-Cola, Nissan, IBM, H&R Block, and Toyota. While discussions on entertainment and educational aspects of virtual worlds pretty much remained the same as previous cluster, focus on technological aspects was reduced the most of all focus areas. It reduced from around 35% to 30%,

Figure 4. Research focus areas for cluster 2

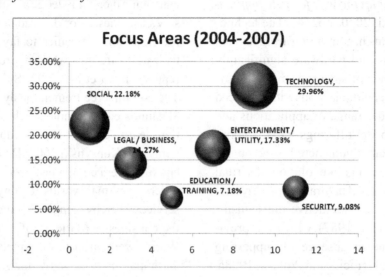

which indicated that while technology remained the biggest discussion theme in these last eight years for the two clusters, its share decreased the most. Figure 4 shows the relative share of different focus areas in this cluster, Appendix 2 details the frequency of words for each area; Table 3 lists the papers that were included in this period.

Cluster 3 (2008-2010)

Consistent with the increasing trend of importance of virtual worlds, this most recent period of two and an half years shown a consistent increase in number of publications in the area of virtual worlds, which increased by around 55% despite having fewer years. The most important trend and emergence was of social issues that sprung

to the topmost theme on virtual worlds research, which increased by 27% over previous period. Virtual worlds are bringing about fundamental and profound changes in patterns of social interaction, relationships and perceptions, which are allowing participants to communicate, establish relationships and acquaintances based on mutual interest rather than geographic proximity. They are eliminating social barriers caused by age, race, gender, geographical location and appearances. Virtual environments are providing a new social environment where youth are playing out issues such as sexuality, identity and a sense of self-worth (Subrahmanyam et al., 2001). Also, Internet as has been considered one of the most important communication tools by adolescents (Gross, 2004).

Table 3. Cluster 2 articles

Cluster 2 (2004 – 2007)
(Chen and Tan 2004; Ferreira and Raffler 2004; Hock Soon and Sourin 2004; Liu, Marchewka et al. 2004; Ong and Mannan 2004; Vahidov and Kersten 2004; Chun and Kim 2005; Çoban and Seçme 2005; Deveci 2005; Kimura and Kanda 2005; Liu, Marchewka et al. 2005; Mania and Robinson 2005; Rust, Kannan et al. 2005; Saha and Marvin 2005; Tahvanainen, Welch et al. 2005; Woerner and Woern 2005; Zhu and Chen 2005; Chen, Huang et al. 2006; Dai, Li et al. 2006; Forte and Power 2006; Kesdogan and Palmer 2006; Kierkegaard 2006; Nguyen, Safaei et al. 2006; Ta and Zhou 2006; Brenton, Hernandez et al. 2007; Contarello and Sarrica 2007; de Sena Caires 2007; Gorge 2007; Hansen, Lowry et al. 2007; Norden and Guo 2007; Pouliquen, Bernard et al. 2007; Qiu, Kok et al. 2007; Salomann, Dous et al. 2007; Saxby 2007; Thatcher, Loughry et al. 2007; Wang 2007; Zhang, Gong et al. 2007)

Figure 5. Research focus areas for cluster 3

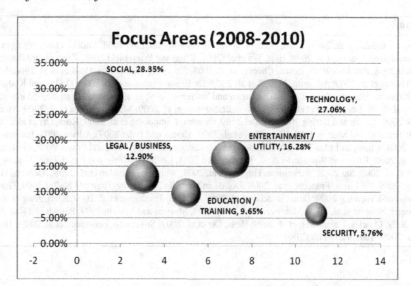

This clearly underscores the emergence of social aspects of virtual worlds and interactions therein in virtual worlds research. Technology continued to remain a major theme, but it also continued to decrease as last period. Business, entertainment and security also decreased by a little margin. Role of educational and training issues in the virtual worlds increased by almost 35% from previous era. This helps us show that companies and universities have actively started to look up to virtual worlds to hold training sessions and conferences. Researchers have also begun to leverage the benefits that these worlds provide in conducting instructional and educational studies. Virtual worlds make lives of educators easier by simplifying and representing *"the increasingly complex and interconnected global society in which they live and work"* (Moore et al., 2007, pp 46), while allowing multiple students to collaborate on the same issue or problem (Antonacci and Modaress, 2005, pp 5). They also allow educators to incorporate experiential and student-centered learning practices into the classroom. At the same time, researchers have ventured into research from domains of business, education and social sciences (Messinger et al., 2009). Examples that strengthen the argument that virtual

worlds are gaining momentum in research community may include:

- The Special issue on "New Ventures in Virtual Worlds," MIS Quarterly, 2008
- A Panel of "Second Life and other Virtual Worlds: A Roadmap for Research" at International Conference on Information Systems 2007, Montreal, Canada 2007
- The Special issue on Virtual Worlds, Database for Advances in Information Systems; Nov 2007; 38, 4
- Virtual Worlds Fall Conference and Expo, October 10 - 11, 2007, San Jose Convention Center in San Jose, California.
- Virtual Worlds Forum Europe 2007, October 23-26, 2007, London, UK.

As a consequence, virtual words offer scholars an interesting set of opportunities for examining social interaction, technology development, adoption and diffusion, business development and operations, and a vast array of other topics of interest to researchers in information systems and other branches of social science (Mennecke et al., 2007).

Table 4. Cluster 3 articles

Cluster 3 (2008 – 2010)
(Adrian 2008; Baldassarri, Cerezo et al. 2008; Chan, Hu et al. 2008; Chang and Man Law 2008; Enders, Hungenberg et al. 2008; Forte and Power 2008; Germanakos, Tsianos et al. 2008; Hsia, Wu et al. 2008; Khan and Wierzbicki 2008; Kierkegaard 2008; Lo 2008; Morse and Raval 2008; Nijholt 2008; Patrikios 2008; Rosen, Cheever et al. 2008; Sai 2008; Walkerdine, Hughes et al. 2008; Walvoord, Redden et al. 2008; Aalberts, Hames et al. 2009; Atkinson, Furnell et al. 2009; De Lucia, Francese et al. 2009; Dodds and Ruddle 2009; Eröz-Tuga and Sadler 2009; Gómez Hidalgo, Sanz et al. 2009; Hanwu and Yueming 2009; Jara, Candelas et al. 2009; Jarmon, Traphagan et al. 2009; Kleij, Jong et al. 2009; Lee, Kozar et al. 2009; Messinger, Stroulia et al. 2009; Mingozzi, Stea et al. 2009; Morgan and Marvin 2009; Parakh and Kak 2009; Piazza and Bering 2009; Poullet 2009; Quarles, Lampotang et al. 2009; Ross, Orr et al. 2009; Silverston, Fourmaux et al. 2009; Thelwall and Marvin 2009; Woo, Choi et al. 2009; Yaman and Polat 2009)(Adrian 2008; Baldassarri, Cerezo et al. 2008; Chan, Hu et al. 2008; Chang and Man Law 2008; Enders, Hungenberg et al. 2008; Forte and Power 2008; Germanakos, Tsianos et al. 2008; Hsia, Wu et al. 2008; Khan and Wierzbicki 2008; Kierkegaard 2008; Lo 2008; Morse and Raval 2008; Nijholt 2008; Patrikios 2008; Rosen, Cheever et al. 2008; Sai 2008; Walkerdine, Hughes et al. 2008; Walvoord, Redden et al. 2008; Aalberts, Hames et al. 2009; Atkinson, Furnell et al. 2009; De Lucia, Francese et al. 2009; Dodds and Ruddle 2009; Eröz-Tuga and Sadler 2009; Gómez Hidalgo, Sanz et al. 2009; Hanwu and Yueming 2009; Jara, Candelas et al. 2009; Jarmon, Traphagan et al. 2009; Kleij, Jong et al. 2009; Lee, Kozar et al. 2009; Messinger, Stroulia et al. 2009; Mingozzi, Stea et al. 2009; Morgan and Marvin 2009; Parakh and Kak 2009; Piazza and Bering 2009; Poullet 2009; Quarles, Lampotang et al. 2009; Ross, Orr et al. 2009; Silverston, Fourmaux et al. 2009; Thelwall and Marvin 2009; Woo, Choi et al. 2009; Yaman and Polat 2009).

CONCLUSIONS AND DISCUSSIONS

It is evident and not surprising that virtual worlds are increasingly becoming popular amongst all cross-sections of the populace, individuals and organizations alike. Improvements in technology – both hardware and software performance and costs – have facilitated fast emergence of complex and near-real experience virtual worlds. There are anticipated several million users of these worlds. It is not just individuals that are joining these worlds, but many real multinational companies have extended their business services to customers through virtual worlds (Salomon 2007). For example, IBM and Cisco have established a customer service centre in one of the most popular virtual world, *Second Life, where* customers can evaluate products and services, get technical help and chat with company representatives, amongst others (Hutcheon, 2007). Due to this, in recent years, they have received significant attention from the businesses and from scholars from almost all disciplines.

There is virtually a virtual world for every aspect of human life including owning a pet, relaxing, vacationing, etc. This has helped increased number of virtual worlds tremendously. Not any longer are the virtual worlds considered only as 3D multiplayer games or chat rooms. They have emerged as a powerful tool for individuals, businesses, governments and educators to further their interests. This has led to increase in research on different phenomena of virtual worlds including users' interaction with the environments, business aspects, security issues, entertainment values, technological challenges and innovations. We looked at over a decade of published research articles in *ScienceDirect* database to explore trends in research focus areas in virtual worlds. We created three time-based clusters from 106 articles published between 2000 and 2010 and carried out content analysis of each cluster to understand the major research themes (six themes as identified and discussed earlier) for each cluster. As we can see in Figure 6, Social aspects of virtual worlds increased the most during last decade, while with improving technologies, the focus on technology decreased the most as did security which often tends to be major issue with newer technologies and experiences and tend to fade out as issues are resolved. Figure 6 shows trend in other themes as well where we observe that research on entertainment and educational aspects remained quite constant.

The most impressive increase in research activity we see in virtual worlds is on education

Figure 6. Trends in research themes during last decade

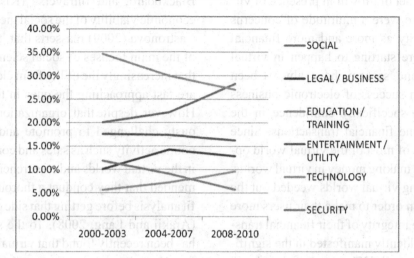

and training that has increased by around 71% in last decade (Figure 7). Numerous educational institutions have opened campuses in these worlds over last few years and the rate at which new ones are opened is very high. Virtual worlds offer unique benefits for training and instructional programs such as flexible spaces for learning, investigation, collaboration and exploration which lend highly effective learning environments. In addition, there are several social aspects of virtual worlds that are novel to study in virtual worlds. So it is not surprising to see that more researchers are studying this aspect of virtual worlds than before. For

the same duration, another emerging trend is that fewer researchers are looking into trust and security issues.

Looking at the future possibilities of the two of the most popular virtual worlds, Second Life and World of Warcraft, Kock (2008) concluded that much talked about and reported benefits of virtual worlds are justified, but that the evolution and reliability of the supporting technology has a long way to go before it matches with the requirements and demand for much wider adoption. More recent research has suggested potential of these worlds for marketing and advertizing (Edery,

Figure 7. Changes in research focus

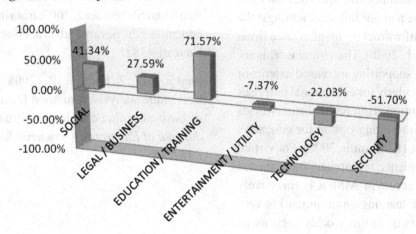

2008). At the onset of growth in presence of virtual worlds there were a multitude of concerns regarding security as more and more financial transactions were starting to happen in virtual worlds. Trust and security have always been major factors in success of electronic business and commerce, specifically confidence in the security of online financial transactions. Since revenue models of most of the virtual world operators included making money in virtual worlds, operators running virtual worlds weeded out the security issues in order to make their users more confident on the integrity of their financial transactions. This evidently manifested in the significant drop, of around 52% over last decade, in discussions in extant literature on security and trust issues. Overall, this study effectively shows how, over most recent decade, research focus has shifted (redistributed) amongst six dominant themes, which presents an interesting story on evolution of the virtual worlds themselves. Over the years we have witnessed, as is also supported by the literature review of this study, that several focus areas that were prominent during a certain period de-emphasized. There have also been several issues that arose during most recent stages of adoption such as technical issues surrounding support for high bandwidth and in-world navigational challenges and difficulties around manipulation and development of avatars (Warburton, 2008; Warburton and Perez-Garcia, 2009). Push for open standards and specifications has also come forth as a major initiative amongst the developers and infrastructure maintenance firms (Livingstone, et al., 2008). The virtual worlds are also looking into supporting increased extents of granularity, particularly for educational purposes that has seen a continued interest in virtual worlds as a viable and interesting option for educators and students alike (Kirriemuir, 2008). For virtual learning environments, researchers have started to use a newer acronym MMOLE (massively multi-user online learning environment) to represent environments within worlds such as as

Blackboard, and Intraverse (Kish, 2007). On economic viability of the social media initiatives, Castronova (2009) reasserts that it has been one of the main focuses of social scientiets; and also that increasingly the utility from electronic goods are fast approaching the ones in the real world. However, despite that, organizations are continuously challenged to promote and expand economic activity such as sales and contract entering in the virtual worlds and researchers have recommended that they conduct a thorough cost-benefit analysis before getting that side of the business (Arakji and Lang, 2008). To the same effect, it has been recently found that virtual worlds suffer from a very low conversion rate (conversion from visits to sales) of around 2-3% (Eisenberg, 2008).

REFERENCES

Aalberts, R., & Hames, D. (2009). The common law and its impact on the Internet. In *Advances in computers* (*Vol. 77*, pp. 299–318). Elsevier. doi:10.1016/S0065-2458(09)01208-X

Adrian, A. (2008). No one knows you are a dog: Identity and reputation in virtual worlds. *Computer Law & Security Report*, 24(4), 366–374. doi:10.1016/j.clsr.2008.03.005

Antonacci, D., & Moderass, N. (2005, February 16). *Second Life: The educational possibilities of a massively multiplayer virtual world (MMVW)*. Retrieved September 2, 2007, from http://connect. educause.edu/library/ abstract/SecondLifeThe-Educati/43821

Arakji, R. Y., & Lang, K. R. (2008). Avatar business value analysis: A method for the evaluation of business value creation in virtual commerce. *Journal of Electronic Commerce Research*, 9(3), 207–218.

Atkinson, S., & Furnell, S. (2009). Securing the next generation: enhancing e-safety awareness among young people. *Computer Fraud & Security*, (7): 13–19. doi:10.1016/S1361-3723(09)70088-0

Bainbridge, W. (2007). The scientific research potential of virtual worlds. *Science, 317*, 472–476. doi:10.1126/science.1146930

Baldassarri, S., & Cerezo, E. (2008). Maxine: A platform for embodied animated agents. *Computers & Graphics, 32*(4), 430–437. doi:10.1016/j.cag.2008.04.006

Bloomfield, R. J. (May 25, 2007). *Worlds for study: Invitation - Virtual worlds for studying real-world business (and law, and politics, and sociology, and....)*. Retrieved from http://ssrn.com/abstract=988984

Bray, D. A., & Konsynski, B. (2007). *Virtual worlds, virtual economies, virtual institutions*. Retrieved from http://ssrn.com/abstract=962501

Brenton, H., & Hernandez, J. (2007). Using multimedia and Web3D to enhance anatomy teaching. *Computers & Education, 49*(1), 32–53. doi:10.1016/j.compedu.2005.06.005

Calongne, C., & Bayne, G. (2007). *Podcast: Using Second Life for immersive learning*. Retrieved September 2, 2007, from http://connect.EDUCAUSE.edu/blog/gbayne/podcastusingsecondli/44967 ((8/22/07)

Castronova, E. (2005). *Synthetic worlds: The business and culture of online games*. Chicago, IL: University of Chicago Press.

Castronova, E. (2006). On virtual economies. *The International Journal of Computer Game Research 3*(2). Retrieved December 18, 2009, from http://www.gamestudies.org/ 0302/castronova/

Castronova, E., Williams, D., Shen, C., Ratan, R., Xiong, L., Huang, Y., & Keegan, B. (2009). As real as real? Macroeconomic behavior in a large-scale virtual world. *New Media & Society, 11*(5), 685. doi:10.1177/1461444809105346

Chan, M.-C., & Hu, S.-Y. (2008). An efficient and secure event signature (EASES) protocol for peer-to-peer massively multiplayer online games. *Computer Networks, 52*(9), 1838–1845. doi:10.1016/j.comnet.2008.03.004

Chang, M. K., & Man Law, S. P. (2008). Factor structure for Young's Internet Addiction Test: A confirmatory study. *Computers in Human Behavior, 24*(6), 2597–2619. doi:10.1016/j.chb.2008.03.001

Chen, K.-T., & Huang, P. (2006). Game traffic analysis: An MMORPG perspective. *Computer Networks, 50*(16), 3002–3023. doi:10.1016/j.comnet.2005.11.005

Chen, L.-D., & Tan, J. (2004). Technology adaptation in e-commerce: Key determinants of virtual stores acceptance. *European Management Journal, 22*(1), 74–86. doi:10.1016/j.emj.2003.11.014

Chun, S.-H., & Kim, J.-C. (2005). Pricing strategies in B2C electronic commerce: Analytical and empirical approaches. *Decision Support Systems, 40*(2), 375–388. doi:10.1016/j.dss.2004.04.012

Çoban, O., & Seçme, G. (2005). Prediction of socio-economical consequences of privatization at the firm level with fuzzy cognitive mapping. *Information Sciences, 169*(1-2), 131–154. doi:10.1016/j.ins.2004.02.009

Contarello, A., & Sarrica, M. (2007). ICTs, social thinking and subjective well-being - The internet and its representations in everyday life. *Computers in Human Behavior, 23*(2), 1016–1032. doi:10.1016/j.chb.2005.08.013

Crisler, K., & Anneroth, M. (2003). The human perspective of the wireless world. *Computer Communications, 26*(1), 11–18. doi:10.1016/S1403-3664(02)00114-7

Dai, K., & Li, Y. (2006). An interactive web system for integrated three-dimensional customization. *Computers in Industry, 57*(8-9), 827–837. doi:10.1016/j.compind.2006.04.017

De Lucia, A., & Francese, R. (2009). Development and evaluation of a virtual campus on Second Life: The case of SecondDMI. *Computers & Education, 52*(1), 220–233. doi:10.1016/j.compedu.2008.08.001

de Sena Caires, C. D. (2007). Towards the interactive filmic narrative--Transparency: An experimental approach. *Computers & Graphics, 31*(6), 800–808. doi:10.1016/j.cag.2007.08.003

Deveci, H. A. (2005). Personal jurisdiction: Where cyberspace meets the real world - Part 1. *Computer Law & Security Report, 21*(6), 464–477. doi:10.1016/j.clsr.2005.09.003

Dodds, T. J., & Ruddle, R. A. (2009). Using mobile group dynamics and virtual time to improve teamwork in large-scale collaborative virtual environments. *Computers & Graphics, 33*(2), 130–138. doi:10.1016/j.cag.2009.01.001

Ducheneaut, N., Moore, R., & Nickell, E. (2007). Virtual third places: A case study of sociability in massively multiplayer games. *Computer Supported Cooperative Work, 16*, 129–166. doi:10.1007/s10606-007-9041-8

Edery, D. (2006). Reverse product placement in virtual worlds. *Harvard Business Review, 84*(12), 24.

Eisenberg, R. (2008). The average conversion rate: Is it a myth? *The ClickZ Network.* Retrieved from http:// www.clickz.com/ showPage.html?page=3628276

Enders, A., & Hungenberg, H. (2008). The long tail of social networking: Revenue models of social networking sites. *European Management Journal, 26*(3), 199–211. doi:10.1016/j.emj.2008.02.002

Epstein, J., & Klinkenberg, W. D. (2001). From Eliza to Internet: A brief history of computerized assessment. *Computers in Human Behavior, 17*(3), 295–314. doi:10.1016/S0747-5632(01)00004-8

Eröz-Tuga, B., & Sadler, R. (2009). Comparing six video chat tools: A critical evaluation by language teachers. *Computers & Education, 53*(3), 787–798. doi:10.1016/j.compedu.2009.04.017

Feridun, M., & Krause, J. (2001). A framework for distributed management with mobile components. *Computer Networks, 35*(1), 25–38. doi:10.1016/S1389-1286(00)00147-X

Ferreira, P., & Raffler, H. (2004). Introduction to the special issue. *Computers & Graphics, 28*(5), 623–624. doi:10.1016/j.cag.2004.06.003

Ficici, S. G., & Pollack, J. B. (1998a). Coevolving communicative behavior in a linear pursuer-evader game. In R. Pfeifer, B. Blumberg, & H. Kobayashi (Eds.), *Proceedings of the Fifth International Conference of the Society for Adaptive Behavior.* Cambridge, MA: MIT Press, 1998.

Ficici, S. G., & Pollack, J. B. (1998b). Challenges in coevolutionary learning: Arms-race dynamics, open-endedness, and mediocre stable states. In C. Adami, R. K. Belew, H. Kitano, & C. E. Talor (eds.), *Proceedings of the Sixth International Conference on Artificial Life.* Cambridge, MA: MIT Press, 1998.

Forte, D., & Power, R. (2006). Ten years in the wilderness, part III: Diogenes on the threshing floor. *Computer Fraud & Security,* (3): 8–12. doi:10.1016/S1361-3723(06)70320-7

Forte, D., & Power, R. (2008). Gazing into a crystal ball presents multiple instances of Déjà Vu: Should we just write a 2008: Year in review now? *Computer Fraud & Security*, (2): 16–19. doi:10.1016/S1361-3723(08)70028-9

Foster, A. L. (2007, July 6). Virtual worlds as social-science labs. *The Chronicle of Higher Education*, *53*(44), 25.

Furlonger, D. (2007, 11 April). Banking on virtual worlds: Threats and opportunities. *Gartner Research Article*. (Gartner ID Number: G00147743).

Gartner Research. (2007, April 24). *Gartner says 80 percent life in the virtual world by the end of 2011*. Retrieved from http://www.gartner.com/it/ page.jsp?id=503861

Germanakos, P., & Tsianos, N. (2008). Capturing essential intrinsic user behaviour values for the design of comprehensive web-based personalized environments. *Computers in Human Behavior*, *24*(4), 1434–1451. doi:10.1016/j.chb.2007.07.010

Glance, N., & Snowdon, D. (2001). Pollen: Using people as a communication medium. *Computer Networks*, *35*(4), 429–442. doi:10.1016/S1389-1286(00)00183-3

Gómez Hidalgo, J. M., & Sanz, E. P. (2009). *Web content filtering. Advances in computers* (*Vol. 76*, pp. 257–306). Elsevier.

Gorge, M. (2007). Security for third level education organizations and other educational bodies. *Computer Fraud & Security*, (7): 6–9.

Greenemeier, L. (2007, July 16). *Virtual worlds, real cheaters*. InformationWeek.

Gross, E. F. (2004). Adolescent Internet use: What we expect, what teens report. *Journal of Applied Developmental Psychology*, *25*, 633–649. doi:10.1016/j.appdev.2004.09.005

Hansen, J. V., & Lowry, P. B. (2007). Genetic programming for prevention of cyberterrorism through dynamic and evolving intrusion detection. *Decision Support Systems*, *43*(4), 1362–1374. doi:10.1016/j.dss.2006.04.004

Hanwu, H., & Yueming, W. (2009). Web-based virtual operating of CNC milling machine tools. *Computers in Industry*, *60*(9), 686–697. doi:10.1016/j.compind.2009.05.009

Hayes, D. L. (2002). Internet copyright: Advanced copyright issues on the Internet -- Part VIII. *Computer Law & Security Report*, *18*(1), 3–10. doi:10.1016/S0267-3649(02)00102-4

Hemp, P. (2006). Avatar-based marketing. *Harvard Business Review*, *84*(6), 48–57.

Herman Group. (2007, March 21). *The futurist*. Retrieved from www.wfs.org

Hock Soon, S., & Sourin, A. (2004). Guest editor's introduction. *Computers & Graphics*, *28*(4), 465–466. doi:10.1016/j.cag.2004.04.001

Hof, R. (2006, 1 May). My virtual life. Business Week. Retrieved October 19, 2009, from http://www.businessweek.com/ magazine/content/06_18/b3982001.htm

Hsia, T.-L., & Wu, J.-H. (2008). The e-commerce value matrix and use case model: A goal-driven methodology for eliciting B2C application requirements. *Information & Management*, *45*(5), 321–330. doi:10.1016/j.im.2008.04.001

Hutcheon, S. (2007, 24 August). IBM expands virtual world presence. *The Age*.

IBM's Institute for Business Value. (2007). *Leadership in a distributed world: Lessons from online gaming*.

Jana, R. (2006, June 27). American Apparel's virtual clothes. *Business Week Online*.

Jara, C. A., & Candelas, F. A. (2009). Real-time collaboration of virtual laboratories through the Internet. *Computers & Education, 52*(1), 126–140. doi:10.1016/j.compedu.2008.07.007

Jarmon, L., & Traphagan, T. (2009). Virtual world teaching, experiential learning, and assessment: An interdisciplinary communication course in Second Life. *Computers & Education, 53*(1), 169–182. doi:10.1016/j.compedu.2009.01.010

Kan, H. Y., & Duffy, V. G. (2001). An Internet virtual reality collaborative environment for effective product design. *Computers in Industry, 45*(2), 197–213. doi:10.1016/S0166-3615(01)00093-8

Kesdogan, D., & Palmer, C. (2006). Technical challenges of network anonymity. *Computer Communications, 29*(3), 306–324. doi:10.1016/j.comcom.2004.12.011

Khan, J. I., & Wierzbicki, A. (2008). Guest editors' introduction: Foundation of peer-to-peer computing. *Computer Communications, 31*(2), 187–189. doi:10.1016/j.comcom.2007.10.038

Kierkegaard, S. (2008). Cybering, online grooming and ageplay. *Computer Law & Security Report, 24*(1), 41–55. doi:10.1016/j.clsr.2007.11.004

Kierkegaard, S. M. (2006). Here comes the cybernators! *Computer Law & Security Report, 22*(5), 381–391. doi:10.1016/j.clsr.2006.07.005

Kim, H. M., Lyons, K., & Cunningham, M. A. (2008). Towards a theoretically-grounded framework for evaluating immersive business models and applications: Analysis of ventures in Second Life. *Journal of Virtual Worlds Research, 1*(1).

Kimura, T., & Kanda, Y. (2005). Development of a remote monitoring system for a manufacturing support system for small and medium-sized enterprises. *Computers in Industry, 56*(1), 3–12. doi:10.1016/j.compind.2004.11.001

Kindberg, T., & Barton, J. (2001). A Web-based nomadic computing system. *Computer Networks, 35*(4), 443–456. doi:10.1016/S1389-1286(00)00181-X

Kirriemuir, J. (2008). Second Life in higher education, medicine and health. *Health Information in the Internet, 64*(1), 6–8. Retrieved September 21, 2010, from http://hii.rsmjournals.com/cgi/content/abstract/64/1/6

Kish, S. (2007). *Second Life: Virtual worlds and the enterprise.* Retrieved September 21, 2010, from http://www.susankish.com/ susan_kish/ vw_secondlife.htm

Kleij, R. d., & Jong, A. D. (2009). Network-aware support for mobile distributed teams. *Computers in Human Behavior, 25*(4), 940–948. doi:10.1016/j.chb.2009.04.001

Kock, N. (2008). E-collaboration and e-commerce in virtual worlds: The potential of Second Life and World of Warcraft. *International Journal of e-Collaboration, 4*(3), 1–13. doi:10.4018/jec.2008070101

Komosinski, M. (2000). The world of framsticks: Simulation, evolution, interaction. *Proceedings of 2nd International Conference on Virtual Worlds*, Paris, France, July 2000, Springer-Verlag

Kotha, S., & Rajgopal, S. (2001). Reputation building and performance: An empirical analysis of the top-50 pure Internet firms. *European Management Journal, 19*(6), 571–586. doi:10.1016/S0263-2373(01)00083-4

Lee, Y., & Kozar, K. A. (2009). Avatar e-mail versus traditional e-mail: Perceptual difference and media selection difference. *Decision Support Systems, 46*(2), 451–467. doi:10.1016/j.dss.2007.11.008

Lehdonvirta, V. (2005). Real-money trade of virtual assets: New strategies for virtual world operators. *Proceedings of Future Play*, Michigan State University, 2005.

Li, H. R., Daugherty, T., & Biocca, F. (2002). Impact of 3-D advertising on product knowledge, brand attitude, and purchase intention: The mediating role of presence. *Journal of Advertising*, *31*(3), 43–57.

Li, J. R., & Khoo, L. P. (2003). Desktop virtual reality for maintenance training: An object oriented prototype system (V-REALISM). *Computers in Industry*, *52*(2), 109–125. doi:10.1016/S0166-3615(03)00103-9

Liu, C., & Marchewka, J. T. (2004). Beyond concern: A privacy-trust-behavioral intention model of electronic commerce. *Information & Management*, *42*(1), 127–142. doi:10.1016/j.im.2004.01.002

Liu, C., & Marchewka, J. T. (2005). Beyond concern--A privacy-trust-behavioral intention model of electronic commerce. *Information & Management*, *42*(2), 289–304. doi:10.1016/j.im.2004.01.003

Livingstone, D., Kemp, J., & Edgar, E. (2008). From multi-user virtual environment to 3D virtual learning environment. *Association for Learning Technology Journal*, *16*(3), 139–150. doi:10.1080/09687760802526707

Lo, S.-K. (2008). The impact of online game character's outward attractiveness and social status on interpersonal attraction. *Computers in Human Behavior*, *24*(5), 1947–1958. doi:10.1016/j.chb.2007.08.001

Lui, T.-W., Piccoli, G., & Ives, B. (2007). Marketing strategies in virtual worlds. *The DataBase for Advances in Information Systems*, *38*(4), 77–80.

MacInnes, I. (2004a). Dynamic business model framework for emerging technologies. *International Journal of Services Technology and Management*, *6*(1), 3–19. doi:10.1504/IJSTM.2005.006541

MacInnes, I. (2004b). *The implications of property rights in virtual worlds*. Paper presented at the Americas Conference on Information Systems, New York, NY. August 6–8.

Maes, P. (1995). Artificial life meets entertainment: Interacting with lifelike autonomous agents. In *Communications of the ACM: Special Issue on New Horizons of Commercial and Industrial AI*, *38*(11), 108-114. ACM Press.

Mania, K., & Robinson, A. (2005). An experimental exploration of the relationship between subjective impressions of illumination and physical fidelity. *Computers & Graphics*, *29*(1), 49–56. doi:10.1016/j.cag.2004.11.007

Mennecke, B. E., Roche, E. M., et al. (2007). *Second Life and other virtual words: A roadmap for research*. Twenty Eighth International Conference on Information Systems, Montreal, Canada.

Messinger, P. R., & Stroulia, E. (2009). Virtual world - Past, present, and future: New directions in social computing. *Decision Support Systems*, *47*, 204–228. doi:10.1016/j.dss.2009.02.014

Messinger, P. R., & Stroulia, E. (2009). Virtual worlds -- Past, present, and future: New directions in social computing. *Decision Support Systems*, *47*(3), 204–228. doi:10.1016/j.dss.2009.02.014

Mingozzi, E., & Stea, G. (2009). EuQoS: End-to-end quality of service over heterogeneous networks. *Computer Communications*, *32*(12), 1355–1370. doi:10.1016/j.comcom.2008.12.013

Mohr, W. (2003). The Wireless World Research Forum--WWRF. *Computer Communications*, *26*(1), 2–10. doi:10.1016/S1403-3664(02)00113-5

Moore, A., Fowler, S., & Watson, C. (2007, September/October). Active learning and technology: Designing change for faculty, students, and institutions. *EDUCAUSE Review, 42*(5), 42–61.

Morgan, G., & Marvin, V. Z. (2009). *Highly interactive scalable online worlds. Advances in computers* (*Vol. 76*, pp. 75–120). Elsevier.

Morse, E. A., & Raval, V. (2008). PCI DSS: Payment card industry data security standards in context. *Computer Law & Security Report, 24*(6), 540–554. doi:10.1016/j.clsr.2008.07.001

Mott, S. (2000). The second generation of digital commerce solutions. *Computer Networks, 32*(6), 669–683. doi:10.1016/S1389-1286(00)00024-4

Nguyen, C. D., & Safaei, F. (2006). Optimal assignment of distributed servers to virtual partitions for the provision of immersive voice communication in massively multiplayer games. *Computer Communications, 29*(9), 1260–1270. doi:10.1016/j.comcom.2005.10.003

Nijholt, A. (2008). Google home: Experience, support and re-experience of social home activities. *Information Sciences, 178*(3), 612–630. doi:10.1016/j.ins.2007.08.026

Norden, S., & Guo, K. (2007). Support for resilient peer-to-peer gaming. *Computer Networks, 51*(14), 4212–4233. doi:10.1016/j.comnet.2007.05.003

Noveck, B. (2004). Unchat: Democratic solution for a wired world. In Shane, P. (Ed.), *Democracy online: The prospects for democratic renewal through the Internet* (pp. 21–34). New York, NY: Routledge.

Ong, S. K., & Mannan, M. A. (2004). Virtual reality simulations and animations in a web-based interactive manufacturing engineering module. *Computers & Education, 43*(4), 361–382. doi:10.1016/j.compedu.2003.12.001

Parakh, A., & Kak, S. (2009). Online data storage using implicit security. *Information Sciences, 179*(19), 3323–3331. doi:10.1016/j.ins.2009.05.013

Patrikios, A. (2008). The role of transnational online arbitration in regulating cross-border e-business - Part I. *Computer Law & Security Report, 24*(1), 66–76. doi:10.1016/j.clsr.2007.11.005

Peppard, J. (2000). Customer relationship management (CRM) in financial services. *European Management Journal, 18*(3), 312–327. doi:10.1016/S0263-2373(00)00013-X

Phan, D. D. (2003). E-business development for competitive advantages: A case study. *Information & Management, 40*(6), 581–590. doi:10.1016/S0378-7206(02)00089-7

Piazza, J., & Bering, J. M. (2009). Evolutionary cyber-psychology: Applying an evolutionary framework to Internet behavior. *Computers in Human Behavior, 25*(6), 1258–1269. doi:10.1016/j.chb.2009.07.002

Pouliquen, M., & Bernard, A. (2007). Virtual hands and virtual reality multimodal platform to design safer industrial systems. *Computers in Industry, 58*(1), 46–56. doi:10.1016/j.compind.2006.04.001

Poullet, Y. (2009). Data protection legislation: What is at stake for our society and democracy? *Computer Law & Security Report, 25*(3), 211–226. doi:10.1016/j.clsr.2009.03.008

Prastacos, G., & Söderquist, K. (2002). An integrated framework for managing change in the new competitive landscape. *European Management Journal, 20*(1), 55–71. doi:10.1016/S0263-2373(01)00114-1

Qiu, Z. M., & Kok, K. F. (2007). Role-based 3D visualisation for asynchronous PLM collaboration. *Computers in Industry, 58*(8-9), 747–755. doi:10.1016/j.compind.2007.02.006

Quarles, J., & Lampotang, S. (2009). Scaffolded learning with mixed reality. *Computers & Graphics, 33*(1), 34–46. doi:10.1016/j.cag.2008.11.005

Reynolds, C. (1987). Flocks, herds and schools: A distributed behavioral model. In *Computer Graphics: Proceedings of SIGGRAPH '87, 21*(4). ACM Press.

Rosen, L. D., & Cheever, N. A. (2008). The impact of emotionality and self-disclosure on online dating versus traditional dating. *Computers in Human Behavior, 24*(5), 2124–2157. doi:10.1016/j.chb.2007.10.003

Ross, C., & Orr, E. S. (2009). Personality and motivations associated with Facebook use. *Computers in Human Behavior, 25*(2), 578–586. doi:10.1016/j.chb.2008.12.024

Rubach, E. (2007, June 31). Parallel worlds. Designweek, (p. 19).

Rust, R. T., Kannan, P. K., et al. (2005). E-service: The revenue expansion path to e-commerce profitability. In *Advances in computers*, volume 64, (pp. 159-193). Elsevier.

Saha, D., & Marvin, V. Z. (2005). Pervasive computing: A vision to realize. In *Advances in computers* (*Vol. 64*, pp. 195–245). Elsevier.

Sai, Y. (2008). Transparent safe. *Decision Support Systems, 46*(1), 41–51. doi:10.1016/j.dss.2008.04.007

Saini, R., & Saxena, P. K. (2000). Internet enabled synergistic intelligent systems and their applications to efficient management of operational organizations. *Information Sciences, 127*(1-2), 45–62. doi:10.1016/S0020-0255(00)00028-1

Salomann, H., & Dous, M. (2007). Self-service revisited: How to balance high-tech and high-touch in customer relationships. *European Management Journal, 25*(4), 310–319. doi:10.1016/j.emj.2007.06.005

Saxby, S. (2002). CLSR Briefing: News and comment on recent developments from around the world. *Computer Law & Security Report, 18*(2), 134–151. doi:10.1016/S0267-3649(02)03020-0

Saxby, S. (2007). News and comment on recent developments from around the world. *Computer Law & Security Report, 23*(2), 125–137. doi:10.1016/j.clsr.2007.01.010

Sheremetov, L., & Arenas, A. G. (2002). EVA: An interactive Web-based collaborative learning environment. *Computers & Education, 39*(2), 161–182. doi:10.1016/S0360-1315(02)00030-1

Silverston, T., & Fourmaux, O. (2009). Traffic analysis of peer-to-peer IPTV communities. *Computer Networks, 53*(4), 470–484. doi:10.1016/j.comnet.2008.09.024

Steinkuehler, C., & Williams, D. (2006). Where everybody knows your (screen) name: Online games as third places. *Journal of Computer-Mediated Communication, 11*(4). doi:10.1111/j.1083-6101.2006.00300.x

Strategy Analytics. (2008). *Interview: Strategy Analytics' Barry Gilbert - 137M virtual worlds users now; 1B by 2017*. Retrieved from http://www.virtualworldsnews.com/2008/06/strategy-analyt.html

Stuurman, K., & Wijnands, H. (2001). Software law: Intelligent agents: A curse or a blessing? A survey of the legal aspects of the application of intelligent software systems. *Computer Law & Security Report, 17*(2), 92–100. doi:10.1016/S0267-3649(01)00203-5

Subrahmanyam, K., Kraut, R., Greenfield, P. M., & Gross, E. F. (2001). New forms of electronic media: The impact of interactive games and the internet on cognition, socialization, and behavior. In Singer, D. L., & Singer, J. L. (Eds.), *Handbook of children and the media* (pp. 73–99). Thousand Oaks, CA: Sage.

Suh, K.-S., & Young, E. L. (2005). The effects of virtual reality of consumer learning: An empirical investigation. *Management Information Systems Quarterly, 29*(4), 674–697.

Ta, D. N. B., & Zhou, S. (2006). A network-centric approach to enhancing the interactivity of large-scale distributed virtual environments. *Computer Communications, 29*(17), 3553–3566. doi:10.1016/j.comcom.2006.05.015

Tahvanainen, M., & Welch, D. (2005). Implications of short-term international assignments. *European Management Journal, 23*(6), 663–673. doi:10.1016/j.emj.2005.10.011

Taxén, G., & Naeve, A. (2002). A system for exploring open issues in VR-based education. *Computers & Graphics, 26*(4), 593–598. doi:10.1016/S0097-8493(02)00112-7

Tay, F. E. H., & Roy, A. (2003). CyberCAD: A collaborative approach in 3D-CAD technology in a multimedia-supported environment. *Computers in Industry, 52*(2), 127–145. doi:10.1016/S0166-3615(03)00100-3

Tewari, G., & Youll, J. (2003). Personalized location-based brokering using an agent-based intermediary architecture. *Decision Support Systems, 34*(2), 127–137. doi:10.1016/S0167-9236(02)00076-3

Thatcher, J. B., & Loughry, M. L. (2007). Internet anxiety: An empirical study of the effects of personality, beliefs, and social support. *Information & Management, 44*(4), 353–363. doi:10.1016/j.im.2006.11.007

Thelwall, M., & Marvin, M. V. (2009). Social network sites: Users and uses. In *Advances in computers* (*Vol. 76*, pp. 19–73). Elsevier.

Tibau, J. (2000). Business teaching in the CIS States. *European Management Journal, 18*(6), 683–691. doi:10.1016/S0263-2373(00)00059-1

Tomlinson, M. (2000). Tackling e-commerce security issues head on. *Computer Fraud & Security*, (11): 10–13. doi:10.1016/S1361-3723(00)11017-6

Tucker, P. (2007). Virtual immortality for virtual eternity. *The Futurist*, 12.

Tynan, D. (2007). *Traveling the Web's third dimension*, (p. 45). PCWorld.com.

Vahidov, R., & Kersten, G. E. (2004). Decision station: Situating decision support systems. *Decision Support Systems, 38*(2), 283–303. doi:10.1016/S0167-9236(03)00099-X

van Dam, A., & Laidlaw, D. H. (2002). Experiments in immersive virtual reality for scientific visualization. *Computers & Graphics, 26*(4), 535–555. doi:10.1016/S0097-8493(02)00113-9

Wagner, M. (2007). *Inside Second Life's data centers*. InformationWeek.

Walkerdine, J., & Hughes, D. (2008). A framework for P2P application development. *Computer Communications, 31*(2), 387–401. doi:10.1016/j.comcom.2007.08.004

Walther, J. (2006). Nonverbal dynamics in computer mediated communication, or:(and the net:('s with you:) and you:) alone. In Manusov, V., & Patterson, M. (Eds.), *The Sage handbook of nonverbal communication* (pp. 461–480). Thousand Oaks, CA: Sage.

Walvoord, A. A. G., & Redden, E. R. (2008). Empowering followers in virtual teams: Guiding principles from theory and practice. *Computers in Human Behavior, 24*(5), 1884–1906. doi:10.1016/j.chb.2008.02.006

Wang, M. (2007). Do the regulations on electronic signatures facilitate international electronic commerce? A critical review. *Computer Law & Security Report, 23*(1), 32–41. doi:10.1016/j.clsr.2006.09.006

Warburton, S. (2008). Loving your avatar: identity, immersion and empathy. *Liquid Learning*. Retrieved September 23, 2010, from http://warburton.typepad.com/liquidlearning/2008/01/loving-your-ava.html

Warburton, S., & Perez-Garcia, M. (2009). 3D design and collaboration in massively multi-user virtual environments. In Russel, D. (Ed.), *Cases on collaboration in virtual learning environments: processes and interactions*. Hershey, PA: IGI Global. doi:10.4018/978-1-60566-878-9.ch002

Warmelink, H. (2009). De opkomst en ondergang van Second Life. *ego, 8*(2), 27-30.

Williams, D., Ducheneaut, N., Xiong, L., Zhang, Y., Yee, N., & Nickell, E. (2006). From tree house to barracks: The social life of guilds in World of Warcraft. *Games and Culture, 1*(4), 338–361. doi:10.1177/1555412006292616

Williams, D., Yee, N., & Caplan, S. (2008). Who plays, how much, and why? A behavioral player census of a virtual world. *Journal of Computer-Mediated Communication, 13*(4), 993–1018. doi:10.1111/j.1083-6101.2008.00428.x

Woerner, J., & Woern, H. (2005). A security architecture integrated co-operative engineering platform for organised model exchange in a Digital Factory environment. *Computers in Industry, 56*(4), 347–360. doi:10.1016/j.compind.2005.01.011

Woo, S. H., & Choi, J. Y. (2009). An active product state tracking architecture in logistics sensor networks. *Computers in Industry, 60*(3), 149–160. doi:10.1016/j.compind.2008.12.001

Woodcock, B. S. (2008). *Charts*. Retrieved June 16, 2010, from http://www.mmogchart.com/charts/.

Yamaguchi, H. (2004). *An analysis of virtual currencies in online games*. Retrieved from http://ssrn.com/abstract=544422

Yaman, D., & Polat, S. (2009). A fuzzy cognitive map approach for effect-based operations: An illustrative case. *Information Sciences, 179*(4), 382–403. doi:10.1016/j.ins.2008.10.013

Yapp, P. (2001). Passwords: Use and abuse. *Computer Fraud & Security*, (9): 14–16. doi:10.1016/S1361-3723(01)00916-2

Yee, N. (2006). The demographics, motivations and derived experiences of users of massively multiuser online graphical environments. *Presence (Cambridge, Mass.), 15*, 309–329. doi:10.1162/pres.15.3.309

Zhang, J., & Gong, J. (2007). Design and development of distributed virtual geographic environment system based on web services. *Information Sciences, 177*(19), 3968–3980. doi:10.1016/j.ins.2007.02.049

Zhu, B., & Chen, B. (2005). Using 3D interfaces to facilitate the spatial knowledge retrieval: A geo-referenced knowledge repository system. *Decision Support Systems, 40*(2), 167–182. doi:10.1016/j.dss.2004.01.007

APPENDIX 1: WORDS FREQUENCY - 2000-2003

		LEGAL		EDUCATION		ENTERTAIN			
SOCIAL		**BUSINESS**		**TRAINING**		**UTILITY**		**TECH**	
ACTIVITIES	189	BUSINESS	116	EDUCATION	57	AVATAR	115	APPLICATION	276
ADDRESS	73	BUYER	47	EDUCATION-AL	48	CAPABILITIES	37	ARCHITECTURE	99
AVATAR	225	CHAIN	57	EXPERIENCE	67	CHARACTER-ISTIC	95	COMMUNICATION	372
BEHAVIOR	151	CLIENTS	76	KNOWLEDGE	53	CHAT	34	COMPONENTS	40
COGNITIVE	78	COMMERCE	25	LEARNING	135	DESIGN	200	COMPUTER	698
COLLABORATIVE	121	COMMERCIAL	17	MULTIMEDIA	56	EXPERIENCE	67	DESIGN	200
COMMUNICA-TION	123	COMPANIES	137	SCHOOL	10	FEATURES	58	DEVELOPMENT	87
COMMUNITY	45	CONSUMER	23	STUDENT	179	FUNCTION	59	DISTRIBUTED	102
ENVIRONMENT	211	COURT	15	STUDIES	176	GAME	253	ENGINEERING	61
EXPERIENCE	67	CUSTOMER	96	TEACHING	20	INDIVIDUAL	147	IMPLEMENTA-TION	53
GROUP	156	ECONOMIC	9	TRAINING	17	INTERACTION	167	INTERFACE	73
HUMAN	147	FIRM	10	VIDEO	82	INTERACTIVE	32	IP	137
IDENTITY	99	INDUSTRY	71		900	MULTIMEDIA	56	MOBILE	66
INDIVIDUALS	148	LAW	47		(5%)	PLAYER	90	MODEL	289
INTERACTION	167	LEGAL	13			PLAYERS	89	MODELING	
INTERACTIVE	32	MANUFACTUR.	49	**SECURITY**		QUALITY	35	NETWORK	410
INTEREST	37	MARKET	62	ACCESS	132	SEARCH	51	NETWORKING	24
LANGUAGE	25	MARKETING	25	ANONYMITY	192	TOOL	66	PERFORMANCE	108
LIFE	65	MEDIA	84	ATTACKER	120	USE	288	PLATFORM	27
MEMBERS	26	ORGANIZA-TION	110	ATTACKS	126	USEFUL	44	PROJECT	57
PEOPLE	163	PRICE	12	CONTROL	136	USER	747	REQUIREMENTS	83
PERSONAL	80	PRODUCT	384	COPYRIGHT	64	VIDEO	82	SERVER	131
PERSONALITY	123	PUBLIC	79	DETECTION	62		2812	SERVICE	423
PRIVATE	48	TRANSACTION	53	ENCRYPTION	61		(18%)	SIMULATION	16
PROTOCOL	72		1617	ID	72			SOFTWARE	144
PUBLIC	79		(10%)	MONITORING	27			SYSTEM	584
RELATIONSHIP	100			PKI	78			TECHNICAL	340
RIGHTS	74			PRIVACY	64			TECHNOLOGIES	571
ROLE	20			PROTECTION	39			WIRELESS	81
SOCIAL	170			REPUTATION	8				5552
SOCIETY	28			RISK	34				(35%)
TOOL	66			SECURE	71				
	3208			SECURITY	235				
	(20%)			SIGNATURE	78				
				TRUST	308				
					1907				
					(12%)				

APPENDIX 2: WORDS FREQUENCY - 2004-2007

		LEGAL		EDUCATION		ENTERTAIN			
SOCIAL		**BUSINESS**		**TRAINING**		**UTILITY**		**TECH**	
ACTIVITIES	198	BUSINESS	341	EDUCATION	181	AVATAR	289	APPLICATION	433
ADDRESS	95	BUYER	116	EDUCATIONAL	37	CAPABILITIES	244	ARCHITECTURE	188
AVATAR	289	CLIENTS	48	EXPERIENCE	130	CHARACTER-ISTIC	108	COMMUNICATION	597
BEHAVIOR	226	COMMERCE	113	KNOWLEDGE	220	CHAT	36	COMPONENTS	111
BEHAVIORAL	91	COMMERCIAL	44	LEARNING	196	DATERS	151	COMPUTER	728
CHILD	22	COMPANIES	157	MULTIMEDIA	239	DATING	176	COMPUTING	71
COGNITIVE	30	CONSUMER	238	SCHOOL	93	DESIGN	260	DESIGN	260
COLLABORATIVE	79	COURT	81	STUDENT	223	EXPERIENCE	130	DEVELOPMENT	298
COMMUNICATION	597	CUSTOMER	268	STUDIES	515	FEATURES	63	DEVICES	96
COMMUNITY	57	ECONOMIC	61	SURVEY	56	FUNCTION	232	DISTRIBUTED	146
ENVIRONMENT	532	FIRM	310	TEACHING	90	GAME	489	ENGINEERING	108
EXPERIENCE	130	INDUSTRY	152	TRAINING	150	INDIVIDUAL	240	IMPLEMENTATION	94
GROUP	287	JURISDICTION	19	VIDEO	51	INTERACTION	180	INTERFACE	148
HUMAN	281	LAW	309		**2181**	INTERACTIVE	122	IP	66
IDENTITY	95	LEGAL	148		**7%**	MULTIMEDIA	239	MOBILE	110
INDIVIDUAL	240	MANUFACTUR.	111			PERFORMANCE	194	MODEL	627
INFLUENCE	72	MARKET	249	**SECURITY**		PLAYERS	233	MODELING	44
INTERACTION	180	MARKETING	84	ACCESS	296	QUALITY	106	NETWORK	628
INTERACTIVE	122	MEDIA	239	ANONYMITY	51	SEARCH	72	NETWORKING	67
INTEREST	142	OPERATIONS	157	ATTACK	135	TOOL	250	PACKET	137
LANGUAGE	95	ORGANIZA-TION	155	ATTACKER	15	USE	568	PERFORMANCE	194
LIFE	77	PAYMENT	20	CONTROL	255	USER	777	PLATFORM	69
MEMBERS	105	PRICE	119	COPYRIGHT	27	VIDEO	51	PROJECT	146
NETWORK	628	PRODUCT	290	CRIMINAL	67	VISUAL	52	PROTOCOL	91
PEERS	38	PUBLIC	88	DETECTION	49		**5262**	REQUIREMENTS	146
PEOPLE	254	STORE	221	ENCRYPTION	40		**17%**	SERVER	393
PERSONAL	367	TRANSACTION	194	INTRUSION	70			SERVICE	645
PERSONALITY	61		**4332**	MONITORING	142			SIMULATION	88
PRIVATE	54		**14%**	PRIVACY	270			SOFTWARE	195
PROTOCOL	91			PROTECTION	116			SYSTEM	1437
PUBLIC	88			REPUTATION	222			TECHNICAL	76
RELATIONSHIP	278			RISK	110			TECHNOLOGY	536
RIGHTS	121			SAFE	99			WIRELESS	122
ROLE	104			SECURE	59				**9095**
SOCIAL	369			SECURITY	428				**30%**
SOCIETY	57			TRUST	305				
TEAM	31				**2756**				
TOOL	150				**9%**				
	6733								
	22%								

APPENDIX 3: WORDS FREQUENCY - 2008-2010

SOCIAL		LEGAL BUSINESS		EDUCATION TRAINING		ENTERTAIN UTILITY		TECH	
		BUSINESS	371	COURSE	146	AVATAR	144	APPLICATION	667
ACTIVITY	521	BUYER	10	EDUCATION	223	CAPABILITIES	36	ARCHITECTURE	109
AVATAR	144	COMMERCE	65	EDUCATIONAL	101	CHARACTER-ISTIC	111	COMMUNICATION	728
BEHAVIOR	727	COMMERCIAL	121	EXPERIENCE	198	CHAT	203	COMPONENTS	108
BEHAVIORAL	100	COMPANIES	252	KNOWLEDGE	478	DESIGN	653	COMPUTER	840
CHILD	394	CONSUMER	198	LEARNING	461	EXPERIENCE	198	COMPUTING	176
COGNITIVE	229	COURT	204	MULTIMEDIA	78	FEATURES	159	DESIGN	653
COLLABORATION	149	CUSTOMER	208	SCHOOL	105	GAME	315	DEVELOPMENT	361
COLLABORATIVE	310	ECONOMIC	108	STUDENT	661	INDIVIDUAL	309	DISTRIBUTED	169
COMMUNICA-TION	728	FIRM	51	STUDY	369	INTERAC-TION	219	ENGINEERING	224
COMMUNITY	111	INDUSTRY	149	SURVEY	166	INTERACTIVE	111	IMPLEMENTA-TION	80
ENVIRONMENT	543	JURISDICTION	189	TEACHING	75	MEDIA	131	INTERFACE	188
EXPERIENCE	198	LAW	933	TRAINING	91	MULTIMEDIA	78	IP	187
GROUP	505	LEGAL	240	VIDEO	315	PLAYER	86	MODEL	783
HUMAN	301	MANUFACTUR.	46		3467	QUALITY	144	NETWORK	741
INDIVIDUAL	309	MARKET	220		(10%)	SEARCH	195	NETWORKING	197
INFLUENCE	175	MARKETING	96			TOOL	445	PERFORMANCE	197
INTERACTION	219	MEDIA	131	SECURITY		USE	1006	PLATFORM	118
INTERACTIVE	111	OPERATIONS	76	ACCESS	193	USEFUL	86	PROJECT	200
LANGUAGE	150	ORGANIZA-TION	249	ANONYMITY	36	USER	1185	PROTOCOL	141
LIFE	273	PAYMENT	123	ATTACK	94	VIDEO	315	REQUIREMENTS	148
MEMBERS	204	PRICE	64	ATTACKER	12	VISUAL	104	SERVER	219
NETWORK	741	PRODUCT	299	CONTROL	316	VIDEO	315	SERVICE	466
PEERS	132	PRODUCTION	100	COPYRIGHT	20	VISUAL	104	SIMULATION	157
PEOPLE	355	PUBLIC	207	CRIMINAL	61		6652	SOFTWARE	281
PERSONAL	200	TRANSACTION	227	DETECTION	38		(16%)	SYSTEM	1328
PERSONALITY	82		4937	ENCRYPTION	24			TECHNICAL	146
PRIVATE	161		(13%)	ID	83			TECHNOLOGIES	715
PUBLIC	207			MONITORING	37			WIRELESS	31
RELATIONSHIP	223			PRIVACY	300				10358
RIGHTS	169			PROTECTION	166	0			(27%)
ROLE	363			REPUTATION	14				
RULES	185			RISK	64				
SOCIAL	740			SECURE	53				
SOCIETY	116			SECURITY	562				
TEAM	330			TRUST	131				
TOOL	445				2204				
	10850				(6%)				
	(28%)								

40

Chapter 3
User Interface Designs, Task Categories and Training

Christina K. Curnow
ICF International, USA

Jeremy A. Henson
ICF International, USA

Robert A. Wisher
Naval Postgraduate School, USA

ABSTRACT

This chapter provides a preliminary framework for learner centered user interface design across a variety of training categories. To arrive at this framework, the authors explore (1) user interface design principles and the extent to which they apply to learning environments, (2) the learner centric psychological principles that should be included in the design of learner interfaces, and (3) methods by which training tasks are categorized. The overarching premise of the framework is that designs that are compatible with the psychology of learning promote learning, and ultimately performance, better than those that do not. This seemingly simple concept is sometimes in conflict with user interface design principles for other purposes, such as general purpose websites or marketing campaigns. The framework results in a notional configuration of 27 learner centered training interfaces, which are analyzed for their relevance to user interface design. The chapter concludes with a call for further research to determine best practices in learner interface design.

INTRODUCTION

Digital information and its delivery are ubiquitous in modern society. From the moment a digital radio or cell phone awakens you, to your daily work routines, to checking on your Facebook friends, our lives are becoming one never-ending interface to the digital world. Advancements, enhancements, and extensions of this trend are relentless. The delivery of education and training content in digital form is clearly part of this trend, as testified by the explosion of the e-learning marketplace. E-learning holds much promise for the training of the workforce, for the education of youth, and

DOI: 10.4018/978-1-61350-516-8.ch003

Copyright © 2012, IGI Global. Copying or distributing in print or electronic forms without written permission of IGI Global is prohibited.

for the development of society (Wisher & Khan, 2010). In Badrul Khan's popular depiction of an e-learning global framework through his octagon model, interface design plays a prominent role (Khan, 2001). The challenge of designing interfaces specific to the needs of the digital learner is worth examining.

The chapter takes a holistic view of this challenge. Our central question concerns the optimal 'user interface' between a learner and learning content. Do user interface design principles for general opertional use apply to learning environments? What factors from a learner-centric perspective should be considered as an underpinning to an ideal interface design for learners? Our examination, then, is from a learning perspective, although from more of a training rather than from an educational point of view. The objective in training is to systematically acquire knowledge, skills, rules, concepts, and attitudes that result in improved performance in another environment. We focus on the application of technologies, specifically information and communications technologies, to bring about this systematic acquisition. What matters for the trainee to interface with digital learning content is our concern.

This chapter is organized into a background section and three main sections. The background section covers learner-centered psychological principles; the user-centrist theme is used throughout the chapter. For our purposes, the user is the learner. A learner centered approach begins with an understanding of how the mind functions, so the natural tendencies of the learner should be factored into designs of the interface to learning content. The background covers some psychological principles of learning centered around the learner rather than the instructor. This analysis is further narrowed to what matters most in training.

The first main section considers relevant aspects from the user-interface-design literature related to simulations, in particular the issue of physical fidelity. The section briefly covers the fidelity question as it relates to reproducing the same cognitive experience by the user/operator/learner. Should the intention be to make the experience and interactions intuitive and efficient, in terms of achieving learning outcomes, or merely replicate the actual environment at a lower cost? The second section, the most extensive, reviews relevant training analysis literature, drawing from the many models that have been proposed for categorical descriptions of the elements of training. The intention is to recognize these contributions and what they can offer to categorical descriptions of learner interfaces. The third section attempts to unite the concepts from the first two sections and form a holistic view of the relationship between interfaces and learning content. This is an ambitious goal, and the limited space allotted for this chapter will allow us to only introduce many of the key areas and examine only a subset of interface configurations. The objective of this chapter is to establish a framework for the many factors that underlie the successful development of the learner interface to digital learning content for the purpose of training.

BACKGROUND

In the past century, significant progress was made in understanding the training of skills and abilities, even performance at an expert level (Clark & Wittrock, 2000). The psychological principles of learning and instruction have led to cognitive models that focus on the critical roles of the learner's cognition, including motivation, memory, comprehension, attention, and the active construction of meaning and understanding (Newell, 1990). These models converge on the human memory system and the processes that attend, transform, store, and retrieve information during learning and later during performance on the job. Note that such models focus on the capacity of the individual to learn and perform, and thus can be viewed from a learner-centered point of view.

Toward the end of the past century, the field of interface design grew from an isolated subarea of ergonomic design to a new area of inquiry driven by software engineering (Shneiderman, 1992). Much of the focus was on human computer interaction, which sought interfaces that were comprehensible, predictable, and controllable. A good deal of the progress in understanding human cognition also contributed to modern views of interfaces to all sorts of devices, as exemplified in Don Norman's stimulating *The Psychology of Everyday Things* (Norman, 1988). It is interesting to note the parallels between guidelines for creating 'user' interfaces to those for creating 'learner' interfaces. Both seek to identify relations between design features and the human information processing system. As we will demonstrate, there are limits to the analogy and some contradictions in what is best for the individual dealing with content through an interface. Our overarching premise is that designs that are consistent with the manner in which the human mind works promote performance and learning better than those that are not.

Learner-Centered Psychological Principles

Nearly two decades ago, the American Psychological Association (APA) announced a set of 14 Learner-Centered Psychological Principles (Alexander & Murphy, 1994; APA, 1993). These 14 principles summarize research from the fields of learning and instruction, motivation, and development, many of which had underpinnings in cognitive psychology. At the same time, cognitive psychology was influencing the field of user interface design, seeking to make users 'smarter' (Norman, 1993). The APA principles address areas such as promoting curiosity and intrinsic motivation, linking new information to old in meaningful ways, providing learner choice and personal control, cultivating social interaction, advancing thinking and reasoning strategies, constructing meaning from experience, and taking into account

learner social and cultural background. These 14 principles have been echoed in many learning theories, particularly those focused on teaching complex material such as cognitive learning strategies (Merrill, Reiser, & Merrill, 1995), constructivism/learner-centered education (Dimock and Boethel, 1999), experiential activities (Van Velsor & Guthrie, 1998), and cognitive flexibility theory (Spiro, Feltovitch, Jacobson, & Coulson, 1992). These 14 principles have significant promise for Web-based instruction (Bonk & Reynolds, 1997) and provide a sound basis for online instruction.

Complementing the learner-centered psychological principles, many educational technologists are advocating the need to shift from instructor-centered to student-centered approaches. Learner-centered pedagogy asks what students need to learn, what their learning preferences are, and what is meaningful to them. Online instruction provides opportunities for learning materials, tasks, and activities to fit individual learning preferences. Of course, the user-as-learner interface is a critical feature and it is often not considered sufficiently in online education and training.

In accordance with the learner-centered movement, online tools should provide opportunities to construct knowledge, actively share and seek information, generate a diverse array of ideas, appreciate multiple perspectives, and engage in social interaction and dialogue. Simply stated, technology rich environments have the capacity to support learner engagement in meaningful contexts. For a more detailed look at the examples, functions, and supporting research for learner-centered environments, see Hannafin and Land (1997).

The 14 principles can be divided into four factors. The factors and related principles are:

1. **Cognitive and metacognitive factors:** the nature of the learning process, the goals of the learning process, the construction of knowledge, strategic thinking, thinking about thinking, and the context of learning.

2. **Motivational and affective factors:** motivational and emotional influences on learning, intrinsic motivation to learn, effects of motivation on learning.

3. **Developmental and social factors:** development within and across physical, intellectual, emotional and social domains, social interactions and interpersonal relations with others.

4. **Individual differences:** in learning, diversity in linguistic, cultural, and social backgrounds, and diagnostic, process, and outcome assessments as an integral part of the learning process. For a more detailed discussion of these principles see Bonk, Wisher, and Lee (2004).

For our purposes, we have selected three principles for inclusion in our crosswalk to heuristics for interface designs and categories of training. A more complete analysis, of course, would include all 14 principles. Multiplying all the possible combinations from the other two sources would involve many thousands of instances, the analysis of which is well beyond the scope of this chapter. Our goal again is to create a framework of the many core elements that form the foundation for interfaces between a learner and training content. The three principles are: Construction of Knowledge – or how the user can link new information with existing knowledge in meaningful ways; Context of Learning – or the environmental factors such as culture, technology, and instructional practices that influence learning; and Individual Differences – the different strategies, approaches, and capabilities for learning that are a function of prior experience and heredity. The fourth area of developmental and social is less related to factors that a training developer or interface designer can directly control and therefore is not addressed here.

USER INTERFACE DESIGNS

Every system has an interface to the user. It may be a simple on-off switch, knobs and dials, or sophisticated screen dialogues to computer systems that determine how people operate and control the system. One common interface design principle is to keep the interface simple and straightforward. Basic functions should be immediately apparent. These suggestions are difficult to refute, unless you are providing training on a system that has already been designed, and which may not have followed the keep-it-simple advice in creating its user interface. This can be the case in simulations of actual equipment usage designed many years ago, such as the control room for a complex operational setting. Do you render an understanding of the mechanics of the system in an easy-to-use interface for the simulation or do you mimic the configuration of the actual system?

The human factors advice on the design of interactive software often applies to either an operating or a learning environment. The methods to develop and assess interfaces, interactive styles, direct manipulation for graphical user interfaces, and design considerations for effective messages, consistent screen design, appropriate colors and so forth can impact the success of users in either environment. There are, however, limitations. For example, Nielsen (1999) identifies ten general principles, really heuristics, for interface design. One heuristic is: Recognition rather than Recall, the rationale being to minimize the user's memory load so that the user should not need to remember information from one part of the dialogue to another. This contrasts with strong evidence from the experimental psychology literature suggesting a different user design in order to enhance learning. Specifically, requiring a user to retrieve some piece of information can directly strengthen the memory for that information and slow the rate of forgetting (Rohrer & Pashler, 2010). At some point, learning depends on remembering information. Ways to facilitate this, rather than avoid it, are keys to learning.

Another counter intuitive example concerns the user interface design heuristic of Nielsen (1999) concerning Aesthetic and Minimalist Design, which advises that dialogues should not contain information which is irrelevant or rarely needed. In multimedia learning, this has been termed a 'seductive detail' or "highly interesting and entertaining information that is only tangentially related to the topic but is irrelevant to the author's intended theme" (Harp & Mayer, 1998, p.1). Its best use in training depends on the intended purpose of the training. Capturing the attention of the learner is important for maintaining learner interest, which in turn leads to deeper processing of information and better learning and transfer. There is evidence that seductive details can have a facilitative effect on transfer of performance from the learning phase to the application phase (Towler et al, 2008). The category of training, then, can override some more general guidelines for interface design.

Fidelity in Design

Interface design is a critical component in simulation that can be used for training. The way in which learners interact with simulated environments can enhance or hinder learning and transfer. While the specific components of a simulator interface will vary greatly depending on the nature of the task that is being trained, one issue that is consistently an issue across all simulator interface designs is that of fidelity. Currently, there is little agreement on what fidelity in simulation is, and how it applies to training (Dahl, Asos, & Svanæs, 2010). Much of the focus of technology developments in simulation is focused on physical fidelity. Physical fidelity is the extent to which a simulator realistically reproduces the aspects of the environment in which the actual task will be conducted (O'Sullivan, Dingliana, Giang, & Kaiser, 2003). While it is intuitively appealing

to consider physical fidelity as an important characteristic of simulation in order to facilitate learning and transfer, a growing body of research has found evidence to the contrary (Hays, Jacobs, Prince, & Salas, 1992). Specifically, some simulations that include rich, high-detail environments (Mania, Badariah, Coxon, & Watten, 2010) and easy-access to task-related information (Waldron, Patrick, Duggan, Banbury, & Howes, 2008) have been shown to reduce knowledge retention and skill transfer to the actual task environment.

One explanation of the disappointing results associated with focusing on physical fidelity is that simulations high in physical fidelity may still not reproduce the cognitive processes associated with a given task. Fidelity with regard to cognitive, affective and psychomotor properties (Bloom, 1956) is called psychological fidelity (Kozlowski & DeShon, 2004). The use of psychological fidelity represents a shift from implicit to explicit modeling of the environment. Physical fidelity is implicit in that it implies that the more accurately an environment is represented physically, the higher degree of task related learning will take place. Alternatively, psychological fidelity is explicit, in that it uses existing theory and systematic analysis of tasks in order to create direct theoretical relationships between aspects of a simulation's design and the task-relevant knowledge, skills, and abilities that will be learned. Kozlowski and DeShon (2004) identified three primary theoretical branches by which this can be accomplished. These include theories, of learning, motivation, and performance, instructional design, and metacognitive theories or heuristics in training of adaptive teams.

The development of a user-interface for a simulation must begin with a thorough cognitive task-analysis (Kozlowski & DeShon, 1999). This process identifies the cognitive processes associated with the task that is to be trained. Once the specific cognitive processes have been identified, the interface and training tasks should be designed in such a way that the cognitive load is reduced for non-task related processes and increased for highly task-related processes. This may seem counterintuitive because relevant training outcomes such as the development of self-efficacy (Bandura, 1997) are related to the successful completion of training tasks (Godstein & Ford, 2002). However, research has indicated that reducing the cognitive load with task-related processes leads to lower retention and skill transfer (Waldron et al., 2008).

As stated before, many design principles and heuristics stress that access to task-related information should be as easy and intuitive as possible. This philosophy may decrease psychological fidelity for tasks in which it is difficult to extract relevant information, thereby reducing skill retention and transfer. As a result, it is recommended to avoid interface design heuristics that encourage this. Alternatively IBM has created a set of eleven "Design Principles for Tomorrow" (Stasko, 1997). These principles stress the congruence of cognitive processes in the user interface with the cognitive processes associated with the task to be trained. These principles are listed below:

1. **Simplicity:** Don't compromise usability for function
2. **Support:** User is in control with proactive assistance
3. **Familiarity:** Build on users' prior knowledge
4. **Obviousness:** Make objects and their controls visible and intuitive
5. **Encouragement:** Make actions predictable and reversible
6. **Satisfaction:** Create a feeling of progress and achievement
7. **Accessibility:** Make all objects accessible at all times
8. **Safety:** Keep the user out of trouble
9. **Versatility:** Support alternative interaction techniques
10. **Personalization:** Allow users to customize
11. **Affinity:** Bring objects to life through good visual design

For our purposes, we have again selected three principles for inclusion in our framework to crosswalk between learner-centered psychological principles and categories of training. A more complete analysis, of course, would include all 11 principles, and other sources of guidelines and heuristics that were not included in this brief review. The three principles selected from the IBM list are: Familiarity – the relationships among user interface objects should allow users to rely on their previous experience in the domain; Versatility – allow users to choose the method of interaction that is most appropriate to their situation; and Affinity – visual design should communicate the function of the user model without ambiguities. The framework is developed later in the chapter.

CATEGORIES OF TASKS

The goal of this section is to present task categorization criteria and subsequent task categories that describe the world of training, at least in terms of tasks. Although there are numerous categorization schemes for tasks, our interest was in isolating those with factors that address whether training can be cost-effectively delivered through technology, and thus require a user interface. We searched a wide range of task categorization methodologies and sought to pick out specific criteria that make one group of tasks unique from another group in terms of how they might best be trained with current instructional practices.

The following review discusses the process and outcomes of a literature search for task classification criteria. This includes academic journals, applied texts and case studies, and military research articles; it covers both empirical and theoretical works independent of the purpose of the classification.

Search Methodology

The literature review took place in multiple steps. First, we prepared a list of journal articles, book chapters, military research reports, and other case studies. These were gathered by searching databases such as PsycINFO, Google Scholar, and the U.S. Military's Defense Technical Information Center. Additionally, we identified case studies by searching the standard Google search engine. Search terms included keywords from e-learning, training task analysis, and training task categories. These terms include task classification models, media selection models, and other factors affecting retention and complexity of tasks. Additional sources were identified by examining prevalent books for chapters pertaining to training, adult education, and job analysis. Results of the searches were screened to determine if they contained information relevant to the objectives of the current literature review.

Articles that presented task classification methodologies were given a more detailed review. Each article was reviewed to determine what, if any, task classification criteria were used. Models with specific criteria are detailed here along with an assessment as to the extent to which the criteria: 1) have the potential to create unique classes that may vary in terms of the media that would be selected for training, 2) produces discrete categories versus general descriptions, 3) are sufficiently important to be included in a categorization schema that will result in a manageable number of categories (so as to not defeat the purpose of creating categories in the first place), 4) Enduring and static - not likely to change in different contexts or environments in the near future.

Results of Search

Numerous examples of task classification criteria are reported in the contemporary literature. Classification systems can be very general in scope or very specific. They also vary in focus and purpose. Listed below are several classification criteria that have been found to be useful when grouping tasks for purposes of job analysis or training development. We should note that there are ample examples of media selection models that recommend delivery media for virtual methods of training, but these are predicated on the assumption of a virtual approach in the first place.

The search resulted in nine broad schemes to describe the world of training:) Levels of analysis; 2) Time and motion analysis; 3) Worker functions, or functional job analysis; 4) Task characteristics; 5) Position analysis questionnaire; 6) Blooms taxonomy; 7) Cognitive task analysis; 8) Level of interaction; 9) Perishability and task retention models. The analysis presented below begins with classification schemes at a top-level view of training, based on how work is organized and how workers function. Characteristics of tasks are then reviewed, including domains, intellectual behaviors, task complexity, interactions during learning, and skill retention dynamics.

Levels of Analysis

Levels of anlaysis is one of the basic ways to describe how work is organized. This classification system is hierarchical, in that each level is made up of units of the next lower classification. An element is the most basic form of classifying work and refers to specific motions that make up tasks. Activities are units of work that are made up of multiple elements. While the more general categories are useful for understanding how work is grouped, training is typically focused on tasks, activities, and elements

Altogether, nine levels of analysis were identified: Branch, Group, Series, Job, Position, Duty, Task, Activity, and Element. For example, Branch is the most general form of work, such as Software Engineering. Position refers to a job this is specific to an individual, such as Programmer, and Activity is composed of multiple elements that make up a more complete unit of work, such as Documentation. This categorization system works well for describing what people do in their jobs but it is not until reaching the Task level that user interface design needs serious consideration.

Time and Motion Analysis

Time and motion analysis categories refer to the amount of time a given task will take as well as what and how many motions are required for the different tasks. Time and motion studies were originally introduced by Frederick Taylor (1911) and still have relevance in today's workplace. Categories such as time and motion seem to fall into a broader construct of task complexity, which would seem to have an impact on how a task needs to be trained and whether it can be trained virtually. Certainly, the Motion category is relevant to user interface design, but not all motions may adequately translate to a design prescription.

Worker Functions (Functional Job Analysis)

Functional Job Analysis focuses primarily on the objects with which people work. Tasks can be categorized depending on whether or not they deal primarily with data (e.g., analyzing a spreadsheet), people (e.g., convincing a customer to buy a product) or things (e.g., filling a sandbag). Furthermore, these categories can be further broken down into levels of each type of object. For example tasks involving data can include activities such as comparing two pieces of data to see if they match (low level) to analyzing complex data and drawing meaningful conclusions (high level). There are three main categories, Data, People, and Things. Within categories, levels of activity include synthesis and analysis for Data, negotiating and supervising for People, and operating and handling for Things. Designing a user interface to train these categories much depends on the context of work.

These categories seem to relate primarily to qualitative differences in the nature of tasks and seem to have a direct relationship to the underlying knowledge, skills and abilities that are needed to perform the tasks. The basic levels of Data, People and Things do seem to provide unique characteristics that would likely lend themselves to different design methods.

Task Characteristics

Many of the task classification schema that are available in the literature focus on creating task lists of what a worker does. The next step is to determine how these tasks are used on the job and to quantify their relationship to one another. This is most commonly done by collecting ratings of the importance and frequency of tasks. Furthermore, at least one case study (Jelley, 2007) used cluster analysis to empirically group similar tasks based on multiple criteria. The task characteristics as used on the job are drawn from four sources. They are described as follows, from Brannick, Levine, & Morgeson (2007): Difficulty to Learn, Difficulty to Perform, Time Spent to Complete; from Jelley (2007): Frequency of Performance, Expected Day-One Proficiency, Importance to Overall Job; from Jonassen, Tessmer, & Hannum (1999): Universality within a Given Job, Criticality or Consequences of Inadequate Performance, Standardization of Performance across Workers; and Rose et al (1985): Perishability or how rapidly a worker loses the ability to perform without practice.

Among the task characteristics we identified, difficulty to learn, perishability and criticality seem to be particularly relevant to designing user interfaces that may have unique attributes to consider. These components seem to fall into a broader category that relates to task complexity.

Position Analysis Questionnaire (PAQ)

The Position Analysis Questionnaire is a computer-scored job analysis method. Tasks are rated based upon several categories and subcategories as described in Brannick, Levine, & Morgeson, 2007, or McCormick, Jeanneret, & Mecham, 1989. The PAQ categories are Information Input (e.g., perceptual activities), Mental Processes (use of stored information), Work Output (use of physical devices), Interpersonal Activities (personal contact), Work Situation and Job Context (physical working conditions). The challenge for user interface design is in assuring that the training can transfer from the learning environment to the working environment, so certain high stress, noisy, crowded environments may not easily be captured in an interface to training content.

As with most of the task classification schema focusing on job analysis, many of the elements of the PAQ relate to how tasks are used on the job, rather than how tasks should be or could be trained. Of course this is the intended purpose of job analysis classification schema. However, there are many pieces from the PAQ that could prove relevant to identifying unique task classes that might need to be handled differently by interface designs for training purposes.

Information input and mental processes relate to the way that a person perceives and processes information while performing a task. Often in training, the fidelity of these processes to the actual job is quite important to ensure training transfer. Processes of this nature warrant consideration when grouping tasks and selecting instructional methods and media.

Interpersonal activities relate to the nature and quality of interaction with people. Interactions with people and the nature of those interactions seem to be a characteristic that would uniquely differentiate a group of tasks and have implications for how they should be trained. Some interactions may be mimicked through virtual training, but

others may be more open-ended and spontaneous requiring a sophistication not yet available.

Work output is geared primarily toward the physical activities required to perform a task, but also has implications for collective tasks in the "coordination of activities" category. Therefore, work output also worthy of further consideration as one of the criteria to include in our task classification.

Bloom's Taxonomy

Bloom's Taxonomy (1956) was developed to describe and categorize learning. It remains a popular scheme to categorize domains of learning. The domains are cognitive, affective, and psychomotor. Cognitive refers to the acquisition of knowledge and the development of skills, affective refers to tasks the involve emotions, motivation, and attitudes, and psychomotor involves tasks the involve physical movement and refined motor skills.

Additionally, Bloom theorized that learning occurred at different levels of intellectual behaviors. The levels described by Bloom vary along a continuum of complexity with knowledge being the least complex and evaluation being the most complex. The levels are listed in Table 1.

The intellectual behaviors detailed in Table 1 relate to progressively greater levels of cognitive processing. These factors relate to overall task complexity and how difficult it is to learn a task, and would seem to have a relationship with how tasks in these categories would need to be trained, which could impact instructional method and media choices; however, the greater implication of these levels is to the learning methodology and instructional design that should be employed rather than the technology itself.

The cognitive, affective, and psychomotor domains identified by Bloom represent qualitatively different modes of learning. These different modes of learning would seem to require different modes and methods of training, which likely has

Table 1. Bloom's levels of intellectual behaviors

Levels	Examples
Knowledge	Defining, labeling, organizing
Understanding	Describing and explaining
Application	Demonstrating and interpreting
Analysis	Appraising, comparing, criticizing
Synthesis	Composing and developing
Evaluation	Arguing and predicting

implications for media selection and interface design (Reiser & Gagné, 1983)..

Cognitive Task Analysis

This type of analysis examines the cognitive processes associated with the completion of tasks. As a part of that process, tasks can be categorized and compared based upon the types of skills associated with them. Specifically, the skills are grouped into automated, representational, and decision making categories. The categories are presented in Table 2.

Instructional Requirements that Limit Instructional Methods

When training tasks, the instructional activities and conditions must include certain elements in order for the intended skills to be transferred. For example, in a fire emergency, individuals are taught to smell for smoke and feel a door for warmth. These factors may or may not be critical in learning a task. If they are critical and if a interface to a virtual training system cannot successfully

replicate these conditions, the likelihood of learning the task is reduced. By the same token, if they are critical, then they must also be replicated in a classroom or field setting. Clark, Bewley, and O'Neil (2006) established a set of three training requirements by which training tasks can be categorized. Sensory mode requirements refer to tasks in which you must taste, touch, or smell something in order to learn the task adequately. If these sensory modes are required to learn a task, they must be present in the training environment. Conditional knowledge requirements address fidelity of a situation. Specifically, if a task takes place in a specific condition (e.g., at night, under water, or high heat), these conditions must be adequately represented in the training environment. Synchronous feedback refers to the ability for training participants to get immediate feedback through the user interface about their actions. This is especially true for complex tasks, during which a coach may be required to stop practice, provide feedback, and demonstrate. The instructional requirements that can limit the use of interfaces include a Sensory Mode Requirement, namely touch, smell, or taste, a Conditional Knowledge

Table 2. Categories of cognitive skills

Category	Description	Example
Automated	Skills that involve little effort or attention	Riding a bicycle
Representational	Skills that involve the use of mental models	Planning a maneuver
Decision Making	The ability to apply general rules and principles to make decisions quickly	Reading channel markers in the water to know if your boat is on course

Requirement, the need for the learning environment of have high fidelity such as gravitational pull for parachute instruction, and a Synchronous Feedback Requirement, the need for immediacy of feedback during training (Clark, Bewley, & O'Neil, 2006).

Level of Interaction

Whether in a classroom setting or through distributed learning, students have multiple levels of interaction in learning any task. Moore (1989) defines three types of interactions in instructional settings: learner-instructor, learner-content, and learner-learner. Each promotes learning, but in classroom environments, the emphasis is traditionally on learner-instructor and learner-content interactions, as knowledge is seen traditionally as flowing towards the learner. More generally, Wagner (1997) defines interactions as reciprocal events requiring two objects and two actions. A feature of effective interactions is that they must result in the transfer of knowledge or a change in intrinsic motivation. In classifying tasks, the breakout of interaction types relate to the 'people level' of worker functions described earlier. Wagner further identifies thirteen types of interactions that can occur in learning environments, presented in Table 3.

More contemporary social constructivist theories of learning, however, point to learner-learner interaction as a key to enhancing learning.

In the classroom, these may occur between training sessions or in other ways uncontrollable by the instructor. A challenge for designers of instructional interfaces is how to support such learning. For collective tasks, interactions between learners (i.e., between team members) is central to task execution.

Perishability and Task Retention Models

More than a century of research on memory has shown that large amounts of forgetting can occur naturally over periods as short as several hours or as long as many years. Furthermore, research has shown that memory for continuous (perceptual-motor) skills is different from memory for discrete (procedural) skills. The task of bicycle riding, for example, may last a lifetime, even after years without practice. This is an example of a continuous perceptual-motor skill. Remembering the correct procedure for changing a flat tire on a bicycle, however, can perish since it is a task with discrete, knowledge-dependent procedures. Organizations makes a large investment in training knowledge-dependent procedures, with thousands of tasks fitting into this category. The issue of retaining task knowledge, therefore, is of vital interest in considering a task categorization scheme.

In the 1980s, the U.S. Army Research Institute undertook an effort to organize and integrate many of the retention research findings into an

Table 3. Types of interactions between learners and instructors

Interaction Types	
to increase willingness to engage in learning	for negotiation of understanding
to increase participation	for teambuilding
to develop communication	for discovery
to receive feedback	for exploration
to enhance elaboration and retention	for clarification of understanding
to support learner/self-regulation	for closure
to increase motivation	

instrument for predicting how rapidly individual procedural tasks are forgotten. The result of this effort is the User's Manual for Predicting Military Task Retention (Rose, Czarnolewski, Gragg,, Austin, & Ford, 1985). The manual, which represents a model of skill retention, was designed to guide a trainer or analyst through a process of numerically rating an individual task on key factors just discussed.

The output is a single score that predicts the decline in performance among soldiers who start out fully proficient. It identifies a curve that gives the percentage of soldiers in a unit who will be able to perform the task correctly after a given interval of no practice. Training managers can use the model to answer questions such as:

- How quickly will a particular task be forgotten?
- Among several tasks, which is most likely to be forgotten or remembered after a given interval?
- When should reacquisition training on a particular task be conducted to keep group performance from falling below an acceptable level?

The task retention model was not designed to address the difficulty of learning a task or how to conduct training. It focuses on task characteristics and does not take into account any techniques or strategies used during initial training or during the retention period to counteract forgetting. However, factors identified in this model provide information about task complexity and the ways that tasks vary in terms of how they are forgotten (and perhaps learned as well). The ten task factors considered by the Task Retention Model are: 1) are job aids used; 2) what is the quality of the job aid; 3) how many steps are required; 4) are the steps ordered; 5) is there built in feedback; 6) is there a time limit; 7)what are the mental requirements (e.g., Blooms level of intellectual behavior); 8) how many facts must be memorized; 9) how

difficult are the facts, terms to remember (e.g., use of mnemonic devices); 10) are there motor control demands.

Summary of Task Categories

The goal of developing a set of categorization criteria for the training of tasks was to identify discrete categories of tasks that vary in terms of training and learner interface design considerations. Ideally, a task classification system should separate tasks on distinct processes that have implications for the mode of instructional delivery (Sugrue & Clark, 2000), which in turn can influence the interface. Depending on the purpose of training, such as regulatory compliance, safety, product familiarity, future performance, long-term retention, different categorical sets can then contribute to issues in designing a learner interface to training content (Robinson, 2007). There may be no best approach, and just as there is overlap between the schemes there is also uniqueness.

Among the factors identified in our literature review, three stand out as particularly important in the context of learner interface design. First based on the work of Rose et al. (1985) is the Perishability of tasks and the underlying complexity of the task. Issues related to how quickly tasks can be forgotten, how frequently they need to be retrained, and how quickly they can be reacquired are important factors to consider in the design phase. The second criteria from cognitive task analysis is Decision Making. Skills that require Decision Making tend to be complex, which creates specific training challenges. Finally, from the instructional requirements category, the Sensory Mode requirement where the sense of touch, smell or touch are required to perform a task clearly has unique training design considerations. While there are certainly additional criteria that warrant further consideration, these three are addressed in our initial framework presented here.

A FRAMEWORK FOR LEARNER-CENTERED DESIGN AND TRAINING TASK CATEGORIES

This final section attempts to unify elements from the reviews. A notional subset of principles and categories have been arbitrarily selected for further consideration in the framework. There were thousands of possibilities, so we have limited our analysis to a notional set of three principals or categories, identified earlier, from each of three fields of inquiry. This leads to 3 x 3 x 3 or 27 separate configurations to evaluate as having relevance to an interface design to digital content for training that is learner-centered, sensitive to design principles, and focused on a particular category of training. The subset of principles and categories seleted are presented in Table 4.

The analysis of the various configurations was accomplished through a consensus building process of independent rater judgments using three judges with a combined experience of more than 50 years in the field of training analysis. Each of the 27configurations, such as Construction of Knowledge by Versatility by Sensory Mode, were rated as having high, medium, or low relevance for an interface. By this, we mean that high relevance configurations should check against the features of a user design for training content, and the medium and low relevance are less important.

The results of this very preliminary analysis are presented below.

High Relevance for Interface Design

- Context of Learning x Familiarity x Sensory Mode
- Context of Learning x Affinity x Sensory Mode
- Construction of Knowledge x Familiarity x Perishability
- Construction of Knowledge x Versatility x Perishability
- Construction of Knowledge x Affinity x Perishability
- Construction of Knowledge x Familiarity x Sensory Mode
- Construction of Knowledge x Versatility x Sensory Mode

Medium Relevance for Interface Design

- Construction of Knowledge x Familiarity x Decision Making
- Construction of Knowledge x Versatility x Decision Making
- Individual Differences x Versatility x Sensory Mode

Table 4. Notional set of considerations for learner-centered training interfaces

Source	Principal or Category
Learner-Centered Psychological	Construction of Knowledge
Learner-Centered Psychological	Context of Learning
Learner-Centered Psychological	Individual Differences
User-Interface	Familiarity
User-Interface	Versatility
User-Interface Training Category	Affinity Perishability (task characteristics)
Training Category	Decision Making (cognitive task analysis)
Training Category	Sensory Mode (instructional reqmts)

- Individual Differences x Familiarity x Perishability
- Individual Differences x Versatility x Perishability
- Individual Differences x Affinity x Perishability
- Context of Learning x Familiarity x Decision Making
- Context of Learning x Affinity x Decision Making
- Context of Learning x Versatility x Decision Making
- Context of Learning x Versatility x Sensory Mode
- Individual Differences x Familiarity x Decision Making
- Construction of Knowledge x Affinity x Decision Making
- Construction of Knowledge x Affinity x Sensory Mode

Low Relevance for Interface Design

- Context of Learning x Familiarity x Perishability
- Context of Learning x Versatility x Perishability
- Context of Learning x Affinity x Perishability
- Individual Differences x Familiarity x Sensory Mode
- Individual Differences x Affinity x Sensory Mode
- Individual Differences x Versatility x Decision Making
- Individual Differences x Affinity x Decision Making

The ratings for these configurations should be applied with caution at this point. Scales need to be developed, rating categories need to be better defined, and outcomes need to be validated. This is the first step in exploring the intricate relation-ships between designs for training that are learner centered, are sensitive to task categories, and consider traditional guidelines on user interface design.

FUTURE RESEARCH DIRECTIONS

The analysis presented here must be considered preliminary. The notional elements represent but a small subset of the many combinations and the rater judgments have not been validated. Future research should systematically manipulate the elements as independent variables in a variety of experimental settings and consider both the immediate learning outcomes and the longer term retention of the training content as an indicator of learning (Wisher, Curnow & Seidel, 2001). It is possible, for example, that the Versatility of an interface when combined with a Construction of Knowledge element of learner centered principles leads to longer retention. Continuing the example, there may be no differences in immediate learning outcomes, but a significant difference in knowledge retention 90 days later. This is of great importance to training since it is transfer to of performance to other environments that is the key to training success.

Much of the research in online learning has focused on educational rather than training programs. The considerations here may not necessarily apply to educational environments, which are much more open ended. Parallel considerations with a revision from task categories to perhaps Bloom's level of intellectual behaviors presented in Table 1 may be the appropriate way ahead. The challenges and opportunities of this volume's theme, including social and cross-cultural dimensions, are broad and deep. Research and its coordination are needed across many multi-disciplinary areas to fully realize the potential of the learner-as-user interface to digital content.

CONCLUSION

There are many facets to designing user interfaces. Much is driven by the purpose of the interface. Much of the literature on interface design stems from the field of software engineering, based on fundamental user analysis, such as the GOMS model, or how to do a task in terms of Goals, Operators, Methods, and Selection Rules (Card, Moran & Newell, 1983). Much of the focusing was on using rather than learner, although one could obviously employ the interface as a stand-alone traning device. This chapter aimed to capture the many popular views of interface design, learner centered principles, and task categories and examine how they intersect and what that may imply for user interface design.

REFERENCES

Alexander, P., & Murphy, P. K. (1994). *The research base for APA's learner-centered psychological principles*. Paper presented at the annual meeting of the American Educational Research Association, New Orleans, Louisiana, USA.

American Psychological Association. (1993). *Learner-centered psychological principles: Guidelines for school reform and restructuring*. Washington, DC: American Psychological Association and the Mid-continent Regional Education Laboratory.

Bandura, A. (1997). *Self efficacy: The exercise of control*. New York, NY: WH Freeman & Company.

Bloom, B. S. (1956). *Taxonomy of educational objectives, handbook I: The cognitive domain*. New York, NY: David McKay, Inc.

Bonk, C. J., & Reynolds, T. H. (1997). Web-based instructional techniques for higher-order thinking, teamwork, and apprenticeship. In Khan, B. H. (Ed.), *Web-based instruction* (pp. 167–178). Ed Tech Pubs.

Bonk, C. J., Wisher, R. A., & Lee, J. (2004). Moderating learner-centered elearning: Problems and solutions, benefits and implications. In Roberts, T. S. (Ed.), *Online collaborative learning: Theory and practice* (pp. 54–85). Hershey, PA: Idea Group Publishing.

Brannick, M. T., Levine, E. L., & Morgeson, F. P. (2007). *Job and work analysis: Methods, research, and applications for human resource management*. Thousand Oaks, CA: Sage Publications.

Card, S., Moran, T., & Newell, A. (1983). *The psychology of human-computer interaction*. Hillsdale, NJ: Lawrence Erlbaum Associates.

Clark, R., & Wittrock, M. C. (2000). Psychological principles of training. In Tobias, S., & Fletcher, J. (Eds.), *Training and retraining: A handbook for business, industry, government, and military* (pp. 51–84). New York, NY: Macmillan Reference USA.

Clark, R. E., Bewley, W. L., & O'Neil, H. F. (2006). Heuristics for selecting distance or classroom settings for courses. In O'Neil, H., & Perez, R. (Eds.), *Web-based learning: Theory, research, and practice*. Mahway, NJ: Lawrence Erlbaum & Associates.

Dahl, Y., Alsos, O. A., & Svanæs, D. (2010). Fidelity consideration for simulation-based usability assessments of mobile ICT for hospitals. *International Journal of Human-Computer Interaction, 26*, 445–476. doi:10.1080/10447311003719938

Dimock, K., & Boethel, M. (1999). *Constructing knowledge with technology*. Austin, TX: Southwest Education Development Lab.

Goldstein, I. L., & Ford, J. K. (2002). *Training in organizations: Needs assessment, development, and evaluation* (4th ed.). Belmont, CA: Wadsworth Publishing.

Hannafin, M. J., & Land, S. (1997). The foundations and assumptions of technology-enhanced, student-centered learning environments. *Instructional Science*, *25*, 167–202. doi:10.1023/A:1002997414652

Harp, S. F., & Mayer, R. E. (1998). How seductive details do their damage: A theory of cognitive interest in science learning. *Journal of Educational Psychology*, *90*, 414–434. doi:10.1037/0022-0663.90.3.414

Hays, R. T., Jacobs, J. W., Prince, C., & Salas, E. (1992). Flight simulator effectiveness: A meta-analysis. *Military Psychology*, *4*, 63–74. doi:10.1207/s15327876mp0402_1

Jelley, R. B. (2007). *Police management job analysis and leadership needs assessment.* Unpublished manuscript, Ontario, CA.

Jonassen, D. H., Tessmer, M., & Hannum, W. H. (1999). *Task analysis methods for instructional design.* Mawah, NJ: Lawrence Earlbaum & Associates.

Khan, B. H. (Ed.). (2001). *Web-based training.* Englewood Cliffs, NJ: Educational Technology Publications.

Kozlowski, S. W. J., & DeShon, R. P. (1999, June). *TEAMSim: Examining the development of basic, strategic, and adaptive performance.*

Kozlowski, S. W. J., & DeShon, R. P. (2004). A psychological fidelity approach to simulation-based training: Theory, research, and principles. In Schiflett, S. G., Elliott, L. R., Salas, E., & Coovert, M. D. (Eds.), *Scaled worlds: Development, validation, and applications.* Burlington, VT: Ashgate.

Mania, K., Badariah, S., Coxon, M., & Watten, P. (2010). Cognitive transfer of spatial awareness states from immersive virtual environments to reality. *ACM Transactions on Applied Perception*, *7*, 1–14. doi:10.1145/1670671.1670673

McCormick, E. J., Jeanneret, P. R., & Mecham, R. C. (1989). *Position analysis questionnaire.* Logan, UT: PAQ Services, Inc.

Merrill, D. C., Reiser, B. J., & Merrill, S. K. (1995). Tutoring: Guided learning by doing. *Cognition and Instruction*, *13*, 315–372. doi:10.1207/s1532690xci1303_1

Moore, M. G. (1989). Three types of interaction. *American Journal of Distance Education*, *3*(2), 1–6. doi:10.1080/08923648909526659

Newell, A. (1990). *Unified theories of cognition.* Cambridge, MA: Cambridge University Press.

Nielsen, J. (1999). *Designing Web usability.* Berkeley, CA: Peachpit Press.

Norman, D. A. (1988). *The psychology of everyday things.* New York, NY: Basic Books.

Norman, D. A. (1993). *Things that make us smart.* Reading, MA: Addison-Wesley.

O'Sullivan, C., Dingliana, J., Giang, T., & Kaiser, M. K. (2003). Evaluating the visual fidelity of physically based animations. *Proceedings of the Association for Computing Machinery's Special Interest Group on Computer Graphics and Interactive Techniques*, *22*, 527–536.

Reiser, R. A., & Gagné, R. M. (1983). *Selecting media for instruction.* Englewood Cliffs, NJ: Educational Technology.

Robinson, P. (2007). Criteria for categorizing and sequencing pedagogic tasks. In del Pilar, M., & Mayo, G. (Eds.), *Investigating tasks in formal language learning.* Tonawanda, NY: Multilingual Matters Ltd.

Rohrer, D., & Pashler, H. (2010). Recent research on human learning challenges conventional instructional strategies. *Educational Research*, *39*, 406–412. doi:10.3102/0013189X10374770

Rose, A., Czarnolewski, M., Gragg, F., Austin, S., & Ford, P. (1985). *Acquisition and retention of soldiering skills (Final Report 671)*. Alexandria, VA: U. S. Army Research Institute for the Behavioral and Social Sciences.

Shneiderman, B. (1992). *Designing the user interface - strategies for effective human-computer interaction* (2nd ed.). Reading, MA: Addison-Wesley Publishing Company.

Spiro, R. J., Feltovich, P. J., Jacobson, M. J., & Coulson, R. L. (1992). Cognitive flexibility, constructivism and hypertext: Random access instruction for advanced knowledge acquisition in ill-structured domains. In Duffy, T., & Jonassen, D. (Eds.), *Constructivism and the technology of instruction*. Hillsdale, NJ: Erlbaum.

Stasko, J. (1997). *Design principles*. Retrieved from http://www.cc.gatech.edu/classes/cs6751_97_winter/Topics/design-princ/

Sugrue, B., & Clark, R. E. (2000). Media selection for training. In Tobias, S., & Fletcher, J. D. (Eds.), *Training and retraining: A handbook for business, industry, government, and the military*. New York, NY. Macmillan Reference, USA.

Taylor, F. W. (1911). *The principles of scientific management*. New York, NY: Harper Bros.

Towler, A., Kraiger, K., Sitzmann, T., Van Overberghe, C., Cruz, J., Ronen, E., & Stewart, D. (2008). The seductive details effect in technology-delivered training. *Performance Improvement Quarterly, 21*, 65–86. doi:10.1002/piq.20023

Van Velsor, E., & Guthrie, V. A. (1998). Feedback intensive programs. In McCauley, C. D., Moxley, R. S., & Van Velsor, E. (Eds.), *The Center for Creative Leadership handbook of leadership development* (pp. 66–105). San Francisco, CA: Jossey-Bass.

Wagner, E. D. (1997). In support of a functional definition of interaction. In Cyrs, T. E. (Ed.), *Teaching and learning at a distance: What it takes to effectively design, deliver and evaluate programs* (pp. 19–26). San Francisco, CA: Jossey Bass. doi:10.1080/08923649409526852

Waldron, S. M., Patrick, J., Duggan, G. B., Banbury, S., & Howes, A. (2008). Designing information fusion for the encoding of visual-spatial information. *Ergonomics, 51*, 775–797. doi:10.1080/00140130701811933

Wisher, R., & Khan, B. (2010). *Learning on demand: ADL and the future of e-learning*. Washington, DC: ADL Initiative.

Wisher, R. A., Curnow, C. K., & Seidel, R. J. (2001). Knowledge retention as a latent outcome measure in distance learning. *American Journal of Distance Education, 15*(3), 20–35. doi:10.1080/08923640109527091

ADDITIONAL READING

Alessi, S. M. (1988). Fidelity in the design of instructional simulations. *Journal of Computer-Based Instruction, 15*, 40–47.

Arthur, W., Bennett, W., Stanush, P., & McNelly, T. (1998). Factors that influence skill decay and retention: A quantitative review and analysis. *Human Performance, 11*(1), 57–101. doi:10.1207/s15327043hup1101_3

Bonk, C. J., & Dennen, V. P. (1999). Teaching on the Web: With a little help from my pedagogical friends. *Journal of Computing in Higher Education, 11*(1), 3–28. doi:10.1007/BF02940840

Burgoon, J. K., Bonito, J. A., Bengtsson, B., Cederberg, C., Lundeberg, M., & Allspach, L. (2000). Interactivity in human-computer interaction: A study of credibility, understanding, and influence. *Computers in Human Behavior, 16*, 553–574. doi:10.1016/S0747-5632(00)00029-7

Colquitt, J. A., LePine, J. A., & Noe, R. A. (2000). Towards integrative theory of training motivation: A meta-analytic path analysis of 20 years of research. *The Journal of Applied Psychology, 85*, 678–707. doi:10.1037/0021-9010.85.5.678

Dede, C. (2007). Reinventing the Role of Information and Communications Technologies in Education. *Yearbook of the National Society for the Study of Education, 106*, 11–38. doi:10.1111/j.1744-7984.2007.00113.x

Dodds, P. V. W., & Fletcher, J. D. (2004). Opportunities for new "smart" learning environments enabled by next generation web capabilities. *Journal of Educational Multimedia and Hypermedia, 13*, 391–404.

Doherty, P. B. (1998). Learner control in asynchronous learning environments. *Asynchronous Learning Networks Magazine, 2*(2), 1–11.

Ericsson, K. A., & Lehmann, A. C. (1996). Expert and exceptional performance: Evidence of maximal adaptation to task constraints. *Annual Review of Psychology, 47*, 273–305. doi:10.1146/annurev.psych.47.1.273

Farr, M. (1987). *The long-term retention of knowledge and skills: A cognitive and instructional perspective*. New York: Springer-Verlag.

Fletcher, J. D., & Tobias, S. (2005). The multimedia principle. In R. E, Mayer (Ed.) *The Cambridge Handbook of Multimedia Learning* (pp 117-133). New York, NY: Cambridge University Press.

Graesser, A. C., Person, N., Harter, D., & TRG (2000). Teaching tactics in AutoTutor. *Proceedings of the workshop on modeling human teaching tactics and strategies at the Intelligent Tutoring Systems 2000 conference*. University of Quebec at Montreal, 49-57.

Hall, B. (1997). *Web-based training cookbook*. New York: Wiley & Sons.

Hays, R. T., & Singer, M. J. (1989). *Simulation fidelity in training system design: Bridging the gap between reality and training*. London, England: Springer-Verlag.

Healy, A., & Bourne, L. Jr. (1995). *Learning and memory of knowledge and skills: Durability and specificity*. Thousands Oaks, CA: Sage.

Hellervik, L. W. (1992). Behavior change: Models, methods, and a review of the evidence. In Dunnette, M. D., & Hough, L. M. (Eds.), *Handbook of industrial and organizational psychology* (2nd ed., *Vol. 3*, pp. 821–895). Palo Alto, CA: Consulting Psychologists Press.

Locke, E., & Latham, G. (2002). Building a practically useful theory of goal setting and task motivation. *The American Psychologist, 57*, 705–717. doi:10.1037/0003-066X.57.9.705

Nardi, B. A. (1996). *Context and Consciousness: Activity Theory and Human-Computer Interaction*. Boston, MA: Massachusetts Institute of Technology.

Nielson, J. (2000). *Designing web usability: The practice of simplicity*. Indianapolis, IN: New Riders Publishing.

Noe, R. A. (2008). *Employee training and development* (4th ed.). New York: Irwin-McGraw.

Northam, G. (2000). *Simulation Fidelity – Getting in Touch with Reality*. Proceedings of the SimTechT annual conference, Sydney, Australia.

Sadasivan, S. (2008). *Effective VR: Interplay of Presence, Perceptions, Fidelity, and Transfer Effects in the Development of Inspection Training Simulators*. Unpublished doctoral dissertation, Clemson, SC.

Schraagen, J. M., Chimpman, S. F., & Shalin, V. L. (2000). *Cognitive Task Analysis*. New York: Routledge Press.

Van Eerde, W., & Thierry, H. (1996). Vroom's expectancy models and work-related criteria: A meta-analysis. *The Journal of Applied Psychology, 81*, 575–586. doi:10.1037/0021-9010.81.5.575

Wetzel, C. D., Radtke, P. H., & Stern, H. W. (1994). *Review of the effectiveness of video media in instruction*. Hillsdale, NJ: Erlbaum.

KEY TERMS AND DEFINITIONS

Affective: In the context of learning, affective refers to tasks that involve emotions, motivation, and attitudes.

Cognitive: In the context of learning, cognitive refers to the acquisition of knowledge and the development of skills.

Individual Differences: The ways in which individual people differ in their behavior, preferences, and abilities.

Physical Fidelity: The extent to which a simulator realistically reproduces the aspects of the environment in which the actual task will be conducted.

Psychological Fidelity: The extent to which a training environment replicates the psychological processes relevant to the successful completion a task in the actual environment.

Psychomotor: In the context to learning, psychomotor refers to tasks that involve physical movement and refined motor skills.

Training: A systematic set of processes implemented with the goal of helping individuals and groups acquire the skills, rules, concepts, and attitudes that result in improved performance in another environment.

Chapter 4

Exploring Past Trends and Current Challenges of Human Computer Interaction (HCI) Design:
What does this Mean for the Design of Virtual Learning Environments?

Fiona Carroll
University of Glamorgan, UK

ABSTRACT

This chapter investigates the potential of aesthetics in the design of Human-Computer Interaction (HCI). In particular, it aims to provide a means by which aesthetics can be applied in photorealistic Virtual Reality (VR) to create engaging experiences. Indeed, this chapter suggests that much can be gained from looking at the aesthetics of photorealistic VR content as opposed to solely looking at the more traditional HCI approaches that have mainly concentrated on the performance and efficiency issues of the technology. The chapter is motivated by the very notion that the aesthetic potential of photorealistic VR content is, and continues to be, underestimated whilst the emphasis on the development of newer and more efficient technologies to create engaging VR experiences increases. Challenging this, the author reports on the results of a comparative analysis performed on two photorealistic virtual environments. These results highlight how both aesthetic form and functionality – efficiency and performance issues – need to be considered in tandem in order to create engaging VR experiences. In demonstrating this, the chapter aims to not only successfully emphasize the experiential side of photorealistic VR, but also to advance the idea of the engaged interaction and in doing so, a new design drive for HCI.

DOI: 10.4018/978-1-61350-516-8.ch004

Copyright © 2012, IGI Global. Copying or distributing in print or electronic forms without written permission of IGI Global is prohibited.

INTRODUCTION

Research shows that aesthetics has the potential to play an intrinsic role in HCI design (Lavie & Tractinsky, 2004; Tractinsky, 1997; Tractinsky, 2004; Tractinsky, 2005; Petersen et al, 2004; Djajadiningrat et al, 2000; Hoffman & Krauss, 2004). By the term *aesthetics*, I mean the process that causes an interaction between the design and the information already stored in the users mind – personal feeling, past experiences, formal knowledge – to expand and/or recombine their existing information and in turn produce a variety of emotions (Csikszentmihalyi & Robinson, 1990). However, in truth, it has taken many years for people like designers, developers, and researchers etc. to fully understand and realize the extent of this potential within HCI. For years the emphasis of the field of HCI has been on usability and particularly efficiency considerations, such as those involving objective performance criteria, time to learn, error rate, and time to complete a task (Lavie & Tractinsky, 2004). Even today, reminiscent of Card et al. (1983) many researchers believe that all HCI requires is a science base of knowledge (built from cognitive psychology and allied sciences) about human performance on which designers then can draw for their designs. However, as Hoffman & Krauss (2004) have pointed out, modern HCI design has placed too much emphasis on performance issues and not enough on other aspects, like aesthetics. In view of this, I propose to closely examine the past trends and current challenges of human computer interaction design. In particular, I will focus on the design of virtual environments that I firmly believe has been left behind in the current HCI movements towards the creation of more holistic experiences. Addressing this, I advocate a shift in focus from performance issues to now showing how aspects like aesthetics can also play a strong role in building people's attitudes and 'engaged' interactions in photorealistic virtual environments. In summary, the following sections aim to illus-trate how a new HCI "design" approach can play an integral part in the design of 'engaging' user interfaces for virtual environments.

PAST TRENDS: HCI AND USABILITY

Human-Computer Interaction is an interdisciplinary subject drawing on knowledge derived from the subject areas of science (physical and social sciences), engineering, and art (Johnson, 1992). This diverse mix of subjects brings with it a broad gathering of interest; however what they all have in common is the understanding that HCI involves the study of interactions between people and computers. The term HCI goes back to the early 1980s when it officially emerged with two main foci: the first on the development of methods and techniques to improve usability; the second on inventing new and more usable software and tools (Carroll, 2001). Even in these early instances, usability can be seen as taking a central role in HCI; so much so, that still today the discipline is portrayed 'as the study and the practice of usability. It is about understanding and creating software and other technology that people will want to use, will be able to use and will find effective when used' (Carroll, 2001, p. xxvii).

As history shows, this desire for usability very quickly became entwined with cognitive psychology theory; it became enthralled with finding out how fast or how easily a user can cognitively interpret the interface in order to efficiently complete a task. In fact, this made such an impact on HCI that researchers are still applying processes that feed into and support this way of designing. For example, over the last ten years, semiotics has started to play a more prominent role in HCI: this idea of the 'coupling of a sign process and a signal process' (Nake & Grabowski in Fishwick, 2006, p. 65) feeds into cognitive theory where 'the notion of the sender and reader in semiotics is not dissimilar to the notion of designer and user or system and user in HCI' (O'Neill, 2005, p. 26). As Nadin (1988) highlights '...to design means to structure systems of signs in such a way as to make possible the achievement of goals', so much so, he believes that all HCI is grounded in semiotics.

However, what seems to have been forgotten or perhaps cast aside until recently is the fact that usability is actually made up of several components. Usability is a collective term for all aspects of an activity's performance that can be affected by the use of technology (Whiteside et al. cited in Newman & Lamming, 1995). As Sutcliffe (1995) points out, an interface has good usability if it can be learned quickly, is easy to operate, can be remembered, and is satisfying. He deconstructs usability into the following components: effectiveness – the measure of how well the system performs in achieving what the user wants to do; learnability – how easy a system is to learn; memorability – the extent to which it reminds the user of previous interactions; and attitude/satisfaction – attitude is the subjective part of usability which quantifies user satisfaction with the system (Sutcliffe, 1995).

Even though HCI has been described as promoting and enabling 'work and other activities to be performed more effectively, efficiently and when performed by people, with more enjoyment and satisfaction' (Johnson, 1992, p. xiv), it has only been in the last few years that the focus on usability has shifted from effectiveness, learnability and memorability issues to also include the satisfaction component. In terms of VR design (and particularly photorealistic VR design) the focus, as we shall see, still remains on performance and efficiency issues. Indeed, the following sections of this chapter aim to broaden this outlook and to develop a more holistic approach to the design of photorealistic VR environments.

CURRENT CHALLENGES: HCI AND DESIGN

As mentioned the main goal of HCI has always been to contribute to the development of more usable digital artifacts (Löwgren & Stolterman, 2004). Today, these goals take on a different perspective as design has started to emerge as a central focus within HCI. In fact, the HCI field has become more and more interested in 'considering systems that people value for purposes other than as tools, we are finding an increasing need to consider aesthetics and other factors that can contribute to the value of a system or an artifact' (Karat & Karat, 2003, p.553). Therefore, it has become essential that HCI designers consider a more holistic approach to understanding usability. They need to consider the learnability, effectiveness and memorability of an interface, but also to consider Sutcliffe's (1995) fourth usability component: satisfaction (1995). The emphasis has now shifted from performance to the user's experience and designers are realizing that they need to explore design as a means of understanding how people feel and their attitudes towards systems.

In actual fact, the goals of HCI and our thoughts and feelings towards the role of technology in our lives has changed from thinking of technology as just a tool for increasing work productivity to now also allowing for its role in the creation of meaningful and valuable experiences. As Zimmerman (2003, p. 1) says 'more recently with the growing acceptance that emotional responses to products and interfaces play a dramatic role in people's perception and evaluation of devices and services, the role for design in HCI has become a little clearer'.

As a result, a new challenge for HCI is teasing out the relationship between the aesthetic and functionality of a system and in particular how to design for 'engaged' interactions. By this we mean all that occurs between the interface and the users' feelings, past experiences, memories, and knowledge that has the power to manipulate the perceptions and actions of the user to create new thoughts and feelings about their interaction with the interface. As Forlizzi (2006, page 1) points out, 'for these reasons, interaction design has developed a larger role within HCI' and for these same reasons, I feel that aspects of experience design could – and indeed should – also play an intrinsic role within HCI and the design of photorealistic VR environments.

Experience Design

Experience Design is a term used to describe an approach for creating successful experiences for people in any medium. Experience of technology refers to something larger than usability or one of its dimensions, such as satisfaction or attitude (McCarthy et al, 2004). It is the overall impression, feelings, interactions that a user has with a product or service. As Shedroff (2005) points out, this approach considers all three spatial dimensions, time, all five common senses, interactivity, as well as customer value and personal meaning. It is about creating experiences beyond just products and services, about creating relationships with individuals, creating an environment that connects on an emotional or value level to the customer (AIGA, 2006).

Until recently, HCI has seemed to have ignored many of these aspects of design, so much so, that experience is now becoming an increasingly important problem for HCI research (Wright et al, 2006) – especially when HCI designers are realizing that the concept of 'experience' is a critical issue for design (Forlizzi et al, 2004). Experience design encompasses traditional HCI design but also takes it further by addressing all aspects of the product, service, and environment and their relationship to the individual. In detail, it 'deals in a holistic manner with all aspects of a user's experience: visual design, interaction design, sound design, animation, industrial design, etc' (Saffer, 2004). It has become concerned with 'developing broader conceptions of usability to encompass enjoyment, engagement,

identity, trust and loyalty' (Blythe et al, 2006). Indeed, by encompassing and considering some of these aspects of experience design, designers can create 'desired perceptions, cognition, and behavior among users, customers, visitors, or the audience' (Jacobson, 2000) which can then enhance the user's experience of the interface or device. However, as already said, VR design seems to be lagging behind; photorealistic VR design, especially, needs to start to think beyond the efficiency issues and the bare cognitive processes of interaction and, like experience design, consider other processes of interaction (such as the 'engaged' interaction) which focus more 'on the interactions between people and products and the experiences that result' (Forlizzi et al, 2004).

VIRTUAL REALITY (VR) AND HCI

The concept of virtual reality has a long history; the search for illusionary visual space can be traced back to antiquity (Grau, 2003). However, the actual VR technology (as recognized today) only dates back about forty years to when researchers first started to consider the computer as a tool for visual display (Kalawsky, 1993). It is highly probable that this spurt of VR development grew from the successful medium of cinema, whose origins, like VR, 'based itself on its ability to show something, it solicits spectator attention, inciting visual curiosity and supplying pleasure through an exciting spectacle' (Elsaesser, 1990, p. 58).

In terms of HCI, VR environments offer a unique medium that allows users 'egocentric perspectives on three dimensional digital worlds' (Stanney, 2003, p. 622). One of its big attractions is that it can provide many opportunities for new kinds of experiences (Scaife & Rogers, 2001). Indeed, it is the perfect medium for the experience design driven HCI discussed above in that it has the potential to encourage an interaction on many different levels – sensually, intellectually, intuitively etc. As Gazzard (2007, p.1) says 'they [virtual worlds] have become increasingly common and diverse in their forms', however, according to Livingston et al. (2006, p. 301), 'there are limitations that have prevented many [VR] systems from being truly useful for participants. One reason is the need to overcome human factor issues'. As Kalawsky (1993) feels VR needs to break free of the early nineties when much more research needed to be undertaken, particularly in the field of human factors.

When one examines the design of virtual environments, one sees two distinct forms: there is the aesthetic notion of designing the desired perceptual responses; and there is the engineering notion of design which involves the creation of plans and models from which to test and build the desired effects (Fencott, 1999b). However, as Fencott (1999b, p. 1) says 'both forms of design are intrinsic to the process of designing effective virtual environments (VEs)' even though at times, the aesthetic tends to be pushed into second place behind the engineering. With regards to this, I am interested in pushing forward the more experiential side of photorealistic VR environments as a means of enhancing user experiences in VR. I am keen to challenge why the emotional aspects of the virtual experience have generally been ignored (Lee, 2007) and why 'the actual nature of the content of virtual environment is [still] rarely considered' (Fencott, 1999a, line 30). The focus in this chapter is therefore on the experiential side of photorealistic VR, and I am interested in what it actually means to 'create a full sensory experience with control of view and narrative development' (Isdale et al., 2002, p.1).

Interacting with VR

'Virtual reality, or virtual environment techniques, will change the way in which man interacts with computer systems' (Kalawsky, 1993, p. 2).

This chapter is primarily concerned with visual interaction in photorealistic VR where participants wear specialized equipment such as head-mounted display (HMD), as an extension of their visual sense to explore the virtual environment. The HMD and head tracker monitor the participant's position and orientation while the stereo imagery provides different views of the virtual environment for each eye. My interest lies in how the participant experiences the photorealistic content as they move around the environment (more so than how the actual VR technology works). Lund & Waterworth (1998) suggest 'a key difference between more tool-like applications (word processors, spreadsheets, etc.) and virtual environments is that users will need more than a functional understanding to interact with virtual environments' (p.1). Virtual environments need to make sense to those who inhabit them; they need to provide meaningful experiences for their inhabitants (Lund & Waterworth, 1998).

One of the most important yet exciting differences between VR and other communications media is that virtual environments can create artificial stimuli for the perceptual systems to interpret rather than making the interpretations for the spectators. It can 'attract visitor's attention through patterns of mediated stimuli which will achieve purpose if the visitor perceives and responds to them as the designer intended' (Fencott, 1999a, p.1). Marsh et al. (2001) describe it as a transparent or invisible style of interaction which keeps them in the flow of their activities and consequently enhances the experiences of participants. Instead of passively interacting and receiving information like readers of a book or participants of a film, participants in a VR environment create their own experiences and narratives. It is their interactive contribution that determines the outcome (Marsh & Wright, 2000). It is this notion of the invisible style of interaction that is driving our work in photorealistic VR design; how to design an 'engaged' interaction which has the power to manipulate the thoughts and feelings of the user to whatever the desired effect.

The VR Environmental Aesthetic Experience

Media artists represent a new type of artist, who not only sounds out the aesthetic potential of advanced methods of creating images and formulates new options of perception and artistic positions in this media revolution, but also specifically researches innovative forms of interaction and interface design, thus contributing to the development of the medium in key areas, both as artists and scientists (Grau, 2003b, p. 3).

Environmental aesthetics can be described as extending 'beyond the narrow confines of the art world and beyond the appreciation of works of art to the aesthetic appreciation of human-influenced and human-constructed as well as natural environments' (Carlson, 2002a, p.1). It is about appreciating environments, and it takes on board the fact that when we appreciate these environments, we are immersed within the object of our appreciation: 'if we move, we move within the object of our appreciation and thereby change our relationship to it and at the same time change the object itself' (Carlson, 2000, p.xvii) We, as appreciators of the environment, become engaged through the senses to become integral parts in the environment itself. It is not only about looking: it is about being in and part of any environment – seeing, hearing, feeling, touching and smelling the environment).

Environmental aesthetics can be applied to natural environments as well as manmade environments (i.e. VR environments) that can range from large landscapes to small and more intimate environments, from ordinary to extraordinary scenes and places. As Berleant defines it, 'an environment is the fusion of an organic awareness of meanings both conscious and unaware of geographical location, of physical presence, personal time, pervasive movement' (1992, p. 34). In terms of the aesthetic experience, an environment is very different from the more traditional art piece, in that 'appreciators are confronted by,

if not intimately and totally immersed in, objects of appreciation that impinge upon their senses, are constantly in motion, are limited in neither time nor space and are of a non predetermined nature and meaning' (Carlson, 2002b, p1).

In terms of photorealistic VR, participants are deceived into believing that the objects in the picture are real and are before them. However, like photography, its aesthetic qualities are not only 'to be sought in its power to lay bare the realities' (Bazin cited in Graham, 1997, p. 102) but also in its capacity to represent objects in a way that is exclusive to VR – visually, tactile, auditory etc – as well as its ability to impose other layers of meaning through choice, technical treatment, framing and layout – through special effects, pose, photogenia and aestheticism (Barthes, 1977, p. 20/21). As Friday (2002) emphasises 'a causal relation with its subject matter may be at the heart of photography [VR], but the photographer [VR designer] has available many means of manipulating and controlling the effects of that causal relation' (p. 72).

Photographers as well as photorealistic VR designers can choose and employ techniques and materials of various types in order to create pictures that draw attention to themselves. As Scruton (1983) points out 'the photographer who aims for an aesthetically significant representation must also aim to control detail: detail being here understood in the wide sense of "any observable fact or feature"' (p. 117). When a photograph or photorealistic VR environment attracts and captures our attention, it does more than merely satisfying our need for visual information: it is the creative use of the medium that attracts our aesthetic interest and 'engages' us.

A photorealistic VR environment, like a photograph, can be designed to encourage the viewer to participate in and perceptually integrate with the content. It can show its subject in a particular light and from a particular viewpoint and subsequently it might reveal things about it that one does not normally observe and, perhaps, that one might not have observed but for the photograph

(Scruton, 1983). It is true, the aesthetic elements of photorealistic VR environments can be patterned to encourage 'continuity' between the viewer and the environment and in doing so, 'engage' them in specific modes of thinking and feeling. As the following study will show the aesthetic form and how it works with the functionality needs to be carefully considered in order to create 'engaging' photorealistic VR experiences.

STUDY: DESIGNING ENGAGING VIRTUAL ENVIRONMENTS

This study investigates the intertwined role of both functionality and form in the design and development of engaging user experiences in virtual

reality (VR). It uses two versions of the same sitting room VR environment: Environment A is a photorealistic static mosaic of a sitting room in a flat in Edinburgh which, when wearing a head mounted display (HMD), allows the user to look 360 degrees around, up and down the room (see Figure 1).

Environment B is also a static mosaic of the same room but this time the color has been saturated at strategically significant areas around the room to encourage the user to look 360 degrees around, up and down the environment (see Figure 2). In detail this dispersion of saturated color in environment B is carefully calculated and chosen to entice the user to look around the room and in doing so to fully engage in the VR experience and also in the creation of a personal visual-narrative.

Figure 1. Environment A

Figure 2. Environment B

A visual-narrative can be defined as pictures that tell a story. These pictures do not depend on a literary component, but are made up of an image or a set of visual elements, which are interwoven with a narrative intent (Coulter-Smith, 2000).

In environment B, the composition and choice of the saturated colors has not only been inspired by the functionality of the VR technology but also by past visual narratives such as Duccio's *Maesta* (1308-11), Masaccio's *The Tribute Money* (1425), Memling's *The Passion of Christ* (1470), and Velasquez's *Las Meninas* (1656) (Carroll, 2008). Following the techniques of these past visual-narratives, particularly Duccio's use of isochromatic patterns and symbolism and Memling's use of artificial color and spatial narrative, the colors have been strategically arranged in environment B to arouse certain thoughts and feelings about the person that lives in the flat. For example the colors are used to arouse youthful, happy, energetic and friendly feelings about the female person who lives there, as well as to highlight certain objects around the room that offer several clues about her character. It is envisioned that the functionality – the ability to look 360 degrees around the room – will work with the saturated colors in the environment to further engage the user in looking around the room and in doing so, figure out the narrative. Indeed, the study aims to show how both the functionality and form of the VR environments working together within a narrative context can create 'engaged' interactions and hence engaging user experiences.

Procedure

Twenty participants, thirteen male and seven female, from a mixed academic background were asked to take part in the study. On arriving at the location of the test, they were asked to familiarize themselves with the VR Kit, especially the HMD and the equipment by trying a sample of an unrelated VR environment for a few minutes.

They were then told briefly about the nature of the test and informed that it would last at the most 30 minutes. Next, they were asked to complete a standard Ishihara Test for Color Blindness. In random order, they were asked to experience, for 5 to 10 minutes, both environment A and environment B of the same flat. During these trials, each participant was asked to talk-aloud and describe their experience. After 'visiting' each environment, they were asked to answer, in writing, the following three questions: Did you enjoy the experience? Why? Were you engaged in the environment? Why? Did it catch your attention and get you involved in the experience? They were then shown both environments again briefly and, elaborating on the written questions, they were asked two similar questions which were recorded using the Digital Audio Tape: Which one did you enjoy the most? Which environment did you find more engaging?

Results

Using a qualitative method of analysis, the aim was to probe into each participant's experience of both environment A and environment B in order to decipher which environment more successfully enhances an 'engaging' user experience. The author uses Berleant's constructs of *Aesthetic Engagement* as a benchmark for analyzing participant's sense of 'engaged' interaction in both environments (Berleant, 1992). It specifically looked at the participant's continuity, perceptual integration and participation in each environment. In that light, the results of the study have proved interesting. The majority of participants felt their attention was captured more in environment B than in the environment A. They reported that they were attracted to the saturated colors; they felt that the objects stood out more; they were noticing more things and in that sense, they were involved more in their surroundings - shown by their looking around and participating:

- 'The first one (Environment B) because I was more curious, some of the colors attract your eyes (i.e. the bag), in the first one I saw it directly and in the second one (Environment A) I had to look for it, it was there but I wouldn't have seen it like that, I saw it directly, in the first, you can show what you want to show it's easier, ya I think the first one engaged you more because its much more curious…' Participant (1)
- 'The second one (Environment B), I could see things more, it was clearer, there was lighter and when I was bending down it was better, seems to be better' Participant (2)
- 'The colors are a bit brighter I can see a lot more things' Participant (4) in the Environment B.
- 'Am the second one (Environment B) I think because more things were jumping out and standing out more, you could have a better nose.' Participant (6)
- 'The second one (Environment B) because it was clearer and more engaging it made me look for things and more details' Participant (8)

It seems that even though both Environment B and Environment A were almost identical, participants were inclined to think that there were fewer objects in Environment A. In fact, the findings show that the saturated colors in Environment B attracted participant's attention to objects that they did not necessarily notice in Environment A. The saturated colors have put an emphasis on certain areas in the room and in doing so, they have subtly persuaded participants to participate, to become involved with each object and then also to look thoroughly at each area around the environment. In addition, the saturated colors have also succeeded in getting participants to feel in certain ways; they are using their senses to create new meanings – perceptual integration – and to build their own impressions. Through the colors, some

of the participants are forming happy, peaceful feelings while others are being more specific when they claim that the colors are giving them more female orientated feelings and impressions.

- 'The first one (Environment B) because of the colors, it is much more colorful and I think it gives you as well as the feeling of happiness that you have more color, more brighter colors, brightness actually thinks it makes you feel much more happy. Much more you know, peaceful feeling, I don't know if that makes sense…a peaceful and colorful environment… if it's not colorful you feel much more sad…' Participant (1)
- 'The feeling of the room gives off a girls feeling…' Participant (7), Environment B
- 'The first thing that occurs to me as I think it's a girl room am I think I can see female clothing lying around but then when I think the colors I immediately felt female.' Participant (13), Environment B

The data also shows that the colors are having a positive impact on the participants; their involvement with the colors is feeding into their impressions of the room. The colors are making them feel more cheered up and happy which in turn are giving them lively and warm impressions of the room.

- 'the feeling from the colors impressed me more' Participant (20), Environment B
- 'it seems a little bit livelier, the room' Participant (4), Environment B
- 'But the first one (Environment A) felt like a dull day so the bright colors would automatically make me feel more cheered up.' Participant (5)

When one probes closer, it is interesting to see how these feelings strongly differ from those felt in Environment A. The following comparisons show a distinct contrast between how participants felt in each environment:

In the Environment B, participant1 felt:

- 'I will say a lively place, there's life here… it's a very relaxed atmosphere, ya its like because it's ordered but not totally ordered it's like everything … ya it's a nice one' Participant (1), Environment B

While in Environment A, participant 1 felt:

- 'It's exactly the same but it looks sad… I still feel comfortable but in the other one I would still have a smile on my face while looking at the bed room but in this one I will just look at it I don't know how to express it, it's a global feeling…its much more sad…' Participant (1), Environment A

In Environment B, Participant 11 felt:

- 'I think I feel warm about this room (Environment B) ah why…the colors of the room, there are many warm colors in the room…the room is small, not many things in the room and warm in my mind, it feels comfortable maybe there is a beautiful girl' Participant (11), Environment B

In Environment A, they felt:

- 'It's very similar but I feel some lonely …am am it's a simple and lonely room' Participant (11), Environment A

In fact, when further investigated, quite a few participants pondered over the contrasting feelings they were receiving from both environments – why they were feeling these?. In many ways Berleant's idea of 'continuity' is beginning to emerge – 'continuity' between environment B and the user's individual and cultural experiences.

- 'got slightly different feelings. it feels am… the first one (Environment B), I keep going back to colors but they were things that stood out first and foremost for me, am they would give me a different impression to the person who lived there, the second one (Environment A) I almost felt the person who lived there was in a, you know, longer relationship, don't really know why, could be to do with things like flamboyance for example the shoes… ya that's it' Participant (5)

- 'I don't know because I thought story for the first environment… if I think the second one (Environment A) is an old story and sad one in the first (Environment B) there is more activity, in the second one I don't know if the place was deserted just a little more deserted not a lot cos there are woman's shoes so in the second one' Participant (17)

In terms of Environment B, it is interesting to see how the feelings, thoughts, and intuitions etc. created by the colors are fusing with the functionality to encourage participants to fully explore the room and, in doing so, to piece together the story. As Participant (1) demonstrates the saturated colors and the consequent feelings aroused are being framed within the 360 degree viewpoint to feed the creation of a narrative. We are beginning to see the happy routine of the person living in Environment B versus the more 'mundane' routine of the person living in Environment A.)

- 'The second one (Environment A) shows you a kind of routine, the first one shows you a happy routine but a more lively, the second one is much more a routine because the colors are always the same' Participant(1)

Indeed, the participants are sensually, intuitively, reminiscently and intellectually interacting with the colors planted strategically in areas 360 degrees around the room, so much so, the happy, warm female feelings that are emerging are seen to feed directly into the building of a narrative. From the impressions the colors have aroused, the majority of participants have started to tease out a female presence. The colors have influenced the participant's judgment on some of the finer details concerning this female character – the colors have made participants feel that the character is quite young:

- 'younger people probably 20's to 30's this time ok' Participant (4), Environment B
- 'I would say the person is probably mid 20's early 30's' Participant (5), Environment B
- 'certainly younger ah...don't know if I would still say that it is rented certainly younger probably 20's am... ya' Participant (18), Environment B
- 'I would say that she is in her late to mid twenties that am...' Participant (7), Environment B

However, in Environment A participants are building different impressions, they feel that the character living in the flat is that bit older:

- 'it kind of an old ladies flat... oh no perhaps not middle aged slightly younger, kinda 30's to 40's maybe' Participant (4), Environment A
- 'I would probably say they were a little bit more reserved... in terms of what they were, maybe reserved is not the right word maybe a little bit ... they are not as flamboyant' Participant (5), Environment A

As the data shows, participants are beginning to form female orientated narratives in environment B, they are creating narratives about a young and even 'beautiful' female, a lively person, who is in a happy routine and living in a comfortable, relaxed flat. In the environment A, participants are reading the opposite; they feel it is about an older and less flamboyant couple who are in a long term relationship and in a routine, who perhaps live simple, lonely and sad lives.

In summary, this study establishes that fifteen out of nineteen participants (one participant was unsure) found Environment B more 'engaging'. Reflecting on the above qualitative data, it is feasible to suggest that the aesthetic qualities of the photorealistic VR environments, in conjunction with the functionality – ability to look 360 degrees around, up and down – have been successful in getting participants to participate, perceptually integrate and create a 'continuity' when compared to Environment A. The study shows that both VR environments allowed participants to look 360 degrees around the room however only when the functionality was interweaved with the aesthetic form did participants engage fully in the user experience. In conclusion, the majority of participants found Environment B more 'engaging' than Environment A.

Discussion

This study has highlighted the important role of the *aesthetic* in the creation of 'engaging' photorealistic VR experiences. In detail, it shows how the *aesthetic* – as expressed in changes of color intensity of certain objects – when intertwined with the functionality of the VR environment has the strength to sway the user's thoughts and feelings in certain directions. In doing so, it confirms the combined power of the functionality and the aesthetics to influence how participants interact with, and feel within photorealistic VR environments, the power to create 'engaging' user experiences. It is this power to 'engage' participants that emphasises the need to rethink the current drive within photorealistic VR development and to start considering how these environments actually make us feel, as opposed to solely looking at what they enable us to do. In terms of HCI, the use of aesthetic takes the general understanding of interaction to a new level, to the 'engaged' interaction and the invisible style of interaction

(Marsh et al, 2001) that has previously been talked about. It takes interaction beyond usability and more towards the experiential, which as seen, introduces many possibilities for new and exciting experiences

FUTURE RESEARCH DIRECTIONS

Emerging from this chapter are thoughts on the future of HCI; in particular the role of *aesthetics* in this future and then the impact this can have on the design of VR environments. Some might ask if we are moving towards a new unified theory of interaction or are we looking at a complementary paradigm to HCI? I have described how aesthetics can indeed work with the functionality of VR system to create more engaged user experiences. However, even though the results suggest strongly that there is an effect worth studying, the future of this work lies in probing this further. It lies in repeating the study with a larger, more diverse group of subjects and teasing out more effective and efficient ways of measurement and evaluation. In doing this, the research will be in a more confidant position to investigate how the 'engaged' interaction fits in with other current research on the aesthetic in HCI – how we might work together towards firmly establishing the role of aesthetics within the field – and then move towards a more complete and unified theory of interaction which includes the 'engaged' interaction.

CONCLUSION

'Good design has always been concerned with the whole experience of interaction. Although most people think that design is about what we see – form, shape, proportion, color and finish – the aesthetic value comes from the whole experience, including gesture and ritual, what we feel and hear perhaps even what we taste and smell' (Moggridge, 1999, p.17).

The power to influence how one might feel – influence what type of experiences they might adhere to – opens the door to endless possibilities of how we might design for certain perceptions, cognition and behaviors amongst users. By demonstrating this, this chapter has highlighted the increasing need for photorealistic VR design to move beyond its fixation with efficiency and performance matters and to consider a more holistic approach that encompasses the senses, intellect, intuition, sentiment, and cultural interpretations. In fact, through the careful delineation of experience design, this chapter has indirectly pushed and promoted a more experience orientated drive for photorealistic VR design. By pursuing the 'engaged' interaction instead of the mere physical interaction, this chapter has not only successfully shown the power of the aesthetic in HCI but also the greater combined power of form and functionality to trigger emotions, associations and intuitions as a means to fuelling the creation of 'engaging' experiences.

REFERENCES

AIGA. (2006). *What is experience design?* (Online). Retrieved from http://www.aiga .org/content.cfm?Contentalias=what_is_ed

Barthes, R. (1977). *Image, music, text*. London, UK: Fontana Paperbacks.

Berleant, A. (1992). *The aesthetics of environment*. Philadelphia, PA: Temple University Press.

Blythe, M., Wright, P., & Mccarthy, J. (2006). Theory and method for experience centred design. In *CHI 2006 – Conference on Human Factors in Computing Systems*, 22-27th April, Montréal, Québec, Canada (pp.1691–1694). New York, NY: ACM Press. (Online). Retrieved from portal.acm. org/ ft_gateway.cfm? Id=1125764&type=pdf

Card, S., Moran, T. P., & Newell, A. (1983). *The psychology of human-computer interaction*. New Jersey: Lawrence Erlbaum Associates.

Carlson, A. (2000). *Aesthetics and the environment – The appreciation of nature, art and architecture.* London, UK: Routledge.

Carlson, A. (2002a). What is environmental aesthetics? Environmental aesthetics. In E. Craig (Ed.), *Routledge encyclopaedia of philosophy.* London, UK: Routledge. (Online). Retrieved from http://www.rep.routledge.com/ article/ M047SECT1

Carlson, A. (2002b). The central philosophical issue of environmental aesthetics: Environmental aesthetics. In E. Craig (Ed.), *Routledge encyclopaedia of philosophy.* London, UK: Routledge. (Online). Retrieved from http://www.rep.routledge.com/ article/M047SECT1

Carroll, F. (2008). The spatial development of the visual-narrative from prehistoric cave paintings to computer games. In Turner, P., Turner, S., & Davenport, E. (Eds.), *Exploration of space, technology, and spatiality: Interdisciplinary perspectives.* Hershey, PA: IGI Global. doi:10.4018/978-1-60566-020-2.ch011

Carroll, J. M. (2001). *Human computer interaction in the millennium.* New York, NY: ACM Press, Addison-Wesley.

Coulter-Smith, G. (2000). *The visual-narrative matrix.* Southampton, UK: Southampton Institute.

Csikszentmihalyi, M., & Robinson, R. E. (1990). *The art of seeing – An interpretation of the aesthetic encounter.* New York, NY: J Paul Getty museum.

Djajadiningrat, J. P., Gaver, W. W., & Frens, W. J. (2000). Interaction relabelling and extreme characters: Methods for exploring aesthetic interactions. In *Proceedings of the Conference on Designing Interactive Systems: Processes, Practices, Methods, and Techniques,* 17-19th August, (pp. 66–71). New York, NY: ACM Press. Retrieved from http://studiolab.io.tudelft.nl/static/gems/publications/00djajdisinte.pdf

Elsaesser, T. (1990). *Early cinema, space frame and narrative.* London, UK: British Film Institute.

Fencott, C. (1999a). *Content and creativity in virtual environment design.* In Virtual Systems and Multimedia, 1-3rd September, Dundee. Scotland: University of Abertay Dundee Publishers (Online). Retrieved from http://www-scm.tees.ac.uk/users/p.c.fencott/vsmm99/welcome.html

Fencott, C. (1999b). *Towards a design methodology for virtual environments.* In King's Manor Workshop: User Centered Design and Implementation of Virtual Environments, 30th September, York. Retrieved from http://www.cs.York.ac.uk/hci/ kings_manor_workshops/UCDIVE/fencott.pdf

Fishwick, P. (Ed.). (2006). *Aesthetic computing.* Cambridge, MA: MIT Press.

Forlizzi, J. (2006). *How do HCI researchers view interaction design?* Retrieved from http://goodgestreet.com/ theory/hcid.html

Friday, J. (2002). *Aesthetics and photography.* London, UK: Ashgate Publishing Limited.

Gazzard, A. (2007). Playing without gaming. In Digital Games: Design and Theory, 14th September, Brunel University, London. Retrieved from http://arts.brunel.ac.uk/ gate/gamesconference/

Grau, O. (2003). *Virtual art – From illusion to immersion.* USA: MIT Press.

Hoffman, R., & Krauss, K. (2004). A critical evaluation of literature on visual aesthetics for the Web. In *Proceedings of the 2004 Annual Research Conference of the South African Institute of Computer Scientists and Information Technologists on IT Research in Developing Countries,* 4-6th October, Stellenbosch (pp. 205-209). South Africa: ACM International Conference Proceeding Series. (Online). Retrieved from http://portal.acm.org/citation.cfm?Id=1035053.1035077

Isdale, J., Daly, L., Fencott, C., & Heim, M. (2002). Content development for virtual environments. In K. M. Stanney, (Ed.), *Handbook of virtual environments: Design, implementation and applications* (pp. 519-532). Lawrence Erlbaum Associates. Retrieved from http://vr.isdale.com/vrtechreviews/vrcontentdev/contentdev4ve_FINALDRAFT.doc

Jacobson, B. (2000). Experience design. *A List Apart: Online Magazine*. Retrieved from http://alistapart.com/articles/experience

Johnson, P. (1992). *Human computer interaction-Psychology, task analysis and software engineering*. Mcgraw-Hill Book Company Europe.

Kalawsky, R. S. (1993). *The science of virtual reality and virtual environments*. Addison-Wesley Publishers.

Karat, J., & Karat, C. M. (2003). The evolution of user-centred focus in the human-computer interaction field. *IBM Systems Journal, 42*(4). Retrieved from http://www.research.ibm.com/ journal/sj/424/karat.html. doi:10.1147/sj.424.0532

Lavie, T., & Tractinsky, N. (2004). Assessing dimensions of perceived visual aesthetics of web sites. *International Journal of Human-Computer Studies, 60,* 269–298. Retrieved from http://www.ise.bgu.ac.il/faculty/ noam/papers/04_tl_nt_ijhcs.pdf#search=%22lavie%2C%20visual%20aesthetics%20of%20web%20sites%22. doi:10.1016/j.ijhcs.2003.09.002

Lee, J. J. (2007). Emotion and sense of telepresence: The effects of screen viewpoint, self-transcendence style, and NPC in a 3D game environment. In *Human Computer Interaction (Intelligent Multimodal interaction Environments)* '07. 22-27 July, Beijing, China (pp. 392-399). Heidelberg, Germany: Springer.

Löwgren, J., & Stolterman, E. (2004). *Thoughtful interaction design – A design perspective on Information Technology*. USA: MIT Press.

Lund, A., & Waterworth, J. A. (1998). *Experiential design: Reflecting embodiment at the human-computer interface*. Retrieved from http://www.informatik.umu.se/ ~jwworth/metadesign.html

Marsh, T., & Wright, P. (2000). *Maintaining the illusion of interacting within a 3D virtual space*. In Presence 2000, 27-28th March, Delft, Netherlands. (Online). Retrieved from http://www.cs.york.ac.uk/hci/inquisitive/ papers/presence00/marsh wright00.pdf

Marsh, T., Wright, P., & Smith, S. (2001). Evaluation for the design of experience in virtual environments: Modelling breakdown of interaction and illusion. *Journal of Cyberpsychology and Behavior, 4*(2), 225–238. Retrieved from http://www.cs.york.ac.uk/hci/inquisitive/ papers/cyberpsy01/cyberpsy01.pdf. doi:10.1089/109493101300117910

Mccarthy, J., & Wright, P. (2004). *Technology as experience*. Massachusetts: MIT Press.

Moggridge, B. (1999). Expressing experiences in design. ACM Digital Library. *Interactions, 6*(4), 17–25. Retrieved from http://delivery.acm.org/10.1145/310000/306430/ p17-moggridge.pdf?Key1=306430&key2= 5164022611&coll= Portal&dl=GUIDE&CFID= 4739955&CFTOKEN=91571747. (30/10/2006).

Nadin, M. (1988). *Interface design: A semiotic paradigm*. Retrieved from http://www.cs.ucsd.edu/users/ goguen/courses/nadin.pdf

Newman, W. M., & Lamming, M. G. (1995). *Interactive systems design*. Addison Wesley Longman Ltd.

Nielsen, J. (2003). *An introduction to usability*. Retrieved from http://www.useit.com/ alertbox/20030825.html

O'Neill, S. (2005). Comparing compatible semiotic perspectives for the analysis of interactive media devices. *Applied Semiotics: A Learned Journal of Literary Research on the World Wide Web, 6*(16). Retrieved from http://www.Chass.toronto.edu/ french/as-sa/ASSA-No16/ Article1en.html

Petersen, M. G., Iversen, O. S., Krogh, P. G., & Ludvigsen, M. (2004). Aesthetic interaction – A pragmatist's aesthetics of interactive systems. In *Designing Interactive Systems: Processes, Practices, Methods, and Techniques,* 10th March, Cambridge, MA (pp. 269–276). New York, NY: ACM Press. Retrieved from http://www.daimi.au.dk/ ~sejer/Home_files/Aesthetic.pdf

Saffer, D. (2004). *Experience design versus interaction design.* (Online). Retrieved from http://lists.interactiondesigners.com/ htdig.cgi/ discuss-interactiondesigners.Com/ 2004-November/003501.html

Scaife, M., & Rogers, Y. (2001). Informing the design of a virtual environment to support learning for children. *International Journal of Human-Computer Studies, 55*(2), 115–143. Retrieved from http://www.informatics.sussex.ac.uk/ research/ groups/interact/publications/ S&R-IJHCS'02.pdf. doi:10.1006/ijhc.2001.0473

Scruton, R. (1983). *The aesthetic understanding.* Carcanet New Press Ltd.

Shedroff, N. (2005a). *Experience design.* Retrieved from http://www.nathan.com/ ed/glossary/index.html

Stanney, K. M. (Ed.). (2003). *International Journal of Human-Computer Interaction.* Lawrence Erlbaum Assoc Inc.

Sutcliffe, A. G. (1995). *Human-computer interface design* (2nd ed.). London, UK: Macmillan Press Ltd.

Tractinsky, N. (1997). *Aesthetics and apparent usability: Empirically assessing cultural and methodological issues.* In CHI 97 – Looking to the Future, 22-27th March, Atlanta, Georgia. Retrieved from http://acm.org/sigchi/chi97/ proceedings/paper/nt.htm

Tractinsky, N. (2004). Towards the study of aesthetics in Information Technology. In *25th Annual International Conference on Information Systems*, 12-15th December, Washington, (pp. 771-780). Retrieved from http://www.ise.bgu.ac.il/faculty/ noam/papers/04_nt_icis.pdf

Tractinsky, N. (2005). *Does aesthetics matter in human computer interaction?* Retrieved from http://mc.informatik.uni-hamburg.de/ konferenzbaende/mc2005/konferenzband/ muc2005_02_tractinsky.pdf

Wright, P., Blythe, M., & Mccarthy, J. (2006). *The idea of design in HCI.* Retrieved from http://www-users.cs.york.ac.uk/ ~pcw/papers/DS VIS%20 paper18_08.pdf

Zimmerman, J. (2003). *Position paper on design in HCI education.* Retrieved from http://www.cs.cmu.edu/ ~johnz/pubs/2003_Interact_pp.pdf

KEY TERMS AND DEFINITIONS

Aesthetic: The object – art/design elements – that causes an interaction between the design and the information already stored in the users mind – personal feeling, past experiences, formal knowledge – to expand and/or recombine their existing information and in turn produce a variety of emotions.

Aesthetic Experience: It is an enriching experience that results from the specific use and grouping of certain art/design elements that sensually attract and arouse the user into the sharing of the information between the design and the user. It is this 'engaged' interaction between the artwork and the user's past experiences, memories, knowledge etc. that has the power to manipulate the perceptions of the user and create new thoughts and feelings.

Engaged Interaction: This occurs between the interface and the users' feelings, past experiences, memories, and knowledge. It has the power to manipulate the perceptions and actions of the user to create new thoughts and feelings about their interaction with the interface.

Engagement: Being involved or drawn in.

Environmental aesthetics: The aesthetic appreciation of human-influenced and human-constructed, as well as natural environments.

Experience Design: Is an approach for creating successful experiences for people in any medium.

Human-Computer Interaction (HCI): The study of interactions between people and computers.

Virtual Reality (VR): A computer generated three dimensional landscape that allows us to expand our physical and sensory powers.

VR Experience: An immersive, illusive – based on or creating an illusion of reality, interactive and self controlling/ creating experience, framed (in the study discussed in this paper) by the used of assistive technology: headgear, gloves, etc.

Chapter 5
Architectural Models for Reliable Multi-User Interfaces

Mario Ciampi
ICAR-CNR, Italy

Antonio Coronato
ICAR-CNR, Italy

Giuseppe De Pietro
ICAR-CNR, Italy

Luigi Gallo
ICAR-CNR, Italy

ABSTRACT

Virtual Environments are complex systems in that they involve the crucial concept of sharing. Users can share knowledge of each other's current activities, environments, and actions. In this chapter, the authors discuss about interaction interoperability, intended to mean the ability of two or more users to cooperate despite the heterogeneity of their interfaces. To allow such interoperability, formal methods to formalize the knowledge and middleware solutions for sharing that knowledge are required. After introducing the state-of-the-art solutions and the open issues in the field, the authors describe a system for providing interaction interoperability among multi-user interfaces. Rather than focusing on the decoupling of input devices from interaction techniques and from interaction tasks, this chapter suggests integrating interactive systems at higher level through an interface standardization. To achieve this aim, the authors propose: i) an architectural model able to handle differences in input devices and interaction tasks; ii) an agent-based middleware that provides basic components to integrate heterogeneous user interfaces. The chapter also presents a case study in which an agent-based middleware is used to support developers in the interconnection of monolithic applications.

DOI: 10.4018/978-1-61350-516-8.ch005

Copyright © 2012, IGI Global. Copying or distributing in print or electronic forms without written permission of IGI Global is prohibited.

INTRODUCTION

In recent years, Virtual Environments (VEs) have become increasingly popular and used for a variety of contexts, such as entertainment, scientific visualization, training, education, art. People from different countries, with different cultures and different languages should be able to collaborate each other in these computer-based simulated environments by using user-centric interfaces. The domain, the task, the input and the output device used have to be considered to provide a usable interface for a specific user in a specific virtual environment. This chapter is focused on interoperability, the ability of two or more software components to cooperate despite differences in language, interface, and execution platform (Wegner, 1997). In greater detail, we discuss interaction interoperability that is the ability of two or more users to cooperate despite differences in input devices and interaction techniques.

To the best of our knowledge, this question has recently been raised in (Ahmed, Gracanin, & Abdel-Hamid, 2008b). In this paper, the authors propose a framework to support interaction interoperability, the main benefit of which is the ability to use ontologies to define interaction tasks and techniques without specifying how these tasks should be accomplished. By using ontologies, the framework binds tasks to the user's preferred interaction techniques and then to available input devices. In other works by the same authors, (Ahmed, Gracanin, Abdel-Hamid, & Matkovic, 2008) and (Ahmed, Gracanin, & Abdel-Hamid, 2008a), the framework capabilities are further described. Interoperability is granted by using a standardized taxonomy built with the Ontology Web Language (OWL). The framework they propose should also be able to choose the best input device for a particular user by analyzing her/his preferences in the interaction. The idea of decoupling interaction techniques from interaction tasks and input devices is also described in (Bowman et al., 2006), in which the authors

explore the integration of different technologies to support co-located collaborations.

From the point of view of an interface programmer, decoupling interaction techniques from input devices may not be worthwhile. As Poupyrev et al. outlined in (Poupyrev, Weghorst, Billinghurst, & Ichikawa, 1998), similar interaction techniques vary depending on the particular implementation. Studies of the particular implementation of a technique may not be easily applied to other implementations of the same technique. Therefore, decoupling interaction techniques from input devices and mixing them according to user patterns could reduce the usability of the interface.

In light of these considerations, assuming that a formal description of interaction tasks is still necessary, we propose to let interaction designers plan ITs coupling them strictly to the particular input devices used. In the approach, we propose that different ITs and input devices are handled in a common framework in the same way as black boxes. We suggest using an agent-based middleware to provide interaction interoperability in Collaborative Virtual Environments (CVEs). This middleware is built upon an architectural model in which the typical system layers have been extended to provide interface standardization between different systems. The aim is to allow both interaction designers to plan ITs, coupling them with the corresponding input devices, and users to collaborate by using the combination of ITs and devices they prefer.

Rather than focusing on the de-coupling of input devices from interaction techniques and from interaction tasks, we suggest integrating interactive systems at higher level through an interface standardization. To achieve this aim, we propose: i) an architectural model able to handle differences in input devices and interaction tasks; ii) an agent-based middleware that provides basic components to integrate heterogeneous user interfaces. We also present a prototype of an agent-based middleware able to support developers in the interconnection of monolithic applications and we introduce tools and languages we have used to formalize the interaction tasks considered in the case study.

The organization of the chapter is as follows. First we discuss about the state-of-the art providing details about the existing systems and middleware solutions for collaborative environments, discussing about the interaction interoperability issue and the formal methods and their application to interactive systems. Then, we describe the architectural model we suggest, introducing an agent-based middleware and its basic components. Finally, we describe a proof-of-concept case study, in which two users collaborate in a virtual environment by using different interaction techniques and input devices.

BACKGROUND

Collaborative Virtual Environments

CVEs can bring together multiple, co-located or remote participants. The number of participants which can simultaneously cooperate with each other deeply influences the design of a collaborative environment. For instance, fully immersive environments well suit to systems with few users (maximum 10), such as SCAPE (Hua et al., 2003) collaborative systems, whereas the existence of many users (farther 100) could lead to devise environments with minimal or no immersion, such as GAZE Groupware (Vertegaal, 1999).

Different issues have to be faced by designers of collaborative virtual environments. The key aspect is providing consistency guarantees to users, despite the high level of responsiveness and interactivity necessary and the experienced network delay. In particular, consistency consists in making participants able to visualize the same virtual objects at the same time. Such issues can be overcome through various techniques, that have been developed in different systems or middleware solutions.

A first technique consists in transmitting update events to all the users as soon as state changes of objects occur. This method is used by DEVA3(Pettifer et al., 2000). A variant of this technique is implemented from several systems, such as COVEN (Normand et al., 1999), and consists in sending update messages to a subset of users on the basis on their proximity. Such update events are typically notified according to the publish/subscribe paradigm model (Ciampi, Coronato & De Pietro, 2008).

Another technique is based on predicting the current location of virtual objects on the basis of their behaviour. According to such a technique, behaviour can be described parametrically. For example, dead reckoning, introduced in DIS, Distributed Interactive Simulation (Sauerborn, 1998), describes movement through time. Basically, dead reckoning aims at estimating users' current positions on the basis of previously determined positions. All such techniques aim at decreasing network traffic and at maintaining high interactivity. Anyway, these techniques don't introduce anomalies, even if users don't have a complete copy of the world.

The technique implemented in CSpray (Pang & Wittenbrink, 1997) transmits raw data to users by means of streaming servers. However, CSpray is not a generic CVE, but it is specialised for specific data. An additional specialised collaborative system is GroupSlicer (Simmross-Wattenberg et al., 2005), which deals with medical data, and is based on replicating actions by sending the commands over the network.

A variant of this technique implemented in CSpray aims at reducing rendering overhead. Instead of transmitting complex geometry data, the streaming server sends pre-rendered 2D textures. This method is implemented in MUVEES (Chen, Yang and Loftin, 2003).

Different communication architectures have been proposed for CVEs, varying from centralized server, multiple servers to peer-to-peer model. In the former one, the only one server represents a single-point-of-failure, whereas the latter ones provide several advantages, such as dependability and decentralized control, even if they are more complex to design and develop.

A number of collaborative systems implement techniques for load balancing, by distributing or replicating objects amongst nodes. Thus, load balancing can be handled with architectures that are based on multiple servers or peer-to-peer. It is managed in DEVA3, Octopus (Hartling, 2003) and RAVE (Grimstead, 2005).

Replicating servers or data is important to provide resilience to collaborative environments designed to support a lot of users. This approach is incorporated in RAVE. Resilience can be coped also by peer-to-peer architectures, by delegating specific peers i) to record all the interactions or ii) to redound object management. The main problem of such an approach is that local users could change their peer at the aim of sending fake information.

Finally, another problem is represented by the lack of common communication protocols, which makes it hard for systems to interact with each other. Middleware solutions such as DIS and HLA, High-Level Architecture (Dahmann, Fujimoto & Weatherly, 1999), implement communication protocols that have been published as IEEE standards, but they are hardly applied in industry mainly for their complexity and their cost.

Interaction Interoperability

Despite the wide availability of input devices and interaction techniques, usually VEs exhibit ad hoc post-WIMP interaction techniques and devices. This is not a surprise since it is a shared vision that diversity in human-computer interfaces is a resource rather than a problem. As stated in (Benford, Snowdon, Colebourne, O'Brien, & Rodden, 1997), it would be impossible to develop a generic interface for every user. In order to be useful, every domain requires a custom design. Bowman et al. (2006) further refine this concept. They state that the key word in the development of

usable user interfaces is specificity. In greater detail, an Interaction Technique (IT), in other words the way of using a physical device to perform an interaction task, should be designed by considering specifically the group of users (and therefore their skills), the tasks they have to perform, the particular application and the input device used.

On the contrary, in reality, in most collaborative environments users are forced to use the same input devices and techniques, nearly always WIMP-based, to interact. For example we can consider the field of telemedicine. In daily clinical practice, each clinician has her/his own skills and uses her/his preferred tools to inspect medical data. Therefore, developing different interfaces for different medical figures can enhance the usability of the interaction with medical datasets.

Nonetheless, collaborative applications are insufficient in handling the heterogeneity of interaction tools. Group-Slicer (Simmross-Wattenberg et al., 2005) is a collaborative extension of the well-known 3D Slicer, a tool for both surgical planning and medical operations. The precondition of the interaction is the use of the same input devices and interaction techniques. The same in (Dev & Heinrichs, 2008), in which the authors describe a middleware environment able to handle heterogeneity of visualization but not of interaction. In (Ryu, Kim, Park, Kwon, & Jeong, 2007) the authors introduce COVE, an extensible framework for collaborative visualization which handles possible conflicts generated by multiple plug-ins that read from the same input device. The main advantage of this framework is that it allows plug-in developers to design ITs by separating their implementation from input devices.

Since every user has her/his preferred formalism and tools, we speculate that in a CVE each user has to be free to use her/his preferred interaction techniques and devices. To allow such heterogeneity in the execution of interaction tasks, interaction formalization plays a primary role. Possible interactions between heterogeneous representations have to be formalized in a common, shared way.

As Wegner states in (Wegner, 1997), there are two main mechanisms for interoperation in this field: interface standardization, which means that each user interface is mapped to a common representation; and interface bridging, which means that there is a two-way map between user interfaces. Interface standardization makes explicit the common properties of interfaces, thereby reducing the mapping task, and separates communication models of user interfaces. On the contrary, interface bridging is more flexible, since it can be tailored to the needs of specific user interfaces.

Formal Methods for Interactive Systems

Formal methods are mathematically based techniques for describing systems architecture, properties and behavior (Wing, 1990). As hardware and software designs grow in size and complexity, current non-formal design methods lead to ambiguous and error-prone specifications. Contrary, formal methods are tools based on logic systems and precise rules of inference that enables the clear and unambiguous specifications of diverse system properties, from architecture composition to real-time constraints. They offer a discipline which complements current methods so designers can successfully meet the demand for high performance systems.

Formal methods cover a broad and diverse set of techniques aimed at improving computer correctness and tools for proving such correctness. Indeed, formal methods are well known techniques able to increase dependability by eliminating errors at the requirements specification and early design stages of the development (Sobel & Clarkson, 2002), (Berry & Tichy, 2003), (Sobel & Clarkson, 2003). On the one hand, they represent the most effective tool to specify requirements in an unambiguous way (Bowen & Stavridou, 1992); that is, they improve fault prevention, which is one of the fault avoidance techniques.

On the other hand, they provide means to verify and validate formally the specifications so that designers are able to detect and remove faults (i.e., apply fault removal techniques) in the early design phases and, contrary to test techniques, without having already realized a prototype of the system (Karlsson et al., 2007; Coronato & De Pietro, in press).

More recently, formal methods are being adopted to assist designer during the testing phase. Indeed, while traditionally these approaches have been seen as rivals, in recent years a new consensus has developed in which they are seen as complementary (Hierons et al., 2009).

Finally, they are also adopted while the system is running to make it able to auto-test (Meyer et al., 2009) and self-verify correctness properties.

While concerning the field of model-based user interface design, task modeling is established as a necessary activity. It is also true that more and more frequently it is required to describe interactions in a precise and unambiguous way. In other world, correctness of interactions may affect the correctness of the entire system. This is also due to the growing number of devices available that makes the design space of interaction techniques very large.

The use of formal models has been proved to be an effective support for the development of interactive systems helping designers to decompose complex applications in smaller manageable parts. As a tool for designing and verifying interactions, it has recently been proposed ICO, Interactive Cooperative Objects, which is an object Petri nets-based formalism (Navarre, Bastide, Schyn, Nedel, & Freitas, 2005). Petri nets are a mathematical representation used to model discrete distributed systems, characterized by places, which are symbolizing states, transitions, which are representing actions, and arcs, which link places and transitions. The state of the system is defined by a distribution of tokens, which flow through places along the

Figure 1. Use of formal models in the development of interactive systems

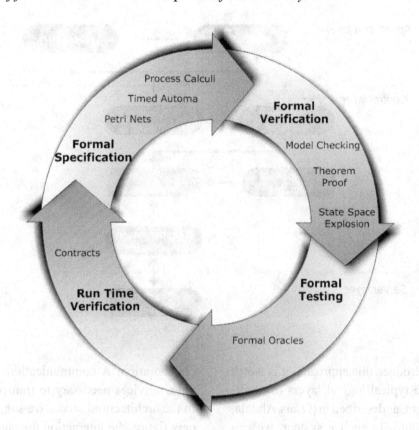

arcs every time transitions are enabled. Object Petri nets attribute a type to each place on the net, allowing thus the use of classes as types and object references as values. Instead, transitions are associated to method invocations.

ICO is an extension of object Petri nets. Basically, ICO is a formal description technique designed to specify, model and implement systems at the aim of describing static aspects of interactive applications. As Human Computer Interaction is event-driven, ICO introduces the notion of interaction events and of user/system relationship. Interaction events enable transitions, whereas user/system relationships consist in: *activations*, aiming at displaying the interaction space of the user; *widgets*, which have the purpose of stating the presentation of objects (e.g. graphical representations or methods to interact with a user

interface); and, *renderings*, which relate a set of widgets to each place or transition in order to make these ones able to render information to the user.

AN APPROACH FOR INTEROPERABLE INTERACTIVE SYSTEMS

Architectural Model

The approach we suggest is to let the user who is in charge of creating the CVE to implicitly formalize, by exposing her/his user interface, the common language that other user interfaces have to speak. Together with the language, the user also has to specify the peculiar interaction rules she/he requests.

Figure 2. Architectural model

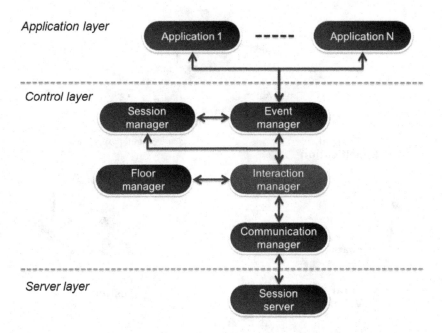

To better introduce this approach, it is worth considering the typical logical layers of a collaborative system, as described in (Osais, Abdala, & Matrawy, 2006). In such a system, we can distinguish three layers: application, control and server (see Figure 2).

The application layer is in charge of intercepting events, providing awareness to users, posting remote events to a manager and interpreting as local the remote events received. The server layer contains the session server, which is in charge of distributing messages to all users. The control layer is the cornerstone of any collaborative system, since it has to replicate state changes to maintain consistency among users, to exchange control information and to replicate signaling messages.

In a control layer, we need several different figures. An event manager performs the required conversion of messages in a common format. A session manager handles sessions, maintaining a list of active participants. A floor manager handles floors that are temporary permissions to access and manipulate resources so regulating

collaboration. A communication manager provides services necessary to transport messages. In the architectural model we suggest, there is a new figure, the interaction manager (see Figure 2). Its main responsibility is to handle transitions between interaction tasks. The interaction manager is interposed between the event manager and the communication manager, since events corresponding to interactions not allowed in a particular context are not further propagated in the system.

This component has to be able to deal with the complexity of post-WIMP interfaces. It works thanks to a formal model of the interaction rules that specifies how interaction tasks are connected and how and when floors are granted. Interaction rules change significantly with the cooperation model. By following the cooperation model proposed in (Margery, Arnaldi, & Plouzeau, 1999), there are three levels of cooperation: level 1 is a basic cooperation level, in which users simply perceive each other in the virtual world; level 2 means that each user can change the scene individually; finally there is level 3 in which users can act on objects in independent ways (3.1) or in a co-dependent way (3.2). Obviously different cooperation levels correspond to different interaction rules.

Agent-Based Middleware

This section presents the key elements of an agent-based middleware infrastructure devised to overcome interoperability issues for CVEs. The middleware has been implemented by an agent infrastructure, since it facilitates the communication between distributed components and provides, at the same time, a certain degree of autonomy (Soldatos, Pandis, Stamatis, Polymenakos, & Crowley, 2007). Such infrastructures, named Multi-Agent Systems (MAS), focus on systems in which intelligent agents interact with each other to cooperate or to solve complex problems (Coronato, De Pietro, & Gallo, 2007). Thus, they are well suited to Collaborative Virtual Environments, where collaboration and problem solving are significant requirements.

The middleware we propose enables users participating in virtual collaborative sessions to use different input devices and interaction techniques. In greater detail, the middleware allows users to interact with each other by visualizing simultaneously the same multimedia objects and replicating on every participant's node the execution of all interaction tasks performed by other participants.

The middleware infrastructure has to aim at: i) sharing a formal description of interaction tasks and a number of interaction rules; ii) handling floor control, by authorizing or not users to perform interaction tasks on multimedia objects; and iii) dispatching event notifications to all participants in order to synchronize the execution of certain tasks.

It is worth noting that formal descriptions of interaction tasks, along with interaction rules, have to be produced by the user who creates the collaborative session. Every participant willing to join the session has to check if she/he has an implementation of those tasks at her/his disposal.

Formal descriptions and interaction rules have to be specified in a shared formal language. For each interaction task, users who want to cooperate have to indicate: i) the typology and number of input and output parameters and ii) the preconditions to be satisfied in order to allow the execution of the task. It is irrelevant how designers implement interaction tasks; it is sufficient that they accomplish the specified requirements.

Middleware architecture consists of a set of components organized in two logical layers, as shown in Figure 3. The Interface layer handles user interactions and implements the interaction tasks requested to participate at a session. The Interoperability layer is the cornerstone of the middleware, since it is in charge of replicating state changes to maintain consistent views.

The components of the middleware architecture are described below:

- *UserInterface*: this component acts as an adaptor and aims at handling interaction events generated by a particular input device while performing interaction tasks. For this reason, each participant has her/his own UserInterface, within which ad hoc developed interaction techniques can be enclosed.
- *CommunicationBroker*: this component is in charge of dispatching messages received from component publishers to component consumers in an asynchronous way according to the publish/subscribe paradigm. The CommunicationBroker plays a central role in the middleware, although its architecture can be distributed.
- *TaskDescriptor*: this component is in charge of archiving and sharing formal descriptions of interaction tasks. The interfaces of UserInterface components have to satisfy such formal descriptions.
- *InteractionManager*: the Interaction-Manager stores and shares the interaction rules. It also ensures that each

Figure 3. Middleware architecture

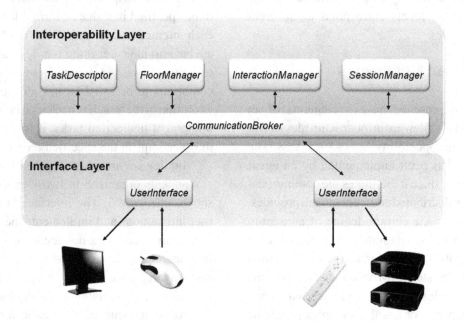

participant has the same visual representation by requiring all users, via the CommunicationBroker, to execute an interaction task launched by a user.

- *FloorManager*: this component handles the concurrency control for shared multimedia objects. Each UserInterface questions the FloorManager to perform an interaction task. The FloorManager grants or refuses the authorization according to the interaction rules shared between participants.

- *SessionManager*: this component allows users to create, join and destroy collaborative sessions by handling a list of participants in a virtual collaborative session. Every participant has to register with such a component to access the system.

A Case Study

A proof-of-concept prototype of middleware has been developed to evaluate the interoperability facilities provided by the agent-based middleware architecture previously described.

As shown in Figure 4, current implementation relies on the Open Agent Architecture (OAA), a framework for constructing Multi-Agent Systems developed at the Artificial Intelligence Centre of SRI International (Martin, Cheyer, & Moran, 1999). OAA is structured so as to minimize the effort involved in creating new agents and wrapping legacy applications. Moreover, OAA facilitates the development of flexible and dynamic agent communities using a wide variety of programming languages. Members of agent communities cooperate with each other in order to perform computation, to retrieve information and to carry out user interaction tasks (Jia & Zhou, 2005).

The OAA-based middleware we have developed enables two users to cooperate in a semi-immersive virtual environment. In greater detail, the application allows them to visualize and interact with 3D anatomical parts reconstructed from CT and MRI images.

Figure 4. Middleware implementation with OAA

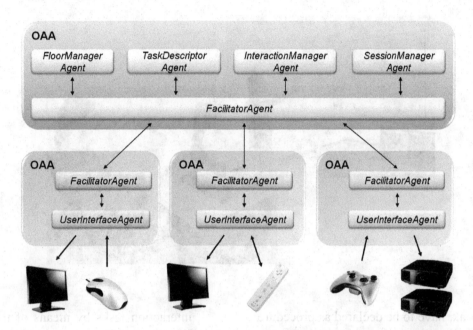

Users can perform two distinct interaction tasks: rotation of a 3D object, which has to be performed in an exclusive way; and pointing at 3D objects, that is moving a 3D cursor in the scene. The two users considered in this scenario use different interaction techniques and input devices: the user on the left of the Figure 5 interacts with a Wiimote, the main controller of the Nintendo Wii console (Nintendo, 2009), whereas the user on the right interacts via a common mouse.

The interaction tasks executed by the two users are implemented differently: the rotation technique of the first user (Wiimote-based interaction) makes use of quaternions as a mathematical notation for representing orientations of objects in three dimensions, whereas the rotation technique of the second user (mouse-based interaction) makes use of three Euler angles. In this scenario, since the first user is assumed to create the collaborative session, quaternions are used as the shared notation. Thus, the adaptor of the second user has to implement the conversion from Euler angles to quaternions.

All components have been implemented as agents, as shown in Figure 4. It is worth noting that an agent has to declare its capabilities, named solvables, in order to join a community of agents. Such solvables establish a high-level interface to the agent, used by a facilitator in communicating with the agent and, most importantly, in delegating service requests to the agent. Such a model is called the delegated computing model in OAA. Two major types of solvables are distinguished: procedure solvables, which describe how agents perform actions, and data solvables, which provide access to a collection of data.

In the following, a description of every agent constituent of the middleware is provided.

- *UserInterfaceAgent*: this agent analyzes input interactions and manages the presentation of multimedia output to the user. Each UserInterfaceAgent implements particular ad hoc developed interaction techniques to perform interaction tasks. These tasks, together with the languages they are able

Figure 5. Case study: Two users interact remotely by using a Wiimote and a mouse respectively.

to speak, have to be declared as procedure solvables to the FacilitatorAgent.

- *FacilitatorAgent*: this agent acts as the CommunicationBroker component. It coordinates agent communications, by maintaining lists of what UserInterfaceAgents can do, that is their solvables. Each UserInterfaceAgent has its own FacilitatorAgent, which delegates service requests to appropriate agents. The FacilitatorAgent implements the publish/subscribe paradigm by means of the OAA's delegated computing model. Each FacilitatorAgent is linked to all the others by means of a root FacilitatorAgent, creating thus a hierarchical configuration. Such a hierarchy has been arranged on two layers, even if it may be organized on more than two.
- *TaskDescriptorAgent*: the TaskDescriptorAgent declares to the FacilitatorAgent a data solvable, in order to archive and share task interfaces written in a formal language. The UserInterfaceAgent that creates the collaborative session sends to the TaskDescriptorAgent the interfaces of

interaction tasks by means of the OAA's Interagent Communication Language (ICL), an interface and communication language designed as an extension of Prolog. In our scenario, the first user specifies the interfaces of the rotation and pointing tasks.

- *InteractionManagerAgent*: the InteractionManagerAgent is a meta-agent that declares a data solvable for the purpose of storing the interaction rules, which have to be specified by UserInterfaceAgents. The aim of such agent is to require every UserInterfaceAgent to execute certain tasks in order to synchronize the visualization among users. This is accomplished by extending the ICO formalism to the agents. Specifically, the notion of object has to be replaced with the concept of agent: an action resulting from a state transition is mapped to an invocation to an agent rather than to an object. This is achieved via the FacilitatorAgent by means of the OAA delegated computing model. For simplicity, in the InteractionManagerAgent of the middleware prototype, the ICO-based interaction rules of the rotation and pointing tasks have been implemented directly as C++ code. Anyhow, several Petri nets interpreters are available (Bastide & Palanque, 1995; Squeak, 2009) and can be used to parse UserInterfaceAgent requests.

- *FloorManagerAgent*: the FloorManagerAgent is an agent that manages the floor control of the objects of the visual representation. The FloorManagerAgent resolves conflicts on the basis of interaction rules that are stored in the InteractionManagerAgent.

- *SessionManagerAgent*: this agent acts as the SessionManager component. It is invoked by other agents to share collaborative sessions or to verify if a participant has the credentials to request the execution of certain tasks.

The object Petri nets-based ICO formalism deserves a further description. Petri nets are a mathematical representation used to model dis-

crete distributed systems, characterized by places, which are symbolizing states, transitions, which are representing actions, and arcs, which link places and transitions. The state of the system is defined by a distribution of tokens, which flow through places along the arcs every time transitions are enabled. Object Petri nets attribute a type to each place on the net, allowing thus the use of classes as types and object references as values.

Instead, transitions are associated to method invocations. ICO extends object Petri nets by adding the notion of interaction events, which enable the transitions.

By using the ICO formalism, the FloorManagerAgent can deduce if an exclusive task has already been executed by a user. Figure 6 reports the ICO-based formalism of interaction tasks considered in the case study scenario. The places Watch and Pointing are initialized with N tokens, where N is the number of participants (N=2 in Figure 5), so a maximum of two users can move their 3D cursor at the same time.

Figure 6. ICO representation of the interaction rules

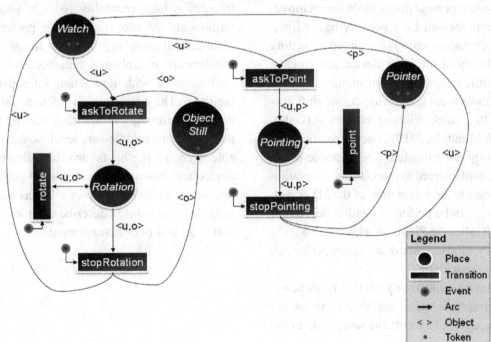

The place ObjectStill is initialized with only one token. If a user < u > asks the FloorManagerAgent to rotate an object, this enables her/him to perform the task only if the token is in the place ObjectStill. In such a case, one token of the place Watch and the token of the place ObjectStill fall into the place Rotation. Until < u > rotates the object < o >, any other user can rotate the object. When < u > stops rotating, the two tokens return to their initial states and the rotation task becomes executable. This configuration ensures the exclusivity of the rotation task. On the other hand, the pointing task is not exclusive. Hence, the initialization of the place Pointer with N tokens, specifying that N pointers < p > are available, guarantees that every user can perform the task.

It is also important that, in the particular case study we have considered, two users exploit different input devices but also different interaction techniques. If performed with the mouse, the pointing task features a fixed 1:1 mapping between the 2D mouse pointer position and 3D cursor position on the image plane (Gallo & Minutolo, 2008). When the Wiimote is used as input device, pointing information is derived by tracking an IR emitter in space (Gallo, De Pietro, Coronato, & Marra, 2008). To manage hand jitters, the Wiimote movements are processed by a velocity-based filter. The control-display ratio is computed according to the velocity of the input device movements, so that a little cursor shift corresponds to a slow Wiimote movement and a wide cursor shift corresponds to a quick Wiimote movement (Gallo, Ciampi, & Minutolo, 2010). Also the rotation task is differently implemented. The Wiimote-based rotation is implemented by mapping the orientation of the device to the orientation of the 3D object, so rotations can be performed with 3 degrees of freedom (Gallo, De Pietro, & Marra, 2008). On the contrary, mouse-based rotations are performed via a virtual trackball.

To grant interoperability, all that is needed is that UserInterfaceAgents are able to speak the same language and execute the same task. In the pointing example, a UserInterfaceAgent communicates the spatial position of the cursor in the three dimensional Cartesian coordinate system, since this is the shared language for the pointing task. Other UserInterfaceAgents receive the pointing event information, understand it since it is in a language they speak, and know how to execute it since they have declared the pointing functionality as one of their procedure solvables.

FUTURE RESEARCH DIRECTIONS

We believe that a crucial challenge in this field is to let users to formalize, in an easy way, clear and unambiguous specifications of diverse properties of interactive systems. Therefore, future research will be focused on building tools to model easily, automatically when possible, the behavior of complex interaction techniques and devices in order to simplify the interface standardization process.

CONCLUSION

In this chapter, we have discussed about the interaction interoperability issue in virtual environments. Moreover, we have presented an architectural model together with an agent-based middleware to enhance collaborative virtual environments with interaction interoperability facilities. The heterogeneity of user interfaces is handled through an interface standardization performed at a middleware level, so each user is able to choose her/his favorite coupling of input device and interaction technique to perform an interaction task. The chapter also has discussed suitable formalisms to describe complex interaction tasks and floor management.

REFERENCES

Ahmed, H. M., Gracanin, D., & Abdel-Hamid, A. (2008a). A framework for interaction interoperability in X3D mobile collaborative virtual environments. In *INFOS '08: Proceedings of the 6th International Conference on Informatics and Systems* (pp. 84–92).

Ahmed, H. M., Gracanin, D., & Abdel-Hamid, A. (2008b). Poster: A framework for interaction interoperability in virtual environments. In *3DUI '08: IEEE Symposium on 3D User Interfaces* (pp. 141–142).

Ahmed, H. M., Gracanin, D., Abdel-Hamid, A., & Matkovic, K. (2008). An approach to interaction interoperability for distributed virtual environments. In *EGVE '08: Short Papers and Posters Proceedings* (pp. 35–38).

Bastide, R., & Palanque, P. A. (1995). A Petri net based environment for the design of event-driven interfaces. In *Petri Nets '95: Proceedings of the 16th International Conference on Application and Theory of Petri Nets* (pp. 66–83). London, UK: Springer-Verlag.

Benford, S., Snowdon, D., Colebourne, A., O'Brien, J., & Rodden, T. (1997). Informing the design of collaborative virtual environments. In *GROUP '97: Proceedings of the International ACM SIGGROUP Conference on Supporting Group Work* (pp. 71–80). New York, NY: ACM.

Berry, D. M., & Tichy, W. F. (2003). Comments on Formal methods application: An empirical tale of software development. *IEEE Transactions on Software Engineering, 29*(6), 567–571. doi:10.1109/TSE.2003.1205183

Bowen, J., & Stavridou, V. (1992). Formal methods and software safety. In H. Frey (Ed.), *SAFECOMP '92: Proceedings of the IFAC Symposium* (pp. 93–98). Pergamon Press.

Bowman, D. A., Chen, J., Wingrave, C. A., Lucas, J. F., Ray, A., & Polys, N. F. (2006). New directions in 3D user interfaces. *The International Journal of Virtual Reality, 5*(2), 3–14.

Chen, J. X., Yang, Y., & Loftin, B. (2003). MU-VEES: A PC-based multi-user virtual environment for learning. In *Proceedings of the IEEE International Symposium on Virtual Reality*, (pp. 163–170). Los Angeles, CA: IEEE Computer Society.

Ciampi, M., Coronato, A., & De Pietro, G. (2008). An asynchronous communication system for pervasive grids. *International Journal of Web and Grid Services, 4*(2), 211–221. doi:10.1504/IJWGS.2008.018888

Coronato, A., & De Pietro, G. (in press). Formal specification of wireless and pervasive healthcare applications. *ACM Transactions on Embedded Computing Systems*.

Coronato, A., De Pietro, G., & Gallo, L. (2007). Automatic execution of tasks in MiPeG. In *GPC '07: Proceedings of the Second International Conference on Advances in Grid and Pervasive Computing* (Vol. 4459, pp. 702–709). Berlin, Germany: Springer-Verlag.

Dahmann, J. S. (1999). The high level architecture and beyond: Technology challenges. *Workshop on Parallel and Distributed Simulation* (pp. 64-70)

Dev, P., & Heinrichs, W. L. (2008). Learning medicine through collaboration and action: Collaborative, experiential, networked learning environments. *Virtual Reality (Waltham Cross), 12*(4), 215–234. doi:10.1007/s10055-008-0099-5

Gallo, L., Ciampi, M., & Minutolo, A. (2010). Smoothed pointing: A user-friendly technique for precision enhanced remote pointing. In *CISIS '10: Proceedings of the international conference on complex, intelligent and software intensive systems*. Los Alamitos, CA: IEEE Computer Society.

Gallo, L., De Pietro, G., Coronato, A., & Marra, I. (2008). Toward a natural interface to virtual medical imaging environments. In *AVI '08: Proceedings of the Working Conference on Advanced Visual Interfaces* (pp. 429–432). New York, NY: ACM Press.

Gallo, L., De Pietro, G., & Marra, I. (2008). 3D interaction with volumetric medical data: Experiencing the Wiimote. In *AMBI-SYS '08: Proceedings of the 1st International Conference On Ambient Media and Systems* (pp. 1–6). Brussels, Belgium: ICST.

Gallo, L., & Minutolo, A. (2008). A natural pointing technique for semi-immersive virtual environments. In *Mobiquitous '08: Proceedings of the 5th Annual International Conference on Mobile And ubiquitous Systems* (pp. 1–4). Brussels, Belgium: ICST.

Grimstead, I. J. (2005). *RAVE - Resource aware visualization environment*. Retrieved from http://users.cs.cf.ac.uk/I.J.Grimstead/RAVE/index.html

Hartling, P., Just, C., & Cruz-Neira, C. (2001). Distributed virtual reality using Octopus. In *Proceedings of IEEE International Symposium on Virtual Reality* (pp. 53–62). IEEE Computer Society.

Hierons, R. M., Bogdanov, K., Bowen, J. P., Cleaveland, R., Derrick, J., & Dick, J. (2009). Using formal specifications to support testing. *ACM Computing Surveys*, *41*(2), 1–76. doi:10.1145/1459352.1459354

Hua, H., Brown, L. D., Gao, C., & Ahuja, N. (2003). A new collaborative infrastructure: Scape. In *Proceedings of the IEEE International Symposium on Virtual Reality*, (pp. 171–179). Los Angeles, CA: IEEE Computer Society.

Jia, W., & Zhou, W. (2005). *Distributed network systems* (*Vol. 15*, pp. 1–13). Springer, US. doi:10.1007/0-387-23840-9_1

Karlsson, D., Eles, P., & Peng, Z. (2007). Formal verification of component-based designs. *Design Automation for Embedded Systems*, *11*(1), 49–90. doi:10.1007/s10617-006-9723-3

Margery, D., Arnaldi, B., & Plouzeau, N. (1999). A general framework for cooperative manipulation in virtual environments. In *Virtual Environments '99: Proceedings of the Eurographics Workshop* (pp. 169–178).

Martin, D., Cheyer, A., & Moran, D. (1999). The open agent architecture: A framework for building distributed software systems. *Applied Artificial Intelligence*, *13*(1/2), 91–128. doi:10.1080/088395199117504

Meyer, B., Fiva, A., Ciupa, I., Leitner, A., Wei, Y., & Stapf, E. (2009). Programs that test themselves. *Computer*, *42*(9), 46–55. doi:10.1109/MC.2009.296

Navarre, D., Bastide, R., Schyn, A., Nedel, L. P., & Freitas, C. M. D. S. (2005). A formal description of multimodal interaction techniques for immersive virtual reality applications. In *INTERACT '05: Proceedings of the Tenth IFIP TC13 International Conference on Human-Computer Interaction* (pp. 170–183). Springer.

Nintendo. (2009, January). *Wiimote*. Retrieved from http://www.nintendo.com/wii/what/controllers/

Normand, V., Babski, C., Benford, S., Bullock, A., Carion, S., & Farcet, N. (1999). The COVEN project - Exploring applicative, technical, and usage dimensions of collaborative virtual environments. *Presence (Cambridge, Mass.)*, *8*(2), 218–236. doi:10.1162/105474699566189

Osais, Y., Abdala, S., & Matrawy, A. (2006). A multilayer peer-to-peer framework for distributed synchronous collaboration. *IEEE Internet Computing*, *10*(6), 33–41. doi:10.1109/MIC.2006.115

Pang, A., & Wittenbrink, C. (1997). Collaborative 3D Visualization with CSpray. *IEEE Computer Graphics and Applications, 17*(2), 32–41. doi:10.1109/38.574676

Pettifer, S., Cook, J., Marsh, J., & West, A. (2000) Deva3: Architecture for a large-scale virtual reality system. In *Proceedings of ACM Symposium in Virtual Reality Software and Technology*, (pp. 33–40). ACM Press.

Poupyrev, I., Weghorst, S., Billinghurst, M., & Ichikawa, T. (1998). Egocentric object manipulation in virtual environments: Evaluation of interaction techniques. *Computer Graphics Forum, 17*(3), 41–52. doi:10.1111/1467-8659.00252

Ryu, S.-H., Kim, H.-J., Park, J.-S., Kwon, Y. W., & Jeong, C.-S. (2007, February). Collaborative object-oriented visualization environment. *Multimedia Tools and Applications, 32*(2), 209–234. doi:10.1007/s11042-006-0066-7

Sauerborn, G. C. (1998). The distributed interactive simulation (DIS) lethality communication server. *Proceedings of 2nd International Workshop on Distributed Interactive Simulation and Real-Time Applications, 19-20*, (pp. 82–85).

Simmross-Wattenberg, F., Carranza-Herrezuelo, N., Palacios-Camarero, C., De La Higuera, J. P. C., & Martin-Fernandez, M. Angel, Aja-Fernandez, S., et al. (2005). GroupSlicer: A collaborative extension of the 3D-Slicer. *Journal of Biomedical Informatics, 38*(6), 431–442. doi:10.1016/j.jbi.2005.03.001

Sobel, A. E. K., & Clarkson, M. R. (2002). Formal methods application: An empirical tale of software development. *IEEE Transactions on Software Engineering, 28*(3), 308–320. doi:10.1109/32.991322

Sobel, A. E. K., & Clarkson, M. R. (2003). Response to Comments on 'formal methods application: An empirical tale of software development. *IEEE Transactions on Software Engineering, 29*(6), 572–575. doi:10.1109/TSE.2003.1205184

Soldatos, J., Pandis, I., Stamatis, K., Polymenakos, L., & Crowley, J. L. (2007, February). Agent based middleware infrastructure for autonomous context-aware ubiquitous computing services. *Computer Communications, 30*(3), 577–591. doi:10.1016/j.comcom.2005.11.018

Squeak. (2009, January). *Etoys.* Retrieved from http://www.squeak.org/

Vertegaal, R. (1999). The GAZE groupware system: mediating joint attention in multiparty communication and collaboration. *Proceedings of the SIGCHI Conference on Human Factors in Computing Systems: The CHI is the Limit*, (pp. 294-301).

Wegner, P. (1997). Interactive software technology. In *The computer science and engineering handbook* (pp. 2440–2463).

Wing, J. M. (1990). A specifier's introduction to formal methods. *Computer, 23*(9), 8–23. doi:10.1109/2.58215

Chapter 6
Information Architecture for the Design of a User Interface to Manage Educational Oriented Recommendations

Olga C. Santos
UNED, Spain & Cadius Community of Usability Professionals, Spain

Emanuela Mazzone
UNED, Spain & Cadius Community of Usability Professionals, Spain

Maria Jose Aguilar
Cadius Community of Usability Professionals, Spain

Jesus G. Boticario
UNED, Spain

ABSTRACT

This chapter presents the information architecture approach for the design of an administration tool for educators to manage educational oriented recommendations in virtual learning environments. In this way, educators can be supported in the publication stage of the e-learning life cycle after recommendations have been designed with the TORMES methodology. The chapter starts introducing relevant background information on recommender systems for e-learning and the rationale for the educators' involvement in the recommendation design process. Afterwards, the chapter comments on the information architecture that supports the user interface design process with user-centered design methods, including the goals to achieve in each of the steps defined. The chapter ends by discussing the application of this approach in different contexts.

DOI: 10.4018/978-1-61350-516-8.ch006

Copyright © 2012, IGI Global. Copying or distributing in print or electronic forms without written permission of IGI Global is prohibited.

INTRODUCTION

In a world where information overload is everywhere, recommender systems (RS) represent a highly-valuable feature: they offer the most relevant products, services or guidance to each specific user's when users have to make choices in daily life situations without sufficient knowledge on the available alternatives (Resnick and Varian, 1997). RS in these domains are usually based on technologies processing previous interactions with the system by a specific user or by similar users. Typical examples of RS are found in commercial services (e.g.: Amazon, YouTube, LastFM). Reviews of RS have been produced in literature where different application domains are identified: e-commerce, web recommender, personalized newspaper, movie recommender, document recommender, information recommender, travel recommender, purchase recommender, music recommender, e-mail filtering, sharing news, netnews filtering, web search filtering (Montaner et al., 2003). The successful implementation of these systems in the e-commerce domain (Schafer, Konstan and Riedl 2001) has motivated their consideration for virtual learning environments (VLE) (Hsu, 2008). The most common approaches focus on providing an automatic process to support students in finding suitable materials (e.g. Shen and Shen, 2004; Al-Hamad et al., 2008; Markellou et al., 2005; Li and Chang, 2005; Hsu, 2008; Schulz et al., 2001; Soonthornphisaj et al., 2006; Ksristofic, 2005,) as an alternative to relying solely on classmates, educators and other sources (Resnick and Varian 1997). However, a recommendation in the e-learning context could be diverse, e.g. as simple as suggesting a web resource, or more interactive (i.e. an on-line activity) such as doing an exercise, reading a posted message on a conferencing system or running an on-line simulation (Zaïane, 2002). One point to be taken into account is that most of the times, recommendations are offered in the form of links recommended (Romero et al, 2007).

The common idea behind the RS in VLE is to overcome the limitations of traditional teaching methods that follow the "one-size-fits-all" approach. In this format, students with different backgrounds are still given the same content at the same time, no matter if it is interesting and useful to their learning (Shen and Shen, 2004), and contents are not dynamic enough to respond effectively to the needs and competences of the learners, resulting in poor learning experiences (Markellou et al., 2005). To increase the learning efficiency, students with different goals and backgrounds should be treated differently by building a model of knowledge and preferences, offering as a result diverse learning experiences to all students with diverse learning preferences (Al-Hamad et al., 2008). Students should not only have access to the most appropriate tools and environments that present information in an engaging manner, but they should also be provided with the appropriate support for the diversity of individual learning styles (Bates and Leary, 2001). Thus, RS within the context of an e-learning platform should take into account not only the user preferences, but also educational aspects of the learning process (Bloch et al., 2003).

The growing success of RS is due to the great potential of new adaptive technologies: the recommendations generated by the system are triggered by real activities and users' behavior in an automated dynamic process. However, recommendations can be automatically created when the users' requirements are clearly defined for the system, which is not the case for RS in the educational domain, where requirements depends on specific educational needs. Therefore, in order to involve the educators in the process of designing educationally oriented recommendations, the *TORMES* methodology has been proposed (Santos and Boticario, 2011a). This methodology follows the standard ISO 9241-210 on Human-centered design for interactive systems and covers the following four activities: (a) description of the context of use based on both individual interviews with educators and data mining analysis from previous courses; (b) requirements specification through the scenario based approach that is used to extract knowledge from the educators and allows identifying recommendation opportunities that can be provided in the scenario outlined to improve the learning experience; (c) creation of design solutions as semantically described recommendations in terms of the corresponding model (Santos and Boticario, 2010), where educators are involved in a focus group to validate and refine the initial set of recommendations elicited; and (d) evaluation of the recommendations designed against the requirements by rating their relevance and classifying them in terms of their scope.

According to the e-learning life cycle (Van Rosmalen et al., 2004) the process of designing educational oriented recommendations takes place during the first stage of the cycle (Santos and Boticario, 2011c). The next stage of the cycle is the administration phase, where the elements involved in the VLE (i.e., users, contents, and services) are to be managed. This includes the recommendations designed with the *TORMES* methodology in the previous stage. For this, an administration tool that bridges the gap between the recommendations' design in terms of the recommendations model and the elements in the VLE is required. The remaining two stages of the e-learning life cycle cover the users' interaction in the learning environment and feedback to the course design.

The originality of the *TORMES* approach lies in the introduction of a 'human touch' through the 'human validation step' needed in an e-learning context where the student–educator relation is involved. This 'manual' step deviates from the initial concept of RS where recommendations are generated and published automatically by using mathematical methods such as collaborative filtering and content-based filtering. This deviation from the RS concept is justified by users needs and has already been suggested in literature. Further information on these issues is provided in the Background section. This need for educators' involvement implies the need of an additional tool where educators can modify, design and experiment recommendations before they are presented to their students (Santos et al., 2009). It addresses two related issues: 1) understanding the needs of learners when receiving recommendations in the e-learning domain, and 2) offering educators a control mechanism on what is recommended to their learners. As a result, educators can benefit from the reduced workload coming from the analysis of the users' interactions and the generation of recommendations regarding platform support with artificial intelligence techniques (Garcia et al., 2009), and at the same time, they can also have visibility and control on what is recommended to their learners within the course (Romero and Ventura, 2007). The process of designing the interface of this tool, based on the user-centered design methodology and with the related conceptual model, should consider five steps in terms of information architecture. These steps are introduced in the corresponding section. This process is based on the user-centered design methodology that counts on social, ethnographic and psychological techniques to obtain patterns that assure cognitive consistency.

Thus, in this chapter, we present some relevant issues on the meaning of a RS in e-learning with special focus on the challenges and opportunities for the user interface design for the end-user administration interface, that is, the user interface used by the educator to manage and control the recommendations process. The next section introduces the relevant background information on RS for e-learning and the rationale for the educators' involvement in the recommendation design process. In particular, after introducing the use of RS in the e-learning context, we review other approaches in literature to produce administration tools to support the functionality of RS in VLE which show that previous experiences of administration tools for adaptive systems, designed without following a user-centered design process, resulted in tools that still require a lot of cognitive effort from the user. Next, the designing approach to be followed is discuss, commenting on available methodologies to design user interfaces for virtual environments. Afterwards, the chapter presents the steps of the information architecture that support the user interface design process with user-centered design methods. The chapter ends with some conclusions as well as discussing the application of this approach in different contexts at three different levels: i) same domain, different scope, ii) same domain, different device, and iii) different domain.

BACKGROUND: ADMINISTRATION INTERFACES FOR RECOMMENDERS IN E-LEARNING

Information overload is a fact in VLE (Markellou et al., 2005). Furthermore, e-learning platforms can be quite complex and involve a variety of elements: the platform itself, the course content, a variety of services (forums, news, etc), some of which are interactive and some other simply delivered (Al-Hamad et al., 2008). The platform is used by a large and heterogeneous set of users. Moreover, the result from e-learning activities is the sheer complexity of the information and the vast size of the data collected, as well as the fact that simple information extraction is not possible (Zaïane, 2002). Following the discussions presented in the introduction, a RS within an e-learning platform can be used as the way to optimize platform's usage by adapting the recommendations to each and every user, without clustering the interface and therefore improving greatly the usability. Moreover, recommendations provide time saving support in the educational context (Schulz et al., 2001). Modalities, purpose and context of learning are in permanent flux. According to new trends, educators have to rethink what teaching means and how to prepare students to become knowledge workers, or workers in a knowledge-based

economy. RS can facilitate the teaching–learning interactions and improve online learners' success. Educators using VLE require non-intrusive and automatic ways to get objective feedback from learners in order to better follow the learning process and appraise the on-line course structure effectiveness (Zaïane, 2002). They should also cope with the lifelong learning approach where more and more citizens are to be supported in their learning at a socially acceptable cost (Schulz et al., 2001).

In this section we discuss the application of RS in e-learning scenarios and review existing user interfaces to support administration and configuration tasks for RS in VLE, which justify the need of an authoring tool that supports the educator's validation step for the recommendations generated.

RS and E-Learning Scenarios

Traditional RS applications follow the two-dimensional user–item paradigm, where items are recommended to users taking into account their preferences to these items or the preferences to these items from similar users. However, this two dimensional paradigm is less suitable for "context-rich" applications, such as traveling or shopping applications. In this type of domains, one may need to consider other dimensions besides item and user. Moreover, in the two-dimensional approach usually the methods are hard-wired by the developers into the RS, they are inflexible and limited in their expressiveness, and, therefore, neglect some possible needs of the users (Adomavicius et al., 2008). In this extended paradigm, there is also a need to empower end-users and other stakeholders by providing them with the tools for expressing recommendations that are of interest to them and provide flexible recommendations capabilities (Koutrika et al., 2008) which consider additional issues, such as the evolving context of the user (Tang and McCalla, 2003). This need of a tool is even more important in this paradigm due to the outstanding complexity. In this sense, (Adomavicius et al., 2008) have proposed a recommendation language based on SQL called REQUEST to allow its users to express in a flexible manner a broad range of recommendations. They propose a multidimensional model that supports additional contextual dimensions that can be tailored to users' own individual needs and, therefore, more accurately reflect their interests. In this way, users can customize recommendations by formulating them in ways that satisfy their personalized needs. This proposal seems a good way to go in the sense that provides a tool for the users to express themselves and can be used to better understand their needs.

Education is a good example of domain where rich contextual information is available. A compilation of up to date practices and challenges in educational RS can be consulted in (Santos and Boticario, 2011d). In this context, RS can be used to help and support both learners and educators during the course. Recommendations in learning environments share the same objective as recommenders for e-commerce applications (i.e. helping users to select the most appropriate item from a large information pool) but have some particularities that have to be taken into account (Tang and McCalla, 2003; Draschler et al., 2007). We have summarized these particularities as follows:

1. *The requirements:* recommendations should be pedagogically guided by educators, not only by learners' preferences, and at the same time, accessibility barriers should be overcome by considering the user preferences and device capabilities
2. *The user predisposition:* learners are not so motivated to continuously provide explicit ratings for each item they access as in e-commerce systems, but in turn they are used to fill in advance information as requested by the institution
3. *The structural context:* educational specifications such as IMS Learning Design and SCORM allow to situate the learner in the course

Moreover, the approach in the e-learning domain is of lower granularity. The goal of RS in this context is usually not to recommend a course from a list of available courses regarding the users' preferences –as done in typical recommending systems, where movies or songs are recommended to a user–, but to recommend actions to the learner while performing the activities designed within a given course. Romero and Ventura (2007) have compared both domains (e-commerce and e-learning) and have identified the differences regarding the domain, the data, the objectives and the techniques.

In this context, the RS, which offer recommendations in the form of links, can be used to enrich the VLE with adaptive navigation support. Adaptive educational hypermedia systems can adaptively sort, annotate, or partly hide the links to make it easier to choose or to recommend to the students where they should go next from where they are at a specific moment. The goal of adaptive navigation support is to help students to find an optimal path through the learning materials (Brusilovsky and Peylo, 2003).

To cope with the contextual richness in e-learning scenarios, the concept of Semantic Educational RS (SERS) has been introduced (Santos and Boticario, 2011b) to describe those RS that extend existing VLE with adaptive navigation support by making a pervasive usage of standards. In particular, SERS depend on (i) a recommendation model; (ii) an open standards-based service-oriented architecture; and (iii) a usable and accessible graphical user interface to deliver the recommendations.

Techniques to Support RS

Several mathematical methods can be applied to generate recommendations and to ensure that the recommended product list meets the customer's need (Lawrence et al., 2001). These methods come from diverse disciplines, such as data mining, knowledge discovery, information retrieval, user modeling, and agent technologies. Usually, in the context of e-learning, personalization is based on web usage mining techniques, which undertake the task of gathering and extracting all data required for constructing and maintaining learners' profiles. Personalization in e-learning applies data mining techniques for discovery and extracting usage information from the Web (Kosala, & Blockeel, 2000). This technique is based on understanding the behavior of each user to discover useful navigation patterns from the interactions recorded and finding hidden trends in learners' behaviour (Zaïane, 2002; Garcia et al., 2009).

The web usage mining process is usually split over time as follows: 1) *off line tasks*, that involve data collection, data cleaning and pre-processing, data integration, data selection and data mining, and 2) *online tasks* that concern the production and evaluation of discovered patterns, and delivery of the recommendations (Markellou et al., 2005). Some authors have introduced the concept of *'integrated web mining'* –where mined patterns are used on the fly by the system- (Zaïane, 2002) as opposed to off-line web mining used by expert users to discover on-line access patterns and to take the appropriate decisions on the course design. In the off-line web mining approach, an aftermath analysis is used to give some hints on how an on-line course is effectively used and how its structure could be improved based on a comparison of the intended usage of the course material vis-à-vis with the real usage tracked in the web log.

The application of algorithms to automatically build user profiles and select the appropriate recommendations have some limitations, especially for dynamic environments like VLE where users' preferences are likely to be subject to change (Shen and Shen, 2004). In this context, these authors also identified the difficulty of i) characterizing and representing user profiles accurately and ii) designing correct methods to compute the similarity between information and user profiles precisely. Thus, they propose that the recommendations produced consider expert

knowledge provided by a domain expert that can be used by the corresponding algorithm. Al-Hamad et al. (2008) share the same approach, and state that to make the recommendations process more accurate, the system should mimic the knowledge of an experienced educator. This knowledge can be expressed –among others- in the form of "if-then-else" type rules. Rule-based RS rely on manually or automatically generate decision rules that are used to recommend items to users. However, it is quite difficult for an educator creating a the course to develop appropriate adaptation models (usually represented using 'if/then' rules). This type of implementation requires considerable knowledge of students' behavior to create such adaptation rules, which will result into an effective adaptation of the presented content together with an appropriate navigation in the course information space (Ksristofic, 2005).

This approach resembles the ideas of the so-called Intelligent Tutoring Systems (ITS). However, the difference between ITS and RS lies in that the former are focused on diagnosing knowledge gaps and misconceptions of the learner performance compared to expert knowledge as stored by the system (i.e. in a close environment). In this case, remediation actions are offered as direct customized instruction or feedback to the students. In turn, RS are considered for open environments where large amounts of information (or actions) exist and the learners are suggested the most appropriate one, considering their individual profiles and performance in the course. Thus, both systems rely on the expertise of the educator, but given their conceptual differences, in the ITS the control is usually given to the system and in the RS the control is always given to the learner.

The above are some of the research works on recommenders for e-learning that provide evidence that a domain expert can improve the recommendation process. Following this, a tool to facilitate the involvement of educators in the process of personalizing the learning experience can be useful for educational RS. This tool is useful to understand the needs of learners when receiving recommendations in the e-learning domain, and to offer educators a control mechanism on what is recommended to their learners, thus helping them to make the interactions during the learning process as simple, meaningful and efficient as possible. Next, we review some of the administration interfaces that have come to our knowledge that involve the educator in improving the intelligence and thus, the efficacy, effectiveness and satisfaction (i.e. the usability), of the system.

End-User Administration Interfaces for RS

In the previous section we have introduced the idea that several mathematical methods –mainly data mining techniques– can be used to extract information from the users' interactions in VLE. Navigational patters can be discovered, and this information can be used by educators to validate the learning models they use as well as the structure of the web site as it is perused by the learners (Zaïane, 2002). Involving users and getting subjective feedback from them is usually considered as a way to adapt the parameters and algorithms used (Farzan and Brusilovsky, 2006). In the education field, the analysis of collaboration and interaction between the actors (students, educators etc.), the artifacts and the environment is a process that can support the understanding of learning, evaluate the educational result and support the design of effective technology (Gassner et al., 2003).

In order to involve educators in the process, the off-line web mining approach can be used. However, it is cumbersome for an educator who does not have extensive knowledge in data mining to use these tools to improve the effectiveness of VLE. Most data mining algorithms need specific parameters and threshold values to tune the discovery process. Nevertheless educators and e-learning site designers are not savvy in the intricate complexities of data mining algorithms (Zaïane, 2001). Moreover, flexible approaches

to allow end-users express user-driven recommendations require good end-user interface (Adomavicius et al., 2008). Most of the current data mining tools –DBMiner, SPSS Clemenitne, Weka- are too complex for educators to use and their features go well beyond the scope of what an educator wants to do. They are not specifically designed and maintained for pedagogical purposes. These tools should have a more easy-to-use interface to simplify the algorithm configuration and execution, as well as specialized visualization facilities to make their results meaningful to educators and courseware designers (Romero and Ventura, 2007).

In order to facilitate the educators' access to the data mined, some specific educational tools have been developed to help educators in analyzing the different aspects of the learning process. For instance, EPRules (Educational Prediction Rules) is an educator-oriented specific visual tool to facilitate the process of discovering interesting prediction rules. In turn, Kristofic (2005) have proposed an authoring tool where adaptation knowledge can be defined by the author that fits in a modular approach for the back-end system designed to produce recommendations in education. As a result, the knowledge discovered by the algorithms is presented to the author, who can make modifications to the domain structure and the contents of the course. Recently, the AHA! adaptive hypermedia system (de Bra and Calvi, 1998) has integrated a data mining tool (Romero et al., 2003) to help the educator carry out the web mining process and support the corresponding recommendation engine (offline approach) in the same e-learning system, so that feedback and results can be directly applied to the courses. The user interface is oriented to discover sequential patterns and to recommend personalized links. Its main window consists of a menu and two information areas. At the top, the information panel that shows general information about the program and algorithms execution. At the bottom, the sequential pattern panel shows the discovered sequences. All the generated recommendation links are shown to the educator so that she can validate them and select which recommendations will be used by the recommender engine. Finally, another example is TADA-Ed, a data mining tool designed to mine primarily data collected in an educational context (Merceron & Yacef, 2005). This tool allows seeing mistakes made by students who do not succeed in finishing exercises as well as concepts involved in these mistakes. At the same time it allows to identify interesting groups of students, like the group of students who make many mistakes with all sorts of concepts without attempting a significant number of exercises, predicting errors in the final exam and thus warn students who are likely to fail. The authors acknowledge that their interface should be made as easy as possible for educators who are not too familiar with new technologies and plan to improve the interface of the tool so it can be used by any educator who has a minimum of computer literacy –the current version can only be used by a educator who understands data mining. However, no improvements have been found in literature at the time of writing this book chapter.

The goal behind the above examples is that educators can manipulate the graphical representations generated, which allow them to gain an understanding of their learners and become aware of what is happening. However, the state of the art in the literature shows that although researchers are aware of the need of an authoring tool for educators that help them in taking control on the adaptive support provided by algorithms plugged in e-learning platforms, the developments focus so far mainly on reducing the complexity of the usage of the algorithms by simplifying the parameters involved. Nevertheless, from our knowledge, no effort has been done from a human-computer interaction point of view to design an authoring tool that is usable for the educator and facilitates the involvement of educators in the process of personalizing the learning experience and understanding the needs of learners when receiving recommendations in the e-learning domain. Such tool will offer them

a control mechanism on what is recommended to their learners, thus helping them to make the interactions during the learning process as simple, meaningful and efficient as possible.

DESIGN APPROACH FOR THE USER INTERFACE TO MANAGE RECOMMENDATIONS

In the previous section we have presented the review of existing approaches for user interfaces that help educators to manage the adaptive navigation support to be offered to their learners by controlling the data mining algorithms. Recommendations for the educational domain are characterized by their complexity, in the sense that the two-dimension (user–item) approach does not suffice. In this section we comment on the particularities regarding the user interface to manage the recommendations and the methodology to design the user interface of the administration tool.

Specific Needs of Recommender System in Virtual Learning Environments

In order to enrich the adaptive navigation support in VLE, recommendations can be provided to offer adaptive navigation support. These recommendations can be designed with the TORMES methodology (Santos et al., 2011a), which has been introduced before. However, once the recommendations have been designed, they have to be inserted into the VLE. In order to manage these recommendations within the VLE, the design of several user interfaces needs to be considered. The authoring tool offers different options, depending on the user role and the type of information managed. Following the model for the management of the recommendations proposed by Santos and Boticario (2010), we defined different possible tasks:

Table 1. Graphical interfaces for RS in e-learning scenarios

Role	View	Manage
System administrator	Show the system performance regarding the recommendations delivery	Configures the recommendations in the different VLE where the RS is used
Educator	Preview of the defined recommendations	**Modifies the recommendations definition**
Learner	Access to the recommendations received	Modify her recommendations' preferences

1. Managing recommendations on different VLE instances (system administrator).
2. Managing the elements that describe the recommendation according to the conceptual model (researcher).
3. Defining and selecting the recommendations to be given to a learner in terms of the recommendations model (educator).
4. Visualizing the results of the recommendation process (any user, but different views).

According to the above tasks, we have identified 6 different interfaces, which combine view and management options for the three main roles in e-learning scenarios, as shown in Table 1.

The view option corresponds to the delivery of the information to the user (end-user interface), while the management option corresponds to the administration interface. In this chapter we focus on the educator administration interface to introduce our approach for designing interfaces for virtual environments. The reason behind this selection is that it is quite a complex interface and, although some approaches have been proposed in the literature, they have not specifically followed a user-centered design methodology. Moreover, a model for recommendations has been proposed -the one defined by Santos and Boticario, (2010)- which can be assimilated to a conceptual model. The structure represented in the model is reflected for example when defining the steps the user has to follow to complete the task on the system (Novak & Godwing, 1988). By combining this conceptual model with user-centered design methods our approach provides greater cognitive consistence than traditional approaches for interface design.

In order to facilitate educators the process of managing recommendations, the first step is to understand the recommendations utility for the learners. A useful recommendation for a learner depends on many factors: i) the user's learning goals, preferences and needs, ii) the progress in the course, and iii) the quality of the contents contributed by other members, etc. Given the complexity of the learning context, it is not possible to design in advance the most appropriate navigation path for each learner in each situation as instructional design theories propose. A suitable navigation has to be dynamically built by taking into account the features of the actual learner and her current and past interactions with the VLE (and those of other users as well, whether they have been successful or not). Recommendations offer a personalized way to guide learners through the wide spectrum of possible actions to take in the course. An adaptive system is required for such a personalized navigation support. In this respect, RS are considered a suitable solution to provide adaptive responses to users' interactions.

In this context, the goal of the administration tool is to offer educators a way to validate and modify the recommendations generated by the algorithms, as well as to introduce new ones designed using the *TORMES* methodology that consider educational needs that may not have been covered during the data mining process. Our main innovation in the approach is the way we have proceeded to come up with the design of the user interface for the educator administration interface for the RS, where we propose the combination of user-centered design methods with conceptual models, as well as the consideration of ergonomic guidelines for the design. Two hypotheses support the rationale for the administration tool: 1) educators feel more comfortable with some sort of control over the recommendations and 2) the human input is useful for the algorithms, to improve the quality and utility of the recommendations generated. The main research challenge in this respect is to understand the behavior of educators while they are working with the students in VLE.

User-Centered Design Methodology

To address the specific needs of this RS interface we followed a user-centered design (UCD) approach (Norman and Draper, 1986), which locates the user as the core of the solution's development process and establishes that "the needs of the users should dominate the design of the interface, and the needs of the interface should dominate the design of the rest of the system". Over a related body of knowledge, Shneiderman (1987) defined eight golden rules of design for facilitating the designer's task and later, Nielsen adapted those criteria as his, widely recognized, heuristic principles for the expert evaluation of a digital interface (Nielsen, 1994).

UCD allows describing the use of the interface in the context of a real situation and in an objective way, not based on personal experience but on inquiries of the field. This way helps to define the features that are necessaries for the solution and the ones that are not as useful as developers or other stakeholders may think. The UCD methods are oriented to the study of the user's needs and profile, taking them into account to define the functions and interaction patterns for an intuitive structure and an easy-to-use solution interface. By interviewing or observing potential users, using techniques based on psychological, ethnographic and statistics data, designers will have a deeper understanding of users' needs and design requirements and offer a human oriented solution. Knowing the solution requirements, and with a user oriented point of view, the designers can establish a metaphor based on a physical context or an object from the real world. This

metaphor is used as a basis to define the design from a conceptual model. The UCD methodology is used to translate a conceptual model in a real world's metaphor, so that digital actions have their reference on daily life activities. This translation allows the user to make the connection between both worlds and gives cognitive consistency to the system's structure and the presentation of the interface.

The methodology proposed for designing the interface for educators to manage the recommendations on an e-learning platform for their learners follows three main stages, adapted from the Usability Professionals' Association (UPA) definition of UCD methodology to the needs of the design at hand. These stages are:

- **Information architecture**: it consists on the analysis of the requirements and objectives of the users by defining use scenarios and user profiles. At the end of this stage all the requirements are covered by a global solution's structure and the main interface navigation is defined with a mock-up interface.
- **Presentation layer**: it is the design phase where all the aesthetics issues are defined (i.e. layout, grid, color code, sizes and typography). This phase also considers the platform restrictions and possibilities, the grids definition, the semantic and ergonomic color code, the visual architecture of the templates, sizes and positions for the elements of the interface, the high fidelity presentation prototypes, the front end development and some usability testing.
- **Behavioral layer:** it comprises the technical development of the solution, covering the templates definitions, the behavior of the interface's components, the back end development, the Web Content Accessibility Guidelines Overview (WCAG) validation for accessibility and the final usability testing.

In this chapter we focus on the Information architecture stage, which includes the following steps: i) user's requirements, ii) conceptual model, iii) mental model and task flow, iv) task based information structure, and v) interaction mock-ups. Next, we comment on each of these steps.

INFORMATION ARCHITECTURE STEPS FOR THE DESIGN OF THE USER INTERFACE

In this section we describe the steps to follow to address the information architecture issues when designing the structure of user interface of the recommendations administration tool. We propose the usage of several techniques on each of the steps defined for this stage. Thus, for each of these steps, we comment on the objective covered, the technique used and the expected outcome when designing the administration tool. The application of these steps to the design of the administration tool is reported in Santos et al. (2012).

Goals to Achieve During the Information Architecture Steps

The information architecture of the user interface aims to address three main goals through the completion of five steps. For the context of a RS administration tool for educators these goals are:

1. Translate the information and data obtained from the users into design requirements.
2. Integrate the conceptual model of a RS with the educator mental model.
3. Produce the interface for the authoring tool according to ergonomic standards based on the conceptual model, its corresponding metaphor derived from the interviews with the users and the visual and cognitive ergonomic guidelines.

These three goals are to be achieved through the five steps of the information architecture detailed in the following sections. Figure 1 illustrates the

Figure 1. Visualization of the information architecture steps

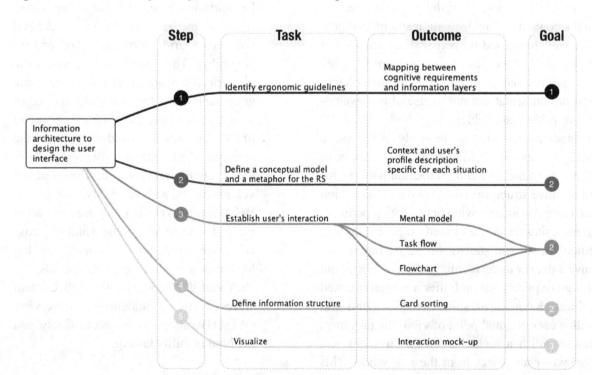

outcomes of the tasks completed in each steps, according to the different goals.

In particular, for each step a specific tasks is defined, which is linked to a certain outcome and covers one of the goals defined above. Next, details for each of the steps are provided.

Step 1: Cognitive and Visual User's Requirements: Ergonomic Guidelines

This step contributes to the achievement of the first goal translating users' needs into design requirements. In this case, the objective is to obtain information about how the educators use the platform, and their technographic (Forrest, 1985) strengths and weakness as well as to identify the opportunities and difficulties perceived by them from the interface. We used two different tools to elicit the design requirements for this user-interface:

1. Ergonomics guidelines for software design according to standards (UNE-EN ISO 9241-1/A1:2002), which describe ergonomic requirements for data displays (i.e. cognitive workload).
2. Categorization of 3 information layers for digital interface defined by W3C standard (W3C, 2007): content, visualization, and behavior. Although these are used to program code, they are also useful to reflect on the cognitive and visual users' requirements as they cover all the elements involved in the user interface.

To obtain the ergonomic guidelines, on one hand, we adapted the UNE guidelines to the three factors of the subjective workload assessment model proposed by O'Donnell and Eggmeier (1986) for the requirements of interfaces, which are i) time pressure, ii) mental effort and iii) emotional stress. On the other hand, we adopted the 3 information layers defined by W3C to identify the elements of the interface, that are involved, which correspond to i) content, ii) visualization and iii) behavior.

We then mapped these three factors that affect the cognitive workload against the three information layers to identify the content, visual and behavioral requirements for the interface. The result of this mapping is presented in Table 2.

Since the mapping refers to generic criteria and references, it does not provide specific rules but it offers suitable directions for the requirements and the potential of the system. The directions suggested in the table below are also supported by a study carried out by Agila (2010) on the appropriate language to use when defining the text for the recommendation to be displayed to the learners, in the sense that the language to use has to be friendly, familiar and motivating.

As a result, according to the UNE-EN ISO 9241-1/A1 and the W3C standard, when applying ergonomic design, the following issues have to be taken into account in order to direct the attention of the users to the educational contents and tasks, rather than the way to use the system:

- The relation between mental model and users' profile.
- Consistency between mental model and visual architecture of the interface.
- Visual ergonomics of interface elements (i.e. using a grid guarantees a clean distribution of the different components).
- Cognitive ergonomics: adapting the process to the users' mental model.
- Visual ergonomics and grid structure.

Table 2 shows the requirements derived by the combination of these 6 factors. By crossing these factors it was possible to take into account all types of content and ergonomic qualities desired for the user interface and thus avoiding to leave out any relevant aspect. Once the cognitive and visual requirements have been considered, the next step deals with the concept definition.

Table 2. *Cognitive and visual user's requirements mapped: Ergonomic guidelines*

	CONTENT	VISUALISATION	BEHAVIOUR
TIME PRESSURE	**a.** When creating a new recommendation, educators start by choosing the algorithm or technique that would generate the recommendation. - i.e. the system can ask them to provide step by step the information needed for creating that specific recommendation manually, or they can have the option of accessing the recommendation automatically created by the system (by web-usage mining). In this case, educators can modify an already existing recommendation and easing the process. **b.** The interface is dynamic and shows to the educator suggestions on building recommendations that take into account students' profile. This optimizes the task of the educators in giving a more personalized education in a virtual environment.	**a.** The interface represents a visual hierarchy of components that matches the mental model of the user. **b.** The visual hierarchy of the contents is based on the proper definition of steps followed by the educator when creating the recommendation for the platform. **b.** Using a frame to define a harmonious distribution of the space help the users to easily scan and read the interface and its items. **c.** The different functionalities of the interface are divided into areas which make them easy to find during the navigation. **d.** The reading and navigation of the interface is made easier by a consistent use of colors, with appropriate contrast ratio and semantic association with the interface items.	**a.** Users are allowed to save unfulfilled recommendations as drafts: - the system will warn users when saving a recommendation that does not comply with all the required information. - in this way, educators can easily retrieve and continue any incomplete tasks. This is the case when they need more time or to search for additional information to define the recommendation. **b.** Allowing users to personalize their interface will ease their use. For example: - shape the visualization of the different content blocks - define interaction for entering data, i.e. predictive writing or automatic grammar check (specifically, when entering text on explaining the reasons behind the recommendations) **c.** The process' navigation is easy and smooth for the educator.
MENTAL EFFORT	**a.** Contextual help on complex tasks, is present to reduce confusion or distraction and therefore the mental effort demand. - Tool-tips are used on elements that are not literally explained, i.e. icons without related label or caption. - Status changes and their effects are warned to the users after they take place with informative messages i.e. *"recommendation sent by mail"*. - When users need to take decisions, the consequences of the available options are specified. i.e. buttons are labeled to detail the action involved on its click. **b.** Users are permanently enabled to retrieve: - pending, recent, frequent, and favorite tasks and documents, - educational objects that have been personalized for individual or groups of students - the tagging system, based on users' language, that reduces users' mental effort to understand process and interact with the system.	**a.** Presentation and location of the messages is appropriated and guarantees their visibility. **b.** The layout of the interface and its items is consistent throughout all the interaction, helping to minimize the user's mental effort. **c.** When a pictorial menu does not include labels due to lack of space, tool-tip alternatives or access to a related caption is provided to reduce users' mental effort and the chance of errors, which increase cognitive load, both mental and emotional	**a.** When presenting emerging layers and other enriched elements, an ergonomic interface considers: - the temporal dimension, and to show only what is needed when it is really needed and therefore to reduce the complexity of the interface. - the efforts required to the users in understanding the interface and its flows, and so, to show the path taken on a breadcrumb that changes on each click.
EMOTIONAL FACTORS	**a.** The language used is familiar to the users and the information is presented in a format adapted to them, according to their performance/task: - Operative: experience in online educational activities - Technical: experience in working with computers or other digital interfaces. Users' ability in handling interfaces with different level of complexity. **b.** Warning and error messages are presented in a colloquial and understandable language for the users. **c.** The interface supports the users in completing their task by presenting one step at a time.	**a.** In order to simplify the process for the users, the design of RS has to focus on functionalities, adapting the scenario to educational tasks and avoid all ornamental elements that may cause distractions.	**a.** Error prone has a friendly interface to increase the motivation of the users in completing complex task. Error prone, explains the error cause or restriction and the instructions needed by the user to continue with the task.

Step 2: Definition of Conceptual Model and Metaphor for Educational RS

Once discussed the ergonomics requirements that has to be addressed in the interface, a real life scenario has to be established. In this step, the objective is to define a real life situation that represents the main concepts and scenarios that will be covered by the functions of the interface. This step adds information obtained from the users to define the user's requirements and achieve the first goal and part of the second one (in combination with the next step), as listed in the previous section.

The proposed technique for this step is to gather user data through scenario-based methods (Rosson & Carroll, 2001) supported by interviews with users, which aim to describe the sequence of actions and events in the context of use: goals, plans, problems and reactions of people in specific circumstances. Scenarios involve the user in describing stories (i.e. scenarios) about the problems taking place in relevant situations in terms of the context, actors with personal motivations, knowledge, capabilities and tools and objects manipulated by the actors. Based on the interviews with users, the conceptual model of the educator's context on her desktop should be defined. The outcomes from the application of the *TORMES* methodology (which designs recommendations for a specific context of use which is previously analyzed) can feed this step.

The advantage about the virtual world is that the personalization of the recommendations is much easier than on the physical world, where difficulties depend on the big amount of learners that would require the delivery of personalized recommendations face to face.

A qualitative approach can be followed to understand the users' context and their requirements (Cooper et al. 2007), which involve the following issues:

i. Context of use: where, when, why and how the product will be used.
ii. Domain knowledge: what do users need to know how to do their jobs.
iii. Current tasks and activities: the ones the product is required to accomplish and the ones it does not support.
iv. Goals and motivation to use the product.
v. Mental model: how users think while doing the task as well as their expectations about the product.
vi. Problems and frustration with current products or analogous system.

From our experience, the following information should be collected from the participants in the interview:

- The description of the problem/challenge
- The context in which occurred (services, course)
- Who is impacted
- How the problem/challenge was detected
- User characteristics that affect the situation
- The solution proposed by the educator
- Solutions that would be desirable
- The severity or the importance of the problem/challenge
- The frequency of the problem/challenge

The resulting information can provide information that allows the design team to propose a user interface model that facilitates the management of the huge quantity of available data with a mathematical accuracy and help the educator distinguish which contents and actions are best for each learner taking into count the motivation level, progress in the course, and educational aspects.

The expected outcome from this step will be different on every case depending on the information gathered and specific requirements. The result will be a description of the context of use from the user's point of view that provides the elements that can be used to represent the recommendations (i.e. the conceptual model) in the user interface. For this purpose, we defined a scenario-based user-centered design process that involves educators to elicit relevant e-learning situations and suitable recommendations to provide in them, which can be obtained by following the TORMES methodology. The information obtained from this process is used to feed the design of the authoring tool. This design of the authoring tool needs to take into account the conceptual model of the users in order to simplify a complex system as the RS is. Thus, it will reflect the conceptual model and the appropriate metaphor for the interaction with the RS.

Step 3: Mental Model, Task Flow and the Information Structure

In this step, the objective is to establish the interactions to be carried out by the user when performing the proposed task, in this case, the management of the recommendations. The outcome of this step integrated with the outcome of the previous step is needed to achieve the second goal of integrating the conceptual model of a RS with the educator mental model.

The mental model can be defined as the prediction of the interactions that the educator would expect to follow when managing the recommendation of content or activity for each one of her learners. Thus, the technique here is to extract the actions (verbs) on the different phrases collected from the interviews with the users from the previous step. These results can be contrasted and complemented with the recommendations model proposed that characterizes the recommendations with metadata information.

The expected outcome is a diagram detailing the mental model and which represents the task flow for the system. It also depends on the functional requirements established on each case. This diagram (flowchart) should represent the interactions to be followed by the educator while using the platform for managing recommendations

for their learners and should explicitly consider the items and the actions available for the typical services in an e-learning platform, where the possibilities for generating content and interacting with existing content should be specified.

Step 4: Task Based Information Structure: The Card Sorting Exercise

The objective of this step is to give a structure to the application and define the process by stages. An open card sorting (Rosenfeld and Morville, 2002) on the recommendations identified in the scenarios can be carried out to help the structuring process to create categories according to the experts' criteria. A card sorting exercise consists on writing the pieces of information to be structured on individual cards, and handing them out to the experts asking them group the ones they considered related. If the card sorting is open, participants have to create categories according to their personal mental model. Thus, each expert makes their own clusters and labels them.

The results of the exercise have to be analyzed both in a quantitative and qualitative way. For the quantitative analysis, the clusters made by each expert can be analyzed by counting the times each item is grouped with another in order to build a symmetric matrix of co-occurrences. The results can then be processed with a statistical suite to obtain the corresponding hierarchical clustering (i.e., a dendrogram).

For the qualitative analysis, the categories resulted from the card-sorting exercise can be compared with existing categories, such as the ones defined in the recommendation model by Santos and Boticario, (2010), computing the percentage of card sorting participants that agreed on that category.

The card sorting results are to be translated into information categories for the filters that the educators should use when managing the recommendations through the user interface. This exercise provides the user's perspective and the

Figure 2. Mock-up for the educator administration interface

qualitative information needed to integrate the interactions that the educator carries out while managing a recommendation to a learner. The information derived from the outcome of this step contributes to the achievement of the second goal of integrating the recommendations conceptual model with the educator mental model.

Step 5: Interaction Mock-Up

The objective of the last step is to represent the structure model and the interaction patterns of the user interface with a visual representation of what the interface will be and how it will look like, called prototype. Prototyping is the most appropriate technique because it is a technique that allows to quickly iterate different solutions, until achieving one that fits and meets the requirements defined in the previous stages.

The expected outcome is a prototype that considers the guidelines proposed in step 1, fol-

lows the task flow defined in step 3, which was in turn extracted from the user's mental model in step 2 and which reflects the information structure obtained in step 4. The mock-up should reflect the simplification of the complexity and minimize the cognitive workload demanded to the users. This final step should integrate all the user's requirements derived from the previous steps: definition of the conceptual and mental models according to the metaphor and the users and ergonomic guidelines. The result of this step addresses the third goal in producing an ergonomic authoring interface for the administration of the educator's recommendations, and in defining as core elements the conceptual model and its metaphor, the mental models elicited from the initial inquiry and the visual and cognitive ergonomic guidelines for the interface's design.

An example of mock-up, obtained following the approach presented in this chapter as described in Santos et al. (2012), is presented in Figure 2 to show the reader what can be an expected result from the design process proposed.

CONCLUSION

There are fields where we can clearly see how the artificial intelligence of a system is improved when it is regarded as complementary to the human cognitive potential. RS, especially in the e-learning context, can be strongly improved with a human oriented approach from the UCD methodology and its information architecture stage, as described in this chapter.

In this sense, we investigated the human role in existing and emerging technologies like RS and VLE. By having intelligent agents working on online data mining in a completely autonomous way, educators would only have to supervise the new recommender links, but not pre-process and apply mining tools (Romero et al., 2007).

As resulted from our field studies, the human intervention in the automated process of the RS is considered essential in the learning domain, where the educator needs to supervise the educational value of the messages directed to students and at the same time students want to be assured of the presence of a human actor beyond the artificial intelligence of the system they interact with. Even if it will require an additional effort for the educators at the beginning, it has been acknowledged that it will contribute in increasing the efficiency of the management of the class and help prevent major setbacks for a smooth completion of the course. Hence, the introduction of a user interface to manage recommendations and the need of a UCD approach to design this interface in a way that is suitable for the specific context at hand.

The UCD methodology was adopted to understand user requirements and elicit recommendations following a user-centered design approach at early stages of the design process, instead of leaving it all to the final usability evaluation phase.

We have presented the information architecture steps that need to be followed to design the

administration tool for educators with ergonomic qualities looking for the improvement of their experience while using the features created to manage educational oriented recommendations in VLE.

The information architecture steps followed are:

- Step 1: Cognitive and visual user's requirements: ergonomic guidelines
- Step 2: Conceptual model definition and metaphor for the RS.
- Step 3: Mental model, task flow and the information structure.
- Step 4: Task based information structure: the card sorting exercise.
- Step 5: Interaction mock-up

The administration tool designed following the UCD methodology, allows educators to manage the recommendations to be offered to the learners, in a user centered and then consistent way. In this way, educators are supported in the publication stage of the e-learning life cycle to manage the definition of the recommendations designed with the TORMES methodology.

Our chapter adds a novel contribution to the research on RS in education because of its multidisciplinary approach in the methodology to produce the design for the user interface. The research presented in this chapter applies UCD approach and related methodologies considering user's needs as the core of system's features. The variety of users, platforms and contexts implies the need of valuing the adaptability of the system in the whole solution's design. RS play an important role in managing this adaptation to a variety of user needs and improving the efficiency of its use.

FUTURE RESEARCH DIRECTIONS

The evaluation of personalized systems is still an open issue in research. The most traditional evaluation methods are based on the assumption

Figure 3. Combinations of design variables

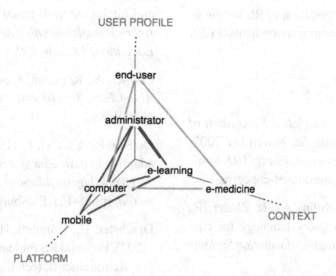

that the system output is the same for each user in every context; therefore the inclusion of personalized output adds complexity when evaluating the system from the user point of view. Moreover, the user-centered evaluation practice of personalized systems is still often perceived as poor, partly due to non-systematically and non-empirically reporting of activities (van Velsen et al., 2008). We intended to avoid the aforementioned issue by adopting a UCD methodology already in the design phase, and benefits from this approach are expected in the subsequent evaluation of the interface.

We have applied this design approach in the e-learning environment because it is one of the most demanding domains, since it needs human intervention to foster and optimize the artificial intelligence of the system. In implementing the RS for the VLE we improved its artificial nature by including the human intelligence factor in the automated process. The process followed helped us to produce a mock-up of the tool that reflects the needs of its users, therefore we intend to apply this process in other digital contexts by using the same UCD approach.

For this exercise we identified three different variables to take into account while designing the solution's interface for any domain:

- The user profile: whether is the end-user, the content administrator, the super-administrator or the content recipient.
- The context we are designing for: which could be, for instance, educational, medical, legal, etc.
- The platform: which can be a personal computer rather than a mobile, digital television, etc.

Figure 3 represents a selection of possible combinations of these three variables, creating different context of use.

In the specific case described in this chapter we focused on the e-learning environment, designing a computer user-interface for educators for an online platform. This approach can be applied to design the user interface for the students both to receive the recommendations and to manage their profile (as we defined in Table 1). Future research will explore the application of the same approach in different domains, for different users profile, using different platforms.

At the same time, another interesting research area in personalized educational contexts is increasing use of mush-up learning environment. This type of educational format is in line with the development of the Web 2.0. and represents an interesting potential application of RS for the so called personalized learning environments (PLE).

REFERENCES

W3C. (2007). *Design principles: Separation of concerns.* Working Draft, 26 November 2007. Retrieved from http://www.w3.org/TR/ html-design-principles/ #separation-of-concerns

Adomavicius, G., Tuzhilin, A., & Zheng, R. (2008). REQUEST: A query language for customizing recommendations. *Information Systems Research, 22*(1).

Agila, M. (2010). *Análisis del lenguaje utilizado en las recomendaciones y explicaciones de un sistema recomendador y su impacto en la decisión del usuario final. Trabajo de Investigación. Doctorado en Inteligencia Artificial Avanzada: Perspectivas Simbólica y Conexionista.* Depto. Inteligencia Artificial. ETSI Informática. UNED.

Al-Hamad, A., Yaacob, N., & Al-Zoubi, A. Y. (2008). Integrating learning style information into personalized e-learning system. *IEEE Multidisciplinary Engineering Education Magazine, 3*(1).

Bates, B., & Leary, J. (2001). Supporting a range of learning styles using a taxonomy-based design framework approach. *Proceedings of the 18th Annual Conference of the Australasian Society for Computers in Learning in Tertiary Education,* 9-12 December, (pp. 45-53).

Blochl, B., Rumershofer, H., & Wob, W. (2003). Individualized e-learning systems enabled by a semantically determined adaptation of learning fragments. In *Proceeding of the 14ᵗʰ International Workshop on Database and Expert Systems Applications,* (pp. 640-645).

Brusilovsky, P., & Peylo, C. (2003). Adaptive and intelligent Web-based educational systems. *International Journal of Artificial Intelligence in Education, 13,* 156–169.

Cooper, A., Reimann, R., & Cronin, D. (2007). *About Face 3 - The essentials of interaction design.* Wiley.

De Bra, P., & Calvi, L. (1998). AHA: A generic adaptive hypermedia system. *Proceedings of the 2nd Workshop on Adaptive Hypertext and Hypermedia,* (pp. 5-12). Pittsburgh.

Drachsler, H., Hummel, H. G. K., & Koper, R. (2007). Personal RS for learners in lifelong learning: Requirements, techniques and model. *International Journal of Learning Technology, 3*(4).

Farzan, R., & Brusilovsky, P. (2006). Social navigation support in a course recommendation system. In *Proceedings of 4th International Conference on Adaptive Hypermedia and Adaptive Web-based Systems.*

Forrest, E. (1985). Segmenting VCR owners. *Journal of Advertising Research, 28*(2).

Garcia, E., Romero, C., Ventura, S., & De Castro, C. (2009). An architecture for making recommendations to courseware authors using association rule mining and collaborative filtering. *User Modeling and User-Adapted Interaction, 19*(1-2), 99–132. doi:10.1007/s11257-008-9047-z

Gassner, K., Jansen, M., Harrer, A., Herrmann, K., & Hoppe, H. U. (2003), Analysis methods for collaborative models and activities. In B. Wasson, S. Ludvigsen, & U. Hoppe (Eds.), *Designing for Change in Networked Learning Environments, Proceedings of CSCL 2003,* (pp. 411-420). Dordrecht, The Netherlands: Kluwer Academic Publishers.

Hsu, M. H. (2008). A personalized English learning recommender system for ESL students. *Expert Systems with Applications, 34*(1), 683–688. doi:10.1016/j.eswa.2006.10.004

Kosala, R., & Blockeel, H. (2000). Web mining research: A survey. *SIGKDD Explorations, 2*(1), 1–15. doi:10.1145/360402.360406

Koutrika, G., Ikeda, R., Bercovitz, B., & Garcia-Molina, H. (2008). Flexible recommendations over rich data. In *Proceedings of the 2008 ACM Conference on Recommender Systems* (RecSys'08), (pp. 203-210). Lausanne, Switzerland, 2008.

Ksristofic, A. (2005). Recommender system for adaptive hypermedia applications. In *Proceeding of Informatics and Information Technology Student Research Conference*, Bratislava, (pp. 229-234).

Lawrence, R. D., Almasi, G. S., Kotlyar, V., Viveros, M. S., & Duri, S. (2001). Personalization of supermarket product recommendations. *Data Mining and Knowledge Discovery, 5*, 11–32. doi:10.1023/A:1009835726774

Li, X., & Chang, S. (2005). A personalized e-learning system based on user profile constructed using information fusion. *DMS, 2005*, 109–114.

Markellou, P., Mousourouli, I., Spiros, S., & Tsakalidis, A. (2005). Using Semantic Web mining technologies for personalized e-learning experiences. *Web-Based Education Conference*, Grindelwald, Switzerland (pp. 461-826).

Merceron, A., & Yacef, K. (2005). Tada-ed for educational data mining. *Interactive Multimedia Electronic Journal of Computer-Enhanced Learning, 7*(1), 267–287.

Montaner, M., Lopez, B., & Lluis, D. J. (2003). A taxonomy of recommender agents on the Internet. *Artificial Intelligence Review, 19*(4), 285–330. doi:10.1023/A:1022850703159

Nielsen, J. (1994). *Usability engineering. Academic Press. Norman, D., & Draper, S. (1986). User centered system design: New perspectives on human-computer interaction.* Hillsdale, NJ: Laurence Erlbaum.

Novak, J. D., & Gowin, D. B. (1984). *Learning how to learn.* Cambridge, UK: Cambridge University Press.

O'Donnell, R., & Eggemeier, F. T. (1986). Workload assessment methodology. In Boff, K. R., Kaufman, L., & Thomas, J. P. (Eds.), *Handbook of perception and human performance.* New York, NY: Wiley.

Resnick, P., & Varian, H. R. (1997). Recommender systems. *Communications of the ACM, 40*, 56–58. doi:10.1145/245108.245121

Romero, C., & Ventura, S. (2007). Educational data mining: A survey from 1995 to 2005. [Elsevier.]. *Expert Systems with Applications, 1*(33), 135–146. doi:10.1016/j.eswa.2006.04.005

Romero, C., Ventura, S., de Castro, C., & de Bra, P. (2003). *Discovering prediction rules in AHA courses!* User Modeling 2003. Pittsburg (USA).

Romero, C., Ventura, S., Delgado, J. A., & De Bra, P. (2007). *Personalized links recommendation based on data mining in adaptive educational hypermedia systems* (pp. 292–306).

Rosenfeld, L., & Morville, P. (2002). *Information architecture for the World Wide Web: Designing large scale websites.* O'Reilly & Associates.

Rosson, M. B., & Carroll, J. M. (2001). *Usability engineering: scenario-based development of human computer interaction.* Morgan Kaufmann.

Santos, O. C., & Boticario, J. G. (2010). Modeling recommendations for the educational domain. In *Proceedings of the 1st Workshop Recommender Systems for Technology Enhanced Learning* (RecSysTEL 2010), Barcelona, Spain, 29–30 September 2010, (pp. 2793–2800).

Santos, O. C., & Boticario, J. G. (2011a). TORMES methodology to elicit educational oriented recommendations. *Lecture Notes in Artificial Intelligence, 6738,* 541–543.

Santos, O. C., & Boticario, J. G. (2011b). Requirements for semantic educational recommender systems in formal e-learning scenarios. *Algorithms, 4*(2), 131–154. doi:10.3390/a4030131

Santos, O. C., & Boticario, J. G. (2011c). Usability in adaptive educational systems. *Workshop on Usability and Educational Technology 2011. Held in Conjunction with the 23rd Conférence Francophone Sur l'Interaction Homme-Machine, Actes Complementaries,* (pp. 93-95). Nice, France.

Santos, O. C., & Boticario, J. G. (2011d). *Educational recommender systems and techniques: Practices and challenges.* Hershey, PA: IGI Global. doi:10.4018/978-1-61350-489-5

Santos, O. C., Martin, L., Mazzone, E., & Boticario, J. G. (2009). Management of recommendations for accessible eLearning platforms: is it a need for learning management system users? In *Proceedings of the 3rd Workshop Towards User Modelling and Adaptive Systems for All (TUMAS-A). In conjunction with the 14th International Conference on Artificial Intelligence in Education* (AIED 200), (pp. 21-22).

Santos, O. C., Mazzone, E., Aguilar, M. J., & Boticario, J. G. (2012). (in press). Designing a user interface to manage recommendations for virtual learning communities. *International Journal of Web Based Communities.*

Schafer, J. B., Konstan, J. A., & Riedl, J. (2001). E-commerce recommendation applications. *Data Mining and Knowledge Discovery, 5,* 115–153. doi:10.1023/A:1009804230409

Schulz, A. G., Hahsler, M., & Jahn, M. (2001). Educational and scientific recommender systems: Designing the information channels of the virtual university. *International Journal of Engineering Education, 17*(2), 153–163.

Shen, L., & Shen, R. (2004). Learning content recommendation service based-on simple sequencing specification. *ICWL, 2004,* 363–370.

Shneiderman, B. (1987). *Designing the user interface: Strategies for effective human-computer interaction.* Addison Wesley.

Soonthornphisaj, N., Rojsattarat, E., & Yim-Ngam, S. (2006). Smart e-learning using recommender system. *International Conference on Intelligent Computing 2006,* (pp. 518-523).

Tang, T., & McCalla, G. (2003). *Smart recommendation for an evolving e-learning system.* Workshop on Technologies for Electronic Documents for Supporting Learning, International Conference on Artificial Intelligence in Education.

UPA – Usability Professionals Association. (2011). *User-centered design methodology.* Retrieved from http://www.usabilityprofessionals.org/upa_publications/ux_poster.html

Van Rosmalen, P., Boticario, J. G., & Santos, O. C. (2004). The full life cycle of adaptation in alfanet elearning environment. *Learning Technology Newsletter, 4,* 59–61.

van Velsen, L., van der Geest, T., Klaassen, R., & Steehouder, M. (2008). User-centered evaluation of adaptive and adaptable systems: a literature review. *The Knowledge Engineering Review, 23*(3), 261–281. doi:10.1017/S0269888908001379

WCAG. (n.d.). *Web content accessibility guidelines overview.* Retrieved from http://www.w3.org/WAI/ intro/wcag.php

Wilson, S., Liber, O., Johnson, M., Beauvoir, P., Sharples, P., & Milligan, C. (2007). Personal learning environments: Challenging the dominant design of educational systems. *Journal of the E-Learning Knowledge Society, 3*, 27–38.

Zaiane, O. (2002). *Building a recommender agent for e-learning systems*. In ICCE 2002.

Zaiane, O. R. (2001) Web usage mining for a better web-based learning environment. In *Proceedings of Conference on Advanced Technology for Education,* (pp. 60–64). Banff, AB, June 2001.

ADDITIONAL READING

AENOR - UNE 139803:2004 http://www.tawdis. net/recursos/ downloads/UNE_139803.pdf

Buxton, B. Sketching User Experiences: Getting the Design Right and the Right Design (Mar 30, 2007). Davidson, M. J., Dove, L., Weltz, J. Mental Models and Usability http://www.lauradove.info/ reports/mental%20models.htm

Dix, A., Finlay, J., Abowd, G., & Beale, R. (1998). *Human-Computer Interaction*. Herfordshire, UK: Prentice Hall Europe.

Garrett, J. J.. The Elements of User Experience: User-Centered Design for the Web (Oct 21, 2002).

International Ergonomics Association. Aug, 2000. http://www.iea.cc/browse.php? contID=what_is_ ergonomics

Krug, Steve. Don't Make Me Think! A Common Sense Approach to Web Usability (2nd edition Aug 28, 2005)

Martin, L., Roldán, D., Revilla, O., Aguilar, M.J., Santos, O. C., Boticario, J.G. (2008) Usability in e-Learning Platforms: heuristics comparison between Moodle, Sakai and dotLRN. OpenACS Conferences, 2008.

McNee, S. M., Riedl, J., & Konstan, J. A. (2006) Being accurate is not enough: How accuracy metrics have hurt RS. In: Extended Abstracts of the 2006 ACM Conference on Human Factors in Computing Systems.

Moggridge, B. Designing Interactions (Oct, 2007)

Morville, Pe. and Rosenfeld, L. Information Architecture for the World Wide Web: Designing Large-Scale Web Sites (Nov 27, 2006).

Norman, D. (1998). *The Psychology of Everyday Things*. MIT Press.

Santos, O. C., & Boticario, J. G. (2008). Users' experience with a recommender system in an open source standard-based learning management system. In proceedings of the 4th Symposium of the WG HCI&UE of the Austrian Computer Society on Usability & HCI for Education and Work (USAB 2008).

Santos, O. C., Martin, L., del Campo, E., Saneiro, M., Mazzone, E., Boticario, J. G., & Petrie, H. (2009b) User-Centered Design Methods for Validating a Recommendations Model to Enrich Learning Management Systems with Adaptive Navigation Support. In: S. Weibelzahl, J. Masthoff, A. Paramythis, and L. van Velsen (Eds.) Proceedings of the Sixth Workshop on User-Centred Design and Evaluation of Adaptive Systems, held in conjunction with the International Conference on User Modeling, Adaptation, and Personalization (UMAP2009), Trento, Italy, June 26th, 2009 (pp. 64-67).

Swearingen, K., & Sinha, R. (2001). An HCI Perspective on RS. In *ACM SIGIR*. Beyond Algorithms.

Tintarev, N., & Masthoff, J. (2007) A Survey of Explanations in RS. In: Uchyigit, G. (ed.) Workshop on RS and Intelligent User Interfaces associated with ICDE 2007, Istanbul, Turkey.

KEY TERMS AND DEFINITIONS

Cognitive Demand: Knowledge and concentration levels required for completing a task.

Cognitive Workload: Knowledge and concentration levels required for completing a task are known as the cognitive demand of the interface. We understand this cognitive demand to become workload when it overcomes the capacity of the user.

Conceptual Model: Where the relation between the steps, are represented by a structure or a diagram that will orient the design of the interface

Ergonomics: (or human factors) Is the scientific discipline concerned with the understanding of interactions among humans and other elements of a system, and the profession that applies theory, principles, data and methods to design in order to optimize human well-being and overall system performance. (International Ergonomics Association. Aug, 2000).

Mental Model: For HCI practitioners, a mental model is a set of beliefs about how a system works. Humans interact with systems based on these beliefs. (Norman, 1988) This makes mental models very important to HCI and its primary objective, usability.

Recommendation: In the context of a VLE, a recommendation can defined as an action to do by the user on an item in the VLE. It consists on a message which contains a link that points to the appropriate object and the associated functionality for the action suggested to be carried out.

Scenario: A description of the context of use from the user's point of view.

Task Flow: The prediction of the steps that the user's would expect to follow using an interface while doing a specific task.

TORMES Methodology: Stands for 'Tutor Oriented Recommendations Modeling for Educational Systems'. This methodology based on the standard ISO 9241-210 on human-centered design for interactive systems and supports educators in the design of educationally oriented recommendations.

Usability: The effectiveness, efficiency and satisfaction with which specified users achieve specified goals in a particular environment. (ISO 9241) (Dix et al., 1998) The standard further defines the components of the usability definition: *Effectiveness*: accuracy and completeness with which specified users can achieve specified goals in a particular environment. *Efficiency* is comprised of the resources expended in relation to the accuracy and completeness of the goals achieved. *Satisfaction* includes the comfort and acceptability of the work system to its users and other people affected by its use.

User Centered Design: Donald Norman uses the term "user-centered design" to describe design based on the needs of the user, leaving aside what he considers to be secondary issues like aesthetics. User-centered design involves simplifying the structure of tasks, making things visible, getting the mapping right, exploiting the powers of constraint, and designing for error (Norman and Draper, 1986).

Chapter 7
Utilizing Cognitive Resources in User Interface Designs

Serkan Özel
Bogazici University, Turkey

ABSTRACT

This chapter focuses on multiple representations and cognitive perspective about presenting information via different modes in user interface design. Research studies indicate that providing accurate representations increases users' recognition of information. Moreover, presentation of one concept in multiple modes improves concept acquisition. Developing an understanding of how concept acquisition occurs requires knowledge about cognitive information processing and brain functioning. Scientific studies related to brain functioning will enlighten the path in front of cognitive psychology while the cognitive psychology research will advance the knowledge base on information processing.

INTRODUCTION

Marois (2005) provided a precise example to demonstrate information storage capabilities of human brain: "During our lifetime, our brain will have amassed 10^9 to 10^{20} bits of information, which is more than fifty-thousand times the amount of text contained in the U.S. Library of Congress, or more than five times the amount of the total printed material in the world!" (p. 30). Despite this limitless capacity, we cannot process every piece of information provided to us or store this information in our long-term memory. The reason for not being able to utilize the whole capacity

of the brain is still a question to be answered. However, researchers are trying to explain how brain functions physiologically and cognitively to process information. While neuroscientists are trying to answer the puzzling questions about the physiological functioning of brain, cognitive researchers study cognitive information processes. Both types of research provide critical information about human learning processes and in particular the ways of integrating multiple modes into user interface design and the effects of this integration on information processing.

Cognitive psychologists drew attention to limited capacity of human brain and the importance of selective utilization of users' cognitive resources for effective presentation (Sweller,

DOI: 10.4018/978-1-61350-516-8.ch007

Copyright © 2012, IGI Global. Copying or distributing in print or electronic forms without written permission of IGI Global is prohibited.

van Merrienboer, & Paas, 1998). Foundation for multimodal designs has been set in the cognitive science literature (Mayer, 2005; Revees et al., 2004). Presenting information in multiple modes utilizing users' cognitive resources effectively is paramount (Baddeley & Hitch, 1974; Clark & Mayer, 2008; Sweller, 1988). If the information about users' cognitive resources is ignored by designers, representation of a concept in multiple modes may interfere with information acquisition. Overloading working memory or presenting users with redundant information may block the knowledge acquisition either by slowing or stopping the information processing. Thus, developing effective presentation models for users becomes a challenge in user interface design. User interface designers have to take the limitations of working memory into consideration when they design user interfaces. Although current theories and empirical research provide designers some guidelines about how to overcome these limitations, future quality design and development research related to the effectiveness of user interfaces and their development is needed to inform designers further about creation of such environments.

HOW HUMAN BRAIN FUNCTIONS

Human brain is the most complicated organ of human body with a myriad of mysteries. Researchers are still trying to figure out how brain functions when it processes information using technological devices such as functional magnetic resonance imaging (fMRI) to measure brain activities during different tasks. One of the critical models developed by neuroscientists about the physiological functioning of brain is the central bottleneck model that analyzes the limitations of human brain in information processing (e.g., Dux, Ivanoff, Asplund, & Marois, 2006; Marois, 2005; Marois & Ivanoff, 2005).

Marois and Ivanoff reported three limitations of working memory derived from the central

bottleneck model: (a) visual short-term memory, (b) attentional blink, and (c) psychological refractory period. Human brain can handle a limited number of objects, which is claimed to be four, in the short-term memory simultaneously, and this limitation of brain is referred to as visual short-term memory. Not only the amount of information processed but also the time required for each process is a limitation for the human brain. This processing time is called attentional blink (Marois). Contrary to the misconception that brain is capable of processing information instantaneously, it takes slightly more than a half second for a brain to process the information presented before the brain is disengaged from it to get ready for the next information (Marois & Ivanoff). Human brain processes information in sequential order and needs time before it starts to process the next information in the queue. This lag is called psychological refractory period (Marois). This knowledge base about brain functioning informs the research in cognitive psychology.

Models employed by information-processing theories of learning and memory posit internal structures for human brain: (a) sensory registers, (b) short-term memory (i.e., working memory), and (c) long-term memory. All the information received through senses (i.e., seeing, hearing, and touching) is sent to sensory registers (Ellis & Hunt, 1983). However, only information that catches the human's attention is transformed into patterns and sent to working memory. This process is called selective perception (Gagne, 1985; Gagne, Briggs, & Wager, 1992). The information selected (attentive selection) in sensory registers by human brain, then, transfers to short-term memory, which is a temporary storage with a limited capacity in terms of the number of items that can be held (Gagne et al.; Marois, 2005). The information in short-term memory is lost unless it is processed or practiced within a short period of time (i.e., 5 to 20 seconds). If the information in working memory is transformed into meaningful form (i.e., semantic encoding), then it can enter long-term memory to be kept for long periods of time (Gagne et al.). Baddeley and Hitch (1974) proposed a model (i.e., working memory model) to explain how working memory functions and transmits information into the long-term memory.

Working Memory

Working memory refers to "a brain system that provides temporary storage and manipulation of the information necessary for such complex cognitive tasks as language comprehension, learning, and reasoning" (p. 556) and stands at "the crossroads between memory, attention, and perception" (Baddeley, 1992, p. 559). Baddeley and Hitch (1974) originally described the working memory as consisting of one main component called *central executive* and two subcomponents, namely *visuospatial sketch pad* and *the phonological loop*. More recently, Baddeley (2000) proposed to add a third subcomponent called *episodic buffer*. The central executive is in charge of coordination of the subcomponents and integration of information coming from these subcomponents. The visuospatial sketch pad is responsible for maintenance and manipulation of visual representations whereas the phonological loop carries the load of storing and rehearsing verbal information. The last subcomponent, episodic buffer, which is controlled by the central executive, acts as a temporary interface between other subcomponents and long-term memory.

The two subcomponents, the phonological loop and the visuospatial sketch pad, can work independently to process information simultaneously. Each system has limited capacity to process information and can process one piece of information at a time. Thus, for more efficient information acquisition these two systems should be utilized simultaneously instead of loading the information on one of the systems. Cognitive load theory emerges as an implication of the working memory model to take advantage of these two subcomponents and provides guidelines for user interface designers.

Cognitive Load Theory

Sweller et al. (1998) stated "Cognitive load theory has been designed to provide guidelines intended to assist in the presentation of information in a manner that encourages learner activities that optimize intellectual performance" (p. 251). Sweller et al. drew attention to the limited capacity of working memory and to the importance of selective use of learners' cognitive resources for effective instruction. Sweller (1994) suggested ineffective user interface designs may interfere with information acquisition by increasing the cognitive load.

Sweller et al. (1998) proposed design principles to reduce cognitive load. *Split-attention effect*, one of the design principles, helps to reduce cognitive load by physically integrating different sources of information in the design in order to lower users' needs of mental integration (Sweller et al.). For example, let us think of a person who is trying to learn how to use software by reading a manual. This person needs to read the manual first and then apply his or her reading to the software. Thus, the process causes the user to split the attention between reading the manual and then applying it to the software. In order to reduce cognitive load, instructions could be read to the user while the user practices them with the software. In this latter case, the information in the manual can be integrated in the software as audio. This integration reduces the cognitive load by letting the user focus on the software while listening to the instructions.

Another design principle suggested by Sweller et al. (1998) was the *modality effect*. This principle suggests incorporating visual and auditory components together to increase the capacity of working memory and decrease the cognitive load (Sorden, 2005). In his recent review of research on the modality effect principle, Mayer (2005) presented an example of a modality effect: Students who received instruction as oral-narration and graphics performed better than students who received instruction as on-screen text and graphics. The oral-narration-and-graphics group could use both auditory and visual channels; whereas, the on-screen-text-and-graphics group's visual channel suffered from being overloaded with two types of visual information.

Various modes in which information is presented form representations. Thus, the theories presented in this section lay the foundation for integrating multiple representations in user interface designs to positively affect usability of the designs. User interfaces have powerful features to combine different modes on a computer screen. However, such environments should be developed by following design principles of working memory, split-attention effect, and modality effect as described by Baddeley and Hitch (1974), and Sweller (1988).

REPRESENTATIONS

User interface designers use various representations to effectively present information. Goldin (2003) broadly defines representation as any configuration of characters, images, or concrete objects that can symbolize or *represent* something else. Representational systems are both internal and external in nature and can be created by forming individual representations such as letters, numbers, words, and real-life objects (Goldin). Kaput (1991) referred to internal representations as "mental structures" and defined them as "means by which an individual organizes and manages the flow of experience." Internal representation systems exist within the mind of the individual and consist of constructs to assist in describing the processes of human learning (Goldin, 1998). On the other hand, external representations are defined as "externalizations of internal systems of thought" (Lesh, 1999, p. 331). Learners use external representations, such as marks on paper, sounds, or graphics on a computer screen, to organize the creation and elaboration of their own mental structures (Cifuentes & Hsieh, 2001).

Unlike internal representation systems, external representation systems can easily be shared with and seen by others.

Multiple Modes of Representation

Multiple modes of representation can be used by user interface designers to enhance usability of interfaces. Most research has shown the importance of using accurate representation in information processing (e.g.; Fennell & Rowan, 2001; Goldin & Shteingold, 2001; Kulm et al., 2007; Perry & Atkins, 2002). However, different representation modes might have differential impact on different users. One mode might be more relevant or effective than another in presenting a specific concept (Ball, 1990). Not only accurate information but also appropriate presentation of information is crucial in user interface designs. Representations that let users actively involve the subject are more effective in concept acquisition rather than the representations which do not support user active involvement. Providing multiple modes of representation goes beyond simply using a single mode in user interface designs (e.g., Gagatsis & Elia, 2004; Suh, Moyer, & Heo, 2005). However, it is important to be cautious about integrating different modes. Providing redundant information with different modes might interfere with acquisition of information (Sweller, 1988).

Translational Skills among Different Modes of Representations

To create user friendly interfaces, user interface designers should provide users with multiple representations of a single concept without relying on a single mode and provide users with an environment that lets users make connections among these representations (Ball, 1990). If user interface designers fail to implement the transitioning among different representations, users might have difficulties with utilizing the interface (Bay, 2001; Cramer, Behr, Post, & Lesh, 1997).

EMPIRICAL RESEARCH IN MULTIMODAL DESIGN

User interface design environments have powerful features to combine different modes together on a computer screen. Research provides evidence that use of multiple modes of representation has positive effects on conveying information (e.g., Fougnie & Marois, 2006; Leahy, Chandler, & Sweller, 2003; Mayer & Moreno, 1998). Fougnie and Marois (2006) performed several experiments to test the capacity of working memory when dual-task is provided. They designed their study to test the effect of different combination of tasks – visual and visual tasks vs. visual and verbal tasks. They concluded that working memory performed better when a visual and verbal task processed concurrently than when two visual tasks processed together (Cohen's $d = 0.75$). Fougnie and Marois' research supports Baddeley and Hitch's (1974) working memory model by providing evidence for presence of two different channels, namely auio an visual channels.

Leahy et al. (2003) designed two experiments in their study to test some hypotheses that were generated based on cognitive load theory. In their first experiment they tested modality effect and split-attention effect by designing an instruction with a graph and explanations of the graph. Neither graph nor explanations would provide complete information alone. That is, both types of information were essential in learning the concept. One group was provided with the graph and written instruction (split-attention effect), while the other group was provided with the graph and oral instruction (modality effect). Modality effect group outperformed the split-attention group (Cohen's $d = 0.81$). That is, instruction was more effective when it utilized both visual and auditory channels of working memory rather than visual channel

only, thereby overloading it. The second experiment was designed to test modality and redundancy effects. Modality effect group was provided with a diagram and instructions next to the diagram, and redundancy effect group was provided with an additional audio instruction that was redundant with the written text instruction. Modality effect group outperformed redundancy effect group (Cohen's $d = 0.66$). The results from this experiment suggested that providing redundant information hindered learning. The results of the two experiments might be considered contradictory to each other. The first experiment shows the inclusion of auditory representation increased the learning, whereas in the second experiment auditory representation interfered with learning. Indeed, these results are not contradictory. Yet, they show the importance of the selection of different modes of representation in designing user interfaces for conveying important information in learning.

In a similar study, Mayer and Moreno (1998) investigated the split-attention effect in multimedia learning. Mayer and Moreno designed an instruction with animation supported by either narration or written text information. Narration group outperformed the written text group (Cohen's $d = 0.93$). According to the cognitive load theory, which was supported by the results of this study, both groups had to split their attention between verbal (either written text or narration) and animation. Because the narration group utilized both visual and auditory channels of working memory, users in this group were able to use their working memory resources more efficiently to learn during the instruction.

Empirical research presented here provided evidence that integrating multiple modes of representation in an efficient way had positive effects on information acquisition. Working-memory model and cognitive load theory have also been supported by the research. Theories and empirical research provide important guidelines for user interface designers about how to design user interfaces for efficient communication with users.

GUIDELINES FOR USER INTERFACE DESIGNERS

Ultimate goal of a user interface is creating efficient schemas in one's brain in order to convey the information provided in the content effectively to the user. The extent of the achievement of this goal is the extent of the efficiency of the interface design. Thus, designers have to carefully design their instructions in such a way that users can process that information efficiently. User interface designers have to take the limitations of working memory into consideration when they design their interfaces. Theories and empirical research provide designers guidelines about how to overcome these limitations. I will provide examples for sample problems in user interfaces and possible solutions for these problems. Each example will be an instruction on teaching operations of fractions. Each user interface will differ based on the presentation of information.

Example I

In this example, a student sees an animation of how to add fractions using a geo-board. Meanwhile the steps for adding fractions were provided in written textual format concurrently with the animation. The problem in this instruction is that student's visual channel is overloaded with two different types of visual information – animation and written steps. This problem is called split-attention effect in cognitive load theory. Student's visual attention is split between two types of visual information resulting in an overload in the visual channel. One solution to this problem is taking some load off from the visual channel and utilizing the auditory channel instead. That is, written textual information can be narrated. Thus, instruction can utilize two channels of working memory thereby avoiding the overload on the visual channel.

Example II

In this example, a narrated animation is used in the instruction on fraction addition to avoid overloading on any channel. However, the instruction in this example is rich in content so the instruction is split into different segments that are presented one after another with a fast pace.

The possible problem in this design of the instruction is overloading both channels, namely visual and auditory, of working memory. Each instruction segment utilizes both channels; however, because of the content rich instruction, both channels are overloaded with several presentations in visual and audio format. The reason for overloading of channels is brain processes information in order, and so it needs time between two processes.

A promising solution to this problem is dividing the instruction into logical segments and providing process times between segments of the instruction. It is possible to give users the control to advance to the next segment of the instruction. Thus, learners will have enough time to process the information in the first segment before moving on to the next segment.

Example III

In this example, the fraction addition instruction is a narrated animation complemented with an attention catcher to catch students' attention. The attention catcher may be background music or audio, a graphic, or an animation.

In this instruction, narration and animation are essential materials for learning whereas attention catcher is an extraneous material which would most likely cause overloading problem in one of the two channels of working memory. Depending of the nature of attention catcher, either auditory or visual channel is overloaded by the extraneous material.

The possible solution is either eliminating the extraneous material from the instruction or moving it to the beginning or between the segments of the instruction. Extraneous materials are not essential for learning; yet, they are interesting materials used to catch learners' attention. Since they are not essential for learning, it is possible to eliminate them in order to avoid overloading the channels of the working memory. However, if instructional designers or educators would want to use some kind of an attention catcher in their instructions, they can provide these attention catchers either at the beginning or between the segments of the instruction. As a result,, extra cognitive load can be avoided.

CONCLUSION

Human brain, which can store almost limitless information, has still secrets to be discovered. Even though human brain has very few limits as storage, there are still limitations in processing information. Scientific studies related to brain functioning will enlighten the path in front of the cognitive psychology while the cognitive psychology research will lead researchers to learn more about information processing. Eventually, emerging theories will guide user interface designers to design more efficient user interfaces utilizing multiple representations.

REFERENCES

Baddeley, A. D. (1992). Working memory. *Science*, *255*, 556–559. doi:10.1126/science.1736359

Baddeley, A. D. (2000). The episodic buffer in working memory. *Trends in Cognitive Sciences*, *4*, 417–423. doi:10.1016/S1364-6613(00)01538-2

Baddeley, A. D., & Hitch, G. J. (1974). Working memory. In Bower, G. H. (Ed.), *The psychology of learning and motivation: Recent advances in learning and motivation* (pp. 47–90). New York, NY: Academic Press.

Ball, D. L. (1990). The mathematical understandings that prospective teachers bring to teacher education. *The Elementary School Journal*, *90*, 449–466. doi:10.1086/461626

Bay, J. (2001). Developing number sense in number line. *Mathematics Teaching in the Middle School*, *6*, 448–452.

Cifuentes, L., & Hsieh, Y. C. (2001). Computer graphics for student engagement in science learning. *TechTrends*, *45*(5), 21–23. doi:10.1007/BF03017083

Clark, R. C., & Mayer, R. E. (2008). *E-learning and the science of instruction: Proven guidelines for consumers and designers of multimedia learning*. San Francisco, CA: Pfeiffer.

Cramer, K., Behr, M., Post, T., & Lesh, R. (1997). *Rational number project: Fraction lessons for the middle grades–level 2*. Dubuque, IA: Kendall/Hunt.

Dux, P. E., Ivanoff, J., Asplund, C. L., & Marois, R. (2006). Isolation of a central bottleneck of information processing with time-resolved fMRI. *Neuron*, *52*, 1109–1120. doi:10.1016/j.neuron.2006.11.009

Ellis, C. E., & Hunt, R. R. (1983). *Fundamentals of human memory and cognition*. Dubuque, IA: Brown.

Fennell, F., & Rowan, T. (2001). Representation: An important process for teaching and learning mathematics. *Teaching Children Mathematics*, *7*, 288–292.

Fougnie, D., & Marois, R. (2006). Distinct capacity limits for attention and working memory: Evidence from attentive tracking and visual working memory paradigms. *Psychological Science*, *17*, 526–534. doi:10.1111/j.1467-9280.2006.01739.x

Gagatsis, A., & Elia, I. (2004). The effects of different modes of representation on mathematical problem solving. In M. J. Høines & A. B. Fuglestad (Eds.), *The 28th Conference of the International Group for the Psychology of Mathematics Education: Vol. 2* (pp. 447-454). Norway: Bergen University.

Gagne, R. M. (1985). *The conditions of learning and theory of instruction*. New York, NY: CBS College.

Gagne, R. M., Briggs, L. J., & Wager, W. W. (1992). *Principles of instructional design* (4th ed.). Belmont, CA: Wadsworth/Thomson Learning.

Goldin, G. A. (2003). Representation in school mathematics: A unifying research perspective. In Kilpatrick, J., Martin, W. G., & Schifter, D. (Eds.), *A research companion to principles and standards for school mathematics* (pp. 275–285). Reston, VA: National Council of Teachers of Mathematics.

Goldin, G. A., & Shteingold, N. (2001). Systems of representations and the development of mathematical concepts. In Cuoco, A. A., & Curcio, F. R. (Eds.), *The roles of representation in school mathematics NCTM yearbook 2001* (pp. 1–23). Reston, VA: National Council of Teachers of Mathematics.

Kaput, J. (1991). Notations and representations as mediators of constructive processes. In von Glasersfeld, E. (Ed.), *Radical constructivism in mathematics education* (pp. 53–74). Boston, MA: Kluwer Academic. doi:10.1007/0-306-47201-5_3

Kulm, G., Capraro, R. M., & Capraro, M. M. (2007). Teaching and learning middle grades mathematics with understanding. *Middle Grades Research Journal, 2,* 23–48.

Leahy, W., Chandler, P., & Sweller, J. (2003). When auditory presentations should and should not be a component of multimedia instruction. *Applied Cognitive Psychology, 17,* 401–418. doi:10.1002/acp.877

Lesh, R. (1999). The development of representational abilities in middle school mathematics. In Sigel, I. E. (Ed.), *Development of mental representation: Theories and applications* (pp. 323–350). Mahwah, NJ: Erlbaum.

Marois, R. (2005). Capacity limits of information processing in the brain. *Phi Kappa Phi, 85,* 30–33.

Marois, R., & Ivanoff, J. (2005). Capacity limits of information processing in the brain. *Trends in Cognitive Sciences, 9,* 296–305. doi:10.1016/j.tics.2005.04.010

Mayer, R. E. (2005). Principles for reducing extraneous processing in multi-media learning: Coherence, signaling, redundancy, spatial contiguity, and temporal contiguity. In Mayer, R. E. (Ed.), *The Cambridge handbook of multi-media learning* (pp. 183–200). New York, NY: Cambridge University Press.

Mayer, R. E., & Moreno, R. (1998). A split-attention effect in multimedia learning: Evidence for dual processing systems in working memory. *Journal of Educational Psychology, 90,* 312–320. doi:10.1037/0022-0663.90.2.312

Nielsen, J. (1994). Heuristic evaluation. In Nielsen, J., & Mark, R. L. (Eds.), *Usability inspection method* (pp. 25–62). New York, NY: John Wiley & Sons.

Perry, J. A., & Atkins, S. L. (2002). It's not just notation: Valuing children's representations. *Teaching Children Mathematics, 9,* 196–201.

Reeves, L. H., Lai, J., Larson, J. A., Oviatt, S., Balaji, T. S., & Buisine, S. (1994). Guidelines for multimodal user interface design. *Communications of the ACH, 47,* 57–59. doi:10.1145/962081.962106

Sorden, S. D. (2005). A cognitive approach to instructional design for multimedia learning. *Informing Science Journal, 8,* 263–279.

Suh, J., Moyer, P. S., & Heo, H. (2005). Examining technology uses in the classroom: Developing fraction sense using virtual manipulative concept tutorials. *Journal of Interactive Online Learning, 3*(4), 1–21.

Sweller, J. (1988). Cognitive load during problem solving: Effects on learning. *Cognitive Science, 12,* 257–288. doi:10.1207/s15516709cog1202_4

Sweller, J. (1994). Cognitive load theory, learning difficulty, and instructional design. *Learning and Instruction, 4,* 295–312. doi:10.1016/0959-4752(94)90003-5

Sweller, J., van Merrienboer, J. J. G., & Paas, F. G. W. C. (1998). Cognitive architecture and instructional design. *Educational Psychology Review, 10,* 251–296. doi:10.1023/A:1022193728205

Chapter 8
Designing Usable Speech Input for Virtual Environments

Alex Stedmon
University of Nottingham, UK

ABSTRACT

Speech is the primary mode of communication between humans, and something most people are able to use on a daily basis in order to interact with other people (Stedmon & Baber, 1999). For over 70 years the potential to interact with machines using speech input has been possible (Ullman, 1987), however it still remains an elusive concept without widespread use or acceptance.

INTRODUCTION

With so many technical advances, especially with the development of computing and distributed interaction technologies, the question remains: why has speech input not matured into a more usable state with far-reaching applications? There are a number of reasons for this:

- Speech recognition technology is still trying to grasp the subtleties of human speech processing, recognition and interaction;
- The uptake of speech input has been slower than might have been expected due to unrealistic user expectations (and marketing promises) about how speech input can be used and what it can achieve;

DOI: 10.4018/978-1-61350-516-8.ch008

- Whilst applications are evolving that use speech input, more tradition input devices are still commonplace.

Input devices are the medium through which users interact with a computer interface and, more specifically in the context of this chapter, a virtual environment (VE) (Stedmon, *et al*, 2003a). Currently, there is an increasing variety of input devices on the market that have been designed for virtual reality (VR) use, such as tradition keyboard, mouse and joystick devices, wands, data-gloves, speech input. With such a variety, there is a danger of users selecting an inappropriate input device which could compromise the overall effectiveness of a VR application and undermine the user's experience and satisfaction.

This chapter discusses the importance of speech input focussing on a number of key areas:

Copyright © 2012, IGI Global. Copying or distributing in print or electronic forms without written permission of IGI Global is prohibited.

- Speech as an input modality for VR applications
- Human factors issues of speech input
- Incorporating speech in the development of VR applications
- Developing a guidance framework for speech input
- Guidelines for speech input

SPEECH AS AN INPUT MODALITY FOR VR APPLICATIONS

Speech is the most natural form of human communication; it is our primary medium of communication for human-human interaction (HHI), which most of us are able to employ in our daily lives from an early age. It is still not fully understood how we learn the subtle rules of syntax and grammar and this is perhaps why it is so difficult to develop such a framework artificially for speech recognition and speech input purposes. What is clear, however, is that speech is a "familiar, convenient, [and] spontaneous part of the capabilities the human brings to the situation of interacting with machines" (Lea, 1980, p.4).

Speech is also the "human's highest-capacity output communication channel" that offers immense potential for human-to-computer communication (Lea, 1980, p.6). Speech also has other inherent advantages over other more conventional interaction modes. Whereas untrained users may find reading, writing, keyboard skills or manual input difficult without prior learning or practise, using speech input (if designed and implemented correctly) can be an intuitive medium for human-machine interaction (HMI).

One of the benefits of speech input is that it can be exploited in situations where other input devices might not be as successful (for example, in the dark or around objects or obstacles). As a medium of communication (sound) and through the medium in which it transfers (air), speech travels omni-directionally without light, in a way

that conventional writing, typing and button pressing are unable to do. As Lea (1980, p.8) states, in "using switches, typewriters, cathode ray tube displays, and even the more unusual graphical input devices ... and joysticks, the user must either be in physical contact with the computer console or terminal or must be orientated in a fixed direction to produce input commands and monitor computer outputs". Speech input therefore presents a basis for remote Human-Machine Interaction (r-HMI) procedures whilst also supporting multi-modal user tasks, through distributed inputs and actions.

Kalawsky (1996) indicates that the design of an input device should match the perceptual needs of the user. As such, the integration of input devices should follow a user needs analysis to map their expectations onto the attributes of an overall VR system. Jacob, *et al*, (1993) recommend that an input device should be natural and convenient for the user to transmit information to a computer. Furthermore, Jacob, *et al*, (1994) suggest that input devices should be designed from an understanding of the task to be performed and the inter-relationship between the task and the input device from the perspective of the user. Building on a sound understanding of user needs, it is important, therefore, to analyse the task in the correct level of detail so that the VR system, and the VE that is developed, supports user interaction and overall application effectiveness. As such, Barfield Baird & Bjorneseth (1998) indicate that a VE input device should account for the type of manipulations a user has to perform, be designed so that it adheres to natural mappings in the way the device is manipulated, and permit movements that coincide with a user's mental model of the type of movement required in a VE. Despite such general recommendations, there are very few established guidelines that detail what is required of an input device in terms of the parameters that pertain to a user and user performance within a VE (Kalawsky, 1996).

There is still much to be understood about the human factors issues involved with both speech input and VR. The use of speech input within VEs is an exciting integration of the two concepts that is not without its challenges. The freedom of speech input can be illustrated by the (subtle) benefit that it can be used 'in the dark and around obstacles'. Within VEs, users are not necessarily in 'darkness' but immersed in a 'virtual reality' where typical 'obstacles' are not necessarily concrete concepts (as in the real world) but anything from the interface and menus they are using or the actual VE they are interacting with. Speech therefore offers the potential to liberate the user and allow a greater degree of freedom to interact with VEs. If a speech metaphor is well designed it can be intuitive, taking the burden of object manipulation, navigation or interaction away from a physical input device, and increasing opportunities for multi-modal interaction.

HUMAN FACTORS ISSUES OF SPEECH INPUT

No strict guidelines exist for the design and development of speech input in VEs (Stedmon, 2003). At a fundamental level within any system application, human factors variables can be divided into four groups as represented in Figure 1.

Within this representation a human (representing user variables) interacts with a machine via displays and controls (representing system variables) to perform a task (representing task variables) within an operational environment (representing environmental variables). Thus, any speech input application should be both designed and evaluated, using:

- *Representative Users:* Within VR applications, users may come from many backgrounds and within collaborative VEs users may interact and communicate using different languages. As such, variables such as age, gender, experience, accent, need to be understood if the overall VR ap-

Figure 1. The principal components of human-machine interaction

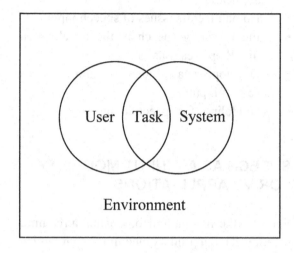

plication and integrated speech input system is to perform properly;

- *Representative Systems:* Speech input technologies are generally be led by the real-world applications market. As such, system variables such as realistic accuracies, response times, dialogue structures, vocabularies, are generally defined by what the conventional market dictates and what technology can deliver. As yet, speech input technologies are not being designed specifically from a VR perspective.

- *Representative Tasks:* Whether in the real world or a virtual world, speech input applications are very much application specific. As such, detailed analysis of the task needs to be carried out to address aspects associated with concurrent or competing tasks, and realistic levels of mental workload, stress, fatigue, to better understand how and where speech input may support the user over more conventional input devices;

- *Representative Environments:* Within VR there are many technical environments that are used to present VEs. These can range from traditional headset or desk-top presentations; through to projection walls and VR CAVEs. In these situations variables such as acoustics and ambient temperature, as well as the presence of any other users, may affect the overall system performance and use acceptance of speech input in VR applications. Within the VE itself, designers have more opportunity to control environmental variables in a way that is not possible in real world speech input applications.

Overall, the success of speech recognition depends on the understanding and integration of user, system, task and environmental variables, all of which have significant effects on overall performance.

INCORPORATING SPEECH IN THE DEVELOPMENT OF VR APPLICATIONS

As with any good design practise, the development of any speech input application should be an iterative process involving both system experts and end-users. In developing particular applications, it is important to recognise that VR may not be the only technology solution. It is important, therefore, to consider from the outset what is already known about VR/VE attributes and consider how they match the application requirements and may compare to alternative technologies (D'Cruz, et al, 2002). Assuming that VR offers a sensible solution, the use of a formal process such as the Virtual Environment Development Structure (VEDS) can assist developers in building an application that satisfies application goals and user requirements, supports task and user analyses, and offers a balanced concept design.

At the beginning of any development process, goals must be defined that provide the driving force of the VE building process. Within an industrial setting, these goals may stem from a problem

within the organisation, such as wastage, high costs or delays, or to increase competitiveness, support training, or reduce design life cycles (D'Cruz, et al, 2002). Through qualitative methods such as structured interviews and focus groups, the initial stages of VE development should assess user requirements, expectations and limitations; which tasks and functions will be completed in the VE; and the allocation of tasks and division of functions within the VE. As such, a VE can be specified in terms of its goals and expected user tasks, in relation to the complexity and balance between interactivity and exploration afforded. This specification should then be agreed by the VE development team and stakeholders (including end users). Further methods can be employed at this stage, such as storyboarding and virtual task analyses, specifying tasks to be performed by the user within the VE. This is a critical component of the VE development process as there are trade-offs between the technical capabilities of VR applications and costs associated with VE complexity (e.g. sensory richness), update rate (e.g. sense of presence and any potential disturbance effects), and interactivity (e.g. numbers of objects that can be manipulated in real-time, and how this is achieved).

Capturing user requirements can support the definition of expected (or unexpected) behaviours that underpin the successful use of a VE. Furthermore, understanding user requirements can also provide a basis for evaluating a VE at a later stage of the design process. For all VE applications, evaluations should be made of both the environments and also their use and usefulness (Wilson, Eastgate, & D'Cruz, 2002). It is possible to divide such evaluations into examinations of validity, outcomes, user experience and process (D'Cruz, et al, 2003). This means that before VE building progresses too far, a more detailed examination can be made of how users will respond to different elements of the VE; utilise its functionality; and comprehend all the interface elements to meet the application goals. As such, a basis can be set for encouraging users to explore a VE and enable them to understand which elements may be interacted with, minimising dysfunctional user behaviour and serious errors.

To answer the typical questions levelled at any new training technology application and to achieve validity and reliability in development and evaluation programmes, it is crucial to invite and incorporate the expertise of the ergonomics and applied psychology community.

During the information gathering stages it is often useful to carry out task and user analyses. Various task analysis techniques (e.g. Kirwan & Ainsworth, 1993; Militello & Hutton, 1998) allow human factors researchers to describe the interactions between users and their environment (real or virtual) at a level of detail that is appropriate to a pre-defined end goal. Due to the limitations of current VR systems it is impossible and sometimes unnecessary to design a VE that reflects every interaction of the real world (Stedmon & Stone, 2001). Task and user analyses help to define the minimum levels of interaction and cues to interactivity that might be needed in the VE before it is built and therefore only the information that affects the user's experience and addresses the goals of the application is necessary.

The task analysis should form an early and central component of any project that takes a human-centred perspective. Indeed, recognition of this has been formalised by the publication of International Standard ISO-13407, *Human-Centred Design Processes for Interactive Systems* (Earthy, *et al,* 2001) which specifies four general principles of human-centred design:

- Ensure active involvement of users and a clear understanding of user and task requirements (including context of use and how users might work with any related future system);

- Allocate functions between users and technology (recognising that today's technology, rather than de-skilling users, can ac-

tually extend their capabilities into new applications and skill domains);

- Ensure iteration of design solutions (by involving users in as many stages of the design and implementation cycle as is practical);

- Ensure the design is the result of a multi-disciplinary input (emphasising the importance of user feedback, but also stressing the need for input from such disciplines as marketing, ergonomics, software engineering, technical authors, etc).

Whilst task analyses can provide an abstraction of the real-world task elements into a corresponding VE, it is only when they are implemented within a coherent framework, such as ISO-13407, that human-centred design issues are fully appreciated (Stedmon & Stone, 2001). Without such a framework there is a risk of specifying or designing a VE system that fails to support the users' understanding of the target application (Stone, 2001).

During the development process, VR application goals, priorities and constraints can be identified and technical problems that may compromise the successful use of speech input in VEs can be addressed. For example, the integration of speech recognition software into the building of VEs can still be problematic as hardware issues associated with microphones (such as sensitivity to background noise and electrical interference) can affect the accuracy of processing speech commands. Furthermore, until the advent of wireless technologies, hand-held and head-mounted microphones could be obtrusive and compromise the versatility, mobility and freedom of using speech input. However, without any general guidelines on the implementation of speech input in VEs, there will always be a lack of consistency and transferability across applications.

DEVELOPING A GUIDANCE FRAMEWORK FOR SPEECH INPUT

Guidelines are a general approach which embody 'good practise' that must be interpreted by designers for a particular problem (Moore, 1998). Guidelines are often used by individuals who do not work within the field of human factors, but need to incorporate such an approach in their work. Guidance therefore needs to be conveyed to non-experts (as well as other human factors experts) in an effective form that they can understand and relate to.

Guidance Framework

Producing generic guidelines is extremely difficult and easily susceptible to 'exceptions disproving the rule' and so it is useful to examine methods of organising guidance. One method of organisation is a tabular matrix, which demonstrates the possibility of organising diverse facets. An example is provided in Table 1.

This matrix illustrates different user groups and links these with system types, task demands, and environmental factors. In this example, user group 1 is linked to system 2, task 2 and environment 5. A profile of 1225 is produced which could relate to specific guidelines for the development, integration and/or use of a particular speech input application (e.g. older users, speaker-independent system, virtual rehabilitation task, in a VE designed to mimic aspects of their home environment).

However, such a matrix could become very complex and prohibitively large due to the scope of factors that need to be incorporated into it and the very specific nature of the sub-classes of each level of the matrix (e.g. different age groups, experience levels, speech styles would compound the matrix). The same could easily happen for system, task and environmental variables, leading to a clumsy organisation of information which would be hard to interrogate and interpret.

A tabular matrix such as this can offer a simple method for organising information if the much of the knowledge is already known. However, speech input is an expanding area of investigation and knowledge building, and more knowledge will need integrating as a greater understanding and awareness is generated through further research and eventually wider use of technologies.

As a result, there could easily be too many very specific profiles which would undermine the generic nature of any guidance structure. A further criticism of such a matrix structure is that it does not allow for inter-relationships to be understood and visualised to a great degree. Therefore, another method of information organisation and visualisation relating information based on pattern languages might offer a solution (Alexander, Ishikawa, & Silverstein, 1977).

Pattern Languages

Pattern languages have been employed in software design where small, stand alone, program seg-

Table 1. Tabular matrix concept

Speech input matrix				Summary
Users	System	Task	Env	
1	1	1	1	Profile 1225: specific guidelines provided
2	**2**	**2**	2	
3	3	3	3	
4	4	4	4	
5 …	5 …	5 …	**5 …**	

ments are developed and re-used as building blocks of larger programs (Moore, 1998). Taking this philosophy forward, pattern language principles could be used to develop human factors guidelines by devolving problem areas into component structures which can then be re-used or re-interpreted to provide different solutions (Stedmon, 2005). In relation to speech input guidelines this organisation of information makes it easier to combine different factors through linked diagrams, rather than developing an exhaustive or ever expanding tabular matrix. An example of a pattern structure could for speech input is represented in Figure 2.

In the figure, six factors are inter-related to form a pattern. There is a degree of structure to the representation as the user group can be decomposed into sub-structures of speech style, experience and accent. These, in turn may be further decomposed (e.g. speech style is decomposed into gender and age). Whilst this implies a degree of hierarchy, it is also important in forming an understanding of how the concepts are inter-related. In this way, as more knowledge is generated, more components can be added or existing components can be further devolved and new links drawn between them. This method

therefore provides a powerful tool for organising information in a more manageable fashion.

The result of the links between the patterns is that a network develops allowing users to generate solutions for a particular problem taken from a number of patterns. The choice of patterns is up to the user in terms of the degree of navigation and level of interrogation, however, the pattern language should be robust enough to provide suitable guidance and solutions without specialised knowledge (Moore, 1998). Indeed, the guidance for using pattern languages is implicit in the description of each pattern. Each pattern should contain a title, context of the problem, factors requiring resolution, and solution strategies (Moore, 1998). Within the factors requiring resolution, links to other associated patterns are provided so that the user can follow these if they feel they are important to the overall problem they are addressing.

The notion of pattern languages aids the development of guidelines as users are less likely to 'miss out' factors they might not have initially considered and are able to navigate through the patterns in order to develop a more comprehensive solution and understanding of the issues. In

Figure 2. Example of a pattern language

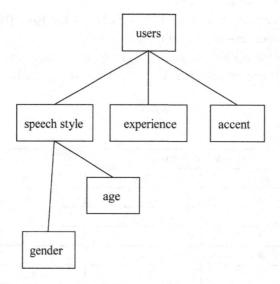

Figure 3. Elaborated pattern language for speech input

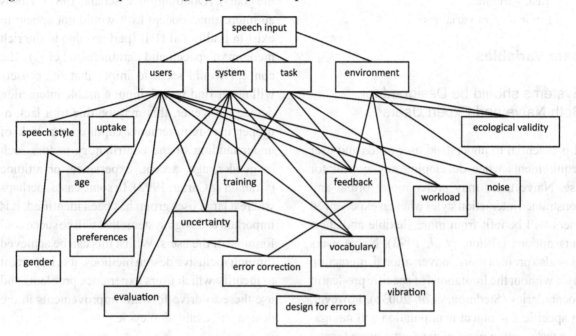

Figure 3, a more elaborate pattern language is presented including many of the factors which will be addressed in relation to developing guidance for speech input.

Whilst this is still not an exhaustive pattern, it represents a number of the factors that impact on the design and use of speech input and the inter-relationships between them. It also allows for further development, as new knowledge and guidelines are generated they can be added and integrated into the framework. It also illustrates the power of pattern languages both in terms of visualising information and also, through the underlying structures that emerge, the organisation of large amounts of information. Pattern languages can be presented as paper based guidelines with quick reference details to navigate through them (Alexander, Ishikawa, & Silverstein, 1977), although it is possible that guidelines could be developed with intelligent support or hyper-text systems to provide assisted navigation and solution generation. It may even be possible to embed them within a VE menu so that users can address

any issues in real-time as they navigate and interact within a VE.

The purpose of investigating pattern languages is to offer a potential method for understanding much of the ad-hoc guidance that exists for speech input. It is beyond the scope of this chapter to develop the patterns any further; however they offer a powerful tool for the systematic development of guidelines in the future.

GUIDELINES FOR SPEECH INPUT

Having proposed a framework for organising guidelines, this section integrates current thought and best practice ideas, supported by research findings, for the future design and development of speech interfaces in VEs. Referring back to the principal components of human-machine interaction (represented in Figure 1) the guidelines are laid out in the following subsections:

- User variables
- Systems variables

- Task variables
- Environment variables

User Variables

Systems should be Designed for Both Naïve and Expert Users

It is essential to understand user needs and user requirements when developing any system for use. Naïve users may prefer more formal and constrained interaction styles whereas experienced users will benefit from more flexible and short cuts options (Dillon, *et al*, 1993). Naïve users may also prefer a more conversational interaction style without the limitations of specific pre-learnt vocabularies (Stedmon, *et al*, 2003b), however, in specific VR object manipulation and navigation tasks, naïve users may adopt a more formal interaction style when they are speaking directly to a recognition interface rather than interacting with other users (Stedmon, *et al*, 2006).

Speech Input should Take Account of the Age of Users

User age can affect the quality and success of speech input systems. Older users may have specific needs due to their slowing of cognitive functioning and difficulty carrying out concurrent tasks (Pattison & Stedmon, 2006) and, as a result, attentional demands should be minimised as far as possible (Rabbitt & Collins, 1989). Relating age to dialogue and interaction pacing, older users will have particular problems with machine-paced systems and so a more user-paced approach should be taken (Graham & Carter, 1998).

Pay Attention to Minority User Groups

The notion of 'goats' and 'sheep' is used to express the idea that speech recognition can generally work for the majority (e.g. the sheep), but that a small proportion of users will encounter problems (e.g.

the goats), (Doddington & Schalk, 1981). This is an interesting concept as it would not appear to exist in traditional HHI (perhaps due to the rich medium of speech and paralinguistic cues). The concept would seem to imply that some users will never find speech input a usable interaction device. However, this may be due to a lack of proper user-requirements capture or a lack of understanding of the contributory factors such as gender, age, accent, experience, or attitude (Graham & Carter, 1998). In some cases, perhaps where a large user group has been identified, it is important to design systems that will be successful for most of the users. Whilst this can be achieved through inclusive design methods, it is important to identify which users experience problems and use these to drive forward improvements in the design and evaluation cycle.

Support User Preferences for Modes of Interaction

Users tend to regard speech input as an 'intelligent servant' rather than a 'dialogue partner' (Baber & Stammers, 1989). As a result, users do not relate to speech input systems in the same way as they do other humans, and this needs to be understood at the outset, if the correct vocabulary and syntax are to be designed into a system. When implementing speech input, it is necessary to understand how users prefer to use it, rather than expect them to learn how to use what has been designed. It has been found that users can find it difficult to navigate in a VE using speech (Stedmon, Griffiths & Bayon, 2004; Stedmon, *et al*, 2006) and in these situations, users may prefer to use conventional input devices if speech is not suited to the task. It is important, therefore, that users are able to use different input devices without affecting the overall HMI process.

System Variables

Choose the Right System

There are a number of factors that need to be considered when identifying the right system to use for an application, such as recognition, users and vocabulary:

- Recognition is generally conducted via isolated, connected or continuous word recognition. Whilst continuous word recognition is the nearest to natural speech, if accuracy is a key task requirement, it may be necessary to employ isolated or connected word recognition;

- In relation to users, systems can be either: user-dependent, user-independent, multiple-user or speaker-adaptive. User-dependent recognition generally gives better performance than user-independent systems but needs to be trained to specific users (which can take time). When systems are designed for more than one user (such as public information services) a speaker-independent system is required as these are designed for general use with little or no training. If the user group are known, then a multiple-user system can be employed with each user training it to their speech style. In the case of speaker adaptive systems, these tend to be single user applications which 'mature' with the user from initial training;

- In terms of vocabularies, these will depend to a large extent on the application speech input is being used for. In HHI, vocabulary is limited only by the knowledge of each human user or constrained by standard operating procedures they work to. In HMI, vocabulary is built into systems and should therefore support user needs and expectations as well as task requirements. Generally, small vocabularies place less

demands on system design (and processing demands), whilst large vocabularies place less demands on users and their cognitive demands.

Vocabulary can be Designed to Take Advantage of Convergence and Habitability

Vocabulary design can take advantage of the phenomenon of 'convergence' (Baber, Johnson & Cleaver, 1997), and 'habitability' (Hone & Baber, 2001). These concepts relate to the tendency of users to adopt the language used by a system or learn what the system will respond to. This occurs in speech input and speech output interactions and is based on HHI principles where speakers adapt various aspects of their speech to that of their conversational partners (Bernstein, 1971). Within VR applications it has been illustrated that even when users were able to use freespeech, their natural style of speaking to a computer interface was in terse commands. This illustrates a degree of expectation in the HMI process in that even though the system did not use speech output, users still used a different style than when speaking to another person (Stedmon, *et al*, 2006). Furthermore, users re-used commands they had previously issued and which had the desired outcome, illustrating a degree of habitability in the HMI process and that interaction style is shaped by user expectations and system performance.

Develop Intuitive Vocabularies

Users will tend revert to pre-learnt and more intuitive words under stress (Baber & Noyes, 1996). This reinforces the requirement for vocabularies to use words that are common, natural and easily remembered (Graham & Carter, 1998). Studies have illustrated that under increased time pressure, users will often revert alternative vocabulary words rather than the required vocabulary (Graham & Baber, 1993). Within VR, the development of intuitive vocabularies can be illustrated where users collectively use a very large vocabulary set, however the most commonly used commands were the most intuitive for navigation and object manipulation for that task (Stedmon, *et al*, 2006). With this knowledge it should be possible to develop a command vocabulary that most users would find intuitive or at least easier to learn than a less common command structure.

Avoid Acoustically Similar Words

Avoiding acoustically similar words will improve recognition accuracy for speech input for HMI processes. For example, in a simple vocabulary set including the digits 0-9 and yes/no, 'oh' is easily confused with 'no' and is often replaced by 'zero' (Jones, *et al*, 1989); letters of the alphabet, particularly the 'e-set' (e.g. b, c, d, e, g) are difficult for speech recognition systems to recognise (Roe, 1994); and "fine" is often confused with "nine" (Mellor, 1996). Possible confusions between words should be identified early on in the design process and the vocabulary designed such that the recognition system is not required to distinguish them and users informed and well-trained in deviations from their natural speech (Jones, Hapeshi & Frankish, 1987).

Avoid the Exacerbation Cycle!

The 'exacerbation cycle' is where users have to keep repeating themselves when a system fails to recognise what they are saying (Tucker & Jones, 1991). In HHI, this cycle is usually broken by the person who is listening asking for clarification or from on-verbal cues leading the speaker to change what they are saying. However, in HMI if an utterance is not recognised it may need to be repeated in a slightly different tone or slight different pace. What occurs, therefore, is that an unreliable recognition system causes frustration or boredom, leading to changes in the user's voice, which compounds the problem leading

to even poorer performance (Graham & Carter, 1998). Within VR, the exacerbation cycle can be a product of the VE design not allowing users to perform specific actions (Stedmon, *et al*, 2006) such as navigating through the VE in a specific manner (e.g. users issuing the command to 'straife right' when user movement was not allowed in this way). It is important, therefore, that both systems and applications take account of failed recognition or user activities so that any prolonged repeated inputs do not become a burden to the user. Ideally the system should be able to mediate user inputs so that they do not become exacerbated.

Poor Performance can Lead to Negative Reinforcement whilst Good Performance can Lead to Positive Reinforcement

It is important that user expectations are supported through the careful design of recognition systems that 'perform as promised' and also that users gain a positive experience from using them. Poor recognition performance or laborious training procedures can lead to reduced motivation to use such systems in the future, whilst a positive experience can lead to enhanced expectations. Within VR, when a system failed to recognise many utterances, users became frustrated (Stedmon, *et al*, 2006), however, users gained a favourable impression of speech input and rated it more positively than users who had used speech input for HHI, or an expert group assessing the potential of speech input (Stedmon, Griffiths & Bayon, 2004).

Design for Errors

Speech input is never 100% accurate. Even in HHI errors of understanding occur and need reconciling. In HMI, users may have repeat an utterance or correct an error if a different word is recognised or a response is interpreted when nothing is said. As such, users must be prepared for the system to make some kind of error and designers must regard errors as inevitable and attempt to design for them (Baber, Stammers, & Usher, 1990). Errors can result from either user or system errors, but error correction should not interrupt the performance of a primary task and should be performed as soon after data or command entry as possible (Stedmon, 2005). As good practise, users should be allowed to repeat mis-recognised commands (Baber, Stammers, & Usher, 1990) and feedback following user or system errors should be constructive and not 'blame' the user (Graham & Carter, 1998). Errors should be easily reversible and the user should never get into an interaction 'cul-de-sac' where it is not possible to correct the error that has occurred (Graham & Carter, 1998). Within VR, this can be a particular problem if the VE has been designed in an inflexible manner. It has been illustrated that if the user gets trapped in an error state, the VR application would eventually crash if the user was unable to issue the correct command (Stedmon, *et al*, 2006). The design of interaction processes needs careful consideration of the ways that errors may occur and how users may react to them and build into the system strategies for overcoming them.

Back-Up Facilities should be Designed and Made Available

As with any primary mode of interaction, some form of back-up is required if it fails to work. Therefore, alternative means of input should always be provided. As speech input is usually introduced when other input devices are already in use, this usually means that these are still available. Indeed, it is often the case that users revert back to traditional input devices if speech input fails to live up to their expectations (Noyes, 2001). There are a number of reasons why such 'back-up' facilities are necessary: they allow input if constant misrecognitions are made by the speech recognition device; they act as a safety measure for important functions; they prevent users being put off the speech recognition device during initial

use; some individuals simply prefer to use manual input; they allow input when the user's voice is busy or fatigued (Hapeshi & Jones, 1988).

Task Variables

In Applications where Time Pressure is High, Interactions should be Short

When multiple tasks are conducted and time pressure is present, short and fast communications minimise the attention and time required to produce and interpret commands, which in turn helps to maintain primary task performance (Stedmon, 2005). This can be achieved by designing vocabularies that are goal directed, imperative and explicit rather that actions using implicit statements which are more common in HHI (Graham & Carter, 1998). Depending on the context of use, some applications deal with discrete tasks that are suited to small vocabularies. However, in a simple VR maintenance task the vocabulary used by different users was still very large and so a degree of vocabulary design and user training would be required in such applications (Stedmon, *et al*, 2006).

Speech Input should not Add to the Interaction Demands

Using a speech recognition system is demanding in itself (Baber, *et al*, 1996), even though users do not always perceive the use of speech input to be demanding (Stedmon, Richardson & Bayer, 2002). A general recommendation, therefore, is that speech systems should be designed to be as undemanding as possible to use (Graham & Carter, 1998). Task demands will not only adversely affect user performance, but they will impact on the performance of the speech recognition system. Therefore, interfaces should be easy to learn, simple and intuitive; and most importantly, they should require minimal attention to be diverted away from the primary task (Graham & Carter, 1998; Stedmon, Richardson & Bayer, 2002).

Allow Users to Control the Pace and Timing of Interaction

Where possible, the pace and timing of dialogues should be controlled by the user. If users feel they are under increased time pressure this may affect their actual speech production (Stedmon & Baber, 1999; Stedmon & Bayer, 2001). In these situations it is important to consider the impact of time pressure where the user may take longer to respond (Stedmon & Baber, 1999) or may revert to pre-learnt vocabularies (Graham & Baber, 1993). Furthermore, it might also be beneficial to incorporate interruption techniques of repeat missed prompt facilities that are under the user's control so that they feel they are controlling the pace of the interaction (Graham & Carter, 1998).

System Initiated Interaction Must not Interfere with Primary Tasks

There will be occasions when a system may initiate an interaction. In such circumstances, it is important that this does not impact on any primary task the user is performing. At crucial task points this could prove distracting, or the user may take longer than normal to respond (Stedmon & Baber, 1999). It is therefore important that a clear task analysis and understanding of dynamic workload factors is incorporated into the implementation of speech input, otherwise in periods of high workload user performance and task efficiency may suffer.

Be Aware that Speech Quality can be Affected by Task Duration

It is important to be aware that voice strength and voice tone can change over a period of time. As such, 'voice drift' may occur and initial recognition templates may begin to fail to recognise subtle changes in speech through vocal fatigue. Fatigue effects can be minimised through regular rest breaks, however, since the performance of speech input may fall to unacceptable levels as a result of fatigue and other task variables, reversion to some non-speech back-up input should be allowed (Graham & Carter, 1998). Another solution to this problem is to use different sets of templates relating to different levels of fatigue or task demands, which can be adopted at different times.

Provide Task Feedback

Feedback on the results of recognition is very important in relation to users monitoring the interaction process. Without the necessary feedback it is easy for users to become 'lost in the transmission' and not be clear what the system has understood or what is about to happen. In HHI feedback is gained directly from what other people say and also from non-verbal cues and paralinguistic features which emphasise what is being said or heard. Many applications can rely on implicit feedback, where a state change is apparent from the instruction that is issued (e.g. turning on a light), however, in cases where a state change is not immediately apparent, or is too subtle for the user to monitor and perceive it has been carried out (e.g. a change in temperature), then explicit feedback is needed. Whether feedback is auditory, visual, or a combination of the two, depends on the task as well as whether the feedback is provided concurrently or terminally (Hapeshi & Jones, 1988). Within VR applications feedback may also be developed within the VE as a state change or even as a vocabulary stream or interface feature that illustrates what the recognition systems is currently doing.

When Evaluating Performance does not Rely just on Recognition Accuracy

Speech input performance is often measured through the recognition accuracy of a system.

Whilst this is important, it is equally important to evaluate user performance, task outcomes, how many errors are made, assistance required, etc, to gain a full appreciation of the system. For example, substitution errors (where something is spoken but something else is recognised) may have more serious outcomes than deletion errors (where something is spoken but nothing is recognised), although deletion errors may cause more frustration to users who have to keep repeating themselves (Stedmon, 2005). Speed is another relevant variable, both in terms of system response time, system processing time and the time required for the user to complete a whole task.

Environment Variables

Speech Input should be Designed with the Task Environment in Mind

The templates that speech recognition systems use to recognise users' speech should be developed and trained in the typical environments that users will be working in. Whilst many VEs might be quite benign (e.g. any disruptive variables can be programmed out in the VE building process), there may still be issues associated with multiple user VEs and or auditory feedback cues that may compromise the speech input processes. Speech input can be trained for specific noise environments so that it performs equally well in both the quiet and noisy conditions so that any problems with failed recognition are minimised (Stedmon & Baber, 1999).

In Collaborative Environments Interaction Initiation Must be Controlled by the User

With various sources of noise occurring in collaborative VEs, speech input must involve some active initiation by the user otherwise the system may pick up on extraneous noise and regard it as a speech input. In many applications user inter-action initiation is conducted via a press-to-talk (PTT) button or specific 'wake up' words used to start the interaction process (Stedmon, 2005). In either case it is important to clarify task needs and user preferences as a PTT button means that users have to manually operate a speech based system, which may interfere with other tasks; or the use of 'wake up' words might become frustrating to experienced users. The act of initiating a dialogue, however may remind the user to revert from an HHI speech style to a more acceptable HMI speech style (Graham & Carter, 1998).

Users should be Trained to Deal with Stressors

Whilst it is not possible to mediate stress in every case, training represents a useful tool in human factors for dealing with some stressors (Baber & Noyes, 1996). As such, training users in effective strategies of using systems and speaking in adverse conditions, might provide a basis for coping with stressors. Another strategy lies in training personnel either in specific stress avoidance tactics or to a high enough standard where users might be able to combine task-units into groups and perform an apparently demanding task with minimal effort (Baber, *et al*, 1996).

Speech Input should be Evaluated in the Task Setting

In much the same way as speech input systems should be trained in the relevant environment they will be used for, recognition systems should also be evaluated in representative task settings (Graham & Carter, 1998). In judging the performance of speech input for VR, evaluations must take place throughout the design cycle and ultimately in the final VE, where in actual use, the user will be subjected to concurrent tasks, time pressure, stressors and fatigue effects.

CONCLUSION

These guidelines are derived from a number of sources and would appear to reinforce widespread 'common sense' conventions and even anecdotal evidence for speech interface use. There is now a need to generate a much better understanding, from a user-centred perspective, and better organisation of guidelines to make them more universally applicable. Only by developing an understanding of how users may want to use a speech interface and the impact of using it has on their performance will it be possible to design an interface that truly meets the expectations of the user and supports task performance.

ACKNOWLEDGMENT

Research presented in this chapter was supported by IST grant 2000-26089: VIEW of the Future; and the Engineering and Physical Sciences Research Council, Project GR/R86898/01: Flightdeck and Air Traffic Control Evaluation.

REFERENCES

Alexander, C., Ishikawa, S., & Silverstein, M. (1977). *A pattern language*. New York, NY: Oxford University Press.

Baber, C., Johnson, G. I., & Cleaver, D. (1997). Factors affecting users' choice of words in speech-based interaction with public technology. *International Journal of Speech Technology, 2*, 45–59. doi:10.1007/BF02539822

Baber, C., Mellor, B., Graham, R., Noyes, J. M., & Tunley, C. (1996). Workload and the use of automatic speech recognition: The effects of time and resource demands. *Speech Communication, 20*, 37–53. doi:10.1016/S0167-6393(96)00043-X

Baber, C., & Noyes, J. M. (1996). Automatic speech recognition in adverse environments. *Human Factors, 38*(1), 142–155. doi:10.1518/001872096778940840

Baber, C., & Stammers, R. B. (1989). Is it natural to talk to computers? An experiment using the Wizard of Oz technique. In Megaw, E. D. (Ed.), *Contemporary ergonomics 1989* (pp. 234–239). London, UK: Taylor & Francis.

Baber, C., Stammers, R. B., & Usher, D. M. (1990). Instructions and demonstrations as media for training new users of automatic speech recognition devices. *Behaviour & Information Technology, 9*(5), 371–379. doi:10.1080/01449299008924251

Barfield, W., Baird, K., & Bjorneseth, O. (1998). Presence in virtual environments as a function of type of input device and display update rate. *Displays, 19*, 91–98. doi:10.1016/S0141-9382(98)00041-9

Bernstein, B. (1971). *Class, codes and control (Vol. 1)*. London, UK: Routledge & Kegan Paul. doi:10.4324/9780203014035

D'Cruz, M., Stedmon, A. W., Wilson, J. R., & Eastgate, R. (2002). *From user requirements to functional and user interface specification: General process*. (University of Nottingham Report No.: IOE/VIRART/01/351).

D'Cruz, M., Stedmon, A. W., Wilson, J. R., Modern, P. J., & Sharples, G. J. (2003). Building virtual environments using the virtual environment development structure: A case study. In *HCI International '03, Proceedings of the 10th International Conference on Human-Computer Interaction, Crete, June 22-27, 2003*. Lawrence Erlbaum Associates.

Dillon, T. W., Norcio, A. F., & DeHaemer, M. J. (1993). Spoken language interaction: Effects of vocabulary size and experience on user efficiency and acceptability. In, G. Salvendy & M. J. Smith (Eds.), *Human-Computer Interaction: Software and Hardware Interfaces, Proceedings of the 5th International Conference on Human-Computer Interaction (HCI International '93)* (pp. 140-145). Amsterdam, The Netherlands: Elsevier Science.

Doddington, G. R., & Schalk, T. D. (1981). Speech recognition: Turning theory into practice. *IEEE Spectrum, 18*(9), 26–32.

Earthy, J., Sherwood Jones, B., & Bevan, N. (2001). The improvement of human-centred processes - Facing the challenge and reaping the benefit of ISO 13407. *International Journal of Human-Computer Studies, 55*, 553–585. doi:10.1006/ijhc.2001.0493

Graham, R., & Baber, C. (1993). User stress in automatic speech recognition. In Lovesey, E. J. (Ed.), *Contemporary ergonomics 1993* (pp. 463–468). London, UK: Taylor & Francis.

Graham, R., & Carter, C. (1998). *The human factors of speech recognition in cars: A literature review (Speech Ideas deliverable 1.1)*. Loughborough, UK: HUSAT Research Institute.

Hapeshi, K., & Jones, D. M. (1988). The ergonomics of automatic speech recognition. *International Reviews of Ergonomics, 2*, 251–290.

Hone, K. S., & Baber, C. (2001). Designing habitable dialogues for speech-based interaction with computers. *International Journal of Human-Computer Studies, 54*(4), 637–662. doi:10.1006/ijhc.2000.0456

Jacob, R., Leggett, J., Myers, B., & Pausch, R. (1993). An agenda for human-computer interaction research: Interaction styles and input/output devices. *Behaviour & Information Technology, 12*(2), 69–79. doi:10.1080/01449299308924369

Jacob, R., Sibert, L., McFarlane, D., & Mullen, P. Jr. (1994). Integrality and separability of input devices. *ACM Transactions on Computer-Human Interaction, 1*(1), 3–26. doi:10.1145/174630.174631

Jones, D. M., Hapeshi, K., & Frankish, C. R. (1987). Human factors and the problems of evaluation in the design of speech systems interfaces. In D. Diaper & R. Winder (Eds.), *People and Computers III. Proceedings of the 3rd Conference of the British Computer Society Human-Computer Interaction Special Group*, (pp. 41-49). Cambridge, UK: Cambridge University Press.

Jones, D. M., Hapeshi, K., & Frankish, C. R. (1989). Design guidelines for speech recognition interfaces. *Applied Ergonomics, 20*(1), 47–52. doi:10.1016/0003-6870(89)90009-4

Kalawsky. R. (1996). *Exploiting virtual reality techniques in education and training: Technological issues.* Prepared for AGOCG. Advanced VR Research Centre: Loughborough University.

Kirwan, B., & Ainsworth, L. K. (1993). *A guide to task analysis*. London, UK: Taylor & Francis.

Lea, W. A. (1980). The value of speech recognition systems. In Lea, W. A. (Ed.), *Trends in speech recognition* (pp. 3–18). Prentice Hall, USA.

Mellor, B. M. (1996). *Options for the evaluation of speech technology in armoured vehicles.* (DRA Report: DRA/CIS(SE1)/377/01/04/AFV/V1.0).

Militello, L. G., & Hutton, R. J. B. (1998). Applied cognitive task analysis (ACTA): A practitioner's toolkit for understanding cognitive task demands. *Ergonomics, 41*(11), 1618–1641. doi:10.1080/001401398186108

Moore, P. (1998). *Embodying human factors guidelines as pattern languages.* (DERA report: DERA/CHS/MID/WP980104/1.0).

Noyes, J. M. (2001). Talking and writing: How natural is human-machine interaction? *International Journal of Human-Computer Studies*, *55*(4), 503–519. doi:10.1006/ijhc.2001.0485

Pattison, M., & Stedmon, A. W. (2006). Inclusive design and human factors: Designing mobile phones for older users. In E. L. Waterworth & J. Waterworth (Eds.), *PsychNology: Special issue – Designing Technology to Meet the Needs of the Older User, 4*(3), 267-284.

Rabbitt, P., & Collins, S. (1989). *Age and design*. Age and Cognitive Performance Research Centre: University of Manchester.

Roe, D. B. (1994). Deployment of human-machine dialogue systems. In Roe, D. B., & Wilpon, J. G. (Eds.), *Voice communication between humans and machines* (pp. 373–389). Washington, DC: National Academy Press.

Stedmon, A. W. (2003). Developing virtual environments using speech as an input device. In C. Stephanidis (Ed.), *HCI International '03, Proceedings of the 10th International Conference on Human-Computer Interaction*, (pp. 1248-1252). Lawrence Erlbaum Associates.

Stedmon, A. W. (2005). *Putting speech in, taking speech out: Human factors in the use of speech interfaces*. University of Nottingham, PhD Dissertation.

Stedmon, A. W., & Baber, C. (1999). Evaluating stress in the development of speech interface technology. In H.-J. Bullinger (Ed.), *HCI International '99. Proceedings of the 8th International Conference on Human-Computer Interaction*, Munich, Germany, 22-27 August 1999, (pp. 545-549). Amsterdam, The Netherlands: Elsevier Science.

Stedmon, A. W., & Bayer, S. H. (2001). Thinking of something to say: Workload, driving behaviour and speech. In Hanson, M. (Ed.), *Contemporary ergonomics 2001* (pp. 417–422). London, UK: Taylor & Francis.

Stedmon, A. W., Griffiths, G., & Bayon, V. (2004). Single or multi-user VEs, manual or speech input? An assessment of de-coupled interaction in virtual environments. *Proceedings of Virtual Reality Design and Evaluation Workshop*, 22-23 January 2004, Nottingham, UK.

Stedmon, A. W., Nichols, S. C., Nicholson, E., Cox, G., & Wilson, J. R. (2003b). *The flightdeck of the future: Perceived urgency of text and speech communications. Proceedings of Human Factors of Decision Making in Complex Systems, September 2003*. UK: Abertay.

Stedmon, A. W., Patel, H., Nichols, S. C., & Wilson, J. R. (2003a). A view of the future? The potential use of speech recognition for virtual reality applications. In McCabe, P. (Ed.), *Contemporary ergonomics 2003* (pp. 289–295). London, UK: Taylor & Francis.

Stedmon, A. W., Richardson, J. R., & Bayer, S. H. (2002). In-car ASR: Speech as a secondary workload factor. In McCabe, P. (Ed.), *Contemporary ergonomics 2002* (pp. 252–257). London, UK: Taylor & Francis.

Stedmon, A. W., Richardson, J. R., & Bayer, S. H. (2002). In-car ASR: Speech as a secondary workload factor. In McCabe, P. (Ed.), *Contemporary ergonomics 2002*. London, UK: Taylor & Francis.

Stedmon, A. W., Sharples, S. C., Patel, H., & Wilson, J. R. (2006). Free-speech in a virtual world: Speech for Collaborative Interaction in a Virtual Environment. *Proceedings of the International Ergonomics Association (IEA): 16th World Congress on Ergonomics*. Maastricht, The Netherlands.

Stedmon, A. W., & Stone, R. (2001). Re-viewing reality: Human factors issues in synthetic training environments. *International Journal of Human-Computer Studies*, *55*, 675–698. doi:10.1006/ijhc.2001.0498

Stone, R.J. (2001). *A human-centred definition of surgical procedures*. European Union Project IERAPSI (Integrated Environment for the Rehearsal and Planning of Surgical Interventions; IST-1999-12175); Work Package 2, Deliverable D2 (Part 1).

Tucker, P., & Jones, D. M. (1991). Voice as interface: An overview. *International Journal of Human-Computer Interaction, 3*(2), 145–170. doi:10.1080/10447319109526002

Ullman, J. R. (1987). Speech recognition by machine. In Gregory, R. L. (Ed.), *The Oxford companion to the mind*. Oxford, UK: Oxford University Press.

Wilson, J. R., Eastgate, R. M., & D'Cruz, M. (2002). Structured development of virtual environments. In Stanney, K. (Ed.), *Handbook of virtual environments*. Lawrence Erlbaum Associates.

Chapter 9
Exploiting the Power of Persistence for Learning in Virtual Worlds

Keysha I. Gamor
ICF International, USA

ABSTRACT

While the age old adage: "Build it and they will come" may ring true to some extent in many cases, it also begs the question: "...But will they come back?" Persistence can describe the continuously existing state of a virtual world, whether anyone is in it and using it or not; it remains as the last person left it. Persistence is a major affordance of virtual worlds—a central characteristic that sets it apart from any other learning medium available in the current instructional design toolkit. This chapter addresses the criticality of exploiting this attribute in order to design the optimal user interface for a meaningful, lasting learning experience in a virtual world.

INTRODUCTION

Developed "through the convergence of social networking, simulation and online gaming" (Gartner, Inc., 2007), a virtual world is an online simulation of either a real or fantasy world environment populated by "avatars", which are pictorial or graphical representations of the human participants. A virtual world can be described as "a synchronous, persistent network of people, represented as avatars, facilitated by networked computers" (Bell, 2008, p. 2). EDUCAUSE, a non-profit association

concerned with leveraging technology to improve higher education, defines a virtual world simply as an "online environment whose "residents" are avatars representing individuals participating online." (The EDUCAUSE Learning Initiative, 2006, p. 1) Still, other definitions which address the specific affordances of 3-D virtual worlds help us understand the potential of the technology as well. Examining popular virtual world applications such as Forterra,, Nexus, OpenSim, Second Life, Teleplace, or VastPark can help frame an understanding of virtual worlds as "online 3-D virtual worlds …within which residents are able to establish identities (avatars), explore, create and

DOI: 10.4018/978-1-61350-516-8.ch009

Copyright © 2012, IGI Global. Copying or distributing in print or electronic forms without written permission of IGI Global is prohibited.

communicate. [Further, a virtual world may] lend itself well to social networking, collaboration and learning" (IEEEE, para. 2).

Crafting meaningful learning experiences has, historically, been a great challenge in situations where context is as important as content. Role playing scenarios, case studies, and discussions are a few of the instructional strategies used to provide a rich, experiential aspect to traditional classroom and e-learning courses. These same strategies can still be used in a virtual world; however, these approaches now have the added benefit of a group dynamic in a persistent, graphically rich space that has a reality outside of the users' imagination; that is co-created rather than dictated; that is simultaneously shared by many users for the purpose of collaboration, rather than accessible to a selected few. Leveraging the significant advances in technology that have yielded faster, cheaper, and more ubiquitous access than even ten years ago, virtual worlds provide for new instructional strategies not possible in traditional learning environments. We can anticipate that virtual worlds are here to stay and to continue to grow as the technology continues to improve. Gartner, Inc. (2009), a leading research firm, identified IT for Green, Social Computing, and Advanced Analytics to be among the Top 10 Strategic Technologies for 2010, and virtual worlds enable these technologies to reach new dimensions through its unique affordances as a collaborative tool. There is no shortage of hype and expectation regarding the Knowledge Revolution, but, in the near future, we can expect faster, cheaper, more stable and more engaging versions of knowledge-sharing technologies, infrastructures, and protocols to emerge. Even more importantly, the technology will become convenient, easy, and reliable (Norris, et. al. 2004). Indeed in the years to come, we expect that virtual worlds will be among the top tools used to conduct business, to participate in meetings and training events, and to socialize.

With more than 300 virtual world products on the market today (Association of Virtual Worlds, 2008) targeting a number of different audiences, and with projections that this number will increase exponentially in the next several years, it is becoming imperative for implementers to be aware of their own functional and technical requirements. Thus, instead of jumping on the virtual world bandwagon "for the cool factor" or "to keep up with the (no possessive, just a simple plural – more than one Jones) Joneses", a clear understanding of the features that most virtual worlds share helps decision-makers identify the unique attributes that may address specific training, education, or performance improvement needs, which will also aid in developing sound instructional design approaches. Understanding why one needs a virtual world, with specific goals, objectives, and functional requirements, will enable organizations to directly benefit from the unprecedented advances in today's virtual worlds, worlds that also provide a comprehensive forum for collaboration.

Virtual Worlds and Distance Learning Challenges

Historically, distance learning theory has been characterized by its focus on the individual learner (Garrison, 2000). The most obvious learning transaction for learners has typically been between the learner and the user interface (Berge, 1995), and thus, historically, giving way to a common complaint by learners of feeling isolated and detached from the institution and their learning peers in traditional distance learning courses (Dickey, 2004; Sheets, 1992; Sweet, 1986). According to a 2009 meta study from the Department of Education: "Students who took all or part of their class online performed better, on average, than those taking the same course through traditional face-to-face instruction (p. 20)." That same study asserts that students who mix online learning with traditional coursework (often referred to as *blended learning*) do even better. While blended learning has typically been considered as the combination of online and traditional face-to-face instruction, the term has been slightly modified to be broader: "a combination of instructor and Web-based training to a blend of many types of interactive content" (Bersin, 2008, p. 4).

The face-to-face component of this "mix" has been credited with filling the void that distance learners tend to experience. The void is also referred to as 'an absence of social presence', and the absence of social presence is part of what causes this distant discomfort that many learners report.

Immersive learning technologies, such as virtual worlds are helping to fill this void and to transform traditional distance learning. According to a study conducted by the United States Air Force, "[d]istance learning will evolve from basic enrollment in computer and web-based courses to virtual learning environments that support online collaboration and classes taught by both live and virtual instructors" (Air Force White Paper, 2008, p. 13). Ted Hoff (2008), IBM CLO, predicts that "[i]n this global, networked world, several technologies including search engines, blogs, podcasts, Web 2.0 applications and virtual worlds such as Second Life will be used for learning (page 47)." Immersive learning technologies have ushered in a new paradigm for distance learning—one that is more community-based and less compartmentalized; one that is more collaborative and less isolating; one that is more discovery-oriented and less dictated. These changes in the distance learning paradigm, among others, will require new instructional approaches in order to optimize these rapidly changing, immersive technologies. Gone are the days of learners being isolated while engaged in a learning event and/or experience. Indeed, as Garrison (2000, p. 13) puts it: "Distance education will be characterized by an adaptability of design before and during the teaching and learning process made possible by affordable and highly interactive communications technology."

Virtual Worlds as Collaborative Tools

With graphically rich tools that support first-person, individual exploration and group collaboration, virtual worlds expand the users' experiences by contextualizing the interactions through the fabric of digital narrative and the user-determined social threads woven by chance and, in some cases, design. Similar to other learning technologies, virtual worlds enable synchronous and asynchronous learning. The attribute of 'co-presence' (being co-located in-world) diminishes one of the most common complaints learners have about distributed or distance learning: Feeling disconnected from other learners. Specifically, virtual worlds facilitate a learner-centered approach wherein learners can determine when and how to navigate through the learning experience. Learners may use virtual worlds asynchronously to familiarize themselves with content; practice processes and procedures; participate in simulations and/or demonstrations; and engage in problem-solving and decision-making activities; conduct self-assessments; and craft self-remediation approaches. Similarly, "learners may also use virtual worlds to test their understanding of content by sharing their views with peers; negotiating meaning/ understanding together with peer groups; examining the impact of others' interpretations in context, thereby supporting problem-identification" (Gamor, 2011, p. 740). Indeed, "…learning is situated and tacit: Problem finding is central to problem solving." (Dede, 2007, p. 11).

These collaborative opportunities are but a few of the ways in which a learning experience in virtual worlds can exploit the strength of the tool. The salient point here is this: research shows that collaboration is a powerful instructional tactic (instructor-planned activities) and learning strategy (learner-initiated activity). Virtual worlds represent an optimal environment for collaboration and co-creation--where "collective problem resolution [is enabled] via mediated interaction" (Dede, 2007, p. 7) because it enables both realistic and representational contexts for learning. Virtual world technology puts the power into the hands of the designer to create a real-life environment as contextually and graphically fictional or realistic as the objectives require. Thus, the potential for loss, harm, and/or unintended discouragement are diminished or eliminated in order to facilitate more in-depth experiences, understanding, awareness, and collaboration.

The 'representational' context, on the other hand, presents an opportunity to accomplish and experience what cannot otherwise be done in the organic world. There is no context other than a virtual world wherein can an individual 'walk through' a wall or become a red blood cell, drill down into a complex data set, or swim in a sea of micro-organisms that you have become and can see with your naked eye. Indeed, through no other medium could such an exploration synchronously accommodate a group of geographically dispersed individuals. Further, in no other context could those same individuals construct an object together in a tangible, graphically rich environment where the geographical dispersion is replaced by a sense of being engaged in fluid interactions much like that experienced in real-life interfaces. Such interactions leave the learners with a perception of having "been someplace", "experienced something first-hand", and "connected with people" (Gamor, 2011, p. 741).

The representational aspect of virtual worlds benefits both the individual and the group interactions. Most virtual worlds have in common six attributes that make this technology unique; Co-creation, Co-existence, Collaboration, Graphical User Interface, Persistence, and Presence. (Virtual World Review, 2009; Federation of American Scientists, 2009). Users generally engage in virtual worlds because they are interested in entertainment, social interaction, education (learning), and/or they simply want a unique experience. Virtual worlds, if well designed, can address all these interests singularly or at the same time. The reasons that lead users to virtual worlds

are important in understanding the value of the virtual world attributes. Figure 1 represents how five of the virtual world attributes share a central attribute: persistence, which all work together to provide the user an environment in which she/he may have her/his interests addressed.

Optimizing each of these intrinsic affordances may lead to a better learning experience. Understanding the *How People Learn* framework (Bransford et. al., 1999) is a useful foundation to consider in the design of any web-based learning experience. The framework is characterized by four optimal learning conditions centered on the learner, knowledge, community and assessment. In Table 1, the affordances of virtual worlds are examined through the lens of Bransford's framework (1999) on how people learn. While some of the affordances supporting Persistence (or the other affordances, for that matter) may not be exclusive to virtual worlds as a technology medium, the concept of persistence, as defined in this chapter, is unique to virtual worlds.

- **Co-existence:** Allows many users to participate simultaneously in a shared environment
- **Graphical User Interface:** Offers visual depiction of and means of interaction with an environment
- **Presence:** Affords real-time interaction; direct and indirect interaction/synchronous and asynchronous interaction
- **Co-creation:** Supports content development or modification
- **Persistence:** Maintains 24/7 existence regardless of user login status; the presence and processing of synchronous and asynchronous interactions and contributions of all avatars and objects within the world.
- **Collaboration:** Encourages development of in-world groups

Figure 1. Affordances of virtual worlds work together with typical user motivations to create a persistent, meaningful learning environment.

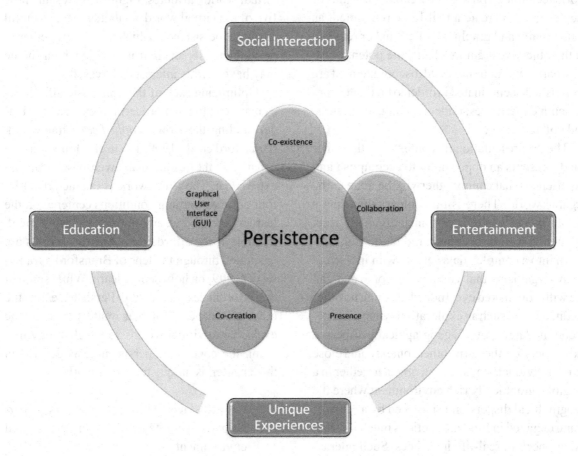

Table 1. How people learn framework and the affordances of virtual worlds (Gamor, 2011, p.742)

How People Learn **Framework***	**Affordances of Virtual Worlds**	**Virtual World Design Considerations**
Learner-centered	Presence Coexistence	Create individual and group activities Plan for synchronous and asynchronous interactions
Knowledge-centered	Graphical User Interface Persistence	Develop interactive objects beyond basic presentation slides and videos Make use of notes, basic building capabilities, and problem-identification activities Look for platforms that enable remote ways to stay connected to the world via communication/ interactions, file portability, asset ownership
Community-centered	Co-creation Collaboration	Include activities and opportunities for multiple perspectives to converge Exploit tried and true instructional strategies that foster collaboration Reward collaboration
Assessment-centered	Persistence Coexistence	Use synchronous/asynchronous learning opportunities Capitalize on avatars, objects, and the environment's persistent nature
		(*Bransford et. al. 1999)

(Gamor, 2011, p. 741; Federation of American Scientists, 2009; Virtual World Review, 2009;)

The author of this chapter determines that "persistence" is a key affordance of virtual worlds which enables meaningful, authentic, and lasting immersive learning experiences. Exploiting persistence, the 24/7, dynamic existence of a virtual world, is where all the other affordances of this technology culminate to create a very powerful, collaborative, teaching and learning tool.

Virtual Worlds and Persistence

While the age old adage: "Build it and they will come" may ring true to some extent in many cases, it also begs the question: "…But will they come back?" At least in virtual worlds, it appears that simply "to exist" in-world is not enough to keep people coming back.

Indeed a 2008 Gartner press release reported that 90% of all corporate initiated virtual worlds fail within 18 months of the launch date. While this study underscores the dangers of the lack of planning, which was apparently the common link among all who failed, it also points out that the "stickiness" of a virtual world is at least as important as the "stickiness" of a web site. The term "sticky" is a common web term used to describe a web site's return visit probability based upon marketing-driven qualities, such as dynamic content, social interaction opportunities, and visual interest. The "stickiness" is a user-centric concept rather than a technology-centric one. Unfortunately, the businesses referred to in the Gartner 2008 Press Release mentioned earlier approached their projects from a technology-centric perspective. "Stickiness" of virtual worlds and web pages is similar in the sense that it is concerned with the following: 1. Retention per visit, 2. Ability to engage users beyond their original purpose, and 3. Repeat or frequency of visits. Virtual worlds, like web sites, should transcend the 'information portal' concept. In fact, Steve Prentice, vice

president and Gartner fellow, put it best when he indicated that web pages have transitioned into web places, requiring more than robust graphics and abandonment of physics. (Gartner, 2008) The Facebook revolution tells us that people want to be connected and engaged to the extent they want, when they want, how they want, and/or with whom they want (or not). In short, users want to interact in some way at their convenience, with or without real people in accordance to their own discretion and within a space that accommodates all the types of interactions they seek.

As the evolution of web site design has progressed, present-day design practices show that pushing information out in a frequent, routine manner is a critical strategy for encouraging repeat visits. Designers have also apparently learned that content which encourages interaction should be available on the web sites. Today's web sites are evident of the realization that in order to make a web site "sticky," there needs to be an ever-present, dynamic quality to keep people interested and to motivate them to return. These designers now realize that they could never really keep up with the demands of the global public by themselves as moderators, facilitators, administrators, web masters, or monitors of web presences. In order to be successful, virtual world designers require these same realizations.

Requirements of and for social media also fuel the criticality of these realizations. In a nutshell, social media enables us to share the burden and the glory associated with a live, dynamic web presence. Social media is also credited with ushering in a new way to stay connected through real-time, mobile communication through a variety of devices; and more importantly, social media capitalizes on the new awareness that the "it takes a village" adage applies to more than just raising a child. Collective knowledge and wisdom, also known as *crowd sourcing*, has pushed the evolution of the Internet from a one-way, information repository to a communication gateway wherein the flow of information and interaction is multidirectional, in real-time, and potentially constant. Designers of virtual world environments will need to learn these lessons from the early maturity stages of the 'webvolution'.

Virtual worlds, in many respects, are affected by the same phenomena that have nudged the Internet's evolution forward; this is a fact that should come as no surprise given that access to most virtual worlds is web-based (not to be confused with browser-based). With this in mind, we may ask, why would a company or organization hang up a shingle in a virtual world and not populate it with things to do, people to see (with whom one can communicate/interact), and/or places to go? Are these not the basic tenants of modern-day web design? While this chapter will not address a one-to-one, direct comparison of the similarities and differences between web sites and virtual worlds, it will address a common denominator that appears to help or hinder success in a 2D or 3D web space: Persistence.

In the context of virtual worlds, the term "persistence" is defined as the continuously existing state of a virtual world, whether anyone is in it and using it or not; it remains as the last person left it. Individuals and groups alike leave behind a 'footprint' of sorts, supporting the notion of a virtual world as a place, not just a space. Persistence is a major affordance of virtual worlds—a central characteristic that sets them apart from any other learning medium available in the current social learning or instructional design toolkit. It could be argued that learning management systems (LMS), like Blackboard, Desire2Learn, or Plateau for instance, do provide some level of persistence via their wiki feature or group assignments. Sans software or hardware failure, LMS 'content' (not interactions) persists from visit to visit. Persistence in the sense of a virtual world should go beyond permanence of the content to include the other elements that lead to a 'sticky' virtual place, a focus on education, entertainment, social interaction, and unique (time and space defying) experiences. This chapter addresses the criticality of exploiting 'persistence' in order to

design an optimal interface for a meaningful, lasting learning experience in a virtual world, one that encourages learning, socializing, and enjoying unique experiences.

To reiterate: the notion of "persistence" in a virtual world refers to the 24/7 existence of the virtual world itself, regardless of the login status of users, and the dynamic nature of the virtual world wherein the virtual world remains as the last person in-world left it (i.e., leaving a 'footprint'). Awareness of these two definitions will aid in developing a solid plan to exploit "persistence" in a virtual world. This section explores the value and power of each perspective on "persistence" as a major affordance of virtual worlds. A closer examination of the meaning of the two-fold definition of "persistence" may help to set the stage for how this affordance can be best exploited to achieve the intended outcomes.

The 24/7 Existence of the Virtual World Itself, Regardless of the Login Status of Users

A learning environment that is 'always open' appeals to the 21st century learner in that it offers the opportunity for the learner to be in control of when and how learning takes place. 'Any time access' is often cited as one of the most valued benefits of distance learning (Keegan, 1986; Knapper, 1988). It stands to reason that this value would hold true for virtual worlds as well. Halvorson (2011), a virtual world researcher, conducted a study to determine the market stickiness of virtual worlds, an interest that was piqued by the astounding failure of corporate virtual world infinitives. His study found that two factors were key criteria contributing to the success of the five selected high traffic Second Life businesses: "Factor 1—The People Factor—the perception of connectedness and equality that [avatars] report feeling with other [avatars participating in the place or] business". (How is this achieved if no one is present?) Factor 2—The Place Factor—the atmospherics of the location perceived by the [business' avatars]"

(p. 18) [How can one engineer an environment compelling enough to become habit-forming?). Halvorson continues by pointing out that "frequency and habit are strong indicators of site stickiness and the People Factor top two items of inclusiveness and equality are strong indicators of community" (p.18). To Halvorson's point, 24/7 access alone is not enough to maintain a robust community, it takes much more engagement. Engagement should be multifaceted to include: other users, objects, the environment itself, external environments and technologies. The virtual world, then, can be conceived as a landscape where the design builds in cognitive flexibility through the multimedia perception of presence, co-existence, co-creation, collaboration, and GUI. How can all these attributes exist all the time? The answer may be hidden in the ways to best exploit the sixth virtual world attribute: Persistence.

The Dynamic Nature of the Ever-Changing Virtual World wherein the Virtual World Remains as the Last Person In-World Left it

Changes in a virtual world are lasting and have consequences just as they do in the organic world. Risk is only as damaging as it's programmed to be—or not. If we look to the e-learning and gaming industries for design lessons-learned, we can test similar elements in the virtual world. Engagement is critical in e-learning and gaming.

How do we foster engagement beyond the 'required minimal participation in a virtual world? What are some strategies from the e-learning and gaming industries that could be brought to bear?

In the organic world, each person is impacted by the people, as well as other organic and non-organic organisms inhabiting their shared space. Take for instance a beautiful, new park. When it opens for the first time, there is little wear and tear or evidence of use, but rather small, seemingly benign traces of human and nonhuman influence. Over time, however, the impact or existence of others becomes more and more

apparent—whether it is through litter or other waste left behind, worn paths in the grass, or mementos removed as souvenirs. The impact of collective actions can be astounding (think real world location: Plastic Island, also known as the Great Pacific Garbage Patch Pacific Trash and the Pacific Trash Vortex....). One plastic bottle tossed into the ocean is only one bottle until it joins the billions of other bottles and other debris people carelessly cast away. In the organic world, it is difficult (if not impossible) to jump off the universal grid completely. Somehow we are all having an impact on our environment no matter how small it may seem to be. Simply being is impactful in some way.

In a virtual world, our presence leaves markers behind as well. Users may have more influence or control over the type of marker they choose to leave behind, but future research is needed to determine the full scope of intentional and unintentional impact of presence in virtual worlds. Indeed, we have the organic world as a living example of the potential impact of our actions; therefore, the virtual world can serve as a test bed for potential actions with little to no real risk, impact, or loss, except that which is virtual. Perception (awareness) of the influence or impact of the others' actions is a critical part of reality; thus, having this capability built into the virtual world is paramount to bridging the virtual world to the real world and enabling transfer of experiences as well as lessons learned. Engineering persistence into the very behaviors of avatars by design is a powerful capability that sets virtual worlds apart from other learning tools.

Understanding the two-fold nature of persistence in virtual worlds enables us to conceptualize its existence, importance, and purpose. Bell (2008) describes the dynamic nature of a persistent world as a great differentiator of virtual worlds from other immersive technologies, such as games and simulations:

[P]ersistence changes the way people interact with other participants and the environment. No

longer is one participant the center of the world but a member of a dynamic community and evolving economy. A participant has a sense the the systems in the space (environment, ecology, economy) exist with or without a participant's presence (p.3).

Developing ways to design learning experiences in order to optimize persistence is important to the success of a virtual world learning activity, event or extended experience.

Selected Instructional Design Theories and Persistence

While there are many instructional design theories that can be applied to virtual worlds, for the purposes of this chapter, this author chooses to focus briefly on constructivist and experiential learning theories and how they may help to frame how the virtual world attributes can be optimized for immersive learning,, with a special emphasis on "persistence".

To date, there is no industry-standard approach for designing learning for virtual worlds; however, conceiving a learning framework should not be so difficult a task, since virtual worlds as multimedia learning tools, embody the elements of constructivist, experiential and cognitively flexible learning experiences. Constructivist learning environments encourage "[l]earners [to] build personal interpretation of the world based on experiences and interactions" ((Dabbagh, 2008; Dede, Clark, Ketelhut, Nelson, & Bowman, 2005; Nelson, Ketelhut, Clarke, Bowman, & Dede, 2005; Delwiche, 2003; Walker, 2009). Authentic contexts serve as the backdrop for meaningful, embedded experiences and interactions, offering the learners the opportunity to construct knowledge from multiple perspectives and situations (Dabbagh, 2008; Jonassen, Grabinger, Harris, 1991; Rheingold, 1991). David Jonassen and colleagues (1994), leaders in constructivist theory and methods, point out that social and cognitive constructivism has significant implications for instructional design;

these implications can also be applied to virtual worlds as constructivist learning environments. Table 2 shows how the affordances of virtual worlds can be used to apply the principles of constructivism. It also depicts how every inherent virtual world characteristic is also intrinsically constructivist, as well as how taking advantage of 'persistence' can expand the application of the specified constructivist principle.

In addition to constructivist theory, Kolb's experiential learning model is also context-and experience-centric. According to Kolb (1984a), Experience is a transformational process that produces knowledge. By fully engaging in and making meaning from an experience, a learner is then able to transform it. In other words, experience offers a "way of knowing" that is personal. As one researcher puts it, "[p]ersonal experience is memorable and meaningful in a way that is unique to the individual. Once an individual has an experience and constructs meaning from it, the knowledge gained is accessible for reflection, sharing or transfer to other situations, contexts, or experiences" (Gamor, 2010, p. 185).

Sound instructional design for virtual worlds should be grounded in, at least, constructivist and experiential learning theories. In so doing, the door is open for enhancing the learner's experience through maximizing the capabilities of the technology itself, especially 'persistence'. In order for virtual worlds to be more than a 'space', they should be dynamic, sticky, alive, indeed, persistent.

Designing for Optimal Persistence

In a learning context, hardly anything is more boring than a virtual learning environment wherein there is no activity, no signs of life, nobody 'home', in a manner of speaking. Virtual worlds for education are like social networking tools in that they are as valuable as the activities taking place in them. If there is no activity, then there is little value. It is akin to the proverbial tree falling in the forest: Does it make a sound if there's no one there to perceive it? While it may theoretically

Table 2. Principles of constructivism for instructional design mapped against virtual world affordances (Gamor, 2010, p. 185)

Principles of constructivism for instructional design (Jonassen, Campbell, & Davidson, 1994)	Affordances of virtual worlds
Offer multiple representations of reality	Collaboration GUI *Persistence* Presence
Represent the inherent complexity of the real world	Coexistence *Persistence*
Emphasize knowledge construction, rather than reproduction	Co-creation *Persistence*
Present authentic tasks, including risk (instruction in context rather than out of context)	Coexistence GUI *Persistence*
Provide real-world, case-based or problem-based learning opportunities, rather than pre-determined, prescriptive instructional sequences	Collaboration *Persistence*
Encourage reflection on experience	Collaboration *Persistence*
Enable context-and content-dependent knowledge construction	GUI Presence *Persistence*
Support "collaborative construction of knowledge through social negotiation, not competition among learners for recognition"	Collaboration Presence Persistence

make a sound whether no one hears it or not, the impact on those not present is the same: nothing. Likewise, if no one is in a virtual world, while it will persist or continue to exist, it will remain unchanged until someone acts upon it. It is in the action where the value endures. Meaningful, collaborative, lasting learning experiences will foster a vibrant, living virtual world. If the virtual world is built, 'they' may come just out of curiosity, but the action, the life of the world, is what will keep them coming back.

In order to optimize one of the greatest strengths of virtual worlds, "persistence", it is important to be aware of the possible interaction types in virtual worlds today. Understanding these interaction types will enable instructional designers to create appropriate activities that provide a well-rounded experience for the learner. Figure 2 illustrates the interaction types that should be considered as part of a design approach.

In addition to interaction types, instructional designers must also be aware of several design principles requiring consideration in order to exploit the power of persistence. Taking advantage of scripting languages and BOT technology is a good place to start. For the purposes of this chapter, scripting is defined as task-specific programming that takes advantage of functionalities of other programs. In other words, it is interpreted by specific software and affects a given application, not the specific computer it's on which the software is running. Scripting languages are generally easier to learn than traditional programming languages and require less code and is 'run' as opposed to being 'executed'. Thus, scripting could be more cost effective, depending upon the programming requirements of the intended task. BOT technology for the purpose of this paper is defined as a virtual world 'robot' that is programmed to carry out automated, simple and repetitive tasks. The physical characteristic of a BOT can be whatever is deemed necessary and effective to achieve the intended goals. For instance, in a case where you have a virtual tour as part of the im-

Figure 2. Avatar interactions in virtual worlds

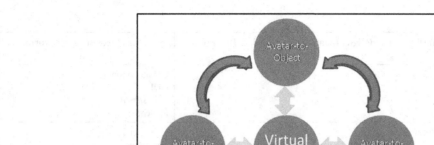

mersive learning experience, a BOT could be the tour guide. The basic tour can follow a predefined path for completing the tour. However, every tour should allow for individual exploration, a basic premise of constructivist theory suggest that learners should be able to plot his or her own path. With this in mind, if it would not interfere with the purpose of the tour, it would be an effective design choice to permit learners to veer off path as portions of the tour intrigue them to conduct further exploration. The BOT could be programmed to meet the learner where he left off or at the next meeting spot. In any case, while a BOT is artificial, it should not be rigidly designed, as this will lead to user frustration. BOTs are persistent entities that are generally created to provide information, offer hints or challenges, or give other support to the learner. Table 3 provides some ideas that could be implemented in order to exploit the power of persistence in virtual worlds. The strategy is first listed and described, and then the level of technical development effort is provided. The point is this: if there is no access to programmers, then one can still exploit the power of persistence by other means. In ideal situations where there is access to programmers and instructional designers, then the virtual world experience

may be optimized by a wider variety of measures. While the following list is certainly not exhaustive, it does provide a range of considerations that could be applied to other instructional strategies or to programming the behavior of the environment, objects, or other inhabitants (BOTS). The critical take-away point is that everything in a virtual world has the potential to be persistent. The value of its persistence is entirely up to the discretion of the designers involved in the project and the avatars participating in the learning experience, for unless the avatars are artificially limited, they too can create dynamic objects that can have impact upon the world.

Table 3 shows only a sampling of how designers can build 'persistence' into the immersive learning experience. Developing creative ways to extend the user's experience can be approached based on the level of technical development one's resources can support. At a minimum, however, a 'low level' approach should be used by implementing thoughtful, creative instructional design strategies.

The purpose of this chapter is to underscore the criticality of exploiting 'persistence' and to provide an overview of how to accomplish that goal. More research is necessary to understand

Table 3. High to low levels of effort to exploiting the power of persistence

Strategy to Exploit Persistence	Strategy Description	Level of Technical Development Effort High/Medium/Low
Scripts	Ensure the virtual world is designed to include scripted, random changes to the environment. Ideally, these changes would be based on user profile information which is linked to the learner's previous performance. However, if this is not possible due to lack of resources, then random scripting will have to suffice.	High
BOTs	Consider using bots to maintain a continuous sense of community and opportunities for some basic levels of interaction 24/7. Determine what kind of BOT you wish to create: Help Desk BOT, Learning facilitator BOT, etc. These autonomous agents can sort, sift, and select; guide, demonstrate, and identify; they can also help, prompt, and support learners. The key take Away here is to determine how to create a BOT that will effectively provide timely information, facilitate discovery, and encourage self-reflection as an iterative activity.	High
Constructivist Activity: Multiple Perspectives	Build in multiple perspectives (around identity, role, and/or context) for each learning objective so that it can be experienced, reviewed and/or practiced as many times as the learner would like.	Medium
Constructivist Activity: Discovery Learning	Challenge learners not only to discover existing problems, but to anticipate potential problems and then create those problems in-world for classmates to solve. Learners must keep a running log of contributions (unless these behaviors are tracked), which can be used for self and group reflection. Individuals and/or groups could develop ePortfolios or vPortfolios to track their own behavior, why they took specific actions, and what their anticipated outcomes. They could then return to the environment to observe and record actual results, noting if any additional actions were taken. The vPortfolio could be part of an overall 'strategy game' designed into the world itself. Researchers describe the ePortfolio as a "digital representation of understanding and performance artifacts that can lead to personal reflection and promote exchange of ideas and encourage feedback" (Lorenzo and Ittelson, 2005). Further, ePortfolios are valued for "being purposeful, progressive, and reflective endeavors" (Gilman, Andrew, and Rafferty, 1995).	Low
Constructivist Activity: Reflection	Incorporate reflective opportunities for individuals and/or groups to discuss their problem identification, solving, and/or creation strategies. This can be accommodated by using built-in social networking tools or add-on, open source or free social networking tools that learners may already be using.	Low
Constructivist Activity: Collaboration	Create a collaborative environment rather than a competitive one. Recognize knowledge acquisition, content understanding, and teamwork by rewarding the collective achievements and peer-support activities, rather than individual mastery. Badges, coins, dollars, or some other 'collectable' or 'gift' could be the reward. Design activities that encourage co-creation. Robbins and Bell (2008) advise that: "While we can read, view, and listen to learning resources, virtual worlds offer a level of experiential learning: • Simulations: (Example: creating and running a business) • Role Play: Taking on an identity as part of the learning process • Building: Creation, Design, Exhibit • Participating in Social Events: (Example: guest visits, conferences, job fairs, socials, campus fairs) (pp. 284 – 285)".	Low-Medium

the time and resource requirements juxtaposed against a sliding scale of 'persistence', based on degree. With sustained effort and the sharing of more research-based lessons learned in the use of virtual worlds for learning, there are sure to be additional discoveries that will inform us how 'persistence' can be leveraged for community building, crowd sourcing, knowledge management, data visualization, social networking, personal learning assistants, and more. Continued advancements in current technologies, such as artificial intelligence, augmented/mixed realities, advanced social media, and mobile technologies, will usher in a seemingly endless flow of possibilities for evolving applications of virtual worlds. Hopefully, worlds will be designed and built to attract and retain, making true the premise of 'build it and they will come'…and come back again and again.

REFERENCES

Association of Virtual Worlds. (2008, August). *The blue book: A consumer guide to virtual worlds*, (4th edition, p. 1). Retrieved on April 12, 2009, from http://www.associationofvirtualworlds. com/ pdf/Blue%20Book%204th%20Edition% 20August%202008.pdf

Bell, M. (2008). Toward a definition of "virtual worlds". *Journal of Virtual Worlds Research, 1*(1), 2-5. Retrieved on February 3, 2009, from http://journals.tdl.org/jvwr/ article/view/283/237

Berge, Z. L., & Collins, M. (Eds.). (1995). *Computer-mediated communication and the online classroom*. Cresskill, NJ: Hampton Press.

Bersin, J. (2008, July). Today's high-impact learning organization. *Chief Learning Officer Magazine*. Retrieved on July 16, 2009, from http:// clomedia.com/articles/ view/today_s_high_im-pact_ learning_organization/1

Bransford, J., Brown, A., & Cocking, R. (1999). *How people learn: Brain, mind experience and school*. Retrieved on November 1, 2008, from http://cde.athabascau.ca/ online_book/pdf/ TPOL_chp02.pdf

Chin, S., & Williams, J. (2006). A theoretical framework for effective online course design. *Journal of Online Learning and Teaching, 2*(1). Retrieved on January 3, 2009, from http://jolt. merlot.org/05007.htm

Dede, C. (2007). Reinventing the role of information and communications technologies in education. *Yearbook of the National Society for the Study of Education, 106*, 11–38. doi:10.1111/j.1744-7984.2007.00113.x

Dickey, M. (2004). The impact of web-logs (blogs) on student perceptions of isolation and alienation in a web-based distance-learning environment. *Open Learning, 19*(3). Retrieved on May 23, 2009, from http://mchel.com/Papers/ OL_19_3_2004.pdf

Federation of American Scientists. (2009). *FAS virtual worlds whitepaper*. Retrieved on March 20, 2009, from http://vworld.fas.org/ wiki/FAS_Vir-tual_Worlds _Whitepaper

Gamor, K. (2010). Adopting virtual worlds in ADL: The criticality of analysis. In Wisher, B., & Khan, B. (Eds.), *Learning on demand: ADL and the future of eLearning*. Alexandria, VA: ADL.

Gamor, K. (2011). What is in an avatar? Identity, behavior, and integrity in virtual worlds for educational and business communications. In Vu, K. P., & Proctor, R. W. (Eds.), *Handbook of human factors in web design* (pp. 739–749). Boca Raton, FL: CRC Press. doi:10.1201/b10855-48

Garrison, R. (2000). Theoretical challenges for distance education in the 21st Century: A shift from structural to transactional issues. *International Review of Research in Open and Distance Learning, 1*(1), 1–17.

Gartner Inc. (2007, April 24). *Press release: Gartner says 80 percent of active Internet users will have a "Second Life" in the virtual world by the end of 2011*. Retrieved on March 20, 2009, from http:// www.gartner.com/it/ page.jsp?id=503861%20

Gartner Inc. (2008b). *Press release: Gartner says 90 per cent of corporate virtual world projects fail within 18 months*. Retrieved March 20, 2009 from http://www.gartner.com/ it/page.jsp?id=670507

Gartner Inc. (2009, October 20). *Press release: Gartner identifies the top 10 strategic technologies for 2010.* Retrieved on November 11, 2009, from http://www.gartner.com/it/page.jsp?id=1210613

Gilman, D. A., Andrew, R., & Rafferty, C. D. (1995). Making assessment a meaningful part of instruction. *NASSP Bulletin, 79*(573), 20–24. doi:10.1177/019263659507957304

Hoff, T. (2008, April). Learning in the 21st century: A brave new world. *CLO Magazine.*

IEEE. (2009). *IEEE islands in Second Life.* Retrieved on May 3, 2009, from http://www.ieee.org/web/volunteers/tab/secondlife/index.html

Jonassen, D. (1991). Evaluating constructivistic learning. *Educational Technology, 31*(10), 28–33.

Jonassen, D. (2000). Toward a meta-theory of problem solving. *Educational Technology Research and Development, 48*(4), 63–85. doi:10.1007/BF02300500

Keegan, D. (1986). *The foundations of distance education.* London, UK: Croom Helm.

Khan, B. H. (2005). *Managing e-learning: Design, delivery, implementation and evaluation.* Hershey, PA: Information Science Publishing. doi:10.4018/978-1-59140-634-1

Knapper, C. (1988). Lifelong learning and distance education. *American Journal of Distance Education, 2*(1), 63–72. doi:10.1080/08923648809526609

Lorenoz, G., & Ittelson, J. (2005). *An overview of e-portfolios.* The EDUCAUSE Learning Initiative, July 2005. Retrieved on December 2, 2008, from http://connect.educause.edu/library/abstract/AnOverviewofEPortfol/39335

Merrill, D. (2007). A task-centered instructional strategy. *Journal of Research on Technology in Education, 40*(1), 5–22.

Norris, D., Mason, J., & Lefrere, P. (2004) Experiencing knowledge. *Innovate, 1*(1). Retrieved November 24, 2009, from http://www.innovateonline.info/index.php?view=article&id=5

Robbins, S., & Bell, M. (2008). *Second life for dummies.* Indianapolis, IN: Wiley Publishing.

Sheets, M. (1992, Spring). Characteristics of adult education students and factors which determine course completion: A review. *New Horizons in Adult Education, 6*(1). Retrieved on October 6, 2009, from http://www.nova.edu/~aed/horizons/vol6n1

Sweet, R. (1986). Student drop-out in distance education: An application of Tinto's model. *Distance Education, 7,* 201-213. Retrieved on October 1, 2009, from http://www.westga.edu/~distance/ojdla/winter84/nash84.htm

The EDUCAUSE Learning Initiative. (2006, June). *7 things you should know about virtual worlds.* Retrieved on June 2, 2009, from http://www.educause.edu/ELI/7ThingsYouShouldKnowAboutVirtu/156818

United States Air Force. (30 January 2008). *White paper: On learning: The future of Air Force education and training.* Air Education and Training Command. Retrieved on June 30, 2009, from http://www.aetc.af.mil/shared/media/document/AFD-080130-066.pdf

U.S. Department of Education, Office of Planning, Evaluation, and Policy Development. (2009). *Evaluation of evidence-based practices in online learning: A Meta-analysis and review of online learning studies.* Retrieved from http://www2.ed.gov/rschstat/eval/tech/evidence-based-practices/finalreport.pdf

Virtual World Review. (n.d.). *What is a virtual world?* Retrieved April 6, 2009, from http://www.virtualworldsreview.com/info/whatis.shtml

Chapter 10

Ontology-Driven Creation of Contents:
Making Efficient Interaction between Organizational Users and Their Surrounding Tasks

Kambiz Badie
Research Institute for ICT (ITRC), Iran

Mahmood Kharrat
Research Institute for ICT (ITRC), Iran

Maryam Tayefeh Mahmoudi
Research Institute for ICT (ITRC), Iran & University of Tehran, Iran

Maryam S. Mirian
Research Institute for ICT (ITRC), Iran & University of Tehran, Iran

Tahereh M. Ghazi
Research Institute for ICT (ITRC), Iran

Sogol Babazadeh
Research Institute for ICT (ITRC), Iran

ABSTRACT

In this chapter, a framework is discussed for creating contents to help significant organizational tasks such as planning, research, innovation, education, development, et cetera be achieved in an efficient way. The proposed framework is based on an interplay between the ontologies of the key segments and the problem context using the linguistically significant notions for each key segment. Once a certain organizational task is faced these notions are adjusted to create a new content filling the new situation. In the chapter, an agent-based architecture is discussed to show how human interaction with his/her surrounding organization can be realized through using this framework.

DOI: 10.4018/978-1-61350-516-8.ch010

Copyright © 2012, IGI Global. Copying or distributing in print or electronic forms without written permission of IGI Global is prohibited.

1. INTRODUCTION

In smart organizations, which in their advanced form can be viewed as learning organizations, users are expected to act as agile and/or smart as possible. Regarding this, taking into account the point that users may need appropriate contents to be helped with their assigned functions, it would be important to provide the essential contents in such a way that the functions allocated to the users due to their organizational tasks, can be performed in a plausible manner. Under such expectation, creating potential contents, to provide sufficient ability for efficient interactions between the knowledge workers in an organization and their organizational tasks, is of high significance. Taking the above point into account, a variety of concerns may exist with respect to the contents in organizations, which should be handled carefully

A. Contents are to be structured on the ground of a kind of interplay between a variety of entities related to different issues such as domain knowledge, problem-context, task model and user model as well.
B. Knowledge on both the task to be performed by users, and the user model itself, should in some way be projected onto the way the essential contents are structured.
C. Some mechanisms are required to assure the essential parameters such as integrity, coherence, validity, soundness,… for the contents within the process of content creation.

Due to the above reasons, it would be necessary to look for a solution that can handle these concerns in terms of appropriate considerations, to organize efficiently the essential background knowledge. To fulfill this, the possible variations of the problems that occur frequently in an organization, should be in some way reflected in the background knowledge in terms of some key concepts that can in some way assure the minimum adequacy required for content. It seems that ontologies, due to their capability in relationalizing the significant concepts in a domain, can be good alternatives in this regard. Obviously, representation in terms of ontology is not only necessary for the domain knowledge, but also for the entities participating in problem context as well as task model and user model.

Having adopted ontological representation in such a way, the problem of creating content for a certain problem context, a certain task and a certain user can be mapped onto the way the corresponding entities in the ontologies of context, task model, and user model are to be carried over into the key concepts in the ontology of domain knowledge, to specify the status/degree of some linguistically significant entities, based on which creation of the entire content can come true in a natural language sense. In our approach, entities such as What, Which, Who, Whom, Where, How, and Why, which address the significant terms with regard to an issue, are selected as the alternatives for these linguistically significant entities. Selection of such entities permits us to have insight into the way the contents belonging to different tasks ought to differ from each other with regard to the key concepts in the domain knowledge ontology. Obviously, due to some difficulties in automated generation of partial contents for these linguistically–significant entities, interaction with a human specialist may come necessary. Another role of the human specialist can be summarized in his/her duty in assuring content's quality in terms of the essential parameters already discussed, based on a periodic screening/editing the intermediate results in content creation.

2. ONTOLOGICAL APPROACH TO REPRESENTING CONTENT DOMAIN KNOWLEDGE AND PROBLEM CONTEXT

2.1 Why Ontological Approach?

The main aim of content creation is to supply appropriate contents based on which various users can receive adequate information to perform their tasks in a reasonable manner. A variety of approaches have been proposed for content creation among which approaches based on information mining, ontology-based reasoning, deductive/rule-based reasoning, analogical/case-based reasoning, and blending (Fauconnier & Turner 1998) (Pereira & Cardoso, 2002), / fusion (Ravi, Yu, Shi, 2009) (Pizzi, Cavazza, Whittaker, Lugrin, 2008) /composition (Mahmoudi & Badie 2004) (Mahmoudi, Badie, Kharrat, Babazadeh, Yadollahi 2008) (Badie, Kharrat, Mahmoudi, Mirian, Babazadeh, Ghazi 2009), are of particular significance. In all these approaches, it is somewhat important to project the requirements of a task and the related content onto the way the key segments in the content are to be formed. Ontologies, as powerful means for representing knowledge, have been shown to be helpful in this regard. Let say, the continuum between the key (major) concepts in an ontology via the existing relations, provides a systematic medium within which parts of the desired content can be generated in a gradual way, taking into account the gradualness with regard to these key concepts in the ontology. Such a gradual-ness has the ability to assure the fineness of the created content, since it assures in a systematic manner what items are to be propounded in a content to make it knowledgeable for the desired purpose. Ontologies for creating content can generally be divided into (i) the one for the key segments in a content that are generally meaningful with no particular emphasis on the application domain, (ii) the one for the problem context, which addresses the conditions under which a task ought to be performed by a content's user, and (iii) the one for the user which addresses the species of the users who may attend an organization with certain peculiarities. With respect to the ontology of problem-context, both focal entities ruling over a problem, and constraints, which limit the scope of applying these focal entities with respect to the possible problems, can be considered.

2.2 Ontology for a Content's Key Segments

As it was discussed, we have to look for the concepts that can be generally meaningful for a content with no particular emphasis on the application domain in which the content's creator is involved. Therefore, those entities should be looked for, which are realized to be consistent for a wide range of possible contents(for helping the users with their tasks in organizations), emphasizing on the aspects such as (i) whether the content has been benefited by a glance of the part to show the genealogy of the problem, (ii) the focal points of the existing approaches to our existing problem (including their strengths &weak-points), (iii) the key point of the ongoing approach, (iv) the way the ongoing approach can show its strengths with regard to the existing problem, (v) the format according to which the ongoing approach can be assessed, and (vi) the new horizons for the ongoing approach with regard to possible application domains that may somewhat be important in the future trend of the existing problem. Regarding the above points, an idea for the ontology of key segments that are to be included in a content, is illustrated in Figure 1. As it is seen from the figure, labels such as "general background", "existing viewpoints", "key issues", "realization/implementation", "comparative analysis & capability interpretation", and "conclusion& prospect anticipation" seem to cover the characteristics discussed above, and are in reality being used by a wide range of knowledge workers in an organization to disseminate results of their works in terms of appropriate contents. An overview of the tasks nature from a cognitive viewpoint, in addition to the above fact, take us to the point that these key segments would be sufficient as the alternatives for the upper layers of the proposed ontology.

Figure 1. The ontology of content's key segments

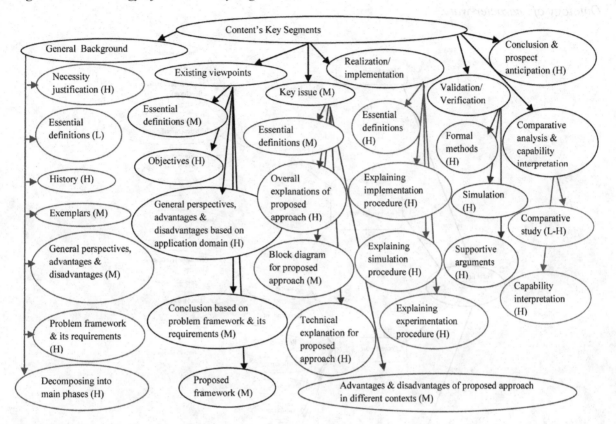

2.3 Ontology for the Problem Context

By the problem context, we mean the conditions under which a task is to be performed by a content's user. Taking this point into account, problem-context can be considered from the viewpoints of (i) focal entities ruling over the problem and (ii) constraints which limit the scope of applying these focal entities with respect to the possible problems that may occur in an organization. With regard to the ontology of focal entities, we are mostly concerned with the four categories of "content-ware", "human-ware", "techno-ware", and "character-ware", which are the basic necessities for an organization.

Obviously, each of these categories may hold its own ontology from the standpoint of certain aspects. For instance, category of content-ware

addresses the possible "tasks and their types", while category of "human-ware" tackles issues such as "roles" and "beneficiaries". Also, category of "techno-ware" includes issues such as "specifications", "standards & benchmarks", "models & algorithms", etc.(Figure2 (a), (b), (c), and(d)). In the meantime category of "character-ware" tackles the possible qualities or characteristics that can be considered with respect to the significant action type entities in the cyber-environment.

The entities under the nodes "human-ware", "techno-ware", "content-ware" and character-ware have been determined according to the general knowledge which exists with regard to respectively, the positions according to which humans tend to contents to help them achieve their tasks, technological entities with respect to the main issues that make sense to the process of task achievement, the task categories themselves

Figure 2. (a) Ontology of human-ware, (b) Ontology of techno-ware, (c) Ontology of content-ware, (d) Ontology of character-ware.

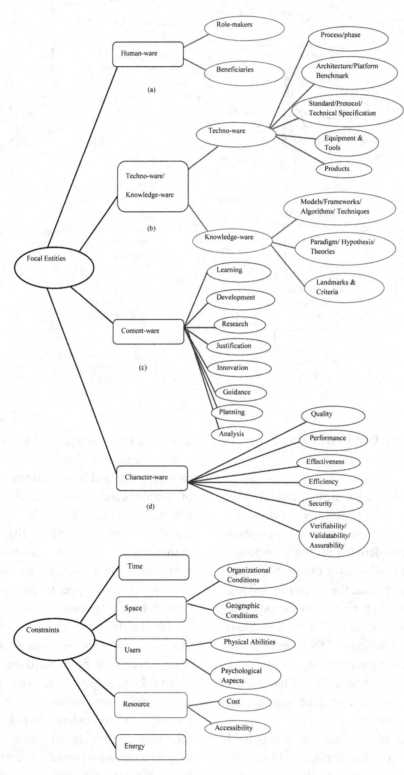

and finally the possible characters that are significant with respect to the existing entities in an organization. Also, with regard to the ontology of constraints, we are primarily concerned with the existing limitations/restrictions with respect to issues such as time, space, energy, and resource, users,... that are essential to performing a task (Figure2 (e)).

Provided the fact that a suitable content is the one including appropriate key segments, and in the meantime being capable of responding satisfactorily to the ongoing problem context, it becomes obvious that the inter-play between the above items can lead us to the point where some petit contents can be systematically created whose assembly can later on yield an appropriate content for the user.

To assure this fact, for each organizational task, a number of nominal values should be pre-agreed for the related key segments, in order to indicate to what extent the linguistically significant notions like "What", "Which", "Where", "When", "Whom", "Who", "Why", and "How" should be tackled to make sound petit contents. Handling these notions calls for a consideration of the problem context with respect to the basic factors of content-ware, human-ware, techno-ware, and character-ware and organizational tasks and key segments as well.

3. GENERATING PETIT CONTENTS

As it was discussed earlier, for each organizational task, a number of nominal values should be pre-agreed for the related key segments, to

indicate to what extent the linguistically significant notions like What, Which, Who, Whom, Where, When, How, and Why should be tackled in order to make sound petit contents for these key segments. Handling these notions calls for a consideration of the problem context with respect to the basic factors such as content-ware, human-ware, techno-ware, and character-ware, which are essential to cyber-environments in general and cyber-learning environment in particular (Smith & Sharif, 2007), (Kumar, Kumar, Dutta, Fantazy, 2007), (Shawyun, 1999), (Henry, 2005). Table 1 indicates the status of these nominal values L, M, and H with regard to the corresponding linguistically significant notions. As is seen from the figure, the higher a nominal value, a higher expectation would exist with regard to the depth of these linguistically significant notions. Let say, comparing M to L, the linguistically significant notion "How" is also called for. Also, comparing H to M, notion "Why", which stands for a deeper explanation should be included in the petit content. The nominal values discussed above are determined according to the average expectation existing with regard to the nature of the ongoing organizational tasks. Some of the major tasks important for an organization are illustrated in Table 2 together with their motivation for content creation. The ground for selecting such items is the analytical & synthetic needs for organization decision-making in general, which have appeared well in the form of appropriate departments/units in many advanced organizations.

It should be mentioned that each task can be conceptualized at different categories, and based upon the type of a category, the status of the cor-

Table 1. Status of the nominal values

Nominal Value	Status of Linguistically Significant notions
L (Low)	Addresses What, Which, Where, When, Who, and Whom
M (Medium)	Addresses What, Which, Where, When, Who, Whom, and How
H (High)	Addresses What, Which, Where, When, Who, Whom, How, and Why

Table 2. Major task categories and their motivations for creating content

Type of Task	Motivation
Planning/ Scheduling	Helping the user do planning through encapsulating the essential requirements for planning in the content.
Research	Helping the user do research through encapsulating the essential requirements for research in the content
Innovation	Helping the user do innovation through encapsulating the essential requirements for innovation in the content
Development/ Optimization/ Improvement	Helping the user do development through encapsulating the essential requirements for development in the content
Education/ Promotion	Helping the user do education through encapsulating the essential requirements for education in the content
Analysis/ Assessment/ Assurance	Helping the user do analysis through encapsulating the essential requirements for analysis in the content.
Guidance	Helping the user do guidance through encapsulating the essential requirements for guidance in the content
Justification	Helping the user do justification through encapsulating the requirements for justification in the content

responding nominal values may differ. In our approach, we do our best to clarify what these organizational tasks would particularly mean in the case of e-learning as a major cyber- application, taking into account the general e-learning framework suggested in (Khan, 2005), (Khan, 2006). Table 3 illustrates the corresponding entities for these tasks according to this framework.

Table 4 illustrates the distribution of the nominal values for the content's key segments with regard to a variety of organizational tasks and the corresponding key segments.

To facilitate the process of organizing the petit contents based on tackling the linguistically significant notions discussed above, Table 5 can be helpful.

According to this table, when a question is propounded for a certain key segment and a certain organizational task, the content generator should refer to the existing aspects in the ontology of Focal Entity, and check which aspects and which entities under such aspects can make sense with respect to the related task, and then if necessary, see which actions out of those already defined, can be meaningful with regard to the key segment

under interest. For instance, if the organizational task is "assessment", and the content generator wants to create a petit content for the key segment "necessity justification", we will have the following findings:

A. With respect to "What is concerned?" ("What Necessity to be Justified?")
   ◦   .. The term "Quality" can be picked out from the ontology of Focal Entity concentrating on "Character-ware" as the working aspect. Coupling of this term with actions such as "Assurance" can yield the composite "Quality Assurance" as the final choice.

B. With respect to "by Who?" ("Who to perform Quality Assurance?")
   ◦   .. The term "Role-maker" can be picked out from the ontology of Focal Entity concentrating on "Human-ware" as the working aspect. No coupling with any action is required in this case.

Table 3. Corresponding entities for major tasks according to general e-learning framework[o]

Type of Task	Correspondence by General e-Learning Framework
Planning/ Scheduling	Management Issues in e-Learning • Content Development Phases
Research	Pedagogical Issues in e-Learning • Instructional Strategies and Blending Strategies using items such as Drill and Practice, Discussion, Interaction, Collaboration, Debate and …, which are more appropriate for research based learning.
Innovation	Pedagogical Issues in e-Learning • Instructional Strategies and Blending Strategies using items such as Demonstration, Tutorials, Storytelling, Role-Playing, Field trips, case study and …, which are more Appropriate for Innovative Learning
Development/ Optimization/ Improvement	Management Issues in e-Learning • Content Development Phases • Evaluation Phases • Generating Revised Materials
Education/ Promotion	Pedagogical Issues in e-Learning • Instructional Strategies • Blending Strategies
Analysis/ Assessment/ Assurance	Evaluation Issues in e-Learning • Evaluation of e-Learning Content Development, Delivery and Maintenance Process • Assessment of Learner Pedagogical Issues in e-Learning • Content, Audience, Goal, Media and Design Approach Analysis
Guidance	Resource Support Issues in e-Learning • Online Support such as Instructional and Counseling Support Interface Design Issues in e-Learning • Page and Site Design • Content Design • Navigation • Accessibility
Justification	Evaluation Issues in e-Learning • Evaluation of Instructional Team, Administrative Support • Learners Support Staff Institutional Issues in e-Learning • Administrative Affairs such as Needs and Readiness Assessment

C. With respect to "for Whom?"("For Whom Quality Assurance to be performed?")

   ° .. The term "Beneficiar" can be picked out from the ontology of Focal Entity concentrating on "Human-ware" again as the working aspect, In this case, there would be no need for any coupling with any action.

D. With respect to "on Which?"("On Which items Quality Assurance is to be performed?")

   ° .. The appropriate terms from the ontology of Focal Entity concentrating on "Content-ware" as the working aspects can be picked out in this regard.

No need would also exist for any kind of coupling with any action.

E. With respect to "Where & When?"("Where & When", Quality Assurance can be satisfactory?")

   ° ..Appropriate terms can be picked out from the ontology of Constraints, concentrating respectively on "Space" and "Time" as working aspects.

Table 4. Status of the nominal values regard to the corresponding organizational tasks

Organizational tasks Content's Key Segments	Research	Development/ Optimization/ improvement	Learning/ Promotion	Justification	Guidance	Innovation	Planning	Analysis/ Assessment/ Assurance
General Background	0.H	0.M	0.L	0.L	0.L	0. M	0.M	0.L
1. Necessity Justification	1.H	1.H	1.H	1.H	1.H	1.H	1.H	1.H
2. Essential definitions	2.L	2.L	2.L	2.L	21.L	2.L	2.L	2.L
3. History	3.H	3.M	3.L	3.L	3.M	3.L	3.M	3.L
4. Exemplars	4.M	4.L	4.H	4.L	4.L	4.L	4.L	4.L
5. General perspectives, advantages & disadvantages	5.M	5.M	5.L	5.L	5.L	5.L	5.M	5.L
6..Problem framework & its requirements	6.H	6.H	6.H	6.H	6.H	6.H	6.H	6.H
7. Decomposing into main phases	7.H	7.H	7.H	7.H	7.H	7.H	7.H	7.H
Existing viewpoints	0.H	0.M	0.H	0.L	0.M	0.M	0.M	0.L
1. Essential definitions	1.M	1.M	1.L	1.L	1.M	1.L	1.M	1.L
2. Objectives	2.H	2.M	2.L	2.L	2.M	2.L	2.M	2.L
3.General perspectives, advantages & disadvantages based on application domain	3.H	3.M	3.L	3.L	3.M	3.L	3.M	3.L
4. Conclusion based on problem framework & its requirements	4.M	4.M	4.L	4.L	4.M	4.L	4.M	4.L
5.Proposed framework	5.M	5.M	5.L	5.M	5.M	5.L	5.M	5.M
Key issue	0.H	0.M	0.M	0.M	0.M	0.M	0.M	0.M
1.Essential definitions	1.M	1.M	1.L	1.L	1.M	1.L	1.M	1.L
2.Overall explanations of proposed approach	2.H	2.H	2.H	2.H	2.H	2.H	2.H	2.H
3. Block diagram for proposed approach	3.M	3.M	3.L	3.M	3.M	3.H	3.M	3.M
4. Technical explanation for proposed approach	4.H	4.H	4.L	4.M	4.H	4.L	4.H	4.M
5. Advantages & disadvantages of proposed approach in different contexts	5.M	5.L	5.M	5.L	5.L	5.L	5.L	5.L
Proposed approach realization/ implementation	0.H	0.M	0.L	0.M	0.L	0.L	0.M	0.M
1. Essential resources	1.H	1.H	1.L	1.L	1.L	1.L	1.H	1.M
2. Explaining implementation procedure	2.H	2.H	2.L	2.H	2.L	2.L	2.H	2.H
3. Explaining simulation procedure	3.H	3.L	3.L	3.L	3.L	3.L	3.L	3.L
4. Explaining experimentation procedure	4.H	4.L	4.L	4.L	4.L	4.L	4.L	4.L
Validation/Verification	0.H	0.M	0.L	0.M	0.L	0.L	0.M	0.H
1. Formal methods	1.H	1.L	1.L	1.M	1.L	1.L	1.M	1.H
2. Simulation	2.H	2.H	2.L	2.M	2.L	2.L	2.H	2.H
3. Supportive arguments	3.H	3.H	3.L	3.H	3.H	3.L	3.H	3.H
Comparative analysis & capability interpretation	0. H	0.M	0.L	0.L	0.M	0.L	0.M	0.L
1.Comparitivestudy	1.L-H	1.L-M	1.L	1.L	1.L-M	1.L	1.L-M	1.L
2. Capability interpretation	2.H	2.M	2.L	2.L	2.M	2.L	2.M	2.L
Conclusion & prospect anticipation	H	H	L	L	H	L	H	L

4. ARCHITECTURE FOR THE PROPOSED APPROACH

4.1 Basic Concepts

Taking into account the specification of the proposed approach to content creation in organizations, and in the meantime the essential interplay between the ontologies of key segments and focal entities, a multi-agent system-based architecture can be conceptualized for the proposed approach (Wooldridge, 2009) (Weiss, 1999). This architecture consists of three prime agents as follows:

Table 5. Remarks for tackling linguistically-significant notions

Linguistically-Significant Notion	Remark
What is concerned	can be picked up from (Focal Entity→Character-ware)
by Who	can be picked up from (Focal Entity→Human-ware→ Role-maker)
for Whom	can be picked up from (Focal Entity→Human-ware→Beneficiar)
on Which	can be picked up from (Focal Entity→Content-ware)
Where/When	can be picked up from (Constraints→Space)/ can be picked up from (Constraints→Time)
How	can be picked up from (Focal Entity→Techno-ware/Knowledge-ware)
Why	can be constructed based on the Advantages& Disadvantages (in the key segment of Key Issue) and all the Human-ware, Content-ware, Techno-ware and Character-ware aspects in Focal Entity

1. An Interplay Performer Agent to manage the inter-play between the ontology of content's key segments and the ontology for the problem-context.
2. A Petit Content Generator Agent to generate local contents for each key segment taking into account the status of the corresponding nominal values.
3. A Content Assembler Agent to assemble together parts (of a petit content) generated for different linguistically significant notions.

Each of these agents is discussed in more details.

4.2 Inter-Play Performer Agent

As explained in section 2.3, we have assumed that a suitable content is the one including appropriate key segments that can facilitate the satisfactory response to the problem context. It is also assumed that the interplay between two sub-ontologies – i.e. content key segments and the problem context, can direct us to the points on how to create systematically some appropriate contents. Content assembling process can therefore result in an appropriate content for the user.

4.3 Petit Content Generator Agent

As stated in section 3, the interplay is explicitly realized through a table of nominal values per every organizational task. These nominal values are pre-specified for every key segment. They stand for level of details that one should extend in his/her explanation about linguistically-significant notions ("What", "Which", "Where", "When", "Whom", "Who", "Why" and "How").

4.4 Content Assembler Agent

As soon as a number of petit contents are generated, the Content Assembler agent puts them together to make a unified content. The sequence of petit contents that are being merged follows natural binding rule: at the beginning more general concepts are presented such as topics about the definition, general background, and necessity justifications and so on. In the middle, the roles involved, the methods, standards and approaches are discussed. At the end, some concluding issues such as advantages/disadvantages are given.

Figure 3. Illustrates a schematic view of the proposed architecture

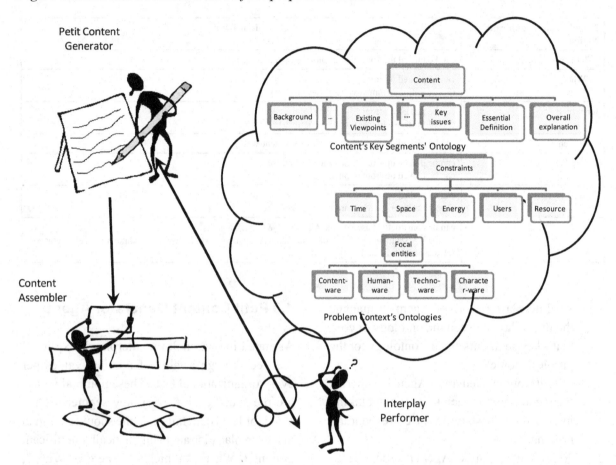

5. SOME EXAMPLES WITHIN THE REALM OF E-LEARNING

5.1 An Example for Generating Content for the Task of Research

The first example to show the capability of the proposed approach to content creation is a case where content is to be created for a user where aim is to do research within a certain scope in the area of e-learning. Taking this point into account, the content should be adjusted such that the user can be helped to make a reasonable approach to his/her steps in research. Our example is to create a content which can guide the researcher to a forum where in he/she can develop a framework for adapting an e-content to learner's conditions/requirements in e-learning environment. Regarding this example, we consider segments such as "Motivation", "Historical Background", "Research Objectives & Scopes", "Major Phases", "Capability Assessment", "Prospect Anticipation", as illustrated in Table 5. These segments have been shown to be meaningful with regard to the task of "research", taking into account aspects like research motivation, history of performed activities, research's objectives &scope, required phases in research, assessing the capability of the research's outcome as well as anticipating the prospects of the corresponding research. The column at the extreme right of the table indicates the key segments according to which the corresponding research proposal's segments can be structured.

Taking the above discussion into account, the petit contents created with regard to some of the segments would be as follows:

A. Motivation's Petit Content

Definitions (L)

- "What is concerned?" ("What is to become subject to Definition?")
  - .. The scale of adaptability between a content's features and user's conditions/requirements (beliefs, desires, intentions, background, …) in an e-learning domain.
- "By Who?" (" Who to perform the related activities?")
  - .. Various characters such as those related to management, sources evaluation, …
- "for Whom?"(" for Whom the related activities to be performed?")
  - .. Stakeholders: such as learning institutes, students, mentors, tutors (teachers), …
- "on Which?"("on Which items the related activities to be performed?"
  - .. A wide variety of contents such as courseware, curriculum, …
- "How? " (" How the related activities to be performed?")
  - .. Using statistical methods for comparative analysis & modeling including simulation, and structured methods such as argumentation.
- "Why?" (" Why the related activities to be performed?")
  - .. Because statistical methods can help realize the advantages & disadvantages for the expected cases regarding the ongoing problem situation, and argumentation can help validate the priority of a method with respect to certain aspects.

Necessity Justification (H)

- "What is concerned?" ("What Necessity to be Justified ?")
  - .. Adaptability Assurance between content's features and user's requirements
- "By Who?" (" Who to Assure the Adaptability?")
  - .. Content generators in organizations, …
- "for Whom?" (" for Whom Adaptability Adjustment to be performed?")
  - .. Beneficiaries such as: staff, students, Instructors, mentors, …
- "on Which" ("on Which items Adaptability Adjustment to be performed?")
  - .. Contents such as: courseware, curriculum, test, …
- "Where & When?" (" Where & When Adaptability Adjustment can be satisfactory?")
  - .. In the learning institutes such as: schools, universities, …
  - .. In the period of content generation, evaluation, planning, …
- "How? " (" How Adaptability Assurance can be performed?")
  - .. Using various adaptation methods including filtering, customization, summarization, classification, enhancement, course allocation, …
- "Why?" (" Why Adaptability Assurance to be performed?")
  - .. Because of an increase in content creation costs, and a decrease in user's Learning Level

5.2 An Example for Generating Content for the Task of Assessment

The Second example to show the capability of the proposed approach to content creation is a case where content is to be created for a user where aim is to do Assessment within a certain scope in the area of e-learning. Taking this point into account, the content should be adjusted such that the user can be helped to make a reasonable approach to his/her steps in assessment. Our example is to create a content which can guide the assessor/ evaluator to a forum where in he/she can develop a framework for adapting an e-content to learner's conditions/ requirements in e-learning environment. Regarding this example, we consider segments such as "General Background", "Key Issue", "Proposed Approach Realization/ Implementation", "Validation/ Verification", as illustrated in Table 4. Taking the above discussion into account, the petit contents created with regard to some of the segments would be as follows.

A. General Background's Petit Content

Essential Definitions (L)

- "What is concerned?" ("What is to become subject to Definition?")
  - ○ .. A framework with regard to Assessment including solutions and routines of e-learning content evaluation in different applications and services .
- "By Who?" (" Who to perform Assessment?")
  - ○ .. Various e-learning experts involved in developing conceptual framework for e-learning requirement necessities.
- "for Whom?" (" for Whom Quality Assurance to be performed?")
  - ○ .. Developers and designers and other stakeholders who intend to present and use physical systems/services.
- "on Which" ("on Which Assessment to be performed?")
  - ○ .. A wide variety of contents and their development process

- "Where & When?" (" Where & When Assessment can be satisfactory?")
  - ○ .. The very phases of content development cycles
- "How? " (" How Assessment to be performed?")
  - ○ .. Using assessment perspectives& strategies from the view-point of learning paradigms& theories such as objectivism, cognitivism and constructivism.
- "Why?" (" Why Quality Assurance to be performed?")
  - ○ .. Because assessment perspectives & strategies from the view-point of learning paradigms can assure the accessibility to the goals & quality of the e-learning environment.

Necessity Justification (H)

- "What is concerned?" ("What Necessity to be Justified ?")
  - ○ .. Quality Assurance of e-learning content for instance in e-learning content production cycle.
- "By Who?" (" Who to Assure the Quality?")
  - ○ ..Various characters such as those involved in content creation like editors, graphic artists, multi-media developers, learning objects specialists (refer to General E-learning Framework) as the instances of Role-makers in Human-ware.
- "for Whom?" (" for Whom Quality Assurance to be performed?")
  - ○ .. Systems administrators, on-line course coordinators, instructor assistants, technical support specialists as the instances of Beneficiaries in Human-ware.
- "on Which" ("on Which items Quality Assurance to be performed?")

- ○ .. Technology requirements, learning objects, sharable content objects (SCO), courseware, as the instances related to content-ware.
- "Where & When?" (" Where & When Quality Assurance can be satisfactory?")
  - ○ .. In trading department of an organization
  - ○ .. When generating e-learning contents for exposing to the users is considered.
- "How? " (" How Quality Assurance can be performed?")
  - ○ Checking both efficiency and effectiveness in content generation process.
- "Why?" (" Why Quality Assurance to be performed?")

E-learning content is an important factor with regard to success or failure of e-learning services. Besides, production and representation of e-learning content is a complicated and expensive process to the extent that attention to the e-learning content status in different processes would be very important. Thus, the ability to assess the e-learning content is an important part of e-learning content design, production and representation processes.

A. Proposed Approach Realization/ Implementation's Petit Content

Explaining Implementation Procedure (H)

- "What is concerned?" ("What items to be considered in implementation of assessment?")
  - ○ .. E-learning content and environment, instructional team, learner support services, ...
- "By Who?" (" Who to implement assessment ?")

- ○ .. Administrators, project managers, instructional designers, editors, interface designers, ...
- "for Whom?" (" for Whom Implementation of Assurance is to be performed ?")
  - ○ .. Instructional teams, business developers, research& design coordinators, copyright coordinators, software vendors, ...
- "on Which" ("on Which Implementation of Assurance is to be performed ?")
  - ○ .. Budgeting, planning, scheduling, presenting, outsourcing projects components,...
- "Where & When?" (" Where & When Assurance is to be Implemented ?")
  - ○ .. Content development cycle, service outsourcing, vendoring cycle, ...
- "How? "(" How Implementation of Assessment to be performed ?")
  - ○ .. Techniques such as α-test, β-test, employing customer feed-backs, project management techniques, ...

6. CONCLUSION

A framework was discussed in this paper to create contents for helping organizational tasks based on an inter-play between the ontologies of the key segments and the problem context. The focal point in this regard is using the linguistically significant notions to be adjusted separately for each key segment once a certain organizational task is faced. An agent-based architecture was then discussed to show how human interaction with his/her surrounding organization can be realized through using this framework. Two examples were discussed, one in the domain of research and the other in the domain of assessment as two organizational tasks, to show how the petit contents belonging to some of the key segments can be created. For the moment, the content for a key segment is generated in such a way that the petit contents generated for different linguistically significant notions are added to each other in a sequential manner with no emphasis on the way they might get blended to produce a coherent content. Employing natural language processing (NLP) techniques to make such a coherence can be viewed as a prime part of future work.

REFERENCES

Badie, K., Kharrat, M., Mahmoudi, M. T., Mirian, M. S., Babazadeh, S., & Ghazi, T. M. (2009). *Creating contents based on inter-play between the ontologies of content's key segments and problem context*. The First International Conference on Creative Content Technologies (CONTENT 2009), Athens/Glyfada, Greece.

Fauconnier, G., & Turner, M. (1998). Conceptual integration networks. *Cognitive Science, 22*(2), 133–187. doi:10.1207/s15516709cog2202_1

Henry, P. (2005). E-learning technology, content and services. *Journal of Education and Training, 43*(4), 249–255. doi:10.1108/EUM0000000005485

Khan, B. (2005). *E-Learning quick checklist*. Information Science Publication.

Khan, B. (2005). *Managing e-learning strategies: Design, delivery, implementation and evaluation*. Information Science Publication. doi:10.4018/978-1-59140-634-1

Khan, B. (2006). *Flexible e-learning in an information society*. Information Science Publication. doi:10.4018/978-1-59904-325-8

Kumar, U., Kumar, V., Dutta, S., & Fantazy, K. (2007). State sponsored large scale technology transfer projects in a developing country context. [Springer.]. *The Journal of Technology Transfer, 32*(6), 629–644. doi:10.1007/s10961-006-8880-7

Mahmoudi, M. T., & Badie, K. (2004). *Content determination for composite concepts via combining attributes' values of individual frames* (pp. 211–215). IKE.

Mahmoudi, M. T., Badie, K., Kharrat, M., Babazadeh Khamaneh, S., & Yadollahi Khales, M. (2008). *Content personalization in organizations via composing a source content model with user model* (pp. 943–949). IC-AI.

Pereira, F. C., & Cardoso, A. (2002). Conceptual blending and the quest for the holy creative process. In *Proceedings of the 2nd Workshop on Creative Systems: Approaches to Creativity in AI and Cognitive Science*, ECAI 2002, Lyon, France.

Pizzi, D., Cavazza, M., Whittaker, A., & Lugrin, J. (2008). Automatic generation of game level solutions as storyboards. *Proceedings of the Fourth Artificial Intelligence and Interactive Digital Entertainment Conference*.

Ravi, J., Yu, Z., & Shi, W. (2009). A survey on dynamic Web content generation and delivery techniques. *Journal of Network and Computer Applications, 32*(5). Elsevier Ltd.

Shawyun, T. (1999). Expectations and influencing factors of IS graduates and education in Thailand: A perspective of the students, academics and business community. *Informing Science, 2*(1).

Smith, R., & Sharif, N. (2007). Understanding and acquiring technology assets for global competition. *Technovation Journal, 27*, 643–649. doi:10.1016/j.technovation.2007.04.001

Weiss, G. (1999). *Multi-agent systems: A modern approach to distributed artificial intelligence*. MIT Press.

Wooldridge, M. (2009). *An introduction to multi-agent systems*, 2nd ed. John Wiley & Sons Pub.

Chapter 11
Unconstrained Walking Plane as Locomotion Interface to Virtual Environment

Kanubhai K. Patel
Ahmedabad University, India

Sanjay Kumar Vij
SVIT, India

ABSTRACT

Locomotion interface with unidirectional as well as omni-directional treadmills creates infinite surface by use of motion floors. But realization of the motion floors requires a bulky or complex drive mechanism, thereby restricting practical use of locomotion interfaces. Secondly, it presents a problem of stability, especially while using these interfaces for simulating virtual walking of visually impaired people for spatial learning through virtual environments. As a result, such devices induce a kind of fear psychosis leading to difficulties in exploring virtual environment and thereby in cognitive map formation. A design of locomotion interface which reduces to a minimum these constraints is presented by first undertaking a literature review of the material existing in the area of locomotion interfaces and computer science. This proposed design of a locomotion interface to the virtual environment for spatial learning is aimed at providing unconstrained walking plane for building improved cognitive map and thereby enhancing mobility skills of persons with limited vision. A major design goal is to allow visually impaired people to walk safely on the device with a limited size, and to give them the sensation of walking on an unconstrained plane.

INTRODUCTION

The device proposed by us uses manual treadmill with handles to provide support, if required, thus allowing walking with assured stability. The structure of the interface, and control mecha-

nism of the device are presented and discussion of advantages and limitations of the interface is given. Different types of locomotion interface to virtual environment with their constraints and benefits are discussed briefly. We believe that by incorporating perspectives from cognitive and experimental psychology, mechanical and

DOI: 10.4018/978-1-61350-516-8.ch011

Copyright © 2012, IGI Global. Copying or distributing in print or electronic forms without written permission of IGI Global is prohibited.

electronics engineering, to computer science, this chapter will appeal to a wide range of audience - particularly computer engineers concerned with assistive technologies; professionals interested in locomotion interface to the virtual environments, including computer engineers, architect, city-planner, cartographer, high-tech artists, and mobility trainer; and psychologists involved in the study of spatial cognition, cognitive behaviour, and human-computer interfaces.

Every year about hundred thousand new blind cases are added to an estimated 314 million visually impaired people in the world, 45 million of them are blind. It includes around 15 million from India. The inability to travel independently around and interact with the wider world is one of the most significant handicaps that can be caused by visual impairment or blindness, second only to the inability to communicate through reading and writing. The difficulties in the mobility of visually impaired people in new or unfamiliar locations are caused by the fact that spatial information is not fully available to them as against it being available to sighted people. Visually impaired people are thus handicapped to gather this crucial information, which leads to great difficulties in generating efficient cognitive maps of spaces and, therefore, in navigating efficiently within new or unfamiliar spaces. Consequently, many blind people become passive, depending on others for assistance. More than 30% of the blind do not ambulate independently outdoors (Clark-Carter, D., Heyes, A., & Howarth, C. (1986); and Lahav, O., & Mioduser, D. (2003).

This constraint can be overcome by providing some means to generate cognitive mapping of spaces and of the possible paths for navigating through these spaces virtually, which are essential for the development of efficient orientation and mobility skills. Reasonable number of repeated visits to the new space leads to formation of its cognitive map subconsciously. Thus, a good number of researchers focused on using technology to simulate visits to a new space for building

cognitive maps. It need not be emphasized that the strength and efficiency of cognitive map building process is directly proportional to the closeness between the simulated and real-life environments. However, most of the simulated environments reported by earlier researchers don't fully represent reality. The challenge, therefore, is to enhance and enrich simulated environment so as to create a near real-life experience.

The fundamental goal of developing virtual learning environment for visually impaired people is to complement or replace sight by another modality. The visual information therefore needs to be simplified and transformed so as to allow its rendition through alternate sensory channels, usually auditory, haptic, or auditory-haptic. One of the methods to enhance and enrich simulated environment is to use virtual reality along with advanced technologies such as computer haptics, brain-computer interface (BCI), speech processing and sonification. Such technologies can be used to provide learning environment to visually impaired people to create cognitive maps of unfamiliar areas.

We aim to present various research studies including ours for communicating spatial knowledge to visually impaired people and evaluating it through non-visual virtual learning environment (NVLE), and thereby enhancing spatial behaviour in real environment. Different types of locomotion interface to virtual environment with their constraints and benefits are discussed briefly. Virtual environment provides for creation of simulated objects and events with which people can interact. Essentially, virtual environment allows users to interact with a computer-simulated environment. Users can interact with a virtual environment either through the use of standard input devices such as a keyboard, joystick and mouse, or through multi-modal devices such as a wired glove, the Polhemus boom arm, or else locomotion interfaces.

A locomotion interface is an input-output device to simulate walking interactions with virtual environments without restricting human mobility in a confined space such as a room. The locomotion interface is used to simulate walking from one location to another location. The locomotion interface can make a person participate actively in virtual environments and feel real spatial sense by generating appropriate unconstrained walking plane or ground surfaces.

The device is needed to be of a limited size, allow a user to walk on it and provide a sensation as if he is walking on an unconstrained walking plane. Locomotion interface with unidirectional as well as omni-directional treadmills create infinite surface by use of motion floors. But realization of the motion floors requires bulky or complex drive mechanism, thereby restricting practical use of locomotion interfaces. Secondly, it presents a problem of stability. As a result, such devices induce a kind of fear psychosis leading to difficulties in cognitive map formation. We have proposed a locomotion interface which reduces to a minimum these constraints. Our proposed design of a locomotion interface to the virtual environment for mobility learning is aimed at building improved cognitive map thereby enhancing mobility skills of persons with limited vision. A major design goal is to allow visually impaired people to walk safely on the device with a limited size, and to give them the sensation of walking on an unconstrained walking plane. The device proposed by us uses manual treadmill with handles to provide support, if required, thus allowing walking with assured stability.

To the best of our knowledge, no researcher has used treadmill-styled locomotion interface to enhance the spatial learning of VIP. Even though in the use of virtual reality with the visually impaired person, the visual channel is missing, the other sensory channels can still lead to benefits for visually impaired people as they engage in a range of activities in a simulator relatively free from the limitations imposed by their disability. In our proposed design, they can do so in safe manner. We describe the design of a locomotion

interface to the virtual environment to acquire spatial knowledge and thereby to structure spatial cognitive maps of an area. Non-visual virtual environment is used to provide spatial information to the visually impaired and prepare them for independent travel. The locomotion interface is used to simulate walking of visually impaired. The device is needed to be of a limited size, allow a user to walk on it and provide a sensation as if he is walking on an unconstrained plane.

The advantages of our proposed device are as follows:

- It solves instability problem during walking by providing supporting rods. The limited width of treadmill along with side supports gives a feeling of safety and eliminates the possibility of any fear of falling out of the device.
- No special training is required to walk on it.
- The device's acceptability is expected to be high due to the feeling of safety while walking on the device. This results in the formation of mental maps without any hindrance.
- It is simple to operate and maintain and it has low weight.

Following questions are addressed in this chapter:

- Does locomotion interface to non-visual virtual learning environment (NVLE) contribute to communicate the spatial knowledge and thereby the formation of a cognitive map of a novel space?
- Does the type of locomotion interface impinge on accuracy of spatial learning?
- Is navigating through treadmill-style locomotion interface less disruptive than navigating via conventional devices?

- Which are the major factors that influence the spatial knowledge communication to visually impaired people through NVLE?
- Which are the factors that mediate for enhancement of the navigation performance of visually impaired people?

We believe that by incorporating perspectives from cognitive and experimental psychology, mechanical and electronics engineering, to computer science, this chapter will appeal to a wide range of audience - particularly computer engineers concerned with assistive technologies; professionals interested in locomotion interface to the virtual environments, including computer engineers, architect, city-planner, cartographer, high-tech artists, and mobility trainer; and psychologists involved in the study of spatial cognition, cognitive behaviour, and human-computer interfaces.

LOCOMOTION INTERFACE

Figure 1 shows the overall diagram of human walking interactions with locomotion interface in computer simulated virtual environments. When a human walks on the locomotion interface, the walking motions of the human are recognized by several sensors such as motion trackers attached to the human body, and force sensors mounted on the locomotion interface. Then, the sensed information is used by the locomotion interface for generation of infinite unconstrained surfaces for continuous walking and the virtual environments for scene update according to motions of the human walking. Then, by feedback of visual and locomotion information, a human can immerse into virtual environments.

Locomotion interface can be used in several application fields such as virtual design, training, exercises, and walking rehabilitation. Locomotion interface can be used to help designers by providing a walk through modeled buildings, airplanes, ships, etc. Moreover, it can be applied to train fire fighters or army personnel, which are very difficult to do in real situations. For entertainment purpose, it can be used for winter sports such as ski and skates as well as general exercise such as promenade. Without locomotion interface, it is difficult to fabricate various terrain models. More applications using locomotion interfaces are well summarized in (Hollerbach, 2002).

Good number of devices has been developed over the last two decades to integrate locomotion interfaces with virtual environments. We have categorized the most common virtual locomotion approaches as follow:

1. Treadmills-style interface (Darken, Cockayne & Carmein, 1997; Hollerbach,

Figure 1. Walking interaction using a locomotion interface

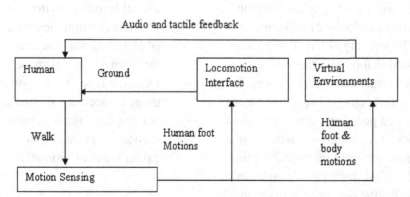

Xu, Christensen, & Jacobsen, 2000; Iwata, & Yoshida, 1999; De Luca, Mattone, & Giordano, 2007),

2. pedaling devices (such as bicycles or unicycles) (Iwata and Fuji, 1996),

3. walking-in-place devices (Sibert, Templeman, Page, Barron, McCune & Denbrook, 2004; Whitten et al, 2008),

4. the motion footpad (Iwata, Yano, Fukushima, & Noma, 2005),

5. actuated shoes (Iwata, Yano, & Tomioka, 2006),

6. the string walker (Iwata, Yano, & Tomiyoshi, 2007), and

7. Finger walking-in-place devices.

Treadmills in general cancel human walking motions by moving belts in the direction opposite to that of the human walking. The Sarcos Treadport (Christensen et. al., 2000) with linear treadmills allows a user to walk, run, and kneel at level ground or slopes. In addition, due to the mechanical tether that provided missing inertial forces, it is not possible to make the acceleration phase of locomotion energetically equivalent to the ground locomotion without applying forces to the body. Darken et al. (Darken et al., 1997) developed omni-directional treadmill (ODT) that is composed of two independent roller-belts, which are made from approximately 3400 separate rollers. But, it was reported that the walking on the ODT was not stable due to a misalignment between the direction of forward motion and the centering motion of the belt. Iwata (Iwata, 1999) developed omni-directional walking device using "Torus Treadmill", which is composed 12 sets of treadmills connected side-by-side and driven in a perpendicular direction. Mechanically, even though these 2D treadmills can allow the user to perform turning motions on these interfaces, they are highly complex and have difficulties in generating fast upright motions.

Wang et. al (Wang et. al., 2003) suggested the powered offset caster transmission to realize the omni-directional motion. Casters are placed on the top of a large piece of cloth material and move the cloth in a planar motion (x, y, and theta). Also, the deformable belt system of ATR's treadmill systems (Noma et. al., 2000) was suggested to allow uneven slopes to be displayed.

The basic idea used in these approaches is that a locomotion interface should cancel the user's self motion in a place to allow the user to move in a large virtual space. A treadmill can cancel the user's motion by moving its belt in the opposite direction. Its main advantage is that it does not require a user to wear any kind of devices as required in some other locomotion devices. However, it is difficult to control the belt speed in order to keep the user from falling off. Some treadmills can adjust the belt speed based on the user's motion. There are mainly two challenges in using the treadmills. The first one is the user's stability problem while the second is to sense and change the direction of walking. The belt in a passive treadmill is driven by the backward push generated while walking. This process effectively balances the user and keeps him from falling off.

The problem of changing the walking direction is addressed by Brooks, F. P. Jr., (1986) and Hirose, M. & Yokoyama, K., (1997), who employed a handle to change the walking direction. Iwata, H. & Yoshida, Y., (1997) developed a 2D infinite plate that can be driven in any direction and Darken, R. P., Cockayne, W.R., & Carmein, D., (1997) proposed an Omni directional treadmill using mechanical belt. Noma, H. & Miyasato, T., (1998) used the treadmill which could turn on a platform to change the walking direction. Iwata, H. & Fujji, T., (1996) used a different approach by developing a series of sliding interfaces. The user was required to wear special shoes and a low friction film was put in the middle of shoes. Since the user was supported by a harness or rounded handrail, the foot motion was canceled passively when the user walked. The method using active footpad could simulate various terrains without requiring the user to wear any kind of devices.

Other than treadmill-style interface, pedaling devices (Brogan, 1997) with an instrumented bicycle was employed to simulate the effect of going up or down hills. Iwata and Fujii suggested sliding machines (Iwata and Fuji, 1996) that utilize shoes with low-friction films on the soles and a brake pad on the toe to stop swing phase. Roston et al. (Roston and Peurach, 1997) proposed a "Whole Body Display" that has 3-dof motions. They utilized 3-dof parallel device driven by sliders. Iwata (Iwata, 1999) developed the "Gait Master" that consists of two 3-dof (x, y, and z) Gough-Stewart Platforms and a turntable. Even though the Gait Master utilized high rigidity and multi-DOF motion of a parallel device, the available stride distance is only 30cm, which is not large enough to allow natural walking with upright walking motion. Schmidt et al. (Schmidt et al., 2002) suggested a serial-parallel hybrid robotic walking simulator for neurological rehabilitation with 3-dof motions of sagittal plane at each foot. The device was composed of 2-dof translational parallel mechanisms, on which an electric motor was used to provide one rotation. Noma (Noma & Miyasato, 1998 and Noma & Miyasato, 1999) suggested the turning strategy to change the walking direction by using a treadmill platform mounted on a turntable. The user's turning motions during walking were canceled by rotating the turntable of the interface according to user's feet motion in swing phase. However, since their device had limitation for rotation angle, the system should stop and return the device to the neutral position when rotation approaches the limit. Bouguila et al. (Bouguila et al., 2003) developed the turntable type locomotion interface which can generate tilt motion with three air cylinders mounted beneath the turntable. But, their device couldn't allow a user to do real walking on the interface since the device couldn't cancel the forward or backward motions as well as lateral motions.

For various surfaces, Slater et al. (Slater et al., 1995) proposed locomotion sensing in virtual environments by "walking in place". Their device was used to recognize the gesture of walking using a position sensor and a neural network. For simulation of various walking surfaces, Hollerbach et al., (Hollerbach et al., 2001) simulated a slope display by utilizing mechanical tether and treadmill since treadmills through their tilt mechanisms are typically too slow to present fast slope changes. Similarly, by adding a force to the waist with a mechanical tether, realistic side slopes and stairs can be simulated (Hayward & Hollerbach, 2002 and Hollerbach, 2003).

MECHANICAL STRUCTURE OF UNCONSTRAINED WALKING PLANE

In order to experience the natural navigation on given virtual environments, the turning motion of the human during walking will be essential to change the walking direction and navigate various routes.

Figure 2 shows the structure of the proposed locomotion interface which is based on thorough

Figure 2 Mechanical structure of unconstrained walking plane. There are three major parts in the figure: (a) A motor-less treadmill, (b) mechanical rotating base, and (c) block containing Servo motor and gearbox to rotate the mechanical base.

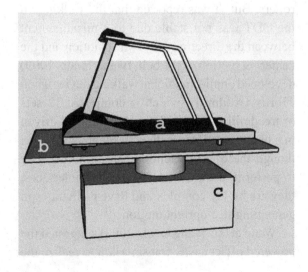

understanding of the human gait. As shown in Figure 2, our device consists of a motor-less treadmill resting on a mechanical rotating base.

In terms of its physical characteristics, our device's upper platform (treadmill) is 54" in length and 30" wide with an active surface 48" X 24". The belt of treadmill contains mat on which 24 stripes along the direction of motion, at a distance of 1" between two stripes are placed. Below each stripe, there are foot position sensors that sense the position and angles of feet. A typical manual treadmill passively rotates as the user moves on its surface, causing belt to rotate backward as the user moves forward. Advantages of this passive (i.e. non-motorized) movement are: (a) to achieve an almost silent device with negligible-noise during straight movement, and (b) the backward movement of treadmill is synchronized with forward movement of user leading thereby jerk-free motion. (c) Also in case of the trainee stopping to walk as detected by non-movement of belt, our system assists and guides the user for further movement. The side handle support provides the feeling of safety and stability to the person which results in efficient and effective formation of cognitive maps.

When user wants to take turn, rotation control system finds out angle through which the platform should be turned, and turns the whole treadmill with user standing on it, on mechanical rotating base, so that the user can place next footstep on the treadmill's belt. The rotation of platform is carried out using a servo motor. Servo motor and gearbox are placed in lower block which is lying under the mechanical rotating base. Our device also provides for safety mechanism through a kill switch, which can be triggered to halt the device immediately in case the user loses control or loses his balance.

The originalities and contributions of our device can be summarized in terms of mechanical, control, and systems as follows;

- Mechanical (hardware)
  - Modular design - single 2-dof planar device
  - Mechanical rotating base - omni-directional locomotion interface
  - More natural foot motions - Reconfigurable footstep size device
  - Control unit - Controls direction and speed of rotation
  - Novel 2-dof parallel mechanisms with single platform for foot motions - More natural foot motions
- Systems (applications)
  - Locomotion interface - 360° Walking simulations by using the single interface.
  - Generation of natural trajectories for normal gait movements of foot
- Control (software)
  - Modular Structure of Software
  - Generalized walking control algorithm of the locomotion interface for natural walking interactions at various walking modes such as turning and side-stepping.

CONTROL PRINCIPLE OF UNCONSTRAINED WALKING PLANE

Belt of treadmill of device rotates in backward or forward direction as user moves in forward or backward direction, respectively, on the treadmill. This is a passive, non-motorized, movement of treadmill. The backward movement of belt of treadmill is synchronized with forward movement of user leading thereby non-jerking motion. This solves the problem of stability. For maneuvering, which involves turning or side-stepping, our Rotation control system rotates the whole treadmill in particular direction on mechanical rotating base.

Human beings subconsciously place their feet at angular direction whenever they intend to take

Figure 3. Rotation of treadmill for veer left turn (i.e. 45°) (a) Position of treadmill before turning (b) after turning

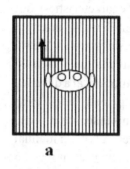

Figure 4. Rotation of treadmill for side-stepping (i.e. 15°) (a) Before side-stepping and (b) after side-stepping

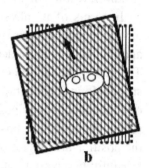

a turn. Therefore the angular positions of the feet on the treadmill are monitored to determine not only user's intention to take a turn, but also the direction and desired angle at granularity of 15°.

Turning

As shown in Figure 3, when foot is on more than three strips then user wants to turn and we should rotate the treadmill. If middle strip of new step is on left side of middle strip of previous footstep then rotation is on left side and if middle strip of new step is on right side of middle strip of previous footstep then rotation is on right side.

Side-Stepping

When both feet are on three strips then compare distance between current and the previous foot positions to determine whether side-stepping has taken placed or not. If it is more than a threshold value, the side-stepping has taken placed otherwise there is no side-stepping as shown in Figure 4. If it is equal or less than maximum gap distance then that is forward step, so no rotation is performed.

After determining the direction and angle of rotation, our software sends appropriate signals to the servo motor to rotate in the desired direction by given angle and, accordingly, the platform rotates. This process ensures that the user places

the next footstep on the treadmill itself, and do not go off the belt.

ALGORITHM FOR TURNING AND SIDE-STEPPING

Our algorithm to find direction and angle of turning is based on (a) number of strips pressed by left foot (nl), (b) number of strips pressed by right foot (nr), (c) distance between middle strips of two feet (dist) and (d) threshold for the distance between middle strips of two feet. The outputs are direction (Left Turn - lt, Right Turn - rt, Left Side stepping - ls, or Right Side stepping – rs) and angle to turn. Different possible cases of turning and sidestepping are shown in Figure 5.

The speed of rotation of the upper platform (r) measured in angle/sec is computed from average foot step size (f) in inches and relative velocity (v) that is speed of walking in feet/sec.

$r = \lambda * f * v$ Here λ is constant.

MODULAR STRUCTURE OF SOFTWARE

The modular structure of software for the unconstrained walking plane is shown in Figure 6. Main Controller is used for the initiating the system,

Figure 5. Various cases of turning and side stepping

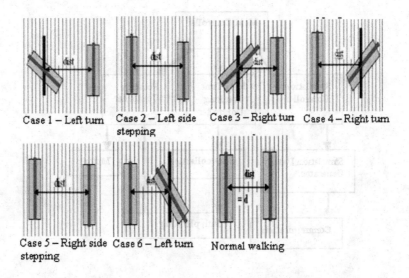

Case 1 – Left turn   Case 2 – Left side stepping   Case 3 – Right turn   Case 4 – Right turn

Case 5 – Right side stepping   Case 6 – Left turn   Normal walking

ALGORITHM

```
1:      If (nl>3) && (dist>d) then   //Case-1
2:      find θ
3:      left_turn = true //i.e. return lt
4:      elseif (nl==3) && (dist>d) then //Case-2
5:      θ = 15°
6:      left_side_stepping = true //i.e. return ls
7:      elseif (nl>3) && (dist<d) then //Case-3, in rare case
8:      find θ
9:      right_turn = true //i.e. return rt
10:     elseif (nr>3) && (dist>d) then //Case-4
11:     find θ
12:     right_turn = true //i.e. return rt
13:     elseif (nr==3) && (dist>d) then //Case-5
14:     θ = 15°
15:     right_side_stepping = true //i.e. return rs
16:     elseif (nr>3) && (dist<d) then //Case-6, in rare case
17:     find θ
18:     left_turn = true //i.e. return lt
19:     end if
```

which activates three controllers meant for different purposes. Real Time Tracking Controller tracks the user and feeds the tracking information to Simulation Controller which maps it to create

virtual reality environment for simulation of the walk as well as that of the locomotion interface.

Data Collection module receives the data of the feet position, while Path Planning module

Figure 6. Modular structure of software for unconstrained walking plane

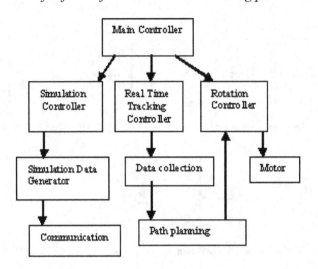

plans out the optimum path for a given source and destination points. On receiving the user's intention to take a turn, the Rotation Controller sends the signal to control the direction of treadmill on a mechanical rotating base.

SYSTEM ARCHITECTURE

Our system allows visually impaired persons to navigate virtually using a locomotion interface. It is not only closer to real-life navigation as against using the tactile map, but it also simulates the distance and the directions more accurately than the tactile maps. The functioning of a locomotion interface to navigate through virtual environment has been explained in previous sections. Computer-simulated virtual environment showing few major pathways of a college is shown in Figure 7. The user (trainee) chooses starting location and destination, and navigates by standing and walking on our locomotion interface physically. The current position indicator (referred to as cursor in this section) moves as per the movement of the user on locomotion interface.

There are two modes of navigation, first is – Guided navigation, that is navigation with system help and environment cues for creating cognitive

map and, second is – Unguided navigation, that is navigation without system help and only with environment cues. During unguided navigation mode, the data of the path traversed by the user (i.e. trainee) is collected and assessed to determine the quality of cognitive map created by the user as a result of training.

In the first mode of navigation, the Instruction Modulator guides the visually impaired person through speech by describing surroundings, guiding directions, and giving early information of a turning, crossings, etc. Additionally, occurrence of various events such as (i) arrival of a junction, (ii) arrival of object(s) of interest, etc. are signaled through vibration using consumer-grade devices and by sound through speakers or headphones. Whenever the cursor is moved onto or near an object, its sound and force feedback features are activated, and a corresponding specific sound or a pre-recorded message is heard by the participant. Participant can also get information regarding orientation and nearby objects, whenever needed, through help keys. The Simulator also generates vibration and audible alert when the participant is approaching any obstacle. During training, the Simulator continuously checks and records participant's navigating style (i.e. normal walk or

Figure 7. Screen shot of computer-simulated 2-D environments

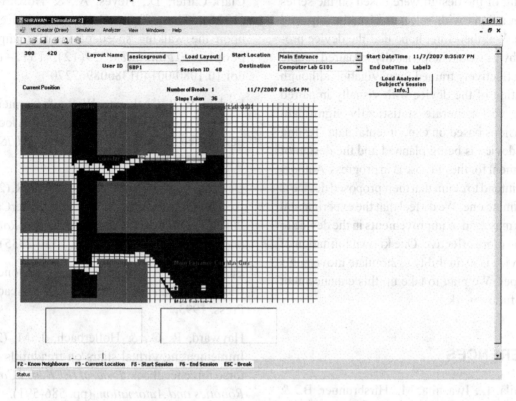

drunkard/random walk) and the path followed by the user when encountered with obstacles.

Once the user gets confident and memorizes the path and landmarks between source and destination, he navigates by using second mode of navigation that is without system's help and tries to reach the destination. The Simulator records participant's navigation performance, such as path traversed, time taken and number of steps taken to complete this task. It also records the sequence of objects encountered on the traversed path and the positions where he seemed to have some confusion (and hence took relatively longer time). The Data Collection module keeps receiving the data from foot position sensors, which is sent to VR system for monitoring and guiding the navigation. Feet position data are also used for sensing the user's intention to take a turn, which is directed to the Motor Planning (Rotation) module to rotate the treadmill.

DISCUSSION AND FUTURE DIRECTIVES

This chapter presents an unconstrained walking plane to facilitate visually impaired persons in developing mental maps of new and unfamiliar places, so that they can navigate through such places with ease and confidence. The proposed device although is of limited size but it gives a user the sensation of walking on an unconstrained plane. Its simplicity of design coupled with supervised multi-modal training facility makes it an effective device for virtual walking simulation. We tried to design a loud-less non-motorized locomotion device that helps user to hear the audio guidance and feedback including contextual help of virtual environment. In fact, absence of mechanical noise reduces the distraction during training thereby minimizing the obstructions in the formation of mental maps. The specifications and detailing of the design were based on the series of interactions with selected visually impaired people. We, therefore, hope that the device proposed by us would help visually impaired people to get effectively trained for navigation although the testing of the device with visually impaired people will generate statistically significant conclusions based on experimental data. Testing of the device is being planned and the design of experiment for the purpose is in progress. Authors do not intend to claim that their proposed device is the ultimate one. We do feel that the experimental results may lead to improvements in the device to become more effective. One known limitation of our device is its inability to simulate movements on slopes. We plan to take up this enhancement in our future work.

REFERENCES

Bouguila, L., Iwashita, M., Hirsbrunner, B., & Sato, M. (2003). Virtual locomotion interface with ground surface simulation. *Proc. of the International Conference on Artificial Reality and Telexistence*, ICAT'03.

Brogan, D. C., Metoyer, R. A., & Hodgins, J. K. (1997). *Dynamically simulated characters in virtual environments* (p. 216). SIGGRAPH Visual Proceedings.

Brooks, F. P., Jr. (1986). Walk through-A dynamic graphics system for simulating virtual buildings. *Proceedings of 1986 Workshop on Interactive 3D Graphics*, (pp. 9-21).

Christensen, R. R., Hollerbach, J. M., Xu, Y., & Meek, S. G. (2000). Inertial-force feedback for the treadport locomotion interface. *Presence (Cambridge, Mass.)*, *9*(1), 1–14. doi:10.1162/105474600566574

Clark-Carter, D., Heyes, A., & Howarth, C. (1986). The effect of non-visual preview upon the walking speed of visually impaired people. *Ergonomics*, *29*(12), 1575–1581. doi:10.1080/00140138608967270

Darken, R. P., Cockayne, W. R., & Carmein, D. (1997). The omni-directional treadmill: A locomotion device for virtual worlds. *Proc. of UIST'97*, (pp. 213-221).

De Luca, A., Mattone, R., & Giordano, P. R. (2007). Acceleration-level control of the CyberCarpet. *2007 IEEE International Conference on Robotics and Automation*, Roma, I, (pp. 2330-2335).

Earnshaw, R. A., Gigante, M. A., & Jones, H. (Eds.). (1993). *Virtual reality systems*. Academic Press, 1993.

Hayward, R. C., & Hollerbach, J. M. (2002) Implementing virtual stairs on treadmills using torso force feedback. *Proc. of IEEE Int'l Conf. on Robotics and Automation*, (pp. 586-591).

Hirose, M., & Yokoyama, K. (1997). Synthesis and transmission of realistic sensation using virtual reality technology. *Transactions of the Society of Instrument and Control Engineers*, *33*(7), 716–722.

Hollerbach, J. M. (2002). Locomotion interfaces. In Stanney, K. M. (Ed.), *Handbook of virtual environments technology* (pp. 239–254). Lawrence Erlbaum Associates, Inc.

Hollerbach, J. M., Checcacci, D., Noma, H., Yanaida, Y., & Tetsutani, N. (2003). Simulating side slopes on locomotion interfaces using torso forces. *Proc. of 11th Haptic Interfaces for Virtual Environment and Teleoperator Systems*, (pp. 247-253).

Hollerbach, J. M., Mills, R., Tristano, D., Christensen, R. R., Thompson, W. B., & Xu, Y. (2001). Torso force feedback realistically simulates slope on treadmill-style locomotion interfaces. *The International Journal of Robotics Research, 20*, 939–952. doi:10.1177/02783640122068209

Hollerbach, J. M., Xu, Y., Christensen, R., & Jacobsen, S. C. (2000). Design specifications for the second generation Sarcos Treadport locomotion interface. *Haptics Symposium, Proc. ASME Dynamic Systems and Control Division, DSC-Vol. 69-2*, Orlando, Nov. 5-10, 2000, (pp. 1293-1298).

Hollins, M. (1989). Blindness and cognition. In *Understanding blindness: An integrative approach*. Lawrence Erlbaum Associates.

Iwata, H. (1999). The Torus treadmill: Realizing locomotion in VEs. *IEEE Computer Graphics and Applications, 19*(6), 30–35. doi:10.1109/38.799737

Iwata, H., & Fujji, T. (1996). Virtual preambulator: A novel interface device for locomotion in virtual environment. *Proc. of IEEE VRAIS'96*, (pp. 60-65).

Iwata, H., Yano, H., Fukushima, H., & Noma, H. (2005). CirculaFloor. *IEEE Computer Graphics and Applications, 25*(1), 64–67. doi:10.1109/MCG.2005.5

Iwata, H., Yano, H., & Tomioka, H. (2006). Powered shoes. *SIGGRAPH 2006 Conference DVD* (2006).

Iwata, H., Yano, H., & Tomiyoshi, M. (2007). *String walker*. Paper presented at SIGGRAPH 2007.

Iwata, H., & Yoshida, Y. (1997). Virtual walk through simulator with infinite plane. *Proc. of 2nd VRSJ Annual Conference*, (pp. 254-257).

Iwata, H., & Yoshida, Y. (1999). Path reproduction tests using a Torus treadmill. *Presence (Cambridge, Mass.), 8*(6), 587–597. doi:10.1162/105474699566503

Lahav, O., & Mioduser, D. (2003). A blind person's cognitive mapping of new spaces using a haptic virtual environment. *Journal of Research in Special Educational Needs, 3*(3), 172–177. doi:10.1111/1471-3802.00012

Lynch, K. (1960). *The image of the city*. Cambridge, MA: MIT Press.

Medina, E., Fruland, R., & Weghorst, S. (2008). Virtusphere: Walking in a human size VR hamster ball. In *Proceedings of the Human Factors and Ergonomics Society 52nd Annual Meeting* (pp. 2102-2106). New York, NY: HFES.

Noma, H., & Miyasato, T. (1998). *Design for locomotion interface in a large scale virtual environment. ATLAS: ATR locomotion interface for active self motion*. 7th Annual Symposium on Haptic Interfaces for Virtual Environment and Teleoperator Systems. The Winter Annual Meeting of the ASME. Anaheim, USA.

Noma, H., & Miyasato, T. (1998). Design for locomotion interface in a large scale virtual environment. ATLAS: ATR locomotion interface for active self motion. *ASME-DSC, 64*, 111–118.

Noma, H., & Miyasato, T. (1999). A new approach for canceling turning motion in the locomotion interface. *ATLAS, ASME-DSC, 67*, 405–407.

Noma, S. Miyasayo, (2000). Development of ground surface simulator for tel-e-merge system. *Proc. of IEEE-Virtual Reality 2000 Conference*, (pp. 217-224).

Roston, G. P., & Peurach, T. (1997). A whole body kinesthetic display device for virtual reality applications. *Proc. of IEEE Int'l Conf. on Robotics and Automation*, (pp. 3006-3011).

Schmidt, H., Sorowka, D., Hesse, S., & Bernhardt, R. (2002). Design of a robotic walking simulator for neurological rehabilitation. *IEEE/RSJ International Conference on Intelligent Robots and Systems*, (pp. 1487-1492).

Shingledecker, C. A., & Foulke, E. (1978). A human factors approach to the assessment of mobility of blind Pedestrians. *Human Factors, 20*, 273–286.

Sibert, L., Templeman, J., Page, R., Barron, J., McCune, J., & Denbrook, P. (2004). *Initial assessment of human performance using the gaiter interaction technique to control locomotion in fully immersive virtual environments. Technical Report.* Washington, DC: Naval Research Laboratory.

Slater, M. (1995). Taking steps: The influence of a walking metaphor on presence in virtual reality. *ACM Transactions on Computer-Human Interaction, 2*(3), 201–219. doi:10.1145/210079.210084

Wang, Z., Bauernfeind, K., & Sugar, T. (2003). Omni-directional treadmill system. *Proc. of 11th Haptic Interfaces for Virtual Environment and Teleoperator Systems*, (pp. 367-373).

Chapter 12
Redefining the Role and Purpose of Learning

Stephen R Quinton
University of New South Wales, Australia

ABSTRACT

In an era marked by rapid change and increasing reliance on digital technologies, there is much evidence to suggest that the learning preferences and goals of today's students have become distinctly different from those of the past. Taken as a whole, it is conceivable that education as we have known it over the past two hundred years is poised on the verge of entering into a new realm of possibilities that will revolutionise accepted views on the role and purpose of learning. If such claims are correct, a highly adaptive, systemic theory of learning may assist to explain the complexities and implications of the present (emergent) and future (unknown) challenges facing educationalists and learners in the coming decade.

This chapter presents a philosophical treatise on how the author envisions the design of electronic learning environments in the future. The uniqueness of the theory of learning to emerge from this exploration lies in its capacity to dynamically adapt and evolve in response to the changing expectations of the teacher and the changing learning needs of the student. It promotes the concept of a continuum of possibilities and opens the way to move beyond the application of a static approach to learning design that is limited in its capacity to satisfy the needs of all, to the adoption of a dynamic, highly adaptable approach that begins to address the specific learning goals of every individual. Thus, educationalists are encouraged to explore what might be possible and not be constrained by current assumptions on how electronic learning environments are currently designed.

BACKGROUND: THE CURRENT STATE OF PLAY

As a general summation, the higher education system has been very successful in transferring skills and competencies for gaining formal qualifications, but has failed to encourage the higher order

analysis, problem solving, and metacognitive thinking skills required to exercise competence in creative and innovation knowledge construction in the twenty-first century. As currently practised, education in general not only has a tendency (often inadvertent) to stifle creativity and innovation, it is also inherently counterproductive to creative thinking.

DOI: 10.4018/978-1-61350-516-8.ch012

Copyright © 2012, IGI Global. Copying or distributing in print or electronic forms without written permission of IGI Global is prohibited.

Unmotivated teachers, irrelevant curriculum, substandard learning environments and uncomfortable conditions all contribute to unsatisfactory learning outcomes. Despite such limitations, many readers would recall that special teacher who was able to connect with our individual learning needs and motivations in a way that was inexplicable yet perceptively transformed the learning experience from a tedious, unrewarding chore to something that was intrinsically fulfilling and life changing. Thus it can be acknowledged that with the 'right' teacher, in the 'right' learning environment, using the 'right' resources, individual learners can be encouraged, motivated, and inspired to be highly creative and innovative.

It is the 'right' combination of components that this chapter will attempt to identify and explore as a theoretical basis for constructing dynamically interactive 'intelligent' electronic learning environments that respond to students' learning needs as and when required. Only then (I believe) will it be possible to inculcate the complex cognitive analysis strategies that enable learners to apply a creative mindset to solving the problems of tomorrow. Whilst it may be countered that creativity can never be taught, at the very least 'creative thinkers' can be better equipped with the cognitive tools required to derive elegant solutions to complex problems.

A more inclusive approach to articulating what 'learning' means is crucial to ensuring successful participation in a world that focuses more and more on the creative production of knowledge. Today's young people exercise their imaginations in ways 'undreamt' of a few years ago. They want (and demand) continuous education and ready access to 'always-on' knowledge. Only sophisticated design models that guide the development of innovative educational delivery practices to provide individualised learning experiences can meet these expectations.

The task of bridging the transition from 'traditional' learning practices to individualised human or electronically facilitated learning is fraught with difficulties as success in meeting learners' needs in a rapidly changing future requires radically different teaching methods, design approaches, and cognition skills. Any attempt to accommodate the skills and preferences of the current generation computer 'literate' student for example, must inevitably compel educational designers to think entirely 'outside the box' and consider real time interaction strategies that are in line with students' expectations and demands.

Such strategies include the provision of 'intelligent' cognition support tools capable of meaningfully interpreting natural language input; the dynamic assembly of customised content to deliver interactive assessment and constructive feedback tailored to students' immediate learning needs; and the capacity for learners to annotate and record ideas that generate user defined (manual) and automatic (dynamic) alternate information and teaching content relative to the current context. In effect, the nature of the learning environment must undergo a dramatic transformation, in particular with regard to the application of distributed information and communications systems, the cultivation of sophisticated metacognitive thinking strategies, and the efficient provision of universal access to high quality learning resources irrespective of device, location and time. In essence, I simply argue there is a need to articulate a new perspective on education as a means of exploring and identifying new strategies for constructing knowledge and solving problems.

INTRODUCTION: CHALLENGES AND OPPORTUNITIES

A major challenge facing educationalists today is to devise advanced learning design methodologies that employ emerging technologies to support the refinement of the essential knowledge creation skills of analysis, problem-solving and metacognition (that encompasses the capacity to apply tacit, experiential knowledge). Proficiency in the application of higher order cognitive competencies to the creative construction of knowledge extends well beyond the transmission of prescribed knowledge and facilitating practice in problem-solving activities.

The task of addressing higher-order learning skills not only extends to the many latent and complex tasks of determining how to model and structure knowledge, but also to identify the relationships that connect defined knowledge structures to selected teaching content while retaining contextual relevance and innate meaning. Resolving the inherent complexities of such obscure abstractions requires an unreserved commitment to: identifying the key properties and relationships that structure knowledge and thereby provide direction on constructing tailored learning strategies and navigational pathways; devising 'intelligent' design approaches to managing and transferring knowledge construction skills; and, enabling the efficient exploitation of digitised teaching resources using dynamic selection and contextualisation strategies.

Given the tenor of the preceding claims, learning solutions in the immediate future should strive to demonstrate a clear pedagogical and technological capacity to interweave all known aspects of the learning process within a highly adaptive (flexible) environment where the focus is on the needs and preferences of all individuals. In addition to improving learning quality and effectiveness, all learning environments regardless of the applied delivery mode, should support the divergent needs of current and past generations, from pre-school through to senior citizens. Equally critical, is research to determine the needs, preferences and propensities of disaffected ethnic groups, disabled people, and the mature aged.

The needs requiring most attention apply to the distinctive attributes of technology use and skills; personal influences and aspirations; values, perceptions and attitudes; and, current and future concerns. Moreover, emphasis must be directed toward identifying and allowing for variations

in learner behaviours, inter-personal communication skills, preferred learning strategies, and intelligence types relative to all generations, interests, and modes of learning. In essence, the individualisation of learning requires an evolving programme of design, experimentation and development augmented by qualitatively and quantitatively distinctive modes of interactive learning resources and just-in-time support.

Ultimately, such learning solutions should facilitate the personal development of all individuals through the provision of dynamically managed and/or self-directed environments that are characterised by flexible, ubiquitous, and individually adaptable delivery modes accessible at any time and from any place. By adding a systemic approach to designing flexible, individual learning solution, the focus of research is redirected towards the creation of new approaches to delivering learning while recognising the emergent need for learners to develop advanced knowledge construction skills that demand entirely new perspectives on the role and purpose of learning.

Instead of requiring learners to follow the same course en masse in the same manner, today's technologies have the capacity to facilitate just-in-time collaboration whilst permitting them to pursue their own individual approaches to learning. Technology can also assist lecturers to collaborate to develop and share resources and teaching strategies; and instead of competing for student numbers, technology can permit institutions to cooperate (internally and externally) to better serve the needs of students. Rather than separate the values and goals of education from the learning aspirations of the individual, the opportunity now exists to hand control back to learners so that they are empowered to learn, understand, and grow in response to their unique preferences, interests, and circumstances.

The problem however, is that in general the present education system is designed for the transmission of prescribed content, thereby making it difficult for many schools and universities to tailor learner-centred approaches such as individualised learning, small group learning, problem-based learning, or many other non-traditional pedagogical approaches. At a time when process skills are increasingly favoured over factual knowledge, skills involving teamwork, problem solving, evaluation, interpretation, application, and interaction have become more difficult to cultivate (Liber, 2004, p 135). Aside from the issue of learning process skills versus factual knowledge, there is also the perennial issue of personal experience versus conceptual understanding as observed as far back as Schopenhauer's time (Magee, 1997, p 6):

The chief drawback of formal education is that it reverses the proper order of experiences and concepts. Concepts have content and significance in so far as they derive from experience and can be cashed back into it. And the trouble with formal education is that it pre-empts experience in this regard by giving us our first knowledge of many of the most important aspects of life not through experience, from which we then abstract and generalise, but through concepts based on other people's abstractions and generalisations to which nothing in our own experience corresponds or can be opposed. So for all of us, reality is bound to be to some extent impeded by the observations and perceptions and of others; and so, therefore, is truly original thinking and insight.

People of all ages now prefer to define their own learning agendas and engage more actively in the learning process. No longer should governments, politicians, and institutions set the agenda: individuals and groups want some say in what and how they learn. The current change in expectations is challenging not just particular beliefs, but also entire belief systems (Mendizza, 2004, p 3). In essence, greater flexibility in accessing learning solutions and how well such solutions meet their needs has become important factors in the minds of learners. A more significant issue is the need for cultural change in the delivery of teaching

and learning. The use of digital technologies to support the learning process has the potential to radically change learning solution design through the introduction of highly interactive, intelligent models of learning.

This chapter does not aim to construct a new theory of learning for the twenty-first century. A task of that magnitude extends well beyond the bounds of a single chapter. Instead, it is argued that the key to achieving real change is to rethink the relationship between learning and information, and once defined, establish the groundwork for advancing such a theory by arguing the need to reconceptualise the design strategies that must be applied to the organisation of instructional information and teaching content. This approach will assist to enhance the learning process and promote the creative construction of knowledge. Alongside this approach there is the potential for the foundation of new theory of learning to emerge as new insights are identified and explored. The question for now however, is "what is the role of information in facilitating the learning process?"

Relationships Define Meaning, Understanding and Knowledge

Providing access to information without the benefit of equipping students with the cognitive skills to convert information into knowledge will prove detrimental to their future learning skills. Today's learners require skills to reflect on new materials, discuss their tentative understandings with others, actively search for additional information in ways that further illuminate or strengthen their understanding and ultimately assist to build conceptual connections to their existing knowledge framework (Brown & Thompson, 1997, p 75). There are other, equally important issues to consider. If graduates are to be proficient in creating new knowledge, then a clear understanding of the relationship between data, information and knowledge is critical. The importance of understanding the relationship between data, information and knowledge is made clear by Megarry (1989, p 50):

Knowledge is not merely a collection of facts. Although we may be able to memorise isolated undigested facts for short while at least, meaningful learning demands that we internalise the information: we break it down, digest it and locate it in our pre-existing, highly complex web of interconnected knowledge and ideas, building fresh links and restructuring old ones.

An examination of how these relationships are derived reveals a useful framework for describing the process of converting data into information and then into knowledge (or knowledge construction). This framework is comprised of three distinct stages of a knowledge construction continuum:

- Raw data that is collected and stored
- Information that is extracted from organised raw data
- Knowledge that is construed from information - by implication, this latter stage involves the cognitive processes of learning and conceptual understanding.

At the level of what we perceive to be reality, data is the given – derived primarily through sensory input. A unit of data represents a fact or statement of an event that is without relationship to other things. It is symbolic as in for example, the statement "it is raining". Information relates to a description, definition, or perspective on data that in some way has been cognitively processed to be useful. It provides answers to the 'what', 'who', 'when', and 'where' questions and embodies an understanding of relationship such as cause and effect. Building on the previous example, we can say "the temperature dropped fifteen degrees and then it started raining". At the next level of "making sense" of data (or interpretation), information becomes the equivalent of data, but nevertheless

is relative to knowledge, which in turn results only from 'higher levels' of conscious adaptation.

Knowledge requires the application of strategy, experience, and method to discern the pattern of relationships that connect information. To derive knowledge requires the application of data and information to determine the answers to the 'how' questions. Once discerned, the cognitive patterns provide a high level of predictability in relation to what has been described and what will happen next. Consider for example the statement "if the humidity is very high and the temperature drops substantially, then the atmosphere is unable to hold the moisture, thus resulting in rain". From this statement we can see that understanding is a cognitive and analytical process through which previously held knowledge is integrated with new information and then synthesised into new knowledge. In other words, it provides an appreciation of the 'why' factor as derived from the available data, information, knowledge, or prior understandings.

Given there are important distinctions to be made between the concepts of data, information and knowledge, the next step is to determine how to manage information (information literacy), and most critically, how information literacy skills can be applied to the conversion of information into knowledge. However, competence in information literacy does not necessarily lead to the ability to understand what information is and how to apply that understanding in productive and creative ways. If for example, we equip people with the skills to discriminate quality information from inaccurate information, then it is clear that a deeper understanding of information types and their distinctive characteristics is essential. We must also accept that the new economy will prescribe an information competency at many levels of abstraction and complexity.

As will become clearer, technology has created a level of complexity that extends well beyond the explanatory scope of the reductionist approach to deriving knowledge. In order to understand, interpret, synthesise, and derive new knowledge, a holistic, systems approach to learning design is required to manage the vast quantities of information that will be generated over the next decade. This added complication poses a dilemma in that it compels us acknowledge one crucial question: how can we even begin to manage such complexity without losing the capacity to construct new knowledge?

The Interconnectedness of Data and Information

Whenever unfamiliar data is encountered, we attempt to attribute meaning in some way by mentally forming associations with other data or information. Take the number '5' for instance. We immediately associate it with other cardinal numbers and determine its relationship is greater than '4' and less than the number '6'. Alternatively, we could consider the word 'time'. Again, the tendency will be to form associations with previously known contexts wherein the word 'time' was found to be meaningful. This act of association might take the form of 'a period of time', 'the time of year', 'take time to smell the roses', or 'we tried several times'. What is implied here is that without context, little or no meaning exists. To compensate for the absence of context, we associate the word or object with a known context, which may or may not prove valid. The point is that once data is given relationship, meaning is attributed and therefore, becomes information.

An explanation of the distinction between data and information in relation to learning and understanding is offered by Capra (1996, p 265). Whenever a fact is regularly encountered in a comparable context, we abstract that fact from the original context and in the process associate the derived meaning with the author's intended meaning. We are so conditioned to this process that the original meaning is somehow assumed to be encapsulated in the fact itself, whilst neglecting to note that the original meaning is embedded

in the context from which the information was originally extracted. The mistake often made is to refer to the derived meaning as information, when by definition a fact (the intended meaning) has become data (the replaced meaning). Thus, there are occasions where our attempts to create context amounts to little more than conjecture.

The extent to which a collection of data can be defined as information is dependent on the associations that can be discerned within the given set (Bellinger, 1997, p 2). This assertion implies that a collection of data for which there is no apparent relationship across the various elements of data is not information. That is to say, information is an understanding of the relationships between data elements, or between elements of data and other information. In effect, information represents an abstraction of ideas. A relational database for example, generates information from the data stored within it. Once deciphered in accordance with predefined rules, a simple message or a complex pattern of data becomes information. Hence, we can state that information is in fact data that has been given meaning by way of recognised relational connections. In other words, information is context dependent. However, we must bear in mind that not all relationships assist to construct useful meaning. The 'meaning' may be of some use, but at the same time is dependent on the individual's prior knowledge.

Whereas information requires an understanding of the relationships that connect data, it generally does not provide a foundation for understanding why the data is what it is, nor an indication as to how that data may change over time. Although information may be relatively static over time, the data it draws meaning from is constantly refined and updated. Thus, because information is dependent on the relationships between data and requires context to give it meaning, information generally holds little implication for the future. Even though as noted, information represents an abstraction of ideas, information itself does not create ideas. Ideas are integrating patterns that are derived through experience, not from information. This is because the human mind operates with ideas or concepts. Information is derived through ideas, not vice versa (Capra, 1996, p 70).

When considered in isolation, concepts can be perceived as conceptual nodes in an interconnected (networked) system of information and media. Representing knowledge as an integrated network of concepts and ideas as opposed to a linear, structured sequence of data and information permits students to discover previously unknown relationships and work through the connections in their own way. Students are enabled to reconstruct the network (or part of it) so that it more closely aligns with their prior cognitive experiences. Although on occasion there may be a need to impose a sequential or hierarchical structure to comply with predefined teaching objectives, some allowance can be given to providing flexibility in terms of individual learning strategies. Moreover, a networked structure of concepts permits students to conduct critical interrogations in order to form new conceptual understandings as prerequisite concepts are mastered. It is possible for example, to provide a networked structure of information in which sections within a document are connected and also interconnected across many separate documents that prompt students to conceptualise and formulate non-linear or multidimensional explorations of the presented teaching content (Harris, 2000, pp 36 - 7).

The implications of the preceding design approach extend well beyond requiring students to proceed through a body of information by observing prescribed pathways in a linear, regulated pace (the once-heralded attributes of computer-aided instruction). Instead, learners focus their investigations on questions informed by their own unique interests and experiences. They are able to proceed through and organise materials so that it makes personal sense, thereby enabling opportunities to test and comprehend their own heuristics. As new understandings emerge, they can discuss their findings with their tutor and their fellow peers.

This flexible 'connectivist' approach to discourse and inquiry has many advantages, not the least of which is the capacity to accommodate diverse personal or cultural learning styles. However, in order to manage this level of autonomy and faculty, learners must be experienced in the explicit use of tutorials, guides, indexes, and reading materials that are designed to provide both a basic grasp of what the textual source contains along with the models or heuristics that can be learned and adapted whilst being actively encouraged to develop as independent thinkers.

Beyond conceptual relationships there are patterns, where pattern is more than just a relation of relationships (Bateson, 1988, pp 9 - 11 and p 29). Pattern embodies a consistency and completeness of relations, which to an extent creates its own unique context. When patterned relationships are discerned amidst a collection of data and information, the potential for deriving meaning is increased. New knowledge is constructed when recognised meanings are cognitively analysed (processed) to interpret the implications inherent within each perceived connection (Bellinger, 1997, p 2). Therefore, the act of deriving meaning can be described as an interpolative and probabilistic process (Bellinger, Castro & Mills, 1997, p 2). Understanding and knowledge emerge through the acts of dialogue, observation, questioning, research, and how information is applied, absorbed, or communicated. That is, the process by which data and information is synthesised into new knowledge requires the application of cognitive, analytical, and language (communication) skills to identify patterns of relationships. New information is generated through the retention of information, ideas, and concepts, which when combined, produces new understandings (Daniel, 1996, p 2; Brown & Thompson, 1997, p 75). It is this process, albeit stated in simplistic terms that results in learning.

The relationship between understanding and knowledge can be compared to the difference between 'learning' and 'memorising'. The learning that assists in the creation of knowledge involves several important processes (Rucker, 1988, p 26). The first applies to the input of information through each of our senses, which is then processed by the human mind. The act of processing involves the generation of new information by posing questions, synthesising new understandings that are then assimilated into the individual's existing cognitive framework and stored as new knowledge. By sending and receiving information, as well as actively processing previously unknown information to construct and store new knowledge, learning is transferred from one individual to another (or to a group of individuals). Complete understanding encompasses the need to comprehend varied perspectives coupled with an ability to explain and a capacity to reason using one's individual knowledge construct. Thus, understanding involves a transformation of meaning based upon associations with personal experience and prior knowledge. It is at this point that the influences of technology on information organisation and knowledge construction require further exploration.

The Inherent Intelligence of Information Networks

The design of most electronic information management and learning delivery systems is motivated by the perceived need to organise information and media in order to facilitate efficient access to learning materials. Their underlying instruction sets and protocols tend to impose explicit organisation on information using preconfigured criteria (although some now permit the capacity to specify alternate organisations). Many electronic learning systems permit explicit (hyper) links to resources predetermined according to external judgements of relevance or importance, effectively pre-structuring and connecting the teaching resources prior to delivery (Rieh, 2002).

In theory, such delivery systems support learning either by overtly directing or cueing users to the next segment of information or to related information. While this method is useful for certain applications, it can also generate confusion and give rise to uninformative results. This is because learning resources designed for one purpose that are (inappropriately) applied to other purposes may contradict or be inconsistent with their original intent and hence, unsuited to learners' needs (Hammer, 2000; Leacock & Nesbit, 2007). Therefore as emphasised earlier, it is important to be aware that application and meaning varies according to context and hence produces variant learning outcomes. Such design may be relevant for example, in instances where the learner is encouraged to apply preferred learning strategies and so construct their own knowledge based on individual goals and interests (Hannafin, 1997, pp 255 - 8).

The benefit of associating apparently incongruous ideas or facts is in learning to discern the connections that support meaningful and useful interpretations, which in turn give rise to novel and insightful understandings. Thus, hyperlinked information and media afford opportunities to exercise effective learning strategies as it assists to highlight ideas and possibilities visually in ways that are not inherent in reading and reflection on print-based materials. Hyperlinks designed with a degree of built-in structure may serve as effective bridges or scaffolds to bring learners to a point where they can create more personal and distinctive organisations of the available materials. Alternatively, hyperlinked learning materials that facilitate varying degrees of unstructured and idiosyncratic exploration provide an indispensable learning strategy for students who are comfortable with independent learning activities. There are however, hidden problems to contend with.

In constantly dealing with large, uncoordinated compilations of electronic information and media, we are habituated over time to believe our knowledge systems are valid (Green, 2005). Consequently, the need to think more critically is ignored. For example, whenever we encounter a familiar sight such as another individual, we often perceive them as male or female without considering other possibilities. Alternatively, when confronted with the unexpected or anomalous such an earthquake, we make judgements or deliberate on what has occurred. In both instances, varying degrees of meaning are added and therefore each encounter leads to new information, albeit in different levels of detail. Regardless of how often or how well information is obtained and subsequently manipulated, at best it is an abstracted representation of ideas. To enable analysis and interpretation, the information presented requires prior knowledge, yet at the same time, presents a useful building block for constructing new knowledge (emergence). By itself, information does not transform into knowledge, but alters the individual's existing knowledge, thereby extending the potential for deriving new knowledge (Stenmark, 2002).

In determining a suitable design model for the delivery of educationally effective information and media, a productive start is to propose that the goal of learning is to assist students to develop 'holistic understanding' through active participation in learning environments modelled on networked systems of learning systems' (Campos, 2004). For such systems to support the cultivation of enhanced learning outcomes, the preferred model for learning design should be composed of multidimensional, multi-levelled, interconnected, and interrelated webs of data, information (including media) and knowledge. Thus, principles of networked ecological systems, self-organisation, and properties of emergence are introduced as integral components of learning environment design (Brown, 2002). In this refined systems model, information and media are not presented in a prescribed format, but instead are structured, destructured, restructured, interwoven and interrelated in highly complex configurations (self-organised) wherein all entities influence each other and the value of any is dependent on the purpose and context to which it is applied. As

a result, meaning, understanding and knowledge do not emerge as unidirectional, sequentially derived outcomes.

If the goal of scholarship and education is to provide accurate insights into reality, then students must be taught to understand that all knowledge believed to be 'real' should not be assumed to be factual and therefore, must be challenged through continual questioning and examination. However, the established strategy for explaining unknown phenomenon is to seek out further information. The problem is that instead of finding that the accumulation of information leads to a more predictable world, many of our assumptions are cast aside as we discover our beliefs are not as immutable as first believed (Dickau, 1999, pp 1 - 2).

As emphasised several times, the most productive learning occurs when new material is readily connected with what are often complex, multiple links of association. The capacity to act intentionally and purposefully on an accumulated understanding of previously derived personal knowledge guides the construction of new knowledge. Through this grounded process, knowledge and understanding catalyse, yielding something that previously did not exist or was not part of the individual's prior experience. Such cognitive action may involve forming an inference, solving problems, responding differentially to complex circumstances, identifying new connections, or articulating new ideas and perspectives. As Tan and Biswas (2007) attest, generating knowledge is what learners do with the information resources provided (or located) as they define their personal learning needs, generate hypotheses, and acquire new understandings. The key factors to note at this stage are that learners naturally construct knowledge as they process information resources, pursue their personal learning goals, construct working hypotheses, and create solutions to the problems at hand.

In attempting to articulate and subsequently derive a personal understanding of new ideas and concepts, learners must actively engage in the process of knowledge construction. One noteworthy, longstanding advocate of this view was Bruner who asserted that the final goal of teaching is to promote the 'general understanding of the structure of a subject matter' (Sprinthall & Sprinthall, 1981, p 281). Bruner reasoned that for learning to be of genuine value it is important for the student to actively form global concepts, build coherent generalisations, and to create what he termed 'cognitive gestalts'. As he explained, for learning to be meaningful, students should be encouraged to search for solutions by exploring alternatives and discovering new relationships. By first understanding the structure of an object or concept it becomes possible to perceive this same structure as an integral part of a greater whole that possess meaningful connections to other areas of knowledge.

For learners to understand the educational purpose of the content presented requires the lecturer and students to reach consensus on the distinctions to be made between data, information and knowledge. In so doing, are equipped to identify the relationships that lead to discernment of meaning. Without meaning, data does not equate to information, which in turn is not the same as knowledge. The implications raised in this statement are crucial to understanding how context may influence the creation of new knowledge. To derive complete understanding and knowledge from a given body of information requires a holistic, (systems) approach to learning where deriving insights into contextual relationships are essential for constructing meaningful, valid connections. To paraphrase Bruner, "you cannot study learning in the abstract and ignore the broader context – the environment in which that learning took place." As Laurillard (1993, p 268) puts it, the term 'holistic' can be applied to describe "an integrated knowledge structure, or an approach to learning that recognises knowledge must be integrated." Thus, it is more appropriate to view the process of knowledge acquisition as an integrated system of distinct sub-processes

each of which are fully dependent upon one another (Shank, 1996, p 173). It is at this point that a systems perspective on learning design begins to take shape.

The construction of new knowledge is not simply the result of the individual's capacity to act intentionally and purposefully on their accumulated experience and understanding. In order to be actively creative and innovative, learners require active encouragement to use their imaginations. To this end, educators must allow students to express their innate thoughts and ideas, and not intentionally or unintentionally stifle such expressions before their imaginations are afforded the right conditions and opportunities to inspire a substantive idea. Whilst it is acknowledged that not every kind of imagining is creative or productive, healthy, or even meaningful, but every attempt at exploring new relationships and meanings brings the individual one step closer to understanding something of the complexity that is the world around us. As will emerge in the pages to follow, the true test of a mature imagination is found in the capacity to follow unrestrained imaginings and then return to the starting point without losing sight of the original learning goal. Once returned, the learner is able to approach the problem under analysis from an entirely new and different perspective. Even young children experience uncontrolled flights of imagination and their play inspires rapid growth in thinking capacity, which the best attempts at training and conditioning can never match. The ability to direct this activity so that they return from flights of fancy to the point of departure with an expanded vision, is something we seldom teach, but is nevertheless the most useful skill we can learn (Dickau, 1999, p 1)

In a free-form learning environment, the role of the teacher is to create the conditions in which the student is encouraged to discern the underlying structure of a given subject. Once such conditions are established, Bruner insisted this type of 'discovery learning' provides a far more permanent and useful understanding of the subject matter than learning based on memorisation and conditioning. When an individual actively seeks to construct knowledge, incoming information is compared with existing cognitive structures. In this way, new meaning is given to existing patterns of organisation and experience which assists the individual to think beyond the information given (Bruner & Anglin, 1973, p 397). Patterns of relationships that lead to the creation of knowledge have a tendency to self-contextualise. That is, the pattern creates its own context, a factor that contrasts with the context dependency that in part, defines information.

Where this chapter is concerned, the question to be resolved is how to underpin the knowledge construction process with the theoretical principles required to devise a design approach for structuring data and information that affords the effective conversion of information into knowledge and in so doing, enhance/reflect/mirror the way the human mind naturally functions (Quinton, 2006). A potentially useful hypothesis is to propose that the goal of learning is to assist students to develop 'holistic understanding' through active participation in learning environments modelled on a networked 'system of learning systems'. To ensure effectiveness in terms of deriving enhanced learning outcomes through higher order thinking, it is argued that such a model should be composed of multidimensional, multi-levelled, interconnected and interrelated networks of data, information and knowledge.

STRUCTURING INFORMATION FOR LEARNING

A well-practiced method for creating artificial associations within electronic text is to organise it into linked nodes that may be as small as a word or a character, or as large as a book or collections of manuscripts. Pre-coded links or hyperlinks allow direct access to alternate information sources re-

gardless of location and format that have the effect of forming subsystems or collections of information. This non-linear form of organising text (and media) transforms the sequential constraints of printed material into a 'meta-structure' enhanced with interconnections and cross-references that provide access to multiple entry points and permit the flexibility to navigate in a manner determined entirely by the reader's interests, curiosity, and experiences (Burbules & Callister, 1996, p 3).

Non-sequentially linked data and information afford an educationally viable option for learning design as it reinforces the skills inherent in the processes of reading and thinking. Learners can construct a unique, personally meaningful, useful interpretation of the displayed learning materials and increase the opportunity to identify new associations from amongst the given data and information. The benefit of learning environments that allow a degree of unstructured and idiosyncratic exploration is in learning to discern the associations that assist to support meaningful and useful interpretations. One design solution is to employ hyperlinked content to prompt learners to apply multiple strategies to enhance their problem solving and information retrieval skills, noting as always that in all complex learning tasks, teacher guidance and modelling exercises a crucial role. Students follow teacher directed pathways through the electronic text, observing and learning how someone with experience searches, collects, and connects information to derive meaning.

Alternatively, hyperlinked pathways could assist teachers and students to focus more on the important learning processes of interpreting and organising information, and less on the acquisition of facts. Either way, students are exposed to a wider range of learning 'possibilities'. A third approach involves the use of 'scaffolding' concepts where the teacher engages learners at an early stage with explicit explanation and guidance, then leads them through a succession of electronic links. The supports are gradually removed as learners gain greater confidence and become more independent in their explorations (Burbules & Callister, 1996, p 16). The more links that are established amongst the given body of material, the greater the exposure to additional relational concepts.

A more radical approach to organising information and media is to consider the possibility that all nodes of information are equal and treated as through there is no hierarchical structure. Hence, no node is considered central or more important than other nodes. From this perspective, learners may form new and previously unimagined associations (links) opening the potential for creativity and innovation in ways that are not possible using print-based materials. The key is to determine the conditions under which it is appropriate to free up and decontextualise each node and thus provide an effective means of identifying useful and novel 'lateral' connections. The optimal representation of knowledge is achieved when one segment of information is connected with as many related concepts as possible. This approach expands the opportunity for deriving a comprehensive understanding of a given concept and its related concepts (Korytkowski & Sikora, 2007, p 713).

Whereas the traditional 'linear' mode of connecting ideas or facts is limited to 'manageable' subsets, the notion of levelling out and equalising all nodes along a continuum of non-hierarchical concepts effectively allows for the number of nodes to be boundless. This is because virtually anything is assumed to be relevant, interesting or important. By drawing on a broader range of sources, the number of potentially useful connective data points is increased considerably, in turn diversifying exposure to include otherwise unknown associations.

The notion of all elements being equal provides a basis for designing learning systems that have the capacity to impose patterns of organisation on existing information (regardless of how it was originally organised – or unorganised) and thus facilitate the learner's capacity to imagine and create new patterns of relationships. In essence, this design model represents a move away from the relatively inflexible, pragmatic, instructivist approach to learning, towards a broader, more open and interpretive exploration of the latent possibilities held within all structured and unstructured information and media. This line of thought will be continued later as a 'continuum of equal possibilities'.

Notwithstanding the potential advantages of unbounded, free form associations, the concern is that unstructured information can lead to undesirable learning experiences. There is the need to recognise the risks in designing electronic learning solutions that provide either too much information with an unbounded structure, or confine learners to a prescribed, inflexible structure that may contain inaccuracies due to the unintended (or even intended) introduction of implicit judgments. Thus, not just any association will serve the learning process. All the while, educators must remain mindful of the fact that there are certain accepted and well-proven conventions and heuristics (Burbules and Callister, 1996, p 5) that promote meaningful and useful interpretations. Ultimately, in order to develop deep understanding, learners sometimes need to make personal choices and at other times, there is a need to impose restrictions.

Care must also be given to avoiding chaos, arbitrariness, as well as the counterproductive and time-consuming exposure to permutations and juxtapositions that are without purpose or application. The meaning of data and information varies from individual to individual due to the innate influences of divergent backgrounds and perspectives that are further complicated by the unique intentions of every learner. The key to successful learning design is to determine when it is appropriate to free up and decontextualise each node of information and so provide an effective means of deriving useful and novel 'lateral' connections. It is only then that the juxtaposition and contradiction of concepts and ideas afford the conditions required to construct knowledge. The question is how to design such solutions whilst ensuring the risks are reduced to a minimum.

Hypertext configured systems have the capacity to impose patterns of organisation on existing information and to facilitate the user's ability to imagine and create new patterns of organisation. In essence, hypertext represents a move away from a relatively inflexible, pragmatic, scientific approach to deriving knowledge towards broader, more open and interpretive explorations that have the potential to produce refined or even new knowledge structures. It is through the cognitive processes of understanding and interpretation rather than the information or knowledge provided that ultimately assists in the learning process. That is, the object of learning is not at all the object per se; it is the process of learning. The symbols we use to interpret reality (words, numbers, and maps) are not the object or event they represent.

As (Ingraham, 2000, p 1) explains, the intellectual challenge is to explore the "limits of interpretation within the potentially infinite play of signification". As will be clarified in the following section, this somewhat lateral perspective clearly moves the process of deriving knowledge beyond the constructivist approach and begins to align with the notion of a continuum of possibilities. Imagine for a moment, a learning environment in which the technology itself assists students to extend their thinking processes to connect with and explore the 'reality of reality' and thus expose the ingrained illusions that have moulded a surrogate reality formed over time in the minds of learners.

A CONTINUUM OF EQUAL POSSIBILITIES

There exists an assumption that digitised information needs to be organised and classified (Peterson, 2006, p 4). In the digital world, there is no requirement for a categorisation or organisational system, which if applied, inherently imposes artificial constraints on how electronic data and information are organised. The application of categorisation strategies to electronic text and media

is incongruous to human thinking as it does not permit sufficient departure from traditional habits of mind and practices to the full extent that is afforded by digital technologies (Shirky, 2006, p1).

What is emerging are ways of organising information that are more organic than current categorisation schemes allow. Two factors make this possible. One as outlined earlier, is the hyperlink, which can point to anything; the other is the tag, which can be used to label anything. The essential strategy is free-form tagging, which is removed from all known categorical constraints. Instead, what is possible in the electronic world are links that act as symbolic connections, aliases, or shortcuts. Taken to its ultimate outcome, if enough links are established, the need for a hierarchical file classification system no longer exists – the links alone are all that is required (Shirky, 2006, p 10). Already the web is demonstrating how significant value can be extracted from complex, disorganised information sets.

The Web is a world where it is possible to allocate a unique identifier to everything. The universal resource locator (URL) provides globally unique identifiers for everything that is directly or indirectly released to the Web. Whenever a URL points to the contents of a webpage, the pointer is direct. If a webpage displays a link to a resource located elsewhere on the Web, the pointer is indirect. For something that does have not a specific location and requires multiple layers of indirection, a uniform resource identifier (URI) is used. Once pointers exist for all elements of a given collection of information, anyone can label each pointer and tag URLs so that they are more useful to their needs without conforming to a top-down organisation scheme (Shirky, 2006, p 16).

In addition to links, the presence of unique labels (tags) allocated to each and every resource regardless of its location (physical or virtual) means that no categorisation/classification strategy is needed. Applied at a global level, the notion of a continuum of possibilities becomes slightly easier to grasp. Not only can resources be uniquely labelled, so too can the links that connect them regardless of whether the configuration is one to one or one to many. The ability to free-form label links combined with the potential for deriving meaning without restriction in the number of interpretations introduces the possibility of generating novel ideas and concepts each time an inquiry is made or unfamiliar information is encountered.

Once such an arrangement is established, then each resource along with all their links can be statically or dynamically metatagged using any strategy deemed appropriate – taxonomy, folksonomy, ontology, or concept analysis. In this way, no file system, predefined categories, and hierarchical structuring need to coexist alongside the link structure. If deemed essential, the unique identifiers in combination with the metatag information permit such organisation. By foregoing formal classification, learners can apply words, numbers, acronyms, concepts – whatever makes sense to them personally, without restriction or regard for any other preference or method. Thus, an enormous amount of user-generated organisational arrangement is made possible. By allowing learners to tag information and then to collaboratively aggregate the tags, more refined, alternate organisational systems emerge that have the effect of assisting individuals to recognise they are providing value to each other, often times without even realising it (Shirky, 2006, p 23). The use of metatags (whether manually or dynamically constructed) as described here allows information, ideas, facts and concepts to be viewed as components of a complex 'neuronal' net, any part of which can trigger any other part.

The foregoing paves the way to considering Pearce's (1974, p 194) description of Piaget's highest form of operational thinking: "the ability to hypothetically consider any state along a continuum of possibilities as potentially equal to any other state, and return to the same state from which the operation began". If an inquiry to discover something unknown is conducted along the lines of what Piaget proposed (and expounded on

by Pearce with his notion of 'reversibility thinking'), then unrealised opportunities for breaking through accepted cognitive boundaries become evident. By conceding that such a seemingly impossible notion may be feasible, new pathways could be opened to empower learners to redefine normalised views of reality and consider new ways of thinking that give rise to unimagined strategies for analysing information and building knowledge. The potential is for the minds of learners to be exposed to new understandings and ideas, new ways of defining what it means to learn, what needs to be learned, and most important, how to learn (Dickau, 1999, p1).

There are no fixed rules, only goals and the possibilities that can be imagined in order to achieve those goals. By possibilities, I refer to a continuum of equal possibilities in which all data, information and knowledge interrelate and interact without structure or favour, and with only one purpose – to facilitate learning in a way that best accommodates learners' individual preferences, values, and needs. While the concept of a continuum of equal possibilities may at first seem antithetical to accepted thinking strategies, consider that even partial acquiescence presents new opportunities to reflect on alternate views and to explore options that in many instances would be dismissed as impractical. Such a model of learning inverts the traditional linear teacher-to-student transmissionist approach, as does it also for the rhetoric of most curriculum frameworks. By encouraging students to process information independently, identify and derive meaningful relationships, recognise patterns of principles and properties, generate new knowledge, and eventually, devise proto-theories or hypotheses to explain why the newly derived connections make sense to them.

A theory of learning that faithfully supports such an approach might also allow for an open systems model for identifying relationships among networked repositories of unorganised information. In this model, there are levels within levels, all interconnected through a complex network of relationships that unite every identifiable element and can be adapted and readapted to form linear, hierarchical and even heterarchical (where connections can be established from many different points to any other position within the overall structure) pathways throughout all system levels.

In a complex system, we know that the solution is out there somewhere; it exists in the informal networks and communications of trust and interdependency that are the day-to-day reality of any large organisation or group. By increasing the number of connections, the greater the likelihood a new idea, concept or understanding will emerge. Once emergence has occurred, a new pattern of understanding is established and is self-evident, albeit only in retrospect (Snowden, 2000, p 20).

Then, because most information repositories are inherently chaotic (witness the results of an Internet search) in that they are mostly independent of context, it is technically feasible to reshape the information (and therefore) the knowledge they contain into a multitude of knowledge structures to accommodate individual cognitive schemas and so encourage wider engagement in a given learning activity. Such structures guide the construction of pathways that learners observe as they strive to comprehend and master an understanding of the core concepts embedded within the displayed information and media. The strategy of turning links on or off (link-hiding) permits the establishment and adaptation to individual pathways. Add to these properties the capacity to automatically organise content in response to user input that prompts learners to recognise emergent properties (through pattern recognition) within complex information systems, then we begin to understand how learners can be exposed to deeper, more comprehensive learning experiences.

If we accept the world is made up of an infinite number of systems in which there are unlimited possibilities, how then it is possible to construct useful knowledge without consuming inordinate amounts of time and eventually risk overwhelm-

ing the learner? Out of practical necessity, any attempt to identify valid connections must be finite in number, whereas in theory all possibilities along a continuum of infinite possibilities are there to be explored. Given such unmanageable potential, we should not assume that valid (useful) connections will always be made nor overlook the fact that there may be zero probability of a valid connection. Another, more productive way to deal with the complex task of managing infinite possibilities is to look to the manner in which the human brain functions.

A useful comparison with the learning model unfolding above can be found in the work of one of the forefathers of hypertext Vannevar Bush (1945, pp 101 - 108). He held the view that 'the structure of hypertext environments parallels and can facilitate the ways in which we learn: non-sequentially, dynamically, and interactively, through associations and by exploration'. Thus, the structure and the function of the brain can be favourably compared to the underlying concepts and principles that explain systems, subsystems, and networks. The view of human thinking that mimics the key properties of networked systems is further strengthened by Bush's argument for applying artificial hyperlinks to electronic text (Bush, 1945, pp 101 - 108):

The human mind...operates by association. Man [sic] cannot hope to fully duplicate this mental process artificially, but he certainly ought to be able to learn from it. One cannot hope to equal the speed and flexibility with which the mind follows an associative trail, but it should be possible to beat the mind decisively in regard to the permanence and clarity of the items resurrected from storage.

From the perspective of constructing an efficient information retrieval mechanism, complete connectivity among all system components is the perfect arrangement. It is not feasible of course to interconnect all information, but as a metaphor, the notion that everything is connected is a useful strategy for inspiring new ideas. Assuming all components within a system are fully interlinked, the task of establishing meaningful relationships or locating useful information is unwieldy to manage and impossible to process, particularly where the goal is to innovate. This is where 'intelligent networks' and globally unique identifiers (URLs) which can be used to point directly, indirectly, or even randomly to indeterminate resources play a crucial role.

INTELLIGENT NETWORKS OF LEARNING OBJECTS

Earlier, hypertext technology was raised as an example of a familiar tool for users of the Internet. A less familiar technology is learning objects – essentially segments of self-contained teaching content that can be interlinked to form a myriad of interrelationships at multiple levels extending from a single character to complete literary works. Content management systems can search, retrieve, and assemble this independent content for any purpose, in any order, recontextualise it, and present it at any level of complexity learner can manage. Thus, the application of a continuum of equal possibilities to exploring the contextual relationships among electronic content becomes technically feasible, opening up unimagined opportunities for learners to look outside the prevailing disciplinary and cultural dimensions to examining the reality that lies within and beyond.

The notion of a fully equalised field of information opens the way for exploring alternate views and to consider new design options. To this end, I refer to the key principles of a systems-based learning model. By discarding the tendency to apply a linear or a hierarchical structure, it is feasible to design a networked system of learning objects comprised of concepts, information, and other resources that interconnect with other sub-systems and systems of objects. In this way, selected learning objects can be assigned to provide a single learning activity, or be interconnected with other objects to form additional learning activities. Networked learning objects can incorporate unlimited multidimensional interrelationships and expose the learner to richer, more productive learning experiences than are attainable using other design models. This is because the information provided by each learning object becomes part of a larger whole, to be explored and analysed in a multitude of ways. A single learning object may be combined with other learning objects to create structured learning activities according to need. A degree course for example, may comprise several units each of which may be made up a number of modules. A module may comprise a tutorial lesson, an assignment, and a test for example. If each of these levels of a traditional course structure were redesigned using learning objects, then this same arrangement could also be viewed as nested systems containing objects and sub-systems of objects.

In effect, there are multiple nested systems made up of learning objects housed within other learning object systems, yet at every level, all remain intact and are therefore independent of each other. Potentially, each learning object may interact with or be interrelated with other objects positioned within its own level, or to objects that are contained within other levels throughout the entire learning environment. In other words, it is possible to combine or recombine learning objects in many different ways to represent the familiar unit, module, or lesson. For example, in a teaching unit that contains a test and an assignment, the unit test may also interact with a grade table held in a database assessment object. Or a unit may contain a learning activity that is also programmed to interact with a video object stored in a separate database repository. The video resource could be used as a navigational tool to assist the leaner to progress through the displayed learning activity. Alternatively, the same video object (or parts thereof) could be reused in another context to support a separate learning activity. As a second alternative, an incorrect response to a question could be programmed to trigger a supplementary learning object to illustrate a complex concept from another perspective. Provision may also be made for what could be loosely described as 'intelligent' response procedures. For example, sub-groups of learning objects could be dynamically assembled to form customised responses based on progress, areas of difficulty, student input, and the need for revision. A number of techniques that can be applied include a capacity to:

- Alert the student to the need for revision and present appropriate alternate material
- Require the student to repeat a certain sequence or even work with alternate material a set number of times
- Dynamically generate customised quizzes, assignments, or activities that correspond to each student's specific needs and competence levels.

The most optimal design is to create objects that have a high degree of interrelatedness and context independence that are combined with support tools and strategies for enhancing the learner's understanding. However, the degree of complexity versus the learner's ease of understanding will be dependent upon the extent of interrelatedness and context independence that is built into the design. As the degree of interrelatedness increases, the higher the likelihood the content will be more context dependent (Bellinger, 1997, p 2). Herein are a number of crucial design issues to consider. A learning object with a high degree of interrelatedness may convey too much information and therefore prove difficult for the learner to comprehend the intended purpose. Conversely, an object that contains an inadequate amount of information with little interrelatedness (therefore context independent) may fail to provide a rewarding learning experience. Consistent with the notion of reusability, the contextual neutrality of reusable learning objects is in itself a barrier to

pedagogical flexibility. The higher the level of contextualisation contained within a given learning object, the greater the difficulty in repurposing or reusing that object for other educational purposes.

The level of understanding expected of the learner is contingent upon the relative quantities of data, information and knowledge provided and the interrelationships established by the content designer to support the development of meta-cognitive thinking skills. The deeper the level of understanding required, the greater the complexity of design and difficulty that will be experienced by the learner. A large concentration of facts for example, may provide little learning value if the amount of meaningful information provided is inadequate. Conversely, the provision of too much information without the provision of basic facts and opportunity for understanding, may cause unnecessary confusion or even prove to be overwhelming. Ideally, an object-based learning activity should provide the correct blend of interrelated data, information, knowledge considered essential to achieving the expected learning outcomes. The interconnectedness of the various components is such that they should form a highly interrelated set of data, information, and knowledge that is not only tailored to student's specific needs in direct accordance with the intended learning outcomes, but also increases the opportunity to generate new ideas through exposure to a continuum of possibilities.

If the preceding example is extended to include a learning object made up of smaller (sub) objects, then the above configuration still applies. However, what is now included is the complexity of forming relationships between selected sub-objects, and the need to ensure each object interrelates with the broader systems levels that as a whole combine to facilitate the intended learning outcomes. In theory, there are no limits to the number of 'system' levels and hence, the degree of flexibility that can be built into this type of learning environment. The limits, if any, will be due to everyday practical teaching needs and time constraints. Not-withstanding the complexities involved, the educational benefit of a more natural (systems) learning approach is highly appealing given the potential for designing highly complex and dynamically adaptable learning experiences.

To illustrate the preceding points further, it is useful to view the act of creativity or knowledge construction as a cognitive activity in which the abstract compilation of previously unrelated mental structures or ideas results in the formation of an emergent whole. Anyone who has experienced that moment where a new idea arises without apparent prior connection would agree that the resultant outcome is often much more than the mere sum of a collection of disconnected thoughts. However, it is not just the sum of the parts that is important, but of comparable significance is the notion of the creative process as an expression of the relationships between the various abstract components. The formation of each new synthesis leads to the emergence of new patterns of relationships with each more complex than the previous, each extending to higher and higher cognitive levels of a mental hierarchy. Koestler's (1978, pp 131 - 33) view is that contrary to popular beliefs, scientific discoveries do not occur by producing something out of nothing. Instead, scientists combine, relate, and integrate known, but previously separate ideas, facts, and associative contexts. The scientist aims to synthesise prior knowledge in a way that adds new levels of understanding to the existing knowledge hierarchy. For some, the synthesis of previously unrelated knowledge may result in what is commonly referred to as the 'aha' effect where apparently disparate bits of information suddenly click into place. At this point new knowledge is realised, and in the process we strive toward higher levels of cognitive understanding.

A WARNING: THE POTENTIAL FOR DISASTER

Piaget's highest form of operational thinking is grounded in a highly developed imaginative capacity. The core foundation of a well-developed and rational imaginative structure is essential for driving creative thought and ideas. To develop this higher order skill, imaginative nurturing throughout the developmental process is essential. Without it, the deeper layers or realms of truly significant insight are not reachable.

Electronic hypertext information offers great potential for extending the learner's mind beyond their current context to consider relationships at the click of a mouse button. The problem with hypertext is that the same author that prepared the main text also predefines the embedded hyperlinks and therefore decides what relationships are embedded before the learner commences reading. The predetermined relationships may or may not be meaningful to the learner, thus elevating the risk of retarding the learning experience rather than enhancing it.

Whenever the learning process involves exploration and discovery, the ambiguity of learning, not teaching gives rise to the potential for chaos. There is no prior experience, expertise or belief system to draw on, and thus the limits to deriving comprehension and understanding are boundless. Such systems are turbulent, they operate under conditions of extreme uncertainty, and so at best learners operate on the edge of chaos, at worst they are paralysed by the chaotic situation (Snowden, 2000, p 3).

In effect, hypertext linked material offers students with less developed cognitive structures, the equivalent of 'calculator-enabled' short cuts for attaining mathematic perception and precision even though they do not have the capacity to fully comprehend how the result was achieved or possess the ability to determine the implications hidden within what appears to be a correct solution (Peterson, 2006, p 4). Despite the author's intent, readers of texts on the Internet become individual interpreters. Without deeper levels of understanding and experience, the learner believes that what has been achieved or imagined is true insight. From a learning perspective, such adverse consequences are a disaster and may prove detrimental to the learner's capacity for effective analytic ability for life. This outcome raises two potential dilemmas. On the one hand, if considering the author's intent, personal interpretations and judgments introduce the likelihood the learner's judgement is incorrect. On the other hand, when multiple interpretations abound and all are afforded equal significance, then at some point the entire system of possibilities will become unusable as it will not be feasible to distinguish accurate meanings.

Technology is providing greater capacity to generate and store large quantities of information. As the power of technology increases, so too does the quantity of information, which leads directly to an expanding need for managing and preserving the human ability for coherent thought. The computer and the information it processes can create a reality that is easily accepted as an independent reality. If this reality is not based on fact, it is clearly inaccurate. Despite this acknowledgement, the human thought process readily constructs another version of reality where no distinction is made between that part of reality created by thought and the part that is independent of thought, or even those parts which are a mixture of both (Bohm, 1995, p4). Therefore, there is a real need to understand how the human mind affects reality, how technology influences thought, and conversely, how technology can empower thought for the better.

If the starting premise is aligned more with the view that absolute truth is not found in ideas and theories, but through imagination and adaptation, then new opportunities for explorations and discovering new ideas can arise in unexpected and exciting ways. The key to success is to ensure the learner remains cognizant of the hidden dangers at all times. Thus, while the potential for disaster must be diligently observed, Mendizza (2004, p 5) provides encouragement to continue pursuit of the goal of unlimited thinking by speculating that "the next frontier in education is moving us away from "content" to a rediscovery of the natural unconditioned state of the mind and its limitless capacity to learn."

CONCLUSION

The liberating power of the new information and communications technologies extends from their capacity to redefine the learning environment in a way that allows individual potential to be truly maximised (Gipson, 1996, p 19). However, technology alone cannot do this. Unless technology is intentionally coupled with reformed educational practice that acknowledges the primacy of the learner rather than the centrality of the lecturer, then its use is limited. In turn, such a shift in thinking permits the teacher to become a facilitator of the student's learning as opposed to being the sole repository and provider of knowledge.

Unrestricted access to information and related technologies provides an opportunity for teachers to develop and devise learning experiences that are tuned to individual needs. More significantly, it affords learners the opportunity to experience both independent and group learning. Thus, the power of technology lies in its capacity to enable individualised learning whilst encouraging participation in co-operative learning environments, a community of learners where learning is the focussed intention, not the incidental outcome.

In the years ahead, greater numbers of users and learners will access material on the web and therefore, more and more information will accumulate around that material. For the most part, this organic, probabilistic approach to deriving meaning from existing information will be about the active use of information that is generated and refined real time as a product of online activities. Such individual sense-making will not involve information from a standard ontology that has been previously produced by an unknown third party that may (intentionally or unintentionally) impose alternate organisational systems. The accumulation and reinterpretation of information coupled with a focus on end use are two key aspects of an ecological approach to building a world of knowledge where hierarchical or any other organisational structures do not need to coexist with the innate relationships, meanings, and possibilities – there is no one correct way to organise and hence the boundaries to imagination are completely removed as are the influences imposed by artificial (human imposed) structures.

Given the increasing complexity of information and knowledge and the potential for technology to generate complete interconnectedness, greater opportunity arises to explore interdisciplinary cross-fertilisation, where even apparently unrelated findings can lead to unexpected ideas. In this example of technological influence on context and relationships, learning is ultimately induced through the cognitive processes of understanding and interpretation. The next frontier in education has little to do with information and a great deal to do with the state of mind that is required to efficiently process information (Mendizza, 2004, p 7).

An understanding of how information is organised or structured can be derived by determining existing associations and/or interrelationships between collections and patterns of information (using principles of systems theory as applied to systems, sub-systems, and networked interrelationships). The application of systems principles to learning design provides the means to identify and define conceptual relationships, which in turn has the effect of fostering deeper insights into the information presented to the learner. This is where novel solutions to practical problems are often found when least expected (McCalla, 2004, pp 4 - 5).

Systems principles represent a plausible theoretical foundation upon which a new, technologically driven model of learning can be established.

Each principle holds the key to devising a range of strategies for recontextualising learning material (configured as learning objects) that assist learners to develop a broader, more holistic perspective as they work on their given course content. Whether applied separately or integrated as appropriate, all principles present new opportunities to design online teaching environments that connect with other subject areas and disciplines to reveal relationships learners may otherwise not have considered. The benefit of course, is to provide the student increased exposure to new opportunities to construct knowledge and in so doing, gradually expand their conceptual schema into wider, more diverse cognitive perspectives. Thus, the significance of learning object technology is further underscored by the fact that it affords considerable flexibility in the design of electronic learning environments.

The design of online environments using learning object technology provides much more than just a new way of organising content and the information it contains, it also holds the potential to influence the meaning of the information provided. As new data and information are presented to the learner, the relationships that had been formed in their minds can be realigned, revealing new insights and unknown aspects that previously were not apparent. It is in this sense, that context and content are interdependent. This of course raises deeper questions about knowledge for as noted, the act of knowing depends upon the meaningful organisation of data and information. Thus, new methods of organisation imply existing forms of knowledge must change in the process. Furthermore, to the extent that learning objects incorporate the capacity to impose patterns of organisation on existing information and to facilitate the learner's ability to imagine new patterns of organisation through the formation of meaningful relationships, it is further argued that the distinctions between accessing and creating new knowledge are becoming unclear. In essence, the educational implications for applying

Korytkowski and Sikora's notion of interrelated learning objects using a more holistic, systems design approach are profound.

For now, the challenge is to design and deliver learning solutions aimed at not just representing knowledge and facilitating navigation through structured or unstructured information and media using complex learning pathways, but also to develop advanced design methodologies that employ emerging technologies to support the refinement of the higher order cognitive skills of analysis, problem-solving, conceptual thinking, and metacognition. Notwithstanding the potential merits of this approach, it is imperative to consider the learner's capacity to undertake independent learning. That is, in order to manage high levels of autonomy and faculty, learners must be experienced in identifying the relationships that connect the available data and information and to apply the insights gained to the construction of models and strategies that will assist them to become adept, independent learners.

In practice, the issues and strategies for designing educationally effective electronic learning environments are highly complex and diverse. Without a thorough examination of the relationships between technology, communication, information, media, human/computer interaction and cognitive development, the full power of ICT as an aid to learning will not be realised. To this end, a core focus of all ICT related educational research should aim to identify and explore the benefits of applying advanced learning strategies, design methodologies and pedagogical innovations to the complex task of delivering learning environments that augment learners' information and media literacy skills and address the goals of all individuals.

As indicated at the outset, this chapter presented a personal vision for the design of electronic learning environments in the future. The design approach proposed during this exploration of technological capacity to empower the learning process lies in the potential to apply the concept of a continuum of possibilities to inform the construction of learning environments that dynamically adapt and evolve in response to the changing expectations of the teacher and the individual learning needs of the student. After reading this chapter, it is my hope that educationalists will be inspired to exercise their imaginations and reflect on what is possible and so extend the boundaries of accepted thinking on the design of electronic learning environments. To encourage and inspire further thinking, the words of Manzini and Cau (1989, p 17) encapsulate the essence of what the preceding synopsis alludes to in relation to fulfilling the potential of human thought and creativity:

Every object made by man is the embodiment of what is at once unthinkable and possible... This interaction, which we refer to as design, is neither simple nor straightforward. There is no broad, free-ranging Thinkable that has only to squeeze into the boundaries of the Possible because the very awareness of those boundaries is a basic element in what can be thought of. On the other hand, thought is not merely the acceptance of known limits. The activities of creation and invention are expressed in the ability to relocate the bounds imposed in other systems of reference, thus creating the new, that which until now has not been thought of and indeed unthinkable. The model one creates of the possible thus becomes a constituent part of creativity.

REFERENCES

Bateson, G. (1988). *Mind and nature: A necessary unity* (pp. 9–11, 29). New York, NY: Bantam Books.

Bellinger, G. (1997). *Knowledge management - Emerging perspectives*. Retrieved on 15th September, 2008, from http://www.systems-thinking.org/ kmgmt/kmgmt.htm

Bellinger, G., Castro, D., & Mills, A. (1997). *Data, information, knowledge, and wisdom*. Retrieved on 15th September, 2008, from http://www.systems-thinking.org/ dikw/dikw.htm

Bohm, D. (1981). *Knowledge & insight*. Retrieved on 15th August, 2008, from http://ttfuture.org/ services/ visionaries/Dbohm/BohmIK.PDF

Bohm, D. (1995). *The limitations of thought*. Retrieved on 15th August, 2008, from http://ttfuture. org/services/ visionaries/Dbohm/BohmLT.pdf

Brown, A., & Thompson, H. (1997). Course design for the WWW - Keeping online students onside. In *14th Annual Conference Proceedings of the ASCILITE. Academic Computing Services*, Curtin University of Technology, Perth, Western Australia (pp. 74-81).

Brown, J. S. (2002). *Growing up digital: How the Web changes work, education, and the ways people learn*. United States Distance Learning Association. Retrieved 20th September, 2008, from http://www.usdla.org/html/journal/ FEB02_Issue/ article01.html

Bruner, J., & Anglin, J. M. (1973). *Beyond the information given - Studies in the psychology of knowing* (p. 397). Toronto, Canada: George J. McLeod Limited.

Burbules, N. C., & Callister, T. A. (1996). Knowledge at the crossroads: Some alternative futures of hypertext learning environments. *Educational Theory*, (Winter): 3.

Bush, V. (1945). As we may think. *Atlantic Monthly*, *176*(1), 101–108.

Campos, M. (2004). A constructivist method for the analysis of networked cognitive communication and the assessment of collaborative learning and knowledge-building. *Journal of Asynchronous Learning Networks*, *8*(2).

Capra, F. (1996). *The Web of life* (p. 70). London, UK: Harper Collins.

Daniel, J. S. (1996). *Mega-universities and knowledge media: Technology strategies for higher education* (p. 2). London, UK: Kogan Page.

Dickau, J. J. (1999). *The known, the unknown, and the unknowable: Are the boundaries of consciousness a fractal?* Retrieved on 30th July, 2008, from http://jond4u.jonathandickau.com/ known.htm

Gipson, S. (1996). *Feral, facsimile of facilitated? Technology serving teaching and learning*. Tridos School Village, Chiang Mai, Thailand: Learning and Teaching: Implications for Gifted and Talented Students.

Green, M. S. (2005). You perceive with your mind: Knowledge and perception. In Darby, D., & Shelby, T. (Eds.), *Hip hop and philosophy* (pp. 6–8). Open Court.

Hammer, D. (2000). Student resources for learning introductory physics. *American Journal of Physics. Physics Education Research Supplement*, *68*(1), 52–59.

Hannafin, M. J. (1997). Resource-based learning environments: Methods and models. In *14th Annual Conference Proceedings of the ASCILITE. Academic Computing Services*, Curtin University of Technology, Perth, Western Australia, (pp. 255–62).

Harris, D. (2000). Knowledge and networks. In Evans, T., & Nation, D. (Eds.), *Changing university teaching: Reflections on creating educational technologies* (pp. 36–37). London, UK: Kogan Page.

Ingraham, B. D. (2000). Scholarly rhetoric in digital media: Post-modernism. *Journal of Interactive Media in Education (JIME)*. Retrieved on 30th July, 2008, from http://jime.open.ac.uk/00/ ingraham/ingraham.pdf

Koestler, A. (1978). Janus – A summing up, (pp. 131–133). Tiptree, Essex, UK: The Anchor Press Ltd.

Korytkowski, P., & Sikora, K. (2007). Creating learning objects and learning sequence on the basis of semantic networks. In R. Wagner, N. Revell, and G. Pernul (Eds). *Lecture Notes in Computer Science Volume 4653/2007, Database and Expert Systems Applications*, (p. 713). Berlin, Germany: Springer.

Laurillard, D. (1993). *Rethinking university teaching: A framework for the effective use of educational technology* (p. 268). London, UK: Routledge.

Leacock, T. L., & Nesbit, J. C. (2007). A framework for evaluating the quality of multimedia learning resources. *Journal of Educational Technology & Society, 10*(2), 44–59.

Liber, O. (2004). Cybernetics: E-learning and the educations system. *International Journal of Learning Technology, 1*(1), 135. doi:10.1504/IJLT.2004.003686

Magee, B. (1997). The philosophy of Schopenhauer. In *Schopenhauer 1788-1860* (On the Fourfold root of the principle of sufficient reason, 1814 -15), (p. 6). Oxford, UK: Clarendon Press: Manzini, E., & Cau, P. (1989). *The material of invention*, (p. 17). Cambridge, MA: MIT Press.

McCalla, G. (2004). The ecological app roach to the design of e-learning environments: Purpose-based capture and use of information about learners. *Journal of Interactive Media in Education: Special Issue on the Educational Semantic Web, 7.* Retrieved 15th November, 2007, from http://www-jime.open.ac.uk/ 2004/7

Megarry, J. (1989). Hypertext and compact discs: The challenge of multimedia learning. In Bell, C., Davies, J., & Winders, R. (Eds.), *Promoting Learning: Aspects of Educational and Training Technology XXII* (p. 50). London, UK: Kogan Page.

Mendizza, M. (2004). *Love of the game: Applying what athletes call the zone to parenting and education* (p. 5). Retrieved 20th February, 2008, from http://www.rethinkingeducation.com/Mendizza.pdf

Mendizza, M. (2006). *The next frontier in education*. Retrieved 20th July, 2008, from http://www.dawntalk.com/NewFiles/Article-Mendizza.html

Pearce, J. (1974). *Exploring the crack in the cosmic egg: Split minds and meta-realities* (p. 194). New York, NY: Washington Square Press.

Peterson, E. (2006). Beneath the metadata: Some philosophical problems with folksonomy. *D-Lib Magazine, 12*(11). Retrieved 15th August, 2008, from http://www.dlib.org/dlib/november06/peterson/11peterson.html

Quinton, S. (2006). Contextualisation of learning objects to derive meaning. Chapter. In Koohang, A., & Harman, K. (Eds.), *Learning objects: Theory, praxis, issues, and trends* (pp. 113–180). Santa Rosa, CA: Informing Science Press.

Rieh, S. Y. (2002). Judgment of information quality and cognitive authority in the Web. *Journal of the American Society for Information Science and Technology, 53*(2), 145–161. doi:10.1002/asi.10017

Rucker, R. (1988). *Mind tools: The mathematics of information* (p. 26). London, UK: Penguin Books.

Shank, R. (1996). *Information is surprises* (p. 173). New York, NY: Touchstone.

Shirky, C. (2006). *Ontology is overrated: Categories, links, and tags. Economics and culture, media and community*. Retrieved 30th September, 2008, from http://shirky.com/writings/ ontology_overrated.html

Snowden, D. J. (2000). Strategies for common sense-making in innovation enabling emergence at the edge of chaos part III. *Journal of Scenario and Strategy Planning, 2*(3).

Sprinthall, R. C., & Sprinthall, N. A. (1981). *Educational psychology: A developmental approach* (p. 281). Reading, MA: Addison-Wesley Publishing Company.

Stenmark, D. (2002). Information vs. knowledge: The role of Intranets in knowledge management. In *Proceedings of HICSS-35*, Hawaii, January, (pp. 7 - 10). IEEE Press.

Tan, J., & Biswas, G. (2007). Simulation-based game learning environments: Building and Sustaining a fish tank. *The First IEEE International Workshop on Digital Game and Intelligent Toy Enhanced Learning,* 2007 (DIGITEL), March, (pp. 73–80).

Chapter 13
Are Web Designers Resisting the Inclusion of Social Cues when Creating Website's User Interface?

Ronan De Kervenoael
Sabanci University, Turkey & Aston University, UK

Christophe Bisson
Kadir Has University, Turkey

Mark Palmer
Birmingham University, UK

ABSTRACT

Using the resistance literature as an underpinning theoretical framework, this chapter analyzes how Web designers through their daily practices, (i) adopt recursive, adaptive, and resisting behavior regarding the inclusion of social cues online and (ii) shape the socio-technical power relationship between designers and other stakeholders. Five vignettes in the form of case studies with expert individual Web designers are used. Findings point out at three types of emerging resistance namely: market driven resistance, ideological resistance, and functional resistance. In addition, a series of propositions are provided linking the various themes. Furthermore, the authors suggest that stratification in Web designers' type is occurring and that resistance offers a novel lens to analyze the debate.

INTRODUCTION

Web site design is often portrayed as a key tool in attracting users and in providing sustainable competitive advantage to online firm (Dailey 2004; Eroglu et al, 2001). In turn, web design is

part of the world of online communication that has recently been the subject of dramatic changes with the introduction of social media (e.g. blogs, Facebook, Twitter, Delicious, LinkedIn). While most of the online marketing research has tended to concentrate on deterministic aspects of website design such as navigation, search, payment,

DOI: 10.4018/978-1-61350-516-8.ch013

Copyright © 2012, IGI Global. Copying or distributing in print or electronic forms without written permission of IGI Global is prohibited.

convenience and generic atmospherics like colors, questions remain over (i) what are social cues online? (ii) who ought to be driving social cues inclusion? (iii) what are the benefits for website designers of introducing social cues? (iv) what are the risks associated with social cue inclusion? And (v) is there any resistance and lack of explicit legitimacy for such inclusion? This chapter tries to answer the last part of this wide area of research namely: Are web designers resisting the inclusion of social cues as they create website user interface? In other words, our paper analyzes: how web designers through their daily practices, adopt recursive, adaptive and resisting behavior regarding the inclusion of social cues online and shape the socio-technical power relationship between designers, clients and users.

The importance of effectively dealing with socially oriented design variables and social capital has been proven to naturally increase international market share as demonstrated by several studies (Constantinides, 2004; Klein, 2003). Nevertheless, this broad literature pays only limited attention to the resistance web designers face while choosing to include or not social capital cues. In particular, social acoustic legitimacy as a multi-dimensional concept ought to be established by all stakeholders prior to designing other more functional website drivers (de Kervenoael at al, 2009). An overall definition of social capital cues has yet to emerge from the literature. As a generic theme social cues are often defined as "a resource that actors derive from specific social structures and then use to pursue their interests; it is created by changes in the relationship among actors" (Baker 1990, p. 619). Another closely related aspect is the process by which social capital is characterized as "the brokerage opportunities in a network" (Burt 1997, p. 355). In our specific context of ICT and web design, social capital can be understood as the bonding [of potentially] similar people and bridging between diverse people, with norms of reciprocity (Dekker and Uslaner 2001; Uslaner 2001). A general definition of social capital and social

cues in an ICT context can then be described as the sum of web experiences including for example: (i) aesthetics, art, (ii) association to user lifestyle symbols including norms, posture, etiquette, gender, politics, religion, and (iii) environmental, personal, cultural grounded reference points. This definition goes beyond the technical aspect of web design and reflects a multi-disciplinary approach. Recent articles in executive management journals have emphasized the critical impact of learning and social networks in driving improved supply chain performance (Postman, 2009; Stuart and Deckert, 1998; Bessant et al, 2003). In practical terms, social cues can take different forms ranging from: sound and music, rich media including photographs and video, icons, apps, RSS, widgets, plug-ins, add-ons, and unfiltered and unmassaged spontaneous information content often including socio cultural traits of minorities, religious factions and political groups. These tools lead to recognized authenticity, transparency and immediacy being attached to the site design interface. In turn, users get a feeling of active engagement in shaping the site strategy, by being listened to and cared about. In particular, these bring about a revolution in participatory communication understanding. In turn, web developers ought to be given a far more central role in the creation and maintenance of the site.

Taking into account the chapter aims, two partial gaps have been identified: first published work often remains at macro level. Setting aside the methods and models of management science, we utilize a micro level practice perspective (Jarzabkowski et al. 2007) that reflect more appropriately the everyday life of web designers. Practice is composed of three interrelated concepts (i) practitioners investigating what people do individually or in group, (ii) practices which represent the large array of tools and mechanisms used to implement day to day strategy and (iii) praxis representing the stream of activities (Whittington, 2007; Palmer & O'Kane, 2007; Jarzabroski et al, 2007). We listen to practitioners in their accomplishment and resistance to the inclusion of social cues online. Second, while users or clients are often under consideration, there has been a lack of concern regarding web designers as the original creators of websites.

This paper argues that it is imperative for web designers to learn about the contested nature of social cues development online, and in particular, the potential role of web designers in shaping the inclusion process before benefiting (or not) from other stakeholders such as clients and users inputs. While social cues and capital are embedded in the offline retail setting and have benefited from centuries of refinement, fashions and trends offering a rich array of cues, displays, signals and reminders; the online environment invariably reveals, increasingly so in the current mass retail sites, a lack of explicit socio-cultural capital. The scale and scope of these potential inclusions thus offers the potential for more complex theoretical insights. The findings of five vignettes with experienced web designers (over 10 years in average) working for firms such as Seesmic and Superonline are presented along with six theoretical propositions.

The following section provides a review of the resistance literature as our theoretical underpinning. Section 3 outlines the methodology. Section 4 presents the exploratory findings and emerging theoretical contributions. Lastly, section 5 concludes and offers insights for management and future research.

LITERATURE REVIEW

Resistance across time has often been described a powerful symbol of human territoriality. In particular, the range of perceived responsibility for any given task is often graded according to different territorial spaces leading to a scale regarding the remit of individual powers. The span of control of any individual stakeholder is then defined and sealed to a great level of details leading to immobility strategies (e.g. job description, con-

tract). Territoriality often relies on classification, prioritization and ranking of task assignment to a specific category of individuals. Territoriality often creates hierarchical views of the world (e.g. red tape), prevents initiatives and creativity between positional levels as a mean to control and impose power and creates de-facto limits among territorial units. Examples include expression such as "mine" and not "yours" and "it is the local regulation", "you may not do this there" (Pile & Keith, 1997). Resistance is subsequently linked to the possibility of territorial changes, power shifts and responsibility evolutions occurring. In the case of ICT adoption, Selwyn (2003) reflects on the individuals' non-use of new technologies in the information age defining resistance to technology as "tactic resistance" and identifying four drivers including: (i) material and cognitive deficiencies, (ii) technophobia as an indicator of technological reticence, (iii) ideological refusal, (iv) diffusion issues. Resistance is then described by Haynes and Prakash (1991, p3) as "those behaviors and cultural practices by subordinates groups that contest hegemonic social formation, that threaten to unravel the strategies of domination. Consciousness need not be essential to its construction".

Accordingly, resistance research has long recognized that technology related product and services face problem situations on a daily basis i.e. in practice. Much existing resistance literature has tended to concentrate on a limited number of areas including: engagement and diffusion (Rogers, 1995), trust (deKervenoael & Aykac, 2008), service experience (Ling, 2008), internationalization (Palmer et al, 2010); sale resistance (Hunt & Bashaw, 1999); consumer resistance (Russel and Russel, 2006), individual resistance to change (Oreg, 2003; Szmigin & Foxall, 1998; Fleming, 2005) and skills for adopters (Marcelle, 2004). Concurrently, resistance has been analyzed in various settings including: political resistance (Watts, 1997), power resistance (Moore, 1997), identity resistance (Banister & Hogg, 2004), managerial

(Lee & Cadogan, 2009), consumption resistance (Clarke et al, 2006), space of resistance, regulatory resistance and cultural resistance (Kozinets & Handelman, 2004).

Furthermore, the traditional resistance literature including Sheth (1981) has developed the concept of 'Habit Resistance'. This line of work was often associated with Mittelsteadt et al. (1976) symbolic adoption or rejection model whereby users may have (i) symbolically rejected an innovation, (ii) accepted but were not able to try and (iii) accepted but decided to postpone trial. As an addition, Gatignon and Robertson (1991) suggested either rejection or postponement depending on individual users may be core in driving non-adoption of an innovation. Context again is strongly related to the characteristics of territoriality. Context in this chapter is understood as "the set of environmental states and settings that either determines an application's behavior or in which an application event occurs and is interesting to the user" (Chen & Kotz, 2000). In other words as presented by Szmigin & Foxall (1998) innovation resistance can be categorized as: rejection, postponement and opposition.

Particularly significant for this chapter is the resistance analysis offered in the strategic alliance literature, whereby resistance is presented as an attitude that demands to "challenge, disrupt or invert prevailing assumptions, discourses and power relations. It can take multiple material and symbolic forms, and its strength, influence and intensity are likely to be variable and to shift over time..." (Collinson, 1994, p49). In other words, following from Palmer et al (2010, p9), and drawing on the work of Ackroyd and Thompson (1999), and Fleming and Spicer (2007), four main expressions of resistance are found to be important namely: refusal, voice, escape and creation:

Resistance as refusal does not follow instruction and overtly blocks the effects of power by undermining the flow of domination rather than attempting to change it. Resistance as voice is to let one be heard by those in control in order to change particular aspects of power relations in favor of those being affected by them. Resistance as escape reflects those mechanisms used to disengage mentally from the workplace such as cynicism, skepticism and misidentification. Resistance as creation refers to the way that alternative identities and discursive systems of representation emerge within the broader flows of domination (Fleming & Spicer, 2007: paraphrased from pages 29-43).

From a technological and website interface design perspective, the four expressions of resistance can be related to the power and relationships among the stakeholders. In the dynamic setting of the online environment, identities, responsibilities, actions and inactions are mediated by the virtual 24/7 aspect of the channel including the participatory element of many sites. Refusal as resistance can be said to reflect (i) the inabilities of certain stakeholders to engage with tasks beyond the technical aspects of the channel or (ii) refusal by other stakeholders to really try to understand the potential and pitfalls of new tools and software. Interestingly, the idea of personalization or one to one communication seems to be understood with the greatest variation. Voice as a resistance can arise (or be stopped) from multiple outlets including: email, blogs, social network sites, second life, video clips among others. The multiplicity of outlets points at various paths and level of responsibilities and territoriality are difficult to control as conventions are yet to emerge on 'appropriate' standards. Escape as resistance allows within any design the voluntary creation of anomalies, unusual naming conventions, graphics or even bugs that may be corrected in the future but aim ultimately at anchoring a rebellion against traditional dull corporate sites. The example of video games, where users need to share tips to progress, is often voluntarily integrated by creative designers. Lastly, creation as resistance may allows web designers to test new concepts and tools while getting instant feedback and growing their area of knowledge and expertise. The online environment allows testing under very specific conditions limited to certain users' categories such as early adopters, mavens and experts.

In parallel, a regular debate among researcher rests on the divergence connecting resistance motivated by personal motivations (internally driven) and motivated by societal and ideological factors (externally driven). For instance, institutional theory is often drawn upon to investigate how institutional framework shape organization's configuration, behavior and action (DiMaggio & Powell, 1983). Studies tend to depict resistance as barriers through a negative bipolarization of the environment whereby many stakeholders are de-facto considered as non-participant. This undermines the implementation aspects and practices in day to day activities (Knights & McCabe, 2000). A particularly notable feature is that stakeholders appearing in similar situations to re-interpret the context on which resistance takes place are arriving at divergent conclusions. In other words, spaces of resistance can be said to be dislocated from the traditional sources of power. In particular, spaces can be visible but are often constituted of hidden and ulterior motives showing the arbitrary of practices. Obstacles and resistance are often portrayed as fixed limits and detached from a dynamic environment of ongoing activities (Palmer et al, 2010). The most challenging aspect of many resistance acts are often the fact that they remain indirect, underground, underlying the importance of other factors in the decision making process (Prasad & Prasad, 2000). A contrasting approach is presented by research concerned with anti-choice behaviors as a positive expression of voluntary anti-consumption. This area of research suggests that grounds for resistance are arising from (i) simplifying decision mechanism (Shaw & Newholm, 2002; Hogg & Michell, 1996); (ii) prioritization of better options (Craig-Lees & Hill, 2002, Piacentini & Banister, 2009); (iii) resistance as a reflection of hidden intention including ethical concerns and environmental principles (Iyer & Muncy, 2009;

Gabriel, 1999). These types of resistances are also portrayed as moral avoidance (Lee et al., 2009 a,b); and (iv) resistance as a coping mechanism (Lazarus & Folkman, 1984).

A number of observations can be made regarding the aforementioned literature. A central assumption to resistance related specifically to ICT lies in the fact that ICT brings its own novel ritual, myths, values and basic conjectures (Schein, 2004). Web designers' local day to day context and histories with previous ICT projects can be said to also have shaped opinions and attitudes towards future inclusion or not of social cues. Decisions regarding designs are usually a tradeoff between increased efficiency and convenience on the one side and decreased personal control over work practice and multitasking expectations on the other side (Castells, 2001; Giddens, 1992). Furthermore, from a marketing perspective the signature tag of the designer ought to increase future prospect. The concept of consideration then becomes relevant as a basis for understanding the contested interactions between stakeholders. Consideration is understood as Ettlinger (2003) as *"Why do people [...] often make decision that result in suboptimal productivity, competitiveness or effectiveness?"*. Many new technologies and practices will then ultimately remain only under consideration but will never be engaged with. In other words, stakeholders need to evaluate the legitimacy of the results of the consideration exercise. Yet, resistances can be very mundane. Following this, while interpreting the findings two sub-concepts ought to be kept in mind. First, the idea of legitimacy understood for our purpose as "a generalized perception or assumption that the actions of an entity are desirable, proper, or appropriate within some socially constructed system of norms, values, beliefs, and definitions" (Suchman, 1995, p. 574). And secondly, the traditional concept of trust defined for our purpose as: 'the extent to which a person is confident in and willing to act on the basis of, the words, actions, and decisions of another' (McAllister, 1995 p.25).

Table 1. Respondents' profile

Name	Position	Experience (year)	Education field	Companies worked for	Nationality
Yael	Web designer	15 years	Ph.D in communication design	Semcor http://www.semcor.net University of Baltimore http://www.ubalt.edu	Israeli
Christophe	Web designer	5 years	Computer engineer	Automa-tech http://www.altix-automa-tech.com Aster association http://www.aster-asso.org	French
Steve	User Interface	7 years	Computer engineer	Seesmic http://www.seesmic.com Sixapart http://www.sixapart.com	French
Jean-Paul	Web designer	13 years	Art, Applied arts	Mengine http://www.mengine.fr Automa-tech Http://www.altix-automa-tech.com	French
Gorkem	Director and Lead Designer	12 years	Art History/Architectural Theory	Emedya http://www.emedya.net Superonline http://www.superonline.com	Turkish

METHODOLOGY

In order to address the aim of this chapter, five web designers, experts with over 10 years in average work experience who are working or have worked in leading companies (such as Seesmic) and across various countries, were recruited and ask through a 60 to 120 minutes semi-structured phone interview their perceptions on the possible resistance drivers resulting in a certain lack of social cue inclusion (see Table 1 for profile). The interviews were structured in three sections: The first set of questions intended to define the general understanding, for each respondent, within his day to day activities, of (i) the meaning of social cues and (ii) the entitlement of web developers 'job'. A definition of the differences between web designers and web developers was asked as an entry point. The second set of questions was aimed at identifying and classifying different types of possible social capital cues currently present online. Each item was then reflected upon as a way to identify potential drivers of resistance. Lastly, questions around the evolution and future

representations of social cues online, the online global attributes and associated technological issues were investigated.

Vignettes through a think aloud techniques were used for each participant (Miles & Huberman, 1994; Preissle et al, 1997) and follow Yin (1994) pattern matching strategy. Behavioral researchers have used vignettes to understand better the basis for complex judgments (Green, 1974; Alexander & Becker, 1978; Rossi & Anderson, 1982; Caro et al, 2009). A variety of titles are employed to categorize vignette survey techniques including conjoint analysis, contingent evaluation method, fractional factorial survey, and stated choice methods (Cavanaugh & Fritzsche, 1985). Constant variable value vignettes (CVVV) were used as all respondents were asked to respond to an identical vignette scenario. Respondents were asked to consider only two options both in the case of a website they were asked to design: (i) Should a manager /firm consider that it is the job of web designers to identify and integrate social cues within the website interface or (ii) should managers / firms continue with their classic designs and systems only. Respondents were asked to consider the situations of hypothetical vignette persons/firms with whom they could identify. Regarding interpretive validity vignette may suffer from low internal validity because of the difficulty in determining whether the participants experience or imagine the context and the independent variables exactly as the researchers intended (Spencer, 1978). Although findings derived from our five vignettes converge. We believe that findings observed should be replicated in field settings with a larger number of observations across different locations.

The findings and analysis proceed concurrently with theorizing, with each vignette having an impact of the procession of others (Merriam, 1998). First, all interviewed were transcribed and translated in English. Second, each interview was analyzed separately as soon as it was conducted. Analysis of early interviews allowed later interviews to benefit from the preliminary insights into the data (Strauss & Corbin, 1990). The data were then analyzed as a whole. A peer evaluation of coding among authors was used whereby each emerging theme was discussed in depth in an iterative spiral process (Flint & Woodruff, 2001). The interviews were guided by concepts and characteristics which emerge from the literature and design to explore participant personal practices and experiences observed across the course of their career. The findings were then re-interpreted in view of the theoretical background with a focus on flexibility and context. A color matrix based data display was designed allowing within and between case similarities to appear (Miles & Huberman, 1994). Constant themes, idiosyncratic situations and linkages between variables were made explicit. The findings presented here remain exploratory and form the pilot of a wider study to be conducted. The letter after each quote identifies which respondent opinion the quote is derived from.

FINDINGS AND DISCUSSION

Market Driven Resistance

The findings first uphold the general differentiation between web designers and web developers. The market, both in term of geographical location of individual web designer and type of sites (i.e. transactional vs informational vs entertainment) were portrayed as a key drivers. Developers were presented as easily outsourced while there was a clear resistance about the applicability of outsourcing a web designer and especially his/her knowledge acquired across his/her career about social cues in specific territorial context. Typically the respondents described each in the following way:

"A web designer makes the graphic and the ergonomic. A web developer makes the code". JP

"A web designer is in charge of the artistic side while the web developer is in charge of programming". C

Interestingly, also the differences were clear on paper, it was more difficult for each individual to classify themselves strictly in a given category. An evolutionary context was presented. Most of them were now managers and had to migrate from one status to the other. It was underlined that a current migration towards the new mobile environment was increasing the complexity and territoriality of the job description. While the typical technical skills required to design on mobile application platforms are similar, a new level of involvedness is required both to fit with the different audiences' lifestyle and the scale and scope of the new devices used to access information (e.g. smart phone, tablet computers) while coping with the new interactivity provided by the spread of touch screen technologies. Similarities with mobile interfaces were echoed with novelty specific to online social media such as Facebook, Twitters and their social corporation applications. These views were expressed and differentiated through the example of retail sites vs entertainment sites. The purpose of a visit was described as nearly opposite with a polarization between efficiency and experiential. For all our respondents, resistance to include social cues in commercial web sites that do not aim at inspiring people but are designed just to make them buy was clear. Resistance was explicit and grounded on a cost benefit analysis for the client. Any social cue integration will need to have a demonstrated impact on the financial bottom line.

"If you make people think too much they buy less. Non commercial or NGOs web site for example can have this goal". JP

"the customers just focus on the product and services. The client focuses on how much money for how much return? Will my customers understand? Will it involve more long term costs?" Y

In particular, it was noticed that a certain resistance emerged regarding the inclusion of social cue while considering website as a homogenous entity. Websites were described as compartmentalized, one page for loyalty actions, one page for feedback, one page for promotion among others. When probing about social cues' characteristics such as inspiration, surprise and excitement, they were perceived to be applicable to only a few pages for any given websites. Moreover, respondents felt that it was not the primary responsibility of designers to decide which page ought to be more socially oriented. Designers were very pragmatic in style. Standard, approved models of design were used again and again. For example:

"If the product is an innovative one, I can try to surprise people to emphasize the innovation, it depends a lot on the client and its products rather than me". JP

Web designers' personality factors such as neuroticism and extraversion recognized in offline sale and service management studies as important were described as largely not present. A status quo situation was explained to have emerged over the year, the internet was created in 1993 quoted one respondent, whereby leaders such as Microsoft, SUN, Apple, IBM create a frame of mind that most designers emulate. It was described as softening the styles variations among web designers. As a legitimating rational, the litigation society from which the Internet has emerged, namely the US was given as a reason not to include any items that may lead to copyright infringement or general lawsuit by specific subgroups within the society.

"We need to follow some standards, it is hard to deviate. Clients are very scared to be sued". Y

"I follow the leaders such as Apple". S

"We aim at being different by making the simplest and easiest of use; follow the model, we have a herd mentality". G

However, change was not described as prescribed. The information volume and its speed of exchange were becoming seamless and growing extremely rapidly. These offer opportunities for social cues that were associated by our respondent with "big files". Compression technologies and images quality increase were depicted as allowing great improvement in the user experiences. Following the trend of Twitter and Facebook, and social networking in general, clients were presented as 'now' asking about possible connections to that type of communication or about the source of these successes. Other websites such as city recommendation for art, culture and gastronomy activities (e.g. Yelp.com) were also mentioned. Overcoming personal fear of social cues, accessing what the buzz out there is currently about was presented as a high priority but curtailed by a lack of social readiness of clients and a lack of fund. Again the majority of websites design (i.e. for local SMEs) was described as 'must be cheap to compete with wizz kid in their garage'.

"We and some clients encourage the development of social network cues as it is trendy, but many of our clients are just local business with a local reach". G

Importantly, unlike Facebook where users can lead easily content development, on a commercial web site, online forums were described as more complicated as they needed to be rigorously controlled. Co-creation was portrayed as virtually not possible. Two types of resistance emerged both from a client perspective in term of readiness to lose control towards letting customers shape discussions on their site and from a design perspective in terms of filtering, updating and most of all answering and participating in the debate in real time.

"In general they are impossible to deal with [user generated content] because of the variety of issues discussed. Who will deal with what? who will have overall control and in particular legal issues?". Y

Interestingly, according to the legislation of some countries a web designer name or logo was not permitted as a mark of signature and recognition (e.g. in France). If the client allows it, the logo of the designer company is put as the only mark of creation. Clients were described as retaining full control of their site and only sub-contracting what was described as a technical service outsourcing. As a consequence for many projects web designers roughly do the same type of work and improve the flow only subsequently to web analytic results. Price is the main differentiating factor as well as timing taking into account the clients and technological constraints. There was resistance by our respondents to invest in long term relationship and risk taking when the web designer was seen as only a tool.

"We all do the same i.e. web 2.0. The logo reflects the client color choice and brand management. We are only tools, not seen as real value added creator. Why should I take the risk under these conditions?". JP

"Five years ago most of web sites were following what was created in USA. The cultural cues spread were then American ones. Nowadays, as the world goes global, they are more social cues to choose from included in websites but many [client and designers] are not ready to take any risk". G

The vignettes demonstrate that designers' social ties impact is low in shaping web site design value added. Drawing from this discussion, we present the following propositions:

P1: Resistance to communicate further about the detail of social cues among stakeholders is preventing the shaping of social capital cues within web sites design.

P2: Stakeholders ought to stop resisting the re-definition of their value added model, whereby designers ought to be more than a simple enabling tool.

Ideological Resistance

In the second phase of the semi-structured interviews, we explored the reasons which legitimate the lack of social cues' and its drivers' inclusion. Web sites were mainly described as minimalists, efficient selling machines and process oriented. The logic behind such a situation was grounded in the possible multiple threats coming from law infringement, competitors and boycott from customers. In addition, it was explaining that the socio-political context of a given location was important and greatly impacting opportunities. Many countries still filter web site information with censure being described as a real danger. While the majority of websites were explained to be designed mainly for a domestic audience, diversity *within* do exist. Web designers' resistance to answer that diversity was made explicit.

"A web site is a 24 hours open window on the world. Hence, you have to be careful to reactions from competitors and e-visitors. There are too many types of American or Turkish to cater for them all ... a simple style is risk free and better for the long term". G

"In certain countries, social opinions are not permitted or accepted, the personal/physical risk will be too high". S

"Our clients do not want to deal with socio-political issues". G

As an illustration to the above issues, gender symbols were regarded as rarely included. Gender was described as a sensitive topic for various reasons including: (i) which symbolic representation to use, (ii) any religious connections, (iii) the place of women in many societies was portrayed as still not clear, (iv) questions were raised by designers on what will be the direct impact on sale? Significantly, it was underlined that web sites were constructed for mass audiences. For example, newsletters were built for all, current and future users. Cost was also mentioned as a rapidly emerging hindrance. In particular, personalization was portrayed as difficult to implement as site become messy or a patchwork of many styles. The only exception given concerns the creation of blogs. Resistance to change and test novel social aspects were apparent. It felt that our respondents were not trained to deal with gender related issues.

"If the product is for one gender, we can include some gender symbols, mainly photographs. But, in general we do not include them as a specific design aim". S

"Cost may increase quickly and may become too high rapidly compared to return – cost vs benefit. I am not sure how to address a mainly women audience?". S

"It becomes a mess very quickly and the web designer is made responsible for other lack of decision. It should not be the designer's job to choose the website gender if any". S

Interestingly, web designers agreed on the fact that personalization was often understood from a supply chain perspective not a user perspective. As such personalization examples were reflected through new web technologies that were employed or not by designers. Products such Ajax (shorthand for asynchronous JavaScript and XML) allowing more interactive sites were described as fashion items. Other sources of inspiration, trend and fashion were again described from a technical deterministic perspective including technology forums and fairs. Moreover, clients were portrayed as not asking specific questions about the trend of fashion underlying weaknesses and myopia towards basic sites.

"The fashion is launched by some companies which launch new technologies e.g AJAX allows specific transparency and sharpness on given page". C

"Web designers get inspired from some research centers of companies, start up. Thereafter, they follow the trend". JP

"In general the clients are not interested in fashion; just some multinational does it a bit". G

P3: to lower designers' resistance towards social cues inclusion, the level of specific social knowledge needed for content creation ought to be re-assessed.

Functional Resistance

In the third phase of the interviews, our respondents described that the main reason for the lack of social cues was the result of long established, process driven mechanisms. Functional resistance to social cues' inclusion appeared at various levels: (i) within the web designer's education process, the resistance to include wider social science subjects within traditional technology related topics were presented as contributing element, (ii) the resistance to alter organizational culture and obligations of many firms was put forwards as another element. In particular, the remit of the marketing department's influences within the client business and between the client business and web designers was described as lacking in clarity. Internal foes and power struggles were often put first before the consideration to include/exclude social cues, (iii) the resistance to bridge the gap between design and implementation of specific cues or conformism to basic structures and rules of design was also described as a resistance bottleneck. These involve an agreement towards deciding what is right or wrong to include as social cue. While many ideas were presented, often derived from other websites viewing, few if any were ever formally adopted and no standardization tended to prevail, (iv) basic technological resistance regarding compatibility issues because of the many access interfaces available were as well declared to be significant.

Regarding education all our respondents did come from different systems in different countries but all systems were described as resisting the inclusion of softer social science topics. Another key characteristic mentioned was the lack of female within the typical web design student cohort as well as teaching faculties. Web design was described to be taught traditionally in engineering school that did not always support other faculties such as visual art, sociology and management. Education was depicted as non-interactive with little contact

with the outside world and lab based applications that were never tested in practice.

"There is a lack of social education within web designers. Most of the time we are self-educated and just focus on the technology". G

"Marketing aspects are rarely taken into account in the education of web designers". JP

P4: There is an inverted U-shaped relationship between resistance to include softer social sciences subject in web designers' education and the inclusion of social cues.

As a second legitimating reason for resisting inclusions of social cue, the client organizational culture was put forwards. Web designers expressed great difficulties in communicating with their clients. Organizational culture regarding online marketing was explained not to have evolved sufficiently. The e-channel was portrayed as the solution to deeper issues (e.g. lack of offline sales growth) without any fundamental evidences making the designer responsible for failure. The vision for online activities was exposed as unclear and lacking in details. Firms by nature were not concerned primarily by art and aesthetics or consumer behavior in general. Functional decision making process was lacking regarding who in the company have the skills and power to accept or reject social cue inclusion and what model ought to be followed.

"It is not very difficult to include social cues but companies' contacts are not often interested. They just have generic macro-information about the site aim". G

"Companies have little interest in artistic representation; this is the cold business world and efficiency". S

"Clients are too powerful and communication as a two way is difficult they are not listening and often do not have the required education to understand the technical and financial implication of social cue's choice". S

Furthermore, relationships between designers and clients were described as not sufficiently developed, hindering potential synergies between technological solutions and the willingness to design more social websites. The lack of decision authority by the client representatives was mentioned as a key reason for not taking any risk and reproducing traditional design interfaces. Neither the web designers nor the client representative leader were in a position to bridge the gap between novel design and implementation of change. In addition, "follow the model", "do not create difficulties" and a certain "herd mentality" were perceived as central elements to future projects. It was recognized that it was not the role of web designers to suggest change a in its client power structure and decision making mechanisms. An ad-hoc mentality was expressed whereby basic structures were put in place and corrected later if required.

"Web designers just look at what is done. Thus, they copy each other". G

"Before making a web site, you need to make a market research. Although it has a cost, the fee you receive for such initiatives do not reflect the effort". JP

"You make a site, then you use Google analytic then you adapt rather than trying to foresee who will come". S

P5: Clients' functional resistance within its own decision making process increases the likelihood for ad-hoc corrections rather than proactive inclusion of social cues.

Lastly, it appeared that technology was still providing a large array of technical constraints including the use of multiple browsers (e.g. Internet Explorer, safari, Mozilla), multiple programming language options, the inclusion of audio and video and the requirement to use related software. Respondents also underlined a lack of knowledge regarding how users are actually accessing websites (e.g. screen size, machine type), with a view that it was probably through a mix of devices that currently do not provide a homogenous experience. This situation was described as today's state of play before the potential inclusion of a larger amount of social cues.

"The browsers do not allow you to do the same things and stuff have to be compatible". C

"As the trend is to use flash to make a web site, your clients want you to use it but what about the user side?" G

P6: Resistance to technological compatibility increases complexity and decreases variety of design and social cues inclusion.

CONCLUSION

The research findings must be read in the light of the study limitation. The data are qualitative and do not lend themselves to formal conclusions. The small size of the sample of experts has, however, allowed us to gain a rich and detailed insight into a generally under-explored area of website interface design linked to power resistance and territoriality among the various stakeholders. Our findings have identified a series of resistance forms and practices namely: market driven, ideological and functional. By highlighting the various sub-factors linking practice to resistance, we have hoped to alert web design's stakeholders and practitioners to the importance of reflecting on and purposefully shaping the future inclusion of social cues.

Our findings mentioned above reveal great opportunities for some proactive, creative and innovative firms to capitalize on the increasing success of social cues online. In this respect, our findings may suggest that a stratification in web designers may be occurring: on the one hand, traditional technically driven designers imitating generic trends may form a group and on the other hand, an emerging breed of 'modern' designers that take advantage of the rising importance of the social media and social cues in the communication process may emerge. Furthermore, we suspect from the findings that the current standing between transactional site and infotainment sites as a legitimating factor for including social cues (or not), may only be artificial and short term. We contend that as user experience grows, users will demand the best possible experiential effect in all their dealing with the channel. The findings indicate that the degree to which social cues could be integrated remains key. In particular, it is worth to notice that the context of web designers is having a great impact. Traditional web design occurs mainly in small firm environment, or start-up context. Designers tend to follow models or a particular culture such as the Microsoft school. Herd mentality and conformism are strong in the industry especially regarding programmers. Significantly, creative work requires more time, resources and risk while the market is requesting efficiency and proven methods. Few firms were described as strong enough to have a clearly defined identity, power structure and online marketing strategy. While characteristics of these and comparable concerns have emerged in prior online retail literature, our conceptualization of these within a resistance framework when dealing with social cues online is unique. Consequently, the findings presented here provide a novel contribution to existing literature on resistance.

The study allows further understanding of web designers' impact in shaping the current de-velopment tools such as Web 3.0, also known as the semantic web or smart web, which includes advanced social capital features socially grounded within consumers' day to day environment and practices. These in turn, will create sustainable differentiation strategies in the profession creating a two tier market whereby some designers are able to provide inimitable value added services within specific markets while other only provide basic technical services.

Of course a topic of the nature is culturally loaded. While the global nature of the online business and globalization of technologies is occurring, an underlying aspect rising from the findings was the hegemonic impact of the USA/ EU as both drivers of new technologies but also standards setter in key areas such as search, navigation and overall efficiency. With the exception of Japan as underlined by our respondents, US/EU standards and understanding of social cues are overwhelmingly shaping the limited amount of social capital cues currently available. At present, very little is known about the new type and possible long term impact of web designers that are emerging from markets such as India and China. Moreover, the overall perception from our experts was that more mechanical ground work was conducted in such location. The rapid pace of the online environment may modify such strategies rapidly.

REFERENCES

Ackroyd, S., & Thompson, P. (1999). *Organizational misbehaviour*. London, UK: Sage.

Alexander, C. S., & Becker, H. J. (1978). The use of vignettes in survey research. *Public Opinion Quarterly, 42*(1), 93–104. doi:10.1086/268432

Baker, W. E. (1990). Market networks and corporate behavior. *American Journal of Sociology, 96*(3), 589–625. doi:10.1086/229573

Banister, E. N., & Hogg, M. K. (2004). Negative symbolic consumption and consumers' dive for self-esteem: The case of the fashion industry. *European Journal of Marketing, 38*(7), 850–868. doi:10.1108/03090560410539285

Bessant, J., Kaplinsky, R., & Lamming, R. (2003). Putting supply chain learning into practice. *International Journal of Operations & Production Management, 23*(2), 167–184. doi:10.1108/01443570310458438

Burt, R. S. (1992). *Structural holes: The social structure of competition.* Cambridge, MA: Harvard University Press.

Caro, D. H., Lenkeit, J., Lehmann, R., & Schwippert, K. (2009). The role of academic achievement growth in school track recommendations. *Studies in Educational Evaluation, 35*(4), 183–192. doi:10.1016/j.stueduc.2009.12.002

Castells, M. (2001). *The internet galaxy: Reflections on the Internet business and society.* Oxford, UK: Oxford University Press.

Cavanagh, G. F., & Fritzsche, D. J. (1985). Using vignettes in business ethics research. In Preston, L. E. (Ed.), *Research in corporate social performance and policy* (pp. 279–293). Greenwich, CT: JAI Press.

Chen, G., & Kotz, D. (2000). *A survey of context-aware mobile computing research,* (p. 16). TR2000-381. Hanover, NH: Dartmouth College.

Claridge, T. (2004). *Social capital and natural resource management.* (Unpublished Thesis). University of Queensland, Brisbane, Australia.

Clarke, I., Hallsworth, A., Jackson, P., de Kervenoael, R., Del Aguila, R. P., & Kirkup, M. (2006). Retail restructuring and consumer choice 1. Long-term local changes in consumer behavior: Portsmouth, 1980-2002. *Environment & Planning A, 38*(1), 25–46. doi:10.1068/a37207

Collinson, D. (1994). Strategies of resistance. In Jermier, J., Knoghts, D., & Nord, W. (Eds.), *Resistance and power in organizations.* London, UK: Sage.

Constantinides, E. (2004). Influencing the online consumer's behavior: The Web experience. *Internet Research, 14*(2), 111–126. doi:10.1108/10662240410530835

Craig-Lees, M., & Hill, C. (2002). Understanding voluntary simplifiers. *Psychology and Marketing, 19*(2), 187–210. doi:10.1002/mar.10009

Dailey, L. (2004). Navigational Web atmospherics: Explaining the influence of restrictive navigation cues. *Journal of Business Research, 57*(7), 795–803. doi:10.1016/S0148-2963(02)00364-8

De Kervenoael, R., & Aykac, D. S. O. (2008). Grey market e-shopping and trust building practices in China. In Kautonen, T., & Karjaluoto, H. (Eds.), *Trust and new technologies.* Cheltenham, UK: Edward Edgar.

De Kervenoael, R., Aykac, D. S. O., & Palmer, M. (2009). Online social capital: Understanding e-impulse buying in practice. *Journal of Retailing and Consumer Services, 16*(4), 320–328. doi:10.1016/j.jretconser.2009.02.007

Dekker, P., & Uslaner, E. M. (2001). Introduction. In Uslaner, E. M. (Ed.), *Social capital and participation in everyday life* (pp. 1–6). London, UK: Routledge.

DiMaggio, P. J., & Powell, W. W. (1983). The iron cage revisited: Institutional isomorphism and collective rationality in organizational fields. *American Sociological Review, 48*, 147–160. doi:10.2307/2095101

Eroglu, S. A., Karen, A. M., & Lenita, M. D. (2001). Atmospheric qualities of online retailing: A conceptual model and implications. *Journal of Business Research, 54*(2), 177–184. doi:10.1016/S0148-2963(99)00087-9

Ettlinger, N. (2003). Cultural economic geography and a relational and microspace approach to trusts, rationalities, networks, and change in collaborative workplaces. *Journal of Economic Geography, 3*, 145–171. doi:10.1093/jeg/3.2.145

Fleming, P., & Spicer, A. (2007). *Contesting the corporation.* Cambridge, UK: Cambridge University Press. doi:10.1017/CBO9780511628047

Flint, D. J., & Woodruff, R. B. (2001). The initiators of changes in customers' desired value: Results from a theory building study. *Industrial Marketing Management, 30*(4), 321–337. doi:10.1016/S0019-8501(99)00117-0

Gabriel, Y. (1999). Beyond happy families: A critical reevaluation of the control resistance-identity triangle. *Human Relations, 52*(2), 179–203. doi:10.1177/001872679905200201

Gatignon, H., & Robertson, T. S. (1991). Innovative decision processes. In Robertson, T. S., & Kassarjian, H. H. (Eds.), *Handbook of consumer behavior* (pp. 316–348). Englewood Cliffs, NJ: Prentice-Hall.

Giddens, A. (1992). *The transformation of intimacy.* Cambridge, MA: Polity Press.

Green, H., & Hof, R. D. (2007). *Picking up where search leaves off.* Retrieved January 15, 2009, from http://www.businessweek.com/ magazine/content/05_15/ b3928112_mz063.htm

Haynes, D., & Prakash, G. (1991). Introduction: The entanglement of power and resistance. In Haynes, D., & Prakash, G. (Eds.), *Contesting power: Resistance and everyday social relations in South Asia.* Berkeley, CA: University of California Press.

Hogg, M. K., & Michell, P. C. N. (1996). Identity, self and consumption: A conceptual framework. *Journal of Marketing Management, 12*(7), 629–644. doi:10.1080/0267257X.1996.9964441

Hunt, K. A., & Bashaw, R. E. (1999). A new classification of sales resistance. *Industrial Marketing Management, 28*(1), 109–118. doi:10.1016/S0019-8501(97)00098-9

Iyer, R., & Muncy, J. A. (2009). Purpose and object of anti consumption. *Journal of Business Research, 62*(2), 160–168. doi:10.1016/j.jbusres.2008.01.023

Jarzabkowski, P., Balogun, J., & Seidl, D. (2007). Strategizing: the challenges of practice perspective. *Human Relations, 60*(1), 5–27. doi:10.1177/0018726707075703

Klein, L. R. (2003). Creating virtual product experiences: The role of telepresence. *Journal of Interactive Marketing, 17*(1), 41–55. doi:10.1002/dir.10046

Knights, D., & McCabe, D. (2000). Ain't misbehavin? Opportunities for resistance under new forms of quality management. *Sociology, 34*(3), 421–436.

Kozinets, R. V., & Handelman, J. M. (2004). Adversaries of consumption: Consumer movements, activism, and ideology. *The Journal of Consumer Research, 31*(3), 691–704. doi:10.1086/425104

Lazarus, R. S., & Folkman, S. (1984). *Stress, appraisal, and coping.* New York, NY: Springer.

Lee, M. S. W., Fernadez, K. V., & Hyman, M. R. (2009a). Anti-consumption: An overview and research agenda. *Journal of Business Research, 62*, 145–147. doi:10.1016/j.jbusres.2008.01.021

Lee, M. S. W., Motion, J., & Conroy, D. (2009b). Anti-consumption and brand avoidance. *Journal of Business Research, 62*, 169–180. doi:10.1016/j.jbusres.2008.01.024

Lee, N., & Cadogan, J. W. (2009). Sales force social exchange in problem resolution situations. *Industrial Marketing Management, 32*(3), 355–372. doi:10.1016/j.indmarman.2008.02.002

Ling, R. (2008). *New tech new ties*. Cambridge, MA: MIT Press.

Marcelle, G. (2004). *Technological learning: A strategic imperative for firms in the developing world*. Cheltenham, UK: Edward Elgar.

McAllister, D. J. (1995). Affect-and cognition-based trust as foundations for interpersonal cooperation in organizations. *Academy of Management Journal, 38*(1), 24–59. doi:10.2307/256727

Merriam, S. (1998). *Qualitative research and case study applications in education*. San Francisco, CA: Jossey-Bass.

Miles, M. B., & Huberman, A. M. (1994). *Qualitative data analysis: An expanded sourcebook*. Newbury Park, CA: Sage Publications.

Mittelstaedt, R. A., Grossbart, S. L., Curtis, W. W., & Devere, S. P. (1976). Optimal stimulation level and the adoption decision process. *The Journal of Consumer Research, 3*, 84–94. doi:10.1086/208655

Moore, D. S. (1997). Remapping resistance: Ground for struggle and the politics of place. In Pile, S., & Keith, M. (Eds.), *Geographies of resistance* (pp. 87–106). London, UK: Routledge.

Oreg, S. (2003). Resistance to change: Developing an individual differences measures. *The Journal of Applied Psychology, 88*(4), 680–693. doi:10.1037/0021-9010.88.4.680

Palmer, M., & O'Kane, P. (2007). Strategy as practice: Interactive governance spaces and the corporate strategies of retail TNCs. *Journal of Economic Geography, 7*, 515–535. doi:10.1093/jeg/lbm015

Palmer, M., Owens, M., & De Kervenoael, R. (2010). Paths of the least resistance: Understanding how motives form in international retail joint venturing. *The Service Industries Journal, 30*(8).

Piacentini, M., & Banister, E. M. (2009). Managing anti-consumption in excessive drinking culture. *Journal of Business Research, 62*, 279–288. doi:10.1016/j.jbusres.2008.01.035

Pile, S., & Keith, M. (1997). *Geography of resistance*. London, UK: Routledge.

Postman, J. (2009). *Social corp: Social media goes corporate*. Berkeley, CA: New Riders.

Prasad, P., & Prasad, A. (2000). Stretching the iron cage: The constitution and implications of routine workplace resistance. *Organization Science, 11*(4), 387–403. doi:10.1287/orsc.11.4.387.14597

Preissle, J., Tesch, R., & LeCompte, M. (1994). *Ethnography and qualitative design in educational research*. Orlando, FL: Academic Press.

Rogers, E. M. (1995). *Diffusion of innovations* (4th ed.). New York, NY: Free Press.

Rossi, P. H., & Anderson, A. B. (1982). The factorial survey approach. In Rossi, P. H., & Nock, S. L. (Eds.), *Measuring social judgments* (pp. 15–67). Beverly Hills, CA: Sage.

Russel, D. W., & Russel, C. A. (2006). Explicit and implicit catalysts of consumer resistance: The effects of animosity, cultural salience and country-of-origin on subsequent choice. *International Journal of Research in Marketing, 23*, 321–331. doi:10.1016/j.ijresmar.2006.05.003

Schein, E. H. (2004). *Organizational culture and leadership*. San Francisco, CA: Jossey-Bass.

Selwyn, N. (2003). Apart from technology: understanding people's non-use of information and communication technologies in everyday life. *Technology in Society, 25*, 99–116. doi:10.1016/S0160-791X(02)00062-3

Shaw, D., & Newholm, T. (2002). Voluntary simplicity and the ethics of consumption. *Psychology and Marketing, 19*(2), 167–185. doi:10.1002/mar.10008

Sheth, J. N. (1981). Psychology of innovation resistance: The less developed concept (LDC) in diffusion research. *Research in Marketing, 4,* 273–282.

Spencer, C. D. (1978). Two types of role playing: Threats to internal and external validity. *The American Psychologist, 33,* 265–268. doi:10.1037/0003-066X.33.3.265

Strauss, A., & Corbin, J. (1990). *Basics of qualitative research: Grounded theory procedures and techniques.* Newbury Park, CA: Sage.

Stuart, F. I., Deckert, P., McCutheon, D., & Kunst, R. (1998). A leveraged learning network. *Sloan Management Review, 39*(4), 81–94.

Suchman, M. C. (1995). Managing legitimacy: Strategic and institutional approaches. *Academy of Management Journal, 20*(3), 571–610.

Szmigin, I., & Foxall, G. (1998). Three forms of innovation resistance: The case of retail payment methods. *Technovation, 18*(6/7), 459–468. doi:10.1016/S0166-4972(98)00030-3

Uslaner, E. M. (2001). Volunteering and social capital: How trust and religion shape civic participation in the United States. In Uslaner, E. M. (Ed.), *Social capital and participation in everyday life* (pp. 104–117). London, UK: Routledge.

Watts, M. (1997). Black gold, white heat: State violence, local resistance and the national question in Nigeria. In Pile, S., & Keith, M. (Eds.), *Geographies of resistance* (pp. 33–67). London, UK: Routledge.

Whittington, R. (2007). Strategy practice and strategy process: Family differences and the sociological eye. *Organization Studies, 28*(10), 1575–1586. doi:10.1177/0170840607081557

Yin, R. (1994). *Case study research: Design and methods.* London, UK: Sage.

KEY TERMS AND DEFINITIONS

Online Social Capital: In the context of ICT, it can be described as the sum of web experiences including for example: (i) aesthetics, art, (ii) association to user lifestyle symbols including norms, posture, etiquette, gender, politics, religion, and (iii) environmental, personal, cultural grounded reference points.

Resistance: Attitude aiming at contesting status quo.

Web Developer: The person in charge of the development and programming aspects of the web site.

Web Site Designer: The person who creates the look and feel of the web site as well as the information architecture.

Chapter 14
Designing Mobile Learning for the User

Mohamed Ally
Athabasca University, Canada

ABSTRACT

There is increasing use of mobile devices around the world to conduct everyday business and to social-ize. As a result, learners will be using mobile devices to access learning materials so that they can learn from anywhere and at anytime. Learning materials must be designed using proven instructional design models and learning theories. This will allow the learning system to provide flexibility in learning and to meet the needs of individual learners. In addition, good user interface design must be followed in mobile learning to allow learners to interact with the learning system and learning materials to facilitate learning from anywhere and at anytime.

INTRODUCTION

There has been a rapid increase in the use of mobile devices such as cell phones, smart phones, tablet PCs, web pads, and palmtop computers by students and individuals in business, education, industry, and society. By the end of 2010 there will be over four billion mobile phones world wide and mobile connection will bypass landline connections. As a result, there will be more access to information and learning materials from anywhere and at anytime, using these mobile devices. The trend in society today is learning and working "on the go" rather than having to be at a specific location

to learn and work. Also, there is a trend towards ubiquitous computing, where computing devices are invisible to the users because of the wireless connectivity of mobile devices. As a result, we are seeing more use of mobile learning in educa-tion and training.

There are many definitions of mobile learning. According to Ally (2004), mobile learning is the use of electronic learning materials with built-in learning strategies for delivery on mobile comput-ing devices to allow access from anywhere and at anytime. O'Malley et al (2003) defined mobile learning as any sort of learning that happens when the learner is not at a fixed, predetermined loca-tion, or learning that happens when the learner takes advantage of the learning opportunities

DOI: 10.4018/978-1-61350-516-8.ch014

Copyright © 2012, IGI Global. Copying or distributing in print or electronic forms without written permission of IGI Global is prohibited.

offered by mobile technologies. Traxler (2005) defined mobile learning as any educational provision where the sole or dominant technologies are handheld or palmtop devices. The definition of mobile learning we will be using in the chapter is "the delivery of learning materials and providing learning support on mobile devices to provide flexibility to the learner so that the learner can learn while they are mobile".

Because of the proliferation of use of mobile technologies around the world, there is a significant interest in mobile learning to provide flexibility in learning. The design of the mobile learning interface from a pedagogical viewport is critical to promote success in learning (Subramanya & Yi, 2006). A systematic framework must be used for the design of mobile learning so that developers produce high quality learning materials that meet the needs of learners. An example of a comprehensive framework for elearning is the one developed by Badrul Khan (2005) which has been used successfully to develop elearning materials globally. This chapter will describe how to design the mobile learning interface and materials for the user using Khan's framework (as shown in Figure 1).

BENEFITS OF MOBILE LEARNING TO THE USER

Mobile learning is accessible across time zones, and location and distance are not issues. In asynchronous mobile learning, students can access their online materials anytime, while synchronous mobile learning allows for real-time interaction between students and instructors. The wireless capability of mobile devices allow users to connect from anywhere and anytime so that they can access learning materials when they want to learn, and from where they want to learn. Mobile devices are small enough to be portable, which allows users to use the device from any location to interact with other users from anywhere, and

Figure 1. Badrul Khan framework for mobile learning (Adapted with permission)

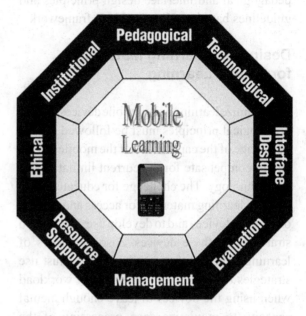

at anytime to share information and expertise, complete a task, or work collaboratively on a project. Learners can use the wireless capability of their mobile devices to access up-to-date and relevant learning materials from the web and to communicate with experts in the field that they are studying. Situated learning, which is the application of knowledge and skills in specific contexts, is facilitated, since learners can complete courses while working on the job or in their own space, and apply what they learn at the same time.

Mobile devices have many benefits because they allow for mobility while learning and working; however, there are some limitations to mobile devices that designers must be aware of when designing learning materials for delivery on mobile devices. Some of the limitations of mobile devices in delivering learning materials include the small screen size for the output of information, small or restricted input devices, low bandwidth, and challenges when navigating through the information. As a result, it is critical that the learning materials and the interface be designed properly for easy access and must include quality learner interaction

(Ally, 2009). The rest of this chapter describes the pedagogical and interface design principles and guidelines based on Khan's (2005) framework.

Designing Learning Materials for Mobile Learning

To maximize learning using mobile devices, proper pedagogical principles must be followed to take advantage of the capabilities of the mobile device and to compensate for the current limitations of the technology. The challenge for educators is to develop learning materials for access and display on mobile devices and to develop user interaction strategies on these devices. Also, designers of learning materials for mobile devices must use strategies to reduce the user's mental workload when using the devices to leave enough mental capacity to maximize deep processing of the learning materials. According to O'Malley et al. (2003), effective methods for presenting information on mobile devices and the pedagogy of mobile learning have yet to be developed. Badrul Khan's (2005) framework (Figure 1) is a promising framework to contribute to the pedagogy of mobile learning and to guide the design, development, and implementation of mobile learning.

Designers of information and learning materials have to aware of the limitations of screen size and input devices when designing for usability. Navigation techniques must allow users of mobile devices to go directly to the information and move back and forth with ease. Information should be targeted to the user needs when they need it and should be presented efficiently to maximize the display on the mobile device. To compensate for the small screen size of mobile devices, learning materials must use rich media to convey the message to the user. For example, rather than present information in text, graphics and pictures can be used to convey the message using the least amount of text. Graphic organizers can be used as the interface to allow users to get the big picture of the lesson and at the same time navigate to any part of the lesson. To present procedures and real life situations, video clips can be used to present real life simulations to the user. Also, the interface must be appropriate for individual users and the software system should have the intelligence to be able to customize the interface based on individual user's preferences. To prepare quality mobile learning materials, designers must of aware of learning theories that can guide development.

Learning Theories to Guide Mobile Learning Development

According to cognitive psychology, learning is an internal process and the amount learned depends on the processing capacity of the user, the amount of effort expended during the learning process (Craik and Lockhart 1972; Craik and Tulving 1975), the quality of the processing, and the user's existing knowledge structure (Ausubel, 1974). These have implications for how learning materials should be designed for mobile devices. Educators must use strategies that allow the user to activate existing cognitive structures and conduct high level processing of the materials. Memory is enhanced when information is represented both in verbal and visual forms (Paivio, 1986). Presenting materials in both textual and visual forms will involve more cognitive processing, resulting in better storage and integration into long term memory (Mayer et al., 2004).

According to constructivism, learners are active during the learning process and they use their existing knowledge to process and personalize the information. Learners interpret information and the world according to their personal reality, and they learn by observation, processing, and interpretation, and then personalize the information into their existing knowledge base (Cooper, 1993). As a result, learning strategies for mobile learning must include strategies to allow students to actively process and internalize the information. Learning is facilitated when learners can contextualize what they learn for immediate application and thus acquire personal meaning. According to Sharples (2000), mobile learning devices allow learners to learn where they are located and in their personal context. Also, mobile learning facilitates personalized learning since learners can learn in their own context from anywhere and anytime.

Design Principles for Mobile Learning

Based on learning theories, the following guidelines are presented for the development of mobile learning materials to maximize the amount learned and to meet the needs of the user.

- Learning materials must be sequenced appropriately to promote learning. Proper sequencing will allow learners to have smooth transition between learning sequence and experience success as they complete the segments of the lesson. Common methods of sequencing include simple to complex, known to unknown, and knowledge to application.

- Learners should be informed of the learning outcomes so that they can plan for their learning sessions, set expectations, and search for resources to achieve the learning outcomes. Mobile learning allows learners to explore and discover additional learning resources because of the connectivity of mobile devices.

- Mobile learning lesson must use evaluation techniques to allow learners to evaluate themselves to determine whether or not they have achieved the learning outcome. This becomes even more important when mobile learning is implemented in a distance education format.

- Feedback should be provided to learners so that they can monitor how they are doing and take corrective action if required. Feedback can be provided immediately with the mobile device and can take dif-

ferent forms such as text, audio, or video because of the multimedia capability of the mobile technology.

- Information should be chunked to prevent overload during processing in working memory for both humans and devices. This is based on Miller's (1956) observation that because of the limited processing capacity in human working memory, materials should be organized in seven plus or minus two chunks. To facilitate efficient processing in working memory, mobile learning materials should present between five and nine items on a screen.

- Learning strategies should be presented in different modes to make use of different parts of the brain to maximize processing for quality learning. Where possible, textual, verbal, and visual information should be presented to encourage encoding. Presenting information in different modes also accommodates individual differences in processing.

- One of the variables that designers tend to ignore when they develop learning materials for mobile devices is the user of the devices. Different users have different learning styles and some users may be more visual while others may be verbal (Mayer & Massa, 2003). Preferences and strategies must be included and information presented in different ways to cater for different learning styles and preferences (Ally & Fahy, 2002). Graphic overviews can be used to cater to users who prefer to get the big picture before they go into the details of the information. For the active learners, information can be presented on the mobile device and then the device will give the user the opportunity to apply the information. For the creative users, there must be opportunities to apply the information in real life applications so that they go beyond what was presented. The learning materials and information have to be designed with the user in mind to facilitate access, learning, and comprehension. Also, the user should have control over what they want to access so that they can go through the learning materials based on their preferred learning styles and other preferences.

- Learning strategies that motivate learners should be included in lessons so that learners can be motivated to learn especially when using mobile technology in distributed learning. According to Keller (1983), instruction should capture and maintain the learners' attention, should be relevant to the learner, should build the learner's confidence, and students should be satisfied with their achievements.

- A major advantage of using mobile technology in education is that students can use the communication capabilities of the technology to communicate with each other and with the teacher or tutor. Collaborative and cooperative learning strategies should be implemented to facilitate coaching and mentoring during learning.

- Learning should be interactive to promote higher-level learning and to establish social presence and to help develop personal meaning. According to Heinich et al. (2002), learning is the development of new knowledge, skills, and attitudes as the learner interacts with information and the environment. Hirumi (2002) proposes a framework of interaction in online learning that consists of three levels. Level one is learner-self interaction, which occurs within learners to help monitor and regulate their own learning. Level two is learner-human and learner-non-human interactions, where the learner interacts with human and non-human resources. Level three is learner-instruction interaction, which consists of activities to achieve a learning outcome. In mobile learning, different types of interaction can be used to facilitate learning. At the lowest level of interaction, there must be learner-interface interaction to allow the learner to access and sense the information. The interface is where learners use their senses to register the information in sensory storage. In mobile learning, the interface is with the mobile device, to access the content and to interact with others. Once learners access the learning materials, there must be learner-content interaction to process the information. Learners navigate through the content to access the components of the lesson, which could take the form of pre-learning, learning, and post-learning activities. Students should be given the ability to choose their own sequence of learning, or should be given one or more suggested sequences. As learners interact with the content, they should be encouraged to problem solve, apply, assess, analyze, synthesize, evaluate, and reflect on what they learn. During the learner-content interaction, learners process the information to transform it from short-term to long-term memory. The higher the level of processing, the more associations are made in the learners' long-term memory, which results in higher-level learning.

- Mobile technologies allow learners to be connected to the outside world and to other learners during the learning process. Hence, learning is taking place in a networked environment (Siemens, 2004). Because of the information explosion, learners should be allowed to explore and research current information. Learners of the future need to be autonomous and independent learners so that they can acquire current information to build a valid and accurate knowledge base.

- Because of globalization, information is not location-specific, and, with the increasing use of telecommunication technologies, experts and learners from around the world can share and review information. Learning and knowledge rests in a diversity of opinions. As a result, learners must be allowed to connect with others around the world to examine others' opinions and to share their thinking with the world. Mobile learning promises to help learners function in a networked world where they can learn at any time and from anywhere (Ally, 2005).

- Because of the information explosion, learners of the future must be willing to acquire new knowledge on an ongoing basis. Mobile learning strategies must give learners the opportunity to research and locate new information in a discipline so that they can keep up-to-date in the field. The Internet is expanding education into a global classroom, with learners, teachers, and experts from around the world. As a result, learners must network with other students and experts to make sure that they are continually learning and updating their knowledge.

INTERFACE DESIGN FOR THE USER OF MOBILE LEARNING

Designers of learning materials for delivery on mobile devices must use effective interface design techniques to make the learning process efficient and flexible to meet the needs of learners. The mobile device interface should cater for users' individual needs since the interface is required to coordinate the interaction between the user and the information (Chong et al., 2004). To compensate for the small screen size of the display of the mobile device, the interface of the mobile device must be designed properly. The interface can be graphical and should present limited information on the screen to prevent information overload in short-term memory. The system should contain intelligent software agents to determine what the user did in the past and adapt the interface for future interaction with the information. The software system must be proactive by anticipating what the user will do next and provide the most appropriate interface for the interaction to enhance learning. Users must be able to jump to related information without too much effort. The interface must allow the user to access the information with minimal effort and move back to previous information with ease. For sessions that are information intense, the system must adjust the interface to prevent information overload.

Some ways to prevent information overload include presenting less concepts on one screen or organizing the information in the form of concept maps to give the overall structure of the information and then presenting the details by linking to other screens with the details. The interface must also use good navigational strategies to allow users to move back and forth between displays. Navigation can also be automatic, based on the intelligence gathered on the user's current progress and needs. Below are key strategies to build the interface and learning materials for mobile learning.

- Because of the small size of current input devices, learning materials must be designed to require minimum input from users. Input can use pointing or voice input devices to minimize typing and writing. Because mobile devices allow information to be accessed from anywhere at anytime, the device must have input and output options to prevent distractions when using the mobile devices. For example, if someone is using a mobile device in a remote location, it may be difficult to type on a keyboard or use a pointing device. The mobile technology must allow the user to input data using voice input or touch screen.

- Intelligent software systems can be built to develop an initial profile of the user and then present materials that will benefit the specific user, based on the user profile. As the intelligent agent interacts with the user, it "learns" about the user and adapts the format of the information, the interface and navigation pattern according to the user's style and needs. Knowing the user needs and style will allow the intelligent software system to access additional materials from the Internet and other networks to meet the user's needs.

- Information and learning materials can be presented to the user in a personalized style or a formal style. In a learning situation, information should be presented in a personalized style since the user of the mobile device may be in a remote location and will find this style more connected and personal. Mayer et al. (2004) found that students who received a personalized version of a narrated animation performed significantly better on a transfer test when compared to students who received a non-personalized, formal version of the narrated animation. They claimed that the results from the study are consistent with the cognitive theory of learning where personalization results in students processing the information in an active way, resulting in higher level learning and transfer to other situations.

- Strategies should be used to allow learners to perceive and attend to the information so that it can be transferred to working memory. Learners use their sensory systems to register the information in the form of sensations so that the information can be process efficiently for transfer. Strategies to facilitate maximum sensation should be used. Examples include the proper loca-

tion of the information on the screen, the use of colors for highlighting, the pacing of the information, and the mode of delivery (audio, visuals, animations, or video). Learners must receive the information in the form of sensations before perception and processing can occur; however, the learner must not be overloaded with sensations, which could be counterproductive to the learning process.

- Information critical for learning should be highlighted to focus learners' attention. For example, headings should be used to organize the details, and formatted to allow learners to attend to and process the details under the headings.

- Learners should be told why they should take the lesson, so that they can attend to the information throughout the lesson. This is critical for motivation and to focus on the learning especially for learners on the move and those who reside in remote locations.

- The difficulty level of the material must match the cognitive level of the learner, so that the learner can both attend to and relate to the material. Links to both simpler and more complicated materials can be used to accommodate learners at different knowledge levels.

- Interface and learning strategies must match the learning style of learners. Students learning styles can be determined by a learning style analysis tool such as the Kolb Learning Style Inventory (Kolb, 1984). Mobile learning materials should include activities for different learning styles, so that learners can select appropriate activities based on their preferred learning style.
  - Concrete-experience learners prefer specific examples in which they can be involved, and they relate to peers more than to people in authority.

They like group work and peer feedback, and they see the instructor as a coach or helper. These learners prefer support methods that allow them to interact with peers and obtain coaching from the tutor.

○ Reflective-observation learners like to observe carefully before taking any action. They prefer that all the information be available for learning, and they see the tutor as the expert.

○ Abstract-conceptualization learners like to work more with things and symbols and less with people. They like to work with theory and to conduct systematic analyses.

○ Active-experimentation learners prefer to learn by doing practical projects and participating in group discussions. They prefer active learning methods and interact with peers for feedback and information. They tend to establish their own criteria for evaluating situations. Adequate supports should be provided for students with different learning styles.

• Because of the limited processing capability of humans, information should be organized or chunked in segments of appropriate and meaningful size to facilitate processing in working memory. A learning session on a mobile device can be seen as consisting of a number of segments sequenced in a pre-determined way or sequenced based on the user needs. Information and learning materials for mobile devices should take the form of information and learning objects which are in an electronic format, reusable, and stored in a repository for access anytime and from anywhere. Information objects and learning objects allow for instant assembly of learning materials by users and intelligent software agents to facilitate just-in-time

learning and information access. Giving learners the ability to access learning materials from electronic repositories will empower the learners to select resources to meet their needs.

• High level concept maps should be used to show the important concepts in the information and the relationship between the concepts, rather than presenting information in a textual format. High level concept maps and networks can be used to represent information spatially so that students can see the main ideas and their relationships (Novak, Gowin, & Johanse 1983). Use of graphics in mobile learning materials will minimize the amount of textual materials students have to read on the small device screen (Tarasewich, 2008).

• For users in remote locations with low bandwidth or with limited wireless access, information that takes a long time to download should be re-designed to facilitate efficient download. For example, low resolution graphics should be used or a description of the graphic should be provided.

CONCLUSION

The proliferation of mobile devices and globalization is determining what students learn, from where and when they learn and how they learn. Mobile devices can be used to deliver information and learning materials to users, but the materials must be designed properly to compensate for the small screen of the devices and the limited processing and storage capacity of users' working memory. Learning materials for delivery on mobile devices must be designed to meet the needs of individual learners and provide flexibility to learn from anywhere and at anytime. The use of global positioning systems (GPS) can determine where users are located and connect them with users in the same location so that they can work collaboratively on projects and help each other on solving problems. The system can also prescribe appropriate learning materials based on the location and context of the learner.

The challenge for designers of learning materials for mobile devices is how to standardize the design for use on different types of devices. Intelligent software agents should be built into mobile devices so that most of the work is done behind the scenes, minimizing input from users and the amount of information presented on the display of the mobile devices. Also, intelligent agents should be built to detect the mobile device the learner is using and format and present the information for the specific device (Chen & Hsu, 2008). This will allow users to use their existing devices, rather than having to purchase new devices.

In the past, the development of learning materials for mobile devices concentrated on the technology rather than the user. Future development of learning materials for mobile devices should concentrate on the user to drive the development and delivery of mobile learning materials. Learning materials need to use multimedia strategies that are information rich rather than being mostly text and should follow sound learning and interface design theories.

While mobile devices have small screens, with the advent of the iPad and similar larger format mobile devices, the limitations are lifting on the amount of information that can be presented comfortably on screen. As mobile technologies advanced there will be significant changes on how users interface with such devices. Sensors within the human body will communicate with the device and there will be increasing use of biometrics (Hook, 2008). Human emotions could determine when learning takes place and there could be direct communication between the human brain and the device. Also, in the future, devices could be embedded in the human body. The challenge to educators is how to design for the rapid changes in technology.

"There is no turning back. Mobile learning will be used increasingly to educate individuals at all levels, anywhere and at anytime, and will be the vehicle to achieve 'education for all'." (Ally, 2010).

REFERENCES

Ally, M. (2004). Using learning theories to design instruction for mobile learning devices. *Mobile Learning 2004 International Conference Proceedings*, Rome, July 2004, (pp. 5-8).

Ally, M. (2009). *Mobile learning: Transforming the delivery of education and training.* Athabasca, Canada: Athabasca University Press.

Ally, M., & Fahy, P. (2002). Using students' learning styles to provide support in distance education. *Proceedings of the Eighteenth Annual Conference on Distance Teaching and Learning*, Madison, Wisconsin, August 2002, (pp. 1-4).

Ally, M., & Lin, O. (2005). An intelligent agent for adapting and delivering electronic course materials to mobile learners. *Proceedings of the International Mobile Learning Conference*, Capetown, South Africa, October 2005, (pp. 1-4).

Ausubel, D. P. (1974). *Educational psychology: A cognitive view*. New York, NY: Holt, Rinehart and Winston.

Chen, C.-M., & Hsu, S.-H. (2008). Personalized intelligent mobile learning system for supporting effective English learning. *Journal of Educational Technology & Society*, *11*(3), 153–180.

Chong, P. H. J., So, P. L., Shum, P., Li, X. J., & Goyal, D. (2004). Design and implementation of user interface for mobile devices. *IEEE Transactions on Consumer Electronics*, *50*(4), 1156–1161. doi:10.1109/TCE.2004.1362513

Cooper, P. A. (1993). Paradigm shifts in designing instruction: From behaviorism to cognitivism to constructivism. *Educational Technology, 33*(5), 12–19.

Heinich, R., Molenda, M., Russell, J. D., & Smaldino, S. E. (2002). *Instructional media and technologies for learning.* NJ: Pearson Education.

Hirumi, A. (2002). A framework for analyzing, designing, and sequencing planned e-learning interactions. *The Quarterly Review of Distance Education, 3*(2), 141–160.

Hook, K. (2008). Knowing, communicating, and experiencing through body and emotion. *IEEE Transactions on Learning Technologies, 1*(4).

Khan, B. H. (2005). *Managing e-learning: Design, delivery, implementation and evaluation.* Hershey, PA: Information Science Publishing. doi:10.4018/978-1-59140-634-1

Khan, B. H. (Ed.). (2007). *Flexible learning in an information society.* Hershey, PA: Information Science Publishing.

Kolb, D. A. (1984). *Experiential learning: Experience as the source of learning and development.* Englewood Cliffs, NJ: Prentice-Hall.

Mayer, R. E., Fennell, S., Farmer, L., & Campbell, J. (2004). A personalization effect in multimedia learning: Students learn better when words are in conversational style rather than formal style. *Journal of Educational Psychology, 96*(2), 389–395. doi:10.1037/0022-0663.96.2.389

Mayer, R. E., & Massa, L. J. (2003). Three facets of visual and verbal learners: Cognitive ability, cognitive style, and learning preference. *Journal of Educational Psychology, 95*(4), 833–846. doi:10.1037/0022-0663.95.4.833

Miller, G. A. (1956). The magical number seven, plus or minus two: Some limits on our capacity for processing information. *Psychological Review, 63*, 81–97. doi:10.1037/h0043158

Novak, J. D., Gowin, D. B., & Johanse, G. T. (1983). The use of concept mapping and knowledge Vee mapping with junior high school science students. *Science Education, 67*, 625–645. doi:10.1002/sce.3730670511

O'Malley, C., Vavoula, G., Glew, J. P., Taylor, J., Sharples, M., & Lefrere, P. (2003). *Guidelines for learning/teaching/tutoring in a mobile environment.* MOBIlearn Project Report. Retrieved October 1, 2010 from http://www.mobilearn.org/results/results.htm

Paivio, A. (1986). *Mental representations: A dual coding approach.* Oxford, UK: Oxford University Press.

Sharples, M. (2000). The design of personal mobile technologies for lifelong learning. *Computers & Education, 34*, 177–193. doi:10.1016/S0360-1315(99)00044-5

Siemens, G. (2004). *A learning theory for the digital age.* Retrieved October 8, 2010, from http://www.elearnspace.org/Articles/connectivism.htm

Subramanya, S. R., & Yi, B. K. (2006). User interfaces for mobile content. *Computer,* (April): 85–87. doi:10.1109/MC.2006.144

Tarasewich, P., Gong, J., Nah, F. F., & DeWester, D. (2008). Mobile interaction design: Integrating individual and organizational perspectives. [IOS Press.]. *Information Knowledge Systems Management, 7*, 121–144.

Traxler, J. (2005). Defining mobile learning. *Proceedings of the 2005 IADIS International Conference,* (pp. 261-266).

Chapter 15
Issues and Challenges Associated with the Design of Electronic Textbook

Elena Railean
Information Society Development Institute, Republic of Moldova

ABSTRACT

This chapter investigates issues associated with the design of an electronic textbook and describes meta-systems learning design (MLD). MLD was founded by the Globalisation G- Anthropology A- Existentialism E paradigm (GAE). This paradigm argues the transition from closed pedagogical systems to more open educational systems. The core element of MLD is the pedagogy of a competence development triggered electronic textbook. The functionality of MLD is assured by a flexible and dynamic instructional strategy. This new strategy provides an operating framework both for teachers and for learners through self-regulation assessment.

The contents of this chapter are framed under three categories: the theoretical approach, pedagogy of competence development and practice. Conclusions are provided at the end.

INTRODUCTION

In this era of social media, all pedagogical systems have been affected by globalization and have become part of a single global educational system (Kalantzis & Cope, 2006; Afanasiev, 2009; Pullen, 2010 etc.). The global educational system became "more open and flexible" (Frick, 2004) than pedagogical system. An instructional based approach has been replaced by a learning based approach. The learning based approach emphasizes "process-oriented teaching" (Bolhus, 2003); "personalizing e-learning" (Bollet&Fallon, 2002); and "learner-centered assessment" (Huba&Freed, 2005). These represent the main criterions of adaptation and accommodation to learner –centred learning environments. As was shown by Midoro (2005, p. 32), a shift from teacher –centred instruction to learner centred instruction is needed to enable student to acquire the new 21st century knowledge

DOI: 10.4018/978-1-61350-516-8.ch015

Copyright © 2012, IGI Global. Copying or distributing in print or electronic forms without written permission of IGI Global is prohibited.

and skills. One of the possible solutions arises from investigation the metasystems approach in study the globalisated learning processes. The proposed solution was resided in GAE paradigm and in didactical model, which seeing learners as knowledge workers acting in physical - virtual learning environment (Railean, 2010a).

The electronic textbook (ET) is one of the main didactical tools (Polat, 2004). Many researchers investigate the design of the electronic textbooks and propose different models based on behaviorism, cognitivism and constructivism theories (Pascoe, Sallis, 1998; Brusilovsky, Schwarz&Weber, 2006; Zaiteva&Popco, 2006; Iasinschii, 2006 etc.). The problem of effectiveness of electronic textbooks for real didactical process is studied with embedded activities on student learning. In his PhD thesis Porter (2011) note that ET, also known as digital texts, e-texts, ebooks, e-books, electronic books, and hypertext books, represent a marriage of a hardcopy book within an electronic environment with software, such as Adobe Acrobat PDF, XML, SGML, HTML files, or hardware, such as a Palm Reader, E-Reader, Sony Reader, and Amazon's Kindle among others. ET are available in different formats, which are portabile, transferabile, and searchabile. Author relates about the importance of the Graphical User Interface; Hypermedia, Hypertext, Multimedia, Usability and user interface.

The design of ET evolves from instructional design to learning design. Instructional design is more related to behaviorism, but learning design – to constructivism. Cooper (1999) observed the shift from bahaviorism to constructivism models of design. Siang&Duffy (2004) describe the evolution of models of learning in design. The learning design models highlight the role of metasystems learning design (MLD). MLD differs from instructional design, which is "a systematic process that is employed to develop education and training programs in a consistent and reliable fashion"(Reiser&Dempsey, 2007). Instructional System Design divides the instruction design

processes into analysis, design, development, delivery and evaluation phases.

The core idea of MLD is that ET is used in complex learning environment, which are "global and local, real and virtual" (Midoro, 2005, p. 42). In such environment ET enables didactical activities to be transformed from passive to active activities. In order to do this, the content of the ET must be customized to each student and needs to have included the hermeneutic dialog. The initial assumption with respect to the value of ET in the complex environment is that hermeneutic dialog has a positive effect on online pedagogical communication through facilitating learning structured in the manner of a well-organized knowledge graph. In such a structure, as compared with alternative structures, it is easier to implement multimedia, hyperlinks, hypertext, audio, video etc. and to form learning outcomes. In addition, the structure of ET can be easy personalized. One possible technology that can be used for this approach is proposed by Railean (2008a), namely, electronic textbooks in an electronic portfolio.

FROM BEHAVIORISM TO CONSTRUCTIVISM ISSUES IN LEARNING DESIGN

In instructional design and instructional system design many models are related to behaviorism, especially to theory of conditioning. According to this theory, studied by H. Ebbinghaus, E. Thorndike, I. Pavlov, W. James, S. Pressey etc., learning can be programmed as stimulus S and response R. The conditioned stimulus is associated with the unconditioned stimulus within the brain, without involving conscious thought. According to Truta (2003) the behavior is a function of external stimuli S, so as $R = f(S)$, where R – is a behavior.

The second, named the theory of operant conditioning, proposed that stimulus S is associated with response through reinforcement I and punishment P. In instructional design the theory is associated within research of R. Hall, K. Spence, D. Wickens, C. Burke, W. Estes, S. Hellyer, K. Lashley, I. Krechevsky, F. Restle, M. Levin etc.

The main idea of operant conditioning theory is reinforcement used in instruction design according to Hall' formula (Atkinson, 1958):

$$_iH_r = M(1 - e^{-iN})$$

where N – the number of practical tasks with reinforcement, i – the parameter of the speed learning, M – the asymptotic value, e – base of natural logarithm and the value of M represent the sum of the crown components:

$$M \in \{S_o, m_{\Delta s}, \Delta t\}$$

where S_o is the state of behavior, $m_{\Delta s}$ - number, intensity and the structure of stimulus and Δt is the time of the difference between stimulus and response.

Evolutionally, the learning in instructional design was interpreted as stochastic processes and in models of learning design was applied the term of probability. So, R. Atkinson, G. Bower, Crothers (1958) demonstrate that in the case when the stimulus S in probe n is reinforced by event j, the probability P of the correct answer in $n + 1$ probe can be calculated by formula:

$$P_{n+1} = \alpha_j P_n + b_j$$ where a_j and b_j are the variables.

The models of learning can be classified in linear and nonlinear. The first linear model was proposed by B. Skinner (1954). In his model is important the immediate feedback and the right answer relevant to the proposed stimulus. After this model, arise the problem of integrity of the stimulus/weight of stimulus associated with pedagogical communication and the studied was turned to process of learning. One relevant example is "a stochastic

model for dialogue systems based on Markov decision process" (Levin, Pieraccini, & Eckert, 1998). Many other examples were described by D. Aristotel, T. Hobbes, J. Locke, D. Hartley, J. Mill, A. Bain, H. Spencer, R. Hall etc. This authors accept the idea that dependence between stimulus and responses can be described as $O \to C \to A$ (where O is the learning object, C –condition of association and A – a new association). On the other hand, Hamme & Glaser (1958) observed that in linear models can be included systems approach. One of the possible models is Gagne's conditions of learning, in which external and internal factors are reflected differently.

From 1986 one can see the shift from programmed to multimedia textbooks. As was noted by Criswell (1989, p. 11) the key elements of instructional design process of the multimedia textbooks are: learners, objectives, methods and evaluation, which can be described in framework for systematic instructional planning. The complete instructional design plan include: assess learning needs for designing an instructional program; state goals, constraints, and priorities that must be recognized; select topics or job tasks to be treated and indicate general purposes to be served; examine characteristics of learners or trainees which should receive attention during planning; identify subject content and analyze task components relating to stated goals and purposes; state learning objectives to be accomplished in terms of subject content and task components; design teaching! learning activities to accomplish the stated objectives; select resources to support instructional activities; specify support services required for developing and implementing activities and acquiring or producing materials; prepare to evaluate learning and outcomes of the program; determine preparation of learners or trainees to study the topic by pretesting them.

Multimedia textbooks provide interactive and adaptive digital resources for teacher – centered environment. In design of multimedia textbooks "scientist would analyze a task, break it down into smaller steps or chunks and use that information to develop instruction that moves from simple to complex building on prior schema" (Mergel, 1998). Knowledge is considered to be declarative and productive. The declarative knowledge is represented in terms of *chunks* (schema-like structures, consisting of an *isa* slot specifying their category and some number of additional slots encoding their contents) and the productive knowledge – productions (special rules), as was noted by Anderson, Reder&Lebiere (1996). The instructional design models are based on different approach to learning: supervised learning, unsupervised learning, semi supervised learning, reinforcement learning etc.

The problem of design became again stringent after 1996, when the globalization and ICT shifts to new paradigm of learning. "New learning paradigm explains the expansion of phenomena of globalisation to learning, as functional structure in powerful learning environment (both physical and virtual). The vitality of the structure justifies that we leave in an Anthropocentric Century, in which human beings is the most significant entity in the universe, because actions and behavior can be easy to be modeling through ICT. In Anthropocentric Age the learner tends to be the centre of physics and virtual networks. But, these networks are, first of all, learning environments." (Railean, 2010*b*).

New paradigm of learning is GAE paradigm (where G – globalisation; A - antropologism and E- existentialism). GAE paradigm of learning emphasizes a new more sophisticated architecture of *savoir,* new principles of learning design, learning centered environments, free, open source and cross-platform, and extensive didactical tools. This is the case of meta-systems. "The meta-systems are distingue from super systems which are nested levels of systems. A meta-systems is a deconstructed super-system and appears as a field out of which systems arise and through which they interoperate and cooperate. A meta-system is an environment or ecosystem for a certain level of system or anti-system pair" (Palmer, 2011, p. 1).

In meta-systems teachers and students need to demonstrate performance in adaptive passing from one to other behavior stages. The best example is how to use learning strategies (such as hands-on learning, group projects and discussions, field trips, simulations, and concept visualization). Such experiences are experimental and intuitive, interactive and adaptive to the environment and need to be configured for all individuals. That is why the globalisated configuration of learning design process engages learner in rational and emotional, practical and whimsical, organized and spontaneous didactical processes related to formal and nonformal environments. It could be argued that only the complex environment provides a real context to apply Gardner's Multiple Intelligence Theory of Learning, which states that "the multiple nature of human intelligence: verbal / linguistic, logical / mathematical, auditory, spatial, kinesthetic, interpersonal and intrapersonal." To be productive, learning design process can be incorporated in metasystems approach of transition.

Consequently, the primary purpose of this chapter is to discuss several concepts that validate the role of the metasystems learning, which can be incorporated in learning metasystems design of electronic textbooks used in open educational systems with complex environments. We will first discuss why self- regulated learning is crucial for learning outcomes in open learning system with complex environments. We next present a learning metasystems design approach developed by the author, discuss issues related to the structure and methods useful for meta-systems which permit to identify the crossprinciples. Lastly, we discuss the pedagogy of competence, the epistemological and methodological dimensions of MLD, the role of computer - based assessment to achieve a synergic effect and why the proposed metasystems approach is most relevant setting to develop self-regulated learning skills.

SELF-REGULATED LEARNING AND ELECTRONIC TEXTBOOKS DESIGN

Various strands of learning theory basically agree that the educational system is an open system. In such a system, learning is self-regulated. Self-regulated learning refers to a learner's "self-generated thoughts, feelings, and actions for attaining academic goals" (Zimmerman, 1998) and it is "a complex interactive process involving not only cognitive self-regulation, but also motivational self-regulation" (Boekaerts, 1997, 1999, 2002). In the self-regulated learning process, students learn to plan their actions and set specific academic goals in order to achieve them. They can anticipate problems that could prevent them from achieving their goals; they are highly self-efficacious, are able to monitor their own academic progress, and to make objective self-assessment judgments about own knowledge, skills and performance.

Electronic textbooks learning design to be used for the open educational systems with complex environment requires self –regulation principle, too. As was noted by Porter (2011) "looking at an electronic textbook as a learning environment with a unique ecological structure allows the textbook to then become a function of constructing meaning with the activities embedded within the book itself. An electronic textbook is more than just a document; it is a system that supports students in performing a task leading to learning, allowing for a repertoire of learning activities and strategies". On the other hand, designing instructional texts' content requires the same basics of a hardcopy textbook – research, drafting, writing, revising, editing, and creating graphics, as well as supplemental educational activities for the students and instructional guidelines for faculty. In practice, we see the need in learning design of the self –regulated skills for future development of metacognition through electronic textbook.

Self-regulated learning is related to metacognition. In the era of social media, both teachers and learners need to develop metacognition as a way to manage complex knowledge process using 'internal regulation', 'external regulation' or a combination of these. According to Bolhus (2003), in 'internal regulation', learners specify their own goals without external guidelines and choose an effective learning strategy; in 'external regulation', learners depend on others to get started or to complete a task; whereas in 'shared regulation' the learner interacts with other systems and different formal/ nonformal environments. Each learner needs to apply own learning strategy that is most suited to their individual needs and style. But, learning strategy involves planning, conscious manipulation, and movement toward an own goal. The restrictions are: cognitive load during problem solving (Sweller, 1988) and the focus of attention. As was shown by Anderson, Reder&Lebiere (1996), the activation of a chunk represent the sum of source activation it receives from the elements currently in the focus of attention, so as:

$$A_i = \sum_J W_J S_{Ji}$$

where Wj is the salience or source activation of element j in the focus of attention, and Sji is the strength of association from element j to i.

Planning and conscious manipulation of the learning strategy highlights the role of computer-based assessment. For this "assessment must be for learning not of learning (i.e. assessment that benefits student learning rather than simply measuring learning achievement; measure understanding not just memory, which is especially important in an information –rich world where being able to remember things is becoming increasingly unimportant but being able to understand and interpret things increasingly more important; be fair, relevant, consistent, innovative, inspired, motivating, regulator, reflective and manageable; be authentic (i.e. asking students to do something that someone in the real world would realistically be asked to do or what to do); be transparent, so that it is clear to students what is expected of them, how their work will be evaluated and how their grade was arrived at; be empowering, so that students feel motivated and involved" (Ellis&Folley, 2011, p. 92).

There are different strategies to promote self –regulated learning in online environments. Harris, Linder&Piiia (2011) state that different self –regulated learning strategies can be readily incorporated in online course. In the case of the open learning system, it has been demonstrated that there is a need for a "flexible, dynamic and instructional strategy" (Railean, 2008b). This strategy is able to provide a powerful learning environment (both real and virtual), in which self- regulated learning develops the competence of the learner. The quality of the learning output depends on input (e.g. the a priori knowledge of the learner, their skills and, the context of this study, the structure of the ET), the metasystem and the nature of the educational system environments. If the learning process is regulated by a dynamic and flexible strategy, the learners become a knowledge worker, acting in real and virtual environments. The perspective of this study is to observe and to describe the synergistic effect (perhaps positive and/or negative).

As was noted by Maria Luisa Sanz de Acedo Lizarraga, Oscar Ardaiz Villanueva&Maria Teresa Sanz de Acedo Baquedano (2011, p. 297), the Internet has undergone a spectacular chance with the appearance of Web 2.0. Web 2.0 dive a voice to individual users through new technologies, applications and values. These changes can be used to allow user to design, modify and save own digital texts and also, to communicate with different learners around the real world. Unfortunately, Web 2.0 technologies support learning, but, not self –regulated learning.

The choice of content as well as organization of material and tasks to obtain the self-regulated learning relies on meaningful learning

and autonomy. In concept of Ausubel' theory of Meaningful Verbal Learning, meaning is created through some form of representational equivalence between language (symbols) and mental context. This theory is validated by Subsumption Theory, which state that when information is subsumed into the learner's cognitive structure it is organized hierarchically. Meaningful learning takes place only if a stable cognitive structure exists. That is why to obtain the effect of self –regulated learning we need well – organized knowledge graph. For self – regulation to occur the knowledge graph need to be design at two levels: a) at correlative subsumption with expectation that new material will be learn like an extension or elaboration of what is already known (on base on a priori knowledge) and 2) derivative subsumption, in which self –regulated learning arise when new material or relationships derived from the existing structure and information can be moved in the hierarchy, or linked to other concepts or information to create new interpretations or meaning.

The next, but not the lasted problem in design of self - regulated learning seems to be the role of feedback. Traditionally, the feedback in learning design is used to achieve understanding of learning objects and to inform learner about errors. To do this, the feedback usually is included in design of pedagogical communication. There are many linear and nonlinear models. One of the most considerable nonlinear models, applied in design of electronic textbook, seems to be Conversation Theory developed by G. Pask. The feedback loop operates both internally and externally. "More specifically, internal feedback is produced by the learner's own monitoring processes when she or he evaluated personal performance, whereas external feedback is provided by other people or events" (Tung&Chin, 2011, p. 197). Both internal and external feedback can be delivered immediately (immediate feedback) or in short time (delayed feedback). Many ICT permit to communicate immediate and delayed feedback: audio conferencing, chatrooms, discussion threads, forums;

e -mail; mailing list; news groups; knowledge network building tools; web conferencing; response pads; whiteboard; shared screen, weblogs, Wikipedia, etc.

METASYSTEMS LEARNING DESIGN APPROACH

Metasystems Learning Design (MLD) is based on metasystems approach. This means that output of learning can be identified using Theory of Metasystem Transition. According to this, we can assume that concept of knowledge, described in terms of Foucauldian's terminology as *savoir,* evolve to competence, described in modern terminology as *savoir –vivre* complex.

Secondly, the structure of the competence can be studied using the structural definition, proposed by F. Heylighen. According to this, the metasystem S' represent an integration of a number of subsystems Si which are normally replicas of some template S to which an unspecified mechanism C is added that controls the behavior and replication of the Si. So, the structure of metasystems represent an integration of a number of subsystems Si which are normally replicas of competence template S to which an unspecified mechanism C is added that controls the behavior and replication of the Si. In our case, the competence template S replicates to subsystems: educational philosophy S', pedagogy S1, psychology S2, cybernetics S3 and management S4. These subsystems correspond to domains that study the concept of competence. The transitions within and of all the subsystems are activated by the mechanisms of variation, selection, and control, which form and maintain the functionality of the meta-system. So, we can see the transition states from inputs (*a priori* knowledge, skills, and competence) to outputs (*a posteori* knowledge, skills, competence) through the self-regulation phase.

The meta-system provides an environment for competence development. The globalised learning environment is the student centred environment. (By student centred environment we means real and virtual environments, which are focused on the student's needs, abilities, interests, and learning styles with the teacher as a facilitator of learning and with the student as a constructor of meaning in the processes of adaptation and accommodation to the globalisated world). So, the meta-system exists just beyond the interfaces of all pedagogical systems with teacher centred environments, either inside of the globalisated educational system. Thus, we can consider that meta-system holds together different interacting objects to form a highly organized structure that permit to develop a competitive structure of competence.

In this era of social media, education represents the planetary culture that has grown out of the developments in information communication technologies. The base for planetary culture is dynamic, interactive and adaptive environment for learning. Thus, as a result of consecutive transitions, a multilevel structure of control arises, which enables complicated forms of meta-system behavior to occur. As a consequence, we can consider the epistemology of globalization (S') to be a syper-system with respect to the subsystems of pedagogy (S1), psychology (S2), cybernetics (S3), knowledge management (S4), as represented in Figure 1.

Metasystems Learning Design is guided by own principles. The principles described core concepts related to philosophy, pedagogy, cybernetics, psychology, and management. From the combination of these, there have emerged new interdependences, which can be summarized as: psychogenesis of knowledge ↔ mental actions ↔ cognitive development. The psychogenesis of knowledge means the initial state of the human cognitive system, where it is ready to initiate new mental actions that will lead to future cognitive development. Mental actions are behavioral actions that are caused by the agent of learning and concrete situation in which they find themselves.

Figure 1. Competence according to theory of metasystem transition

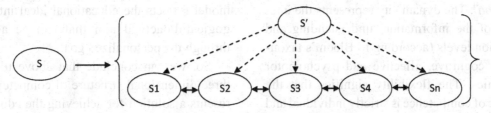

According to Galperin's theory (2000) concerning the development of mental actions need to have logical and materialistic forms. Thus, mental actions are functional actions and constitute the core of didactical activity. The functionality of mental actions is determined by self-regulated learning processes, stabilized through immediate and delayed feedback that is provided at the mental action stage, and realized in a powerful learning environment.

The MLD principles have been identified through own metasystem method. This method consists of the following: 1) the identification of reference concept with respect to the related domain (in our case the *educational ideal*); 2) the identification of the subdomains that study the proposed concept using the method of ideal type (in our case, education philosophy, pedagogy of competence development, cybernetics of open systems (based on *Open System Theory*), developmental psychology (composed by bioecological theory of human development and quantum psychology), and knowledge management); 3) a comparative analysis of the rules and principles that characterize each subsystem that together form the initial state of the metasystem; and 4) the identification of the core crossprinciples.

As result, was identified six main crossprinciples: *principles of self–regulation* (the automatic regulation of learning process through activation of metacognition using didactical and psychological methods, cybernetics techniques and management systems); *principle of personalization* (the individualization of learning objects through increased formation of the individuals as a self and as a member of global learning community); *principle of feedback diversity* (electronic educational context needs to be evaluated through immediate and delayed feedback); *principle of clarity* (the formation of structural skeleton content with powerful interconnected concepts); *principle of dynamism and flexibility* (the learner' active inclusion in elaboration the ET content on order to provide the competence development skills) and *principle of ergonomic* (computer based leaning and computer based assessment is guided by ergonomic interfaces and ergonomic places of work.).

The teaching, learning, and assessment strategies and methods, which will integrate the proposed principles into electronic textbook design, can be described using the model of competence pedagogy. In concept of competence pedagogy the competence-building model integrates three components: "*savoir-dire, savoir-faire* and *savoir-être*" (Minder, 2003). The component *savoir-dire* (which is equivalent to *savoir*) represents theoretical and verbal knowledge; *savoir-faire* represents methods, techniques, procedures, and learning strategies; and *savoir-être* represents wishes, affectivity, emotions, and motivations.

The conceptual structure of competence building can be represented graphically through topographic methods. Such a structure is characterized by complexity, dynamicity, and flexibility. The complexity represents the succession of the stages of '*knowledge → competence → expert level*' implemented in the managerial chain: '*in-*

formation → understanding → application → evaluation'. The dynamicity represents the integration of the information, understanding and application levels (according to Bloom's taxonomy) in cognitive, affective and psychomotor taxonomies. The flexibility signifies that the structure of competence is strictly individual and can be formed only after each individual has been included in the learning process. As will be shown in Figure 2, from the three-dimensional perspective, the structure of competence can be represented by the vectors OA, OB, and OC, whose maximum length corresponds to the taxonomic level that each vector represents. For example, the length of the vector OA equals 6 (which corresponds to Bloom's taxonomical levels); the OB vector equals 7 (which corresponds to Simpson's taxonomical levels); and the length of OC equals 5 (which corresponds to Krathwohl's taxonomical levels). The resulting vector $\overrightarrow{OE}$ (savoir - vivre) represents the sum of vectors: $\overrightarrow{OA}$, $\overrightarrow{OB}$, and $\overrightarrow{OC}$ has the co-ordinates $\overrightarrow{OE} = (6, 5, 7)$.

This interpretation describes a core concept of the new didactical model for electronic textbook design: the competence needs to be developed at teacher *P* and learner *I* levels. Digital content that is developed in line with this new didactical model reflects the educational ideal into pedagogical/didactical aim that can be achieved through the personalized goal.

So, we can conclude that above illustrated three-dimensional structure of competence represents a solution for achieving the educational ideal, which equates to achieving: professionalism, global thinking, and cultural pluralism. That is why a new didactical model needs to be implemented at the pedagogical and at the didactical levels.

1. At the pedagogical level, the digital content is designed to form the macrostructure of knowledge that represents the final form of competence or, in other words, the self-regulated competence of the learner.

2. At the didactical level, the digital content is designed to enable the learner to achieve the curricula and personal objectives, as specific objectives, that include: calculating, writing, list, defining, selecting, naming, comparing, solving, etc.

The design of the context to achieve certain pedagogical and didactical levels determines the managerial processes that are used to incorporate

Figure 2. The structure of competence according to LMD

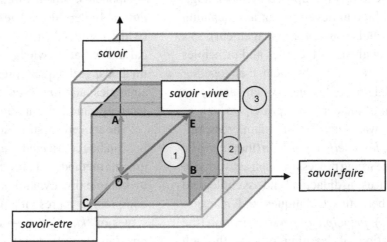

the overall pedagogical/didactical aims into a learner's personalized aims. These managerial processes function at two levels:

- In terms of pedagogical/didactical goals, through objectives that are realized using digital content and the computer-based self-assessment,
- In terms of personalized goals, through computer-based self-assessment.

To be effective, the *pedagogical / didactical goals* is achievement through informational / communicational, cognitive and assessment processes, which need to be developed according to knowledge management rules, as is shown in Figure 3.

Knowledge management circle show evidence of the interdependences established between pedagogic and management subsystems. Such interdependence can be represented

$$\alpha^{l} = k\alpha, \ \beta^{l} = k\beta, \ \gamma^{l} = k\gamma$$

$$\delta^{l} = k\delta$$

$\alpha =$, $\beta =$, $\gamma =$, $\delta =$ and k – the coefficient of proportionality $0 \leq k \leq 1$

(). Using the above mentioned interdependences, one can observe that LMD define the theory and practice of elaboration the complex didactical processes. These complex process integrate *informational / communicational* (limited by α), *cognitive activity* (limited by β) and *computer based self-assessment processes* (limited by γ).

THE EPISTEMOLOGICAL AND METHODOLOGICAL DIMENSIONS

LMD demonstrate evidence of two dimensions: *epistemological* (define learning outcomes) and *methodological* (add value of methods of learning). Both dimensions need to be archive through educational dynamic and flexible strategy. So, is demonstrating that learning includes *dynamic and flexible knowledge, skills and competence* related to variables: *savoir-dire, savoir-faire, savoir-être* in *savoir-vivre*. Such a conceptual structure can be used to manage knowledge through: 1) *theoretical methods* (that represent the integration of the principles into the functional structure with affordance to archive learning outcomes) and 2) *practical methods* (used by user and complying with the stages of the ET development process).

For its practical application that strategy employs:

Figure 3. The role of knowledge management in LMD

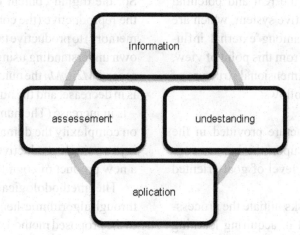

- Communication/information strategies – the learner plays a central role in learning by personalizing the content, guided more les by the teacher;
- Cognitive activity strategies– the learner gains knowledge, skills and competence; learn and apply new methods, procedures, and techniques for individual, group, collaborative, and co-operative working;
- Computer based assessment strategies – the learner is involved both in computerized self-assessment and new forms of summative assessment.

To be applied for electronic textbook design the strategies are guided during knowledge management phases. That is to say, communication/information strategies enable to achieve the pre-planned pedagogical functions; cognitive activity strategies are achieved through cognitive, affective, and psychomotor actions; and assessment strategies – through assessment principles. The common formula for achieved the strategies described is $Y = D(X)$, where Y – is the pedagogical or didactical goal, X – personal goal and D indicates the strategies (processes) of transforming the pedagogical/educational goal into a personalized goal. In this formula, the role of the assessment strategies is the most critical. The assessment strategies exploit the ability of the digital context to be used for self-regulation. Through self-regulation, the real and potential states of the human cognitive system, which are affected by interactions among external influences, can be explained. From this point of view, the nucleus of the three-dimensional structure of competency operates as follows:

- The knowledge structure provided in the digital content acts upon the human cognitive system at the level of goal-oriented influences,
- The incorporated tasks initiate the processes that are involved in acquiring learning outputs as transitory processes from the current psychological state (initial quantum level) to the potential psychological state (intermediate or final quantum level),
- All psychopedagogical mechanisms are involved in these processes,

In the dynamic and flexible education strategy all processes that conduct to the development of the learning outcomes are hierarchical. Let us analyse this processes deeper, studying the competence formation. In the initial phase, the prototype of the competence structure has the shape of an optimized knowledge graph.

At an intermediary phase, the knowledge graph is expanded through additions and automations (By additions we mean the processes of personalization the digital context planned and provided by teacher, and by automations – the processes of computer based self -assessment). In the final stage, the resulting structure of learning outputs is evaluated on the basis of the characteristics of the final educational product.

The methodological dimension is represented by the way in which the didactical activities are integrated into functional structures that assure the efficiency of the communication/information, cognitive activity and assessment processes. The proposed model of design is to consider the first phase equivalent to the first module (named M1), the second phase – to the second module M2, etc. So, the digital content of M1 incorporate from the reproductive (the content is recalled from the memory) to productive tasks (the learner construct own understanding using concept mapping). The second *M2, .. Mn* the number of reproductive tasks is in decrease, and the number of productive tasks – is in increase (The number of modules depends on complexity the domain). The final stage there is just a single productive task (the learner creates a new product of cognitive activity).

The methodological actions are projected through algorithmic-heuristic method. According to the proposed method, the algorithmic activities can be developed using curricula objectives that, in main cases, affordance to savoir (according to Bloom's taxonomy), whereas the heuristic activities are implemented through productive tasks, which correspond to the development of the behavioral skills. The productive tasks can be obtained only if the digital content will integrate savoir – faire with *savoir – être*. The action verbs can be identified using Krathwohl and Simpson taxonomies. This integrative method promotes the gradual development of the heuristic activities by reducing the algorithmic activities simultaneously.

COMPUTER- BASED ASSESSMENT AND SYNERGISTIC EFFECT

It is important to understand the role of computer-based assessment in our nonlinear model. We expect to obtain the synergistic effect during self-regulated learning. In our opinion, the synergistic effect occurred when all didactical processes that are triggered through the ET functioning together produce a result which is not independently obtainable. For this case, practically firstly was fount the relevant conditions to obtain the synergistic effect. Then, we consider that learning outcomes can be ascertained through computerized assessment. For this purpose, the assimilation coefficient was design taken into account the formula $K\alpha=\alpha/p$ (where $K\alpha$ is the assimilation coefficient, α is the number of test operations executed correctly, and p is the total number of test operations). According to Bespalco (1987) the one test operation corresponds to one psychological operation needed to solve the problem within the assessment process. For example, to solve the task $2 + 2 = 4$ the learner will apply 2 test operations, to recall the number and to apply the mathematical operation from long term memory.

Theoretically, $K\alpha$ is established within the range $0 \leq K\alpha \leq 1$. If the $K\alpha \geq 0.7$ the teaching process is considered to be completed. By teaching processes we mean teaching in the zone of proximal development, designing the scaffold learning activities and mediating of learning experiences. If $K\alpha \geq 0.7$, the learner achieve self-regulated competence and in system is viewed the synergistic effect. As result, $K\alpha \geq 0.7$ can be considered an indicator that the teaching process is finished and the self-regulated processes have been initiated. In other cases, the teaching process can be corrected through mediating or intelligent and adaptive tutoring within the electronic learner centred environment.

The methodological dimension of educational dynamic and flexible strategy can be validated, if will be taken into consideration of the following:

1. The diversity of reusable learning objects N, where $N = \left\{ N_1, N_2, N_3, N_4 \right\}$. So, using the description provided by Haughey & Muirhead (2011), we can consider that:

   a. N_1 is a learning object with function to introduce new concepts, extend learning by providing new means for presenting curricular material and support new types of learning opportunities not available in a classroom environment

   b. N_2 is a learning object with function to provide reinforcement to existing skills

   c. N_3 is a learning object with function to illustrate concepts that are less easily explained through traditional teaching methods

   d. N_4 is a learning object with function to provide enrichment activities for gifted and highly motivated students.

2. The abstraction level (β)), which defines a way of hiding the implementation details of a particular set of functionality. Using the Bespalco study, we can model the ET at:

Table 1. The correlation between diversity of ET, parameters and diagnostic criteria of content

ET type	N	β	α	γ	δ	$K\alpha$	$K\iota$ (min)
Didactic ET	N1	$\beta1 - \beta4$	α_4	$\gamma3$	Fluent	> 0,7	15-20
Declarative ET	N2	$\beta1 - \beta3$	α_3	$\gamma2$	-	0,7>Kα>0,3	-
Dogmatic ET	N3	$\beta1 - \beta2$	α_2	$\gamma1$	0,5	> 0,3	38
Monographic ET	N4	$\beta2$	α_1	-	-	-	Unlimited

a. phenomenological level ($\beta1$) – in the digital content are used everyday language;

b. qualitative level ($\beta2$) – in the digital content are included same scientific data;

c. quantitative level ($\beta3$) - the learning outcomes are hidden in educational models;

d. axiomatic level ($\beta4$) – the educational model include, at least one, abstraction layer (for example, Open Graphics Library) .

3. The level of assimilation (α), which defines the level of assimilation of the content. According to Bespalco (2007), this level can be either reproductive or productive. Therefore, the assimilation level can be:

a. level $\alpha1$ – the learner assimilates the data presented in a logically manner;

b. $\alpha2$ – the learner is involved in cognitive activity processes (e.g. through immediate feedback or interactive content);

c. $\alpha3$ – the learner is involved in learning that is guided in scaffolding way;

d. $\alpha4$ – the learner is involved in the personalized construction of the content.

4. The level of automation (ι), which defines the time required to learn the digital content. Traditionally, the level of automation is established in range: $0 \leq K\iota \leq 1$ (where

0 represents the minimal time required, 1 represents the level of automation necessary (for disciplines that require fluency in thinking) and 0.5 corresponds to disciplines that require only fluency in reading or traditional problem solving.

5. Assimilation awareness (γ), which defines the quality of the assimilation with regard to the following levels:

a. $\gamma1$ – knowledge from the studied domain is needed for rationalizing/ reasoning with information provided;

b. $\gamma2$ – knowledge from similar domains is needed for reasoning with data;

c. $\gamma3$ – interdisciplinary knowledge is needed for reasoning with data that required solving critical problems in research, innovation or professional practice.

According to the proposed table, the diversity of the electronic textbooks include: *didactic, declarative, dogmatic* and *monographic*. The design of the didactic electronic textbook has a lot of common with the design of printed textbook: pedagogical aim (objective) →tools (content) →actions (tasks) → results (assessment). However, the design of frames emphases the role of interactivity, adaptive frame based on flexibility and dynamicity and encourages constructivism learning practice. On the other hand, computer based assessment increase the power of feedback in achievement of the learning outcomes, if will be used for synergetic effect.

Declarative design of electronic textbook is based on management chain, realized by pedagogical aim (objective) →tools (hypertext, hypermedia, multimedia) → actions (computer based task) →results (immediate feedback). The design encourages cognitivist learning practice, expercially through interactive pedagogical scenarious and allows students to discover the world of the learning objects. Simulating, the learning flexibility and dynamicity of hypertext allow user to manipulate with different pedagogical scenarios in own way.

Dogmatic design of electronic textbook has many things in common with the design of intelligent tutorials. The core of learning design is formula: stimulus→ response→ reinforcement. The diversity of frames are included in the concept of design the educational models and/or pedagogical agents, that „models" the didactic activity of the most qualified tutor, but synergistic effect cannot be obtained.

Monographic design of the ET excludes two components: actions and results. On the other hand, if the frame is designed according to learner cognitive structure, the digital structure of text, which incorporate hermeneutic dialogue serve as a guide for achievement the core structure of competence. This structure will be reinforcement through self-computer assessment.

THE DIDACTIC PROCESSES TRIGGERED ELECTRONIC TEXTBOOK

As described above, the processes, which are triggered electronic textbook, can be classified as: communication/information processes, cognitive activity processes, and assessment processes. The communication/information processes represent the transfer of data, information and knowledge from the source (tutor/mentor, learner/group of learners, environment) to the recipient (the learner and/or digital content) over time through a transmitter (for example, the e-Learning platform, instructional system, networked computer). The models of integrated processes triggered electronic textbook can be represented as following in Figure 4.

In the proposed model *mE* represent the diversity of the electronic textbook (that can be viewed at the level of teacher and at the level of student). The level of formalization the knowledge, skills and competence is equivalent to level of abstraction, which can be designed at phenomenological, qualitative, quantitative and axiomatic levels.

Figure 4. The model of integrated processes triggered electronic textbook

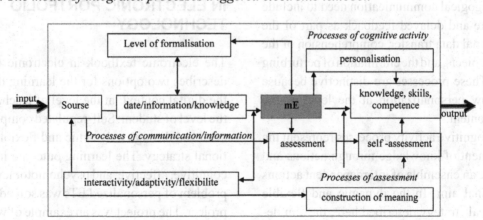

The communication processes are characterized by interactivity, dynamicity, reciprocity, and self-regulation, whereas the information processes are high speed, heterogeneous and accessible. During the informational processes need to be taken into consideration, that the store of short-term memory is 7±2 items. That is why; the result of the information processes is localized in sensory memory and/or short term memory as data, but the result of communicational processes – in working memory as information and knowledge. The knowledge differs from information, because the knowledge is deposited in well-organized schemas. This capacity can be increased through a chunking process - a phenomenon whereby individuals have grouping the responses when performing a memory task. Other solution is the concept map – a graphical tool for organizing and representing knowledge. The affordance of concept mapping, validated by Ausubel's Theory of Learning, is based on idea that learning is the assimilation of new concepts/propositions into existing concept and propositional frameworks held by the learner, while knowledge structure refer to own cognitive structure.

If the information is significant for learner the data is mediated and integrated into long term memory (during the communication processes). The long term memory encodes information semantically. On the other hand, the quality of long term memory associations depends on getting sufficient sleep between training and test. The pedagogical communication need to include immediate and delayed feedback as part of the bidirectional data transfer, comprehension of the learning objects, and the elimination of perturbing factors. These processes are distinctive because they allow personalization at the level of the learner content.

The cognitive activity processes represent the development of knowledge through actions and constitute an ensemble of interdependent actions with a final aim. In the dynamic and flexible educational strategy described here, the aim determines the curricular objectives. Teaching and evaluation activities are developed on the basis of these objectives. Each teaching and evaluation activity is accomplished through teaching, learning, and evaluation actions. These actions are evaluated through a set of indicators (the starting point, the ending point, the subject of the action, and the target of the action). The transposition of goals in the cognitive processes is triggered by the integration in the EM of the functions of the actions.

Computerized assessment is characterized by diversity of feedback. There are two rules that must be followed: 1) the task must be written as a set of rational steps and 2) the tasks must be as clear as possible. From the psycho-pedagogical perspective, the human brain analyses a task on multiple levels. If the task is too complex, the learner will not try to solve it. However, if the task is too simple, the learner will become bored and will not have enough motivation to initiate the cognitive processes. To maintain the processes it is necessary to engage learners actively.

The challenges in computerized assessment, associated with the design of electronic textbook, are the following: 1) the assessment can be done using traditional (*face –to face*) and virtual (*online*) methods of assessment; 2) assessment is individual, group, and collaborative.

THE ELECTRONIC TEXTBOOK IN ELECTRONIC PORTFOLIO TECHNOLOGY

The electronic textbook in electronic portfolio describes two options for the learning design of the digital context: at the level of teacher and at the level of student. Self-regulated competence is achieved through a dynamic and flexible educational strategy. The learning outcome integrates cognitive, affective, and psychomotor levels. The problem of personalized ETs was solved through project. The project was an example of where the context of the ET acts as a generator of data for self-regulated learning and permit to obtain the synergetic effect. That was shown that first module can serves as a prototype for self-regulated learning. The good prototype provides the learners with all the possibilities to develop learning outcomes.

The Figure 5 shows the first and final phase of electronic textbook development. At the first phase the digital content is planned. During this phase the concepts are associated in modules, paragraphs and themes (using the technique of matrix and knowledge graphs). Then, the initial structures of digital content are placed in learning environment (for example, in knowledge content management system). After then, the learner is engaged in the didactic process. The didactic process, incorporated in digital context, is personalized according to *a priori* student knowledge and skills. The process of personalization is guided by the teacher.

To achieve the reference point in the system, named the coefficient of assimilation, the digital content is completed by computer based assessment. For the effective learning design we developed five tests, which correspond to five chapters. The computer based tests are generated from data base of items. Each test includes at least 30 operations of test provided for 20 minutes.

The modern educational technology and learning design allow students to construct their unique understanding of learning objects through multiple sources within one context/delivery method. As was noted by Porter (2011), an electronic textbook is more than just a document; it is a system that supports students in performing a task leading to learning, allowing for a repertoire of learning activities and strategies. Taking into consideration these ideas, we can see that electronic textbook interface learning design could be pre-planned by teacher and developed by each student individually. In this case, a user interface rules will be directed to human –computer interaction through using hypermedia, hypertextual menus and/or multimedia file. The key elements such us: learnability, efficiency, memorability, errors that a user makes when using, and satisfaction of use, which describe usability within an electronic document, will be associated with student cognitive style and his/her level of formalization the learning objects.

CONCLUSION

We hypothesize that the metasystems learning design will become widespread in the near future and that it will replace instructional design and instructional system design models. The

Figure 5. Electronic textbooks in electronic portfolio

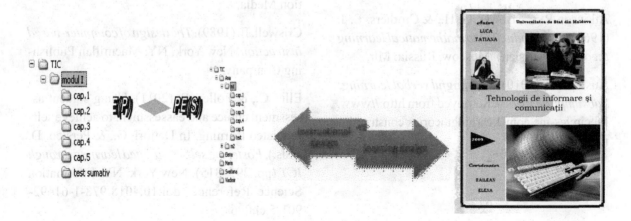

application of ETs enables the development of the self-regulated learning environment. Such environments permit to keep motivation and to develop metacognition.

ACKNOWLEDGMENT

I would like to acknowledge the contributions of my scientific advice Gheorghe Rudic (Centre of Modern Pedagogy, Canada); my colleagues Donatella Persico and Djuliana Detorri (Jenova Institute of Didactical Technologies, Italy) and of Felix Hamsa –Lup (Amstrong University) to the development processes of this paper. This project is supported by research grants provided in part by European Commission (Grant IMG 3004-2004), JTEL Winter School on Advanced Learning (2010) and J. William Fulbright Foreign Scholarship (2011).

REFERENCES

Afanasiev, U. (1997). *The informatization of education as global problem on the crossroad of century*. Retrieved from http://www.yuriafanasiev.ru/articles/ magazines_1997_156.htm

Anderson, J., Rreder, L., & Lebiere, C. (1996). Working memory: Activation limitations on retrieval. *Cognitive Psychology*, *30*, 221–256. doi:10.1006/cogp.1996.0007

Atkinson R. C., Bower, G. H., & Crothers, E. J. (1969). *An introduction to mathematical learning theory*. (in Russian). Moscow, Russia: Mir.

Ausubel, D. (2010). *Meaningful verbal learning: Subsumption theory*. Retrieved from http://www.lifecircles-inc.com/ Learningtheories/constructivism/ausubel.html

Bespalco, B. P. (2007). Параметры и критерии диагностической цели. В: Образовательные технологии [Parameters and criteria for the diagnostic purpose]. *Instructional Technologies*, *1*, 19–34.

Boekaerts, M. (1997). Self-regulated learning: A new concept embraced by researchers, policy makers, educators, teacher and students. *Learning and Instruction*, *7*(23), 161–168. doi:10.1016/S0959-4752(96)00015-1

Boekaerts, M. (1999). Self - regulated learning: Where we are today? *International Journal of Educational Research*, *3*, 161–186.

Boekaerts, M. (2002). Bringing about change in the classroom: strengths and weaknesses of self regulated learning approach. *Learning and Instruction*, *2*, 589–604. doi:10.1016/S0959-4752(02)00010-5

Boekaerts, M., & Minnaert, A. (1999). Self - regulation with respect to informal learning. *Educational Research*, *31*, 533–544.

Bolhus, S. (2003). Toward process-oriented teaching for self -directed lifelong learning: A multidimensional perspective. *Learning and Instruction*, *13*, 327–347. doi:10.1016/S0959-4752(02)00008-7

Bollet, R., & Fallon, S. (2002). *Personalising e - learning. Educational Media International* (pp. 545–549). International Council for Education Media.

Criswell, E. (1989). *The design of computer-based instruction*. New York, NY: Macmillan Publishing Company.

Ellis, C., & Folley, S. (2011). Using student assessment choice and eassessment to achieve self-regulated learning. In Dettori, G., & Persico, D. (Eds.), *Fostering self–regulated learning through ICT* (pp. 295–315). New York, NY: Information Science Reference. doi:10.4018/978-1-61692-901-5.ch006

Ertmer, P., & Newby, T. (1993). Behaviorism, cognitivism, constructivism: Comparing critical features from an instructional design perspective. *Performance Improvement Quarterly, 6*(4), 50–72. doi:10.1111/j.1937-8327.1993.tb00605.x

Frick, T. (1998). *Restructuring education through technology*. Retrieved from http://education. indiana.edu/%7Efrick/fastback/fastback326. html#journey

Hall, A. (1987). *Metasystems methodology: A new synthesis and unification*. Pergamon Press.

Harris, B., Reinhard, W., & Pilia, A. (2011). Strategies to promote self –regulated learning in online environments. In Dettori, G., & Persico, D. (Eds.), *Fostering self–regulated learning through ICT* (pp. 295–315). New York, NY: Information Science Reference. doi:10.4018/978-1-61692-901-5.ch008

Haughey, M., & Muirhead, B. (2011). *Evaluating learning objects for schools*. Retrieved from http://www.ascilite.org.au/ajet/ejist/ docs/vol8_no1/fullpapers/ eval_learnobjects_school.hm

Heylighen, F. (1995). *(Meta)systems as constraints on variation-A classification and natural history of metasystem transitions*. Retrieved from http://pespmc1.vub.ac.be/ Papers/MST-ConVar.pdf

Huba, M., & Freed, J. (2005). *Learner-centered assessment on college campuses: Shifting the focus from teaching to learning*. Needham Heights, MA: Allyn and Bacon.

Kalantzis, M., & Cope, B. (2008). *New learning: Elements of a science of education*. Port Melbourne, Canada: Cambridge University Press.

Kalyuga, S., Chandler, P., & Sweller, J. (2000). Incorporating learner experience into the design of multimedia instruction. *Journal of Educational Psychology, 92*, 126–136. doi:10.1037/0022-0663.92.1.126

Koulopoulos, T., & Frappaolo, C. (2000). *Smart things to know about knowledge management*. Padstow, UK: T. J. International Ltd.

Levin, E., Pieraccini, R., & Eckert, W. (1998). *Using Markov decision process for learning dialogue strategies*. Acoustics, Speech and Signal Processing. Retrieved from http://ieeexplore.ieee.org/xpl/ freeabs_all.jsp?arnumber=674402

Lizarraga, M. L., Villanueva, O. A., & Baquedano, M. T. (2011). Self–regulation of learning supported by Web 2.0 Tools: An example of raising competence on creativity and innovations. In Dettori, G., & Persico, D. (Eds.), *Fostering self – regulated learning through ICT* (pp. 295–315). New York, NY: Information Science Reference.

Mergel, B. (1998). *Instructional design & learning theory*. Retrieved from http://www.usask.ca/education/ coursework/802papers/mergel/ brenda.htm#Cognitivism

Midoro, V. (2005). *A common European framework for teachers' professional profile in ICT for education*. MENABO Didactica.

Novak, D., & Carias, A. (2006*). The theory underlying concept maps and how to construct and use them*. Retrieved from http://cmap.ihmc.us/publications/ researchpapers/theorycmaps/theoryunderlyinconceptmaps.htm

Palmer, K. D. (2002). *Advanced meta-systems theory for metasystems engineers*. Retrieved from http://holonomic.net/sd01V04.pdf

Porter, P. (2011). *Effectiveness of electronic textbooks with embedded activities on student learning*. Ph.D. dissertation, Capella University, United States -- Minnesota. Retrieved from Dissertations & Theses: Full Text. (Publication No. AAT 3397091).

Pullen, D. L., & Cole, D. R. (2009). *Multiliteracies and technology enhanced education: Social practice and the global classroom.* Hershey, PA: Information Science Reference. doi:10.4018/978-1-60566-673-0

Railean, E. (2008). Aspects of teaching and learning processes in the closed and open didactical systems. *Learning Technology Newsletter, 10*(4).

Railean, E. (2008). Electronic textbooks in electronic portfolio: A new approach for the self-regulated learning. *Proceedings of 9th International Conference on Development and Application Systems,* Suceava (Romania), (pp. 138-141).

Railean, E. (2010a). A new didactical model for modern electronic textbook elaboration. *Proceeding of ICVL 2010 Conference,* (pp. 121-129).

Railean, E. (2010b). *Metasystems approach to research the globalized pedagogical processes. Annals of Spiru Haret University* (pp. 31–50). Mathematics-Informatics Series.

Reiser, R., & Dempsey, J. (2007). *Trends and issues in instructional design.* Upper Saddle River, NJ: Pearson Education, Inc.

Roberts, T. (2006). *Self, peer, and group assessment in e-learning.* Hershey, PA: Information Science Publishing. doi:10.4018/978-1-59140-965-6

Skinner, B. (1954). The science of learning and the art of teaching. *Harvard Educational Review, 24*(2).

Smith, W., & Moore, J. (1970). *The learning process and programmed instruction.* New York, NY: Halt, Runehalt and Winston Inc.

Sweller, J. (1988). Cognitive load during problem solving: Effects on learning. *Cognitive Science, 12,* 257–285. doi:10.1207/s15516709cog1202_4

Zhang, L. (2002). *Knowledge graph theory and structural parsing.* Enschede, The Netherlands: Twente University Press.

Zimmerman, V. J. (1998). Academic studying and the development of personal skill: A self regulatory perspective. *Educational Psychology, 33,* 73–86.

Zimmerman, V. J., & Schunk, D. H. (Eds.). (2001). *Self-regulated learning and academic achievement: Theoretical perspectives.* Mahwah, NJ: Lawrence Erlbaum Associates.

Chapter 16
Using a Blueprint in the Design of Instruction for Virtual Environments

Mauri Collins
StRebel Design, LLC, USA

ABSTRACT

Other chapters in this book discuss the design and development of interfaces for virtual worlds. This chapter will discuss the instructional design aspects of designing learning in virtual worlds. The use of virtual worlds is a relatively new phenomenon in education and, like many innovations that have preceded them, they are a new and intriguing tool to be mastered by both student and instructor alike. While bounded by a computer screen, virtual worlds have many of the affective components of everyday life and familiar-looking environments, where real life rules pertain, can be created to transfer learning, and both formal and informal learning can take place (Jones & Bronack, 2007).

INTRODUCTION

The first prerequisite to designing learning in virtual worlds is experience in the virtual world that you have chosen, or the one that your institution has made available to you. As an instructor or designer, you need to be comfortable in the environment you will be working in, and sometimes this takes many hours of personal exploration and experimentation. Once you are thoroughly familiar with the interface, you will be able to operate through it, rather than focusing all your

concentration on managing it. You will discover that the experience of virtual worlds is very similar to the real world. You have, through your avatar, a sense of presence and immediacy – you feel as if you are really there, interacting in real time. You can move around, interact with other persons and with artifacts, and communicate in several modes including text and voice and scripted body language (Jones & Bronack, 2007)

When considering the use of a virtual world for your class, your first consideration should be what the "return on investment" will be for both you and your students. To master a virtual world takes many hours of practice – will that investment

DOI: 10.4018/978-1-61350-516-8.ch016

Copyright © 2012, IGI Global. Copying or distributing in print or electronic forms without written permission of IGI Global is prohibited.

be worth it to your students? Is instructional time in a virtual world the best choice for your content? If your aim is to pass along information and you want to lecture or demonstrate, or your content is static (why not use a web page?) or your lesson isn't designed to be interactive, then there are many other ways of presenting information that don't require the heavy investment of teaching/learning in a virtual world. Sitting in a virtual world classroom that replicates a real classroom, listening to a lecture and viewing slides that resolve very slowly on a screen is rarely a good use of a virtual world, unless the presentation is brief and intended to set up a learning activity that the students will then get up out of their chairs and pursue.

Students who pursue their education at a distance frequently experience of a sense of isolation from other students. In virtual worlds the sense of "presence" can have a great emotional and social impact – beyond the common benefit of looking at a three-dimensional model of a building or a super-size model of a giant squid (Aldrich, 2009). Students can come early to class meetings and visit, much as they might do in a physical classroom, and linger afterwards to continue their discussions.

In a virtual world you can build – or have built for you – spaces for students to learn in that would be prohibitively expensive in the real world – or too dangerous to allow students to work in (Jones & Bronack, 2007). Students can be immersed in authentic environments and actively work together to solve problems, using the customary problem-solving patterns for their discipline. They can research and build artifacts and environments at little or no cost or explore their virtual world and find environments that others have already created. In some virtual worlds various communities have researched and created cities and towns from different historical periods, complete with authentic looking buildings and artifacts. Residents and visitors dress in period clothing and often speak in the dialect of the time. Contemporary settings have been created by different language groups and students can be assigned to seek out and interact

with native language speakers to practice their conversational skills (Aldrich, 2009).

Instructional design for virtual worlds has a lot in common with instructional design for traditional educational settings, provided they include interactive and immersive learning. For those who are used to collaborative learning and the building of learning communities, instructional design for virtual worlds will feel natural and straightforward. You can design "lecture courses" for virtual worlds but it would be a waste of the interactive resources available to you.

This chapter presents a relatively straightforward instructional design framework that stresses the alignment of learning outcomes, learning activities, and assessment/feedback (Berge, 2002). It focuses on student learning rather than instructional input and, because it is a structural model, can be used in most, if not all, disciplines. The model states that learning/performance outcomes should be stated for the student, learning resources provided, learning activities designed to help the student move from their entry level to the stated learning/performance outcomes, interaction among the students and continuing assess ent and feedback so that students are confident they are meeting the learning outcomes. The model does not specify what the learning/performance outcomes, learning activities, nor assessments should be, only that those elements should be present and aligned with each other.

The model is phrased in language familiar to most faculty who have taught in the traditional classroom. This model recognizes that, in most settings, faculty are responsible for designing their own classroom, online or virtual world courses, with the assistance, sometimes, of technical personnel. This model is designed to assist instructors to continuously improve their skills in designing their own courses It is not designed to turn the instructor into a professional instructional designer nor keeping them dependent on others.

In higher education, the most common model for online and distance course development involves faculty designing and redesigning their own courses by themselves, and sometimes with the help of technology resource persons. At the very least, teaching and learning in virtual worlds requires a different kind of course presentation compared to typical classes. The use of mediated course delivery in the form of teaching and learning in virtual worlds can serve as a catalyst for rethinking and redesigning the whole teaching and learning environment, not just turning existing web-based course materials into note cards and more web-pages. The role of the instructor, the instructional methods used, and learners' practice activities must be changed to take advantage of your chosen virtual world's characteristic strengths. For instance, teaching and learning in virtual worlds is well-suited for building, exploring, experimenting, communication, collaboration, and information acquisition, but not for reading long text files on screen (Network, 2003) in the form of lectures in text chat, or sitting through powerpoint slides.

The important questions regarding learning in virtual worlds are not those that focus on technology choices, although these are important. Students and instructors will have a most unsatisfactory experience, if they don't have a broadband connection and late-model equipment. They also need to master the virtual world interface, which is sometimes not intuitive.

The most important questions that should be asked concern what constitutes good teaching and learning. Faculty members often do not have the philosophical or practical knowledge regarding the systematic design of instruction to have asked or answered these important questions. This chapter presents a model of instructional design that was developed by a faculty development specialist to assist faculty to restructure their own courses for online teaching and learning (Collins & Berge, 2003) and has been updated for teaching and learning in virtual worlds.

Instructional design is a discipline that uses systematic processes involving the use of learning and instructional theory to insure educational quality and optimal student learning environments. General principles of learning and instruction are translated into plans for instructional materials and learning activities (Willis, 2003). At the heart of effective improvement of teaching in any medium (classroom, online, in virtual worlds, etc.) is an ongoing process of self-evaluation and incorporating feedback from others, including students. Whether this is the first time a faculty member has thought seriously about teaching a course or it is a veteran instructor rethinking a course, an opportunity exists to improve teaching and learning. The faculty member must articulate what the learning goals for the course are, how the course materials will be presented and indicate how students will interact with course resources, the instructor, and with other students. The faculty member knows the subject matter and often has experience with the student audience and where in the scope and sequence of the course content students persistently have problems with concepts or processes.

Focus on Key Principles First

There are hundreds of different instructional design models (Seels & Glasgow, 1998), that can be used in the design of online instruction some focusing on behaviorism, cognitivism, or constructivism, and they are presented at various levels of detail. The focus of this chapter and the design model it describes is on the continuous improvement of the faculty member's skills in designing their own courses, rather than turning the instructor into someone having the same skills as professional instructional designers

Faculty new to teaching and learning in virtual worlds can profitably consider how they are currently teaching their course or how they teach in the classroom, to determine their teaching style and what they consider their responsibilities as a professor to be. Their personal style can make it more or less difficult to accept the necessary "information dispenser" to "learning facilitator" transition that the move to online venues advantages. When teaching and learning is moved online, faculty roles change (Berge, 1996). Embedded implicitly or explicitly in this process are fundamental principles that generally apply regardless of the faculty member's educational philosophy. For instance:

- Faculty should provide clear guidelines for three kinds of interaction: student with content, student with other students and student with instructor (Moore, 1989).
- Well-designed discussion assignments facilitate meaningful cooperation among students, the sharing of experience and transfer of learning between classroom and their lives.
- Students should build their course projects throughout the learning term, centered around their own content and subject to frequent feedback
- Instructors need to provide two types of feedback: information feedback and acknowledgment feedback.
- Online courses need frequent deadlines and checkpoints to assist students to pace their learning through the course.
- All assignments and practice activities should be relevant and contribute to student learning outcomes.
- Challenging tasks, sample cases, and praise for quality work communicate high expectations.
- Allowing students to choose project topics encourages a sense of ownership of learning and incorporates diverse views into online courses

The above list includes modifications of the "Seven Principles of Good Practice in Undergraduate Education" (Chickering & Gameson, 1987) made by Graham et. al. (2001) for online courses. Depending upon the individual faculty member,

some of these principles may be emphasized more than others, but all are based on a half century of educational research (Chickering & Reisser, 1993) and have served as a framework to help faculty members improve their teaching practices.

An Outcomes-Based Model for eLearning

The structural model presented here can be used to plan a half hour virtual world excursion, a training workshop, a 10 minute piece of computer-based training, or a 16 week course. This is because the model focuses on providing a structure and framework into which almost any content can be planned. Since this model allows faculty who are designing their own courses a lot of latitude in their instructional choices, faculty using the model have not felt the course design and development process hampers their creativity or academic freedom. This model is also consistent with the tenets of Outcome-based Assessment (Zundel, et al., 2000). While we realize some authors draw distinctions among some or all of the following terms, for our purposes here "outcome-based assessment" includes assessment concepts such as "criterion-referenced," "competence-based," "performance-based," and "competency-based".

Increasingly, many applied disciplines such as engineering, business, accounting, and the health care professions are being called upon by industry and licensing bodies to train students for specific tasks that will be faced in the workplace. Such specific instruction calls for specific assessment. Outcome-based assessment is one of four components of an educational process that includes:

1. Defining educational targets - outcomes definition;
2. Doing things to achieve the targets - helping students reach outcomes (teaching);
3. Checking to see that targets are being met - assessment (outcome-based assessment);

4.   Changing actions to ensure that targets are being met or, in some situations, modifying targets so they are achievable - responding to assessment results

The course design model presented here divides the course design process into five aspects and while described in a linear fashion here for clarity and convenience, it actually represents an iterative process. These aspects are

*   Content
*   Performance/Learning Outcomes
*   Learning resources
*   Learning and Practice Activities
*   Interaction/Discussion
*   Assessment/feedback

The accompanying worksheet (the Course Module BluePrint) is divided into columns that represent each of these aspects. It would be valuable for you to print out several copies of the BluePrint and as you read the rest of this description of the course design elements you will be making notes, to start to fill in at least one of the worksheets. The BluePrint is a simple, landscape 2 row by 6 column table in a word processor and can be easily reproduced.

For the purpose of this discussion, we will assume that you are designing classes or instructional units for a course that meets once each week. If you conduct more than one class meeting each week, then you will eventually build a set of BluePrints for each course meeting. Your first worksheet should describe, in general terms, what will occur at the course level each week. Then, for each week, take another worksheet and describe in more detail the learning outcomes, learning resources, learning activities, interactions and assessments. Course design is an iterative process so you can expect to revisit each column many times and in apparently random order during the process. You can work onscreen in a wordprocessor if you choose, but you can work equally well in pencil

on printed sheets. Some instructors have used the smallest pad of "post-it" notes so they could pick them up and move them around as needed.

A word of advice – constantly check the alignment of objectives/outcomes, learning activities and assessments. Is there something written as an outcome for which there is no corresponding assessment, or which cannot be assessed (like 'understand' or 'appreciate')? Are there learning activities scheduled that do not pertain to the learning outcomes or do not provide the students an opportunity to practice towards the assessments? Are there activities for which no discussion is planned?

USING THE COURSE BLUEPRINT

The following section will describe the elements of the model in detail. While the columns on the worksheet are described below from left to right, you do not have to proceed through your course design in a linear fashion. You may have a favorite learning activity for a particular unit and enter that first, then write the appropriate learning outcomes and assessment statements, and afterwards add the necessary learning resources. When one worksheet page is devoted to each learning unit/module/lesson, you can easily re-number units to change their order in the course, if you discover that improves the logical flow through the material. Some instructors choose to use one sheet for each learning outcome in a unit, as they prefer to work in great detail; others use the barest outline with several outcomes to a sheet. Try to keep each outcome and their attendant resources, activities, interactions and assessments on a single line – it really does help to you to see the relationships.

UNIT TITLE AND TOPICS

The content that the students will be expected to cover needs to be divided into logical "chunks" to fit across the learning term. Sometimes this coincides with the content arrangement of the textbook chosen for the course. In other courses, the units may coincide with the steps in a project that the students are expected to develop or a particular sequence of skills to be mastered, with resources being provided to help students at each project step. Decide how you will divide your content across your learning units and fill that information in the first column of however many sheets you will need. Later you can spread all your units out on a flat surface and check to make sure that all content is covered.

LEARNING/PERFORMANCE OUTCOMES

Learning outcomes provide the student with a clear statement of measurable performances that will be required of them at the end of the period of instruction. Learning outcomes at the course level are often cumulative and stated broadly as "goals", with the final result being the sum of meeting a number of interim learning outcomes. These interim outcomes are often written for each session or unit of a course and can be assessed individually or when demonstrated as part of a final assessment event. Learning outcomes assist you to design your instruction, as course design should begin with the end in mind. The choice of learning resources made available to the students, the learning and practice activities required of the students in the application of the concepts they are learning, the kinds of interaction required and the choice of appropriate assessments are all aligned with those outcomes.

Learning outcomes are statements that specify, in measurable or observable terms, what students are required to demonstrate (i.e., apply their knowledge to) at the end of a unit of instruction—a learning session; course; program. The terms "learning outcomes" and "performance outcomes" are used interchangeably in this model, with the

caveat that learning must be expressed by observable performance of some kind.

One difficult concept for many instructors to grasp is that learning and performance outcomes describe a course of study in terms of the learner's gain or output rather than in terms of the instructor's teaching or input. Teaching inputs are easily under instructor control, but student learning is not. When learning outcomes are stated at the beginning of a course of study, students then acquire knowledge and apply it to practice so that the outcome assessment measures the students' mastery of those performance outcomes. There are no surprises.

Instructors commonly state objectives in terms of ensuring a student "understands" or "appreciates" a particular topic. "Understanding" and "appreciating" are cognitive activities, so are difficult to see or to measure. How will a student know, and can demonstrate when they have reached an acceptable level of understanding or appreciation? How will the instructor know or not? On what can feedback be given to the student? In a properly stated performance outcome, the student may be asked to perform some action, describe/perform a process, identify and distinguish between several different elements, build an artifact or environment, compare two opposing views, reflect on personal experience, use specific cognitive or manual tools and/or equipment, explain a concept, re-design an object, collect and/or evaluate data, use or derive an equation, etc. There are a number of action verb lists that can be consulted when writing performance outcomes that translate cognitive outcomes into observable performances (see, for example, Kizlik, 2010).

LEARNING RESOURCES

These are all the "content resources" that students will have to assist them in the accomplishment of their learning tasks. Resources can be in any form of media, such as paper (textbooks, study guides, readings etc.), video/audio, or in a myriad of electronic formats. They can also include the instructor, other students, their fellow workers, or family members. They can also be in the form of processes and procedures that they learn and will apply, for example, such as how to solve equations, how to conjugate verbs, how to build artifacts and use textures, how to debug a C++ program, or the components of a business plan and how to build one. Not all resources need to be provided by the instructor; it is an excellent learning activity for students to seek out and share their own resources. In virtual worlds, many resources are provided by the infrastructure and students can use, or buy, resources that they will use "in-world".

It is often useful to list separately as resources many of the items that have traditionally been considered as learning activities. Why? Because students are acquiring raw materials from which they build intellectual, motor, and affective knowledge and skills they will use during their practice to reach the learning outcomes.

Information is "course content"—raw material found in resources such as books, videos, lectures, or interactions with others. In and of itself, information has little value to a particular student unless that student uses the resource to create something, including intellectual structures, (though practice) or to do something.

Processes and procedures are not what most instructors think of as resources, but as instructional outcomes. The acquisition of processes and procedures is, however, not usually the final endpoint in instruction. At work there are a myriad "how to" processes and procedures to be learned and applied. Once learned, these become resources for a worker and some can be applied across applications, or used to extrapolate from one application to another.

The same kind of process learning occurs in a college classroom. What is the process for analyzing character and plot in short stories? What are the processes for creating a storefront or orientation trail in a virtual world? What is the

process for cleaning a four-color press? What is the process for creating a lithograph? What is the procedure to follow "to prepare a stained section for microscopic examination?" What procedure do you follow to solve quadratic equations? What process do you use to estimate the load-bearing strength of steel beams using virtual world gravity? Students learn the process steps by observation, personal study (reading or watching a video), or some other method. Still, the knowledge acquisition should precede using the process to achieve some ultimate outcome.

LEARNING/PRACTICE ACTIVITIES

Students need to apply the knowledge they are acquiring. They need to practice this application in the same forms as their final assessments, and each practice exercise may mark successive steps towards that goal. In virtual worlds students spend a lot of time learning how to navigate, use their cameras and manipulate objects and artifacts, before they can do much of anything else.

Student learning falls into two general levels: "learning to be" and "learning what and how" (Brown & Duguid, 2000). Learning to be a member of their discipline or profession involves using discipline/profession appropriate vocabulary and problem-solving methods to address issues of concern to their discipline or profession. This can be accomplished by instructor-planned discussion, papers, reports, case studies, and by working alongside faculty in an apprentice mode. In virtual worlds, student avatars can dress appropriately for their chosen profession and engage in activities and discourse in a safe environment that they may have, themselves, created.

Learning "what and how" involves learning to correctly manipulate the tools, both material and cognitive, that are common to the student's discipline or profession. This can range from practicing writing memorandums and reports using specified content and formats, performing medical procedures, building learning environments, to creating financial and risk management plans, designing and building computer chips or dissecting frogs. Consistent practice in the style of their final assessments allows both students and instructors to monitor learning during the instructional unit and provides early warning of misconceptions or learning difficulties.

Students need to practice using processes and procedures if they are to result long term learning. This sometimes starts with hygienic instances—the tidy problems in the text book. As skills and knowledge develop, the cases can be scaled up to very untidy, real-life problems, and this is an area in which virtual worlds can excel. Other instructors like to start out with authentic, messy problems, helping students to solve intermediate problems as they are discovered. Either way may work, depending on student characteristics and other factors. Try both until experience can guide your design.

Sometimes practice activities are intellectual processes—how to think through a problem, for instance, or how to take and react from a particular ideological stance. Students can be given problems to solve and "show their work," or they can be asked to take one side in a debate, or write a paper from a particular viewpoint, or build artifacts or environments for particular audiences or activities. To develop a case for or against an issue, inquiry requires students to critically think and research various points of view other than their own. In many practical and applied courses this is easily addressed. A process that a student must learn may be to "develop and print black and white film in the darkroom." So where does the student practice? In the dark room! If a student is required to learn how quenching works with metals, and the effects of different temperatures and quenching mediums, where do they practice? In the lab! If students are required to learn sociological principles, where do they go after they have read the book and watched the video? Into their lives and their memories to see if they can match theory with practice.

When creating activities for students in virtual worlds, you need to be very specific about what you want your students to do. Often students are distracted while in-world and have a hard time focusing and following verbal instructions. Step-by-step instructions should be written out for each activity in-world and given to the students on note cards, put on sign boards in their learning area, or distributed ahead of time via email or the course learning management system. Activity instructions prepared ahead of time can also be copy-and-pasted into the Chat function so that students can scroll back if they lose their place, or forget what they have been asked to do.

There are many resources to suggest activities appropriate for students in virtual worlds

INTERACTION/DISCUSSION

Interaction, especially in the form of discussion (Brookfield, 2004) is a special form of learning activity, so it is a key activity that should be deliberately planned into a course. One of the instructor's jobs is to provide an environment or forum where student reactions to their learning activities can be discussed. Within their own learning community students can rehearse their understanding and ask questions in relative safety from embarrassment or harm that might be found in public spaces. This is also a place where students can practice the language of their discipline, making vocabulary tests unnecessary. Students should be required to use the language and terminology of their discipline correctly, both in the way questions are asked and by following the instructor's modeling.

Often students need reflection time after in-world activities, as they are on cognitive overload managing their avatar inworld. This discussion can take place by something as simple as an email discussion list or in the discussion forums of whatever learning management system is available. Text chat is complex to manage inworld as many different threads can quickly emerge; voice chat suffers from the same limitations as classroom discussion: limited time and too many people to be heard. Effort should be made to include all avatars in discussion activities.

When using the design model BluePrint for planning interaction, the questions that become the key discussion starters are listed. If the students are going to interact with each other in teams or groups, these groups are identified too, along with other activities they will be doing.

The curriculum of an online course should be designed to cause dialogue among the students. During online discussions, the participants collect information and send it to the virtual classroom for comments, critiques and more discussion. In order to generate this type of information, students must actively seek out the required material. The synergy of the discussion is itself a learning tool. With that in mind, much of the information presented to the class can come from the participants themselves. (ION 2003, n.p.)

Through discussion and interaction with others, the students share their experiences, try out different ways of looking at their own experiences and those of others, explore multiple perspectives and views that often conflict with their own and make a firm connection between theory and their own practice. They can practice the discipline or profession-specific cognitive problem-solving methods they are learning, and express the results in the language of their discipline or profession.

ASSESSMENT/FEEDBACK

The questions to be asked concerning the creation of assessments include what types of assessment are going to allow the students to demonstrate that they have acquired the necessary competences or attained the performance outcomes for the course. Is student learning going to be assessed only at the middle and/or the end of the learning term?

Will students be assessed continually by assigning graded activities, homework, discussions, quizzes or tests, on a weekly basis and the grades will be summed across the semester, or will they be assessed using a portfolio or final project, or in some other way?

Structuring feedback is a key component of designing effective instruction. Feedback can take the form of instructor to student, student to instructor, and student to student interactions. The more opportunities for feedback in all these forms throughout the learning process, the more opportunities students have to assess their own performance and to make changes and corrections in their learning or performance strategies.

It is critical to make sure that assessments and practice activities are congruent with each other and with the learning objectives. There is no point in having the students practice in ways different to those that will be used for their assessments or practice that which will not be assessed. If students are learning a manual process, for instance, a pencil-and-paper test may be used to determine if they know the steps in the process or the appropriate applications of the process, when to use that process instead of some other, and the criteria for choice. But, if it is a manual skill they are to acquire, then they must at some point demonstrate it manually (such as creating an artifact inworld).

Students' critical thinking/understanding/learning can be assessed in the tangible products of cognitive activity such as what they write and post in the discussion conferences, and in other written assignments. The instructor cannot see what is going on inside the students' heads until they make their learning manifest in some way. So, the instructor must design specific assessments—write a paper, develop a plan, build an artifact, use scripts and textures, locate and use appropriate learning environments, complete a project, document a process, make a machinima of specific performances—that allow the students to demonstrate they have acquired the competences designed into the course.

Feedback: Feedback used as assessment permits students to correct their practice and often through successive approximations, more closely match the standards and expectations set for them by the instructor, or they have set for themselves.

The goals of feedback in e-learning may include some or all of the following:

- Ensuring accuracy of content acquisition, performance, and understanding
- Providing guidance, coaching, and modeling of the learning goals
- Facilitating social interchange and building relationships
- Increasing student motivation and maintaining the focus of the learning activities
- Linking the learning goals of the course to relevancy in the workplace
- Providing evidence for certification of credit
- Providing information helpful for improving the course now and in the future (Berge, 2002).

Feedback is dependent on interaction. Both feedback and interaction are central to meeting the expectations of teachers and learners in education and therefore are primary goals of the educational process.

USING YOUR BLUEPRINTS

What do you do with your BluePrints, once you have completed them? Spread them out on a large flat surface and make sure that each column has an entry. Look at your outcomes – does each outcome have associated resources, activities, interaction and assessment? It is so much easier to make changes to a course of instruction when it is in BluePrint form than when you are deep

in the development process, both inworld and in your learning management system.

If you have the opportunity, share your blueprints with colleagues or the helpful faculty development people at your institution. Instructors have also shared BluePrints with senior or graduate students to get their reactions. BluePrints are also appropriate documents to share with curriculum committees or whatever body approves new or revised courses.

If you are fortunate to have access to the services of an instructional designer then your BluePrints will very clearly show what you have in mind for your course and they can base their suggestions on a clear understanding of your plans. If you have access to the service of instructional developers then, they, too, will benefit from receiving a copy of your BluePrints so they know exactly what your course will need.

If you have to develop the course yourself, you will find the BluePrints to be invaluable as you set up your course in your learning management system and plan your inworld sessions. Check off each item on your BluePrint as you enter them into your unit agendas. BluePrints make an excellent outline for a "This Week" or "This Meeting" page with the column headings down the left hand side of the page with your entries under them – then the students will know exactly what to expect for each course unit.

CONCLUSION

Thoughtful consideration regarding what students must demonstrate to the instructor and themselves to show their mastery of the course learning outcomes is a key to effective course development. The instructor needs to decide what students should be able to show that they can do after the learning event. Then they can focus on what activities will make the learning meaningful, relevant and transferable. Aligning the learning activities and assessment with those learning outcomes is the secret to effective planning in course development. This is true for any instruction, regardless of where it is delivered, or by what means.

REFERENCES

Aldrich, C. (2009). *Learning online with games, simulations, and virtual worlds*. San Francisco, CA: Jossey-Bass.

Berge, Z. L. (1996). *Changing roles in higher education: Reflecting on technology Collaborative Communications Review* (pp. 43–53). McLean, VA: International Teleconferencing Association.

Berge, Z. L. (2002). Active, interactive and reflective elearning. *Quarterly Review of Distance Education, 3*(2).

Brookfield, S. D. (2004). Discussion. In Galbraith, M. W. (Ed.), *Adult learning methods: A guide for effective instruction* (3rd ed., pp. 209–226). Malabar, FL: Robert E. Kreiger Publishing Company.

Brown, J. S., & Duguid, P. (2000). *The social life of information*. Boston, MA: Harvard Business School Press.

Chickering, A. W., & Gameson, Z. (1987). Seven principles of good practice in undergraduate education. *AAHE Bulletin, 39*(7), 3–7.

Chickering, A. W., & Reisser, L. (1993). *Education and identity*. San Francisco, CA: Jossey-Bass.

Collins, M. P., & Berge, Z. L. (2003). Using instructional design for faculty development in a post-secondary, technology-enhanced environment. *Educational Technology, 46*(6), 21–27.

Graham, C., Cagiltay, K., Lim, B., Craner, J., & Duffy, T. M. (2001). *Seven principles of effective teaching: A practical lens for evaluating online courses*. The Technology Source. [Online.] Retrieved from http://ts.mivu.org/ default. asp?show=article&id=839

Graziano, A., Higgins, R. A., Hislop, D. W., & Moore, K. (2000). *A changing focus in higher education? Outcome-based assessment*. Retrieved from http://www.shu.ac.uk/schools/ ed/ pgclt/1999-2000/resources/task1/ presentations/ almerindo-richard-donald-kathie/home.htm

ION (Illinois Online Network and the Board of Trustees of the University of Illinois). (2003). *Alternatives to the online lecture*. Retrieved from http://illinois.online.uillinois.edu/ IONresources/ instructionaldesign/ alternative.html

Jones, J. G., & Bronack, S. C. (2007). Rethinking cognition, representations, and processes in 3D online social learning environments. In Gibson, D., Aldrich, C., & Prensky, M. (Eds.), *Games and simulations in online learning: Research and development frameworks*. Hershey, PA: Information Science Publishing. doi:10.4018/9781599047980. ch010

Kizlik, B. (2003.) *Definitions of behavioral verbs for learning objectives*. Retrieved from http:// www.adprima.com/ verbs.htm

Kizlik, B. (2010). *Definitions of behavioral verbs for learning objectives*. Retrieved July 13, 2010, from http://www.adprima.com/ verbs.htm

Moore, M. G. (1989). Three types of interaction. *American Journal of Distance Education, 3*(2), 1–6. doi:10.1080/08923648909526659

Network, I. O. (2003). *Alternatives to the online lecture*. Retrieved July 12, 2010, from http://illinois.online.uillinois.edu/ IONresources/instructionaldesign/ alternative.html

Ryder, M. (2003). *Instructional design models*. Retrieved from http://carbon.cudenver.edu/~mryder/itc_data/idmodels.html

Seels, B., & Glasgow, Z. (1998). *Making instructional design decisions* (2nd ed.). Upper Saddle River, NJ: Prentice Hall.

Seels, B. B., & Glasgow, Z. (1998). *Making instructional design decisions*. Upper Saddle River, NJ: Prentice Hall.

Willis, B. (2003). *Distance education at a glance: Guide #3*. Retrieved from http://www.uidaho.edu/eo/dist3.html

Zundel, P. E., Needham, T. D., Richards, E. W., Kershaw, J. A., Daugharty, D. A., & Robak, E. W. (2000). Fostering competency with outcome-based assessment. In M. R. Ryan & W. B. Kurtz (Eds.), *Third Biennial Conference on University Education in Natural Resources*. Retrieved from https://www.cnr.usu.edu/ quinney/files/uploads/UENR3.pdf#page=98

APPENDIX: COURSE BLUE PRINT

Module #, Title, Topic(s)	Learning Outcomes	Learning Resources	Learning Activities	Discussion Topics	Assignments for Assessment
What content do you want to cover in this unit?	*At the end of this unit, what do you want students to demonstrate they have learned how to do?*	*What are the resources that students will have to work with? (Text book(s), readings, videos, recorded lectures. web sites etc.)*	*What, and how do you want students to practice, using the Resources to meet the Learning Outcomes?*	*What discussion / interactions would allow students to demonstrate movement towards Learning Outcomes?*	*What evidence must students present to show they have met the learning outcomes? What will the student be graded on?*

Chapter 17
Design and Robots for Learning in Virtual Worlds

Michael Vallance
Future University Hakodate, Japan

ABSTRACT

The meme of the physical university is changing and moving swiftly, due mostly to virtual technological developments, towards the "multi-versity" where Higher Education Institutes will exist in both the real world and a virtual space: a term this chapter names "augmented education." Augmented education requires innovation in technology that can deliver new ways of learning. Therefore, virtual worlds that support effective experiential learning need to be designed beyond merely established real world replication. The concern for researchers and educational practitioners is the need to provide evidence-based frameworks for tasks of measurable complexity that result in verifiable learning in an augmented virtual world. In an attempt to develop a framework for science education this chapter summarizes the theoretical and technical progress of research in the iterative, leaner centered design of virtual tools and associated tasks for evidencing the processes of learning (witnessed as measurements of six cognitive processes and four knowledge dimensions) of participants communicating the programming of LEGO robots within a virtual world.

INTRODUCTION: AUGMENTED EDUCATION

The inception of augmented education has become a realistic image scenario for university futures. The blending of real and virtual is becoming accepted as augmented reality is placed into the hands of consumers in the form of iPhone Apps such as 'Layar' and 'Acrossair'. Moreover, virtual worlds such as Second Life and MMORPG games such as 'World of Warcraft' have assisted the progress of a virtual presence that supplements real persona. Augmentation is not the sole domain of consumers though. Researchers systematically develop scenarios and images of education as transformative and sometimes disruptive futures (Vallance & Wright, 2010). Virtual institutes will consequently evolve to 24/7 open access quite similar to current service offered such as iTunesU, MIT Open Courseware, Open University UK,

DOI: 10.4018/978-1-61350-516-8.ch017

Copyright © 2012, IGI Global. Copying or distributing in print or electronic forms without written permission of IGI Global is prohibited.

Kaplan University, and many others. The meme of the physical 'uni-versity' is consequently changing and moving swiftly, due mostly to virtual technological developments, towards the 'multi-versity' where Higher Education Institutes will exist in both the real world and a virtual space. The worry for university traditionalists and its administrative bureaucrats is enormous. The concern for researchers though is to design educationally effective spaces and produce metrics that provide evidence of learning in the augmented institutes.

The focus of this chapter is on augmentation. Augment is a transitive verb which is defined as meaning to make greater, as in size, quantity, strength, and to enlarge. Engelbart uses this term to emphasize the role of technology in a human context; technology is to be designed to increase human capabilities, to extend them in imagined and unimagined ways, to change the basic character of communities, and to make these more effective. The components of an augmented system are the bundle of all things that can be added to what a human is genetically endowed with, the purpose of which is to augment these basic human capabilities in order to maximize the capabilities that a human organization can apply to the problems and goals of human society. Augmentation systems have always existed; they have often been developed unconsciously. Throughout history, augmentation systems have emerged as a result of continuing socio-cultural capability (Ambron & Hooper, 1988).

To enable an augmented education scenario, research in the 'informed use' (Towndrow & Vallance, 2004) of technology for educational purposes highlights the need to go beyond the replication of traditional, didactic practices to an appropriation of digital communication (Warschauer, 1999) facilitated by a constructivist pedagogy (Jonassen & Land, 2000) to support purposeful tasks (Martin & Vallance, 2008). The subsequent convergence of instructivism, constructionism, and social and collaborative learning towards a cohesive 'Conversational Framework' (Laurillard,

2002) will then provide opportunities for learners to take "a more active role in learning and for tutors to support learning activities in multimodal ways" (deFreitas & Griffiths, 2008, p.17). Learning is thus considered to be a "process whereby knowledge is created through the transformation of experience" (Kolb, 1984, p.41). deFreitas and Neumann (2009) suggest that the appeal, immersivity, and immediacy of virtual worlds can support this 'experiential learning' but education requires a re-consideration of how, what, when, and where we learn. deFreitas and Neumann (2009) use Dewey's (1934) concept of inquiry (pre-reflection, reflection, and post-reflection) to posit that learners' virtual experiences, their use of multiple media, the transactions and activities between peers, and the facilitation of learner control between them will lead to 'transactional learning' which "aims to support deeper reflection upon the practices of learning and teaching" (deFreitas and Neumann, 2009; 346) which arguably leads to "wider opportunities for experiential learning" (*ibid*). As deFreitas (2008) asserts, "In order to achieve this next step two related aspects are required: the first is developing better metrics for evaluating virtual world learning experiences, and the second is developing better techniques for creating virtual learning experiences (e.g. frameworks, approaches and models)" (p.11). Therefore, there needs to be a move from the commonly seen replication of existing practice towards the exploitation of the unique pedagogical affordances offered by emerging technologies (Cuban, 1992). In other words, virtual worlds must create a synthetic experience that "support learning by augmenting, replacing, creating or managing a learner's actual experience with the world" (Cannon-Bowers & Bowers, 2008; p.318). Therefore, synthetic learning environments such as virtual worlds need to combine the key elements of learning theories and technologies.

In the early days of modern educational technology adoption (circa 1980's) the development of associated software was termed Programmed

Instruction where computer usage simply supported the repeat and practice drills associated with the behaviorist pedagogy at that time (Higgins & Johns, 1984). In recent years there has been an acknowledgement that pedagogically-focused technology 'engagement' is more effective than simply 'integrating' technology into existing practices (Selwyn, 2011). Of course over many years there has been a recognition of the need for pedagogically driven technology (Sandholtz, Ringstaff & Dwyer, 1997). Consequently, after much investment in implementing technology in education worldwide (Vallance, 2008), there now appears to be an emphasis on the learner as technology informant. This has led to an approach for educational technology engagement called 'learner centered design' (Soloway, Guzdial & Hay, 1994). Learner centered design takes into account theories and practice of learning which subsequently informs the appropriation of the developing technology. It takes into account current tenets of a social constructivist theory of learning which include active construction of meaning, situated cognition or context for learning, discourse for developing understanding, and scaffolding for supporting the learner's progression. Learners are provided opportunities to make meaning of what they are doing, and reflect upon the knowledge acquired. With learner centered design, the focus of technology development is thus on the learner and not the technology. Such experiential learning provides learners with opportunities to engage with problems that require the retrieval of prior knowledge, offer multiple perspectives of problems and solutions, and facilitate a challenging process which leads to an achievable outcome. Learning does not occur in isolation but involves communication, cooperation and collaboration with fellow learners and experts (Kolb, 1984). In this Vygotskian social constructivist learning perspective, personal interpretation, decision-making and community cooperation fosters long-term understanding and transference of learned concepts. In summary, the construction of knowledge requires learners (of science or other subjects) to be actively involved in designing and shaping the learning process.

RESEARCH METHOD

In order to determine the effectiveness of a learner centered design process and associated learning an instrument to measure success (or otherwise) is required. For over forty years Bloom has provided a valid and reliable taxonomy that has allowed educators to visualize teaching objectives and perceived learning together with the associated notation, categorization and assessment of aims (Bloom, 1956; Anderson, Krathwohl, Airasian, Cruicshank, Mayer, Pintrich, Raths, & Wittrock, 2001). In Bloom's taxonomy, a range of learning objectives are presented as cognitive functions that enable cognitive learning, that is, "… recall or recognition of knowledge and the development of intellectual abilities and skills" (Bloom, 1956, p.7). The six categories associated with the cognitive processes identified in Anderson et al's revised taxonomy are remember, understand, apply, analyze, evaluate and create. (Anderson et al, 2001). Supporting the cognitive processes are four general types of knowledge that include factual knowledge, conceptual knowledge, procedural knowledge, and metacognitive knowledge (*ibid*). A strength of this neo-Bloomian taxonomy is that it provides a visualization of a relationship between both cognitive processes and knowledge; see Table 1. Bloom's revised taxonomy grid. It allows researchers and practitioners to sort out complexities and identify gaps where none may have been previously acknowledged. Bloom's taxonomy has been widely adopted and extensively cited as a useful way of framing what happens in a potential learning situation.

Given the validity and reliability of this instrument it was decided to explore the degree to which activities in virtual worlds are likely to provoke behaviors which can be located within the neo-

Table 1. Bloom's revised taxonomy grid.

Cognitive Process	Knowledge			
	Factual - knowledge of discrete, isolated, content elements	Conceptual - knowledge of more complex, organised forms such as classifications, categories, principles, generalizations, theories, models and structures	Procedural - knowledge of how to do something	Meta-cognitive - knowledge about cognition in general as well as awareness of and knowledge about one's own cognition
Remember - retrieve relevant information form long-term memory				
Understand - construct meaning from instructional messages, including oral, written, and graphic communication				
Apply - carry out or use a procedure in a given situation				
Analyze - break material into constituent parts and determine how parts relate to one another and to an overall structure or purpose				
Evaluate - make judgments based on criteria and standards				
Create - put elements together to form a coherent or functional whole, reorganize elements into a new pattern or structure				

Bloomian taxonomy. The research project was conceived to facilitate an exploration of this by studying the communicative exchanges between, and within, teams during problem solving tasks. Closed and highly defined tasks seemed most likely to provide the necessary comparability and empirical data to determine the success of task completion. To satisfy this criteria, the programming of a robot to navigate mazes of varying complexity was adopted. Reviewing the research literature, Barker and Ansorge (2007) found that teaching robotics: is an effective tool for teaching science, engineering, and technology; students who have engineered and programmed robots are exposed to other disciplines that are important for robotics, science and engineering; there is exposure to real-world conditions with multiple possible solutions; effective teamwork is a significant

outcome; and that female students respond positively to working with robots. The research was thus designed to observe the iterative process of learning in a virtual world which would in turn support the development of transferable metrics and framework for meaningful education with tangible, quantifiably measured outcomes,

The robot selected for the programming tasks was LEGO robot 8527 supported by the LEGO Mindstorms NXT software version 1.1. LEGO robot 8527 was adopted due to its simplicity and potential for sensors to be added as the learner centered design and research task framework developed (Vallance, Martin, Wiz, & van Schaik, 2009). The instructions for the design of LEGO robot 8527 is available at http://preview.tinyurl.com/yfw75s2,

In order to quantify each task complexity the programming the LEGO robot required a determination of an action and a vector. Adopting Barker and Ansorge's criteria the first important variable of task difficulty in this context was defined as the minimum number of discrete maneuvers required to successfully navigate a given maze. For example, a maze requiring five distinct maneuvers such as a forward move, a left turn, a forward move, a right turn and then a final forward move, was defined as a maze of complexity level five. Successfully navigating this maze would be no different in level of intrinsic difficulty to navigating a maze requiring a right turn, a forward move, a right turn, a forward move and then a left turn. Mazes with differing levels of intrinsic difficulty could therefore be provided for participants to facilitate true comparisons of like with like and to act as the problem specification dependant variable (Vallance, Martin, Wiz & van Schaik, 2010).

The metrics proposed for assessing the experiment adopted Olsen and Goodrich's (2003) criteria of Task Effectiveness (TE), Interaction Effort (IE), frequency of course navigation, and time requirement for successful course completion. Communication between groups was carried out using synchronous interactive virtual technologies and all communication was digitally captured, transcribed and analyzed using the approach described in Vallance et al. (*ibid*). The quantitative data set (i.e. Task Effectiveness (TE) - the number of commands successfully programmed into the robot, and Interaction Effort (IE) – the amount of time required to interact with the robot (Olsen & Goodrich, 2003) were merged with personalized 'meaning' of data collected via a qualitative data set; i.e. the follow up interviews and digital capture of participants on task. Combining both quantitative and qualitative data sets reduces bias (Brown, 1992).

Figure 1. Robot 8527

IMPLEMENTATION: LEARNER CENTERED DESIGN FOR ROBOT TASKS IN A VIRTUAL WORLD

The participants in this research programmed robots to navigate courses designed by others remotely located, and subsequently modified the program to improve navigation on successive attempts. Prior to implementing the tasks, communication and robot programming, a virtual learning space was designed using a learner centered design approach merged with a futures studies method that supports the development of possible, probable and preferable futures through the use of scenarios (Vallance & Wright, 2010). This involves an analysis, a critique and a panoramic view of present designs in order to facilitate a discussion and an ownership of the change process.

An originally designed Second Life learning space consisted of two levels with transparent walls. The lower level space was used as a sandbox (the term used in Second Life for avatars to learn how to construct and modify objects). A media presenter with images previously uploaded was also available for avatars to use. The media presenter was essentially a presentation screen con-

Figure 2. Solution is programmed to NXT Mindstorms software and transferred to the LEGO robot

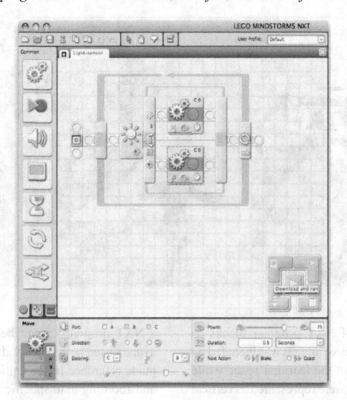

nected to a virtual laptop. Pressing the keyboard on the laptop changed the image on the presenter. Avatars could upload images from their own inventory. The second level provided tools for the LEGO experiments. Again, a media presenter was available. Next to the media presenter was a video streaming screen. This enabled live video to be streamed from a student's physical working area via a video camera connected to a networked computer. The screen also displayed fixed images in a similar way to the aforementioned presenter. The feedback from the participants in attempting to solve initial tasks and program the LEGO robot to follow a particular circuit indicated that this space was limiting though. The virtual world did not utilize any unique tools and merely replicated a real world experience. Cuban (1992) has recognized similar developments in many early stages of technology use in education circumstances. According to Cuban the stage of this learner

centered design would be considered 'replication' and thus no change in educational circumstance: zero order change. For technology to have an impact on education change it needs to 'explore' (first order change) and then 'innovate' (second order change).

The next stage may be considered an exploratory stage of the learner centered design. The design by the students enabled individual avatars to place and move blocks on the virtual floor. These blocks were graphical representations of the NXT Mindstorms software blocks required to build the program required to navigate the LEGO robot. On the sides (named Options Walls by the students) of the second level of the virtual structure were images of the NXT configuration panels. These were displayed so that students could point and focus on specific configurations that needed to be inputted in order to program specifically detailed operations of the robots. In

Figure 3. Initial learner centered design of virtual space for undertaking tasks

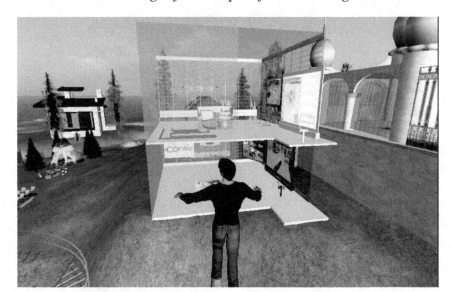

summary, the use of NXT program blocks as manipulative, interactive images was included on the horizontal floor of the learning space while NXT block variables were represented as vertical images. During the implementation the avatars would meet on the second level and together re-construct their NXT program. Figure 4 illustrates a NXT program circuit being constructed. The avatars used both voice and text to communicate, made reference to the Options Wall by pointing and zooming in to specific configuration panels, constructed new NXT objects (using the 'Shift and drag' computer operation), and moved the NXT objects to construct the program required

Figure 4. Participants (as avatars) collaborating in the upper level of the initial design

Figure 5. Creating NXT program objects within the virtual world

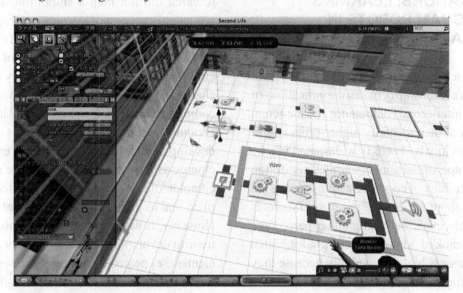

to upload to the LEGO robot. Figure 5 details the creation of the NXT program objects within the virtual world.

Once this virtual learning space had been built, sixteen (16) tasks were implemented: the initial seven (7) were utilized for practice; data was collected from the remaining nine (9). Each iteratively more difficult task aimed to challenge students to communicate a construction process leading to a successful outcome; that is, program a LEGO robot to follow a specified circuit of movements and turns. Communication between participants (in this case, N=8) was supported by the virtual world chat facility and the behavior of participants' avatars in the environment. Each team had to design the maze of an identical robot on the floor of their laboratory using adhesive tape. Next, one team's task was to act as 'learners' and create a robot program (using the MindStorms software) to follow the maze that the other (teaching) team had designed. The learning team used the information provided in an attempt to solve the robot programming problem. The teaching team used their robot to run the program on the taped maze to establish its success, and were encouraged to offer feedback via the Second Life

environment to the learning team when the robot executed an incorrect maneuver and in answer to questions from the learning team (Vallance & Martin, 2011).

Over 60 hours of video of participants communicating in the real world was recorded. This data was transcribed and analyzed using Transana (http://www.transana.org/) and TAMS Analyzer (http://tamsys.sourceforge.net/) software. Screen captures of all actions in the virtual world were also recorded and aligned to the real world video data recordings. The coding for the analysis was, as mentioned previously, the cognitive processes and knowledge dimension of Bloom's taxonomy. Initial indications from our data suggest that the nature and defined difficulty of learning tasks can be used to create metrics for designing and evaluating learning scenarios in immersive virtual environments that can be articulated within Bloom's revised taxonomy. This is discussed in the next section.

OBSERVATIONS: LEARNING TO PROGRAM ROBOTS IN A VIRTUAL WORLD

Higher Education assessment schemes presume an ordered relationship between the indications of increasing intellectual competence and the actual acquisition of incrementally higher-order cognition by individuals. There is widespread use by many educators of assessment schemes based on an ordered hierarchy of cognitive activity, where the judgments about the learning progress of students is commonly expressed using either percentage marks or ranked alphanumeric grades. Such schemes possess high face-validity because they appear to represent common-sense descriptions of learning progression. Given this assumption there is thus a direct inference that cognitive processes develop linearly from low-order thinking (such as 'remember') to high order thinking (such as 'create'). If this is to be believed, tasks of progressively increasing complexity should facilitate learning along a progressively increasing path, as illustrated in Figure 6. However, the data in this

research did not map a smooth developmental sequence or process of learning (see Figures 7 and 8). These observations are elaborated upon below.

Given the steadily rising level of task difficulty and students' increasing mastery of the more challenging tasks as evidenced by their ability to complete them with fewer errors and in less time, Bloom's taxonomy would suggest that some developmental pattern should be expected to emerge as the procedural knowledge required to complete them came to be more effectively applied and as student accomplishment increased. However, it was surprising to see no consistent trend or development in the frequency with which elements appeared over time in the sessions. The relative frequency with which particular kinds of cognition appeared in the data (e.g. 'applying procedural knowledge') was not patterned as tasks progressed and difficulty increased (see Figure 7). Moreover, the relative frequency with which the different elements of cognition appeared in the data (e.g. 'applying conceptual knowledge') did not present itself as a linear or rising percentage of what might have been expected in a devel-

Figure 6. Activity as percentage of each task – expected outcomes

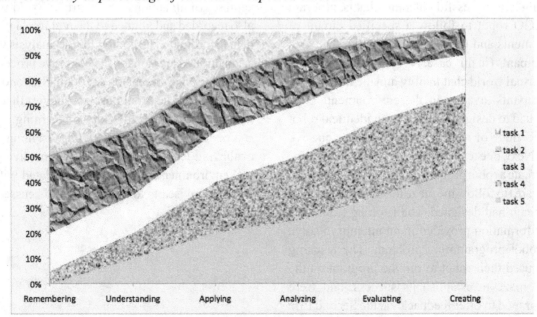

Figure 7. Activity as percentage of each task – procedural knowledge

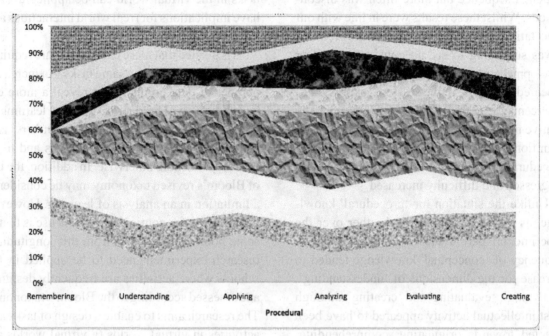

Figure 8. Activity as percentage of each task – conceptual knowledge

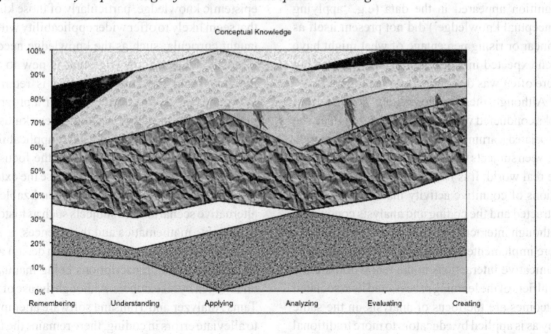

opmental sequence but more often was discontinuous. Whilst these results were in line with our expectations and given the nature of the set tasks, it was surprising to see no consistent trend or development in the frequency with which elements appeared over time in the sessions, expressed as a percentage of the total session activity. The relative frequency with which particular kinds of cognition appeared in the data (e.g. 'applying procedural knowledge') was not patterned as tasks progressed and difficulty increased.

Unlike the situation for 'procedural' knowledge, as sessions followed each other over the experimental period the observed cumulative frequency of 'conceptual' knowledge tended to increase for the dimensions of 'understanding', 'analyzing', 'evaluating' and 'creating' although most intellectual activity appeared to have been directed towards originating, comprehending, understanding and developing such knowledge rather than to applying it. However, as was found with 'procedural' knowledge, the relative frequency with which the different elements of cognition appeared in the data (e.g. 'applying conceptual knowledge') did not present itself as a linear or rising percentage of what might have been expected in a developmental sequence but more often was discontinuous (see Figure 8).

Although these outcomes are derived from tasks conducted within a virtual environment, the associated learning and communicative interaction between subjects was conducted synchronously in the real world. It is from the real world manifestations of cognitive activity that data have been extracted and the coding and analysis conducted. Although interactive collaborative learning tasks were implemented in the virtual world, the communicative interactions in the real world are the signifiers of the learning process and its associated outcomes are the focus of analysis, in the same way as is applied by educators to more traditional encoded expressions of learning (written work, discussions, presentations, portfolios, etc.). Interactions within and outcomes from the learning tasks in the virtual world can be applied to (and have implications for) real world interactions and learning contexts.

It is posited that more participants are required though to undertake the same tasks. An increased number of data points might reveal a more cohesive pattern. The data shows that learning is not as structured or uniform as Bloom's revised taxonomy suggests so more students and more data may illustrate otherwise. In addition, the use of Bloom's revised taxonomy may be considered a limitation in an analysis of learning. However, the rationale for continuing with its use is that at some point the outcomes from this longitudinal research experiment need to be applied in the schools where activities are frequently designed and assessed according to the Bloom's taxonomy. The research aims to enable a design of tasks and activities in virtual worlds (a virtual worlds activity metrics framework) that will meet specific learning (or assessment) criteria based upon the experiments we have conducted.

The taxonomy could be broadened to include epistemic knowledge, particularly of those kinds that seem likely to offer wider applicability within taught curricula: such as the knowledge needed to create subject knowledge that is new to the individual and the knowledge that is required in order to be able to decide whether a proposition, argument or theory is valid. These kinds of epistemic knowledge would have applicability in communicative contexts beyond the focus of the present research and could increase the extent to which our findings may be generalizable to alternative scenarios and subjects such as history, geography, mathematics and the sciences.

A further limitation in the research design was the coding of the transcriptions being manually undertaken by researchers. Although the use of the Tams Analyzer and Transana software attempted to alleviate errors in coding, there remains the fact that the researchers could only 'interpret' what they perceived to be going on given the textual and video evidence available. The transcriptions were of participants discussing how to work through the set tasks. Linking the transcripts to the captured videos attempted to visually interpret the discussions within the parameters of the Bloom's taxonomic elements. These discussions were not necessarily explicit expressions of learning though. The analysis in this research therefore remains an interpretation, despite procedures to enhance academic rigor, such as linking video to transcribed text, returning to the video and text (via the aforementioned software) to confirm specific taxonomic elements, and checking inter-rater reliability of the researchers. This was particularly challenging when interpreting between Procedural and Conceptual knowledge, hence the value of the augmented data observation. The researchers were attempting to interpret thinking and learning from the participants' spoken communication. This is a constraint of the research that needs to be overcome in the next iteration.

The process of a learner centered design approach to educational usage of virtual worlds has been presented. The design supported a research project that attempted to record instances of learning by enabling participants to experience tasks of increasing difficulty. The following section will summarize the planned developments that support the learner centered design process.

FUTURE DIRECTIONS: CONTINUING THE LEARNER CENTERED DESIGN PROCESS

As mentioned previously, real change in educational practices through the informed use of technology requires 'innovation' which Cuban (2002) terms second order change. It is posited that the learner centered design approach and associated iterative technical developments in this research has illustrated innovation in action. The advancement has not halted though. For instance, during the research, the participants made the decision to transfer the project from the Second Life

virtual world to a dedicated open source virtual space . The main reasons were not to do with the limitations of task design or their implementation, but more pragmatic. Second Life leasing was deemed expensive, the virtual world would occasionally be unavailable due to updates by Linden Labs, there was concern by administrators of the research funding about privacy and the worry about undesirable individuals somehow accessing our space, and there was a feeling of a lack of ownership over the designs and recorded data. The solution was to reflect upon the previous experiences by researchers and participants and opt for a more flexible alternative. Open Simulator (commonly referred to as OpenSim, an open source multi-platform, multi-user 3D application server) was chosen and Reaction Grid (see http://outpost.reactiongrid.com) selected as the service for locating the virtual space. Reaction Grid's service and server space are much cheaper than Second Life. The support has been excellent as enthusiastic virtual world developers respond quickly and offer advice. Hippo software (see http://www.osgrid.org/elgg/pg/utilities/software) for the Macintosh computers has been installed in order to access the new virtual world. The privacy issue has been resolved which, in turn, reassures administrators that the student participants are 'safe' in the OpenSim virtual world. This new stage of the learner centered design enabled a number of innovative tools to be created and customized by the participants.

One of the most unique tools designed and programmed by the participants in the OpenSim virtual world (named Future University on the OpenSim Grid) is the ability to move a graphical representation of the LEGO robot object and leave a trail of the circuit as evidence (see Figure 9). This is in contrast to the previous virtual space where only NXT program blocks were manipulated. The 'virtual robot' allows participants to enhance the collaboration in the design and solution of maze tasks which need to be later programmed to the

Figure 9. Robot movement controllers (Left-Right-Forward-Backward) leaves a trail, and recording data via a virtual iPad to an online database

Mindstorms NXT software and the physical robot in the real world.

An innovative method for collecting and collating data has been implemented in the form of a graphical iPad; named Blooms Pad (see Figure 8). In the virtual world this allows specific instances of Bloom's taxonomic elements to be selected by the participants at pre-determined periodic time intervals. This data is then directly transferred to a database that records and time-stamps each instance of selected cognitive process. The data can then be graphed immediately after each task in order to analyze current task effectiveness and participant learning, and then develop the next task; resulting in an iterative development in level of difficulty. Of course, the initial challenge is for participants to become familiar with the lexis associated with each of the Bloom's taxonomic elements and would thus need appropriate training. However, the next task can then be designed given the results from the participants as opposed to an interpretation by researchers. This will result in further iterative development in level of task complexity. The challenge though is to create new tasks that will

further the data for subsequent analysis using Bloom's taxonomy. By adding to the existing data it is anticipated an evidence-based framework can be developed that will inform practitioners how to best implement tasks that require specific curriculum learning aims in virtual spaces.

To support this anticipated iteration of task complexity within the learner centered design process, a telemetry device will be connected to the virtual world via a host computer. This will enable movements of the 'virtual robot' to be directly transferred to the 'real life robot'. The movements will therefore be synchronized from virtual to real. To enable such interaction the program translation will be undertaken using LabVIEW software from National Instruments (http://www.ni.com/labview/). This 'virtual to real' simultaneous movement has much potential for simulations of robot usage such as at nuclear plants. It will also further challenge researchers in education to design new tasks alongside learners in order to further evidence cognitive processes, knowledge, and learning. These developments represent the innovation of second order change required for augmented education in the 21st Century.

CONCLUSION

This chapter has demonstrated the theoretical and pragmatic progress of three years of research in the learner centered design and iterative development of metrics for evidencing the processes of learning (witnessed as measurements of Bloom's six cognitive processes and four knowledge dimensions) within virtual worlds. Metrics for learning have been recorded, analyzed and interpreted from tasks that involved problem solving, communication and collaboration in a virtual space. The context for the iteratively designed and quantifiably measured tasks has been the programming of LEGO Mindstorms robots to follow predefined mazes. The chapter has detailed the innovative utilization of virtual technologies and a unique method for collecting and collating the research data. It is proposed that the revealed dynamics between the neo-Bloomian taxonomic elements and the developed metrics will provide insights into the nature of effective pedagogy supported by learner centered design in virtual learning and teaching environments. By adding to the existing data it is anticipated an evidence-based framework can be developed that will inform practitioners on how to best design and implement tasks that require specific curriculum learning aims in virtual spaces.

ACKNOWLEDGMENT

The author wishes to acknowledge the contributions of fellow researchers: Stewart Martin and Paul van Schaik of Teesside University UK, Charles Wiz of Yokohama National University, Japan and Takushi Homma of Future University Hakodate, Japan. The current research is supported by the JAIST grant 00423781.

REFERENCES

Ambron, S., & Hooper, K. (1988). *Interactive multimedia: Visions of multimedia for developers, educators & information providers*. Washington: Microsoft Press.

Anderson, L. W., Krathwohl, D. R., Airasian, P. W., Cruicshank, K. A., Mayer, R. E., & Pintrich, P. R. ... Wittrock, M. C. (2001) *A taxonomy for learning, teaching and assessing: A revision of Bloom's taxonomy of educational objectives*. New York, NY: Longman.

Barker, S. B., & Ansorge, J. (2007). Robotics as means to increase achievement scores in an informal learning environment. *Journal of Research on Technology in Education*, 39(3), 229–243.

Bloom, B. S. (Ed.). (1956). *Taxonomy of educational objectives, the classification of educational goals. Handbook 1: Cognitive domain*. New York, NY: McKay.

Brown, A. L. (1992). Design experiments: theoretical and methodological challenges in creating complex interventions in classroom settings. *Journal of the Learning Sciences*, 2(2), 141–178. doi:10.1207/s15327809jls0202_2

Cannon-Bowers, J. A., & Bowers, C. A. (2008). Synthetic learning environments. In Spector, J. M., Merril, M. D., van Merrienboer, J., & Driscoll, M. P. (Eds.), *Handbook of research on educational communications and technology* (3rd ed.). New York, NY: Lawrence Erlbaum Associates.

Cuban, L. (1992). Curriculum stability and change. In Jackson, P. W. (Ed.), *Handbook of research on curriculum* (pp. 216–247). New York, NY: Macmillan.

Cuban, L. (2002). *Oversold & underused. Computers in the classroom*. Cambridge, MA: Harvard University Press.

de Freitas, S. (2008) *Serious virtual worlds: A scoping study.* JISC publications. Retrieved March 14, 2009, from http://www.jisc.ac.uk/ publications/publications/ seriousvirtualworldsreport.aspx

de Freitas, S., & Griffiths, M. (2008). The convergence of gaming practices with other media forms: What potential for learning? A review of the literature. *Learning, Media and Technology, 33*(1), 11–20. doi:10.1080/17439880701868796

deFreitas, S., & Neumann, T. (2009). The use of exploratory learning for supporting immersive learning in virtual environments. *Computers & Education, 52,* 343–352. doi:10.1016/j.compedu.2008.09.010

Dewey, J. (1938). *Experience & education.* New York, NY: Touchstone.

Higgins, J., & Johns, T. (1984). *Computers in language learning.* London, UK: Collins.

Jonassen, D. H., & Land, S. M. (2000). *Theoretical foundations of learning environments.* Mahwah, NJ: Lawrence Erlbaum Associates.

Kolb, D. A. (1984). *Experiential learning: Experience as the source of learning and development.* Englewood Cliffs, N.J.: Prentice-Hall.

Laurillard, D. (2002). *Rethinking university teaching. A conversational framework for the effective use of learning technologies.* New York, NY: Routledge. doi:10.4324/9780203304846

Martin, S., & Vallance, M. (2008). The impact of synchronous inter-networked teacher training in Information and Communication Technology integration. *Computers & Education, 51,* 34–53. doi:10.1016/j.compedu.2007.04.001

Martin, S., Vallance, M., van Schaik, P., & Wiz, C. (2010). Learning spaces, tasks and metrics for effective communication in Second Life within the context of programming LEGO NXT Mindstorms TM robots: towards a framework for design and implementation. *Journal of Virtual Worlds Research, 3*(1).

Olsen, D. R., & Goodrich, M. A. (2003). *Metrics for evaluating human-robot interactions.* Retrieved March 14, 2009, from http://icie.cs.byu.edu/ Papers/RAD.pdf

Sandholtz, J. M., Ringstaff, C., & Dwyer, D. C. (1997). *Teaching with technology: Creating student-centered classrooms.* New York, NY: Teachers College Press.

Selwyn, N. (2011). *Schools and schooling in the digital age. A critical analysis.* London, UK: Routledge.

Soloway, E., Guzdial, M., & Hay, K. E. (1994). Learner centered design: The challenge for HCI in the 21st century. *Interaction, 1,* 36–48. doi:10.1145/174809.174813

Towndrow, P. A., & Vallance, M. (2004). *Using Information Technology in the language classroom* (3rd ed.). Singapore: Longman.

Vallance, M. (2008). Beyond policy: Strategic actions to support ICT integration in Japanese schools. *Australasian Journal of Educational Technology, 24*(3), 275–293.

Vallance, M., Martin, S., Wiz, C., & van Schaik, P. (2009). LEGO Mindstorms for informed metrics in virtual worlds. In *Proceedings of Human Computer Interaction (HCI) 2009 - People and Computers XXIII,* Cambridge University, UK, (pp. 159-162). Cambridge, UK, Sept. 2009.

Vallance, M., Martin, S., Wiz, C., & van Schaik, P. (2010, January - March). Designing effective spaces, tasks and metrics for communication in Second Life within the context of programming LEGO NXT Mindstorms™ robots. *International Journal of Virtual and Personal Learning Environments*, *1*(1), 20–37. doi:10.4018/jvple.2010091703

Vallance, M., & Wright, D. L. (2010). Japanese students' digitally enabled futures images: A synergistic approach to developing academic competencies. In Mukerji, S., & Tripathi, P. (Eds.), *Cases on technological adaptability and transnational learning: Issues and challenges*. Hershey, PA: IGI Global. doi:10.4018/978-1-61520-779-4.ch009

Warschauer, M. (1999). *Electronic literacies: Language, culture, and power in online education*. Mahwah, NJ: Lawrence Erlbaum Associates.

ADDITIONAL READING

Baker, E. L., Gearhart, M., & Herman, J. L. (1993). Evaluating the Apple Classrooms of Tomorrow: The UCLA evaluation studies. Retrieved February 9, 2007, from http://www.cse.ucla.edu/ CRESST/Reports/TECH353.pdf.

Cuban, L. (2003). *Why is it so hard to get good schools?* New York: Teachers College Press.

Dede, C. (2005). Planning for neomillennial learning styles: Implications for investments in technology and faculty. In Oblinger, D. G., & Oblinger, J. L. (Eds.), *Educating the net generation* (pp. 15.11–15.22). Educause.

Dewey, J. (1938). *Experience & Education*. New York: Simon & Schuster.

Dror, I. E. (2007). Gold mines and land mines in cognitive technology. In Dror, I. E. (Ed.), *Cognitive Technologies and the Pragmatics of Cognition*. UK: John Benjamins.

Field, M., Vallance, M., & Yamamoto, T. (2008) *Crossing the Discipline Divide: Building Learning Contexts*. In Proceedings of World Conference on Educational Multimedia, Hypermedia and Telecommunications 2008 (pp. 84-89). Vienna, Austria, June 2008.

Fullan, M. G., & Stiegelbauer, S. (1991). *The New Meaning of Educational Change* (2nd ed.). New York: Teachers College Press.

Hicks, D. (2002). *Lessons for the Future: The Missing Dimension in Education*. London: Routledge Falmer. doi:10.4324/9780203219331

Inayatullah, S. (2005). *Questioning the Future: Methods and Tools for Organizational and Societal Transformation* (2nd ed.). Taiwan: Tamkang University Press.

Jarmon, L., Traphagan, T., Mayrath, M., & Trivedi, A. (2009). Virtual world teaching, experiential learning, and assessment: An interdisciplinary communication course in Second Life. *Computers & Education*, *53*, 169–182. doi:10.1016/j.compedu.2009.01.010

Jennings, N., & Collins, C. (2008). Virtual or Virtually U: educational institutions in Second Life. *International Journal of Social Sciences*, *2*(3), 180–186.

Kress, G., & Van Leeuwen, T. (2001). *Multimodal Discourse: The Modes and Media of Contemporary Communication*. London: Arnold.

Lewin, K. (1951). Field Theory. In *Social Science*. New York: Harper & Row.

Morrison, K. (1998). *Management Theories For Educational Change*. Thousand Oaks: Sage Publications.

Niemitz, M., Slough, S., Peart, L., Klaus, A. D., Leckie, R. M. & St. John, K. (2008). Interactive virtual expeditions as a learning tool: the school of rock expedition case study. *Journal of multimedia and hypermedia*, 17(4), 561-580.

Polak, F. (1973). *The Image of the Future*. New York: Elsevier Scientific Publishing.

Slaughter, R., & Bussey, M. (2006). *Futures Thinking for Social Foresight*. Taiwan: Tamkang University Press.

Thornburg, D. D. (1991). *Edutrends 2010. Restructuring, technology, and the future of education*. USA: Starsong.

Towndrow, P. A. (2007). *Task design, implementation and assessment: Integrating information and communication technology in English language teaching and learning*. Singapore: McGraw-Hill.

Trochim, W. M. K. (2005). *Research methods. The concise knowledge base*. USA: Atomic Dog Publishing.

Vallance, M., & Wright, D. L. (2010). The Futures Studies Toolbox and iPod Touch: Digitally Enabled Futures Images for the Japanese University 2020 Project. *The International Journal of Interdisciplinary Social Sciences, 5*(Issue 5), 261–274.

Vygotsky, L. (1986). *Thought and Language*. Cambridge, MA: MIT Press.

Wiz, C., & Vallance, M. (2008). Real world activities in virtual worlds. *Modern English Teacher, 17*(1), 57–61.

Ying, X. Z., & Hui, Z. S. (2002). Where is the Technology Induced Pedagogy? Snapshots from Two Multimedia EFL Classrooms. *British Journal of Educational Technology, 33*(1), 39–52. doi:10.1111/1467-8535.00237

KEY TERMS AND DEFINITIONS

Augmentation: Augment is a transitive verb which is defined as meaning to make greater, as in size, quantity, strength, and to enlarge.

Bloom's Revised Taxonomy: A classification of learning objectives.

Cognitive Processes: The performance of some specific cognitive activity that affects mental contents; the process of thinking.

Learner Centered Design: A move away from technology's ease-of-use issues and toward the development of a learner's comprehension and expertise.

LEGO Mindstorms: A hardware and software kit including sensors and cables for programming LEGO robots.

OpenSim: An open source multi-platform, multi-user 3D application server used to create a virtual environment.

Virtual Worlds: A computer-mediated reality which presents the user with an experience which can impact the real world.

Chapter 18
An Interface Design Evaluation of Courses in a Nursing Program using an E-Learning Framework:
A Case Study

Brenda Tyczkowski
University of Wisconsin Green Bay, USA

Eric Bauman
Clinical Playground, LLC, USA

Susan Gallagher-Lepak
University of Wisconsin Green Bay, USA

Christine Vandenhouten
University of Wisconsin Green Bay, USA

Janet Resop Reilly
University of Wisconsin Green Bay, USA

ABSTRACT

Interface design refers to the overall look and feel of an e-learning program by the end user (Hall, as cited in Khan, 2005). Initially designed for corporate use, the World Wide Web as it is now known surfaced in the early 1990s. Individual use grew rapidly in the 1990's, with "online users doubling or tripling every year" (When Guide, n.d.). Online degree granting educational programs slowly developed. An early fully online RN (Registered Nurse) to BSN (Bachelor of Science in Nursing) program was the Collaborative Nursing Program (CNP) in Wisconsin. The CNP, now called the "BSN@Home" program, started in 1995, to serve associate degree and diploma prepared nurses throughout the state of Wisconsin desiring

DOI: 10.4018/978-1-61350-516-8.ch018

Copyright © 2012, IGI Global. Copying or distributing in print or electronic forms without written permission of IGI Global is prohibited.

a baccalaureate degree in nursing. This statewide program continues to be delivered collaboratively by five University of Wisconsin (UW) nursing programs (UW-Eau Claire, UW-Green Bay, UW-Madison, UW-Milwaukee, and UW-Oshkosh). A critical look at interface design in this program was undertaken with methods and outcomes detailed below.

INTRODUCTION

The BSN@Home program at UW-Green Bay is a unique collaboration that has been highly successful and allows adult learners across the state access to BSN completion and flexibility in taking online courses. Although the curriculum and courses have been revised over the years, the focus has been primarily on the quality and content of individual courses. Review of courses across the curriculum has primarily focused on critical content required to meet professional nursing standards and has not focused on the user perspective. A review of the interface design of the BSN@Home courses has not previously been undertaken. Being an online program, the BSN@HOME faculty is challenged to stay abreast of and integrate the latest in educational technology and health care informatics.

Review and evaluation of the interface design of the BSN@Home program was undertaken in 2010, using the E-Learning Framework (Khan, 2005). A case study of the process is detailed in this chapter.

BACKGROUND

Nursing and E-learning

Online enrollment is growing at meteoric rates and at higher rates than overall higher education enrollments (Greer, 2010; Allen & Seaman, 2011). Nursing programs, especially RN to BSN programs, are well suited for online learning and have been part of the growth boom. The BSN@Home program is a unique collaboration among five UW nursing programs to deliver an RN to BSN

program. Associate Degree or diploma prepared nurses enrolled in the program need to complete general education credits, nursing support courses and core nursing courses. A "home school" model is used, whereby students apply to any of the five UW programs and follow the specific academic requirements of their chosen home school.

Five core nursing courses (18 credits) are shared among the UW partners and form the majority of nursing credits required. Each UW campus developed and continues to be responsible for teaching one of the five core courses in the program. Although subcommittees developed course objectives, each core nursing course was developed by an instructor with the assistance of an instructional designer. Over the years, courses have been revised in an iterative manner. Although a consistent UW technology support service has been used to assist with development and maintenance of courses, a formal brand was not established across courses at the onset. Fairly high turnover of instructional designers has impacted consistency within the program design. A BSN@Home Steering Committee, composed of one representative from each campus, provides a structure for collaboration and curriculum review.

There are new challenges facing health care educators everywhere and many of the changes are driven by forces outside of health care academia. Health care informatics is the powerful combination of knowledge and methods from healthcare, computer, library and statistical sciences with the latest information technology (Johns Hopkins, n.d.). Recent incentives, including the American Recovery and Reinvestment Act of 2009, encourage meaningful use of health information technology by 2014 and have fueled a spike in nursing and health informatics (American Recovery and

Re-investment Act, n.d.). Nursing has been a leader and role model for other health professions, by bringing current informatics information to both practice and education (Weaver, Delaney, Weber & Carr, 2010). One example is the Technology Informatics Guiding Educational Reform (TIGER) initiative, with the goal to encourage nurses and nursing students to "fully engage in the unfolding digital era of healthcare" (TIGER Summit, n.d.). Currently in phase three, TIGER is integrating its recommendations to the nursing and health community via creation of a Virtual Learning Center (VLC). It is hoped that the VLC will help overcome a major barrier in informatics education: limited access to information systems and technology. The TIGER VLC showcases innovative, effective, and exemplary approaches of using technology-enabled health care delivery (TIGER Summit Virtual Demo, n.d.).

In an effort to engage nursing students in the digital age of healthcare, the University of Wisconsin (UW) - Madison, in collaboration with the four UW nursing campuses, received a U.S Department of Health and Human Services, Health Systems and Research Administration (HRSA) federal grant to enhance nursing informatics in undergraduate nursing education through an innovative approach to faculty development. Titled the Wisconsin Technology Enhanced Collaborative Nursing Education (WI-TECNE) Grant, this five year grant (2006-2011) involved a minimum of six faculty scholars from each of the five campuses each year (WI-TECNE Grant, n.d.). The following nursing informatics topics were covered through monthly interactive video meetings and annual conferences: Telehealth and informatics; Mechanical simulators; Virtual simulations; Problem based case learning; and E-learning (WI-TECNE Grant, n.d.).

Interface Design using an E-Learning Framework

Prior to Year 5 (E-Learning focus) of the grant, the planning committee of nursing professors

Figure 1. The e-learning framework

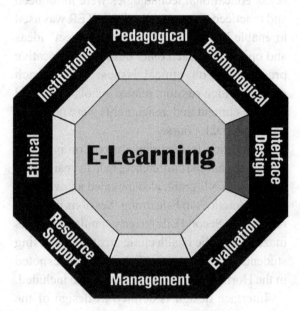

and instructional designers from UW-Green Bay searched for an e-learning framework for the year of faculty development. The textbook *Managing E-Learning Strategies* by Badrul Khan (2005) and its e-learning framework was chosen. The eight dimensions of e-learning in Khan's framework are pedagogical, technological, interface design, evaluation, management, resource support, ethical and institutional concerns. WI-TECNE scholars were exposed to all dimensions of e-learning throughout the year of learning. To evaluate faculty scholar's perceptions and awareness of each of the eight dimensions, a brief electronic survey was conducted using questions from the Khan E-Learning Framework (see Figure 1). Sample questions from the E-learning Framework, related to interface design (Khan, 2005), are listed in the Appendix.

A two dimensional virtual learning environment (VLE) faculty development course was created using the Desire to Learn (D2L) platform. The course housed scholarly activities and information from the year. WI-TECNE scholars were enrolled in this course as virtual students. In addition to the VLE, WI-TECNE scholars were further immersed in the e-learning student role as select educational technologies were introduced and practiced. For example, TWITTER was used to enable WI TECNE scholars to "tweet" ideas and opinions to each other during a provocative presentation on ethical issues. Before each monthly video session, related scholarly journal articles, content and assignments were posted in the online D2L course.

In addition to featuring a report on interface design, the annual conference, held in year five of the WI TECNE grant, also included an overview of best practices in E-learning. Sessions included reports on a Second Life poverty simulation, ethics maze and public health clinic created for nursing students; a variety of other E-learning topics noted in the Horizon Report (2011) were also included.

Interface design is defined as design of the software (in this case D2L) where the focus is on ease of the user's experience. The E-learning dimension of interface design was addressed through a formal analysis of the five core online courses taught in the BSN@HOME collaborative. Such an analysis was aimed at identifying strengths and areas for improvement of the program. Based on both student and faculty perspectives, there was a strong need for evaluation of the program interface design.

Student Perspective

Students' knowledge, expectations and coping strategies for technology problems are the key to understanding their experience in the courses. A successful online platform design will bring harmony between the designers' ideas and the needs of the students (Ahmed, McKnight & Oppenheim, 2009). Student input is sought at the end of each course regarding the individual course but input about the students' overall experiences in the core courses as a whole had never been sought. Another source of valuable student feedback has been virtual student meetings (VSM), an on-line discussion board, opened for the purpose of soliciting student feedback on a variety of program and course specific topics. Though not specifically solicited, during the 2009 VSM (Virtual Student Meeting, 2009), several students expressed concerns related to the design of online courses. Comments included:

"Our discussions/lessons are fragmented..."

"I am not sure why, but I do know that each on-line course has been different from the next, and this can be very frustrating...this would include presentation of the course, how to maneuver the discussion area and understand the assignment due dates and where to place the completed assignment..."

"...frustration with not having a unified online format..."

Students in the BSN @ Home program may take the five core nursing courses in any order. In each course there is typically a mix of students new to both the program and to online learning, as well as students who have completed much of their coursework and are quite comfortable with online learning. Courses in the BSN@ Home program are delivered in the D2L platform (Desire2Learn, n.d.). While each course contains an overview about using D2L, students are not required to utilize this tool prior to beginning coursework. Each course must then be designed to meet the needs of students, whose experience with E-learning ranges from novice to expert user.

Nursing students, as consumers of education services, are savvy purchasers in a "consumer-driven and competitive environment" (Coonen, 2008, p. 118). A growing number of students are adult learners, who seek to improve their career by returning to school for a baccalaureate degree. These students "expect results" (Coonan, 2008, p. 118). If nursing education is a product, then it needs to be a partnership between those who design the product (course designers), those who purchase the product (students) and those who deliver the product (faculty). It behooves the BSN@Home program to put forth a program that facilitates learning, satisfies the needs of the students and prepares nurses to enhance their skill level in the work environment. With that in mind, it was logical that an evaluation of the usability of the courses should be undertaken.

Faculty Perspective

Courses in the BSN@Home program are developed by each lead instructor, using the services of a single course designer for the program. Each instructor has the "academic freedom" to develop the course in the manner they feel appropriate. The American Association of University Professors (AAUP) (n.d.) defines academic freedom as "teachers are entitled to freedom in the classroom in discussing their subject". The scope of that principle is clear enough in the traditional physical classroom with four walls, a floor, and a ceiling. But the concept of "classroom" must be broadened to reflect the realities of the virtual classroom. The "classroom" must indeed encompass all sites where learning occurs—web sites, home pages, discussion boards, listservs, etc.

Well-intentioned, but often isolated, faculty perpetuates "functional silos" (Baker, 2005). In doing so, they develop course content and deliver the content to fit their individual ideas about how to best do so. This relative independence in the development of a single course from remaining core courses "obscures any meaningful view of the institution as a whole…valuable employee time and resources within a silo are misspent protecting the silo from blame by those outside, rather than exploring collaborative approaches to problems" (Baker, 2005).

Course faculty in the BSN@Home program is free to present course materials in the online environment, as they see fit. While course designers handle all of the core courses and offer suggestions to faculty regarding course design, there has never been a strong set of expectations

for similarity of course design put forth to the faculty. Over the years each course has been developed following the individual faculty vision of the course, rather than in a uniform fashion. Faculty members in the BSN@Home program are located in five geographic locations across Wisconsin. Most faculty have access to only the course they teach. Though there is a program steering committee and a program director, there has not been an initiative to explore collaborative approaches to course design and delivery.

Students want timely access to information on the network, to help them interpret information and maximize its value (Skiba, 2011). Lecturing online with PowerPoint slides has little place in meeting these needs. Chickering and Ehrmann (1996) indicate that faculty needs to be reminded to "bypass materials that are purely of a didactic nature, instead searching for those that are interactive, problem-oriented, and relevant to real-world issues and that evoke student motivation". Despite knowledge of these changing needs, it is all too easy to fall back into the pattern of teaching, using strategies that are not congruent with student expectations. Faculty is often dependent on course designers to bring awareness of new technologies and incorporate these technologies into the core courses.

Top trends in online education described by Skiba (2011, p. 44), a prolific author in nursing technology education, include:

- "People expect to be able to work, learn and study wherever and whenever they want to. The abundance of resources and relationships made easily accessible via the internet is increasingly challenging us to revisit our roles as educators in sense-making, coaching and credentialing.
- The world of work is increasingly collaborative, giving rise to reflection about the way student projects are structured.

• The technologies we use are increasingly cloud-based, and our notions of IT support are decentralized."

These trends have implications for the BSN@ Home program. The role of the educator is changing from that of knowledge disseminator to that of coach and mentor (Skiba, 2011). In view of this shift, and coupled with the knowledge that students expressed concerns about the cohesiveness of the delivery of the course content, the core courses of the BSN@Home program bear re-evaluation.

When the silos in education are spanned to deliver high-quality distance education, efforts must be coordinated between lead instructors of each core course and the instructional designer. These longstanding silos will be broken down when leadership provides compelling and positive visions of the possibilities (Baker, 2005). Breaking down the silos requires faculty and design staff to have a clear understanding of each other's areas of expertise and a willingness to develop mutually shared goals (Miller, Jones, Graves & Cullinan Sievert, 2010).

Student concerns, course development that occurred in silos, and a growing awareness of the changing role of both faculty and course design, all converged to create the realization that the interface design portion of the WI-TECNE Grant (n.d.) could serve as a catalyst for review and change in the BSN@Home program.

Usability Perspective

Analysis of online course design is often guided by a review of usability heuristics (Joshi, Arora, Dai, Price, Vizar & Sears, 2004). A heuristic evaluation is "a usability inspection method for computer software that helps to identify usability problems in the user interface (UI) design. It specifically involves evaluators examining the interface and judging its compliance with recognized usability principles (the "heuristics")" (Usability, n.d.).

Several heuristic systems are noted in the literature, including those developed by Molich and Nielsen (Usability, n.d.) and Quality Matters (QM) (Quality Matters, n.d.). The decision was made to use the heuristics developed by Khan (2005), since the *E-Learning Framework* was being used as a framework for the exploration of e-learning in year 5 of the WI-TECNE grant.

Human computer interaction (HCI) is the investigation of human and machine interface issues, which is also known as usability design evaluation (Joshi, Arora, Dai, Price, Vizar & Sears, 2004). There are two main approaches to conducting a usability design evaluation: empirical and heuristic analytical. The empirical approach involves conducting tests where real users are observed using the software. In contrast, the heuristic analytical approach utilizes experts, who assess the usability by applying established theories and principles (Ahmed, McKnight & Oppenheim, 2009). Utilizing a "double" usability expert, with expertise in both usability evaluation and in the content area, was found to significantly increase the performance of the testing (Ahmed, et al., 2009). The heuristic analytical evaluation method identifies problems in a timely manner (Joshi, Arora, Dai, Price, Vizar & Sears, 2004).

The year-5 WI-TECNE planning committee and BSN@Home program steering committee agreed to the concept of conducting a usability study of the interface design of the program, as part of the WI-TECNE grant. The determination was made that a heuristic approach for the review and evaluation of the core courses in the BSN@Home program would be sought, using the E-Learning Framework (Khan, 2005) for the primary focus of the evaluation, with consideration to be given to other salient points as appropriate to the evaluation.

Several consultants were considered, and ultimately, two experts were engaged to review the five core courses making up the BSN@Home curriculum. One of the experts was considered a "double" usability expert, as a registered nurse with a master's degree in nursing education and a PhD in adult curriculum and instruction, with a focus on technology enhanced learning. The second expert, with a background in social work and a master's degree and expertise specific to educational technology, was a doctoral candidate in curriculum and instruction focusing on adult education and technology enhanced learning.

Prior to review of the five courses, the experts had discussions with faculty who taught and authored some of the five courses. These discussions sought to understand learner perceptions of the courses and in general focused on human interaction and interface with the delivery of the courses through the D2L web-based learning platform. Feedback conveyed that, based on anecdotal information provided to faculty from students, learner perceptions were focusing on a facet that would later be described by the evaluators as flow. Flow came to represent the intuitive or logical nature of transition of one topic to another and how students interacted with the courses within the E-learning platform.

There is support in the literature regarding the importance of consistency and ease of use, or flow. Herzberg, et al., (2008) identified the following five essential usability characteristics, described

as vital for any study of Human Computer Interaction (HCI).

- **Learnability:** The user can rapidly begin to work with the system
- **Efficiency:** The user attains a high level of productivity
- **Memorability:** It is easy to return to the system after some time of non-use
- **Low Error Rate:** Users are prevented from making errors and errors do not have devastating consequences
- **Satisfaction:** The system is pleasant to use

With this background in mind, evaluation of the interface design of the core courses in the BSN@Home program commenced.

METHOD OF EVALUATION FOR THE INTERFACE DESIGN

An evaluation rubric was developed based on a preliminary review of the five WI-TECNE courses, Khan's *E-Learning Framework* (2005), expertise of the reviewers associated with educational technology and other contemporary learning theories

Figure 2. The evaluation rubric titled eLearning Course Assessment

	Consistency & Coherence	Content Management	Engagement	Curriculum Design
B R A N D I N G	• Between Courses • Within a Course • Coherence Validity	• Volume +/- • Flow • Setting of expectations	• Personal • Team or Group • Professional Identity or acculturation	• Objective Clarity • Objectives are well represented throughout the course • Designed for online medium
	Score 0-1-2-3-4-5	Score 0-1-2-3-4-5	Score 0-1-2-3-4-5	Score 0-1-2-3-4-5

Human Interface

Level of Technology/Leveraging of Technology   © EB Bauman & DW Simkins 2011 including *Socially Situated Cognition* (Gee, 2003), *Designed Experience* (Squire, 2006; Squire, Giovanetto, DeVane, & Durga, 2005), and *Ecology of Culturally Competent Design* (Games and Bauman, 2011; Bauman, 2010). The evaluation rubric, the eLearning Course Assessment (Figure 2), focuses on four categories: consistency and coherence, content management, engagement curriculum and design.

Rubric

The rubric illustrated in Figure 2 was used to determine an in-category score. No assumptions about category weight or cumulative score were determined for this evaluation of the core nursing courses. Rather, this evaluation rubric provided a starting point for further discussion and evaluation of these courses and other distributed courses taking advantage of distributive learning technology focusing on E-learning and web-based learning templates. The review focused on identifying strengths and weaknesses within each course relative to other courses in the curriculum.

The top header of the rubric is titled "Human Interface" to reflect the primary aim of determining how well the courses communicated their content to learners; in other words how people interacted with the electronic learning platform. Four columns or main categories are included in the evaluation rubric: consistency and coherence, content management, engagement curriculum and design. Each of these columns represents a different facet of human interface and descriptors are listed for each facet. In addition, a proposed scoring system is provided so that a quantitative analysis of each category can be scored and compared among multiple evaluators. A Likert-style scoring schemata was proposed (range 0 – 5). In this scoring schemata zero represents the lowest possible score, where descriptive elements for the category are not present and five represents the highest category score (all descriptive elements are present and well represented).

The left hand side bar of the rubric is titled "Branding" and reflects course faculty and learner feedback, and overall analysis of the courses by the evaluators of the need for a consistent product or experience across BSN@Home program. To this end, branding came to represent an overarching facet regardless of whom or where courses were designed. The footer in the rubric titled level of "technology/leveraging of technology" is present to help evaluators remain grounded in the realm of educational technology as opposed to an evaluation focusing on a traditional lecture or classroom environment.

EVALUATION FINDINGS

Coherence and Consistency

Coherence and consistency are measures of the level of standardization. Good practice for online learning involves maintaining a much higher level of standardization than one might consider necessary for offline learning. This is in part to help offset the increased complexity for the student taking an online course, who must deal with technology issues, a more complex schedule, and for adult learners, who are often balancing school work with responsibilities of jobs and families. There are choices to be made in how best to present course content though online instruction, and coherence and consistency chart how well these decisions are maintained throughout a course and a curriculum (Bauman & Simkins, 2011).

The challenges associated with online learning are not the same as those in face-to-face coursework. As students become more familiar with online learning, variations in style and format of instruction may become less of an impediment, but even expert participants in online learning have come to expect greater structure in the delivery of online coursework than would be generally expected in a face-to-face course (Bauman & Simkins, 2011; Khan, 2005, p201ff).

By using a standard online learning platform such as D2L, faculty and educational designers are assisted in developing a brand by using standardized templates that serve as a "wrapper" for course material. This wrapper, as in the case of D2L, includes a navigation bar on the left hand side of the window, a top menu bar, and two common orientation units. These are successful features of D2L that help students navigate the online course environment in a consistent manner across any given course and among a cadre of related courses that make up an area of study.

Beyond the "wrapper" of the course material supported by a platform like D2L, one must attend to the level of variation that can occur across courses. Variation can be common in instructional curricula that collect independently created lessons, and may be an indicator that academic freedom is being maintained as policy. Though uniformity in online courseware is desirable, it should never be imposed at the cost of effective pedagogy. While internal coherence within a given course is relatively easy to maintain, variations occurring across the courses can be more difficult to attend to, particularly when courses are created across different campuses and leverage the broad experience of many faculty and instructional designers. Evidence of coherence validity is present when clear objectives that are identified in each unit and lesson are carried out throughout the course. Further, the tools necessary to meet curriculum objectives, such as the way students access the internet, should be consistent from lesson to lesson and course to course. Students should be using the same tools repeatedly, whether downloading readings, evaluating video, or engaging in online activities. Unusual tasks should be explained well, and the grounds for assessing successful completion of the coursework should be consistent across the online curriculum (Bauman & Simkins, 2011).

When creating a curriculum, as opposed to a collection of lessons, it is important to maintain a high level of coherence among the courses. Given

the realities and desirability of academic freedom, some variation in coherence is expected and is generally acceptable to accommodate the varying academic styles of course faculty. In courses that include core curricula, in this case core nursing courses, it generally is helpful to work toward a more unified structure for courses, but not if doing so threatens the unity of each individual course or the primacy of the learning process (Bauman & Simkins, 2011).

Coherence and consistency were evaluated within courses and across courses. It was found that each course had good Coherence Validity within individual courses. Each course had clear objectives identified in each unit, and lesson and objectives were addressed throughout the lessons. Working through each lesson, it was found that the same tools (e.g. discussion boards and drop boxes) were available both within and among courses. Unusual tasks were explained well, and the grounds for assessing successful completion of the coursework were well within the customary standards of higher education.

Standardization across courses in a curriculum enhances the quality of the curriculum. Due to the relatively low level of immediate feedback in online learning, it is often helpful for even experienced students to experience a coherent appearance, interface, and statement of learning goals and expectations and structure of content (Khan, 2005, p201ff). Although the courses are "templated" within the D2L platform, it was found that the courses had a very different look and feel from each other. There was a lack of internal consistency across the cadre of courses. There was less structural consistency between courses within the on-line curriculum, particularly in regards to grading. For example, some courses used points to assign grades (e.g., discussion posts equal 10 points each), essentially eliminating weighting, while others used weighting to assign grades to individual assignments (e.g., discussion posts equal 20% of course grade). It was recommended that a higher level of coherence among the courses be developed while maintaining academic freedom and style differences (Bauman & Simkins, 2011).

When variation is in the service of learning, as with the inclusion of video examples, virtual world experiences, and mixed synchronous and asynchronous discussion models, the variation should be preserved. When it is not serving a useful purpose for learning, it may be a distraction. As such, the variation may add to the already increased complexity and responsibility imposed upon the student in online learning environments (Khan, 2005).

Content Management

Aspects of content management reviewed included access to course materials, course expectations and flow. In an online learning setting, it is critical that students have ready and ongoing access to the materials they will require to successfully complete a course and the overarching curriculum. Students need ongoing access to the syllabus, technical support documents, instructional media, grades and other assessments of their work, and discussion forums. These elements allow the student to schedule their work, collaborate with others, find answers to questions and maintain organization within the complex online coursework environment.

One of the challenges to content management focuses on assisting learners to be successful given the didactic volume, expectations and flow of course work. From this perspective, online courses and courses leveraging electronic content management systems must insure that students are oriented to the e-learning environment. Hosting a course in an e-learning environment is often asynchronous and does not allow for instant interaction among teachers and learners. Each brand of e-learning environment is likely to include some intuitive design elements, but will also include some variation. The e-learning environment is a created environment. Students should not be expected to understand the advantages and limi-

tations of created environments without explicit orientation and explanation of the experiences faculty hope to facilitate for learners in e-learning spaces (Bauman, 2007; Bauman, 2010; Bauman & Games, 2011; Games & Bauman, 2011). The facets or descriptors evaluated in the category of content management included the following; volume, flow, and setting expectations.

Flow was previously discussed, and refers to how topics within courses relate to not only one another, but how they relate to other courses. Feedback is not always immediate and is often asynchronous in the online learning environment. Therefore, it is important that lessons within a course prepare learners for later course modules and success in other courses found within the curriculum.

When considering the second area of content management, volume, the amount of content is considered. The evaluators sought to compare the amount of content in any given course to the credit value assigned to the course. In addition, the amount of course content of any given course was compared to other courses in the curriculum. Faculty should pay close attention to the amount of didactic content they include in online courses. Faculty sometimes include and require relatively large reading lists in online courses, because doing so seems value added and is relatively easy to do in an e-learning platform. In online courses, there are often no textbooks to purchase, and gone are the days of preparing hard copy for students to purchase. The absence of physical reading material as a cue to volume means that teachers must make critical decisions about what is required and what may be seen as supplemental didactic material.

The final area considered under content management was the setting of expectations. In the e-learning environment, setting of expectations is very important for learner success. This in part also relates to the likelihood that asynchronous communication will take place between students and faculty. Setting clear expectations related to grading and the time students will need to devote to achieve optimal learning should be made explicit in each course and should be consistent across courses. This is of paramount importance in a series of courses such as the five core courses described in this chapter because learners will see the courses as a single branded curriculum. Students should never be penalized because they do not understand assignments or are confused when trying to negotiate expectations from course to course within a branded curriculum. When expectations are not clear or are inconsistent, students, particularly returning adult students, are likely to become confused and frustrated.

In review of the courses, access to course content was found at times to be very challenging across courses. The program reviewed had no standard across courses for delivering readings and other course content. While some of the courses require less work on the part of the student to access course content (e.g., articles posted directly in the course), other courses require the student to engage in a relatively complex process of retrieving course materials from other sites (e.g., use e-reserves on another UW campus). While this process may at times have the learning goal of teaching research process, this objective was not stated among the learning goals. Also, the more cumbersome methods of accessing course materials are, in part, cumbersome because they are idiosyncratic (Bauman & Simkins, 2011).

A common access point and location for all learning materials would be helpful. Unless there is an overriding reason for complicating access to course material, it would be quite useful for students to be able to directly access all materials from the lessons found across all courses through a single access point, a central virtual resource for all course materials. Materials could link to the central database of materials, segmented by course in the curriculum, allowing for students to engage with texts outside of their current course, exploring connections across the curriculum and expanding their understanding of nursing as a field (Bauman & Simkins, 2011).

Each course reviewed did a good job of setting in-course expectations, but expectations for courses were not consistent across the cadre of courses. As mentioned in the coherence and consistency section, while individual courses succeeded in setting expectations within the course, they do not represent their expectations in similar ways across all of the courses. Further, courses did not achieve a sense of balance related to demands on students. For many students in the D2L target audience, the need to balance demands of work and home with school work requires the students to know how much time they should expect to spend on their coursework. The evaluated courses are either weighted as three or four credit hours. A student would and should assume that the relative course load among all 3-credit courses will be comparable and the same being true for 4-credit courses. While an exact balancing of coursework is not feasible, inconsistency among the credit weighting of the courses was noted. Paying careful attention to credit weighting among the courses helps to prepare students for optimal success. Reevaluation of course expectations and work load is recommended to ensure that credit offered is consistent within the schemata of all five of the core courses. If reevaluation of courses in terms of credit hours is not feasible, providing a mechanism for communicating to students the relative work required by each course would allow students to allocate sufficient time to maximize their chance of success. In general, it is recommended that courses be reevaluated for credit assignment from time to time as curriculum is updated and revised and as new professors are assigned to courses.

The high level structure of the courses introduces the student to each course in a consistent manner (left hand navigation). The overall course structure provided by the D2L course wrapper shared by the lessons in the curriculum was found to be largely successful in assisting students with navigating the courses, whether they choose to work linearly through each course, or choose to navigate though courses non-linearly. This is facilitated by the inclusion of some navigational standards within and across courses. The overall course structure, units, and lessons are consistently identified and readily accessible by students. It is clear what linear order the student should follow so that future learning can build on prior knowledge, and it is clear how students can quickly access a summary assessment of their performance to date in the course. These are intuitive and helpful guides for new students, and follow standards that will be familiar to those experienced in online learning environments.

The first two D2L introductory units of the courses serve as reference guides on how to use D2L. It may be helpful to include a statement for learners pointing out that these sections remain constant throughout the courses. These are helpful lessons, providing a necessary introduction for students new to D2L and a useful refresher for returning students. If students are returning for many courses, sometimes more than one in a semester, it may be helpful to mention that these units are identical throughout the curriculum. It might also be useful to include a change report that would indicate when each unit last changed. This way returning students would be appraised of potential changes to the first two units since their last enrollment in courses using the D2L environment. The note could be brief, as there is little investment in a student reviewing the material (Bauman & Simkins, 2011).

Engagement

All coursework requires students to take responsibility for their own education, but learning theory strongly supports learning environments that support and encourage high levels of student interaction with the course material. A student who is engaged in learning activities that they find meaningful, enjoyable, or interesting will tend to excel over those who do not. Student engagement can be encouraged by developing coursework that is in tune with and aware of a variety of learning styles. Vygotsky (1978) discusses engagement as

lying within the student's zone of proximal development, the area in which they can succeed, but only with assistance from professors, peers, readings and other media (Bauman & Simkins, 2011; Merriam & Caffarella, 2007; Vygotsky, 1978).

Personal engagement refers to how an individual learner is interacting with the course. This is the most traditional facet in the category of engagement. In general, it refers to what is asked of the student in terms of his or her personal commitment and interaction with the course material and assignments.

Team or group engagement reflects the level of interaction among members who are simultaneously enrolled in a given course. Team or group engagement is more challenging to facilitate in online environments because the very nature of an asynchronous environment does not support or allow for groups of students to cohabitate in the same space at the same time, to interact with one another as they would in a traditional laboratory, classroom, or clinical setting. The more powerful form of group engagement occurs when learners share an experience together and then as a group engage in debriefing of the experience that will challenge established perceptions. Reflection as an active part of learning is a tenant of various forms of experiential learning (Schön, 1983, Kolb, 1984).

Activities that facilitate experiences that model and drive professional identity or acculturation are perhaps the most powerful type of learner engagement. This is particularly true as students move into new clinical, academic, and leadership roles based in part on their academic achievement (Gee, 2003). Assignments should be translational. This is a particularly salient point for returning adult students. Assignments should be meaningful in a way that informs future practice and promotes a path to mastery within the profession (Benner, Tanner & Chesla, 2009). It is the case that novices may not be in the position to identify how a given assignment promotes mastery or is in some way translational. However, when this is the case, the curriculum should include pearls or narrative that contextually situates assignments for learners so that these lessons foreshadow future experience and the role that the now student will later fulfill in a professional context.

Engagement elements reviewed included individual learner perspective, group interaction, and professional acculturation. All coursework requires students to take responsibility for their own education. Learning theory strongly supports learning environments that facilitate high levels of student interaction with the course material.

From the individual learner perspective, it was found to be easy to engage the courses. Directions and student expectations within each course encouraged students to take an active learner role. With few exceptions, course content was explicit and accessible. Course materials such as readings and videos corresponded well with individual sections and lessons.

There were required group activities in all of the core courses. However, in general the group activities require students to engage in a group discussion, but do not ask them to collaborate in a way that works towards consensus. Group activities are an important part of professional acculturation. This said the group activities most often incorporated into the curricula includes asking students to participate in online group discussions with one another. Group discussions provide an environment for students to interact with one another, but without direction this level of interaction can be relatively superficial. Collaborative assignments that encourage consensus or compromise require a deeper form of peer-to-peer engagement and responsibility. Peer-to-peer collaboration that leads to the development of consensus and compromise building skills situated within the profession, in this case nursing, and essential to the professional acculturation process.

Group activities in general did not drive professional acculturation. Acculturation into the nursing profession is an essential component of nursing education. Returning associate degree nurses must come to understand what it means to be a professional nurse, or what it means to move from one level of academic preparation to another. The academic environment should provide learners with the social and professional expectations of the cohort they are seeking to join (Gee, 2003). In this way, those activities that provide interaction and experiences that allow or push students to interact with practicing clinicians in authentic professional environments will be the most powerful. Learning from experience and later using past experiences to inform decision making and clinical practice is associated with various well known and supported experiential learning theories including Benner's novice-to-expert model of clinical nursing practice (Benner, 1984; Benner, Tanner, & Chesla, 2009; Kolb, 1984; Schön, 1983).

Curriculum Design

The development of curriculum is challenging, even preparing for a single lecture, workshop, or lab experience is time consuming and can take an inordinate amount of resources. When developing web-based courses this task is to a large extent very frontloaded. There is greater need to anticipate students' reaction to a curriculum and their ability to meet course benchmarks and ultimately have a successful learning experience.

Beyond the individual lessons, learning is enhanced if there is curricular coherence. A strong online curriculum includes clear objectives that form a complete body of work. Meeting objectives in one course should prepare students for success in other courses within the curriculum. An online environment that allows for the simplification of the learning process by providing consistent and simple access to course materials by leveraging existing web-based or e-learning tools is attending to the advantages and power of modern learning technology at the level of curriculum design (Bauman & Simkins, 2011).

Institutions that are relative novices to online and now virtual learning environments must address what types of courses and objectives are best suited for E-learning. The goal with e-learning is not to reinvent the nostalgia of the correspondence course. Online courses and those courses leveraging virtual environments should be specifically designed to leverage the educational technology and the many opportunities associated with distributed multi-media learning. When evaluating e-learning courses an analysis of the appropriateness of content for technology should be considered. A mismatch in these variables will often leave both faculty and students disappointed and frustrated.

As with any sound design, an evaluation plan must be considered from the outset (Khan, 2005, figure 1, page 380). Khan suggests that not only should we evaluate the products but also the people and processes involved in e-learning. While the main emphasis of e-learning evaluation falls on the shoulders of content and design experts, one would be remiss to exclude both formal and informal evaluation of e-learning interface design by the end user, namely students.

Faculty and designers alike should consider the degree to which course design enhances or detracts from student learning. Questions to consider include: 1) Is the interface design learner-centric?, 2) To what extent does the interface design promote learning and ultimately better student performance?, and 3) Is the design aesthetically pleasing or distracting to the learner? These are all important considerations when designing courses, and particularly series of courses taken by learners as part of the larger curriculum.

Elements of curriculum design reviewed across courses included clarity and use of objectives and overall design for the online medium. Beyond the style and content of individual lessons, learning is enhanced if there is curricular coherence. At a minimum, objective clarity should be present at the curriculum, lesson, and unit level. Clear objectives need to be carried through the lesson plans themselves. A strong online curriculum will make use of online tools not only for good pedagogy, but also to help organize and guide

learners through the curriculum process (Bauman & Simkins, 2011).

The courses surveyed largely achieved the required level of proactive preparation for student learning, but there is room for ongoing improvement. The courses reviewed also represent an interesting challenge for the professors teaching them. The core courses in the BSN@Home program were developed by different professors across multiple campuses, but have essentially been branded as a product of the UW System. Finding an ongoing balance between academic freedom and a consistent student experience will be crucial to maintaining a good learning environment for participating students.

When several courses, in this case five courses, are offered as a series that meet requisite coursework in a "single" system there is an expectation that the courses are going to be similar in presentation, effort, and workload. There is an inherent challenge to attending to academic freedom (individual professors and campuses), while also recognizing that these courses represent a UW System brand. In general, it was felt that the courses evaluated were good courses that represented relevant content and built on one another from courses to course. This said inconsistent expectations across courses being represented by the same brand might be confusing for students. Finding a way to standardize student expectations, workload, and evaluation processes may enhance the learner experience across courses. Strengthening the brand may be one way to accomplish this.

The most successful courses outlined objectives clearly and concisely. The best examples outlined objectives in the syllabus section and again for each section/lesson. The review of the courses and the D2L platform found the left hand navigation tool to be very useful. Courses that offered consistency in navigation and that emphasized objectives throughout the architecture offered an intuitive user interface and degree of elegance.

Grading across the courses was not consistent. It might be helpful to establish a single grading system that remains consistent across all of the courses. If it is not possible to use a single grading system for all five courses, it would be helpful if each course provided a more explicit and detailed explanation of grading within the syllabus. The reviewers support faculty and staff academic freedom, but also understand the power of branding as it relates to students expectations of a given program.

Content for courses did not always seem to leverage advantages of online learning environments. Online learning environments address the challenges of time and place, in this case leveraging the UW System brand by supporting students across the state. Online learning environments have the potential to bring in new students to grow enrollments in markets not currently served and meet the UW System goal of increasing the number of per capita state residents who have earned a college degree.

In summary, attention to design elements such as page/site design, content design, ease of navigation, and accessibility is critical. Feedback from learners provides a valuable source of information with the potential to result in continuous course and curricular improvement, increased learner satisfaction, and increased enrollments by recruitment of new students by satisfied customers.

PLAN FOR IMPROVING INTERFACE DESIGN

Elements of Interface Design Change

Three critical roles of interface design include providing: 1) learner orientation to instructional content, 2) navigational tools to access content and instructional strategies, and 3) feedback to the learner (Lohr, 2000). In order to more effectively evaluate how the course assists the learner to interact with the course learning system, it is

important to include questions that address each of these design elements. Questions to address page and site design, content design and navigation can be added to course evaluation tools (mid- or end of semester) to evaluate each of these elements in a manner that are relevant to the learner (Khan, 2005).

Areas of concern and recommendations identified in the interface design review were divided into two groups: 1) "quick fix" changes (changes involving only one or two of the courses and/or relatively small and easy) and, 2) Changes requiring greater time and/or resources.

Quick Fixes

Greater consistency across courses could be implemented easily in syllabi format, and accessing of course materials. Syllabi could have, for example, a consistent "grades" page in syllabi and/or use of similar rubrics. It is recommended that greater consistency be used in terms of where course materials (textbook readings, other readings, videos, web sites, etc.) are located in the course and how they are accessed. Similar headings could be used across courses for course materials.

Clearer statements of the time commitment students should expect to make for each course (hours per week) are needed. Additionally, insertion of language at the beginning of the two orientation sections indicating that these two sections are the same in all of the online nursing courses is recommended. Although these sections are important, students will not need to read them as carefully the second time around.

More Involved Fixes

One area that will require more time and effort to change is that of improvement in the consistency of course structure and composition. A balance must be struck between the need for consistency and the need to allow for academic freedom. While some variation between courses is expected, this variation should be based on sound pedagogical rationale.

Achieving greater consistency in terms of access to course materials, especially e-materials, will need to be considered. Establishing a single point of entry for all e-materials used by all of the program courses is recommended. Materials would be linked through a central database. Achieving this in each of the core courses is a complex process, involving faculty input, copyright concerns, library resources, course designer input and so forth. If research is intended to be part of a lesson, then this should be made explicit in the lesson objectives and perhaps the syllabus.

Another recommendation from the review was the refinement of group exercises, to move them from simple discussion to a greater level of collaboration and consensus-building or compromise-building. This change is stressed not simply on general pedagogical grounds, but specifically on grounds of professional acculturation. A more in-depth review of all group exercises will need to be undertaken by faculty in order to achieve this.

The recommendation was made that objectives be spelled out in the syllabus and also noted in the individual units and lessons. While a relatively straightforward change to make, the magnitude of the change comes in awareness of the number of places this would need to be set up and cross-checked, in order to achieve consistency and accuracy. For that reason, implementing this change cannot be done quickly.

Standardizing the evaluation and grading processes across the core courses was another suggestion resulting from the review. As noted in the review, scales and measures vary across the five schools. Achieving consensus on this matter will require extensive discussion by the BSN@Home Steering Committee and faculty teaching the core courses. The review primarily addresses the benefit of having a single grading scale for all of the courses and similar layout in the grades area of all courses. However, consistency in other respects is also suggested, including how

descriptions of grades are given in the syllabus, rubrics, nomenclature, layout of the grades page in the syllabus, etc. These are all issues that will require a thorough and consistent review of each of the core courses, with consensus agreement about how to best proceed.

The last area raised by the review is the need to strengthen the connection to the UW brand and the BSN@Home program. In fact, other similar collaborative UW programs, such as the University of Wisconsin Sustainable Management program (UW Sustainable Management, n.d.), have developed strong brand presence which is clearly evident across the curriculum. Developing a comparable brand presence for the BSN@Home program will require concentrated efforts and resources.

Course Evaluation

Traditional course evaluation miss the mark with E-learning. Course evaluations have traditionally focused on student evaluation of the instructor, however in e-learning environments; the instructor is just one part of the larger e-learning environment (Khan, 2005). Traditional course evaluation methods often miss critical elements of interface design. While they may measure elements such as student's perceptions of course organization, and accomplishment of learner objectives, they do not address the details needed to effectively evaluate course interface design elements (e.g. page and site design, accessibility, ease of navigation, etc.)..

For some, issues of interface design can be so distracting that learning is blocked. For example, if students are unable to navigate through course documents, they may miss key information such as due dates for course assignments. A consistent layout or format can enhance student learning through consistent use of site design elements, content relevant markers (icons, buttons, images, etc.), and multimedia components.

It is customary for students to evaluate each of their courses at the end of the semester. Some students will rate courses based on whether or not they liked the content. In other words, students opine whether or not the subject matter appealed to them. In other cases, students may evaluate courses based on the mechanism or style of delivery. Students often are not in the position to make accurate judgments about the importance of course content, because they lack the expertise to know what will be of importance as they graduate from student to novice to expert. They are however, well positioned to provide keen insight about the style and method of delivery. This is particularly true as educators continue to leverage technology as a mechanism for distributed education.

Further, today's traditional students come with a high and sophisticated level of media literacy, and contemporary expectations of how higher education ought to engage them as learners. Many students are more comfortable in digital and distributed environments than their faculty. This said nursing often attracts returning adult students who are generally seeded amongst the more traditionally aged students. Returning adult students in general often have different perceptions and expectations about educational processes (Merriam & Caffarella, 1999). These students may, but do not always have different levels of media literacy and even program expectations than their younger counterparts (Prensky, 2010).

While student perceptions of content and delivery can be biased based on the above discussion, student evaluations can identify trends worth investigating as part of any one course or cadre of courses existing within or across a given curriculum.

Informal learner feedback, while often not scheduled, can provide valuable feedback to course faculty. Student questions throughout the course and particularly at the beginning of the course may provide clues to interface design flaws. Comments such as "I cannot tell when assignments are due?" Or "I cannot open the link to the website" may identify design concerns that may be addressed and corrected when discovered. Some instruc-tors provide an opportunity for ongoing student feedback via e-mail or even through the use of a virtual "course suggestion box".

CONCLUSION

Limited attention has been given to the interface design of courses across a program of study. Interface design is the evaluation of course effectiveness, from the users' perspective. Interface design is an important part of developing and maintaining a robust curriculum that meets individual course objectives, but more importantly in meeting program objectives. Engaging in a review of interface design using the E-Learning Framework (Khan, 2005) afforded the BSN@Home program the opportunity to establish a continuous quality improvement mechanism to enhance learner outcomes. Quality will be improved by strengthening the consistency and coherence, content management, engagement and curriculum and design aspects of the program. Through close collaboration between the BSN@Home steering committee, faculty and course designers, findings of the review will be incorporated into subsequent course development. Well-designed courses and curriculum has the potential to improve student learning, confidence and satisfaction.

REFERENCES

Ahmed, S. M. Z., McKnight, C., & Oppenheim, C. (2009). A review of research on human-computer interfaces for online information retrieval systems. *The Electronic Library, 27*, 96–116. doi:10.1108/02640470910934623

Allen, E., & Seaman, J. (2011). *Online nation: Five years of growth in online learning.* Retrieved from http://sloanconsortium.org/ publications/survey/online_nation

American Association of University Professors (AAUP). (n.d.). *Academic freedom and electronic communications*. Retrieved from http://www.aaup.org/ AAUP/pubsres/policydocs/ contents/ electcomm-stmt.htm

American Recovery and Reinvestment Act. (n.d.). *About the act*. Retrieved from http://www.recovery.gov/ About/Pages/The_Act.aspx

Baker, J. (2005). *Span the silos for comprehensive distance education*. Retrieved from http://www.educause.edu/blog/ jbaker/spanthesilosforcomprehensivedi/165064

Bauman, E. (2007). *High fidelity simulation in healthcare*. Ph.D. dissertation, The University of Wisconsin–Madison, United States. Dissertations & Theses @ CIC Institutions database. (Publication no. AAT 3294196 ISBN: 9780549383109 ProQuest document ID: 1453230861)

Bauman, E. (2010). Virtual reality and game-based clinical education. In K. B. Gaberson, & M. H> Oermann (Eds.), *Clinical teaching strategies in nursing education* (3rd ed). New York, NY: Springer Publishing Company.

Bauman, E. B., & Games, I. A. (2011). Contemporary theory for immersive worlds: Addressing engagement, culture, and diversity. In Cheney, A., & Sanders, R. (Eds.), *Teaching and learning in 3D immersive worlds: Pedagogical models and constructivist approaches*. Hershey, PA: IGI Global. doi:10.4018/978-1-60960-517-9.ch014

Bauman, E. B., & Simkins, D. W. (2011). *TECNE interface design analysis of online nursing courses*. Unpublished manuscript, University of Wisconsin Green Bay, Green Bay, Wisconsin.

Benner, P. (1984). *From novice to expert: Excellence and power in clinical nursing practice*. Menlo Park, CA: Addison-Wesley.

Benner, P., Tanner, C., & Chesla, C. (2009). *Expertise in nursing: Caring, clinical judgment, and ethics*. New York, NY: Springer Publishing Company.

Chickering, A. W., & Ehrmann, S. C. (1996). Implementing the seven principles: Technology as lever. *AAHE Bulletin, October*, (pp. 3-6). Retrieved from http://www.tltgroup.org/ programs/ seven.html

Coonan, P. (2008). Educational innovation: Nursing's leadership challenge. *Nursing Economics, 26*, 117–121.

Desire2Learn (D2L). (n.d.). *Website*. Retrieved from http://www.desire2learn.com/

Games, I., & Bauman, E. (2011). Virtual worlds: An environment for cultural sensitivity education in the health sciences. *International Journal of Web Based Communities, 7*(2), 187–205. doi:10.1504/IJWBC.2011.039510

Gee, J. P. (2003). *What videogames have to teach us about learning and literacy*. New York, NY: Palgrave-McMillan.

Grant, W. I.-T. E. C. N. E. (n.d.). *Wisconsin technology enhanced nursing education grant*. Retrieved from http://research.son.wisc.edu/ tecne/index.html

Greer, J. (2010). *Study: Online education continues its meteoric growth*. Retrieved from http://www.usnews.com/education/ online-education/ articles/ 2010/01/26/study-online- education-continues-its-meteoric-growth

Guide, W. (n.d.). *When did the Internet start?* Retrieved from http://www.whenguide.com/ when-did-the-internet-start.html

Herzberg, D., Marsden, N., Kubler, P., Leon-hardt, C., Thomanek, S., Jung, H., & Becker, A. (2008). Specifying computer-based counseling systems in health care: A new approach to user-interface and interaction design. *Journal of Biomedical Informatics, 42*, 347–355. doi:10.1016/j.jbi.2008.10.005

Johns Hopkins Bloomberg School of Public Health. (n.d.). *About the program*. Retrieved from http://www.jhsph.edu/dept/hpm/certificates/informatics/whatis.html

Joshi, A., Arora, M., Dai, L., Price, K., Vizer, L., & Sears, A. (2009). Usability of a patient education and motivation tool using heuristic evaluation. *Journal of Medical Internet Research, 11*(4). doi:10.2196/jmir.1244

Khan, B. (2005). *Managing e-learning strategies*. Hershey, PA: Information Science Publishing. doi:10.4018/978-1-59140-634-1

Kolb, D. (1984). *Experiential learning: Experience as the source of learning and development*. Upper Saddle River, NJ: Prentice Hall.

Lohr, L. (2000). Designing the instructional interface. *Computers in Human Behavior, 16*(2), 161–182. doi:10.1016/S0747-5632(99)00057-6

Matters, Q. (n.d.). *Program FAQ*. Retrieved from http://www.qmprogram.org/faq

Merriam, S. B., & Caffarella, R. S. (1999). *Learning in adulthood: A compressive guide* (2nd ed.). San Francisco, CA: Jossey-Bass.

Miller, L. C., Jones, B. B., Graves, R. S., & Cullinan Sievert, M. (2010). Merging silos: Collaborating for information literacy. *Journal of Continuing Education in Nursing, 41*, 267–272. doi:10.3928/00220124-20100401-03

Prensky, M. (2010). *Teaching digital natives: Partnering for real learning*. Corwin Press.

Report, H. (2011). *2011 Horizon report*. Retrieved from http://www.educause.edu/ Resources/2011 HorizonReport/223122

Schön, D. A. (1983). *The reflective practitioner: How professionals think in action*. New York, NY: Basic Books.

Skiba, D. (2011). On the horizon: Emerging technologies for 2011. *Nursing Education Perspectives, 32*(1), 44–46. doi:10.5480/1536-5026-32.1.44

Squire, K. (2006). From content to context: Videogames as designed experience. *Educational Researcher, 35*(8), 19–29. doi:10.3102/0013189X035008019

Squire, K., Giovanetto, L., DeVane, B., & Durga, S. (2005). From users to designers: Building a self-organizing game-based learning environment. *TechTrends, 49*(5), 34–42. doi:10.1007/BF02763688

Summit, T. I. G. E. R. (n.d.). *About us*. Retrieved from http://tigersummit.com/ About_Us.html

Summit, T. I. G. E. R. (n.d.). *Virtual demo*. Retrieved from http://tigersummit.com/ Virtual_Demo_New.html

University of Wisconsin. (n.d.). *Sustainable management*. Retrieved from http://sustain.wisconsin.edu/

University of Wisconsin-Green Bay. (2009). *Virtual student meeting minutes, Fall*.

Usability. (n.d.). *Heuristic evaluations*. Retrieved from http://www.usability.gov/ methods/test_refine/heuristic.html

Vygotsky, L. (1978). *Mind in society*. Cambridge, MA: Harvard University Press.

Weaver, C. A., Delaney, C. W., Weber, P., & Carr, R. L. (Eds.). (2010) *Nursing and informatics for the 21st century: An international look at practice, education and EHR trends. 2nd ed*. Chicago, IL: Healthcare Information and Management System Society (HIMSS) and American Medical Informatics Association (AMIA). Retrieved from http://www.himss.org/ content/files/nursinginformaticsexcerpt.pdf

APPENDIX

Sample Interface Design Questions

Page and Site Design:
Are course elements easy to navigate? Find?
Does the course use a variety of visual enhancements to maintain learner attention? (Use of color, varying brightness, captions and headings, etc.)?
Are colored graphics or text used and if so, does printing course materials in black and white impact interpretation of the content?
Are there visual cues that help to mark where they are or where they have been in the course?
Are there links to helpful resources (e.g., writing lab, program website, etc.)?
Content Design:
Is the syllabus logically organized?
Does the course calendar identify the focus of each unit/week?
Is the content organized in a meaningful way?
Are headings used to signify movement from one content or unit to the next? Is there consistency in titles and headings between the course assignments, drop box, and grade book? (in other words, are these titled consistently?)
Are assignment due dates clearly identified?
Are reading assignments clearly identified?
Is it clear how grades are established (points, weighting of assignments, use of rubrics)?
Navigation:
Is course content presented in an attractive, easy to read manner?
Am I able to open course documents (pdf, word, other)?
Does it take an excessive amount of time to download documents?
Are audio and video components appropriate and relevant? Do these enhance your understanding of the course content?
Is there a text alternative to audio and vice versa for students with disabilities?
Am I able to navigate back to the course if a link takes me outside of the course website?

(Khan, 2005)

Compilation of References

Aalberts, R., & Hames, D. (2009). The common law and its impact on the Internet. In *Advances in computers* (*Vol. 77*, pp. 299–318). Elsevier. doi:10.1016/S0065-2458(09)01208-X

Ackroyd, S., & Thompson, P. (1999). *Organizational misbehaviour*. London, UK: Sage.

Adomavicius, G., Tuzhilin, A., & Zheng, R. (2008). REQUEST: A query language for customizing recommendations. *Information Systems Research, 22*(1).

Adrian, A. (2008). No one knows you are a dog: Identity and reputation in virtual worlds. *Computer Law & Security Report, 24*(4), 366–374. doi:10.1016/j.clsr.2008.03.005

Afanasiev, U. (1997). *The informatization of education as global problem on the crossroad of century*. Retrieved from http://www.yuriafanasiev.ru/articles/magazines_1997_156.htm

Agila, M. (2010). *Análisis del lenguaje utilizado en las recomendaciones y explicaciones de un sistema recomendador y su impacto en la decisión del usuario final. Trabajo de Investigación. Doctorado en Inteligencia Artificial Avanzada: Perspectivas Simbólica y Conexionista*. Depto. Inteligencia Artificial. ETSI Informática. UNED.

Ahmed, S. M. Z., McKnight, C., & Oppenheim, C. (2009). A review of research on human-computer interfaces for online information retrieval systems. *The Electronic Library, 27*, 96–116. doi:10.1108/02640470910934623

Ahmed, H. M., Gracanin, D., & Abdel-Hamid, A. (2008a). A framework for interaction interoperability in X3D mobile collaborative virtual environments. In *INFOS '08: Proceedings of the 6th International Conference on Informatics and Systems* (pp. 84–92).

Ahmed, H. M., Gracanin, D., & Abdel-Hamid, A. (2008b). Poster: A framework for interaction interoperability in virtual environments. In *3DUI '08: IEEE Symposium on 3D User Interfaces* (pp. 141–142).

Ahmed, H. M., Gracanin, D., Abdel-Hamid, A., & Matkovic, K. (2008). An approach to interaction interoperability for distributed virtual environments. In *EGVE '08: Short Papers and Posters Proceedings* (pp. 35–38).

AIGA. (2006). *What is experience design?* (Online). Retrieved from http://www.aiga.org/ content.cfm?Contentalias=what_is_ed

Aldrich, C. (2009). *Learning online with games, simulations, and virtual worlds*. San Francisco, CA: Jossey-Bass.

Alexander, C., Ishikawa, S., & Silverstein, M. (1977). *A pattern language*. New York, NY: Oxford University Press.

Alexander, C. S., & Becker, H. J. (1978). The use of vignettes in survey research. *Public Opinion Quarterly, 42*(1), 93–104. doi:10.1086/268432

Alexander, P., & Murphy, P. K. (1994). *The research base for APA's learner-centered psychological principles*. Paper presented at the annual meeting of the American Educational Research Association, New Orleans, Louisiana, USA.

Al-Hamad, A., Yaacob, N., & Al-Zoubi, A. Y. (2008). Integrating learning style information into personalized e-learning system. *IEEE Multidisciplinary Engineering Education Magazine, 3*(1).

Allen, E., & Seaman, J. (2011). *Online nation: Five years of growth in online learning*. Retrieved from http://sloanconsortium.org/ publications/survey/online_nation

Ally, M. (2009). *Mobile learning: Transforming the delivery of education and training*. Athabasca, Canada: Athabasca University Press.

Ally, M. (2011 in press). Designing mobile learning for the user. In Khan, B. H. (Ed.), *User interface design for virtual environments: Challenges and advances*. Hershey, PA: IGI Global.

Ally, M. (2004). Using learning theories to design instruction for mobile learning devices. *Mobile Learning 2004 International Conference Proceedings*, Rome, July 2004, (pp. 5-8).

Ally, M., & Fahy, P. (2002). Using students' learning styles to provide support in distance education. *Proceedings of the Eighteenth Annual Conference on Distance Teaching and Learning*, Madison, Wisconsin, August 2002, (pp. 1-4).

Ally, M., & Lin, O. (2005). An intelligent agent for adapting and delivering electronic course materials to mobile learners. *Proceedings of the International Mobile Learning Conference*, Capetown, South Africa, October 2005, (pp. 1-4).

Ambron, S., & Hooper, K. (1988). *Interactive multimedia: Visions of multimedia for developers, educators & information providers*. Washington: Microsoft Press.

American Association of University Professors (AAUP). (n.d.). *Academic freedom and electronic communications*. Retrieved from http://www.aaup.org/ AAUP/pubsres/ policydocs/ contents/electcomm-stmt.htm

American Psychological Association. (1993). *Learner-centered psychological principles: Guidelines for school reform and restructuring*. Washington, DC: American Psychological Association and the Mid-continent Regional Education Laboratory.

American Recovery and Reinvestment Act. (n.d.). *About the act*. Retrieved from http://www.recovery.gov/ About/ Pages/The_Act.aspx

Anderson, J., Rreder, L., & Lebiere, C. (1996). Working memory: Activation limitations on retrieval. *Cognitive Psychology*, 30, 221–256. doi:10.1006/cogp.1996.0007

Anderson, L. W., Krathwohl, D. R., Airasian, P. W., Cruicshank, K. A., Mayer, R. E., & Pintrich, P. R. … Wittrock, M. C. (2001) *A taxonomy for learning, teaching and assessing: A revision of Bloom's taxonomy of educational objectives*. New York, NY: Longman.

Antonacci, D., & Moderass, N. (2005, February 16). *Second Life: The educational possibilities of a massively multiplayer virtual world (MMVW)*. Retrieved September 2, 2007, from http://connect.educause.edu/library/ abstract/SecondLifeTheEducati/43821

Arakji, R. Y., & Lang, K. R. (2008). Avatar business value analysis: A method for the evaluation of business value creation in virtual commerce. *Journal of Electronic Commerce Research*, 9(3), 207–218.

Association of Virtual Worlds. (2008, August). *The blue book: A consumer guide to virtual worlds*, (4th edition, p. 1). Retrieved on April 12, 2009, from http://www.associationofvirtualworlds.com/ pdf/Blue%20Book%20 4th%20Edition% 20August%202008.pdf

Atkinson, S., & Furnell, S. (2009). Securing the next generation: enhancing e-safety awareness among young people. *Computer Fraud & Security*, (7): 13–19. doi:10.1016/S1361-3723(09)70088-0

Atkinson R. C., Bower, G. H., & Crothers, E. J. (1969). *An introduction to mathematical learning theory*. (in Russian). Moscow, Russia: Mir.

Ausubel, D. P. (1974). *Educational psychology: A cognitive view*. New York, NY: Holt, Rinehart and Winston.

Ausubel, D. (2010). *Meaningful verbal learning: Subsumption theory*. Retrieved from http://www.lifecircles-inc.com/ Learningtheories/constructivism/ausubel.html

Baber, C., Johnson, G. I., & Cleaver, D. (1997). Factors affecting users' choice of words in speech-based interaction with public technology. *International Journal of Speech Technology*, 2, 45–59. doi:10.1007/BF02539822

Baber, C., Mellor, B., Graham, R., Noyes, J. M., & Tunley, C. (1996). Workload and the use of automatic speech recognition: The effects of time and resource demands. *Speech Communication*, 20, 37–53. doi:10.1016/S0167-6393(96)00043-X

Baber, C., & Noyes, J. M. (1996). Automatic speech recognition in adverse environments. *Human Factors, 38*(1), 142–155. doi:10.1518/001872096778940840

Baber, C., Stammers, R. B., & Usher, D. M. (1990). Instructions and demonstrations as media for training new users of automatic speech recognition devices. *Behaviour & Information Technology, 9*(5), 371–379. doi:10.1080/01449299008924251

Baber, C., & Stammers, R. B. (1989). Is it natural to talk to computers? An experiment using the Wizard of Oz technique. In Megaw, E. D. (Ed.), *Contemporary ergonomics 1989* (pp. 234–239). London, UK: Taylor & Francis.

Baddeley, A. D. (1992). Working memory. *Science, 255,* 556–559. doi:10.1126/science.1736359

Baddeley, A. D. (2000). The episodic buffer in working memory. *Trends in Cognitive Sciences, 4,* 417–423. doi:10.1016/S1364-6613(00)01538-2

Baddeley, A. D., & Hitch, G. J. (1974). Working memory. In Bower, G. H. (Ed.), *The psychology of learning and motivation: Recent advances in learning and motivation* (pp. 47–90). New York, NY: Academic Press.

Badie, K., Kharrat, M., Mahmoudi, M. T., Mirian, M. S., Babazadeh, S., & Ghazi, T. M. (2009). *Creating contents based on inter-play between the ontologies of content's key segments and problem context.* The First International Conference on Creative Content Technologies (CONTENT 2009), Athens/Glyfada, Greece.

Bainbridge, W. (2007). The scientific research potential of virtual worlds. *Science, 317,* 472–476. doi:10.1126/science.1146930

Baker, W. E. (1990). Market networks and corporate behavior. *American Journal of Sociology, 96*(3), 589–625. doi:10.1086/229573

Baker, J. (2005). *Span the silos for comprehensive distance education.* Retrieved from http://www.educause.edu/blog/jbaker/spanthesilosforcomprehensivedi/165064

Baldassarri, S., & Cerezo, E. (2008). Maxine: A platform for embodied animated agents. *Computers & Graphics, 32*(4), 430–437. doi:10.1016/j.cag.2008.04.006

Ball, D. L. (1990). The mathematical understandings that prospective teachers bring to teacher education. *The Elementary School Journal, 90,* 449–466. doi:10.1086/461626

Banathy, B. H. (1995). Developing a systems view of education. *Educational Technology, 35*(3), 53–57.

Bandura, A. (1997). *Self efficacy: The exercise of control.* New York, NY: WH Freeman & Company.

Banister, E. N., & Hogg, M. K. (2004). Negative symbolic consumption and consumers' dive for self-esteem: The case of the fashion industry. *European Journal of Marketing, 38*(7), 850–868. doi:10.1108/03090560410539285

Barfield, W., Baird, K., & Bjorneseth, O. (1998). Presence in virtual environments as a function of type of input device and display update rate. *Displays, 19,* 91–98. doi:10.1016/S0141-9382(98)00041-9

Barker, S. B., & Ansorge, J. (2007). Robotics as means to increase achievement scores in an informal learning environment. *Journal of Research on Technology in Education, 39*(3), 229–243.

Barry, B. (2002). *ISD and the e-learning framework.* Retrieved January 24, 2003, from http://www.wit.ie/library/webct/isd.html

Barthes, R. (1977). *Image, music, text.* London, UK: Fontana Paperbacks.

Bastide, R., & Palanque, P. A. (1995). A Petri net based environment for the design of event-driven interfaces. In *Petri Nets '95: Proceedings of the 16th International Conference on Application and Theory of Petri Nets* (pp. 66–83). London, UK: Springer-Verlag.

Bates, B., & Leary, J. (2001). Supporting a range of learning styles using a taxonomy-based design framework approach. *Proceedings of the 18th Annual Conference of the Australasian Society for Computers in Learning in Tertiary Education,* 9-12 December, (pp. 45-53).

Bateson, G. (1988). *Mind and nature: A necessary unity* (pp. 9–11, 29). New York, NY: Bantam Books.

Bauman, E. B., & Games, I. A. (2011). Contemporary theory for immersive worlds: Addressing engagement, culture, and diversity. In Cheney, A., & Sanders, R. (Eds.), *Teaching and learning in 3D immersive worlds: Pedagogical models and constructivist approaches.* Hershey, PA: IGI Global. doi:10.4018/978-1-60960-517-9.ch014

Bauman, E. (2007). *High fidelity simulation in healthcare.* Ph.D. dissertation, The University of Wisconsin – Madison, United States. Dissertations & Theses @ CIC Institutions database. (Publication no. AAT 3294196 ISBN: 9780549383109 ProQuest document ID: 1453230861)

Bauman, E. (2010). Virtual reality and game-based clinical education. In K. B. Gaberson, & M. H> Oermann (Eds.), *Clinical teaching strategies in nursing education* (3rd ed). New York, NY: Springer Publishing Company.

Bauman, E. B., & Simkins, D. W. (2011). *TECNE interface design analysis of online nursing courses.* Unpublished manuscript, University of Wisconsin Green Bay, Green Bay, Wisconsin.

Bay, J. (2001). Developing number sense in number line. *Mathematics Teaching in the Middle School, 6,* 448–452.

Bedard-Voorhees, A., & Dawley, L. (2008). *Evaluating SL course experience: A learner's evaluation and faculty response.* Retrieved November 12, 2008, from http://www.aect.org/ SecondLife/08-archives.asp

Bell, M. (2008). Toward a definition of "virtual worlds". *Journal of Virtual Worlds Research, 1*(1), 2-5. Retrieved on February 3, 2009, from http://journals.tdl.org/jvwr/article/view/283/237

Bellinger, G. (1997). *Knowledge management - Emerging perspectives.* Retrieved on 15th September, 2008, from http://www.systems-thinking.org/ kmgmt/kmgmt.htm

Bellinger, G., Castro, D., & Mills, A. (1997). *Data, information, knowledge, and wisdom.* Retrieved on 15th September, 2008, from http://www.systems-thinking.org/ dikw/dikw.htm

Benford, S., Snowdon, D., Colebourne, A., O'Brien, J., & Rodden, T. (1997). Informing the design of collaborative virtual environments. In *GROUP '97: Proceedings of the International ACM SIGGROUP Conference on Supporting Group Work* (pp. 71–80). New York, NY: ACM.

Benner, P. (1984). *From novice to expert: Excellence and power in clinical nursing practice.* Menlo Park, CA: Addison-Wesley.

Benner, P., Tanner, C., & Chesla, C. (2009). *Expertise in nursing: Caring, clinical judgment, and ethics.* New York, NY: Springer Publishing Company.

Berge, Z. L., & Collins, M. (Eds.). (1995). *Computer-mediated communication and the online classroom.* Cresskill, NJ: Hampton Press.

Berge, Z. L. (1996). *Changing roles in higher education: Reflecting on technology Collaborative Communications Review* (pp. 43–53). McLean, VA: International Teleconferencing Association.

Berge, Z. L. (2002). Active, interactive and reflective elearning. *Quarterly Review of Distance Education, 3*(2).

Berleant, A. (1992). *The aesthetics of environment.* Philadelphia, PA: Temple University Press.

Bernstein, B. (1971). *Class, codes and control (Vol. 1).* London, UK: Routledge & Kegan Paul. doi:10.4324/9780203014035

Berry, D. M., & Tichy, W. F. (2003). Comments on Formal methods application: An empirical tale of software development. *IEEE Transactions on Software Engineering, 29*(6), 567–571. doi:10.1109/TSE.2003.1205183

Bersin, J. (2008, July). Today's high-impact learning organization. *Chief Learning Officer Magazine.* Retrieved on July 16, 2009, from http://clomedia.com/articles/ view/ today_s_high_impact_ learning_organization/1

Bespalco, B. P. (2007). Параметры и критерии диагностической цели. В: Образовательные технологии [Parameters and criteria for the diagnostic purpose]. *Instructional Technologies, 1,* 19–34.

Bessant, J., Kaplinsky, R., & Lamming, R. (2003). Putting supply chain learning into practice. *International Journal of Operations & Production Management, 23*(2), 167–184. doi:10.1108/01443570310458438

Blochl, B., Rumershofer, H., & Wob, W. (2003). Individualized e-learning systems enabled by a semantically determined adaptation of learning fragments. In *Proceeding of the 14th International Workshop on Database and Expert Systems Applications,* (pp. 640-645).

Bloom, B. S. (1956). *Taxonomy of educational objectives, handbook I: The cognitive domain.* New York, NY: David McKay, Inc.

Bloom, B. S. (Ed.). (1956). *Taxonomy of educational objectives, the classification of educational goals. Handbook 1: Cognitive domain.* New York, NY: McKay.

Bloomfield, R. J. (May 25, 2007). *Worlds for study: Invitation - Virtual worlds for studying real-world business (and law, and politics, and sociology, and....).* Retrieved from http://ssrn.com/abstract=988984

Blythe, M., Wright, P., & Mccarthy, J. (2006). Theory and method for experience centred design. In: *CHI 2006 – Conference on Human Factors in Computing Systems,* 22-27th April, Montréal, Québec, Canada (pp.1691–1694). New York, NY: ACM Press. (Online). Retrieved from portal.acm.org/ ft_gateway.cfm? Id=1125764&type=pdf

Boekaerts, M. (1997). Self-regulated learning: A new concept embraced by researchers, policy makers, educators, teacher and students. *Learning and Instruction, 7*(23), 161–168. doi:10.1016/S0959-4752(96)00015-1

Boekaerts, M. (1999). Self - regulated learning: Where we are today? *International Journal of Educational Research, 3,* 161–186.

Boekaerts, M. (2002). Bringing about change in the classroom: strengths and weaknesses of self regulated learning approach. *Learning and Instruction, 2,* 589–604. doi:10.1016/S0959-4752(02)00010-5

Boekaerts, M., & Minnaert, A. (1999). Self - regulation with respect to informal learning. *Educational Research, 31,* 533–544.

Bohm, D. (1981). *Knowledge & insight.* Retrieved on 15th August, 2008, from http://ttfuture.org/services/visionaries/Dbohm/BohmIK.PDF

Bohm, D. (1995). *The limitations of thought.* Retrieved on 15th August, 2008, from http://ttfuture.org/services/visionaries/Dbohm/BohmLT.pdf

Bolhus, S. (2003). Toward process-oriented teaching for self -directed lifelong learning: A multidimensional perspective. *Learning and Instruction, 13,* 327–347. doi:10.1016/S0959-4752(02)00008-7

Bollet, R., & Fallon, S. (2002). *Personalising e - learning. Educational Media International* (pp. 545–549). International Council for Education Media.

Bonk, C. J., & Reynolds, T. H. (1997). Web-based instructional techniques for higher-order thinking, teamwork, and apprenticeship. In Khan, B. H. (Ed.), *Web-based instruction* (pp. 167–178). Ed Tech Pubs.

Bonk, C. J., Wisher, R. A., & Lee, J. (2004). Moderating learner-centered elearning: Problems and solutions, benefits and implications. In Roberts, T. S. (Ed.), *Online collaborative learning: Theory and practice* (pp. 54–85). Hershey, PA: Idea Group Publishing.

Boshier, R., Mohapi, M., Moulton, G., Qayyum, A., Sadownik, L., & Wilson, M. (1997). Best and worst dressed web courses: Strutting into the 21st Century in comfort and style. *Distance Education, 18*(2), 327–348. doi:10.1080/0158791970180209

Bouguila, L., Iwashita, M., Hirsbrunner, B., & Sato, M. (2003). Virtual locomotion interface with ground surface simulation. *Proc. of the International Conference on Artificial Reality and Telexistence,* ICAT'03.

Bowen, J., & Stavridou, V. (1992). Formal methods and software safety. In H. Frey (Ed.), *SAFECOMP '92: Proceedings of the IFAC Symposium* (pp. 93–98). Pergamon Press.

Bowman, D. A., Chen, J., Wingrave, C. A., Lucas, J. F., Ray, A., & Polys, N. F. (2006). New directions in 3D user interfaces. *The International Journal of Virtual Reality, 5*(2), 3–14.

Brannick, M. T., Levine, E. L., & Morgeson, F. P. (2007). *Job and work analysis: Methods, research, and applications for human resource management.* Thousand Oaks, CA: Sage Publications.

Bransford, J., Brown, A., & Cocking, R. (1999). *How people learn: Brain, mind experience and school.* Retrieved on November 1, 2008, from http://cde.athabascau.ca/ online_book/pdf/TPOL_chp02.pdf

Bray, D. A., & Konsynski, B. (2007). *Virtual worlds, virtual economies, virtual institutions.* Retrieved from http://ssrn.com/abstract=962501

Brenton, H., & Hernandez, J. (2007). Using multimedia and Web3D to enhance anatomy teaching. *Computers & Education*, *49*(1), 32–53. doi:10.1016/j.compedu.2005.06.005

Brogan, D. C., Metoyer, R. A., & Hodgins, J. K. (1997). *Dynamically simulated characters in virtual environments* (p. 216). SIGGRAPH Visual Proceedings.

Brookfield, S. D. (2004). Discussion. In Galbraith, M. W. (Ed.), *Adult learning methods: A guide for effective instruction* (3rd ed., pp. 209–226). Malabar, FL: Robert E. Kreiger Publishing Company.

Brooks, F. P., Jr. (1986). Walkthrough-A dynamic graphics system for simulating virtual buildings. *Proceedings of 1986 Workshop on Interactive 3D Graphics*, (pp. 9-21).

Brown, J. S., & Duguid, P. (2000). *The social life of information*. Boston, MA: Harvard Business School Press.

Brown, A. L. (1992). Design experiments: theoretical and methodological challenges in creating complex interventions in classroom settings. *Journal of the Learning Sciences*, *2*(2), 141–178. doi:10.1207/s15327809jls0202_2

Brown, A., & Thompson, H. (1997). Course design for the WWW - Keeping online students onside. In *14th Annual Conference Proceedings of the ASCILITE. Academic Computing Services*, Curtin University of Technology, Perth, Western Australia (pp. 74-81).

Brown, J. S. (2002). *Growing up digital: How the Web changes work, education, and the ways people learn*. United States Distance Learning Association. Retrieved 20th September, 2008, from http://www.usdla.org/html/journal/ FEB02_Issue/article01.html

Bruner, J., & Anglin, J. M. (1973). *Beyond the information given - Studies in the psychology of knowing* (p. 397). Toronto, Canada: George J. McLeod Limited.

Brusilovsky, P., & Peylo, C. (2003). Adaptive and intelligent Web-based educational systems. *International Journal of Artificial Intelligence in Education*, *13*, 156–169.

Burbules, N. C., & Callister, T. A. (1996). Knowledge at the crossroads: Some alternative futures of hypertext learning environments. *Educational Theory*, (Winter): 3.

Burt, R. S. (1992). *Structural holes: The social structure of competition*. Cambridge, MA: Harvard University Press.

Bush, V. (1945). As we may think. *Atlantic Monthly*, *176*(1), 101–108.

Calder, J., & McCollum, A. (1998). *Open and flexible learning in vocational education and training*. London, UK: Kogan Page.

Calongne, C., & Bayne, G. (2007). *Podcast: Using Second Life for immersive learning*. Retrieved September 2, 2007, from http://connect.EDUCAUSE.edu/blog/ gbayne/ podcastusingsecondli/44967 ((8/22/07)

Campos, M. (2004). A constructivist method for the analysis of networked cognitive communication and the assessment of collaborative learning and knowledge-building. *Journal of Asynchronous Learning Networks*, *8*(2).

Cannon-Bowers, J. A., & Bowers, C. A. (2008). Synthetic learning environments. In Spector, J. M., Merril, M. D., van Merrienboer, J., & Driscoll, M. P. (Eds.), *Handbook of research on educational communications and technology* (3rd ed.). New York, NY: Lawrence Erlbaum Associates.

Capra, F. (1996). *The Web of life* (p. 70). London, UK: Harper Collins.

Card, S., Moran, T., & Newell, A. (1983). *The psychology of human-computer interaction*. Hillsdale, NJ: Lawrence Erlbaum Associates.

Carlson, A. (2000). *Aesthetics and the environment – The appreciation of nature, art and architecture*. London, UK: Routledge.

Carlson, A. (2002a). What is environmental aesthetics? Environmental aesthetics. In E. Craig (Ed.), *Routledge encyclopaedia of philosophy*. London, UK: Routledge. (Online). Retrieved from http://www.rep.routledge.com/ article/M047SECT1

Carlson, A. (2002b). The central philosophical issue of environmental aesthetics: Environmental aesthetics. In E. Craig (Ed.), *Routledge encyclopaedia of philosophy*. London, UK: Routledge. (Online). Retrieved from http:// www.rep.routledge.com/ article/M047SECT1

Caro, D. H., Lenkeit, J., Lehmann, R., & Schwippert, K. (2009). The role of academic achievement growth in school track recommendations. *Studies in Educational Evaluation*, *35*(4), 183–192. doi:10.1016/j.stueduc.2009.12.002

Carroll, J. M. (2001). *Human computer interaction in the millennium*. New York, NY: ACM Press, Addison-Wesley.

Carroll, F. (2008). The spatial development of the visual-narrative from prehistoric cave paintings to computer games. In Turner, P., Turner, S., & Davenport, E. (Eds.), *Exploration of space, technology, and spatiality: Interdisciplinary perspectives*. Hershey, PA: IGI Global. doi:10.4018/978-1-60566-020-2.ch011

Castells, M. (2001). *The internet galaxy: Reflections on the Internet business and society*. Oxford, UK: Oxford University Press.

Castronova, E. (2005). *Synthetic worlds: The business and culture of online games*. Chicago, IL: University of Chicago Press.

Castronova, E., Williams, D., Shen, C., Ratan, R., Xiong, L., Huang, Y., & Keegan, B. (2009). As real as real? Macroeconomic behavior in a large-scale virtual world. *New Media & Society*, *11*(5), 685. doi:10.1177/1461444809105346

Castronova, E. (2006). On virtual economies. *The International Journal of Computer Game Research 3*(2). Retrieved December 18, 2009, from http://www.gamestudies.org/ 0302/castronova/

Cavanagh, G. F., & Fritzsche, D. J. (1985). Using vignettes in business ethics research. In Preston, L. E. (Ed.), *Research in corporate social performance and policy* (pp. 279–293). Greenwich, CT: JAI Press.

Chan, M.-C., & Hu, S.-Y. (2008). An efficient and secure event signature (EASES) protocol for peer-to-peer massively multiplayer online games. *Computer Networks*, *52*(9), 1838–1845. doi:10.1016/j.comnet.2008.03.004

Chang, M. K., & Man Law, S. P. (2008). Factor structure for Young's Internet Addiction Test: A confirmatory study. *Computers in Human Behavior*, *24*(6), 2597–2619. doi:10.1016/j.chb.2008.03.001

Chen, K.-T., & Huang, P. (2006). Game traffic analysis: An MMORPG perspective. *Computer Networks*, *50*(16), 3002–3023. doi:10.1016/j.comnet.2005.11.005

Chen, L.-D., & Tan, J. (2004). Technology adaptation in e-commerce: Key determinants of virtual stores acceptance. *European Management Journal*, *22*(1), 74–86. doi:10.1016/j.emj.2003.11.014

Chen, C.-M., & Hsu, S.-H. (2008). Personalized intelligent mobile learning system for supporting effective English learning. *Journal of Educational Technology & Society*, *11*(3), 153–180.

Chen, G., & Kotz, D. (2000). *A survey of context-aware mobile computing research*, (p. 16). TR2000-381. Hanover, NH: Dartmouth College.

Chen, J. X., Yang, Y., & Loftin, B. (2003). MUVEES: A PC-based multi-user virtual environment for learning. In *Proceedings of the IEEE International Symposium on Virtual Reality*, (pp. 163–170). Los Angeles, CA: IEEE Computer Society.

Cheon, J., & Grant, M. M. (2009). Are pretty interfaces worth the time? The effects of user interface types on web-based instruction. *Journal of Interactive Learning Research*, *20*(1), 5–33.

Chickering, A. W., & Gameson, Z. (1987). Seven principles of good practice in undergraduate education. *AAHE Bulletin*, *39*(7), 3–7.

Chickering, A. W., & Reisser, L. (1993). *Education and identity*. San Francisco, CA: Jossey-Bass.

Chickering, A. W., & Ehrmann, S. C. (1996). Implementing the seven principles: Technology as lever. *AAHE Bulletin, October*, (pp. 3-6). Retrieved from http://www.tltgroup.org/ programs/seven.html

Chin, K. L., & Kon, P. N. (2003). Key factors for a fully online e-learning mode: A Delphi study. In G. Crisp, D. Thiele, I. Scholten, S. Barker & J. Baron (Eds.), *Interact, integrate, impact: Proceedings of the 20th Annual Conference of the Australasian Society for Computers in Learning in Tertiary Education*, Adelaide, 7-10 December 2003.

Chin, S., & Williams, J. (2006). A theoretical framework for effective online course design. *Journal of Online Learning and Teaching, 2*(1). Retrieved on January 3, 2009, from http://jolt.merlot.org/05007.htm

Chong, P. H. J., So, P. L., Shum, P., Li, X. J., & Goyal, D. (2004). Design and implementation of user interface for mobile devices. *IEEE Transactions on Consumer Electronics*, *50*(4), 1156–1161. doi:10.1109/TCE.2004.1362513

Christensen, R. R., Hollerbach, J. M., Xu, Y., & Meek, S. G. (2000). Inertial-force feedback for the treadport locomotion interface. *Presence (Cambridge, Mass.)*, *9*(1), 1–14. doi:10.1162/105474600566574

Chun, S.-H., & Kim, J.-C. (2005). Pricing strategies in B2C electronic commerce: Analytical and empirical approaches. *Decision Support Systems*, *40*(2), 375–388. doi:10.1016/j.dss.2004.04.012

Ciampi, M., Coronato, A., & De Pietro, G. (2008). An asynchronous communication system for pervasive grids. *International Journal of Web and Grid Services*, *4*(2), 211–221. doi:10.1504/IJWGS.2008.018888

Cifuentes, L., & Hsieh, Y. C. (2001). Computer graphics for student engagement in science learning. *TechTrends*, *45*(5), 21–23. doi:10.1007/BF03017083

Claridge, T. (2004). *Social capital and natural resource management*. (Unpublished Thesis). University of Queensland, Brisbane, Australia.

Clark, R. C., & Mayer, R. E. (2008). *E-learning and the science of instruction: Proven guidelines for consumers and designers of multimedia learning*. San Francisco, CA: Pfeiffer.

Clark, R. E., Bewley, W. L., & O'Neil, H. F. (2006). Heuristics for selecting distance or classroom settings for courses. In O'Neil, H., & Perez, R. (Eds.), *Web-based learning: Theory, research, and practice*. Mahway, NJ: Lawrence Erlbaum & Associates.

Clark, R., & Wittrock, M. C. (2000). Psychological principles of training. In Tobias, S., & Fletcher, J. (Eds.), *Training and retraining: A handbook for business, industry, government, and military* (pp. 51–84). New York, NY: Macmillan Reference USA.

Clark-Carter, D., Heyes, A., & Howarth, C. (1986). The effect of non-visual preview upon the walking speed of visually impaired people. *Ergonomics*, *29*(12), 1575–1581. doi:10.1080/00140138608967270

Clarke, I., Hallsworth, A., Jackson, P., de Kervenoael, R., Del Aguila, R. P., & Kirkup, M. (2006). Retail restructuring and consumer choice 1. Long-term local changes in consumer behavior: Portsmouth, 1980-2002. *Environment & Planning A*, *38*(1), 25–46. doi:10.1068/a37207

Çoban, O., & Seçme, G. (2005). Prediction of socio-economical consequences of privatization at the firm level with fuzzy cognitive mapping. *Information Sciences*, *169*(1-2), 131–154. doi:10.1016/j.ins.2004.02.009

Collins, M. P., & Berge, Z. L. (2003). Using instructional design for faculty development in a post-secondary, technology-enhanced environment. *Educational Technology*, *46*(6), 21–27.

Collinson, D. (1994). Strategies of resistance. In Jermier, J., Knoghts, D., & Nord, W. (Eds.), *Resistance and power in organizations*. London, UK: Sage.

Constantinides, E. (2004). Influencing the online consumer's behavior: The Web experience. *Internet Research*, *14*(2), 111–126. doi:10.1108/10662240410530835

Contarello, A., & Sarrica, M. (2007). ICTs, social thinking and subjective well-being - The internet and its representations in everyday life. *Computers in Human Behavior*, *23*(2), 1016–1032. doi:10.1016/j.chb.2005.08.013

Coonan, P. (2008). Educational innovation: Nursing's leadership challenge. *Nursing Economics*, *26*, 117–121.

Cooper, A., Reimann, R., & Cronin, D. (2007). *About Face 3 - The essentials of interaction design*. Wiley.

Cooper, P. A. (1993). Paradigm shifts in designing instruction: From behaviorism to cognitivism to constructivism. *Educational Technology*, *33*(5), 12–19.

Coronato, A., & De Pietro, G. (in press). Formal specification of wireless and pervasive healthcare applications. *ACM Transactions on Embedded Computing Systems*.

Coronato, A., De Pietro, G., & Gallo, L. (2007). Automatic execution of tasks in MiPeG. In *GPC '07: Proceedings of the Second International Conference on Advances in Grid and Pervasive Computing* (Vol. 4459, pp. 702–709). Berlin, Germany: Springer-Verlag.

Coulter-Smith, G. (2000). *The visual-narrative matrix*. Southampton, UK: Southampton Institute.

Craig-Lees, M., & Hill, C. (2002). Understanding voluntary simplifiers. *Psychology and Marketing*, *19*(2), 187–210. doi:10.1002/mar.10009

Cramer, K., Behr, M., Post, T., & Lesh, R. (1997). *Rational number project: Fraction lessons for the middle grades–level 2*. Dubuque, IA: Kendall/Hunt.

Crisler, K., & Anneroth, M. (2003). The human perspective of the wireless world. *Computer Communications, 26*(1), 11–18. doi:10.1016/S1403-3664(02)00114-7

Criswell, E. (1989). *The design of computer-based instruction*. New York, NY: Macmillan Publishing Company.

Csikszentmihalyi, M., & Robinson, R. E. (1990). *The art of seeing – An interpretation of the aesthetic encounter.* New York, NY: J Paul Getty museum.

Cuban, L. (2002). *Oversold & underused. Computers in the classroom*. Cambridge, MA: Harvard University Press.

Cuban, L. (1992). Curriculum stability and change. In Jackson, P. W. (Ed.), *Handbook of research on curriculum* (pp. 216–247). New York, NY: Macmillan.

D'Cruz, M., Stedmon, A. W., Wilson, J. R., & Eastgate, R. (2002). *From user requirements to functional and user interface specification: General process.* (University of Nottingham Report No.: IOE/VIRART/01/351).

D'Cruz, M., Stedmon, A. W., Wilson, J. R., Modern, P. J., & Sharples, G. J. (2003). Building virtual environments using the virtual environment development structure: A case study. In *HCI International '03, Proceedings of the 10th International Conference on Human-Computer Interaction, Crete, June 22-27, 2003*. Lawrence Erlbaum Associates.

Dabbagh, N. H., Bannan-Ritland, B., & Silc, K. (2000). Pedagogy and Web-based course authoring tools: Issues and implications. In Khan, B. H. (Ed.), *Web-based training* (pp. 343–354). Englewood Cliffs, NJ: Educational Technology Publications.

Dahl, Y., Alsos, O. A., & Svanæs, D. (2010). Fidelity consideration for simulation-based usability assessments of mobile ICT for hospitals. *International Journal of Human-Computer Interaction, 26*, 445–476. doi:10.1080/10447311003719938

Dahmann, J. S. (1999). The high level architecture and beyond: Technology challenges. *Workshop on Parallel and Distributed Simulation* (pp. 64-70)

Dai, K., & Li, Y. (2006). An interactive web system for integrated three-dimensional customization. *Computers in Industry, 57*(8-9), 827–837. doi:10.1016/j.compind.2006.04.017

Dailey, L. (2004). Navigational Web atmospherics: Explaining the influence of restrictive navigation cues. *Journal of Business Research, 57*(7), 795–803. doi:10.1016/S0148-2963(02)00364-8

Daniel, J. S. (1996). *Mega-universities and knowledge media: Technology strategies for higher education* (p. 2). London, UK: Kogan Page.

Darken, R. P., Cockayne, W. R., & Carmein, D. (1997). The omni-directional treadmill: A locomotion device for virtual worlds. *Proc. of UIST'97*, (pp. 213-221).

Davies, A., & Dalgarno, B. (2008). Learning fire investigation the clean way: The virtual experience. In Hello! Where are you in the landscape of educational technology? *Proceedings ASCILITE Melbourne 2008*. Retrieved from http://www.ascilite.org.au/conferences/ melbourne08/procs/davies.pdf

De Bra, P., & Calvi, L. (1998). AHA: A generic adaptive hypermedia system. *Proceedings of the 2nd Workshop on Adaptive Hypertext and Hypermedia*, (pp. 5-12). Pittsburgh.

de Freitas, S., & Griffiths, M. (2008). The convergence of gaming practices with other media forms: What potential for learning? A review of the literature. *Learning, Media and Technology, 33*(1), 11–20. doi:10.1080/17439880701868796

de Freitas, S. (2008) *Serious virtual worlds: A scoping study*. JISC publications. Retrieved March 14, 2009, from http://www.jisc.ac.uk/ publications/publications/seriousvirtualworldsreport.aspx

De Kervenoael, R., Aykac, D. S. O., & Palmer, M. (2009). Online social capital: Understanding e-impulse buying in practice. *Journal of Retailing and Consumer Services, 16*(4), 320–328. doi:10.1016/j.jretconser.2009.02.007

De Kervenoael, R., & Aykac, D. S. O. (2008). Grey market e-shopping and trust building practices in China. In Kautonen, T., & Karjaluoto, H. (Eds.), *Trust and new technologies*. Cheltenham, UK: Edward Edgar.

De Luca, A., Mattone, R., & Giordano, P. R. (2007). Acceleration-level control of the CyberCarpet. *2007 IEEE International Conference on Robotics and Automation*, Roma, I, (pp. 2330-2335).

De Lucia, A., & Francese, R. (2009). Development and evaluation of a virtual campus on Second Life: The case of SecondDMI. *Computers & Education, 52*(1), 220–233. doi:10.1016/j.compedu.2008.08.001

de Sena Caires, C. D. (2007). Towards the interactive filmic narrative--Transparency: An experimental approach. *Computers & Graphics, 31*(6), 800–808. doi:10.1016/j.cag.2007.08.003

Dede, C. (2007). Reinventing the role of information and communications technologies in education. *Yearbook of the National Society for the Study of Education, 106*, 11–38. doi:10.1111/j.1744-7984.2007.00113.x

deFreitas, S., & Neumann, T. (2009). The use of exploratory learning for supporting immersive learning in virtual environments. *Computers & Education, 52*, 343–352. doi:10.1016/j.compedu.2008.09.010

Dekker, P., & Uslaner, E. M. (2001). Introduction. In Uslaner, E. M. (Ed.), *Social capital and participation in everyday life* (pp. 1–6). London, UK: Routledge.

del Galdo, E. M., & Nielsen, J. (Eds.). (1996). *International user interfaces*. New York, NY: John Wiley & Sons.

Desire2Learn (D2L). (n.d.). *Website*. Retrieved from http://www.desire2learn.com/

Dev, P., & Heinrichs, W. L. (2008). Learning medicine through collaboration and action: Collaborative, experiential, networked learning environments. *Virtual Reality (Waltham Cross), 12*(4), 215–234. doi:10.1007/s10055-008-0099-5

Deveci, H. A. (2005). Personal jurisdiction: Where cyberspace meets the real world - Part 1. *Computer Law & Security Report, 21*(6), 464–477. doi:10.1016/j.clsr.2005.09.003

Dewey, J. (1938). *Experience & education*. New York, NY: Touchstone.

Dickau, J. J. (1999). *The known, the unknown, and the unknowable: Are the boundaries of consciousness a fractal?* Retrieved on 30th July, 2008, from http://jond4u.jonathandickau.com/ known.htm

Dickey, M. (2004). The impact of web-logs (blogs) on student perceptions of isolation and alienation in a web-based distance-learning environment. *Open Learning, 19*(3). Retrieved on May 23, 2009, from http://mchel.com/Papers/ OL_19_3_2004.pdf

Dillenbourg, P., Schneider, D. K., & Synteta, P. (2002). Virtual learning environments. In A. Dimitracopoulou (Ed.), *Proceedings of the 3rd Hellenic Conference on Information & Communication Technologies in Education* (pp. 3-18). Kastaniotis Editions, Greece.

Dillon, T. W., Norcio, A. F., & DeHaemer, M. J. (1993). Spoken language interaction: Effects of vocabulary size and experience on user efficiency and acceptability. In, G. Salvendy & M. J. Smith (Eds.), *Human-Computer Interaction: Software and Hardware Interfaces, Proceedings of the 5th International Conference on Human-Computer Interaction (HCI International '93)* (pp. 140-145). Amsterdam, The Netherlands: Elsevier Science.

DiMaggio, P. J., & Powell, W. W. (1983). The iron cage revisited: Institutional isomorphism and collective rationality in organizational fields. *American Sociological Review, 48*, 147–160. doi:10.2307/2095101

Dimock, K., & Boethel, M. (1999). *Constructing knowledge with technology*. Austin, TX: Southwest Education Development Lab.

Djajadiningrat, J. P., Gaver, W. W., & Frens, W. J. (2000). Interaction relabelling and extreme characters: Methods for exploring aesthetic interactions. In *Proceedings of the Conference on Designing Interactive Systems: Processes, Practices, Methods, and Techniques*, 17-19th August, (pp. 66–71). New York, NY: ACM Press. Retrieved from http://studiolab.io.tudelft.nl/static/ gems/publications/00djajdisinte.pdf

Doddington, G. R., & Schalk, T. D. (1981). Speech recognition: Turning theory into practice. *IEEE Spectrum, 18*(9), 26–32.

Dodds, T. J., & Ruddle, R. A. (2009). Using mobile group dynamics and virtual time to improve teamwork in large-scale collaborative virtual environments. *Computers & Graphics, 33*(2), 130–138. doi:10.1016/j.cag.2009.01.001

Drachsler, H., Hummel, H. G. K., & Koper, R. (2007). Personal RS for learners in lifelong learning: Requirements, techniques and model. *International Journal of Learning Technology, 3*(4).

Ducheneaut, N., Moore, R., & Nickell, E. (2007). Virtual third places: A case study of sociability in massively multiplayer games. *Computer Supported Cooperative Work, 16*, 129–166. doi:10.1007/s10606-007-9041-8

Dux, P. E., Ivanoff, J., Asplund, C. L., & Marois, R. (2006). Isolation of a central bottleneck of information processing with time-resolved fMRI. *Neuron, 52*, 1109–1120. doi:10.1016/j.neuron.2006.11.009

Earnshaw, R. A., Gigante, M. A., & Jones, H. (Eds.). (1993). *Virtual reality systems.* Academic Press, 1993.

Earthy, J., Sherwood Jones, B., & Bevan, N. (2001). The improvement of human-centred processes - Facing the challenge and reaping the benefit of ISO 13407. *International Journal of Human-Computer Studies, 55*, 553–585. doi:10.1006/ijhc.2001.0493

Edery, D. (2006). Reverse product placement in virtual worlds. *Harvard Business Review, 84*(12), 24.

Eisenberg, R. (2008). The average conversion rate: Is it a myth? *The ClickZ Network.* Retrieved from http:// www. clickz.com/ showPage.html?page=3628276

Ellington, H. (1995). Flexible learning, your flexible friend. In Bell, C., Bowden, M., & Trott, A. (Eds.), *Implementing flexible learning* (pp. 3–13). London, UK: Kogan Page.

Ellis, C. E., & Hunt, R. R. (1983). *Fundamentals of human memory and cognition.* Dubuque, IA: Brown.

Ellis, C., & Folley, S. (2011). Using student assessment choice and eassessment to achieve self-regulated learning. In Dettori, G., & Persico, D. (Eds.), *Fostering self–regulated learning through ICT* (pp. 295–315). New York, NY: Information Science Reference. doi:10.4018/978-1-61692-901-5.ch006

Elsaesser, T. (1990). *Early cinema, space frame and narrative.* London, UK: British Film Institute.

El-Tigi, M. A., & Khan, B. H. (2001). Web-based learning resources. In Khan, B. H. (Ed.), *Web-based training* (pp. 59–72). Englewood Cliffs, NJ: Educational Technology Publications.

Emami, H., Aqdasi, M., & Asousheh, A. (2008). Key success factors in e-learning in medical education. *Journal of Medical Education, 12*(3), 81–89.

Enders, A., & Hungenberg, H. (2008). The long tail of social networking: Revenue models of social networking sites. *European Management Journal, 26*(3), 199–211. doi:10.1016/j.emj.2008.02.002

Epstein, J., & Klinkenberg, W. D. (2001). From Eliza to Internet: A brief history of computerized assessment. *Computers in Human Behavior, 17*(3), 295–314. doi:10.1016/S0747-5632(01)00004-8

Eroglu, S. A., Karen, A. M., & Lenita, M. D. (2001). Atmospheric qualities of online retailing: A conceptual model and implications. *Journal of Business Research, 54*(2), 177–184. doi:10.1016/S0148-2963(99)00087-9

Eröz-Tuga, B., & Sadler, R. (2009). Comparing six video chat tools: A critical evaluation by language teachers. *Computers & Education, 53*(3), 787–798. doi:10.1016/j.compedu.2009.04.017

Ertmer, P., & Newby, T. (1993). Behaviorism, cognitivism, constructivism: Comparing critical features from an instructional design perspective. *Performance Improvement Quarterly, 6*(4), 50–72. doi:10.1111/j.1937-8327.1993.tb00605.x

Ettlinger, N. (2003). Cultural economic geography and a relational and microspace approach to trusts, rationalities, networks, and change in collaborative workplaces. *Journal of Economic Geography, 3*, 145–171. doi:10.1093/jeg/3.2.145

Farzan, R., & Brusilovsky, P. (2006). Social navigation support in a course recommendation system. In *Proceedings of 4th International Conference on Adaptive Hypermedia and Adaptive Web-based Systems.*

Fauconnier, G., & Turner, M. (1998). Conceptual integration networks. *Cognitive Science, 22*(2), 133–187. doi:10.1207/s15516709cog2202_1

Federation of American Scientists. (2009). *FAS virtual worlds whitepaper.* Retrieved on March 20, 2009, from http://vworld.fas.org/ wiki/FAS_Virtual_Worlds_Whitepaper

Fencott, C. (1999a). *Content and creativity in virtual environment design.* In Virtual Systems and Multimedia, 1-3rd September, Dundee. Scotland: University of Abertay Dundee Publishers (Online). Retrieved from http://www-scm.tees.ac.uk/users/ p.c.fencott/vsmm99/welcome.html

Fencott, C. (1999b). *Towards a design methodology for virtual environments*. In King's Manor Workshop: User Centered Design and Implementation of Virtual Environments, 30th September, York. Retrieved from http://www.cs.York.ac.uk/hci/kings_manor_workshops/UCDIVE/fencott.pdf

Fennell, F., & Rowan, T. (2001). Representation: An important process for teaching and learning mathematics. *Teaching Children Mathematics, 7,* 288–292.

Feridun, M., & Krause, J. (2001). A framework for distributed management with mobile components. *Computer Networks, 35*(1), 25–38. doi:10.1016/S1389-1286(00)00147-X

Ferreira, P., & Raffler, H. (2004). Introduction to the special issue. *Computers & Graphics, 28*(5), 623–624. doi:10.1016/j.cag.2004.06.003

Ficici, S. G., & Pollack, J. B. (1998a). Coevolving communicative behavior in a linear pursuer-evader game. In R. Pfeifer, B. Blumberg, & H. Kobayashi (Eds.), *Proceedings of the Fifth International Conference of the Society for Adaptive Behavior.* Cambridge, MA: MIT Press, 1998.

Ficici, S. G., & Pollack, J. B. (1998b). Challenges in coevolutionary learning: Arms-race dynamics, open-endedness, and mediocre stable states. In C. Adami, R. K. Belew, H. Kitano, & C. E. Talor (eds.), *Proceedings of the Sixth International Conference on Artificial Life.* Cambridge, MA: MIT Press, 1998.

Fishwick, P. (Ed.). (2006). *Aesthetic computing.* Cambridge, MA: MIT Press.

Fleming, P., & Spicer, A. (2007). *Contesting the corporation.* Cambridge, UK: Cambridge University Press. doi:10.1017/CBO9780511628047

Flint, D. J., & Woodruff, R. B. (2001). The initiators of changes in customers' desired value: Results from a theory building study. *Industrial Marketing Management, 30*(4), 321–337. doi:10.1016/S0019-8501(99)00117-0

Forlizzi, J. (2006). *How do HCI researchers view interaction design?* Retrieved from http://goodgestreet.com/theory/hcid.html

Forrest, E. (1985). Segmenting VCR owners. *Journal of Advertising Research, 28*(2).

Forte, D., & Power, R. (2006). Ten years in the wilderness, part III: Diogenes on the threshing floor. *Computer Fraud & Security, (3):* 8–12. doi:10.1016/S1361-3723(06)70320-7

Forte, D., & Power, R. (2008). Gazing into a crystal ball presents multiple instances of Déjà Vu: Should we just write a 2008: Year in review now? *Computer Fraud & Security, (2):* 16–19. doi:10.1016/S1361-3723(08)70028-9

Foster, A. L. (2007, July 6). Virtual worlds as social-science labs. *The Chronicle of Higher Education, 53*(44), 25.

Fougnie, D., & Marois, R. (2006). Distinct capacity limits for attention and working memory: Evidence from attentive tracking and visual working memory paradigms. *Psychological Science, 17,* 526–534. doi:10.1111/j.1467-9280.2006.01739.x

Frick, T. (1998). *Restructuring education through technology.* Retrieved from http://education.indiana.edu/%7Efrick/fastback/fastback326.html#journey

Friday, J. (2002). *Aesthetics and photography.* London, UK: Ashgate Publishing Limited.

Furlonger, D. (2007, 11 April). Banking on virtual worlds: Threats and opportunities. *Gartner Research Article.* (Gartner ID Number: G00147743).

Gabriel, Y. (1999). Beyond happy families: A critical reevaluation of the control resistance-identity triangle. *Human Relations, 52*(2), 179–203. doi:10.1177/001872679905200201

Gagatsis, A., & Elia, I. (2004). The effects of different modes of representation on mathematical problem solving. In M. J. Høines & A. B. Fuglestad (Eds.), *The 28th Conference of the International Group for the Psychology of Mathematics Education: Vol. 2* (pp. 447-454). Norway: Bergen University.

Gagne, R. M. (1985). *The conditions of learning and theory of instruction.* New York, NY: CBS College.

Gagne, R. M., Briggs, L. J., & Wager, W. W. (1992). *Principles of instructional design* (4th ed.). Belmont, CA: Wadsworth/Thomson Learning.

Gallo, L., & Minutolo, A. (2008). A natural pointing technique for semi-immersive virtual environments. In *Mobiquitous '08: Proceedings of the 5th Annual International Conference on Mobile And ubiquitous Systems* (pp. 1–4). Brussels, Belgium: ICST.

Gallo, L., Ciampi, M., & Minutolo, A. (2010). Smoothed pointing: A user-friendly technique for precision enhanced remote pointing. In *CISIS '10: Proceedings of the international conference on complex, intelligent and software intensive systems.* Los Alamitos, CA: IEEE Computer Society.

Gallo, L., De Pietro, G., Coronato, A., & Marra, I. (2008). Toward a natural interface to virtual medical imaging environments. In *AVI '08: Proceedings of the Working Conference on Advanced Visual Interfaces* (pp. 429–432). New York, NY: ACM Press.

Gallo, L., De Pietro, G., & Marra, I. (2008). 3D interaction with volumetric medical data: Experiencing the Wiimote. In *AMBI-SYS '08: Proceedings of the 1st International Conference On Ambient Media and Systems* (pp. 1–6). Brussels, Belgium: ICST.

Games, I., & Bauman, E. (2011). Virtual worlds: An environment for cultural sensitivity education in the health sciences. *International Journal of Web Based Communities, 7*(2), 187–205. doi:10.1504/IJWBC.2011.039510

Gamor, K. (2011). Signs and guideposts: Creating successful virtual world experiences. In G. Vincenti & J. Braman (Eds.) *Multi-User Virtual Environments for the Classroom: Practical Approaches to Teaching in Virtual Worlds.* Hershey, PA: IGI Global.

Gamor, K. (2011). What is in an avatar? Identity, behavior, and integrity in virtual worlds for educational and business communications. In Vu, K. P., & Proctor, R. W. (Eds.), *Handbook of human factors in web design* (pp. 739–749). Boca Raton, FL: CRC Press. doi:10.1201/b10855-48

Gamor, K. (2010). Adopting virtual worlds in ADL: The criticality of analysis. In Wisher, B., & Khan, B. (Eds.), *Learning on demand: ADL and the future of eLearning.* Alexandria, VA: ADL.

Garcia, E., Romero, C., Ventura, S., & De Castro, C. (2009). An architecture for making recommendations to courseware authors using association rule mining and collaborative filtering. *User Modeling and User-Adapted Interaction, 19*(1-2), 99–132. doi:10.1007/s11257-008-9047-z

Garrison, R. (2000). Theoretical challenges for distance education in the 21st Century: A shift from structural to transactional issues. *International Review of Research in Open and Distance Learning, 1*(1), 1–17.

Gartner Inc. (2007, April 24). *Press release: Gartner says 80 percent of active Internet users will have a "Second Life" in the virtual world by the end of 2011.* Retrieved on March 20, 2009, from http://www.gartner.com/it/page.jsp?id=503861%20

Gartner Inc. (2008b). *Press release: Gartner says 90 per cent of corporate virtual world projects fail within 18 months.* Retrieved March 20, 2009 from http://www.gartner.com/ it/page.jsp?id=670507

Gartner Inc. (2009, October 20). *Press release: Gartner identifies the top 10 strategic technologies for 2010.* Retrieved on November 11, 2009, from http://www.gartner.com/ it/page.jsp?id=1210613

Gartner Research. (2007, April 24). *Gartner says 80 percent life in the virtual world by the end of 2011.* Retrieved from http://www.gartner.com/it/ page.jsp?id=503861

Gassner, K., Jansen, M., Harrer, A., Herrmann, K., & Hoppe, H. U. (2003), Analysis methods for collaborative models and activities. In B. Wasson, S. Ludvigsen, & U. Hoppe (Eds.), *Designing for Change in Networked Learning Environments, Proceedings of CSCL 2003,* (pp. 411-420). Dordrecht, The Netherlands: Kluwer Academic Publishers.

Gatignon, H., & Robertson, T. S. (1991). Innovative decision processes. In Robertson, T. S., & Kassarjian, H. H. (Eds.), *Handbook of consumer behavior* (pp. 316–348). Englewood Cliffs, NJ: Prentice-Hall.

Gazzard, A. (2007). Playing without gaming. In Digital Games: Design and Theory, 14th September, Brunel University, London. Retrieved from http://arts.brunel.ac.uk/ gate/gamesconference/

Gee, J. P. (2003). *What video games have to teach us about learning and literacy.* New York, NY: Palgrave-McMillan.

Germanakos, P., & Tsianos, N. (2008). Capturing essential intrinsic user behaviour values for the design of comprehensive web-based personalized environments. *Computers in Human Behavior*, *24*(4), 1434–1451. doi:10.1016/j.chb.2007.07.010

Giddens, A. (1992). *The transformation of intimacy.* Cambridge, MA: Polity Press.

Gilbert, P. K. (2002). *The virtual university an analysis of three advanced distributed leaning systems.* Retrieved February 24, 2004, from http://gseacademic.harvard.edu/~gilberpa/homepage/portfolio/ research/pdf/edit611.pdf

Gilman, D. A., Andrew, R., & Rafferty, C. D. (1995). Making assessment a meaningful part of instruction. *NASSP Bulletin*, *79*(573), 20–24. doi:10.1177/019263659507957304

Gipson, S. (1996). *Feral, facsimile of facilitated? Technology serving teaching and learning.* Tridos School Village, Chiang Mai, Thailand: Learning and Teaching: Implications for Gifted and Talented Students.

Glance, N., & Snowdon, D. (2001). Pollen: Using people as a communication medium. *Computer Networks*, *35*(4), 429–442. doi:10.1016/S1389-1286(00)00183-3

Goldin, G. A., & Shteingold, N. (2001). Systems of representations and the development of mathematical concepts. In Cuoco, A. A., & Curcio, F. R. (Eds.), *The roles of representation in school mathematics NCTM yearbook 2001* (pp. 1–23). Reston, VA: National Council of Teachers of Mathematics.

Goldin, G. A. (2003). Representation in school mathematics: A unifying research perspective. In Kilpatrick, J., Martin, W. G., & Schifter, D. (Eds.), *A research companion to principles and standards for school mathematics* (pp. 275–285). Reston, VA: National Council of Teachers of Mathematics.

Goldstein, I. L., & Ford, J. K. (2002). *Training in organizations: Needs assessment, development, and evaluation* (4th ed.). Belmont, CA: Wadsworth Publishing.

Gómez Hidalgo, J. M., & Sanz, E. P. (2009). *Web content filtering. Advances in computers* (*Vol. 76*, pp. 257–306). Elsevier.

Goodear, L. (2001). *Cultural diversity and flexible learning.* Presentation of Findings 2001 Flexible Learning Leaders Professional Development Activity. South West Institute of TAFE. Australia. Retrieved February 24, 2004, from http://www.flexiblelearning.net.au/ leaders/events/pastevents/2001/ statepres01/papers/l_goodear.pdf

Gorge, M. (2007). Security for third level education organizations and other educational bodies. *Computer Fraud & Security*, (7): 6–9.

Graham, R., & Carter, C. (1998). *The human factors of speech recognition in cars: A literature review (Speech Ideas deliverable 1.1).* Loughborough, UK: HUSAT Research Institute.

Graham, R., & Baber, C. (1993). User stress in automatic speech recognition. In Lovesey, E. J. (Ed.), *Contemporary ergonomics 1993* (pp. 463–468). London, UK: Taylor & Francis.

Graham, C., Cagiltay, K., Lim, B., Craner, J., & Duffy, T. M. (2001). *Seven principles of effective teaching: A practical lens for evaluating online courses.* The Technology Source. [Online.] Retrieved from http://ts.mivu.org/default.asp?show=article&id=839

Grant, W. I.-T. E. C. N. E. (n.d.). *Wisconsin technology enhanced nursing education grant.* Retrieved from http://research.son.wisc.edu/ tecne/index.html

Grau, O. (2003). *Virtual art – From illusion to immersion.* USA: MIT Press.

Graziano, A., Higgins, R. A., Hislop, D. W., & Moore, K. (2000). *A changing focus in higher education? Outcome-based assessment.* Retrieved from http://www.shu.ac.uk/schools/ ed/pgclt/1999-2000/resources/task1/ presentations/almerindo-richard-donald-kathie/home.htm

Green, M. S. (2005). You perceive with your mind: Knowledge and perception. In Darby, D., & Shelby, T. (Eds.), *Hip hop and philosophy* (pp. 6–8). Open Court.

Green, H., & Hof, R. D. (2007). *Picking up where search leaves off.* Retrieved January 15, 2009, from http://www.businessweek.com/ magazine/content/05_15/b3928112_mz063.htm

Greenemeier, L. (2007, July 16). *Virtual worlds, real cheaters.* Information Week.

Greer, J. (2010). *Study: Online education continues its meteoric growth*. Retrieved from http://www.usnews.com/education/ online-education/articles/ 2010/01/26/study-online- education-continues-its-meteoric-growth

Grimstead, I. J. (2005). *RAVE - Resource aware visualization environment*. Retrieved from http://users.cs.cf.ac.uk/I.J.Grimstead/RAVE/index.html

Gross, E. F. (2004). Adolescent Internet use: What we expect, what teens report. *Journal of Applied Developmental Psychology*, *25*, 633–649. doi:10.1016/j.appdev.2004.09.005

Guide, W. (n.d.). *When did the Internet start?* Retrieved from http://www.whenguide.com/ when-did-the-internet-start.html

Hall, A. (1987). *Metasystems methodology: A new synthesis and unification*. Pergamon Press.

Hammer, D. (2000). Student resources for learning introductory physics. *American Journal of Physics. Physics Education Research Supplement*, *68*(1), 52–59.

Hannafin, M. J., & Land, S. (1997). The foundations and assumptions of technology-enhanced, student-centered learning environments. *Instructional Science*, *25*, 167–202. doi:10.1023/A:1002997414652

Hannafin, M. J. (1997). Resource-based learning environments: Methods and models. In *14th Annual Conference Proceedings of the ASCILITE. Academic Computing Services*, Curtin University of Technology, Perth, Western Australia, (pp. 255–62).

Hansen, J. V., & Lowry, P. B. (2007). Genetic programming for prevention of cyberterrorism through dynamic and evolving intrusion detection. *Decision Support Systems*, *43*(4), 1362–1374. doi:10.1016/j.dss.2006.04.004

Hanwu, H., & Yueming, W. (2009). Web-based virtual operating of CNC milling machine tools. *Computers in Industry*, *60*(9), 686–697. doi:10.1016/j.compind.2009.05.009

Hapeshi, K., & Jones, D. M. (1988). The ergonomics of automatic speech recognition. *International Reviews of Ergonomics*, *2*, 251–290.

Harp, S. F., & Mayer, R. E. (1998). How seductive details do their damage: A theory of cognitive interest in science learning. *Journal of Educational Psychology*, *90*, 414–434. doi:10.1037/0022-0663.90.3.414

Harris, B., Reinhard, W., & Pilia, A. (2011). Strategies to promote self –regulated learning in online environments. In Dettori, G., & Persico, D. (Eds.), *Fostering self – regulated learning through ICT* (pp. 295–315). New York, NY: Information Science Reference. doi:10.4018/978-1-61692-901-5.ch008

Harris, D. (2000). Knowledge and networks. In Evans, T., & Nation, D. (Eds.), *Changing university teaching: Reflections on creating educational technologies* (pp. 36–37). London, UK: Kogan Page.

Hartling, P., Just, C., & Cruz-Neira, C. (2001). Distributed virtual reality using Octopus. *In Proceedings of IEEE International Symposium on Virtual Reality* (pp. 53–62). IEEE Computer Society.

Haughey, M., & Muirhead, B. (2011). *Evaluating learning objects for schools*. Retrieved from http://www.ascilite.org.au/ajet/ejist/ docs/vol8_no1/fullpapers/ eval_learnobjects_school.hm

Hayes, D. L. (2002). Internet copyright: Advanced copyright issues on the Internet -- Part VIII. *Computer Law & Security Report*, *18*(1), 3–10. doi:10.1016/S0267-3649(02)00102-4

Haynes, D., & Prakash, G. (1991). Introduction: The entanglement of power and resistance. In Haynes, D., & Prakash, G. (Eds.), *Contesting power: Resistance and everyday social relations in South Asia*. Berkeley, CA: University of California Press.

Hays, R. T., Jacobs, J. W., Prince, C., & Salas, E. (1992). Flight simulator effectiveness: A meta-analysis. *Military Psychology*, *4*, 63–74. doi:10.1207/s15327876mp0402_1

Hayward, R. C., & Hollerbach, J. M. (2002) Implementing virtual stairs on treadmills using torso force feedback. *Proc. of IEEE Int'l Conf. on Robotics and Automation*, (pp. 586-591).

Hedberg, J. G., Brown, C., Larkin, J. L., & Agostinho, S. (2001). Designing practical websites for interactive training. In Khan, B. (Ed.), *Web-based training*. Englewood Cliffs, NJ: Educational Technology Publications.

Heinich, R., Molenda, M., Russell, J. D., & Smaldino, S. E. (2002). *Instructional media and technologies for learning*. NJ: Pearson Education.

Hemp, P. (2006). Avatar-based marketing. *Harvard Business Review*, *84*(6), 48–57.

Henry, P. (2005). E-learning technology, content and services. *Journal of Education and Training, 43*(4), 249–255. doi:10.1108/EUM0000000005485

Herman Group. (2007, March 21). *The futurist*. Retrieved from www.wfs.org

Herzberg, D., Marsden, N., Kubler, P., Leonhardt, C., Thomanek, S., Jung, H., & Becker, A. (2008). Specifying computer-based counseling systems in health care: A new approach to user-interface and interaction design. *Journal of Biomedical Informatics, 42*, 347–355. doi:10.1016/j.jbi.2008.10.005

Heylighen, F. (1995). *(Meta)systems as constraints on variation-A classification and natural history of meta-system transitions*. Retrieved from http://pespmc1.vub.ac.be/ Papers/MST-ConVar.pdf

Hierons, R. M., Bogdanov, K., Bowen, J. P., Cleaveland, R., Derrick, J., & Dick, J. (2009). Using formal specifications to support testing. *ACM Computing Surveys, 41*(2), 1–76. doi:10.1145/1459352.1459354

Higgins, J., & Johns, T. (1984). *Computers in language learning*. London, UK: Collins.

Hirose, M., & Yokoyama, K. (1997). Synthesis and transmission of realistic sensation using virtual reality technology. *Transactions of the Society of Instrument and Control Engineers, 33*(7), 716–722.

Hirumi, A. (2002). A framework for analyzing, designing, and sequencing planned e-learning interactions. *The Quarterly Review of Distance Education, 3*(2), 141–160.

Hock Soon, S., & Sourin, A. (2004). Guest editor's introduction. *Computers & Graphics, 28*(4), 465–466. doi:10.1016/j.cag.2004.04.001

Hof, R. (2006, 1 May). My virtual life. Business Week. Retrieved October 19, 2009, from http://www.businessweek.com/ magazine/content/06_18/b3982001.htm

Hoff, T. (2008, April). Learning in the 21st century: A brave new world. *CLO Magazine*.

Hoffman, R., & Krauss, K. (2004). A critical evaluation of literature on visual aesthetics for the Web. In *Proceedings of the 2004 Annual Research Conference of the South African Institute of Computer Scientists and Information Technologists on IT Research in Developing Countries, 4-6th October, Stellenbosch* (pp. 205-209). South Africa: ACM International Conference Proceeding Series. (Online). Retrieved from http://portal.acm.org/ citation.cfm?Id=1035053.1035077

Hogg, M. K., & Michell, P. C. N. (1996). Identity, self and consumption: A conceptual framework. *Journal of Marketing Management, 12*(7), 629–644. doi:10.1080/0267257X.1996.9964441

Hollerbach, J. M., Mills, R., Tristano, D., Christensen, R. R., Thompson, W. B., & Xu, Y. (2001). Torso force feedback realistically simulates slope on treadmill-style locomotion interfaces. *The International Journal of Robotics Research, 20*, 939–952. doi:10.1177/02783640122068209

Hollerbach, J. M. (2002). Locomotion interfaces. In Stanney, K. M. (Ed.), *Handbook of virtual environments technology* (pp. 239–254). Lawrence Erlbaum Associates, Inc.

Hollerbach, J. M., Checcacci, D., Noma, H., Yanaida, Y., & Tetsutani, N. (2003). Simulating side slopes on locomotion interfaces using torso forces. *Proc. of 11th Haptic Interfaces for Virtual Environment and Teleoperator Systems*, (pp. 247-253).

Hollerbach, J. M., Xu, Y., Christensen, R., & Jacobsen, S. C. (2000). Design specifications for the second generation Sarcos Treadport locomotion interface. *Haptics Symposium, Proc. ASME Dynamic Systems and Control Division, DSC-Vol. 69-2*, Orlando, Nov. 5-10, 2000, (pp. 1293-1298).

Hollins, M. (1989). Blindness and cognition. In *Understanding blindness: An integrative approach*. Lawrence Erlbaum Associates.

Hone, K. S., & Baber, C. (2001). Designing habitable dialogues for speech-based interaction with computers. *International Journal of Human-Computer Studies, 54*(4), 637–662. doi:10.1006/ijhc.2000.0456

Hook, K. (2008). Knowing, communicating, and experiencing through body and emotion. *IEEE Transactions on Learning Technologies, 1*(4).

Hsia, T.-L., & Wu, J.-H. (2008). The e-commerce value matrix and use case model: A goal-driven methodology for eliciting B2C application requirements. *Information & Management*, *45*(5), 321–330. doi:10.1016/j.im.2008.04.001

Hsu, M. H. (2008). A personalized English learning recommender system for ESL students. *Expert Systems with Applications*, *34*(1), 683–688. doi:10.1016/j.eswa.2006.10.004

Hua, H., Brown, L. D., Gao, C., & Ahuja, N. (2003). A new collaborative infrastructure: Scape. In *Proceedings of the IEEE International Symposium on Virtual Reality*, (pp. 171–179). Los Angeles, CA: IEEE Computer Society.

Huba, M., & Freed, J. (2005). *Learner-centered assessment on college campuses: Shifting the focus from teaching to learning*. Needham Heights, MA: Allyn and Bacon.

Hunt, K. A., & Bashaw, R. E. (1999). A new classification of sales resistance. *Industrial Marketing Management*, *28*(1), 109–118. doi:10.1016/S0019-8501(97)00098-9

Hutcheon, S. (2007, 24 August). IBM expands virtual world presence. *The Age*.

IBM's Institute for Business Value. (2007). *Leadership in a distributed world: Lessons from online gaming.*

IEEE. (2009). *IEEE islands in Second Life*. Retrieved on May 3, 2009, from http://www.ieee.org/web/volunteers/tab/secondlife/index.html

Ingraham, B. D. (2000). Scholarly rhetoric in digital media: Post-modernism. *Journal of Interactive Media in Education (JIME)*. Retrieved on 30th July, 2008, from http://jime.open.ac.uk/00/ ingraham/ingraham.pdf

ION (Illinois Online Network and the Board of Trustees of the University of Illinois). (2003). *Alternatives to the online lecture*. Retrieved from http://illinois.online.uillinois.edu/ IONresources/instructionaldesign/ alternative.html

Isdale, J., Daly, L., Fencott, C., & Heim, M. (2002). Content development for virtual environments. In K. M. Stanney, (Ed.), *Handbook of virtual environments: Design, implementation and applications* (pp. 519-532). Lawrence Erlbaum Associates. Retrieved from http://vr.isdale.com/vrtechreviews/ vrcontentdev/content-dev4ve_FINALDRAFT.doc

Iwata, H. (1999). The Torus treadmill: Realizing locomotion in VEs. *IEEE Computer Graphics and Applications*, *19*(6), 30–35. doi:10.1109/38.799737

Iwata, H., Yano, H., Fukushima, H., & Noma, H. (2005). CirculaFloor. *IEEE Computer Graphics and Applications*, *25*(1), 64–67. doi:10.1109/MCG.2005.5

Iwata, H., & Yoshida, Y. (1999). Path reproduction tests using a Torus treadmill. *Presence (Cambridge, Mass.)*, *8*(6), 587–597. doi:10.1162/105474699566503

Iwata, H., & Fujji, T. (1996). Virtual preambulator: A novel interface device for locomotion in virtual environment. *Proc. of IEEE VRAIS'96*, (pp. 60-65).

Iwata, H., & Yoshida, Y. (1997). Virtual walk through simulator with infinite plane. *Proc. of 2nd VRSJ Annual Conference*, (pp. 254-257).

Iwata, H., Yano, H., & Tomioka, H. (2006). Powered shoes. *SIGGRAPH 2006 Conference DVD* (2006).

Iwata, H., Yano, H., & Tomiyoshi, M. (2007). *String walker*. Paper presented at SIGGRAPH 2007.

Iyer, R., & Muncy, J. A. (2009). Purpose and object of anti consumption. *Journal of Business Research*, *62*(2), 160–168. doi:10.1016/j.jbusres.2008.01.023

Jacob, R., Leggett, J., Myers, B., & Pausch, R. (1993). An agenda for human-computer interaction research: Interaction styles and input/output devices. *Behaviour & Information Technology*, *12*(2), 69–79. doi:10.1080/01449299308924369

Jacob, R., Sibert, L., McFarlane, D., & Mullen, P. Jr. (1994). Integrality and separability of input devices. *ACM Transactions on Computer-Human Interaction*, *1*(1), 3–26. doi:10.1145/174630.174631

Jacobson, B. (2000). Experience design. *A List Apart: Online Magazine*. Retrieved from http://alistapart.com/articles/experience

Jana, R. (2006, June 27). American Apparel's virtual clothes. *Business Week Online*.

Jara, C. A., & Candelas, F. A. (2009). Real-time collaboration of virtual laboratories through the Internet. *Computers & Education*, *52*(1), 126–140. doi:10.1016/j.compedu.2008.07.007

Jarmon, L., & Traphagan, T. (2009). Virtual world teaching, experiential learning, and assessment: An interdisciplinary communication course in Second Life. *Computers & Education*, *53*(1), 169–182. doi:10.1016/j.compedu.2009.01.010

Jarzabkowski, P., Balogun, J., & Seidl, D. (2007). Strategizing: the challenges of practice perspective. *Human Relations*, *60*(1), 5–27. doi:10.1177/0018726707075703

Jelley, R. B. (2007). *Police management job analysis and leadership needs assessment.* Unpublished manuscript, Ontario, CA.

Jia, W., & Zhou, W. (2005). *Distributed network systems* (*Vol. 15*, pp. 1–13). Springer, US. doi:10.1007/0-387-23840-9_1

Johns Hopkins Bloomberg School of Public Health. (n.d.). *About the program.* Retrieved from http://www.jhsph.edu/dept/hpm/certificates/ informatics/whatis.html

Johnson, P. (1992). *Human computer interaction- Psychology, task analysis and software engineering.* Mcgraw-Hill Book Company Europe.

Jonassen, D. H., Tessmer, M., & Hannum, W. H. (1999). *Task analysis methods for instructional design.* Mawah, NJ: Lawrence Earlbaum & Associates.

Jonassen, D. (1991). Evaluating constructivistic learning. *Educational Technology*, *31*(10), 28–33.

Jonassen, D. (2000). Toward a meta-theory of problem solving. *Educational Technology Research and Development*, *48*(4), 63–85. doi:10.1007/BF02300500

Jonassen, D. H., & Land, S. M. (2000). *Theoretical foundations of learning environments.* Mahwah, NJ: Lawrence Erlbaum Associates.

Jones, D. M., Hapeshi, K., & Frankish, C. R. (1989). Design guidelines for speech recognition interfaces. *Applied Ergonomics*, *20*(1), 47–52. doi:10.1016/0003-6870(89)90009-4

Jones, J. G., & Bronack, S. C. (2007). Rethinking cognition, representations, and processes in 3D online social learning environments. In Gibson, D., Aldrich, C., & Prensky, M. (Eds.), *Games and simulations in online learning: Research and development frameworks*. Hershey, PA: Information Science Publishing. doi:10.4018/9781599047980.ch010

Jones, M. G., & Farquhar, J. D. (1997). User interface design for Web-based instruction. In Khan, B. H. (Ed.), *Web-based instruction* (pp. 239–244). Englewood Cliffs, NJ: Educational Technology Publications.

Jones, D. M., Hapeshi, K., & Frankish, C. R. (1987). Human factors and the problems of evaluation in the design of speech systems interfaces. In D. Diaper & R. Winder (Eds.), *People and Computers III. Proceedings of the 3rd Conference of the British Computer Society Human-Computer Interaction Special Group*, (pp. 41-49). Cambridge, UK: Cambridge University Press.

Joshi, A., Arora, M., Dai, L., Price, K., Vizer, L., & Sears, A. (2009). Usability of a patient education and motivation tool using heuristic evaluation. *Journal of Medical Internet Research*, *11*(4). doi:10.2196/jmir.1244

Kalantzis, M., & Cope, B. (2008). *New learning: Elements of a science of education.* Port Melbourne, Canada: Cambridge University Press.

Kalawsky, R. S. (1993). *The science of virtual reality and virtual environments.* Addison-Wesley Publishers.

Kalawsky. R. (1996). *Exploiting virtual reality techniques in education and training: Technological issues.* Prepared for AGOCG. Advanced VR Research Centre: Loughborough University.

Kalyuga, S., Chandler, P., & Sweller, J. (2000). Incorporating learner experience into the design of multimedia instruction. *Journal of Educational Psychology*, *92*, 126–136. doi:10.1037/0022-0663.92.1.126

Kan, H. Y., & Duffy, V. G. (2001). An Internet virtual reality collaborative environment for effective product design. *Computers in Industry*, *45*(2), 197–213. doi:10.1016/S0166-3615(01)00093-8

Kao, D., Tousignant, W., & Wiebe, N. (2000). A paradigm for selecting an institutional software. In D. Colton, J. Caouette, & B. Raggad (Eds.), *Proceedings ISECON 2000, v 17* (p. 207). Philadelphia, PA: AITP Foundation for Information Technology Education.

Kaput, J. (1991). Notations and representations as mediators of constructive processes. In von Glasersfeld, E. (Ed.), *Radical constructivism in mathematics education* (pp. 53–74). Boston, MA: Kluwer Academic. doi:10.1007/0-306-47201-5_3

Karat, J., & Karat, C. M. (2003). The evolution of user-centred focus in the human-computer interaction field. *IBM Systems Journal, 42*(4). Retrieved from http://www.research.ibm.com/journal/sj/424/karat.html. doi:10.1147/sj.424.0532

Karlsson, D., Eles, P., & Peng, Z. (2007). Formal verification of component-based designs. *Design Automation for Embedded Systems, 11*(1), 49–90. doi:10.1007/s10617-006-9723-3

Keegan, D. (1986). *The foundations of distance education.* London, UK: Croom Helm.

Kesdogan, D., & Palmer, C. (2006). Technical challenges of network anonymity. *Computer Communications, 29*(3), 306–324. doi:10.1016/j.comcom.2004.12.011

Khan, B. H. (2005). *Managing e-learning: Design, delivery, implementation and evaluation.* Hershey, PA: Information Science Publishing. doi:10.4018/978-1-59140-634-1

Khan, B. H. (2005a). *E-learning Quick checklist.* Hershey, PA: Information Science Publishing.

Khan, B. H. (Ed.). (2007). *Flexible learning in an information society.* Hershey, PA: Information Science Publishing.

Khan, J. I., & Wierzbicki, A. (2008). Guest editors' introduction: Foundation of peer-to-peer computing. *Computer Communications, 31*(2), 187–189. doi:10.1016/j.comcom.2007.10.038

Khan, B. H. (Ed.). (2001). *Web-based training.* Englewood Cliffs, NJ: Educational Technology Publications.

Khan, B. H. (2005). *Managing e-learning: Design, delivery, implementation and evaluation.* Hershey, PA: Information Science Publishing. doi:10.4018/978-1-59140-634-1

Khan, B. (2005). *E-Learning quick checklist.* Information Science Publication.

Khan, B. (2005). *Managing e-learning strategies: Design, delivery, implementation and evaluation.* Information Science Publication. doi:10.4018/978-1-59140-634-1

Khan, B. (2006). *Flexible e-learning in an information society.* Information Science Publication. doi:10.4018/978-1-59904-325-8

Khan, B. H. (2005). *Managing e-learning: Design, delivery, implementation and evaluation.* Hershey, PA: Information Science Publishing. doi:10.4018/978-1-59140-634-1

Khan, B. H. (Ed.). (2007). *Flexible learning in an information society.* Hershey, PA: Information Science Publishing.

Khan, B. (2005). *Managing e-learning strategies.* Hershey, PA: Information Science Publishing. doi:10.4018/978-1-59140-634-1

Khan, B. H., Cataldo, L., Bennett, R., & Paratore, S. (2007). Obstacles encountered during e-learning. In Khan, B. H. (Ed.), *Flexible learning in an information society* (pp. 307–320). Hershey, PA: Information Science Publishing.

Khan, B. H., & Ealy, D. (2001). A framework for web-based authoring systems. In Khan, B. H. (Ed.), *Web-based training* (pp. 355–364). Englewood Cliffs, NJ: Educational Technology Publications.

Khan, B. H., & Smith, H. L. (2007). A program satisfaction survey instrument for online students. In Khan, B. H. (Ed.), *Flexible learning in an information society* (pp. 321–338). Hershey, PA: Information Science Publishing. doi:10.4018/9781599043258.ch030

Khan, B. H., & Vega, R. (1997). Factors to consider when evaluating a Web-based instruction course: A survey. In Khan, B. H. (Ed.), *Web-based instruction* (pp. 375–380). Englewood Cliffs, NJ: Educational Technology Publications.

Khan, B. H., Waddill, D., & McDonald, J. (2001). Review of Web-based training sites. In Khan, B. H. (Ed.), *Web-based training* (pp. 367–374). Englewood Cliffs, NJ: Educational Technology Publications.

Khan, B. H. (2003). Do we fit in the virtual education plan? *Daily Star, 4*(206). Retrieved November 23, 2010, from http://www.thedailystar.net/2003/12/24/d312241601108.htm

Kierkegaard, S. (2008). Cybering, online grooming and ageplay. *Computer Law & Security Report, 24*(1), 41–55. doi:10.1016/j.clsr.2007.11.004

Kierkegaard, S. M. (2006). Here comes the cybernators! *Computer Law & Security Report, 22*(5), 381–391. doi:10.1016/j.clsr.2006.07.005

Kim, H. M., Lyons, K., & Cunningham, M. A. (2008). Towards a theoretically-grounded framework for evaluating immersive business models and applications: Analysis of ventures in Second Life. *Journal of Virtual Worlds Research, 1*(1).

Kimura, T., & Kanda, Y. (2005). Development of a remote monitoring system for a manufacturing support system for small and medium-sized enterprises. *Computers in Industry, 56*(1), 3–12. doi:10.1016/j.compind.2004.11.001

Kindberg, T., & Barton, J. (2001). A Web-based nomadic computing system. *Computer Networks, 35*(4), 443–456. doi:10.1016/S1389-1286(00)00181-X

Kirriemuir, J. (2008). Second Life in higher education, medicine and health. *Health Information in the Internet, 64*(1), 6–8. Retrieved September 21, 2010, from http://hii.rsmjournals.com/cgi/content/abstract/64/1/6

Kirwan, B., & Ainsworth, L. K. (1993). *A guide to task analysis*. London, UK: Taylor & Francis.

Kish, S. (2007). *Second Life: Virtual worlds and the enterprise*. Retrieved September 21, 2010, from http://www.susankish.com/ susan_kish/vw_secondlife.htm

Kizlik, B. (2003.) *Definitions of behavioral verbs for learning objectives*. Retrieved from http://www.adprima.com/ verbs.htm

Kizlik, B. (2010). *Definitions of behavioral verbs for learning objectives.* Retrieved July 13, 2010, from http://www.adprima.com/ verbs.htm

Kleij, R. d., & Jong, A. D. (2009). Network-aware support for mobile distributed teams. *Computers in Human Behavior, 25*(4), 940–948. doi:10.1016/j.chb.2009.04.001

Klein, L. R. (2003). Creating virtual product experiences: The role of telepresence. *Journal of Interactive Marketing, 17*(1), 41–55. doi:10.1002/dir.10046

Knapper, C. (1988). Lifelong learning and distance education. *American Journal of Distance Education, 2*(1), 63–72. doi:10.1080/08923648809526609

Knights, D., & McCabe, D. (2000). Ain't misbehavin? Opportunities for resistance under new forms of quality management. *Sociology, 34*(3), 421–436.

Kock, N. (2008). E-collaboration and e-commerce in virtual worlds: The potential of Second Life and World of Warcraft. *International Journal of e-Collaboration, 4*(3), 1–13. doi:10.4018/jec.2008070101

Koestler, A. (1978). Janus – A summing up, (pp. 131–133). Tiptree, Essex, UK: The Anchor Press Ltd.

Kolb, D. A. (1984). *Experiential learning: Experience as the source of learning and development*. Englewood Cliffs, NJ: Prentice-Hall.

Komosinski, M. (2000). The world of framsticks: Simulation, evolution, interaction. *Proceedings of 2nd International Conference on Virtual Worlds*, Paris, France, July 2000, Springer-Verlag

Korytkowski, P., & Sikora, K. (2007). Creating learning objects and learning sequence on the basis of semantic networks. In R. Wagner, N. Revell, and G. Pernul (Eds). *Lecture Notes in Computer Science Volume 4653/2007, Database and Expert Systems Applications*, (p. 713). Berlin, Germany: Springer.

Kosala, R., & Blockeel, H. (2000). Web mining research: A survey. *SIGKDD Explorations, 2*(1), 1–15. doi:10.1145/360402.360406

Kotha, S., & Rajgopal, S. (2001). Reputation building and performance: An empirical analysis of the top-50 pure Internet firms. *European Management Journal, 19*(6), 571–586. doi:10.1016/S0263-2373(01)00083-4

Koulopoulos, T., & Frappaolo, C. (2000). *Smart things to know about knowledge management*. Padstow, UK: T. J. International Ltd.

Koutrika, G., Ikeda, R., Bercovitz, B., & Garcia-Molina, H. (2008). Flexible recommendations over rich data. In *Proceedings of the 2008 ACM Conference on Recommender Systems* (RecSys'08), (pp. 203-210). Lausanne, Switzerland, 2008.

Kozinets, R. V., & Handelman, J. M. (2004). Adversaries of consumption: Consumer movements, activism, and ideology. *The Journal of Consumer Research, 31*(3), 691–704. doi:10.1086/425104

Kozlowski, S. W. J., & DeShon, R. P. (2004). A psychological fidelity approach to simulation-based training: Theory, research, and principles. In Schiflett, S. G., Elliott, L. R., Salas, E., & Coovert, M. D. (Eds.), *Scaled worlds: Development, validation, and applications*. Burlington, VT: Ashgate.

Kozlowski, S. W. J., & DeShon, R. P. (1999, June). *TEAM-Sim: Examining the development of basic, strategic, and adaptive performance*.

Krug, S. (2006). *Don't make me think: A common sense approach to Web usability*. Berkeley, CA: New Riders.

Ksristofic, A. (2005). Recommender system for adaptive hypermedia applications. In *Proceeding of Informatics and Information Technology Student Research Conference*, Bratislava, (pp. 229-234).

Kuchi, R., Gardner, R., & Tipton, R. (2003). *A learning framework for information literacy and library instruction programs at Rutgers University Libraries. Recommendations of the Learning Framework Study Group*. Rutgers University Libraries.

Kulm, G., Capraro, R. M., & Capraro, M. M. (2007). Teaching and learning middle grades mathematics with understanding. *Middle Grades Research Journal*, *2*, 23–48.

Kumar, U., Kumar, V., Dutta, S., & Fantazy, K. (2007). State sponsored large scale technology transfer projects in a developing country context. [Springer.]. *The Journal of Technology Transfer*, *32*(6), 629–644. doi:10.1007/s10961-006-8880-7

Lahav, O., & Mioduser, D. (2003). A blind person's cognitive mapping of new spaces using a haptic virtual environment. *Journal of Research in Special Educational Needs*, *3*(3), 172–177. doi:10.1111/1471-3802.00012

Laurillard, D. (1993). *Rethinking university teaching: A framework for the effective use of educational technology* (p. 268). London, UK: Routledge.

Laurillard, D. (2002). *Rethinking university teaching. A conversational framework for the effective use of learning technologies*. New York, NY: Routledge. doi:10.4324/9780203304846

Lavie, T., & Tractinsky, N. (2004). Assessing dimensions of perceived visual aesthetics of web sites. *International Journal of Human-Computer Studies*, *60*, 269–298. Retrieved from http://www.ise.bgu.ac.il/faculty/ noam/ papers/04_tl_nt_ijhcs.pdf#search=%22lavie% 2C%20 visual%20aesthetics%20of%20web%20sites%22. doi:10.1016/j.ijhcs.2003.09.002

Lawrence, R. D., Almasi, G. S., Kotlyar, V., Viveros, M. S., & Duri, S. (2001). Personalization of supermarket product recommendations. *Data Mining and Knowledge Discovery*, *5*, 11–32. doi:10.1023/A:1009835726774

Lazarus, R. S., & Folkman, S. (1984). *Stress, appraisal, and coping*. New York, NY: Springer.

Lea, W. A. (1980). The value of speech recognition systems. In Lea, W. A. (Ed.), *Trends in speech recognition* (pp. 3–18). Prentice Hall, USA.

Leacock, T. L., & Nesbit, J. C. (2007). A framework for evaluating the quality of multimedia learning resources. *Journal of Educational Technology & Society*, *10*(2), 44–59.

Leahy, W., Chandler, P., & Sweller, J. (2003). When auditory presentations should and should not be a component of multimedia instruction. *Applied Cognitive Psychology*, *17*, 401–418. doi:10.1002/acp.877

Lee, Y., & Kozar, K. A. (2009). Avatar e-mail versus traditional e-mail: Perceptual difference and media selection difference. *Decision Support Systems*, *46*(2), 451–467. doi:10.1016/j.dss.2007.11.008

Lee, M. S. W., Fernadez, K. V., & Hyman, M. R. (2009a). Anti-consumption: An overview and research agenda. *Journal of Business Research*, *62*, 145–147. doi:10.1016/j.jbusres.2008.01.021

Lee, M. S. W., Motion, J., & Conroy, D. (2009b). Anti-consumption and brand avoidance. *Journal of Business Research*, *62*, 169–180. doi:10.1016/j.jbusres.2008.01.024

Lee, N., & Cadogan, J. W. (2009). Sales force social exchange in problem resolution situations. *Industrial Marketing Management*, *32*(3), 355–372. doi:10.1016/j.indmarman.2008.02.002

Lee, J. J. (2007). Emotion and sense of telepresence: The effects of screen viewpoint, self-transcendence style, and NPC in a 3D game environment. In *Human Computer Interaction (Intelligent Multimodal interaction Environments)* '07. 22-27 July, Beijing, China (pp. 392-399). Heidelberg, Germany: Springer.

Lehdonvirta, V. (2005). Real-money trade of virtual assets: New strategies for virtual world operators. *Proceedings of Future Play*, Michigan State University, 2005.

Lesh, R. (1999). The development of representational abilities in middle school mathematics. In Sigel, I. E. (Ed.), *Development of mental representation: Theories and applications* (pp. 323–350). Mahwah, NJ: Erlbaum.

Levin, E., Pieraccini, R., & Eckert, W. (1998). *Using Markov decision process for learning dialogue strategies*. Acoustics, Speech and Signal Processing. Retrieved from http://ieeexplore.ieee.org/xpl/ freeabs_all.jsp?arnumber=674402

Li, H. R., Daugherty, T., & Biocca, F. (2002). Impact of 3-D advertising on product knowledge, brand attitude, and purchase intention: The mediating role of presence. *Journal of Advertising, 31*(3), 43–57.

Li, J. R., & Khoo, L. P. (2003). Desktop virtual reality for maintenance training: An object oriented prototype system (V-REALISM). *Computers in Industry, 52*(2), 109–125. doi:10.1016/S0166-3615(03)00103-9

Li, X., & Chang, S. (2005). A personalized e-learning system based on user profile constructed using information fusion. *DMS, 2005*, 109–114.

Liber, O. (2004). Cybernetics: E-learning and the educations system. *International Journal of Learning Technology, 1*(1), 135. doi:10.1504/IJLT.2004.003686

Ling, R. (2008). *New tech new ties*. Cambridge, MA: MIT Press.

Liu, C., & Marchewka, J. T. (2004). Beyond concern: A privacy-trust-behavioral intention model of electronic commerce. *Information & Management, 42*(1), 127–142. doi:10.1016/j.im.2004.01.002

Livingstone, D., Kemp, J., & Edgar, E. (2008). From multi-user virtual environment to 3D virtual learning environment. *Association for Learning Technology Journal, 16*(3), 139–150. doi:10.1080/09687760802526707

Lizarraga, M. L., Villanueva, O. A., & Baquedano, M. T. (2011). Self–regulation of learning supported by Web 2.0 Tools: An example of raising competence on creativity and innovations. In Dettori, G., & Persico, D. (Eds.), *Fostering self – regulated learning through ICT* (pp. 295–315). New York, NY: Information Science Reference.

Lo, S.-K. (2008). The impact of online game character's outward attractiveness and social status on interpersonal attraction. *Computers in Human Behavior, 24*(5), 1947–1958. doi:10.1016/j.chb.2007.08.001

Lohr, L. (2000). Designing the instructional interface. *Computers in Human Behavior, 16*(2), 161–182. doi:10.1016/S0747-5632(99)00057-6

Lohr, L., Falvo, D., Hunt, E., & Johnson, B. (2007). Improving the usability of web learning through template modification. In Khan, B. (Ed.), *Flexible learning* (pp. 186–197). Educational Technology Publications.

Lorenoz, G., & Ittelson, J. (2005). *An overview of e-portfolios*. The EDUCAUSE Learning Initiative, July 2005. Retrieved on December 2, 2008, from http://connect.educause.edu/ library/abstract/ AnOverviewofEPortfol/39335

Löwgren, J., & Stolterman, E. (2004). *Thoughtful interaction design – A design perspective on Information Technology*. USA: MIT Press.

Lui, T.-W., Piccoli, G., & Ives, B. (2007). Marketing strategies in virtual worlds. *The DataBase for Advances in Information Systems, 38*(4), 77–80.

Lund, A., & Waterworth, J. A. (1998). *Experiential design: Reflecting embodiment at the human-computer interface*. Retrieved from http://www.informatik.umu.se/ ~jwworth/ metadesign.html

Lynch, K. (1960). *The image of the city*. Cambridge, MA: MIT Press.

MacInnes, I. (2004a). Dynamic business model framework for emerging technologies. *International Journal of Services Technology and Management, 6*(1), 3–19. doi:10.1504/IJSTM.2005.006541

MacInnes, I. (2004b). *The implications of property rights in virtual worlds*. Paper presented at the Americas Conference on Information Systems, New York, NY. August 6–8.

Maes, A., Van Geel, A., & Cozijn, R. (2006). Signposts on the digital highway. The effect of semantic and pragmatic hyperlink previews. *Interacting with Computers, 18*, 265–282. doi:10.1016/j.intcom.2005.05.004

Maes, P. (1995). Artificial life meets entertainment: Interacting with lifelike autonomous agents. In *Communications of the ACM: Special Issue on New Horizons of Commercial and Industrial AI, 38*(11), 108-114. ACM Press.

Magee, B. (1997). The philosophy of Schopenhauer. In *Schopenhauer 1788-1860* (On the Fourfold root of the principle of sufficient reason, 1814 -15), (p. 6). Oxford, UK: Clarendon Press: Manzini, E., & Cau, P. (1989). *The material of invention*, (p. 17). Cambridge, MA: MIT Press.

Mahmoudi, M. T., & Badie, K. (2004). *Content determination for composite concepts via combining attributes' values of individual frames* (pp. 211–215). IKE.

Mahmoudi, M. T., Badie, K., Kharrat, M., Babazadeh Khamaneh, S., & Yadollahi Khales, M. (2008). *Content personalization in organizations via composing a source content model with user model* (pp. 943–949). IC-AI.

Mania, K., & Robinson, A. (2005). An experimental exploration of the relationship between subjective impressions of illumination and physical fidelity. *Computers & Graphics, 29*(1), 49–56. doi:10.1016/j.cag.2004.11.007

Mania, K., Badariah, S., Coxon, M., & Watten, P. (2010). Cognitive transfer of spatial awareness states from immersive virtual environments to reality. *ACM Transactions on Applied Perception, 7*, 1–14. doi:10.1145/1670671.1670673

Marcelle, G. (2004). *Technological learning: A strategic imperative for firms in the developing world*. Cheltenham, UK: Edward Elgar.

Margery, D., Arnaldi, B., & Plouzeau, N. (1999). A general framework for cooperative manipulation in virtual environments. In *Virtual Environments '99: Proceedings of the Eurographics Workshop* (pp. 169–178).

Markellou, P., Mousourouli, I., Spiros, S., & Tsakalidis, A. (2005). Using Semantic Web mining technologies for personalized e-learning experiences. *Web-Based Education Conference*, Grindelwald, Switzerland (pp. 461-826).

Marois, R. (2005). Capacity limits of information processing in the brain. *Phi Kappa Phi, 85*, 30–33.

Marois, R., & Ivanoff, J. (2005). Capacity limits of information processing in the brain. *Trends in Cognitive Sciences, 9*, 296–305. doi:10.1016/j.tics.2005.04.010

Marsh, T., Wright, P., & Smith, S. (2001). Evaluation for the design of experience in virtual environments: Modelling breakdown of interaction and illusion. *Journal of Cyberpsychology and Behavior, 4*(2), 225–238. Retrieved from http://www.cs.york.ac.uk/hci/inquisitive/ papers/cyberpsy01/cyberpsy01.pdf. doi:10.1089/109493101300117910

Marsh, T., & Wright, P. (2000). *Maintaining the illusion of interacting within a 3D virtual space*. In Presence 2000, 27-28th March, Delft, Netherlands. (Online). Retrieved from http://www.cs.york.ac.uk/hci/inquisitive/ papers/presence00/marsh wright00.pdf

Martin, D., Cheyer, A., & Moran, D. (1999). The open agent architecture: A framework for building distributed software systems. *Applied Artificial Intelligence, 13*(1/2), 91–128. doi:10.1080/088395199117504

Martin, S., & Vallance, M. (2008). The impact of synchronous inter-networked teacher training in Information and Communication Technology integration. *Computers & Education, 51*, 34–53. doi:10.1016/j.compedu.2007.04.001

Martin, S., Vallance, M., van Schaik, P., & Wiz, C. (2010). Learning spaces, tasks and metrics for effective communication in Second Life within the context of programming LEGO NXT MindstormsTM robots: towards a framework for design and implementation. *Journal of Virtual Worlds Research, 3*(1).

Matters, Q. (n.d.). *Program FAQ*. Retrieved from http://www.qmprogram.org/faq

Mayer, R. E., & Moreno, R. (1998). A split-attention effect in multimedia learning: Evidence for dual processing systems in working memory. *Journal of Educational Psychology, 90*, 312–320. doi:10.1037/0022-0663.90.2.312

Mayer, R. E., Fennell, S., Farmer, L., & Campbell, J. (2004). A personalization effect in multimedia learning: Students learn better when words are in conversational style rather than formal style. *Journal of Educational Psychology, 96*(2), 389–395. doi:10.1037/0022-0663.96.2.389

Mayer, R. E., & Massa, L. J. (2003). Three facets of visual and verbal learners: Cognitive ability, cognitive style, and learning preference. *Journal of Educational Psychology, 95*(4), 833–846. doi:10.1037/0022-0663.95.4.833

Mayer, R. E. (2005). Principles for reducing extraneous processing in multi-media learning: Coherence, signaling, redundancy, spatial contiguity, and temporal contiguity. In Mayer, R. E. (Ed.), *The Cambridge handbook of multimedia learning* (pp. 183–200). New York, NY: Cambridge University Press.

McAllister, D. J. (1995). Affect-and cognition-based trust as foundations for interpersonal cooperation in organizations. *Academy of Management Journal, 38*(1), 24–59. doi:10.2307/256727

McCalla, G. (2004). The ecological approach to the design of e-learning environments: Purpose-based capture and use of information about learners. *Journal of Interactive Media in Education: Special Issue on the Educational Semantic Web, 7*. Retrieved 15th November, 2007, from http://www-jime.open.ac.uk/ 2004/7

Mccarthy, J., & Wright, P. (2004). *Technology as experience*. Massachusetts: MIT Press.

McCormick, E. J., Jeanneret, P. R., & Mecham, R. C. (1989). *Position analysis questionnaire*. Logan, UT: PAQ Services, Inc.

Medina, E., Fruland, R., & Weghorst, S. (2008). Virtusphere: Walking in a human size VR hamster ball. In *Proceedings of the Human Factors and Ergonomics Society 52nd Annual Meeting* (pp. 2102-2106). New York, NY: HFES.

Megarry, J. (1989). Hypertext and compact discs: The challenge of multimedia learning. In Bell, C., Davies, J., & Winders, R. (Eds.), *Promoting Learning: Aspects of Educational and Training Technology XXII* (p. 50). London, UK: Kogan Page.

Mello, R. (2002, June). 100 pounds of potatoes in a 25-pound sack: Stress, frustration, and learning in the virtual classroom. *Teaching With Technology Today, 8*(9). Retrieved February, 2004, from http://www.uwsa.edu/ttt/articles/mello.htm

Mellor, B. M. (1996). *Options for the evaluation of speech technology in armoured vehicles*. (DRA Report: DRA/CIS(SE1)/377/01/04/AFV/V1.0).

Mendizza, M. (2004). *Love of the game: Applying what athletes call the zone to parenting and education* (p. 5). Retrieved 20th February, 2008, from http://www.rethinkingeducation.com/ Mendizza.pdf

Mendizza, M. (2006). *The next frontier in education*. Retrieved 20th July, 2008, from http://www.dawntalk.com/ NewFiles/Article-Mendizza.html

Mennecke, B. E., Roche, E. M., et al. (2007). *Second Life and other virtual words: A roadmap for research*. Twenty Eighth International Conference on Information Systems, Montreal, Canada.

Merceron, A., & Yacef, K. (2005). Tada-ed for educational data mining. *Interactive Multimedia Electronic Journal of Computer-Enhanced Learning, 7*(1), 267–287.

Mergel, B. (1998). *Instructional design & learning theory*. Retrieved from http://www.usask.ca/education/coursework/802papers/mergel/ brenda.htm#Cognitivism

Merriam, S. (1998). *Qualitative research and case study applications in education*. San Francisco, CA: Jossey-Bass.

Merriam, S. B., & Caffarella, R. S. (1999). *Learning in adulthood: A compressive guide* (2nd ed.). San Francisco, CA: Jossey-Bass.

Merrill, D. C., Reiser, B. J., & Merrill, S. K. (1995). Tutoring: Guided learning by doing. *Cognition and Instruction, 13*, 315–372. doi:10.1207/s1532690xci1303_1

Merrill, D. (2007). A task-centered instructional strategy. *Journal of Research on Technology in Education, 40*(1), 5–22.

Messinger, P. R., & Stroulia, E. (2009). Virtual world - Past, present, and future: New directions in social computing. *Decision Support Systems, 47*, 204–228. doi:10.1016/j.dss.2009.02.014

Messinger, P. R., & Stroulia, E. (2009). Virtual worlds -- Past, present, and future: New directions in social computing. *Decision Support Systems, 47*(3), 204–228. doi:10.1016/j.dss.2009.02.014

Meyer, B., Fiva, A., Ciupa, I., Leitner, A., Wei, Y., & Stapf, E. (2009). Programs that test themselves. *Computer*, *42*(9), 46–55. doi:10.1109/MC.2009.296

Midoro, V. (2005). *A common European framework for teachers' professional profile in ICT for education.* MENABO Didactica.

Miles, M. B., & Huberman, A. M. (1994). *Qualitative data analysis: An expanded sourcebook.* Newbury Park, CA: Sage Publications.

Militello, L. G., & Hutton, R. J. B. (1998). Applied cognitive task analysis (ACTA): A practitioner's toolkit for understanding cognitive task demands. *Ergonomics*, *41*(11), 1618–1641. doi:10.1080/001401398186108

Miller, G. A. (1956). The magical number seven, plus or minus two: Some limits on our capacity for processing information. *Psychological Review*, *63*, 81–97. doi:10.1037/h0043158

Miller, L. C., Jones, B. B., Graves, R. S., & Cullinan Sievert, M. (2010). Merging silos: Collaborating for information literacy. *Journal of Continuing Education in Nursing*, *41*, 267–272. doi:10.3928/00220124-20100401-03

Mingozzi, E., & Stea, G. (2009). EuQoS: End-to-end quality of service over heterogeneous networks. *Computer Communications*, *32*(12), 1355–1370. doi:10.1016/j.comcom.2008.12.013

Mittelstaedt, R. A., Grossbart, S. L., Curtis, W. W., & Devere, S. P. (1976). Optimal stimulation level and the adoption decision process. *The Journal of Consumer Research*, *3*, 84–94. doi:10.1086/208655

Moggridge, B. (1999). Expressing experiences in design. ACM Digital Library. *Interactions*, *6*(4), 17–25. Retrieved from http://delivery.acm.org/10.1145/310000/306430/p17-moggridge.pdf?Key1=306430&key2=5164022611&coll=Portal&dl=GUIDE&CFID=4739955&CFTOKEN=91571747. (30/10/2006).

Mohr, W. (2003). The Wireless World Research Forum--WWRF. *Computer Communications*, *26*(1), 2–10. doi:10.1016/S1403-3664(02)00113-5

Montaner, M., Lopez, B., & Lluis, D. J. (2003). A taxonomy of recommender agents on the Internet. *Artificial Intelligence Review*, *19*(4), 285–330. doi:10.1023/A:1022850703159

Moore, A., Fowler, S., & Watson, C. (2007, September/October). Active learning and technology: Designing change for faculty, students, and institutions. *EDUCAUSE Review*, *42*(5), 42–61.

Moore, M. G. (1989). Three types of interaction. *American Journal of Distance Education*, *3*(2), 1–6. doi:10.1080/08923648909526659

Moore, D. S. (1997). Remapping resistance: Ground for struggle and the politics of place. In Pile, S., & Keith, M. (Eds.), *Geographies of resistance* (pp. 87–106). London, UK: Routledge.

Moore, P. (1998). *Embodying human factors guidelines as pattern languages.* (DERA report: DERA/CHS/MID/WP980104/1.0).

Morales, T. (2002). *Virtual doctors: A growing trend avoid waiting at doctor's office.* Retrieved October 21, 2010, from http://www.cbsnews.com/stories/2002/06/21/earlyshow/saturday/main513017.shtml

Morgan, G., & Marvin, V. Z. (2009). *Highly interactive scalable online worlds. Advances in computers* (Vol. 76, pp. 75–120). Elsevier.

Morse, E. A., & Raval, V. (2008). PCI DSS: Payment card industry data security standards in context. *Computer Law & Security Report*, *24*(6), 540–554. doi:10.1016/j.clsr.2008.07.001

Mott, S. (2000). The second generation of digital commerce solutions. *Computer Networks*, *32*(6), 669–683. doi:10.1016/S1389-1286(00)00024-4

Nadin, M. (1988). *Interface design: A semiotic paradigm.* Retrieved from http://www.cs.ucsd.edu/users/goguen/courses/nadin.pdf

Navarre, D., Bastide, R., Schyn, A., Nedel, L. P., & Freitas, C. M. D. S. (2005). A formal description of multimodal interaction techniques for immersive virtual reality applications. In *INTERACT '05: Proceedings of the Tenth IFIP TC13 International Conference on Human-Computer Interaction* (pp. 170–183). Springer.

Network, I. O. (2003). *Alternatives to the online lecture.* Retrieved July 12, 2010, from http://illinois.online.uillinois.edu/IONresources/instructionaldesign/alternative.html

Newell, A. (1990). *Unified theories of cognition*. Cambridge, MA: Cambridge University Press.

Newman, W. M., & Lamming, M. G. (1995). *Interactive systems design*. Addison Wesley Longman Ltd.

Nguyen, C. D., & Safaei, F. (2006). Optimal assignment of distributed servers to virtual partitions for the provision of immersive voice communication in massively multiplayer games. *Computer Communications*, *29*(9), 1260–1270. doi:10.1016/j.comcom.2005.10.003

Nielsen, J. (1999). *Designing Web usability*. Berkeley, CA: Peachpit Press.

Nielsen, J. (1994). *Usability engineering. Academic Press. Norman, D., & Draper, S. (1986). User centered system design: New perspectives on human-computer interaction.* Hillsdale, NJ: Laurence Erlbaum.

Nielsen, J. (1994). Heuristic evaluation. In Nielsen, J., & Mark, R. L. (Eds.), *Usability inspection method* (pp. 25–62). New York, NY: John Wiley & Sons.

Nielsen, J. (2003). *An introduction to usability*. Retrieved from http://www.useit.com/ alertbox/20030825.html

Nijholt, A. (2008). Google home: Experience, support and re-experience of social home activities. *Information Sciences*, *178*(3), 612–630. doi:10.1016/j.ins.2007.08.026

Nintendo. (2009, January). *Wiimote.* Retrieved from http://www.nintendo.com/ wii/what/controllers/

Noma, H., & Miyasato, T. (1998). Design for locomotion interface in a large scale virtual environment. ATLAS: ATR locomotion interface for active self motion. *ASME-DSC*, *64*, 111–118.

Noma, H., & Miyasato, T. (1999). A new approach for canceling turning motion in the locomotion interface. *ATLAS, ASME-DSC*, *67*, 405–407.

Noma, H., & Miyasato, T. (1998). *Design for locomotion interface in a large scale virtual environment. ATLAS: ATR locomotion interface for active self motion.* 7th Annual Symposium on Haptic Interfaces for Virtual Environment and Teleoperator Systems. The Winter Annual Meeting of the ASME. Anaheim, USA.

Noma, S. Miyasayo, (2000). Development of ground surface simulator for tel-e-merge system. *Proc. of IEEE-Virtual Reality 2000 Conference,* (pp. 217–224).

Norden, S., & Guo, K. (2007). Support for resilient peer-to-peer gaming. *Computer Networks*, *51*(14), 4212–4233. doi:10.1016/j.comnet.2007.05.003

Norman, D. A. (1988). *The psychology of everyday things*. New York, NY: Basic Books.

Norman, D. A. (1993). *Things that make us smart*. Reading, MA: Addison-Wesley.

Normand, V., Babski, C., Benford, S., Bullock, A., Carion, S., & Farcet, N. (1999). The COVEN project - Exploring applicative, technical, and usage dimensions of collaborative virtual environments. *Presence (Cambridge, Mass.)*, *8*(2), 218–236. doi:10.1162/105474699566189

Norris, D., Mason, J., & Lefrere, P. (2004) Experiencing knowledge. *Innovate*, *1*(1). Retrieved November 24, 2009, from http://www.innovateonline.info/ index. php?view=article&id=5

Novak, J. D., & Gowin, D. B. (1984). *Learning how to learn*. Cambridge, UK: Cambridge University Press.

Novak, J. D., Gowin, D. B., & Johanse, G. T. (1983). The use of concept mapping and knowledge Vee mapping with junior high school science students. *Science Education*, *67*, 625–645. doi:10.1002/sce.3730670511

Novak, D., & Carias, A. (2006*). The theory underlying concept maps and how to construct and use them.* Retrieved from http://cmap.ihmc.us/publications/ researchpapers/ theorycmaps/ theoryunderlyinconceptmaps.htm

Noveck, B. (2004). Unchat: Democratic solution for a wired world. In Shane, P. (Ed.), *Democracy online: The prospects for democratic renewal through the Internet* (pp. 21–34). New York, NY: Routledge.

Noyes, J. M. (2001). Talking and writing: How natural is human-machine interaction? *International Journal of Human-Computer Studies*, *55*(4), 503–519. doi:10.1006/ijhc.2001.0485

O'Malley, C., Vavoula, G., Glew, J. P., Taylor, J., Sharples, M., & Lefrere, P. (2003). *Guidelines for learning/teaching/tutoring in a mobile environment*. MOBIlearn Project Report. Retrieved October 1, 2010 from http://www.mobilearn.org/ results/results.htm

O'Sullivan, C., Dingliana, J., Giang, T., & Kaiser, M. K. (2003). Evaluating the visual fidelity of physically based animations. *Proceedings of the Association for Computing Machinery's Special Interest Group on Computer Graphics and Interactive Techniques, 22*, 527–536.

O'Donnell, R., & Eggemeier, F. T. (1986). Workload assessment methodology. In Boff, K. R., Kaufman, L., & Thomas, J. P. (Eds.), *Handbook of perception and human performance*. New York, NY: Wiley.

Olsen, D. R., & Goodrich, M. A. (2003). *Metrics for evaluating human-robot interactions*. Retrieved March 14, 2009, from http://icie.cs.byu.edu/ Papers/RAD.pdf

O'Neill, S. (2005). Comparing compatible semiotic perspectives for the analysis of interactive media devices. *Applied Semiotics: A Learned Journal of Literary Research on the World Wide Web, 6*(16). Retrieved from http://www.Chass.toronto.edu/ french/as-sa/ASSA-No16/ Article1en.html

Ong, S. K., & Mannan, M. A. (2004). Virtual reality simulations and animations in a web-based interactive manufacturing engineering module. *Computers & Education, 43*(4), 361–382. doi:10.1016/j.compedu.2003.12.001

Oreg, S. (2003). Resistance to change: Developing an individual differences measures. *The Journal of Applied Psychology, 88*(4), 680–693. doi:10.1037/0021-9010.88.4.680

Osais, Y., Abdala, S., & Matrawy, A. (2006). A multi-layer peer-to-peer framework for distributed synchronous collaboration. *IEEE Internet Computing, 10*(6), 33–41. doi:10.1109/MIC.2006.115

Paivio, A. (1986). *Mental representations: A dual coding approach*. Oxford, UK: Oxford University Press.

Palmer, M., & O'Kane, P. (2007). Strategy as practice: Interactive governance spaces and the corporate strategies of retail TNCs. *Journal of Economic Geography, 7*, 515–535. doi:10.1093/jeg/lbm015

Palmer, K. D. (2002). *Advanced meta-systems theory for metasystems engineers*. Retrieved from http://holonomic.net/sd01V04.pdf

Palmer, M., Owens, M., & De Kervenoael, R. (2010). Paths of the least resistance: Understanding how motives form in international retail joint venturing. *The Service Industries Journal, 30*(8).

Pang, A., & Wittenbrink, C. (1997). Collaborative 3D Visualization with CSpray. *IEEE Computer Graphics and Applications, 17*(2), 32–41. doi:10.1109/38.574676

Parakh, A., & Kak, S. (2009). Online data storage using implicit security. *Information Sciences, 179*(19), 3323–3331. doi:10.1016/j.ins.2009.05.013

Patrikios, A. (2008). The role of transnational online arbitration in regulating cross-border e-business - Part I. *Computer Law & Security Report, 24*(1), 66–76. doi:10.1016/j.clsr.2007.11.005

Pattison, M., & Stedmon, A. W. (2006). Inclusive design and human factors: Designing mobile phones for older users. In E. L. Waterworth & J. Waterworth (Eds.), *PsychNology: Special issue – Designing Technology to Meet the Needs of the Older User, 4*(3), 267-284.

Pearce, J. (1974). *Exploring the crack in the cosmic egg: Split minds and meta-realities* (p. 194). New York, NY: Washington Square Press.

Peppard, J. (2000). Customer relationship management (CRM) in financial services. *European Management Journal, 18*(3), 312–327. doi:10.1016/S0263-2373(00)00013-X

Pereira, F. C., & Cardoso, A. (2002). Conceptual blending and the quest for the holy creative process. In *Proceedings of the 2nd Workshop on Creative Systems: Approaches to Creativity in AI and Cognitive Science*, ECAI 2002, Lyon, France.

Perry, J. A., & Atkins, S. L. (2002). It's not just notation: Valuing children's representations. *Teaching Children Mathematics, 9*, 196–201.

Petersen, M. G., Iversen, O. S., Krogh, P. G., & Ludvigsen, M. (2004). Aesthetic interaction – A pragmatist's aesthetics of interactive systems. In *Designing Interactive Systems: Processes, Practices, Methods, and Techniques*, 10th March, Cambridge, MA (pp. 269–276). New York, NY: ACM Press. Retrieved from http://www.daimi.au.dk/ ~sejer/Home_files/Aesthetic.pdf

Peterson, E. (2006). Beneath the metadata: Some philosophical problems with folksonomy. *D-Lib Magazine, 12*(11). Retrieved 15th August, 2008, from http://www.dlib.org/dlib/november06/ peterson/11peterson.html

Pettifer, S., Cook, J., Marsh, J., & West, A. (2000) Deva3: Architecture for a large-scale virtual reality system. In *Proceedings of ACM Symposium in Virtual Reality Software and Technology*, (pp. 33–40). ACM Press.

Phan, D. D. (2003). E-business development for competitive advantages: A case study. *Information & Management*, *40*(6), 581–590. doi:10.1016/S0378-7206(02)00089-7

Piacentini, M., & Banister, E. M. (2009). Managing anti-consumption in excessive drinking culture. *Journal of Business Research*, *62*, 279–288. doi:10.1016/j.jbusres.2008.01.035

Piazza, J., & Bering, J. M. (2009). Evolutionary cyberpsychology: Applying an evolutionary framework to Internet behavior. *Computers in Human Behavior*, *25*(6), 1258–1269. doi:10.1016/j.chb.2009.07.002

Pile, S., & Keith, M. (1997). *Geography of resistance*. London, UK: Routledge.

Pimentel, J. R. (1999). Design of net-learning systems based on experiential learning. *Journal of Asynchronous Learning Networks*, *3*(2), 64-90. Retrieved June 11, 2002, from http://www.aln.org/publications/ jaln/v3n2/ v3n2_pimentel.asp

Pizzi, D., Cavazza, M., Whittaker, A., & Lugrin, J. (2008). Automatic generation of game level solutions as storyboards. *Proceedings of the Fourth Artificial Intelligence and Interactive Digital Entertainment Conference.*

Porter, P. (2011). *Effectiveness of electronic textbooks with embedded activities on student learning.* Ph.D. dissertation, Capella University, United States -- Minnesota. Retrieved from Dissertations & Theses: Full Text. (Publication No. AAT 3397091).

Postman, J. (2009). *Social corp: Social media goes corporate*. Berkeley, CA: New Riders.

Pouliquen, M., & Bernard, A. (2007). Virtual hands and virtual reality multimodal platform to design safer industrial systems. *Computers in Industry*, *58*(1), 46–56. doi:10.1016/j.compind.2006.04.001

Poullet, Y. (2009). Data protection legislation: What is at stake for our society and democracy? *Computer Law & Security Report*, *25*(3), 211–226. doi:10.1016/j.clsr.2009.03.008

Poupyrev, I., Weghorst, S., Billinghurst, M., & Ichikawa, T. (1998). Egocentric object manipulation in virtual environments: Evaluation of interaction techniques. *Computer Graphics Forum*, *17*(3), 41–52. doi:10.1111/1467-8659.00252

Prasad, P., & Prasad, A. (2000). Stretching the iron cage: The constitution and implications of routine workplace resistance. *Organization Science*, *11*(4), 387–403. doi:10.1287/orsc.11.4.387.14597

Prastacos, G., & Söderquist, K. (2002). An integrated framework for managing change in the new competitive landscape. *European Management Journal*, *20*(1), 55–71. doi:10.1016/S0263-2373(01)00114-1

Preissle, J., Tesch, R., & LeCompte, M. (1994). *Ethnography and qualitative design in educational research*. Orlando, FL: Academic Press.

Prensky, M. (2010). *Teaching digital natives: Partnering for real learning*. Corwin Press.

Pullen, D. L., & Cole, D. R. (2009). *Multiliteracies and technology enhanced education: Social practice and the global classroom*. Hershey, PA: Information Science Reference. doi:10.4018/978-1-60566-673-0

Qiu, Z. M., & Kok, K. F. (2007). Role-based 3D visualisation for asynchronous PLM collaboration. *Computers in Industry*, *58*(8-9), 747–755. doi:10.1016/j.compind.2007.02.006

Quarles, J., & Lampotang, S. (2009). Scaffolded learning with mixed reality. *Computers & Graphics*, *33*(1), 34–46. doi:10.1016/j.cag.2008.11.005

Quinton, S. (2006). Contextualisation of learning objects to derive meaning. Chapter. In Koohang, A., & Harman, K. (Eds.), *Learning objects: Theory, praxis, issues, and trends* (pp. 113–180). Santa Rosa, CA: Informing Science Press.

Rabbitt, P., & Collins, S. (1989). *Age and design*. Age and Cognitive Performance Research Centre: University of Manchester.

Railean, E. (2010b). *Metasystems approach to research the globalized pedagogical processes. Annals of Spiru Haret University* (pp. 31–50). Mathematics-Informatics Series.

Railean, E. (2008). Aspects of teaching and learning processes in the closed and open didactical systems. *Learning Technology Newsletter, 10*(4).

Railean, E. (2008). Electronic textbooks in electronic portfolio: A new approach for the self-regulated learning. *Proceedings of 9th International Conference on Development and Application Systems,* Suceava (Romania), (pp. 138-141).

Railean, E. (2010a). A new didactical model for modern electronic textbook elaboration. *Proceeding of ICVL 2010 Conference,* (pp. 121-129).

Ravi, J., Yu, Z., & Shi, W. (2009). A survey on dynamic Web content generation and delivery techniques. *Journal of Network and Computer Applications, 32*(5). Elsevier Ltd.

Reeves, L. H., Lai, J., Larson, J. A., Oviatt, S., Balaji, T. S., & Buisine, S. (1994). Guidelines for multimodal user interface design. *Communications of the ACH, 47,* 57–59. doi:10.1145/962081.962106

Reiser, R. A., & Gagné, R. M. (1983). *Selecting media for instruction.* Englewood Cliffs, NJ: Educational Technology.

Reiser, R., & Dempsey, J. (2007). *Trends and issues in instructional design.* Upper Saddle River, NJ: Pearson Education, Inc.

Report, H. (2011). *2011 Horizon report.* Retrieved from http://www.educause.edu/ Resources/2011HorizonReport/223122

Resnick, P., & Varian, H. R. (1997). Recommender systems. *Communications of the ACM, 40,* 56–58. doi:10.1145/245108.245121

Reynolds, C. (1987). Flocks, herds and schools: A distributed behavioral model. In *Computer Graphics: Proceedings of SIGGRAPH '87, 21*(4). ACM Press.

Rieh, S. Y. (2002). Judgment of information quality and cognitive authority in the Web. *Journal of the American Society for Information Science and Technology, 53*(2), 145–161. doi:10.1002/asi.10017

Robbins, S., & Bell, M. (2008). *Second life for dummies.* Indianapolis, IN: Wiley Publishing.

Roberts, T. (2006). *Self, peer, and group assessment in e-learning.* Hershey, PA: Information Science Publishing. doi:10.4018/978-1-59140-965-6

Robinson, P. (2007). Criteria for categorizing and sequencing pedagogic tasks. In del Pilar, M., & Mayo, G. (Eds.), *Investigating tasks in formal language learning.* Tonawanda, NY: Multilingual Matters Ltd.

Roe, D. B. (1994). Deployment of human-machine dialogue systems. In Roe, D. B., & Wilpon, J. G. (Eds.), *Voice communication between humans and machines* (pp. 373–389). Washington, DC: National Academy Press.

Rogers, E. M. (1995). *Diffusion of innovations* (4th ed.). New York, NY: Free Press.

Rohrer, D., & Pashler, H. (2010). Recent research on human learning challenges conventional instructional strategies. *Educational Research, 39,* 406–412. doi:10.3102/0013189X10374770

Romero, C., & Ventura, S. (2007). Educational data mining: A survey from 1995 to 2005. [Elsevier.]. *Expert Systems with Applications, 1*(33), 135–146. doi:10.1016/j.eswa.2006.04.005

Romero, C., Ventura, S., Delgado, J. A., & De Bra, P. (2007). *Personalized links recommendation based on data mining in adaptive educational hypermedia systems* (pp. 292–306).

Romero, C., Ventura, S., de Castro, C., & de Bra, P. (2003). *Discovering prediction rules in AHA courses!* User Modeling 2003. Pittsburg (USA).

Romiszowski, A. J. (2004). How's the e-learning baby? Factors leading to success or failure of an educational technology innovation. *Educational Technology, 44*(1), 5–27.

Rose, A., Czarnolewski, M., Gragg, F., Austin, S., & Ford, P. (1985). *Acquisition and retention of soldiering skills (Final Report 671).* Alexandria, VA: U. S. Army Research Institute for the Behavioral and Social Sciences.

Rosen, L. D., & Cheever, N. A. (2008). The impact of emotionality and self-disclosure on online dating versus traditional dating. *Computers in Human Behavior, 24*(5), 2124–2157. doi:10.1016/j.chb.2007.10.003

Rosenfeld, L., & Morville, P. (2002). *Information architecture for the World Wide Web: Designing large scale websites*. O'Reilly & Associates.

Ross, C., & Orr, E. S. (2009). Personality and motivations associated with Facebook use. *Computers in Human Behavior*, *25*(2), 578–586. doi:10.1016/j.chb.2008.12.024

Rossi, P. H., & Anderson, A. B. (1982). The factorial survey approach. In Rossi, P. H., & Nock, S. L. (Eds.), *Measuring social judgments* (pp. 15–67). Beverly Hills, CA: Sage.

Rosson, M. B., & Carroll, J. M. (2001). *Usability engineering: scenario-based development of human computer interaction*. Morgan Kaufmann.

Roston, G. P., & Peurach, T. (1997). A whole body kinesthetic display device for virtual reality applications. *Proc. of IEEE Int'l Conf. on Robotics and Automation*, (pp. 3006-3011).

Rubach, E. (2007, June 31). Parallel worlds. Designweek, (p. 19).

Rucker, R. (1988). *Mind tools: The mathematics of information* (p. 26). London, UK: Penguin Books.

Russel, D. W., & Russel, C. A. (2006). Explicit and implicit catalysts of consumer resistance: The effects of animosity, cultural salience and country-of-origin on subsequent choice. *International Journal of Research in Marketing*, *23*, 321–331. doi:10.1016/j.ijresmar.2006.05.003

Russell, D. (Ed.). (2010). *Cases on collaboration in virtual learning environments: Processes and interactions*. Hershey, PA: IGI Global.

Rust, R. T., Kannan, P. K., et al. (2005). E-service: The revenue expansion path to e-commerce profitability. In *Advances in computers*, volume 64, (pp. 159-193). Elsevier.

Ryder, M. (2003). *Instructional design models*. Retrieved from http://carbon.cudenver.edu/ ~mryder/itc_data/idmodels.html

Ryu, S.-H., Kim, H.-J., Park, J.-S., Kwon, Y. W., & Jeong, C.-S. (2007, February). Collaborative object-oriented visualization environment. *Multimedia Tools and Applications*, *32*(2), 209–234. doi:10.1007/s11042-006-0066-7

Saffer, D. (2004). *Experience design versus interaction design*. (Online). Retrieved from http://lists.interaction-designers.com/ htdig.cgi/discuss-interactiondesigners.Com/ 2004-November/003501.html

Saha, D., & Marvin, V. Z. (2005). Pervasive computing: A vision to realize. In *Advances in computers* (*Vol. 64*, pp. 195–245). Elsevier.

Sai, Y. (2008). Transparent safe. *Decision Support Systems*, *46*(1), 41–51. doi:10.1016/j.dss.2008.04.007

Saini, R., & Saxena, P. K. (2000). Internet enabled synergistic intelligent systems and their applications to efficient management of operational organizations. *Information Sciences*, *127*(1-2), 45–62. doi:10.1016/S0020-0255(00)00028-1

Salomann, H., & Dous, M. (2007). Self-service revisited: How to balance high-tech and high-touch in customer relationships. *European Management Journal*, *25*(4), 310–319. doi:10.1016/j.emj.2007.06.005

Saltzbert, S., & Polyson, S. (1995, September). Distributed learning on the World Wide Web. *Syllabus*, *9*(1), 10–12.

Sandholtz, J. M., Ringstaff, C., & Dwyer, D. C. (1997). *Teaching with technology: Creating student-centered classrooms*. New York, NY: Teachers College Press.

Santos, O. C., & Boticario, J. G. (2011a). TORMES methodology to elicit educational oriented recommendations. *Lecture Notes in Artificial Intelligence*, *6738*, 541–543.

Santos, O. C., & Boticario, J. G. (2011b). Requirements for semantic educational recommender systems in formal e-learning scenarios. *Algorithms*, *4*(2), 131–154. doi:10.3390/a4030131

Santos, O. C., & Boticario, J. G. (2011d). *Educational recommender systems and techniques: Practices and challenges*. Hershey, PA: IGI Global. doi:10.4018/978-1-61350-489-5

Santos, O. C., Mazzone, E., Aguilar, M. J., & Boticario, J. G. (2012). (in press). Designing a user interface to manage recommendations for virtual learning communities. *International Journal of Web Based Communities*.

Santos, O. C., & Boticario, J. G. (2010). Modeling recommendations for the educational domain. In *Proceedings of the 1st Workshop Recommender Systems for Technology Enhanced Learning* (RecSysTEL 2010), Barcelona, Spain, 29–30 September 2010, (pp. 2793–2800).

Santos, O. C., & Boticario, J. G. (2011c). Usability in adaptive educational systems. *Workshop on Usability and Educational Technology 2011. Held in Conjunction with the 23rd Conférence Francophone Sur l'Interaction Homme-Machine, Actes Complementaries,* (pp. 93-95). Nice, France.

Santos, O. C., Martin, L., Mazzone, E., & Boticario, J. G. (2009). Management of recommendations for accessible eLearning platforms: is it a need for learning management system users? In *Proceedings of the 3rd Workshop Towards User Modelling and Adaptive Systems for All (TUMAS-A). In conjunction with the 14th International Conference on Artificial Intelligence in Education* (AIED 200), (pp. 21-22).

Sauerborn, G. C. (1998). The distributed interactive simulation (DIS) lethality communication server. *Proceedings of 2nd International Workshop on Distributed Interactive Simulation and Real-Time Applications, 19-20,* (pp. 82–85).

Saxby, S. (2002). CLSR Briefing: News and comment on recent developments from around the world. *Computer Law & Security Report, 18*(2), 134–151. doi:10.1016/S0267-3649(02)03020-0

Saxby, S. (2007). News and comment on recent developments from around the world. *Computer Law & Security Report, 23*(2), 125–137. doi:10.1016/j.clsr.2007.01.010

Scaife, M., & Rogers, Y. (2001). Informing the design of a virtual environment to support learning for children. *International Journal of Human-Computer Studies, 55*(2), 115–143. Retrieved from http://www.informatics.sussex.ac.uk/research/groups/interact/publications/S&R-IJHCS'02.pdf. doi:10.1006/ijhc.2001.0473

Schafer, J. B., Konstan, J. A., & Riedl, J. (2001). E-commerce recommendation applications. *Data Mining and Knowledge Discovery, 5,* 115–153. doi:10.1023/A:1009804230409

Schein, E. H. (2004). *Organizational culture and leadership.* San Francisco, CA: Jossey-Bass.

Schmidt, H., Sorowka, D., Hesse, S., & Bernhardt, R. (2002). Design of a robotic walking simulator for neurological rehabilitation. *IEEE/RSJ International Conference on Intelligent Robots and Systems,* (pp. 1487-1492).

Schön, D. A. (1983). *The reflective practitioner: How professionals think in action.* New York, NY: Basic Books.

Schulz, A. G., Hahsler, M., & Jahn, M. (2001). Educational and scientific recommender systems: Designing the information channels of the virtual university. *International Journal of Engineering Education, 17*(2), 153–163.

Scruton, R. (1983). *The aesthetic understanding.* Carcanet New Press Ltd.

Seels, B., & Glasgow, Z. (1998). *Making instructional design decisions* (2nd ed.). Upper Saddle River, NJ: Prentice Hall.

Selwyn, N. (2003). Apart from technology: understanding people's non-use of information and communication technologies in everyday life. *Technology in Society, 25,* 99–116. doi:10.1016/S0160-791X(02)00062-3

Selwyn, N. (2011). *Schools and schooling in the digital age. A critical analysis.* London, UK: Routledge.

Shank, R. (1996). *Information is surprises* (p. 173). New York, NY: Touchstone.

Sharples, M. (2000). The design of personal mobile technologies for lifelong learning. *Computers & Education, 34,* 177–193. doi:10.1016/S0360-1315(99)00044-5

Shaw, D., & Newholm, T. (2002). Voluntary simplicity and the ethics of consumption. *Psychology and Marketing, 19*(2), 167–185. doi:10.1002/mar.10008

Shawyun, T. (1999). Expectations and influencing factors of IS graduates and education in Thailand: A perspective of the students, academics and business community. *Informing Science, 2*(1).

Shedroff, N. (2005a). *Experience design.* Retrieved from http://www.nathan.com/ed/glossary/index.html

Sheets, M. (1992, Spring). Characteristics of adult education students and factors which determine course completion: A review. *New Horizons in Adult Education, 6*(1). Retrieved on October 6, 2009, from http://www.nova.edu/~aed/horizons/vol6n1

Shen, L., & Shen, R. (2004). Learning content recommendation service based-on simple sequencing specification. *ICWL, 2004*, 363–370.

Sheremetov, L., & Arenas, A. G. (2002). EVA: An interactive Web-based collaborative learning environment. *Computers & Education, 39*(2), 161–182. doi:10.1016/S0360-1315(02)00030-1

Sheth, J. N. (1981). Psychology of innovation resistance: The less developed concept (LDC) in diffusion research. *Research in Marketing, 4*, 273–282.

Shingledecker, C. A., & Foulke, E. (1978). A human factors approach to the assessment of mobility of blind Pedestrians. *Human Factors, 20*, 273–286.

Shirky, C. (2006). *Ontology is overrated: Categories, links, and tags. Economics and culture, media and community*. Retrieved 30th September, 2008, from http://shirky.com/writings/ ontology_overrated.html

Shneiderman, B. (1992). *Designing the user interface - strategies for effective human-computer interaction* (2nd ed.). Reading, MA: Addison-Wesley Publishing Company.

Shneiderman, B. (1987). *Designing the user interface: Strategies for effective human-computer interaction.* Addison Wesley.

Sibert, L., Templeman, J., Page, R., Barron, J., McCune, J., & Denbrook, P. (2004). *Initial assessment of human performance using the gaiter interaction technique to control locomotion in fully immersive virtual environments. Technical Report.* Washington, DC: Naval Research Laboratory.

Siemens, G. (2004). *A learning theory for the digital age.* Retrieved October 8, 2010, from http://www.elearnspace.org/ Articles/connectivism.htm

Silverston, T., & Fourmaux, O. (2009). Traffic analysis of peer-to-peer IPTV communities. *Computer Networks, 53*(4), 470–484. doi:10.1016/j.comnet.2008.09.024

Simmross-Wattenberg, F., Carranza-Herrezuelo, N., Palacios-Camarero, C., De La Higuera, J. P. C., & Martin-Fernandez, M. Angel, Aja-Fernandez, S., et al. (2005). GroupSlicer: A collaborative extension of the 3D-Slicer. *Journal of Biomedical Informatics, 38*(6), 431–442. doi:10.1016/j.jbi.2005.03.001

Singh, H. (2003). Building effective blended learning programs. *Educational Technology, 44*(1), 5–27.

Skiba, D. (2011). On the horizon: Emerging technologies for 2011. *Nursing Education Perspectives, 32*(1), 44–46. doi:10.5480/1536-5026-32.1.44

Skinner, B. (1954). The science of learning and the art of teaching. *Harvard Educational Review, 24*(2).

Slater, M. (1995). Taking steps: The influence of a walking metaphor on presence in virtual reality. *ACM Transactions on Computer-Human Interaction, 2*(3), 201–219. doi:10.1145/210079.210084

Smith, R., & Sharif, N. (2007). Understanding and acquiring technology assets for global competition. *Technovation Journal, 27*, 643–649. doi:10.1016/j.technovation.2007.04.001

Smith, W., & Moore, J. (1970). *The learning process and programmed instruction.* New York, NY: Halt, Runehalt and Winston Inc.

Snowden, D. J. (2000). Strategies for common sense-making in innovation enabling emergence at the edge of chaos part III. *Journal of Scenario and Strategy Planning, 2*(3).

Sobel, A. E. K., & Clarkson, M. R. (2002). Formal methods application: An empirical tale of software development. *IEEE Transactions on Software Engineering, 28*(3), 308–320. doi:10.1109/32.991322

Sobel, A. E. K., & Clarkson, M. R. (2003). Response to Comments on 'formal methods application: An empirical tale of software development. *IEEE Transactions on Software Engineering, 29*(6), 572–575. doi:10.1109/TSE.2003.1205184

Soldatos, J., Pandis, I., Stamatis, K., Polymenakos, L., & Crowley, J. L. (2007, February). Agent based middleware infrastructure for autonomous context-aware ubiquitous computing services. *Computer Communications, 30*(3), 577–591. doi:10.1016/j.comcom.2005.11.018

Soloway, E., Guzdial, M., & Hay, K. E. (1994). Learner centered design: The challenge for HCI in the 21st century. *Interaction, 1*, 36–48. doi:10.1145/174809.174813

Soonthornphisaj, N., Rojsattarat, E., & Yim-Ngam, S. (2006). Smart e-learning using recommender system. *International Conference on Intelligent Computing 2006*, (pp. 518-523).

Sorden, S. D. (2005). A cognitive approach to instructional design for multimedia learning. *Informing Science Journal, 8*, 263–279.

Spencer, C. D. (1978). Two types of role playing: Threats to internal and external validity. *The American Psychologist, 33*, 265–268. doi:10.1037/0003-066X.33.3.265

Spiro, R. J., Feltovich, P. J., Jacobson, M. J., & Coulson, R. L. (1992). Cognitive flexibility, constructivism and hypertext: Random access instruction for advanced knowledge acquisition in ill-structured domains. In Duffy, T., & Jonassen, D. (Eds.), *Constructivism and the technology of instruction*. Hillsdale, NJ: Erlbaum.

Spiro, R. J., Collins, B. P., & Ramchandran, A. R. (2007). Modes of openness and flexibility in cognitive flexibility hypertext learning environments. In Khan, B. H. (Ed.), *Flexible learning in an information society*. Hershey, PA: Information Science Publishing. doi:10.4018/9781599043258.ch002

Sprinthall, R. C., & Sprinthall, N. A. (1981). *Educational psychology: A developmental approach* (p. 281). Reading, MA: Addison-Wesley Publishing Company.

Squeak. (2009, January). *Etoys*. Retrieved from http://www.squeak.org/

Squire, K. (2006). From content to context: Videogames as designed experience. *Educational Researcher, 35*(8), 19–29. doi:10.3102/0013189X035008019

Squire, K., Giovanetto, L., DeVane, B., & Durga, S. (2005). From users to designers: Building a self-organizing game-based learning environment. *TechTrends, 49*(5), 34–42. doi:10.1007/BF02763688

Stanney, K. M. (Ed.). (2003). *International Journal of Human-Computer Interaction*. Lawrence Erlbaum Assoc Inc.

Stasko, J. (1997). *Design principles*. Retrieved from http://www.cc.gatech.edu/classes/ cs6751_97_winter/Topics/design-princ/

Stedmon, A. W., Nichols, S. C., Nicholson, E., Cox, G., & Wilson, J. R. (2003b). *The flightdeck of the future: Perceived urgency of text and speech communications. Proceedings of Human Factors of Decision Making in Complex Systems, September 2003*. UK: Abertay.

Stedmon, A. W., & Stone, R. (2001). Re-viewing reality: Human factors issues in synthetic training environments. *International Journal of Human-Computer Studies, 55*, 675–698. doi:10.1006/ijhc.2001.0498

Stedmon, A. W., & Bayer, S. H. (2001). Thinking of something to say: Workload, driving behaviour and speech. In Hanson, M. (Ed.), *Contemporary ergonomics 2001* (pp. 417–422). London, UK: Taylor & Francis.

Stedmon, A. W., Patel, H., Nichols, S. C., & Wilson, J. R. (2003a). A view of the future? The potential use of speech recognition for virtual reality applications. In McCabe, P. (Ed.), *Contemporary ergonomics 2003* (pp. 289–295). London, UK: Taylor & Francis.

Stedmon, A. W., Richardson, J. R., & Bayer, S. H. (2002). In-car ASR: Speech as a secondary workload factor. In McCabe, P. (Ed.), *Contemporary ergonomics 2002* (pp. 252–257). London, UK: Taylor & Francis.

Stedmon, A. W. (2003). Developing virtual environments using speech as an input device. In C. Stephanidis (Ed.), *HCI International '03, Proceedings of the 10th International Conference on Human-Computer Interaction*, (pp. 1248-1252). Lawrence Erlbaum Associates.

Stedmon, A. W. (2005). *Putting speech in, taking speech out: Human factors in the use of speech interfaces*. University of Nottingham, PhD Dissertation.

Stedmon, A. W., & Baber, C. (1999). Evaluating stress in the development of speech interface technology. In H.-J. Bullinger (Ed.), *HCI International '99. Proceedings of the 8th International Conference on Human-Computer Interaction*, Munich, Germany, 22-27 August 1999, (pp. 545-549). Amsterdam, The Netherlands: Elsevier Science.

Stedmon, A. W., Griffiths, G., & Bayon, V. (2004). Single or multi-user VEs, manual or speech input? An assessment of de-coupled interaction in virtual environments. *Proceedings of Virtual Reality Design and Evaluation Workshop*, 22-23 January 2004, Nottingham, UK.

Stedmon, A. W., Sharples, S. C., Patel, H., & Wilson, J. R. (2006). Free-speech in a virtual world: Speech for Collaborative Interaction in a Virtual Environment. *Proceedings of the International Ergonomics Association (IEA): 16th World Congress on Ergonomics*. Maastricht, The Netherlands.

Steinkuehler, C., & Williams, D. (2006). Where everybody knows your (screen) name: Online games as third places. *Journal of Computer-Mediated Communication, 11*(4). doi:10.1111/j.1083-6101.2006.00300.x

Stenmark, D. (2002). Information vs. knowledge: The role of Intranets in knowledge management. In *Proceedings of HICSS-35*, Hawaii, January, (pp. 7 - 10). IEEE Press.

Stone, R. J. (2001). *A human-centred definition of surgical procedures*. European Union Project IERAPSI (Integrated Environment for the Rehearsal and Planning of Surgical Interventions; IST-1999-12175); Work Package 2, Deliverable D2 (Part 1).

Strategy Analytics. (2008). *Interview: Strategy Analytics' Barry Gilbert - 137M virtual worlds users now; 1B by 2017*. Retrieved from http://www.virtualworldsnews.com/ 2008/06/strategy-analyt.html

Strauss, A., & Corbin, J. (1990). *Basics of qualitative research: Grounded theory procedures and techniques*. Newbury Park, CA: Sage.

Stuart, F. I., Deckert, P., McCutheon, D., & Kunst, R. (1998). A leveraged learning network. *Sloan Management Review, 39*(4), 81–94.

Stuurman, K., & Wijnands, H. (2001). Software law: Intelligent agents: A curse or a blessing? A survey of the legal aspects of the application of intelligent software systems. *Computer Law & Security Report, 17*(2), 92–100. doi:10.1016/S0267-3649(01)00203-5

Subrahmanyam, K., Kraut, R., Greenfield, P. M., & Gross, E. F. (2001). New forms of electronic media: The impact of interactive games and the internet on cognition, socialization, and behavior. In Singer, D. L., & Singer, J. L. (Eds.), *Handbook of children and the media* (pp. 73–99). Thousand Oaks, CA: Sage.

Subramanya, S. R., & Yi, B. K. (2006). User interfaces for mobile content. *Computer*, (April): 85–87. doi:10.1109/MC.2006.144

Suchman, M. C. (1995). Managing legitimacy: Strategic and institutional approaches. *Academy of Management Journal, 20*(3), 571–610.

Sugrue, B., & Clark, R. E. (2000). Media selection for training. In Tobias, S., & Fletcher, J. D. (Eds.), *Training and retraining: A handbook for business, industry, government, and the military. New York, NY*. Macmillan Reference, USA.

Suh, K.-S., & Young, E. L. (2005). The effects of virtual reality of consumer learning: An empirical investigation. *Management Information Systems Quarterly, 29*(4), 674–697.

Suh, J., Moyer, P. S., & Heo, H. (2005). Examining technology uses in the classroom: Developing fraction sense using virtual manipulative concept tutorials. *Journal of Interactive Online Learning, 3*(4), 1–21.

Summit, T. I. G. E. R. (n.d.). *About us*. Retrieved from http://tigersummit.com/ About_Us.html

Summit, T. I. G. E. R. (n.d.). *Virtual demo*. Retrieved from http://tigersummit.com/ Virtual_Demo_New.html

Sutcliffe, A. G. (1995). *Human-computer interface design* (2nd ed.). London, UK: Macmillan Press Ltd.

Sweet, R. (1986). Student drop-out in distance education: An application of Tinto's model. *Distance Education, 7*, 201-213. Retrieved on October 1, 2009, from http://www.westga.edu/~distance/ ojdla/winter84/nash84.htm

Sweller, J. (1988). Cognitive load during problem solving: Effects on learning. *Cognitive Science, 12*, 257–288. doi:10.1207/s15516709cog1202_4

Sweller, J. (1994). Cognitive load theory, learning difficulty, and instructional design. *Learning and Instruction, 4*, 295–312. doi:10.1016/0959-4752(94)90003-5

Sweller, J., van Merrienboer, J. J. G., & Paas, F. G. W. C. (1998). Cognitive architecture and instructional design. *Educational Psychology Review, 10*, 251–296. doi:10.1023/A:1022193728205

Sweller, J. (1988). Cognitive load during problem solving: Effects on learning. *Cognitive Science, 12*, 257–285. doi:10.1207/s15516709cog1202_4

Szmigin, I., & Foxall, G. (1998). Three forms of innovation resistance: The case of retail payment methods. *Technovation, 18*(6/7), 459–468. doi:10.1016/S0166-4972(98)00030-3

Ta, D. N. B., & Zhou, S. (2006). A network-centric approach to enhancing the interactivity of large-scale distributed virtual environments. *Computer Communications, 29*(17), 3553–3566. doi:10.1016/j.comcom.2006.05.015

Tahvanainen, M., & Welch, D. (2005). Implications of short-term international assignments. *European Management Journal, 23*(6), 663–673. doi:10.1016/j.emj.2005.10.011

Tan, J., & Biswas, G. (2007). Simulation-based game learning environments: Building and Sustaining a fish tank. *The First IEEE International Workshop on Digital Game and Intelligent Toy Enhanced Learning, 2007* (DIGITEL), March, (pp. 73–80).

Tang, T., & McCalla, G. (2003). *Smart recommendation for an evolving e-learning system*. Workshop on Technologies for Electronic Documents for Supporting Learning, International Conference on Artificial Intelligence in Education.

Tarasewich, P., Gong, J., Nah, F. F., & DeWester, D. (2008). Mobile interaction design: Integrating individual and organizational perspectives. [IOS Press.]. *Information Knowledge Systems Management, 7,* 121–144.

Taxén, G., & Naeve, A. (2002). A system for exploring open issues in VR-based education. *Computers & Graphics, 26*(4), 593–598. doi:10.1016/S0097-8493(02)00112-7

Tay, F. E. H., & Roy, A. (2003). CyberCAD: A collaborative approach in 3D-CAD technology in a multimedia-supported environment. *Computers in Industry, 52*(2), 127–145. doi:10.1016/S0166-3615(03)00100-3

Taylor, F. W. (1911). *The principles of scientific management*. New York, NY: Harper Bros.

Tewari, G., & Youll, J. (2003). Personalized location-based brokering using an agent-based intermediary architecture. *Decision Support Systems, 34*(2), 127–137. doi:10.1016/S0167-9236(02)00076-3

Thatcher, J. B., & Loughry, M. L. (2007). Internet anxiety: An empirical study of the effects of personality, beliefs, and social support. *Information & Management, 44*(4), 353–363. doi:10.1016/j.im.2006.11.007

The EDUCAUSE Learning Initiative. (2006, June). *7 things you should know about virtual worlds*. Retrieved on June 2, 2009, from http://www.educause.edu/ELI/7ThingsYouShouldKnowAboutVirtu/156818

Thelwall, M., & Marvin, M. V. (2009). Social network sites: Users and uses. In *Advances in computers* (Vol. 76, pp. 19–73). Elsevier.

Tibau, J. (2000). Business teaching in the CIS States. *European Management Journal, 18*(6), 683–691. doi:10.1016/S0263-2373(00)00059-1

Tomlinson, M. (2000). Tackling e-commerce security issues head on. *Computer Fraud & Security,* (11): 10–13. doi:10.1016/S1361-3723(00)11017-6

Towler, A., Kraiger, K., Sitzmann, T., Van Overberghe, C., Cruz, J., Ronen, E., & Stewart, D. (2008). The seductive details effect in technology-delivered training. *Performance Improvement Quarterly, 21,* 65–86. doi:10.1002/piq.20023

Towndrow, P. A., & Vallance, M. (2004). *Using Information Technology in the language classroom* (3rd ed.). Singapore: Longman.

Tractinsky, N. (1997). *Aesthetics and apparent usability: Empirically assessing cultural and methodological issues*. In CHI 97 – Looking to the Future, 22-27th March, Atlanta, Georgia. Retrieved from http://acm.org/sigchi/chi97/ proceedings/paper/nt.htm

Tractinsky, N. (2004). Towards the study of aesthetics in Information Technology. In *25th Annual International Conference on Information Systems*, 12-15th December, Washington, (pp. 771-780). Retrieved from http://www.ise.bgu.ac.il/faculty/ noam/papers/04_nt_icis.pdf

Tractinsky, N. (2005). *Does aesthetics matter in human computer interaction?* Retrieved from http://mc.informatik.uni-hamburg.de/ konferenzbaende/mc2005/konferenzband/ muc2005_02_tractinsky.pdf

Traxler, J. (2005). Defining mobile learning. *Proceedings of the 2005 IADIS International Conference,* (pp. 261-266).

Tucker, P. (2007). Virtual immortality for virtual eternity. []. Retrieved from www.wfs.org]. *The Futurist*, 12.

Tucker, P., & Jones, D. M. (1991). Voice as interface: An overview. *International Journal of Human-Computer Interaction*, *3*(2), 145–170. doi:10.1080/10447319109526002

Tynan, D. (2007). *Traveling the Web's third dimension*, (p. 45). PCWorld.com.

U.S. Department of Education, Office of Planning, Evaluation, and Policy Development. (2009). *Evaluation of evidence-based practices in online learning: A Meta-analysis and review of online learning studies.* Retrieved from http://www2.ed.gov/rschstat/ eval/tech/ evidence-based-practices/ finalreport.pdf

Ullman, J. R. (1987). Speech recognition by machine. In Gregory, R. L. (Ed.), *The Oxford companion to the mind*. Oxford, UK: Oxford University Press.

United States Air Force. (30 January 2008). *White paper: On learning: The future of Air Force education and training*. Air Education and Training Command. Retrieved on June 30, 2009, from http://www.aetc.af.mil/ shared/media/ document/ AFD-080130-066.pdf

University of Wisconsin. (n.d.). *Sustainable management*. Retrieved from http://sustain.wisconsin.edu/

University of Wisconsin-Green Bay. (2009). *Virtual student meeting minutes, Fall*.

UPA – Usability Professionals Association. (2011). *User-centered design methodology*. Retrieved from http://www.usabilityprofessionals.org/ upa_publications/ ux_poster.html

Usability. (n.d.). *Heuristic evaluations*. Retrieved from http://www.usability.gov/ methods/test_refine/heuristic.html

Uslaner, E. M. (2001). Volunteering and social capital: How trust and religion shape civic participation in the United States. In Uslaner, E. M. (Ed.), *Social capital and participation in everyday life* (pp. 104–117). London, UK: Routledge.

Vahidov, R., & Kersten, G. E. (2004). Decision station: Situating decision support systems. *Decision Support Systems*, *38*(2), 283–303. doi:10.1016/S0167-9236(03)00099-X

Vallance, M. (2008). Beyond policy: Strategic actions to support ICT integration in Japanese schools. *Australasian Journal of Educational Technology*, *24*(3), 275–293.

Vallance, M., Martin, S., Wiz, C., & van Schaik, P. (2010, January - March). Designing effective spaces, tasks and metrics for communication in Second Life within the context of programming LEGO NXT Mindstorms™ robots. *International Journal of Virtual and Personal Learning Environments*, *1*(1), 20–37. doi:10.4018/jvple.2010091703

Vallance, M., & Wright, D. L. (2010). Japanese students' digitally enabled futures images: A synergistic approach to developing academic competencies. In Mukerji, S., & Tripathi, P. (Eds.), *Cases on technological adaptability and transnational learning: Issues and challenges*. Hershey, PA: IGI Global. doi:10.4018/978-1-61520-779-4.ch009

Vallance, M., Martin, S., Wiz, C., & van Schaik, P. (2009). LEGO Mindstorms for informed metrics in virtual worlds. In *Proceedings of Human Computer Interaction (HCI) 2009 - People and Computers XXIII*, Cambridge University, UK, (pp. 159-162). Cambridge, UK, Sept. 2009.

van Dam, A., & Laidlaw, D. H. (2002). Experiments in immersive virtual reality for scientific visualization. *Computers & Graphics*, *26*(4), 535–555. doi:10.1016/S0097-8493(02)00113-9

Van Rosmalen, P., Boticario, J. G., & Santos, O. C. (2004). The full life cycle of adaptation in alfanet elearning environment. *Learning Technology Newsletter*, *4*, 59–61.

van Velsen, L., van der Geest, T., Klaassen, R., & Steehouder, M. (2008). User-centered evaluation of adaptive and adaptable systems: a literature review. *The Knowledge Engineering Review*, *23*(3), 261–281. doi:10.1017/S0269888908001379

Van Velsor, E., & Guthrie, V. A. (1998). Feedback intensive programs. In McCauley, C. D., Moxley, R. S., & Van Velsor, E. (Eds.), *The Center for Creative Leadership handbook of leadership development* (pp. 66–105). San Francisco, CA: Jossey-Bass.

Vertegaal, R. (1999). The GAZE groupware system: mediating joint attention in multiparty communication and collaboration. *Proceedings of the SIGCHI Conference on Human Factors in Computing Systems: The CHI is the Limit*, (pp. 294-301).

Virtual World Review. (n.d.). *What is a virtual world?* Retrieved April 6, 2009, from http://www.virtualworldsreview.com/ info/whatis.shtml

Vygotsky, L. (1978). *Mind in society*. Cambridge, MA: Harvard University Press.

W3C. (2007). *Design principles: Separation of concerns*. Working Draft, 26 November 2007. Retrieved from http://www.w3.org/TR/ html-design-principles/ #separation-of-concerns

Wagner, M. (2007). *Inside Second Life's data centers*. InformationWeek.

Wagner, E. D. (1997). In support of a functional definition of interaction. In Cyrs, T. E. (Ed.), *Teaching and learning at a distance: What it takes to effectively design, deliver and evaluate programs* (pp. 19–26). San Francisco, CA: Jossey Bass. doi:10.1080/08923649409526852

Waldron, S. M., Patrick, J., Duggan, G. B., Banbury, S., & Howes, A. (2008). Designing information fusion for the encoding of visual-spatial information. *Ergonomics*, *51*, 775–797. doi:10.1080/00140130701811933

Walkerdine, J., & Hughes, D. (2008). A framework for P2P application development. *Computer Communications*, *31*(2), 387–401. doi:10.1016/j.comcom.2007.08.004

Walther, J. (2006). Nonverbal dynamics in computer mediated communication, or:(and the net:('s with you:) and you:) alone. In Manusov, V., & Patterson, M. (Eds.), *The Sage handbook of nonverbal communication* (pp. 461–480). Thousand Oaks, CA: Sage.

Walvoord, A. A. G., & Redden, E. R. (2008). Empowering followers in virtual teams: Guiding principles from theory and practice. *Computers in Human Behavior*, *24*(5), 1884–1906. doi:10.1016/j.chb.2008.02.006

Wang, M. (2007). Do the regulations on electronic signatures facilitate international electronic commerce? A critical review. *Computer Law & Security Report*, *23*(1), 32–41. doi:10.1016/j.clsr.2006.09.006

Wang, Z., Bauernfeind, K., & Sugar, T. (2003). Omni-directional treadmill system. *Proc. of 11th Haptic Interfaces for Virtual Environment and Teleoperator Systems*, (pp. 367-373).

Wann, J., & Mon-Williams, M. (1996). What does virtual reality NEED? Human factors issues in the design of three-dimensional computer environments. *International Journal of Human-Computer Studies*, *44*, 829–847. doi:10.1006/ijhc.1996.0035

Warburton, S., & Perez-Garcia, M. (2009). 3D design and collaboration in massively multi-user virtual environments. In Russel, D. (Ed.), *Cases on collaboration in virtual learning environments: processes and interactions*. Hershey, PA: IGI Global. doi:10.4018/978-1-60566-878-9.ch002

Warburton, S. (2008). Loving your avatar: identity, immersion and empathy. *Liquid Learning*. Retrieved September 23, 2010, from http://warburton.typepad.com/ liquidlearning/2008/01/loving-your-ava.html

Warmelink, H. (2009). De opkomst en ondergang van Second Life..*ego, 8*(2), 27-30.

Warschauer, M. (1999). *Electronic literacies: Language, culture, and power in online education*. Mahwah, NJ: Lawrence Erlbaum Associates.

Watts, M. (1997). Black gold, white heat: State violence, local resistance and the national question in Nigeria. In Pile, S., & Keith, M. (Eds.), *Geographies of resistance* (pp. 33–67). London, UK: Routledge.

WCAG. (n.d.). *Web content accessibility guidelines overview*. Retrieved from http://www.w3.org/WAI/ intro/wcag.php

Weaver, C. A., Delaney, C. W., Weber, P., & Carr, R. L. (Eds.). (2010) *Nursing and informatics for the 21st century: An international look at practice, education and EHR trends. 2nd ed*. Chicago, IL: Healthcare Information and Management System Society (HIMSS) and American Medical Informatics Association (AMIA). Retrieved from http://www.himss.org/ content/files/nursinginformaticsexcerpt.pdf

Wegner, P. (1997). Interactive software technology. In *The computer science and engineering handbook* (pp. 2440–2463).

Weiss, G. (1999). *Multi-agent systems: A modern approach to distributed artificial intelligence*. MIT Press.

Whittington, R. (2007). Strategy practice and strategy process: Family differences and the sociological eye. *Organization Studies, 28*(10), 1575–1586. doi:10.1177/0170840607081557

Williams, R., & Tollett, J. (2006). *The non-designer's web book: An easy guide to creating, designing, and posting your own website* (3rd ed.). Berkeley, CA: Peachpit Press.

Williams, D., Ducheneaut, N., Xiong, L., Zhang, Y., Yee, N., & Nickell, E. (2006). From tree house to barracks: The social life of guilds in World of Warcraft. *Games and Culture, 1*(4), 338–361. doi:10.1177/1555412006292616

Williams, D., Yee, N., & Caplan, S. (2008). Who plays, how much, and why? A behavioral player census of a virtual world. *Journal of Computer-Mediated Communication, 13*(4), 993–1018. doi:10.1111/j.1083-6101.2008.00428.x

Willis, B. (2003). *Distance education at a glance: Guide #3.* Retrieved from http://www.uidaho.edu/ eo/dist3.html

Wilson, S., Liber, O., Johnson, M., Beauvoir, P., Sharples, P., & Milligan, C. (2007). Personal learning environments: Challenging the dominant design of educational systems. *Journal of the E-Learning Knowledge Society, 3,* 27–38.

Wilson, J. R., Eastgate, R. M., & D'Cruz, M. (2002). Structured development of virtual environments. In Stanney, K. (Ed.), *Handbook of virtual environments.* Lawrence Erlbaum Associates.

Wing, J. M. (1990). A specifier's introduction to formal methods. *Computer, 23*(9), 8–23. doi:10.1109/2.58215

Wisher, R., & Khan, B. H. (Eds.). (2010). *Learning on demand: ADL and the future of e-learning.* Alexandria, VA: Advanced Distributed Learning.

Wisher, R., & Khan, B. (2010). *Learning on demand: ADL and the future of e-learning.* Washington, DC: ADL Initiative.

Wisher, R. A., Curnow, C. K., & Seidel, R. J. (2001). Knowledge retention as a latent outcome measure in distance learning. *American Journal of Distance Education, 15*(3), 20–35. doi:10.1080/08923640109527091

Woerner, J., & Woern, H. (2005). A security architecture integrated co-operative engineering platform for organised model exchange in a Digital Factory environment. *Computers in Industry, 56*(4), 347–360. doi:10.1016/j.compind.2005.01.011

Woo, S. H., & Choi, J. Y. (2009). An active product state tracking architecture in logistics sensor networks. *Computers in Industry, 60*(3), 149–160. doi:10.1016/j.compind.2008.12.001

Woodcock, B. S. (2008). *Charts.* Retrieved June 16, 2010, from http://www.mmogchart.com/charts/.

Wooldridge, M. (2009). *An introduction to multi-agent systems,* 2nd ed. John Wiley & Sons Pub.

Wright, P., Blythe, M., & Mccarthy, J. (2006). *The idea of design in HCI.* Retrieved from http://www-users.cs.york.ac.uk/ ~pcw/papers/DS VIS%20paper18_08.pdf

Yamaguchi, H. (2004). *An analysis of virtual currencies in online games.* Retrieved from http://ssrn.com/abstract=544422

Yaman, D., & Polat, S. (2009). A fuzzy cognitive map approach for effect-based operations: An illustrative case. *Information Sciences, 179*(4), 382–403. doi:10.1016/j.ins.2008.10.013

Yapp, P. (2001). Passwords: Use and abuse. *Computer Fraud & Security,* (9): 14–16. doi:10.1016/S1361-3723(01)00916-2

Yee, N. (2006). The demographics, motivations and derived experiences of users of massively multiuser online graphical environments. *Presence (Cambridge, Mass.), 15,* 309–329. doi:10.1162/pres.15.3.309

Yin, R. (1994). *Case study research: Design and methods.* London, UK: Sage.

Zaiane, O. (2002). *Building a recommender agent for e-learning systems.* In ICCE 2002.

Zaiane, O. R. (2001) Web usage mining for a better web-based learning environment. In *Proceedings of Conference on Advanced Technology for Education,* (pp. 60–64). Banff, AB, June 2001.

Zhang, J., & Gong, J. (2007). Design and development of distributed virtual geographic environment system based on web services. *Information Sciences, 177*(19), 3968–3980. doi:10.1016/j.ins.2007.02.049

Zhang, L. (2002). *Knowledge graph theory and structural parsing*. Enschede, The Netherlands: Twente University Press.

Zhang, J., Khan, B. H., Gibbons, A. S., & Ni, Y. (2001). Review of web-based assessment tools. In Khan, B. H. (Ed.), *Web-based training* (pp. 137–146). Englewood Cliffs, NJ: Educational Technology Publications.

Zhu, B., & Chen, B. (2005). Using 3D interfaces to facilitate the spatial knowledge retrieval: A geo-referenced knowledge repository system. *Decision Support Systems, 40*(2), 167–182. doi:10.1016/j.dss.2004.01.007

Zimmerman, V. J. (1998). Academic studying and the development of personal skill: A self regulatory perspective. *Educational Psychology, 33*, 73–86.

Zimmerman, V. J., & Schunk, D. H. (Eds.). (2001). *Self-regulated learning and academic achievement: Theoretical perspectives*. Mahwah, NJ: Lawrence Erlbaum Associates.

Zimmerman, J. (2003). *Position paper on design in HCI education*. Retrieved from http://www.cs.cmu.edu/~johnz/pubs/2003_Interact_pp.pdf

Zundel, P. E., Needham, T. D., Richards, E. W., Kershaw, J. A., Daugharty, D. A., & Robak, E. W. (2000). Fostering competency with outcome-based assessment. In M. R. Ryan & W. B. Kurtz (Eds.), *Third Biennial Conference on University Education in Natural Resources*. Retrieved from https://www.cnr.usu.edu/ quinney/files/uploads/UENR3.pdf#page=98

About the Contributors

Badrul H. Khan is a world-renowned educator, author, speaker, and consultant in the field of distance education. He has17 years of experience in developing and managing distance education programs. Professor Khan has the credit of first coining the phrase Web-based instruction and popularizing the concept through his 1997 best-selling Web-Based Instruction book, which paved the way for the new field of e learning. His Managing E-Learning book has been translated into 14 languages. He contributed to the development of US virtual education policies organized by the White House Office of Science and Technology Policy and the Naval Postgraduate School, the National Educational Technology Plan by the US Department of Education, and the Review of Joint Professional Military Education organized by the Joint Chiefs of Staff. He served as contributing and consulting editor of nine prestigious international learning journals & magazines. He is a past president of the International Division of the Association for Educational and Communication Technology (AECT). He authored and coauthored 11 books/ manuals and over 100 papers in the field of e-learning and distance learning. He delivered keynote speeches in more than 50 international e learning and distance learning conferences. He is the founder of McWeadon Education (a professional development institution). He previously served as the founding Director of the Educational Technology Leadership (ETL) graduate cohort program at The George Washington University, the founding Director of the Educational Technology (ET) graduate program at the University of Texas, Brownsville, and an Instructional Designer and Evaluation Specialist in the School of Medicine at Indiana University, Indianapolis. Dr. Khan has served as a consultant to distance education, learning development and human resource development projects at: (a) the World Bank, (b) the US Federal Government, (c) the Asian Development Bank, and (d) various academic institutions and corporations in the U.S. and throughout the world. For more info, please visit his personal Website: http://BadrulKhan.com/.

* * *

Maria Jose Aguilar is an interaction designer, focused on information architecture and pattern definitions for websites and applications. She graduated as graphic designer, and now works as senior user experience designer at Tuenti Technologies.

Mohamed Ally is Professor and Director of the Centre for Distance Education at Athabasca University, Canada. He obtained his Ph.D. from the University of Alberta, Canada. His current areas of research include mobile learning, e-learning, and the use of information and communication technology in training and education. Dr. Ally is Past-President of the International Federation of Training and Development

Organizations (IFTDO) and is one of the Founding Directors of the International Association of Mobile Learning (IamLearn). Dr. Ally chaired the Fifth World Conference on Mobile Learning and co-chaired the First International Conference on Mobile Libraries. He recently edited 3 books on the use of mobile technology in education, training, and libraries.

Kambiz Badie received all his degrees from Tokyo Institute of Technology, Japan, majoring in pattern recognition. Within the past years, he has been actively involved in doing research in a variety of issues, such as machine learning, cognitive modeling, systemic knowledge processing, and knowledge creation in general, and analogical knowledge processing, experience modeling, and modeling interpretation process in particular, with emphasis on creating new ideas, techniques, and contents. Out of the frameworks developed by Dr. Badie, "interpretative approach to analogical reasoning," "viewpoint oriented manipulation of concepts," and "compositional adaptation based on merging solution graphs" are particularly mentionable as novel approaches to creative idea generation, which in the meantime have a variety of applications in developing novel scientific frameworks as well as creating potential education and research support contents. Dr. Badie is one of the active researchers in the areas of interdisciplinary and transdisciplinary studies in Iran, and has a high motivation for applying intelligent/ cognitive modeling methodology to the human issues. Currently, he has become interested in modeling the process of phenomenological experience as a step to promoting pedagogical quality in cyber-space. At present, he is a member of the scientific board of IT Research Faculty at Research Institute for ICT, an advisor to center's director in IT affairs, an affiliated Professor at Faculty of Engineering Science in the University of Tehran, and in the meantime, the Editor-in-Chief of *International Journal of Information & Communication Technology* (IJICT) being published by Research Institute for ICT.

Christophe Bisson is an Assistant Professor of Management Information System at Kadir Has University, Turkey. He received his PhD from the University of Aix-Marseille, France. He is interested in decisional processes online/offline and decision systems. He is the President of the Internationally Accepted Marketing Standards and Editor in Chief of the *International Journal of Marketing Principles and Practices.*

Jesus G. Boticario is Professor of several courses at UNED concerning Artificial Intelligence subjects at the Computer Science School. He has been an invited speaker at national and international conferences, forums and institutions. He has published over 200 research articles. He has participated in 18 R&D funded projects (Spain, USA, EU). He is currently Head of aDeNu research group, Scientific coordinator in European and National funded projects in the areas of e-learning and e-inclusion, and Program Committee member at national and international conferences. He has co-chaired international workshops in the areas of user modeling and accessibility. He is reviewer of research projects and international journals. He has held several positions at UNED in the ICT area.

Fiona Carroll is a Lecturer currently working at the University of Glamorgan in Wales, UK. She comes from a strong academic background holding a PhD in computing with research interests within the fields of Human Computer Interaction, interaction design, experience design, and virtual reality. Prior to her current position, she worked on numerous research projects demonstrating a proven proficiency in a wide range of research and design methods. She has many years experience both working in and teaching design and technology and to date, has produced an extensive yet diverse list of publications. She advocates an innovative approach to user experience research and design focusing on how people and computers can engage in meaningful and effective activities and experiences.

Rui Chen is an Assistant Professor of Information Systems at Ball State University. He earned his Ph.D. in Management Science and Systems from State University of New York at Buffalo. His research interests are in the areas of information assurance, emergency management, social networks, coordination and collaboration, and information technology outsourcing. Some of his publications have appeared in *Communications of the ACM, Communications of the AIS, Decision Support Systems, Journal of the AIS,* and other journals. He received an Advanced Certificate in Information Assurance from National Center of Excellence in Information Systems Assurance Research and Education (CEISARE). He is also a Microsoft Certified System Engineer (MCSE) and Database Administrator (MCDBA).

Mario Ciampi is a research fellow at the Institute of High Performance Computing and Networking (ICAR) of the National Research Council of Italy (CNR). His main topics of interest are in the area of eHealth and medical image processing and visualization. He received a MSc in Computer Engineering from the University of Naples Federico II and a Ph.D. degree in Information Technology Engineering at the University of Naples Parthenope. He serves as a member of the editorial board of several journals and of the program committee of numerous international conferences.

Antonio Coronato is a researcher at the Institute of High-Performance Computing and Networking (ICAR) of the National Research Council of Italy (CNR). His research focuses on pervasive computing and component-based architectures. Coronato received an M.Sc. in computer engineering from Federico II University in Naples. He serves as a member of the editorial board of several journals and of the program committee of numerous international conferences. He is a member of the ACM.

Christina K. Curnow is a Vice President at ICF International (ICF) and is the director ICFs Workforce Research Center. She holds a Ph.D. in Industrial and Organizational Psychology from the George Washington University. Dr. Curnow has over 15 years of experience conducting research and evaluations related to training, and much of her work has addressed training in virtual learning environments. In this capacity, she has worked with federal agencies, the U.S. military, state governments, and local governments. Dr. Curnow's research has been published in peer reviewed journals and presented at national conferences. Her expertise has helped provide organizations with actionable, innovative, and data driven solutions to their workforce challenges.

Luigi Gallo is a researcher at the Institute of High Performance Computing and Networking (ICAR) of the National Research Council of Italy (CNR). His research focuses on human interface aspects of 3D visualization. Luigi Gallo received an M.Sc. in Computer Engineering from the University of Naples Federico II and a Ph.D. degree in Information Technology Engineering at the University of Naples Parthenope. He serves as a member of the editorial board of several journals and of the program committee of numerous international conferences. He is a professional member of ACM and a featured member of KES Intelligent Systems Society.

Keysha I. Gamor earned her Ph.D. in Education, with concentrations in Instructional Systems Design (ISD) and Organizational Learning, from George Mason University in Fairfax, Virginia. Dr. Gamor owns and serves as Managing Partner of KG2 Consulting. She is recognized for her research, publications, and other contributions in virtual worlds (VWs), immersive learning, and mobile technologies. With more than 15 of experience in teaching, ISD, adult education, research & training, Dr. Gamor remains active in her areas of interest by serving on the board of the United States Distance Learning Association (USDLA), on the editorial board of the American Educational Research Association's Applied Research in Virtual Environments Special Interest Group (AERA ARVEL SIG), and on the advisory boards of GameTech and the Federal Consortium for Virtual Worlds—to name a few. She was also named as one of the top three people in VWs by the Association of Virtual Worlds.

Tahereh Mirsaeed Ghazi has a M.Sc. degree in Information Technology Management from the AmirKabir University of Technology. Within the past years, she has been involved in a variety of research works at Knowledge Management & e-Organizations Group in IT Research Faculty of Research Institute for ICT (ex ITRC) working on issues like intelligent systems in e-learning and knowledge management and assessment issues in learning organization. She has participated in supervision of several research and development projects associated with e-learning and e-content as well. At present, she is a researcher at Knowledge Management & e-Organizations Group in IT Research Faculty of Research Institute for ICT.

Manish Gupta is currently an executive in a US-based large financial institution in Buffalo, NY, USA. He received his Bachelor's degree in Mechanical Engineering from Institute of Engineering and Technology, Lucknow, India; PhD and MBA in Information Systems from State University of New York, Buffalo, NY, USA. He has more than twelve years of experience in information systems, security policies, and technologies. He has co-authored or co-edited 6 books in the area of information security, ethics, and assurance. He has published more than 50 research articles in leading journals, conference proceedings, and books including *DSS, ACM Transactions, IEEE*, and *JOEUC*. He has received best paper award and PhD student achievement. He holds several professional designations including CISSP, CISA, CISM, ISSPCS, and PMP.

Jeremy A. Henson is an Associate at ICF International (ICF). During his tenure at ICF, he has worked on several projects for government agencies that involve training development, simulation, and practical implementation of virtual worlds. In addition, Mr. Henson has experience with both public and private organizations in the areas of job analysis, personnel selection, and organizational development. He is currently a Ph.D. candidate in Central Michigan University's Industrial/Organizational Psychology program and is completing his doctoral dissertation on leadership in organizations.

Ronan de Kervenoael is an Assistant Professor of Marketing at Sabanci University, Turkey. He received his PhD from Sheffield University UK. He is interested in choice, anti-choice, and resistance. His work is published in *Environment and Planning A, World Development, Journal of Industrial Relation, The Service Industries Journal*, and *International Journal of Retail and Distribution Management*.

Sogol Babazadeh Khamaneh holds a B.Sc. degree in Computer Engineering from Islamic Azad University in Tehran. She joined Knowledge Management & e-Organizations Group in IT Research

Faculty of Research Institute for ICT (ex ITRC) in 2002. She had been involved in a number of R&D projects on constituting databases for telecommunications by text mining, content personalization for smart organizations, conceptual ontology design for e-learning contents, and evaluating and optimizing contents for e-services. At present, she is a researcher at Knowledge Management & e-Organizations research Group in IT Research Faculty of Research Institute for ICT.

Mahmood Kharrat received his MS degree in Biomedical Engineering from the University of Tehran, Iran. Out of the research activities conducted by M. Kharrat, "representation & utilization of the ontology of learning content" and" hybridizing user model and learning style" are particularly mentionable due to their wide applications in automating tutoring purposes. Within the past years, he has been actively involved in doing research in a variety of issues, such as IT Applications and Services in general and e-learning, intelligent tutoring system, organizational learning, and knowledge management in particular. He is a member of the scientific board of IT Research Faculty at Research Institute for ICT(ex ITRC). At present he is the head of Knowledge Management & e-Organization Research Group and in the meantime an Adjunct Lecturer of Foundations of Information Technology in the University of Tehran.

Maryam Tayefeh Mahmoudi is a Ph.D candidate at Department of Machine Intelligence in the University of Tehran majoring in Artificial Intelligence with emphasis on intelligent organization of educational contents. Within the past years, she has been involved in a variety of research works at Knowledge Management & e-Organization Research Group of IT Research Faculty at Research Institute for ICT (ex ITRC), working on issues like automatic generation of ideas and contents, decision support systems for research & education purposes, as well as conceptualization of IT research projects. She is a co-author of the book entitled "Strangification: A New Paradigm in Knowledge Processing & Creation" and also the co-author of many research papers in different journals and proceedings of conferences. At present, she is a researcher at Knowledge Management & e-Organizations Group in IT Research Faculty of Research Institute for ICT, and in the meantime an Adjunct Lecturer of Computer Engineering subjects in the University of Tehran.

Emanuela Mazzone is a researcher in Interaction Design (ID) with a PhD on co-design methods for designing children's technologies from the University of Central Lancashire (UK). Since 2002 she has been participating, coordinating, delivering, and publishing on ID research projects. She works with aDeNu research group at UNED (Spain), being responsible for usability aspects of accessible ICT for education.

Maryam S. Mirian has recently received her Ph.D. degree from University of Tehran, majoring in Artificial Intelligence and Robotics focusing on control learning for artificial agents and robots. Since 2003 she has been working with Knowledge Management & e-Organizations Group in IT Research Faculty of Research Institute for ICT (ex ITRC) focusing on various areas such as text mining, learning organizations, ontological research content generation, and knowledge networking where she has been able to publish a number of research papers in both journals and proceedings of conferences. Her main research interests include learning through mixture of experts, knowledge extraction from experts, learning under uncertainty, and reinforcement learning. She is currently a faculty member in Research

Institute for ICT and at the same time an Adjunct Lecturer in the Faculty of Electrical and Computer Engineering in Shahid Beheshti University.

Serkan Özel is an Assistant Professor in the Department of Primary Education at Bogazici University in Turkey. His research interests include integrating technology in teaching and learning, specifically of mathematics, effect of cognitive psychology in designing and developing learning environment, and representational systems in mathematics.

Mark Palmer is a Reader in Marketing at Birmingham Business School, Birmingham University. His research explores the contested process of retail corporate strategizing and market development. This work is published in the *Journal of Economic Geography, European Journal of Marketing, Journal of Marketing Management, Environment and Planning A,* and the *Journal of Strategic Marketing.*

Kanubhai K. Patel is an Assistant Professor at the Schools of ICT of Ahmedabad University, Ahmedabad, India. He was previously a faculty member at GLS ICA, Gujarat University, Ahmedabad. He is pursuing PhD degree from the Faculty of Technology at Dharmsinh Desai University, Nadiad. He received his MCA from Gujarat Vidyapith, Ahmedabad in June 1997. His research interests include assistive technology, spatial cognition, human-computer interaction, and virtual learning environments. He has authored over thirteen publications, including three refereed journal papers and three book chapters. He has also authored a book – "Data Structures: Theory and Problems."

Giuseppe De Pietro is a senior researcher at the Institute of High Performance Computing and Networking (ICAR) of the National Research Council of Italy (CNR). He is a grant Professor of Information Systems at the Second University of Naples. His research interests cover pervasive computing, and multimodal and virtual reality environments. He serves as a member of the editorial board of several journals and of the program committee of numerous international conferences. He is member of the IEEE.

Stephen Quinton is a specialist in the fields of education, educational technology, information technology, and information systems with more than twenty-five years experience in the higher education sector. His qualifications include a Bachelor of Education, a Master of Education, and a Doctor of Philosophy from the University of Western Australia, all majoring in online education. He has extensive knowledge and expertise in the use of educational technologies for improving learning and enhancing learners' understanding and metacognitive thinking skills. His research aims to design educationally effective software systems that assist learners to identify concepts and form new cognitive associations from which to synthesise information and create knowledge. He has worked on many research programmes and projects that have focused on the application of learning theory, pedagogical strategy and practice, online educational design, Human Computer Interface (HCI) design, and dynamic content (learning object) assembly methods to the delivery of ICT supported learning environments.

Elena Railean is a doctoral candidate at the State University of Moldova and a researcher at the Academy of Science of Moldova. She was written the book "Methodology of educational software" and over 53 articles in theory and practice of Educational Technology. She writes at the intersection of philosophy of learning, cybernetic pedagogy, competence pedagogy, quantum psychology, and knowledge management. The focus of her research is to investigate the metasystems approach of learning processes, knowledge based design, principles of writing and assessment in digital semantic workspaces. Elena is author of new didactical model for electronic textbook development, which affordance is to develop the core structure of competence through dynamic and flexible instructional strategy.

Janet Resop Reilly completed her Doctoral degree (DNP) at Case Western University in Cleveland, Ohio. She is an Assistant Professor in the Professional Program in Nursing at the University of Wisconsin in Green Bay, teaching in a collaborative online RN to BSN program, offered through five campuses of the University of Wisconsin System. Dr. Reilly coordinated a year of faculty development across the five campuses on e-learning, funded by a federal Health Resources and Systems Administration (HRSA) grant (1 U1KHP07714-01-00). Interface design was featured content during the faculty development year. For details, see: https://research.son.wisc.edu/tecne/year5.htm

Olga C. Santos is the R&D Technical Manager of aDeNu Research Group at UNED. She has a PhD in Artificial Intelligence. Her current research interest focuses on taking into account recommendation strategies to provide open source educational-accessible user-centred e-learning services for learners. She has been involved in over a dozen research projects, published over a hundred papers in various international conferences and journals, and co-chaired workshops and conferences related to topics from her research.

Alex W Stedmon, MIEHF, CPsychol FRSA, is a Lecturer and Course Director of the MSc Human Factors in the Faculty of Engineering at the University of Nottingham. He is a Registered Ergonomist, Chartered Psychologist and Fellow of the Royal Society for the encouragement of Arts, Manufactures and Commerce. With a background in Sociology & Psychology he completed a PhD in the Human Factors investigating speech input for real world and virtual reality applications. He has published extensively in areas such as aviation, military training systems, transport applications, and augmented and virtual reality. He has worked on key EU projects developing novel interaction metaphors for virtual reality applications such as VIEW of the Future (VIEW: IST 2000-26089), Project IRMA (FP5-G1RD-CT-2000-00236) and, more recently, Sound AND Tangible Interfaces for Novel product design (SATIN: FP6-IST-5-034525).

Brenda Tyczkowski RN MSN is a Lecturer in the Professional Program in Nursing at the University of Wisconsin Green Bay (UWGB). She is also the Academic Director for a proposed program in Health Information Management and Technology (HIMT) at UWGB. Brenda is a candidate for a Doctorate of Nursing Practice (DNP) at the University of Kansas Medical Center. Her professional experience includes serving as a director of nursing in a long-term care facility, working as the director of training and implementation for a company that sold electronic health records (EHR) and serving in a supervisory role for the state of Wisconsin in the Bureau of Nursing Home Resident Care, Division of Quality Assurance.

Michael Vallance is a Professor at Future University Hakodate (FUN), Japan. He has a Doctorate in Education from Durham University and a Master's Degree in Computer Assisted Learning from Stirling University, UK. He has been involved in educational technology design, implementation, research, and consultancy for over fifteen years, working closely with Higher Education Institutes, schools, and media companies in UK, Singapore, Malaysia, and Japan. The virtual worlds research is funded by the

UK Prime Minister's Initiative (PMI2) and the Japan Advanced Institute of Science and Technology (JAIST). He is also the co-founder of the International Virtual Environments Research Group (http://www.iverg.com). His website is at http://www.mvallance.net.

Sanjay K. Vij received his PhD degree from IIT, Bombay, in 1974. He is currently a Director in the Department of CE-IT-MCA, Sardar Vallabhbhai Patel Institute of Technology (SVIT), Vasad. His research interests include text mining, knowledge management, and NLP. He has authored over twenty publications, including over seven refereed journal papers and two book chapters. He is a registered PhD guide with Dharmsinh Desai University, Nadiad. He is Member Board of Studies at MS University, Baroda and Dharmsinh Desai University, Nadiad. He had been a panel of experts/advisor in GSLET and GPSC. He is reviewer in couple of peer reviewed journals. He has been Chairman of Computer Society of India, Vadodara Chapter.

Index

3D-CAD technology 22, 36

A

ad-hoc mentality 220
Aesthetic Engagement 67
Aesthetic Experience 65, 74
Affinity 46, 53-54
American Association of University Professors
    (AAUP) 289, 302
American Psychological Association (APA) 43, 55,
    252
asynchronous JavaScript and XML (Ajax) 218
Augmentation 268-269, 284
augmented education 268-269, 280

B

Bachelor of Science in Nursing (BSN) 285-286,
    288-292, 298, 300-301
behaviorism 235, 237, 253, 257
blended learning 4, 14, 143
Bloom's Taxonomy 270-271, 275, 278, 284
BluePrints 255, 259, 263-264
BOTs 151-152
brain-computer interface (BCI) 172
BSN@Home 285-286, 288-292, 298, 300-301

C

CAI - See Computer-Assisted Instruction.
central executive 117
Co-creation 145, 149, 217
Co-existence 145, 149
cognitive activity 202, 245-246, 248-250, 263, 276,
    278, 284
Cognitive Demand 114
cognitive gestalts 194
cognitive load theory 115, 117, 119-120, 123

Cognitive Processes 45-46, 50, 63, 189, 197, 204,
    250, 268, 270, 275-276, 280-281, 284
cognitive psychology 43, 61, 115-116, 121-122,
    228, 252
Cognitive resources 115-117
Cognitive Workload 103, 107, 114
cognitivism 168, 235, 237, 253, 257
Collaboration 14, 27, 32, 34, 37, 82-83, 89-91, 98,
    142-145, 149, 187, 257, 270, 279, 281, 286-
    287, 297, 300-301
collaborative learning 22, 35, 55, 206, 256, 269, 278
Collaborative Nursing Program (CNP) 285
Collaborative Virtual Environments 30, 77-79, 81,
    83, 88-90
communication/information processes 249
competence-based 258
Computer-Assisted Instruction 2
Computer-Based Training (CBT) 2, 258
Conceptual Model 94, 100-102, 105-108, 114, 222
Constant variable value vignettes 214
Construction of Knowledge 43-44, 53-54, 187-188,
    270
Constructivism 51, 150, 152, 197, 206, 269-270,
    302
constructivist pedagogy 269
content analysis 16, 21, 23, 26
Content Assembler Agent 165
Content creation 156-158, 161, 164, 166-168, 218
content resources 260
content-ware 159-161, 163, 169
Context of Learning 43-44, 53-54, 59, 95
cooperative learning 230
course content 9, 95, 204, 257, 261, 289-290, 292,
    294-295, 297, 301
criterion-referenced 258
crowd sourcing 147, 153
CSpray 78, 91
CVEs - See Collaborative Virtual Environments.
CVVV - See Constant variable value vignettes.